D0585975

IN THE
RING

A Commonwealth Memoir

DON McKINNON

To my wife Clare and five children
Margaret, Peter, Stuart, Cameron and James

LANCASHIRE COUNTY LIBRARY	
3011812599781 1	
Askews & Holts	08-Mar-2013
909.097124 MCK	£20.00

Plate section image credits
Image 2 (page i, bottom) © Paul Popper Ltd/Getty Images
Image 3 (page ii, top) © The New Zealand Herald
Image 7 (page iii, bottom left) © Garrick Tremain
Image 18 (page viii, top) © Heriot-Watt University

All other images are © and reproduced by kind permission of the Commonwealth Secretariat

First published 2013 by Elliott and Thompson Limited
27 John Street, London WC1N 2BX
www.eandtbooks.com

ISBN: 978-1-908739-26-1

Text © Don McKinnon 2013

The Author has asserted his right under the Copyright, Designs and Patents Act, 1988, to be identified as Author of this Work.

All rights reserved. No part of this publication may be reproduced, stored in or introduced into a retrieval system, or transmitted, in any form, or by any means (electronic, mechanical, photocopying, recording or otherwise) without the prior written permission of the publisher. Any person who does any unauthorized act in relation to this publication may be liable to criminal prosecution and civil claims for damages.

9 8 7 6 5 4 3 2 1

A CIP catalogue record for this book is available from the British Library.

Printed and bound in the UK by TJ International

Typeset by Marie Doherty

Contents

Acknowledgements

I put off writing this book in the same way some people put off riding a horse for the first time. It's unfamiliar, could be uncomfortable and there's always a chance you'll fall flat on your face.

In my eight years in London, I kept notes about the things I did, the people I met and the dramas in which I was involved. In the back of my mind, I imagined some generous, highly-skilled writer coming along and saying 'I'll write your book and we'll both make a lot of money!' Or perhaps in fifty years' time the notes would be found and someone would make sense of them. After leaving the Commonwealth, I gave a lecture in late 2008 and someone asked me when my book would be out. It wasn't the first time the question had been posed but this questioner warned me that if I didn't write my account of my time as Secretary-General someone else might, and I might not agree with their version.

That jibe was enough to stir my competitive spirit. I talked with my wife Clare and my academic brother Malcolm and they gave me good advice and encouragement. I took the plunge – or rather I got on my literary horse.

Writing a book was, for me, a new experience. Surrounded by a decade of personal and official diaries, briefs, press releases, speeches, news cuttings and emails, I thought long and hard about where to start. I have always devoured political biographies, noting the great disparity in quality between them. Some writers had started with their diaries in front of them, and moved through them mechanically, with little texture or colour added beyond what was already in the public domain. Others relied heavily on pictures, with little of great substance in the narrative. The ones I really enjoy are those that deal with interesting and challenging issues in depth and provide genuinely new insights. That was my starting point and I hope this book delivers.

The Commonwealth is an amazing, much loved yet much misunderstood organisation. Within the Commonwealth Secretariat, among the London-based staff and those abroad, there are many people who are daily improving the lives of thousands. Their stories are not always easy to write about nor can they always compete with the breaking news stories of the day.

I had to weigh up what to include in this book and what to leave out. I chose to shed more light on issues that had already been in the public domain because inevitably there was an incomplete picture to finish. These issues had also taken up most of my managerial time.

One key message I want to emphasise, in the arena of foreign relations, is that no person and certainly no country likes to be told what to do by an outsider, another country or organisation. I was constantly pushing uphill in this regard. I can understand the reaction of people who demand that someone DO SOMETHING when they witness atrocities or cruelty on their TV screens. Yet sometimes doing something to soothe an outraged public can be counterproductive, and I know that it is rare that a person or country changes their way when threatened with a communiqué or at the point of a gun. What helps most is direction, encouragement, time, more time, and then some more time – most of my stories here are about those marathons, not headlining sprints. It is inevitable then that many of the good works of Commonwealth staff and consultants won't get mentioned, but I can assure them they are not forgotten.

On a practical note, I have virtually no keyboard skills so my first drafts were all in longhand. I was not completely hopeless with technology though and would scan and email these pages to a number of people who I employed to decipher my writing and get it typed up. These included my daughter-in-law Kere, who did a huge amount of work. Jessa and Nicola at the Auckland War Memorial Museum, where I was CEO 2010–11, did similar work at home, after hours. Our friend Francine in London pitched in when needed, along with some typists in Auckland. My wife Clare, a professional journalist and writer, was a constant support, offering typing, editing, and second opinions despite protesting she still could not read my writing after nearly two decades of marriage. It would have been too easy to lean on her all the time and for the book to dominate both our lives, so I was glad to spread the load and maintain a happy marriage.

In compiling the content of this book, I owe a lot to former staff members who read and commented on areas of special interest and responsibility. Winston Cox, Syed Sharfudin, Matthew Neuhaus, Professor Ade Adfuye, Juliet Solomon and Albert Mariner gave generously of their time. Commonwealth scholar Harshan Kumarashingham, and the doyen of Commonwealth academics, Professor David McIntyre of Christchurch, added valuable thoughts and perspective. The writings of my predecessors Arnold Smith in *Stitches in Times*, Sir Shridath Ramphal in *Inseparable Humanity*, and Chief Emeka Anyaoku in *The Inside Story* were informative. There was also the great historical perspective of Lord Elton in the 1945 publication *Imperial Commonwealth* and the more contemporary *State of Africa* by Martin Meredith, and Geoff Hill's *The Battle for Zimbabwe*. Long-time Commonwealth journalist and watcher Derek Ingram had useful comments on most issues after 45 years of writing and Hilary McEwan in the Secretariat's archives dug out relevant bits of information well beyond my reach.

Geoff Walker, former CEO of Penguin Books in New Zealand, brought all his publishing knowledge and editing skills to the fore and moulded my long discourses into something more readable and saleable. The penultimate draft was read by brother Malcolm and Clare, and both further nuanced my text.

By chance, my hairdresser Ola Jafar at Truefitt and Hill in London introduced me to another of her clients, Lorne Forsyth of the publisher Elliott and Thompson, and the rest as they say is history. I am grateful also to Olivia Bays, Jennie Condell, Marie Doherty, Mark Ecob and James Collins for their work on various aspects of the book's production.

Don McKinnon
Auckland, New Zealand
December 2012

Foreword

by Madeleine Albright, US Secretary of State 1997–2001

During the 1990s, Don McKinnon and I served concurrently; he as New Zealand's foreign minister, I as America's secretary of state. Despite the vast geographical separation, we met regularly and talked often while working together on behalf of the many goals our two countries shared in the Asia Pacific and across the globe. In the process of grappling with similar challenges from somewhat different angles, we became warm friends. This was to my benefit because Don is both charming and well informed. He is as interesting a conversationalist as he is a writer, and his opinions – thoughtfully expressed – carry much weight. It is little wonder that he has earned a place in the top tier of world diplomats. Many international figures carve out a particular region in which they can be counted as expert; Sir Donald McKinnon is one of the few who is respected everywhere.

As Don would be the first to admit, however, respect does not always translate into affection. During his career, he made his share of enemies among the dictators, *faux* democrats, neocolonialists and hypocrites who occupied positions of authority in various governments. Even by them, he was known for saying what he thought, honestly and without grandstanding. He is not the kind of person who will pick a fight simply to prove a point, but neither will he shy from confrontation when an important principle is at stake. I saw these attributes first-hand when we joined forces on such matters as support for Aung San Suu Kyi and the pro-democracy opposition in Burma, the liberation of East Timor from Indonesia, and the development of economic reforms in the wake of the 1998 Asian financial crisis. Don McKinnon's was rarely the loudest voice in any multilateral discussion, but his ideas were often the most sensible, coolly pointing in the direction of practical and positive action.

The rising stature of the New Zealand diplomat was recognised when, in 2000, he was elected Secretary-General of the Commonwealth, a 54-member organisation with historic ties to Great Britain and representing about a quarter of the world's population. *In the Ring* gives a fascinating insider's account of the succeeding eight years, and of McKinnon's effort to ride herd on a group of nations held together by little more than a name, some connection to the English language, and a passion for cricket.

The two decades since the Cold War's end have been derided – like Churchill's rejected pudding – for possessing no overriding theme. As Don McKinnon quickly discovers, this shortcoming has made life harder for those presiding over international organisations because priorities are no longer clear-cut and a sense of common purpose is difficult to establish. The temptation is strong for states to turn to a body such as the Commonwealth only when convenient and at other times to pay it little heed, gradually diminishing its capabilities. McKinnon does not offer a magic solution for these perils, but he does demonstrate how – through a combination of diligence, creativity and spine—one can move forward nonetheless.

The rich diversity of the Commonwealth, coupled with the competing historical narratives favoured by its various members, would test any leader. As a New Zealander, Don McKinnon was well positioned to communicate with all the factions in his flock, but only if he was perceived as being his own man. That required an attentive ear, an open mind, and a sense of responsibility not only to the organisation's giants – Great Britain, India and Australia – but to small and impoverished states as well.

In theory, and to an extent in practice, Commonwealth members are bound by their pledge to uphold democratic institutions and values. Any country that strays too far from that vow may find itself the subject of critical discussion, unwelcome fact-finding delegations, and partial or full suspension of the right to participate in Commonwealth activities. The group's problem states are naturally a concern for its leader and their stories provide the grist for the majority of chapters in this insightful memoir. Readers may observe from a front-row seat as Don McKinnon strives to ease political turbulence in Zimbabwe, mend fences following a coup in Pakistan, referee a dispute between two rival leaders (both women) in Bangladesh, and tamp down ethnic-based violence in Fiji. The book offers us a chance to travel with the Secretary-General as he makes his rounds – summoning the best from leaders in Guyana, trying to convince the king of Swaziland that political freedom has merit, and sharing concerns about the future with Pacific Islanders, whose tiny homelands face the possibility of extinction from climate change.

Adding piquancy to these accounts is Don's skill in sketching the personalities of those – great and not-so-great – with whom he is called upon to practise his trade. Although unafraid to give discredit where it is due, especially to the pompous and long-winded, he has warm words for many and is observant above all. The formal head of the Commonwealth is not the Secretary-General, but Her Majesty Queen Elizabeth, whose capacity for purposeful conversation on a multitude of topics earns the author's praise. As for Prince Charles, he had to deal with the sensitive question of whether he would – upon his mother's death or abdication – automatically succeed her as head of the Commonwealth. Sir Don McKinnon had to remind officials in London that the position is one agreed upon by leaders, and that British nostalgia for the days of Empire was not universally shared. This meant that the Prince should travel and show his interest in Commonwealth matters, but without seeming to campaign or to anticipate the question of how quickly a succession might occur.

During the eight years that serve as the focus of this book,

Don is constantly trying to persuade leaders to do what is right for their countries. More often than not, he succeeds, but there are disappointments. In writing about Zimbabwe, the diplomat's fairness is on full display as readers are urged to take history into account before judging the government's controversial land policies. However, the transformation of Robert Mugabe from anti-colonial hero to intolerant dictator was a source of personal sorrow to Don, whose relationship with the man deteriorated abruptly. Pakistan proved another headache when its strong-willed President, Pervez Musharraf, insisted on serving simultaneously as the uniformed chief of the military. As someone who also had official dealings with Musharraf, I can vouch for the accuracy of Don McKinnon's assessment. Musharraf had the intelligence and – for a time – the popularity to lead his country in a more democratic direction, but his contempt for civilians made him unwilling to delegate and reluctant to relax his hold on power. In the end he destroyed himself and caused considerable harm to his country.

As a young man, Don McKinnon yearned to be a farmer, beginning by wrangling horses and cattle in Wyoming to sheep ranches in New Zealand. In maturity, he devoted himself to public service and rose steadily through the ranks from parliamentarian to become his country's longest-serving foreign minister, then the fourth Secretary-General of the Commonwealth (complete with knighthood), and finally world statesman. Throughout this vertiginous journey, he kept his sense of balance and dry humour. He writes in this journal with the same flair that he brought to each of his many jobs, showing an eye for detail, the ability to penetrate quickly to the heart of any subject, and a sincere desire to make the best of an imperfect world. I trust that you will find him as I do: excellent company, indeed.

Madeleine Albright
Washington DC, May 2012

Introduction

'The Commonwealth makes the world safe for diversity'
– Nelson Mandela, after his release from twenty-seven years of
imprisonment, 1990

'The best ever post-graduate course in politics'
– Former Prime Minister Lee Kwan Yew of Singapore on the leaders'
Retreat at the Commonwealth Heads of Government Meeting (CHOGM)

'It's the best club in the world!'
– The former President of Malawi, Dr Hastings Banda, on why he loved
being a member of the Commonwealth

'The Commonwealth's big enough for all of us'
– Her Majesty Queen Elizabeth II, Head of the Commonwealth,
on her family's deepening involvement in the Commonwealth

'It is easy to define what the Commonwealth is not'
– Arnold Smith, the first Secretary-General of the Commonwealth
(he added that trying to do so was 'indeed quite a popular pastime')

Naturally, there have been those who have taken an altogether contrary view. Shortly after he led Zimbabwe out of the Commonwealth in 2003, President Robert Mugabe described the Commonwealth as 'a mere club. It has become like *Animal Farm*, where some members are more equal than others.'

Yes, the Commonwealth is an organisation that means many things to many people. It's the world's oldest international political association of states, yet when I became Secretary-General it was still struggling to establish a clear identity, and perhaps it still is.

What is the Commonwealth, how has it evolved and where is it heading? After eight years at the helm, I could just about predict the questions I would get from any audience I was addressing.

From the bluebloods of Great Britain: 'Why do we have to have the European Union when we've got the Commonwealth?' Or from another, older Commonwealth member country: 'How on earth did Mozambique ever become a member?' Or from the exasperated middle-aged-plus: 'Why can't the Commonwealth do more about Mugabe?' From a student in a developing country: 'Why aren't there more Commonwealth scholarships for my country?' Or, 'How can I get to be the Secretary-General?'

The last question, asked many times, always pleased me as it suggested a bright young person thinking well beyond their normal horizons.

International organisations have sprung up all over the world since the Second World War. Although a number existed pre-1940, the record of the League of Nations gave few people confidence in such bodies. But as transport became easier and people moved more freely, countries with common interests began to formalise their relationships among the like-minded. Country groups came together for reasons of region, religion, security, language and culture.

The modern Commonwealth's beginnings go back to the nineteenth century, when Canada, Australia, South Africa and New Zealand (and, from 1922, the Irish Free State) achieved self-government, which in the early twentieth century was termed 'dominion status'. The Balfour Report of 1926 declared that these countries, and Great Britain, were to be 'equal in status, in no way subordinate one to another in any aspect of their domestic or external affairs'. Though united by a common allegiance to the Crown they freely associated as members of the British Commonwealth of Nations.

Regular meetings of prime ministers date from 1907, but the modern multiracial Commonwealth we know today is very much a product of the decolonisation process from the 1940s to the 1970s, which saw dozens of former British colonies achieve independence.

With India, Pakistan and Ceylon becoming independent in 1947–8, the London Declaration of 1949 dropped 'British' in front of 'Commonwealth of Nations' and discarded the term 'dominion' in favour of 'Commonwealth member'.

When India declared that it wished to adopt a republican form of government while remaining in the Commonwealth, a constitutional crisis had to be addressed. It was agreed that when India became a republic it would remain a member, and in place of allegiance to the Crown it would recognise the monarch as head of the Commonwealth. Thus Queen Elizabeth II is head of the Commonwealth, but India is still a republic, along with a majority of members.

So emerged a new organisation born of the former Empire, now having eight members, which was to build up to fifty-four members by the time I became Secretary-General in 2000. As my friend and long-time expert on the Commonwealth Professor David McIntyre has observed, the organisation changed from being a small, white, imperial club to a large, multicultural, international association.

Many countries either linked to Britain or to another Commonwealth country decided it was an organisation they wished to join or could not afford not to join. A total of thirty-eight of the fifty-three members do not have Queen Elizabeth II as head of state, but recognise her as head of the Commonwealth. A very small number, notably Mozambique, Rwanda and Cameroon, have been accepted as members of the Commonwealth in recent times even though they are not former British colonies; at one time a part of Papua New Guinea, South-west Africa (now Namibia), Rwanda, Samoa, part of Cameroon and Tanganyika (part of modern-day Tanzania) were in fact former German colonies. On the other hand, some independent former British colonies such as Aden (now Yemen), Palestine and Jordan, Egypt, Sudan and Burma (now Myanmar) elected not to join.

The Commonwealth has no written constitution. Many leaders, and in fact Queen Elizabeth II herself, have referred to the concept of family as a partial explanation for the Commonwealth's continuing existence. The Commonwealth exists because its members feel they have a natural, family-style connection. They have a shared past and in the main a shared common language and institutions.

The Secretary-General position was established in 1965. A year earlier, at the Commonwealth prime ministers' meetings in London, the President of Ghana, the very ambitious Kwame Nkrumah, had proposed that there be an independent secretariat for the organisation, answerable to all member governments collectively.

This proposal was not universally welcomed, especially by a group now disparagingly referred to as the 'old white Commonwealth', namely the United Kingdom, Australia, Canada, South Africa and New Zealand. I believe that there were some at the time who did not expect the Commonwealth to survive this diplomatic stand-off. Newer members were unhappy with what they saw as the old members' preoccupation with the Cold War. The more pressing issue for the Commonwealth, declared Dr Nkrumah and others, was decolonisation and the gap between the First World and the Third. What was needed was a secretariat to provide the association with administrative strength and the ability to coordinate policy. The United Kingdom, Canada and Australia were all strongly against. New Zealand was silent, but in the end the old guard decided they should go with the new members, and so the line was crossed.

Many people believe, and I certainly agree with them, that the most significant advance in the evolution of the modern Commonwealth as we know it today was this setting up of the Secretariat in 1965. Until that year the management of the organisation had been firmly entrenched in the British Cabinet Office and the Commonwealth Relations Office, part of the Whitehall complex of government departments in London.

The first Secretary-General was former Canadian diplomat Arnold Smith, who began work in August 1965. Smith wrote cogently and somewhat self-effacingly about this period. What had emerged was the reluctance of the older group to have any obstacle between them and the British government. For the newer members it was about separating themselves a little more from the machinery and civil servants of the former colonial master. A secretariat central to the organisation, serving all equally, would principally assist their economic development.

Despite the intensity of the debate, and continuing rear-guard resistance from the Commonwealth Relations Office, the Commonwealth now had a full-time Secretariat. And thirty-five years after the establishment of the Secretariat, it was my job to steer it through the first decade of the new millennium.

Early arguments over the status of the office of Secretary-General ranged from those who wanted just a secretary to those who wanted someone to work more independently. In fact, at the time of writing I still hear comments from some governments that the incumbent should be more Secretary and less General. But more on this later.

My predecessors, my successor and I, however, appreciated the fact that the Secretary-General would have a rank akin to a senior high commissioner. He or she would rank as an equal with leaders at the conference table and would be employed by the Secretariat. These last two points were strongly and unsuccessfully resisted by the British in 1965. They preferred that the Secretary-General sit in the middle of the circle of leaders on his or her own – so there could be no direct contact during meetings – and they insisted that they, through their Commonwealth Relations Office, be the employer. A second unsuccessful proposal.

As with many international organisations where governments are the shareholders, there is rarely agreement on the qualifications or characteristics of the chief executive or even senior staff members. Invariably they will oscillate between wanting a strong, forthright person, and wanting someone who will 'just take the minutes'.

Nevertheless, there's a job to be done, and on many issues the Secretary-General just has to do what he or she thinks best as there are many unexpected situations that do not fit easily into what's known as 'the area of responsibility' or have not been mandated by leaders of government or the ministers.

The Commonwealth for which I have the highest level of familiarity has for over sixty years been getting these things right, but nothing ever remains static.

CHAPTER 1

A Rather Unusual Route

Although I was often introduced as an international diplomat, I would usually hasten to correct that by stating that most diplomats had high academic qualifications, were multilingual and had spent a lifetime in the job. I possessed none of those characteristics.

I came from a reasonably well-off but not by any means wealthy family. My father was a professional soldier who became a general, and my mother was from a pioneering Wellington, New Zealand family. From a very early age, influenced by summer stays on an uncle's farm in the Manawatu district of New Zealand, I wanted to be a farmer.

My first real job, at age seventeen, was working on cattle, horse and dude ranches in Wyoming and Montana. This was possible because my family was living in the United States, where my father was the New Zealand Defence Attaché in Washington DC, that most beautiful city. I graduated from Woodrow Wilson high school there in June 1956, and Big Horn Wyoming was the beginning of a twenty-year trek in the world of agriculture. That stay was an introduction to the great American West and the pastoral splendour of Wyoming, and to have fun riding horses twelve hours a day and getting paid for it was a bonus.

Our family – myself, parents and four younger siblings – returned to New Zealand in 1957, and I was soon working as a roustabout and later shepherd on a 3,500-acre sheep and beef farm. This job was deemed to be near the bottom of the farming ladder and you were expected to work your way up to head shepherd, stock manager and finally manager. Each shepherd spent nearly all day on horseback monitoring 1,500-plus sheep and fifty or more beef cattle. For an eighteen-year-old it was all good fun and a steep learning curve. We were great meat eaters, and it was my job to kill and dress the sheep required for eating. But you learned first on the animals that were killed for the dogs to eat before you graduated to the carcass intended for human consumption. After a few months I could produce a respectable carcass of near-supermarket quality. We had tough horses, and they needed to be tough. This was very rough country, and I often carried a sheep back to our home base on the saddle in front of me.

Soon the government intervened. Conscription for all eighteen-year-olds was still the law, so after eighteen months I did four months of army training, passing an officer's selection board, and was posted to an artillery unit. Then it was back to farming. My father, however, was convinced I should go to university, something I resisted strongly because it would stop me farming and earning money and would make no difference to my pay at the end. Nevertheless, the pressure of his wisdom eventually sunk in, so aged twenty-two I enrolled in a two-year diploma course at what was then Canterbury Agricultural College, now Lincoln University. That was very enjoyable even if, for me, not academically successful. But in the process of studying, partying and playing rugby, I was elected the vice-president of the Students' Association.

This first foray into politics was interesting, stimulating and some fun. Politics is a drug for many, and the addiction can be very strong. I was always interested but not, I believe, addicted. However, having lived impressionable teenage years in Washington DC in the 1950s, watched the McCarthy hearings on television, stood in Pennsylvania Avenue to watch the

Eisenhower second inauguration and been friends with the sons and daughters of congressmen and White House officials, I couldn't help developing a fascination with politics.

I read *The Washington Post*, *Time* and *Newsweek*, and was completely mesmerised in 1960 by Allen Drury's great book on Washington politics, *Advise and Consent*. With a father who was a senior army officer back in Wellington, politics seemed to always permeate family discussions. Former New Zealand politician John A. Lee's book, *Children of the Poor*, was a fascinating read and an insight into New Zealand political history.

After Lincoln, I went into the back blocks of Taihape, again as a shepherd, with the firm idea of some day owning a farm of my own. It was a slow climb up that ladder, but finally I got to manage a farm north of Auckland in 1964.

With a new job, and newly married to Tricia Moore of Taihape, this seemed like the most appropriate move towards farm ownership, but little did I know then that the local community of the East Coast Bays and my involvement in the Junior Chamber of Commerce (or Jaycees, as they were known) were to slowly change my direction. An involvement with the Auckland Debating Association, teaching communication skills for nine years to prison inmates at the Paremoremo maximum security prison and joining a political party sparked many new interests, as well as a desire to do more and be more involved in getting things done and reshaping the local community.

During a long, cold winter in 1969, probably after listening to too many flattering comments about my abilities, I became a candidate for the National Party in the 1969 election.

I was a candidate for only seven weeks prior to the November election day, but I found the whole campaign most exhilarating. I enjoyed all of it: meeting people, street-corner speeches, arguing against opponents and advocating what a government in New Zealand should be doing. The big topics were the Vietnam War, industrial stoppages and the usual array of education, health and social welfare issues.

Yes, I had caught the political bug, even though I didn't win the seat; I was a candidate again in 1972, when I was also unsuccessful but succeeded in pegging back my opponent's majority. In 1975 my wife and I had four children under ten and a big mortgage on a new property, and I had lost money on the cattle market. I had left day-to-day farming, as it was never going to deliver any wealth, and had started to work part-time in the property business. So being a candidate again in 1975 was out of the question. Of course, it was the very year my National Party won big.

In 1978 a surprising opportunity emerged when a new electorate called Albany was created in response to the constant population growth on Auckland's North Shore. With no sitting member of Parliament staking a claim to this winnable seat, I soon had a team set up to help me win.

Others thought the same, and fourteen prospective candidates lined up to seek the nomination, four of whom would ultimately become members of Parliament in subsequent elections. Having had two unsuccessful campaigns behind me that had taught me a lot, I believed I knew how to go about winning the nomination, and that I did.

So it was that on 27 February 1978, the day of my thirty-ninth birthday, I became the National Party candidate for the seat of Albany in the Auckland region. The speech to the selection committee was probably the most important speech I could ever have given, as winning launched me onto a totally new life trajectory which, with many ups and downs, has taken me to the present day.

No one can be prepared or even serve an apprenticeship to be an MP. You learn on the job, and if you enjoy the life and have some ambition, you slowly climb the greasy political pole. It's a massive change for anyone who suddenly arrives in Parliament.

Some adjust easily, some thrive in this new environment and there are always a few that just never fit in.

I guess I adjusted in reasonable time and soon began to do things in an efficient way. There is always more to do in any twenty-four-hour period than you have time for, so you do have to become a good time manager and become efficient with people and paper.

The institution that I joined was very male-dominated. The senior people in the government were predominantly Second World War veterans; some had been prisoners of war. They had served their country, so in some respects they had a more balanced if slightly sceptical attitude to political life than we new and enthusiastic members. We wanted electorate offices and a twenty-four-hour schedule of meeting people, and we would be available to open any sandpit in a kindergarten. We seriously wanted change from the very managed New Zealand economy of the 1960s and 70s, and so slowly we sowed the seeds of an economic policy which was more market-orientated than that which our own right-of-centre party had been deploying for most of the post-war years.

My own first argument within our governing party caucus involved questioning the right of the postal service to compete directly with the private sector couriers who had emerged in the environment of an inefficient Post Office. They were doing what the Post Office should have been doing, and doing it very efficiently. The result was positive, as the government changed its policy and the Post Office was told to leave the private couriers alone. Other colleagues brought forward similar initiatives, and slowly our party moved into a more enlightened era.

However, there were some things the leadership under Sir Robert Muldoon was reluctant to do, so we became divided as a party and lost the 1984 election. But then the left-of-centre new Labour government that followed us moved quite violently to the right and did many of the things that should have been the prerogative of our National Party.

I slowly moved through the ranks of the parliamentary party, becoming a whip in 1980, the chief whip in 1981, the deputy leader in 1987 and, on our party winning the election in 1990, the deputy prime minister. I had understudied the health portfolio for three years and was very ready to become minister of health. However, my Prime Minister had other ideas and asked me to become minister for foreign affairs and trade. This was another life-changing event. I held the portfolio for more than nine years, the longest of anyone in that portfolio ever in New Zealand.

It was life-changing, and where did I begin? As a parliamentarian you have lots of bits of knowledge across a wide range of governmental activities, but when you become a minister not only are you the face of that portfolio, you also have to know it thoroughly. The Ministry of Foreign Affairs in Wellington had about 600 staff and some forty-five missions around the world. The staff were some of the brightest and best out of our universities, and now they had a minister who had been to an agricultural university, without any academic success, and was about to learn on the job. In political terms the best I had done in this area was to attend a conference of Commonwealth parliamentarians in Kenya in 1983. However, I dived into the job with enthusiasm and some deserved modesty. It entailed a lot of travel, a lot of getting to know fellow foreign ministers and their key officials, but most importantly moving on the policy issues upon which the party had campaigned.

Repairing a fractured relationship with the United States brought about by the nuclear issue, which had declared New Zealand 'Nuclear Free', was at the top of the list. However, it was only after six months in the job that I realised that this issue seemed to permeate every other issue. Wherever I went the first question from a fellow foreign minister was, 'How are you getting along with the US?', as all knew that this relationship was an important cornerstone of a country's foreign policy. It was not worth being offside with the United States.

Of course, the nuclear issue had been divisive in New Zealand.

Within the Foreign Affairs team there were those who were immensely proud of this stance and defended it robustly. Others thought it was one of the more stupid things New Zealand had ever done and just held their counsel. I was caught. It was a government policy which I didn't think was that sensible and so I made it clear that, yes, we would adhere to it, it was there, but we were not marketing this policy to the world.

The other was the relationship we had with South Africa and the imminent end of apartheid. In New Zealand, a rugby-dominated country, playing sport with South Africa led to pressure from those who felt that only the total international isolation of South Africa would bring about internal political changes. We were a very divided country on that topic as well; unfortunately, as we learned from the impact it had on other issues, we were playing with fire.

Very soon the benefits of multilateralism became apparent to me. I quickly realised that many of these meetings with my peers held the potential to transact very useful other business. Via APEC (Asia-Pacific Economic Cooperation), the ASEAN (Association of Southeast Asian Nations) Post-Ministerial Conference, the Pacific Islands Forum and, of course, the Commonwealth, there was much fertile ground for bilateral meetings as well as for keeping up with issues and their background. The UN is the one place where you can and should be able to meet everyone you need to at the General Assembly in September (although it's so chaotic with 190-plus leaders or ministers and entourages that if you meet half of those you wish to, that will be regarded as successful).

The challenges of policy-making were fascinating. To convert the aspirations of a political party in opposition to workable policy is always a demanding exercise. I soon found that most Foreign Affairs officials took great delight in stretching their minds across the possibilities within these aspirations. It seemed as much an intellectual challenge, a mental exercise, as a means to an end. It would be an understatement to say I was well served by officials. Those I worked with put in extraordinary hours when required. They all worked hard, thought clearly and knew how to get the optimum result. As a small country you just don't have the battalions to threaten anyone; you must get the intellectual work right, and thereafter it is hard graft. Then it's a question of using the maximum leverage you can among your range of contacts around the globe.

The New Zealand Ministry of Foreign Affairs was, and still is, an essentially career department. Many join from university and stay there for most of their working life. If there was one deficiency I felt needed remedying, it was the need for these very competent people to get out and tell the public what they were doing. I suggested to the successive chief executives Graeme Ansell, Richard Nottage and Neil Walter that all returning ambassadors should get on the speaking circuit – Rotary, the Chambers of Commerce and other luncheon clubs, the Institute of International Affairs and the trade bodies handling New Zealand's large commodity exports – and tell people what was going on in the world. To keep talking to New Zealanders, I later initiated a series of seminars around New Zealand educating people on how to deal and trade with Asia. There seemed to me to be a strong need to get to know Asia and its people because of the expanding influence they would have on New Zealand in the future. We were successful in Asia, but for most Kiwis it was alien territory.

These seminars, however, were so successful that we then, with the help of the private sector, set up Asia 2000, the name suggesting we should achieve much by the year 2000. This organisation has now evolved into the Asia New Zealand Foundation and is still the principal body helping New Zealanders to understand Asia.

I also initiated the establishment of the New Zealand Institute for Strategic Studies to encourage independent debate on foreign and defence policy topics, the funding for which came from Foreign Affairs and Defence. In doing so I created a group that would often challenge our foreign policy, but at least they did so with more intellectual strength than the peace groups the media would normally turn to for a contrary opinion.

For me, reaching out to the community is important, if only to inform the taxpayers how their dollars are spent.

We campaigned actively and successfully for a non-permanent seat on the UN Security Council, which brought to the fore many foreign policy issues we would not otherwise have needed to be concerned about. Having a drink at the Libyan mission in New York to get their support was all part of the job at hand. The issues in the former Yugoslavia, Somalia and Rwanda, in particular, were very demanding. Working with our key officials we often had to make overnight decisions – and get it right.

There's a curious thing about foreign ministers all over the world: the longer you are there, the more senior you become and the more wisdom you are perceived to have. This obviously helps, because even from a small country, it gives you more clout. By 1995 I was one of the long stayers and found that getting doors opened was much easier. I did not contemplate beating the seventeen-year record of Hans Dietrich Genscher of West Germany or Dr Velayati of Iran, and I was probably a bit lucky to make it into a third three-year term in 1996.

The Commonwealth came dramatically to my attention when New Zealand hosted the Commonwealth Heads of Government Meeting (CHOGM) in Auckland in 1995. As foreign minister I had to play a significant role in most events. Strange as it may seen, foreign ministers were not major players in the Commonwealth family. The CHOGM was all about leaders getting together every two years, and there were many other ministerial meetings – finance, education, health, youth, sports, women's and other ministers all got together. But there appeared no specific need for foreign ministers to be involved, even though the foreign ministries did all the legwork for many of the meetings.

Having chaired the meeting in Auckland on small states and become a member of the Commonwealth Ministerial Action Group (CMAG – see Chapter 3), I started to get to know a little about the breadth, depth and value of this truly global organisation.

At the Edinburgh CHOGM in 1997 it was put to me quite seriously that I should stand for the job of Secretary-General, which would be decided at the next CHOGM in South Africa in 1999. That timing would also coincide with the next General Election in New Zealand. The thought captured my imagination, so I talked to a few of the people I met in my travels as foreign minister and soon ascertained I had some support.

Early in 1998 I felt there were three possibilities open to me, assuming that by 1999 I would have been New Zealand's foreign minister for nine years and many would think it was time for a change. As with most jobs, after a number of years you start to see some things come round for the third or fourth time.

So these were the options: I could challenge for the job of Secretary-General, which would start in April 2000; I could leave politics after the November 1999 elections and look for a new challenge, probably in business; or I could stay in Parliament, though if my party was still in government I would seek a domestic portfolio.

If we went into opposition – could I again face years of negativity? No, I would resign from Parliament and have a rest for a while, or take the advice of former Secretary of State James Baker and just sniff the roses.

I decided the Commonwealth job was worth pursuing. I was reasonably well known, I was named Foreign Minister of the Year in 1998 by the magazine *World Forum* and I had worked hard to get a settlement to the civil war on the island of Bougainville in Papua New Guinea. So I went about contacting key players, prime ministers, presidents and foreign ministers whom I knew, seeking their views and their support.

All were very good. Tofilau Eti, the then Prime Minister of Samoa, said he would get all the Pacific behind me, as did Prime Minister Owen Arthur of Barbados for the Caribbean. My ministry, however, suggested I should run a low-key campaign, presumably protecting me and them if I lost. I said, 'No, I've run campaigns, we go out big and tell the world. We'll always listen but we'll look confident.'

Another two prospective candidates emerged, who soon dropped to one – Farooq Sobhan, a former Bangladesh Secretary of Foreign Affairs. There was a feeling among many it was Asia's turn, even though the Commonwealth did not designate 'turns'. Although a Bangladesh candidate would get support in Asia, much would depend on which way Africa would go, and the chance of other candidates emerging could not be discounted.

Plans were prepared, a travel schedule developed and people were asked to speak up on my behalf. Amid all this, a curious and interesting parallel activity was taking place, with parliamentary colleague and former New Zealand Prime Minister Mike Moore seeking to be the new director general of the World Trade Organization (WTO).

International political positions are aggressively sought after, so two people from the same country seeking such positions was going to be a problem. The organisations were quite different, but given the trade-offs that go on in this arena, this was a risk for me. As most Commonwealth countries are part of the WTO, many would be asked to vote for two New Zealanders. Mike Moore was part of the Labour opposition, but he had done enough travelling and talking to people that he was able to prove to the government he had a good chance. Would they therefore back him and give him financial and personal support? The vote on the WTO position would be in August–September 1999 and the Commonwealth in November 1999; being part of the second vote might therefore be harder for me.

There was a little discussion about this in the Prime Minister's department, and I was invited to have a candid conversation with my party leader and Prime Minister, Jenny Shipley, who generously said I was the priority, 'and we have no obligation to fund Mike Moore'. This was not easy. She was giving me the option to pull the plug on Mike's campaign for the only reason that it was my ministry that would be funding his campaign. I knew his campaign would be used against mine, especially by my opponent. How many jobs did New Zealand want? I knew many would take the easy option of one vote for New Zealand and one vote for someone else. But around that time, at the end of 1998, I did feel I was gaining ground and it would be churlish of me to cut him out of his race.

So I took a deep breath and said, 'No, we'll run both campaigns.' We did, and New Zealand won both.

By now I was getting to know a lot about the Commonwealth – its role, the funding, the projects and the challenges – and I was becoming very excited thinking of the opportunities there, and the difference one could make to people all over the world. One phrase that kept coming back to me, uttered by a number of leaders when calling on them, was: 'We don't really make enough use of our Commonwealth membership.'

My campaign ran steadily (but not secretly) for a while until October 1998, when the Prime Minister launched it publicly in Wellington. We were able to say where our support was, where we believed it would continue to come from and how I had a very good chance of winning the contest.

'Was I the best candidate?' asked the New Zealand media. 'Probably not,' I replied, 'but I believe at this stage I am the most electable.'

It is amazing the way all these top political jobs are filled. There are no job advertisements, no job applications, no screening process, no psychometric testing, no submitted material, no formal interviews, no trial period. It's about which country you're from, how many supportive heads of other governments will back you, your previous five to ten years – and you must look about right. When jobs such as the head of the United Nations,

International Monetary Fund or World Bank emerge there is always an attempt by many to have more of the professional and less of the political brought to bear on the process. But as long as the sun rises in the morning, the international body realpolitik just wants to do things its own way and won't allow another. Another strong element is that of political people picking other political people – or 'I only trust one of my own kind'. However, as many political people will not know the candidate personally, it is for their diplomats to assess and provide advice. So a key to winning is not to get offside with diplomats anywhere.

For too many people, including some political leaders, the Commonwealth was defined by what it might have been thirty years before. I decided we had to ensure not only that people were brought up to date but also that the key to the modern-day Commonwealth's survival was relevance and credibility: *relevant* in that the work the Commonwealth was doing was contemporary, useful and met members' needs, and *credible* in that the work could stand up to the highest international scrutiny. We had to be truly internationally competitive and stand up for our values. Having been a member of CMAG, I had been able to see just what some leaders would do to stay in power rather than trust the people to an election.

I soon found a good network of supporters in Africa, even including Zimbabwe, who said they would support me because they saw me as the better candidate. But – and there were many buts – this assurance was often followed by: 'But if the Malaysians put up a candidate, we'd feel bound to support them.'

I probably heard that ten times, and that's the way international politics works. The Malaysians had made considerable investments throughout Africa, earning a lot of goodwill, and that is hard to beat. So I can honestly say that right up to the actual election at the CHOGM in Durban in November 1999 I would not have been surprised by the last-minute appearance of a smiling Malaysian candidate fully supported by Dr Mahathir, the Prime Minister of Malaysia. Maybe it was the financial crisis, or perhaps Mahathir felt he had lost his Midas touch, but none appeared. Dr Mahathir did try what I thought was a dubious end run by asking the Commonwealth Secretariat to circulate a one-page piece of paper calling for all leaders at the CHOGM to support the candidate from Bangladesh. The Secretariat wisely refused to do so.

It was a long but relatively efficient campaign. I campaigned for the Secretary-General's job while I was travelling doing my job as a foreign minister, and in fact I made only two side trips that I would not have otherwise made. There was another reason I was pleased to contain my travels as far as possible. My first marriage had ended, and in 1995 I had married journalist Clare de Lore. Our son James was born in February 1998, as this campaign was really getting off the ground, and I wanted to be home whenever possible.

As the campaign came to an end I felt we were ahead. The best estimates of my head counter Simon Gimson (a diplomat and at one time my press secretary) were all twelve Pacific votes, at least ten Caribbean, two in South-east Asia, none in South Asia, three in Europe and more than half of the nineteen in Africa. Of course this was just one of the two campaigns run by our Foreign Affairs people.

A real weakness in our campaign was to be the absence of New Zealand's Prime Minister from the Durban CHOGM due to the New Zealand elections. This absence always sends its own negative signal and creates some doubts as to commitment. Her place was taken by Sir Douglas Graham, the New Zealand justice minister, a good friend with the appropriate gravitas, who was well equipped to lead and was strongly helped by skilled officials.

So after a long journey – from wrangler to shepherd, farm manager, farm consultant, real estate agent, property developer, member of Parliament and foreign minister – I was elected the fourth Commonwealth Secretary-General, to take office in April 2000.

In the course of the next eight years I travelled widely, met many important and fascinating people and soon realised that you could make a difference to people's lives by ensuring the right policies were pursued to their conclusion.

Although I was untrained in a world normally inhabited by diplomats, the one area in which I had a minor advantage was that of agriculture. I had never expected this subject to play a big part in diplomacy, but knowledge of farming, recognising plants, understanding soil types and assessing the health of the land and animals is second nature to one who has spent a lot of time on the land. Observing the land carefully tells you stories about the people and how they engage with the land. The small but fertile holdings in Malawi that I viewed from the air and on the ground could tell me reasonably accurately just how much people had to eat and the state of their health. From the deserts of Botswana to the lush vegetation in the Caribbean, there wasn't a country in which the state of the land did not reveal interesting information.

CHAPTER 2

A Gracious Presence

**'The most important contact between nations is usually
contact between people'**
Queen Elizabeth II on the Commonwealth, in a speech in Westminster
Hall on the occasion of her 60th year on the throne

'Well, now that you've got the job you'd better meet She
Who Must Be Obeyed,' said my foreign affairs assistant
Simon Gimson. He was, of course, referring to the head of the
Commonwealth, Queen Elizabeth II, for whom he had worked
in Buckingham Palace for four years on secondment from the
New Zealand Ministry of Foreign Affairs.

We were in Durban at the 1999 Commonwealth Heads of
Government Meeting (CHOGM), and the leaders had gone off
to the Retreat. This was the occasion on which leaders left the
main conference venue and went off to a 'secluded' place, without officials, for informal interaction with no one taking notes.
It was conceived by former Canadian Prime Minister Pierre
Trudeau, who rightly believed there was a need for leaders to be
on their own, if only to discuss how to deal with difficult senior
civil servants. Incidentally, at the Malta CHOGM in 2005 I was
pleased during one session to hear Shaukat Aziz, the Pakistan
Prime Minister, say that the Retreat, with only the leaders and
no officials present, was the best international meeting he had
ever attended. It's always good to hear such comments, and he

wasn't on his own. It is never easy to explain to people that this Commonwealth convention was an amazing opportunity for leaders to be candid and genuinely enjoy each other's company. I'm sure that a poll taken among leaders would find that this part of the CHOGM would be the last thing they would give up. The Retreat segment has since been imported into many international summits, including APEC (Asia-Pacific Economic Cooperation) and the Pacific Islands Forum.

On this occasion, the Queen hosted a function for all those remaining, mostly foreign ministers and senior officials. I had met the Queen on a few occasions before and always came away with the feeling that people don't see her the way she naturally is. She is a person who smiles easily, laughs a lot and would have to be the world's expert on handling small talk and on moving away graciously from a difficult and boring situation. In the eight years as Secretary-General, I must have had meetings with the Queen more than thirty times, and every meeting I enjoyed.

So from among a small group of people at the Durban function, there she emerged, probably the most photographed face in the world.

'How do you do?' she said with a smile. 'And congratulations, it was a long campaign. And when are you coming to London?'

'Thank you so much and, well, probably March,' I replied.

'Well, yes. Not too soon, you would wish to avoid the winter,' she said with a chuckle. Then after a little more small talk, she moved on.

Then the Duke of Edinburgh moved into view. 'My word,' he said during the handshake. 'Foreign minister for nine years. That's pretty good.' Always straight to the point.

I did get to London late in March 2000, ready to take on the job. In a pre-induction meeting, I was introduced to what would be an ongoing concern during my time in the job: the outgoing Secretary-General Chief Emeka Anyouku of Nigeria, going through his handover list, said it was very important to keep close to the royal family, and to ensure that the Prince of Wales, who seemed to keep his distance, was kept up to date.

Before I went to London I believed, like most assertive, egalitarian Kiwis, that in this day and age the monarchy could not and would not survive for much longer. I thought that the long-running democratic pressures for greater equality would eventually see it fade away. But after nearly nine years of living in London, of having significant contact with many close to the royal family and even members of the family themselves, I can see this institution more than outliving me, my children and my grandchildren.

Why the change of heart? First, you have to acknowledge that the monarchy is part of the fabric of society in the United Kingdom and has been so for more than 900 years. So it is not something alien, it's part of the make-up of the country.

Second, it provides a balance to the elected democratic structures, which can only come about through several hundred years of living with each other through good and bad times and without causing surprises. It does give people a level of comfort, which leads to my next point.

Third, as most people now put politicians below the category of used-car salesmen, the public does need someone in supposed authority to look up to, to provide balance. The unchanging nature of the monarchy and the sense of decency shown by the Queen help to answer that need.

Fourth, you cannot ignore the huge number of people who are part of her estate in Britain, who've been drawn into it by various levels of patronage, from jobs through to non-titular honours, knighthoods and peerages. Most of these people not only believe in the institution, they also give it active support. Presumably, the House of Lords in its present form would need to disappear if the monarchy was set aside. For me, as I now see it, the monarchy brings all these elements together.

Fifth: from within, the management of the monarchy is mostly superb. There is no easily opened doorway; instead, there is managed and controlled rationing of access to the monarchy, designed to help sustain its enduring value. Errors are few.

And sixth, never underestimate the value to tourism of the foot guards and the mounted guards in their resplendent uniforms standing outside royal palaces and on horses in Whitehall, or parading to and from the barracks beside Hyde Park – they are perpetually photographed (and even propositioned) – and the pageantry provided on special occasions such as the 2011 royal wedding. These overt and rather quirky public displays of support for the monarch are an attractive and colourful addition to the story.

For all these reasons, I believe the monarchy as an institution will not fade away. I believe that it provides differentiation, and creates national comfort and pride. I also believe it is capable of surviving a weak monarch, as it has done in the past.

The Queen herself has been magnificent. I believe that Prince Charles, who gets mixed reviews and has had a long apprenticeship, will be more comfortable as king than as a prince-in-waiting, and William has made his mark most comprehensively. So the individuals we are familiar with today will not let it subside.

Many people say they would never accept an honour, and that may be true. But enough of them do so to make honours much sought after. The range of honours is wide, and the title of lord or knight is respected by many, thus adding to the numbers of those who will ensure the monarchy's longevity. Also, over the years, many successful and no-longer-illustrious members of Parliament have been willing to give up a seat in the Commons – and thus their regular democratic voting right – and be sent to the Lords, thus permitting their party leader to introduce valuable new talent.

Further, one cannot ignore the role the Queen plays as head of state. Meeting (and farewelling) high commissioners, judges, cabinet ministers and ambassadors takes a huge burden off the executive head of state – the prime minister. It's the perfect job-sharing team. Not only the Queen but also a number of other royals of lesser rank are always available to attend. Finally, adding value to the British economy and enhancing exports is another well-known royal function.

In all my meetings with many Commonwealth heads of government about who will take over as head of the Commonwealth after the Queen, there has invariably been a circuitous discussion that canvasses all the alternatives and eventually goes the full circle and returns to the British monarch. Many Commonwealth leaders have met and had discussions with Her Majesty and few come away other than impressed by her interests, her enquiring mind and her genuine warmth for people. None, therefore, seem to feel she should be replaced.

African leaders, for example, have made it clear to me that they don't feel diminished by the Queen of their former colonial power being head of the Commonwealth. I recall one saying he felt that 'having the British monarch as head of the Commonwealth gave us something no other organisation has'. Another said, 'We are all different in our own way, why should we say no to the next king?'

It's a curious safety valve, and rarely tested – but it's there.

I do believe that overall, weighing up the pluses and minuses, the strengths and the weaknesses, the monarchy will not change much other than very slowly in the next fifty years – unless the monarchy wants to. And it's hard to envisage that occurring.

So have I personally been bought off (with a knighthood in 2009) by too-close association? Well, maybe I've been influenced a little. But I'm mindful of a Swahili proverb: 'If you take something away from people you must replace it with something of value.' Replacing the monarchy with an elected presidency would in my opinion leave most British people feeling short-changed.

After a few weeks in the job, a time was set for my first official meeting with Her Majesty. On the appointed day my driver took me down to Buckingham Palace. The car had to push its way through the tourists, through the gates, through the arch and across the yard to the portico, delivering me onto the red carpet. Then I was given instructions from a shiny-faced army aide-de-camp to go in, bow, shake hands, sit down, talk, shake hands, bow and go out, no need to walk out backwards!

The doors opened, I was announced, the Queen was smiling so I smiled too – and forgot to bow – and we shook hands. Suddenly I remembered that I wasn't just a citizen of a realm where she was the head of state – I was actually representing fifty-four countries, of which thirty-eight did not recognise her as head of state, although they acknowledged her as head of the Commonwealth.

It is a well-respected convention that one does not disclose details of meetings with the Queen, and I benefited from that mutual confidence as much as anyone. What I would say is that Her Majesty was probably the most knowledgeable person on the Commonwealth over the long term that I have ever met. She always showed well-informed interest in and concern about issues, which added a valuable dimension to our discussions. She has clearly displayed the commitment of a lifetime.

On that occasion we had a relaxed, engaging and informative chat, just as two people. She was warm, gracious and often funny. She was very interested in Zimbabwe, from where I had just returned, and regaled me with stories of some former Commonwealth leaders she had met. At one stage I thought, what an amazing book she could write. All those people who've been sitting in this chair, going back to 1953: Winston Churchill, Jawaharlal Nehru, Kenneth Kaunda, Robert Menzies and, in later years, some real bandits such as Ceauşescu (my words not hers) and others.

The twenty minutes stretched to half an hour and then, after a farewell shake of hands and a very warm smile, I was walking out of the room. It was a most fascinating and unforgettable experience.

Soon after this I had my first meeting with Prime Minister Tony Blair. I never felt Tony really warmed to the Commonwealth. He was thrown into the deep end by having to host a CHOGM soon after taking on the job, and wasn't impressed by what he saw. Ever after, I think he put the Commonwealth in the same category as fox-hunting: it belonged to another age, it wasn't really 'New Labour'.

Nevertheless, he was generous to me, and Cherie and Clare got on well, both juggling official life with the demands of small children and busy husbands. Zimbabwe was high on Tony's agenda, and he concluded our meeting by saying, 'You tell us what you want and we'll try to get it for you.' If only the Foreign and Commonwealth Office (FCO) senior officials had heard that and were as generous.

Within a few months I received word from one of the Buckingham Palace courtiers that the Queen Mother would like to meet me, so it was arranged that I would call on her one morning at Clarence House, just a stone's throw from Marlborough House, where our offices were situated. Clarence House, which adjourns St James's Palace, had been the Queen Mother's residence since 1954 and is now the residence of the Prince of Wales and the Duchess of Cornwall. A few days later the invitation was raised to a lunch with the Queen Mother and extended to include Clare.

Other guests included a British couple who lived in France; Princess Margaret, who arrived late; Sir Alastair Aird, a royal courtier who had been with the Queen Mother for years and was almost a caricature of himself; and Lady Angela Oswald, the lady-in-waiting.

Yes, said the Queen Mother, the Commonwealth was very

dear to her heart. 'Lots of wonderful people went out there,' meaning of course New Zealand, Australia, South Africa, Canada and Rhodesia. I was always amused by the English habit of referring to such countries as 'out there'. Everywhere was 'out'.

I sat with the Queen Mother as she chatted knowledgeably about places she had visited while our glasses were regularly filled. Then Clare had a turn alongside her before we went to lunch. Then there was more conversation about people she had known and her travels. After a couple of hours we got up and she walked us around the lower floor of Clarence House, where the walls were covered mostly with photos and paintings of racehorses. We had a brief discussion about a family of foxes in the high-walled garden, and concluded the tour close to the front door.

'Now, don't forget to look after the family,' said the Queen Mother as we departed. 'Oh,' I said. 'Clare and James?' 'No, no, the old Commonwealth family.'

And that really said it all. After all, her era was from the 1920s through to the 1950s. The Commonwealth, or strictly up to 1949 the *British* Commonwealth, rested in her mind more as what it had been than as what it was now. No one could fail to be charmed by this remarkable woman, but nearly three hours for a luncheon, I thought – that will be hard to keep up.

Sir Robin Janvrin, the Queen's private secretary, came to see me at Marlborough House to speak about the role of the Commonwealth in the Queen's 50th Jubilee of 2002. Robin was a former naval officer and then a diplomat before he joined the Palace. He was a very smart operator, quite unflappable, with a commonsense view of the contemporary Commonwealth, politics and the art of the possible.

I said that for such an event to be successful I hoped there could be a linkage between the Jubilee and the Manchester Commonwealth Games in 2002, when there could well be a number of Commonwealth heads of government visiting. These days heads of government could not afford to travel for merely social occasions. If, however, a prime minister or president intended to attend the opening of the Commonwealth Games, discuss economic issues with the UK prime minister or ministers, attend a Jubilee dinner for the Queen, take the salute at a full Commonwealth tattoo, then go on to one or two other European capitals for trade purposes, that would be productive and therefore more acceptable to the folks back home.

The point I was making was that if the Palace or the British government wished to host a gala dinner, including Commonwealth heads of government, it would not be desirable to have only half there, and they would presumably not all be able to come. This was an aspect of Commonwealth politics not fully understood by those who never left Whitehall (although this didn't apply to Robin Janvrin) and whose view of Britain's position in the world was more applicable to the nineteenth and early twentieth centuries. Gone were the days of summoning leaders to London. That now seems to be Washington's role.

The sensitive issue of the management of succession when the Queen died was frequently discussed. Who would then be the head of the Commonwealth? On one visit to Nigeria, I had a very useful one-on-one discussion with President Obasanjo. The President was a big man in Africa. He had, through military means, overthrown a corrupt regime and returned the country to democracy. Regretfully that didn't last, and some years later there was another military coup led by General Sani Abacha. Obasanjo was jailed and only released in 1998, but went on to win the election in 1999. A quick but deep thinker, he summed up the issue of succession well:

Commonwealth leaders could argue for days about the position, propose a former leader, based on where they came from, how long would it be for – and then we would have to take turns, region by region. That will become unnecessarily political. We don't feel so small that we have to reject the monarchy to feel big. The monarchy is equally part of our heritage, as is our common law judicial system and our parliamentary system. It keeps the Commonwealth unique.

He went on: 'After the death of the Queen you, Secretary-General, must talk to all heads of government to establish a consensus around the new king, and announce it. We don't want to be put in a position of scrutiny by the public or the media, and certainly we don't want to be confronted with anything resembling a vote on the issue.'

I talked to many heads of government about this sensitive subject, always privately, always just the two of us. After going round the full circle of the arguments, the various options, all tended to end up in the same place as President Obasanjo. By my departure in April 2008 I was glad the issue had not arisen.

Not long after, I had my first meeting with the Prince of Wales at his residence-cum-office in St James's Palace. It was 50 metres from Marlborough House. He seldom enjoyed a good press, but was well-briefed and entertaining. I found him a most engaging dinner companion, telling amusing stories, many against himself. According to our records in the Secretariat, he had not been very involved in Commonwealth activities in recent years, and knowing how anyone gets out of date on issues unless you're dealing with them regularly, I decided we had to pull him closer into the fold.

Thus began the development of a programme that would renew his interest without in any way usurping the role of his mother – or, more importantly, giving the impression that this was part of a campaign to let her retire from Commonwealth activities. I know Her Majesty will be there until the end, but

anyone in their eighties can be unwell or temporarily unfit to
travel, and the Prince of Wales, as an obvious stand-in, should be
familiar with the contemporary Commonwealth and its leaders.
This was one of my central concerns during my whole period in
office and I had many fruitful discussions with him.

It was soon after this meeting that I got into an unnecessary
argument with the very nationalistic British media. It began with
my comment to a journalist that the Prince of Wales did not
automatically become head of the Commonwealth on the death
of the Queen. The position was one decided on by heads of
government. That became a media headline and a subsequent
short-term frenzy.

It was deemed an insult to the Prince and to the monarchy. Questions were asked in the Commons and the Lords.
Baroness Amos, answering for the foreign secretary in the
Lords, responded that of course Her Majesty wanted her successor to be the head of the Commonwealth. But she also recognised
the correctness of my statement that it was for Commonwealth
leaders to decide.

St James's Palace issued a statement saying that, in fact, the
Secretary-General was correct. Still, the public discussion wasn't
really welcomed in many quarters.

An invitation to dinner and an overnight stay at Windsor Castle
on 10 April 2001 was one of the great experiences in a life where
we got to enjoy many special events over the years. Clare and
I arrived there late one June afternoon, joining the other guests
in cars outside the main gates where, for reasons I will mention
shortly, there was a horde of paparazzi flashing cameras at every
car that passed. After casual pre-dinner drinks with the Queen
and the Duke, we retired to our room to freshen up and change
into formal evening wear. We found, as we had been warned by

friends who had once enjoyed the same experience, that all our bags had been unpacked and some clothes pressed, and a maid had 'drawn a bath' for Clare. Some guests to such an occasion, we were told, bought a new wardrobe for fear a maid would have to see and touch some older underwear.

There were a number of other guests, and where we were seated seemed to reflect how we ranked. I was one away from the Queen, alongside Cardinal Cormac Murphy-O'Connor, Archbishop of Westminster. On the other side of me sat Sophie, Countess of Wessex, who had just emerged from a rather messy scam set up by the *Daily Mail*. This had clearly left her rather bruised, and this was the first time she had come face to face publicly with her in-laws since the scandal erupted, hence the turnout of paparazzi hoping to capture her arrival at the castle. Despite her problems, she put on a brave face and was a very pleasant dinner companion.

After dinner, the Queen invited Clare and me to view some of the collections she held in the library at Windsor Castle. Among them were the first-ever decimal currency notes and coins from New Zealand in 1967, photos of the royal tour of New Zealand in 1901 and, of interest to me, a letter written by the first Duke of Marlborough, carried from southern Germany by a soldier from Virginia, to Queen Anne in 1704, announcing his win at the Battle of Blenheim. It was 12.30 a.m. before we all, including the Queen, retired to bed. This queen, I thought, will go on for ever. Beyond one hundred, like her mother.

Strengthening the links between the Commonwealth and the Prince of Wales continued to be a focus. My thoughts were that the Prince needed to engage with Commonwealth heads whenever they came to London. I wanted prime ministers or presidents to have the chance to meet the Prince, and get to know him beyond the image portrayed in the news media. I was pleased then to be invited to St James's Palace in 2001 to have a chat with the Prince, just prior to a meeting he was to have with the Pacific high commissioners at New Zealand House. This was the first of a series of meetings with regional groups of high commissioners that allowed them to have an informed discussion with the Prince about the challenges of their countries as well as hearing from him about his Prince's Trust. In many cases there was a synergy between the two as the Trust was looking for useful, sustainable projects in developing Commonwealth countries, particularly small islands.

I wanted to make some changes at Marlborough House, most notably by flying the flags of Commonwealth countries visibly and prominently along the southern or Mall boundary of the Marlborough House grounds. I recall one particular discussion. 'Look,' I said, 'you folk all know the warm feeling you get when you see the Union Jack flag flying in a foreign country?' To nods of approval, I went on. 'Well, Marlborough House is the headquarters of the Commonwealth. Commonwealth taxpayers are paying to be there and paying for the programmes, and they too would like to see their flags flying as Commonwealth members. And why not?'

The message got through. But it wasn't the end of the flag issue, which thereafter continued to rumble through the corridors of English Heritage, the Georgian Society, the Victorian Society, Royal Parks and Westminster City Council. It was all about changing the appearance of a royal palace, which the diehards considered unacceptable. Most gave up their mumbled objections when they knew that the Queen supported the move and that Buckingham Palace wasn't objecting. The big surprise was Westminster finally telling us we did not even need planning or building consent to go ahead.

The only disappointment over the flag issue was that, after member states applauded the news that their individual flags would all be flying, they then discovered that they would have to pay £1,000 each to see it achieved. Even for seasoned diplomats, writing out an unbudgeted cheque would always be a problem.

I made a trip, with Clare, to Balmoral Castle in 2001 to talk with Her Majesty about the upcoming CHOGM in Australia in 2002. Having heard a little about this vast estate of 26,000 hectares, and knowing that the Queen had some good horses, I asked her private secretary if I could go for a ride while there and see the estate. That was agreed, so riding boots (short Australian ones) and a pair of jeans were popped into my bag alongside the official papers.

Balmoral had a distinctly relaxed feel, and it was easy to see why the Queen is happy there, able to indulge her love of the countryside and switch off from the more formal life of Buckingham Palace. Princess Margaret joined us in the sitting room before lunch, wheeled in by an assistant. A few months earlier, she'd scalded her feet in a bath, an accident that had been widely reported. She was clearly unwell, and the Queen was touchingly kind and caring in her conversation with her younger sibling. Three or four other guests came for lunch, which was as relaxed as I've ever seen the Queen and the Duke. Both Clare and I later agreed that this was a couple who enjoyed each other's company and had a great friendship preserved over many years of marriage, despite the pressures of being constantly in the public gaze.

After lunch the Queen said, 'I hear you are going for a ride on our Highland ponies.' 'Yes. If you don't mind,' I replied. 'Oh no. You'll enjoy it. We've picked out a good horse for you. We know how heavy you are!' I was impressed by the background intelligence that produced this information.

So off I went with the royal blessing, accompanied by the daughter of the farm manager, or factor, as they are known. Around the hills above the castle, we rode for about an hour and a half. The contour of the land was like the New Zealand hill country, a rugged landscape with many conifers; we spotted some flighty deer and you could get a nice cold drink in a stream. I tried every gait and could not fault the sturdy pony. What a contrast, I thought – from central London to the Highlands of Scotland, from planes and cars to a good riding horse and lots of fresh air.

Back at the stables, I clambered off and started to unhitch the saddle when a voice about 20 metres away said, 'I suppose you'll now need a car ride back to the castle,' – this from a smiling Queen. 'No, ma'am. Not at all. I can still walk.' Meanwhile, Clare, who doesn't ride, had done an extensive tour of the property in a Land Rover, with one of the ladies-in-waiting. We both returned to London later that day having had another memorable experience of royal hospitality.

Princess Margaret died in February 2002. I had met her only three times and never found her as easy to converse with as her older sister. I hand-wrote two condolence letters, one to the Queen and one to the Queen Mother, and had them delivered.

Later that day I noticed that all flags in the immediate area were at half-mast except for a trial new one in the corner of the Marlborough House garden. I asked security why it wasn't down. They said they could not shift the flag. I had a look and saw there was no halyard. I went back to the car, got a spanner, undid the bolt at the bottom of the pole and lowered the whole flagpole with flag intact to the ground. Honour was saved. The press criticism would have been too much.

Then in March, only a month later, the Queen Mother died. Our family was on holiday in Portugal at the time and I did numerous phone interviews with various media about her life and times from a Commonwealth perspective. The Queen Mother lay in state in Westminster Hall and many thousands stood in long lines to pay their last respects. We were able to slip in a side door to do the same after we returned to

London and attended her funeral, our second royal funeral in a month.

We had our second lunch with the Prince and, this time, the high commissioners of East and West African countries. All went well. We were welcomed with a rather overlong speech by High Commissioner Dr George Kirya of Uganda. After each high commissioner had given a three-to-four-minute summary of his own country's challenges, my Ugandan friend got up again, saying as he had previously spoken as the dean of the corps, he would now speak for Uganda.

After ten minutes, the Prince was rolling his eyes. But we made it to the end and I indicated to our guest that we wouldn't let that happen again. We wanted discussion and debate, questions seeking answers, not long academic speeches.

The FCO people once again wanted to talk about the succession. Having been with the Queen a number of times recently and noted her robust health, I knew this wasn't a pressing concern. She seemed very healthy and always at ease with herself. Nevertheless, the FCO asserted, there had to be a plan.

'No,' I said. 'You can't possibly expect Commonwealth leaders to give their consent for the new king to be head of the Commonwealth within twenty-four hours when Charles the King-to-be is expected to give the oath of allegiance within the accession proclamation.' It was fine back in 1953 when there were only eight countries, and it was all sewn up when Nehru assented, I said. But not now.

I knew many heads of government would come to the funeral or memorial service, but they would not wish to have a meeting on that subject alone. The process of conferring on this issue could be initiated only by me, or by a subsequent Secretary-General, by phoning round and establishing if in fact there was a consensus. Certainly, by the coronation it would be known. There were unknown factors that would have to be considered, including the recent activities of the Prince of Wales or the likelihood of an election in one of the Commonwealth countries in which the role of the monarchy might be a divisive campaign issue.

There was also a new generation of leaders emerging who might have a totally different attitude, so there was work to be done. I just knew there was a need for the Prince of Wales to get out and about in Commonwealth countries. I also believed that there were many opportunities for the Prince of Wales to speak at the five or six ministerial meetings we had every year. Leaders must feel they know and are in a political comfort zone with the king-to-be.

The Queen keeps rude good health so, even though she is in her 80s, it's hard to imagine the world without her. It's well known that there is an agreed funeral plan for the Queen and other members of the Royal Family, so that Palace and government officials are prepared for 'the unthinkable' and the remarkably efficient British system of pageantry and protocol can be activated. I have attended three royal funerals and two royal weddings and given all the challenges of media, foreign dignitaries and large crowds, these events went seamlessly. They were planned to the finest detail and it paid off.

As Palace officials have long had to plan for the Queen's death, I also had to give some thought to what might happen in relation to the role of head of the Commonwealth when that day came. It is not an inherited role so, while the Prince of Wales would automatically become king, there would have to be a process for managing a transition to head of the Commonwealth. If it happened on my watch, the process would be along these lines: I would see if there was a consensus among Commonwealth leaders in favour of the Prince of Wales. If this was quickly apparent, an announcement could be made before the Queen's funeral and it could subsequently be included in the new sovereign's titles. If there was no consensus, the issue could be held over until the next Commonwealth Heads of Government meeting. I am thankful I never had the task of implementing a head of Commonwealth transition.

I went to dinner at 11 Downing Street, towards the end of 2003. It was my first time at the official residence of the chancellor of the exchequer, then Gordon Brown. It is always surprising, given the street view, just how spacious these places are, with the reception and dining rooms easily catering for large numbers. It was a pleasant gathering of some twenty people mostly from the commercial and political domains, including the guest of honour, the Italian finance minister.

At one point, Gordon said to his guest: 'You've met Don over here,' as he gestured in my direction, and continued: 'He's head of the British Commonwealth.' I laughed and said, 'Sorry, Gordon, wrong on two counts. The Queen is the head, and the British Commonwealth died in 1949 before you were born.' The Italian laughed and Gordon smiled at his error.

A few years later, on becoming Prime Minister, Gordon became a very good friend of the Commonwealth, but I remember thinking at the time, my goodness, we still have a long way to go.

I once made a special visit to the heart of Britain's military training establishment, Sandhurst at Camberley, Surrey, where the two princes, William and Harry, did their training. I was there to address the assembled cadets. You cannot help but be impressed with the history of these military universities, and are reminded of it by all the photos and pictures that adorn the walls and the regimental flags in some special rooms. Coming also from a military family and temporarily having been a soldier, it wasn't an alien setting for me.

I also saw something I had not seen in years: a hard-bitten sergeant-major dressing down young officers. 'Sir, you will not run in the corridor, *sir*!' And the memorable line: 'I will call you "sir" because I have to. You will call me "sir" to prove you're not imbecilic, *sir*.'

It was a good stimulating evening and I got lots of good questions after my speech to the cadets.

An extremely pleasant official duty was attending the wedding of Prince Charles and Camilla Parker Bowles in April 2005. Prior to the day, there had been uncertainty as to where the wedding was to take place. In the end, Clare and I joined about 800 others at St George's Chapel, Windsor Castle, for the service after the civil nuptials at the local town hall. We sat among the many governors general and some other Commonwealth leaders. Opposite us, actor Rowan Atkinson looked in character as Mr Bean during the singing of hymns and even managed to sit down and stand up at the wrong time, causing everyone around us a small chuckle.

The reception that followed produced an upswell of goodwill towards a man who had gone though years of embarrassment by way of lurid headlines about the breakdown of his marriage to Princess Diana and his love for Camilla. Now they were man and wife and there was a palpable sense of relief among guests, family and the couple themselves.

During the reception I got a friendly little royal wave and so moved across to the Queen. She was chatting with her senior farm staff, which enabled her to introduce me: 'Don used to farm in New Zealand. He'll understand your problems with the heifers.'

A little later the Duke of Edinburgh told me that he had discovered some cousins in Germany the previous week that he had not known existed. 'Absolutely amazing, these chaps scurrying around Bavaria.'

In November 2007, the Prince of Wales and the Duchess of Cornwall visited Kampala in Uganda for the CHOGM after some other Commonwealth interaction with leaders and ministers. It proved to be well worth the effort. The Prince was a great hit with schoolchildren, participated in the Foreign Ministers' Forum and made a good impression with Commonwealth civil society groups.

The Prince made useful contact with a wide range of other Commonwealth organisations. He seemed to be smiling most of the time, and genuinely engaged. The Duchess, relatively new then to the rigours of foreign visits, came across as a warm and down-to-earth woman, and it helped establish her firmly by her husband's side and win her acceptance from Commonwealth leaders. Clare and I enjoyed the last evening of the CHOGM, after the Queen's departure, chatting over dinner with the Prince and Duchess, hosted by President Museveni and his wife, Janet.

In a chat with the new foreign secretary, David Miliband, in July 2007 about the role of the Prince of Wales, I said that the pressure must be maintained to keep up Commonwealth member country visits. Miliband wasn't aware that the role of head of the Commonwealth wasn't an inherited position. I thought at the time, you've got to keep these ministers focused, because the FCO machine, with its very EU and USA orientation, will just keep grinding away, doing what it wants to do.

At the end of my term Clare and I invited the Queen and the Duke to our residence in Mayfair for a farewell lunch in March 2008. We were delighted they accepted, especially as according to the Palace it was the first time in more than seven years that they had been to a private house in London. Clare organised

Peter Gordon, the well-known New Zealand chef, to cater for the lunch. He didn't tell his two waiting staff who they were serving or even where they were going until a few minutes before they arrived. As they pulled up outside our place, one of them told Peter she'd been to our house before, obviously a bit disappointed it was only us she was going to be serving. The other apparently thought George Clooney might be there. Both were happily taken aback to find it was to be the Queen and the Duke.

It was very easy and relaxing, with security deliberately kept to a minimum and unobtrusive so as not to draw attention to the visitors. A drink, a chat about the garden and talk over lunch about the two young princes, the New Zealand Army (my late father's portrait in his general's uniform hung on the wall), wines of New Zealand, the 2007 CHOGM host President Museveni of Uganda, Rwanda and favourite TV programmes. At the appropriate time, the dark green Jaguar returned to our front door. The Queen was given a bouquet of flowers by our son James, then ten, and allowed home from his school over the road for ten minutes to perform this duty. We hadn't told him who was coming to lunch or why he was coming home from school for a short time, so when he went back and told his teachers and classmates what he'd been doing they were naturally a little sceptical! Peter Gordon and his staff met and shook hands with the Queen and Duke and we saw them into their car. They disappeared in virtual anonymity into the London traffic for the three-minute drive back to Buckingham Palace.

And so to my final call on the Queen. There had been speculation among my senior staff that, like my two predecessors, this was when I would receive a knighthood from the Queen. I thought otherwise, knowing Helen Clark, then Prime Minister of New Zealand, was opposed to titular honours and would not welcome their return in any form in New Zealand.

I told the Queen I was returning with my family to New Zealand but would come back from time to time. I was both a fifth-generation New Zealander and a British citizen, having been born in London while my New Zealand parents were based there, but was determinedly Kiwi in every respect including my choice of passport. She then took me over to a table where there were two signed photographs, one of her and one of the Duke, for me to take home, commenting with a small smile that it was 'not much for eight years' service'. With a bigger smile, she then gave me a very attractive letter opener, saying she was not sure what I would use it for – or against. A warm handshake and then we agreed we would meet again before long at the Ed Hillary Memorial Service at Windsor. By that time I was out of office by a few weeks but I had known Sir Ed and Lady Hillary for many years and was attending in a personal capacity.

The Queen did not knight me that day but she did two things that reassured me she thought I'd done my best in the job. One was a simple but telling comment in the speech to Commonwealth leaders in Uganda, where she paid me a tribute and ended by saying, 'We will miss you.'

The other came by way of a registered letter to my home in New Zealand from Buckingham Palace in January 2009. I was asked if I would accept from the Queen a GCVO, Knight Grand Cross of the Victorian Order. I was genuinely taken aback. I had been asked in November 1999 if I would accept a knighthood from the Queen, on the recommendation of the New Zealand government, in recognition of my services as an MP and minister of the Crown. I declined that offer, on the eve of my departure for my new job in London, as I had been supportive of the review and eventual abolition of titular honours in New Zealand. I would have felt uncomfortable and a little hypocritical accepting the offered GNZM. I had no such reservations about a personal honour from the Queen, not tied to my country or hers, entirely within her discretion. I asked that the announcement be made on Commonwealth Day, in March, and returned to the UK in July that year for a private investiture in the Queen's apartments in Buckingham Palace.

Queen Elizabeth II is an amazing and impressive lady. Commonwealth people everywhere have benefited from her quiet but firm leadership. There has never been anybody during her lifetime with such a commitment to the Commonwealth, its peoples and its aspirations. She promised as such in 1952 and has never been found wanting. I could not have had a better 'boss'.

CHAPTER 3

Facing the Challenges

There had been a widespread view for some time that the structure of the Commonwealth was preventing it from facing up to some of the most important issues involving its members. One of the main events in the development of the modern Commonwealth took place four years before I became Secretary-General, although as New Zealand's foreign minister I was closely involved. It was the Commonwealth's answer to the fundamental question: how should nations respond when other member countries act in ways that transgress Commonwealth values and principles?

What should be the Commonwealth's response when there are military coups in member states, when elections are delayed or abandoned, when countries imprison and even execute citizens who dissent? Should the modern Commonwealth even attempt to meet these challenges? Or should it remain, in the words of Dr Hastings Banda (quoted in the Introduction), merely 'the best club in the world'?

The majority of members have been very clear in recent years that a more active role is the one that should be followed. There was a widespread view among members that we needed some new mechanism or body that could act fast and flexibly and address issues as they arose. In essence, the Commonwealth needed to be strengthened. Being the best club in the world wasn't enough.

An important first step had been setting up the office of Secretary-General. Thirty years later, in November 1995, came the decision to establish the Commonwealth Ministerial Action Group, soon universally known as CMAG. Since then CMAG has played a vital and valuable role in strengthening the values of the Commonwealth.

CMAG has not been without controversy. For some, it's an organisation that never does enough nor is tough enough. To others it's grossly unfair that this organisation appears to be able to act as investigator, prosecutor and judge on a state that appears to violate Commonwealth principles. Some say it's an organisation that has far too much power and authority, others that it's not aggressive enough.

Of all the current international political organisations only the Pacific Islands Forum (PIF) has a similar facility. No Commonwealth members seek to be on CMAG's agenda. Yet most agree that CMAG has determinedly and effectively upheld Commonwealth principles. As I explain elsewhere in the book, the mere threat of being placed on the CMAG agenda has in itself been enough to deter certain nations from behaving in a particular way.

Some would discard it, others would give it more authority, but for all its deficiencies it has, in my opinion, played a very valuable role in strengthening the values of the Commonwealth within its membership.

It's doubtful that such an organisation could have been put together so rapidly, so comprehensively, if it had not been for the infamous actions of General Sani Abacha, the military dictator of Nigeria, who on 10 November 1995 summarily executed thirteen people, including the well-known writer Ken Saro-Wiwa.

Whether General Abacha knew that Commonwealth leaders were all meeting in New Zealand (he clearly had no intention of attending) for their biennial Commonwealth Heads of

Government Meeting (CHOGM) at that time, or whether he just didn't care, has not been established. What is known is that despite appeals to the Nigerian foreign minister, Tom Ikimi, when he was in Auckland by a number of Commonwealth leaders or ministers such as myself, the executions went ahead.

Commonwealth leaders were disturbed, some were furious and President Nelson Mandela was reportedly incandescent with rage.

In the few months before the CHOGM, I had been talking to other foreign ministers about the need to put pressure on the Nigerian government over the lack of democracy and the abuse of human rights that was occurring. I had hoped to obtain consent from the Commonwealth leaders to have an ongoing contact group of ministers who would continue to press for prisoner releases in Nigeria and a return to democracy.

Admittedly, the Commonwealth was used to Nigeria's rollercoaster style of governance, in and out of military dictatorships; but it was a big and important African country, and a very early and strongly committed member of the Commonwealth.

However, it was due to the force of Mandela's personality, no doubt reflecting his own period as a political prisoner, that thoughts of a contact group got swept away when leaders at the CHOGM Retreat in 1995 at Millbrook, in the South Island of New Zealand, decided to suspend Nigeria from the Commonwealth. Following that, a permanent group of foreign ministers was set up to continue to monitor the situation. It became known as the Commonwealth Ministerial Action Group, or CMAG.

Officials then spent time drafting how CMAG would operate to bring Nigeria back to being a full member. The key phrase that was ultimately adopted as a basis for CMAG action was that an errant country 'has persistently violated Commonwealth values and principles'. CMAG has met regularly since that time, dealing with issues and suspensions from Nigeria and Sierra Leone to Pakistan, Fiji and Zimbabwe.

Legal purists will find many weaknesses in its setting up, structure, modus operandi and resolutions. In strictly legal terms they would be right, but it has to be recognised that CMAG is a political group. Its membership is made up not of officials but of current foreign ministers, who are expected to address political issues rather than legal ones.

One would normally expect such an organisation to have rules and penalties for those who breach the rules clearly set out and adopted in advance. But not so the Commonwealth.

Let's go back a few years.

From the Second World War to the mid-1960s, Commonwealth prime ministers held most of their meetings in London, where discussions were very general and economics-orientated. It wasn't until the landmark CHOGM in Singapore in 1971 that the leaders debated and accepted a 'Declaration of Principles', which set out the values that all would agree to and abide by. Thenceforth, CHOGMs were held every two years at different locations.

Then fast-forward to the CHOGM in Harare, Zimbabwe, in 1991, when the leaders were focusing again on the issue of values, principles and generally what they all stood for. They acknowledged that the Singapore principles had stood the test of time over twenty years, but the challenge in that year was to apply these principles to the contemporary situation. The Harare Commonwealth Declaration was accordingly adopted. Ironically, it was carefully managed through the meeting by the then chair, none other than President Robert Mugabe, who a decade later would be found to be a serious transgressor, much to his chagrin and to the disappointment of his fellow leaders.

Having reconfirmed the principles to which the Commonwealth was committed, the leaders went on to underline the fundamental political values underpinning democratic governments: judiciaries, human rights, equal opportunities and so on. The need was for all to receive the benefits of development, protect the environment, fight drug trafficking, help small states and support the UN and other international institutions.

All Commonwealth organisations were to help advance these goals, including equality for women, access to education for all, a stable international framework, sound economic policies and adequate flow of resources from developed to developing countries. This wasn't the full list, but it provides a general idea of what was expected.

One area where some member countries, not so wedded to these principles, wished to give themselves more flexible boundaries was in the sensitive area of governance. They appeared happy to highlight the universality of the principles, but they wished to include references to 'democratic processes and institutions which reflect national circumstances'. For some it was clearly a case of 'We'll do it our way.' Not surprisingly, this was to be used by some as a defence against the indefensible. Nevertheless, the declaration was wide-ranging and comprehensive and created high but not impossible expectations.

Now back to 1995 at Millbrook Lodge in New Zealand. Having decided to suspend Nigeria from all Commonwealth activity, and also to place Sierra Leone and The Gambia on the agenda of the Commonwealth Ministerial Action Group (CMAG) – a lesser charge whereby surveillance and contact was maintained – the leaders then accepted what came to be formally known as the Millbrook Commonwealth Action Plan on the Harare Commonwealth Declaration. The document highlighted the key parts of the Harare Declaration, to do with advancing fundamental Commonwealth political values, promoting sustainable development and facilitating consensus-building.

Then in a new departure, to give substance to the Nigerian suspension, a section was added entitled 'Measures in response to violations of Harare Principles', followed by eight points designed to 'encourage the restoration of the Harare Principles' – in other words, a return to democracy. Three of those points referred to either levels of suspension or other measures.

The declaration then called for the creation of a 'Commonwealth Ministerial Action Group' as a mechanism for the implementation of those required measures. In this way the Millbrook document became a set of guidelines used by the Ministerial Action Group when reaching decisions.

Of course, not every perceived violation of a Commonwealth principle is a square hole awaiting a square peg. For years afterwards, through many CMAG meetings, there was continuing debate about definitions, on what had gone before, on what should be done, on the ability to act – and, of course, on the repercussions.

If a legal purist were to try to find a clear strand of legal thinking, which began with the origins of the Commonwealth and then took in the Singapore, Harare and Millbrook Declarations, he or she would be struggling. The key point is that it can be ascertained in all of these developments that they are *political* documents, written by politicians for political purposes. Thus it soon became apparent to the first group of eight foreign ministers meeting as CMAG that, on the margins of violations by Commonwealth countries, what is best for country A may not be suitable for country B.

Seventeen years on from the setting up of CMAG, we can therefore conclude that when it comes to a group of member states within an organisation such as the Commonwealth wishing to highlight a democratic deficiency or even punish one of their own, a CMAG might not always be the best possible mechanism. But I do believe that globally it's the best to date.

From CMAG's very first meeting held in Marlborough House in December 1995, it became apparent that whatever the issue or problem on the agenda, the members, all being foreign ministers, would approach things differently, and certainly never bureaucratically. In all my time of involvement, first as a minister and later as Secretary-General, it was clear that the country or government under scrutiny could generally depend on a little more support from its geographical neighbours or those of a similar ethnicity or religious background. The feeling would be conveyed that 'We know them better and we know how to deal with them.' As ministers got to know each other and began to better understand each other, the chemistry of the meetings improved. It often followed that the outcomes were of a productive rather than a punitive nature.

At the first meeting of CMAG in 1995, there was a lengthy discussion about who should be chair of the group. As CMAG had been set up in New Zealand, there was a strong case for me to be in the chair. On the other hand, all the countries that had been placed on the agenda – Nigeria, Sierra Leone and The Gambia – were African. So there was strong support for the foreign minister of Zimbabwe, Stan Mudenge, to take the position. He was backed by South Africa and Ghana, with tentative support from Jamaica.

After some discussion the elderly freedom fighter and ANC activist Alfred Nzo, the South African foreign minister, said: 'Don, we like you very much, but we think Stan's the right man now.' Given later events, it was an interesting choice. There was nothing more for me to say and so it was concluded. The Secretary-General, Chief Emeka Anyaoku, then nominated me as the vice-chair.

That turned out to be one of the easier issues compared with the dealings we had with Foreign Minister Tom Ikimi of Nigeria and President Jammeh of The Gambia.

Members agreed to receive written submissions on the issues in front of CMAG where appropriate and to review its modus operandi whenever necessary. So from the beginning CMAG was saying not only 'This is the way we'll do it now', but also 'That may change depending on circumstances.'

At the beginning, Nigeria was the most serious matter before the ministers. No one was prepared to forgive General Abacha for the executions. After all, they had been the catalyst that had prompted the creation of CMAG in the first place. After much discussion, ministers agreed to a series of restrictions on Nigeria's Commonwealth participation. If all else failed, it would move for further actions, which would have financial consequences. It concluded by observing that the underlying objective was to get that country back to democracy and full Commonwealth membership.

While at the CHOGM in New Zealand, the leaders, as mentioned earlier, also voiced their concerns about The Gambia and Sierra Leone, but they were not suspended from the Commonwealth. Knowing that both countries were under significant military influence, which could not be ignored, the heads in their wisdom agreed that they should suffer some penalty for their democratic deficiencies, Sierra Leone being under the de facto control of one Johnny Paul Koroma, and President Jammeh having taken power at the point of a gun. So they were 'put on the CMAG agenda', meaning they would be under constant surveillance, which was not appreciated by President Jammeh.

Due to the continuing deterioration of the situation in Sierra Leone, and the appalling aggressive behaviour of the Revolutionary United Front (RUF) led by Foday Sankoh in Sierra Leone, that country, in July 1997, was 'suspended from the councils of the Commonwealth'. This was a category of restriction that did not allow Sierra Leone to attend Commonwealth meetings, but it could remain as a member. It also meant that Nigeria would not be totally isolated as the sole transgressor.

As the CMAG had already decided to send a small mission to The Gambia to hurry them along towards an election, they also decided to send a five-minister mission to Nigeria. Ghana, Jamaica, Malaysia, New Zealand and Zimbabwe were the members. Needless to say, the idea of a group of ministers descending on Abuja to criticise General Abacha and the regime was likely to be too much for the latter to stomach.

We knew we were in for a long game. At the same time the Nigerian diplomatic machine was in full gear, letting it be known to the African members in CMAG – Ghana, South Africa and Zimbabwe – as well as to the Secretary-General that they expected to be treated as befitted the most senior, most populous and economically the near-strongest of the African family – not as some small, juvenile and weak renegade. The offer of a CMAG visit was emphatically rejected.

So ministers concluded, after much debate, to up the pressure by considering a series of smart sanctions aimed at the leadership on visas, education outside Nigeria, sporting bans and downgrading of diplomatic missions.

There was also a feeling among the group that it would be useful to signal the next tranche of restrictions that would be taken if there was no adequate response. They then announced they were prepared to go further by having discussions with the European Union, the United States and the United Nations to bring about some collective restrictions on banking, overseas-held assets and air links.

So now CMAG was being put to the test, the pressure was working. On 24 and 25 June 1996, Tom Ikimi led a delegation into a Marlborough House meeting of CMAG. Nothing was going to stop him giving the ministerial group a broadside of his views. How dare anyone, least of all fellow foreign ministers, have the temerity to criticise and judge Nigeria? I have to admit it was an Oscar-winning performance, but I couldn't help reflecting on those many people in Nigeria who had been killed or summarily detained.

It was the first close-up encounter I had had with a group of well-educated Nigerians of this kind. They emphasised in subtle and not-so-subtle ways their inherent belief in their supremacy – not just within West Africa or Africa, but on the world stage. They had perfected the speech, the body language and the humour, all set off in those beautiful flowing robes.

It wasn't just Minister Ikimi but the whole entourage who made it clear that the Commonwealth had made a huge mistake suspending such an important country. But for the fact that they placed great emphasis on the value of the Commonwealth, they probably would not be there.

Of course, we were eternally grateful for this dialogue, but most of us remained very sceptical. Was it likely that President Abacha would be prepared to move towards democratic elections and thus possibly put himself out of a job? We doubted it.

At this CMAG meeting we were conscious that our discussions about The Gambia and Sierra Leone were equally important to the citizens of those countries. At that time we were pleased that the transition programmes in The Gambia were working and that the parliamentary elections in Sierra Leone had passed with a degree of optimism, even if the marauding RUF was still a problem.

But only months later at the meeting of CMAG on 28 August 1996, ministers were to feel The Gambia had slipped backwards when the government banned certain political parties and personalities from the upcoming elections. CMAG was now beginning to better understand that President Jammeh wanted perpetually tight controls, total predictability and political enemies out of the way. They decided that the ban had to be rescinded or no observers would be sent to monitor the elections.

It does seem a characteristic of many military leaders – those who gain power at the point of a gun – that they do not necessarily translate into democrats. They don't really trust the people. After all, military training is all about controlling a situation, not leaving things to chance and not wishing for surprises. Combined with this seems to be the thought that if you live by the gun so you can die by the gun, so you never lie easy in bed. President Jammeh, however, could not bring himself to walk out of the Commonwealth, and so began a tortuous process of negotiation,

with Jammeh conceding only a little at a time. We had serious
doubts about his real commitment to the Commonwealth.

From 18 to 21 November 1996 a CMAG group of ministers
and officials visited Abuja in the hope of making some progress with the Nigerians. There we received the full treatment
of Nigerian hospitality: efficient facilitation through Lagos and
later into Abuja, time for informal discussions and even some
friendly back-slapping, but not without their constant assertive
persuasiveness. There were long explanations of why the military
had to take over a 'failing state' – and how it would take time to
prepare for an election. Despite all the delays, we were assured
that its election transition programme was on target for elections
in late 1998, some two years away.

When I was invited to sit beside Foreign Minister Tom Ikimi
at a lunch break he asked me how long it would be before the
suspension was lifted. I said Nigeria had a long way to go, particularly in getting the democratic structure right and in releasing
all these people who were dubiously detained. He then surprised
me by saying, 'If I released some of them today, will it make a
difference?'

Well, I thought, what a question. Is he serious? Does he have
the authority? And could he deliver? Or was this just another
piece of gamesmanship? Knowing I had to leave for Manila
at 3 p.m. I said, 'If you go back into the meeting and tell
everyone the release dates, I'm sure that will be well received.'
I didn't attend the rest of the meeting, and Ikimi's stance
remained unchanged.

That wasn't the only thing that didn't go smoothly. My New
Zealand staff member Kirsty Graham and I were driven to Abuja
airport and dropped off at the lounge, only to discover that no
one was there. No officials, no security, no aircraft, no airline
staff, not even any cleaners. The only sign of life was a dog trot-
ting across the runway.

After many phone calls, none of them successful, we heard
a plane. A corporate jet taxied up. The gentleman who alighted

from the flight deck walked over and said he was contracted to fly to Lagos and was I Baron Chalker? I said, 'If you're flying to Lagos, I certainly am Baron Chalker.' I had to pick up a Lufthansa flight to Frankfurt from Lagos in three hours' time. The plane looked airworthy, and the flight deck crew looked professional and competent. There appeared to be no alternative.

I did not think that Baroness Lynda Chalker, who was attending as a Foreign Office minister in place of Foreign Secretary Malcolm Rifkind, whom I had left with the CMAG delegation in Abuja, could possibly need this aircraft tonight. If she did, it could always come back to get her. So we gratefully boarded and slumped back in the first-class seats. It was particularly nice after take-off to be offered a large gin and tonic, of which Kirsty and I consumed more than one.

At about this time there was praise for what CMAG and the Commonwealth were doing, but some exasperation that other organisations were not doing more. All agreed it was a deteriorating situation in Nigeria; respect for the law had gone, and the path back to democracy looked bleak. Some were urging that we get tougher, which provided CMAG with a useful platform from which to pursue its objective. No one was able to discern any credible progress.

On 8 June 1998, President Sani Abacha died of a heart attack. This dictator, who had been close to the centre of successive governments since the 1960s, who had fleeced the country of some US$4 billion, died in the company of a couple of prostitutes who allegedly gave him an apple laced with cyanide. Someone will know the full story, and no doubt it will emerge some day. But with the death of this fifty-four-year-old soldier things suddenly started to happen that were music to CMAG's ears.

The head of the armed forces, General Abdulsalami Abubakar, became head of state and immediately announced there would be elections in February 1999, with a new president inaugurated in

June. He had released many political prisoners, including General Obasanjo, who on his release said 'the Commonwealth without CMAG is nothing' and praised the group for its perseverance, which had assisted his release. At an October 1998 CMAG meeting, Tom Ikimi had been replaced by Ignatius Olisemeka, a very experienced player. He outlined the programme by which Nigeria could return to democracy and also thanked CMAG for its determination.

Sierra Leone posed CMAG with very serious problems because for a long period it was essentially government-less. Everyone was crossing their fingers that there could be reconciliation between the government of Tejan Kabbah and the RUF from the time Sierra Leone was put on the agenda in 1995 and later suspended from the councils on 11 July 1997. The UK foreign secretary called for reconciliation between the two groups, which, laudable though it was, caused me to wonder why we in the West expected this to happen quickly and easily in a developing country. If I had been involved in supporting a long period of killing, maiming, assaulting or raping a defined group of people in my own country, or been on the receiving end of such actions, to just move to have meetings of reconciliation after a peace agreement might have been too much to stomach. Yet from my time of meeting many from Sierra Leone who had lost family or limbs or homes during this protracted civil war, I came to admire these people for their endurance of such physical suffering, and the forgiveness they were prepared to grant. Maybe there was just no alternative in this post-civil war period.

Once the government of Tejan Kabbah was back in office from 10 March 1998 and therefore the country was no longer deemed to be in serious violation of Commonwealth principles, CMAG tasked the Secretariat with continuing involvement in reconstruction, and suspension was lifted on 9 October 1998; however, at the request of President Kabbah, CMAG remained engaged in a supportive role. 'We don't wish to be forgotten' were his words.

By October 1999 all was ready for us to give a second report to CHOGM leaders, this time in Durban, South Africa. We were well prepared – until General Musharraf decided that as head of the Pakistan armed forces he would take over the democratically elected government of his country. From then on Pakistan proved a continuing problem for CMAG and the Commonwealth. This persisted throughout my time as Secretary-General, as I discuss in detail in Chapter 7.

A military coup in a member state leaves few doubts among CMAG members about their expected response. Thus a special meeting was called on 18 October, only a week after the coup. It was not a long debate, but members saw no alternative but to 'suspend from the councils of the Commonwealth' – despite the fact that the coup had been bloodless and that many people were actually rather pleased it had happened. A mission led by Canadian Foreign Minister Lloyd Axworthy and including Billie Miller of Barbados, Victor Gbeho of Ghana and Musa Hitam of Malaysia was asked to visit Pakistan and do what it could to hasten the country's return to democracy.

CMAG was now reaching a new level of maturity. The group was working well together and it was accepted by all Commonwealth members as having a major role to play. For those on the receiving end of its interventions, CMAG was proving to be a group that could not be ignored. This was just as well because after the Lloyd Axworthy mission had made it very clear what was expected of the Pakistan military regime, the Commonwealth became *persona non grata* in Islamabad for a time. The military leaders of Pakistan had regularly run the government since independence in 1947 and virtually saw this intervention as business as usual. Why should anyone be surprised? They certainly felt that they didn't need to be lectured by anyone. CMAG played a key role (and, I believe, a useful one) in the suspension of Pakistan from the Commonwealth from 1999 to 2005, and again in November 2007 (see Chapter 7).

At the CHOGM in Durban in November 1999, the heads of government gave CMAG their full endorsement and encouragement. They also asked for an overall review of CMAG's mandate, and to replace as members New Zealand with Australia and Ghana with Nigeria. It was also decided that no country should serve more than two terms. This did not please the United Kingdom or Canada (the former, of course, hoping for a United Nations Security Council-style 'permanent status'). But that was not how other countries saw it.

For me, having now departed CMAG membership as a minister, I was elected at the CHOGM to be the Secretary-General and hence took up my new role within the group. I was clearly familiar with CMAG's history since its inception.

My new chief of staff Amitav Banerji, a highly trained diplomat from India, as a member of the Political Affairs Division within the Secretariat had also followed CMAG from its inception and was well placed to follow through as a most useful adviser to me, as he knew all the players. He and I survived together for the full eight years, which was rather remarkable and most useful for me. We immediately discussed the make-up, strengths and weaknesses of the new CMAG membership.

I called the first meeting together in May 2000 and was pleased that it took no time in establishing that the group would accept Foreign Ministers Mompati Merafhe of Botswana as the chair, and Billie Miller from the Caribbean as vice-chair. Both were excellent choices. Merafhe was an experienced, well-balanced former army officer who was rock-solid on people's rights. Miller was as strong a human rights advocate as you would find. Tun Musa Hitam, from Malaysia, had indicated his willingness to be the chair, but he wasn't a foreign minister. Musa's status as 'Special Envoy of the Malaysian Prime Minister' meant that he sat a little differently and to one side of all the other ministers, so the support was not forthcoming. However, I can say that Musa Hitam's contribution to CMAG was outstanding over a six-year period. He was always very concise and asked the most penetrating questions. His commitment to human rights never deviated from his moral compass. This was perhaps not quite what Malaysian Prime Minister Dr Mahathir expected.

So the first meeting got under way, and all the principal issues were straightforward. What the ministers wanted to talk about, however, was Zimbabwe, which was not on the agenda but was picked up under 'any other business'.

Zimbabwe was an area on which the ministers were not always united. Their views ranged from 'Do we have a mandate to have such a discussion?' to 'Surely we can talk about anything?' and 'Should we not wait until our leaders have decided what we can discuss?' Well, discuss it they did, even though there was no mention of the discussion in the concluding statement (see Chapter 5).

And so began a long, tortuous – and in the end not very productive – relationship between CMAG, myself and the Zimbabwe government or, more precisely, President Robert Mugabe. In fact, the first threat came immediately from Foreign Minister Mudenge: 'If CMAG discusses Zimbabwe there'll be no cooperation from us.' The intricacies of the Zimbabwe issue are discussed in more detail in Chapters 5 and 6.

The next issue to test CMAG's effectiveness was Fiji in May 2000, where a group of citizens led by one George Speight had locked up members of the Fiji Parliament, dividing them along racial lines in two rooms in the Parliament buildings.

It will be known by many that for about a hundred years the Fiji Islands had had a population evenly divided between the indigenous, mostly Melanesian peoples and the Indian community, brought from South Asia to work the sugar plantations. They never lived easily together and soon the uneasy peace exploded with the first coup against an Indo-Fijian government in 1987. Peace was established but it was never truly peaceful. Now here was another coup.

Once again a special CMAG crisis meeting was held on 6 June 2000, followed by immediate suspension of Fiji from the councils of the Commonwealth. It was also decided to dispatch a ministerial mission consisting of the chair, Merafhe from Botswana, Foreign Minister Alexander Downer from Australia, Musa Hitam from Malaysia and also Phil Goff, my successor as New Zealand foreign minister.

For a while no one was too sure who was really behind the coup leader George Speight, but there was much gossip in Suva that it was all rather sudden after a number of indigenous Fijians got together and decided they just could not stomach the leadership of Prime Minister Mahendra Chaudhry, a former tough trade unionist and an Indo-Fijian. It was the third coup in Fiji in fourteen years. When I visited with Sergio de Mello, a Brazilian diplomat later killed in Iraq, to see if we could break the deadlock (see Chapter 10), Speight was on a high, and it would be a while before he came back to earth. Later Speight was effectively sidelined, then jailed and put on trial for treason.

Ratu Sir Kamisese Mara, independent Fiji's first leader, was now President again, but formally only until 29 May, when he resigned but still retained authority. It wasn't until 13 July that Ratu Josefa Iloilo took over as President. I knew how difficult and prickly he was about anyone lecturing him on what to do. But it had to be done. I knew I had to get someone there who could get alongside him but who carried no baggage and could steer him into an appropriate course of action. No New Zealander, Australian, British or Pacific Islander would be even let in the door. I spoke to President Mbeki of South Africa, chair of the Commonwealth, telling him who and what I wanted, and he invited me to contact three of his judges. These were people that Ratu Mara could not easily criticise in advance. I did talk to them and the one that appealed to me was Justice Pius Langa. He was head of the South African constitutional court, had fought against apartheid, was highly regarded in legal circles and had done some peace-making in Lesotho. So with his and Mbeiki's consent, and with the assistance of my two staff members, Langa went to Fiji in December 2000.

As I predicted, Ratu Mara would not be easy. 'What does this African man know about Fiji?' he was heard to say in his intimidating way. But Justice Langa had a huge intellect, was patient and smiled a lot. Eventually, Ratu Mara and other Fijians came round to believing that this man was pretty good. In all Langa made six visits. Each was difficult and movement was incremental, but slowly progress was made. So by June 2001 the Commonwealth was invited to observe elections the government agreed to have in August 2001, and following a reasonably positive report, suspension was lifted on 20 December, although Fiji remained on the agenda of CMAG. The coup is discussed in more detail in Chapter 10.

Parallel to all these events was the work of a High Level Review Group, which had been asked by leaders to assess how the Secretariat and particularly CMAG could function better. As two members of this group were Zimbabwean and Tanzanian, there was a strong push by them to ensure that short of a military coup, CMAG had no entitlement to intrude into any of the workings of a member state. This group spent a lot of time on this issue, but I'm sad to say that at the end not much had changed to enhance CMAG's role. I would, however, give President Mbeki credit for not allowing CMAG to be pulled backwards to a position of impotence, as some were seeking to do.

By March 2001 the issue of Zimbabwe was at the centre of all Commonwealth discussion. The majority of ministers wanted to do something. CMAG discussed a number of options – an Eminent Persons' Group, special envoys, ministerial groups – wishing at all times to keep out of the Zimbabwe–United Kingdom crossfire, on issues highlighted daily in the British

press. Whatever was done would not be welcome, but that was
no reason to sit and wait.

I cite this as an example of foreign ministers having the inherent political sensitivity to know how far they could push an issue.
It was always evident that whenever an official took the place of
a minister, that person would present their government line, then
sit back. CMAG ministers were prepared to debate with give
and take, but in the end they had to feel right politically about a
position and know they were all together.

Just how far CMAG could and should go remained a constant
subject of discussion, particularly on Zimbabwe. In a forceful
statement to the March 2001 CMAG meeting, Merafhe made
a profound comment. He said there appeared to be a far too
strict interpretation by some of Millbrook: 'In all my reading of
both Harare and Millbrook, there are no explicit restrictions,
there has been too narrow an interpretation, we must look at
the principal values, from Singapore to Harare to Milbrook.' He
went on to say, 'We have a strong position, we can move with
confidence.' Billie Miller responded in agreement: 'Mudenge [the
previous chair] had a very narrow interpretation. We must break
out of those constraints.'

From an African and an African-Caribbean, this was music to
the ears of Australia's Alexander Downer, Jack Straw, the newly
appointed UK foreign secretary, and John Manley, Canada's foreign minister. CMAG now moved smoothly and determinedly to
a more demanding level of expectation. The time had ended for
Zimbabwe not to be on the agenda.

The pre-CHOGM CMAG meeting in Coolum in March 2002
wanted to come down heavily on Zimbabwe and included words
such as 'suspension' in the draft communiqué. Of course, these
were fighting words to the African members. However, among
the African leaders, in particular President Obasanjo of Nigeria,
there was real worry about how this complicated Zimbabwe

issue would pan out. All knew there was a problem, all found it embarrassing, yet none wanted to be seen to be criticising a fellow African, particularly one such as Robert Mugabe, whose front-line-state credentials were above criticism.

It was Obasanjo who, on hearing that CMAG was about to recommend suspension, and knowing that the Zimbabweans would detonate as a result, promptly proposed the formation of a troika, being the former, present and future chairs of CHOGMs (Mbeki, Howard, Obasanjo) to take over the issue (for the setting up and workings of the troika, see Chapters 5 and 6).

From that point on CMAG played a secondary role, as following the flawed presidential election a few weeks later (9–11 March in 2002), Zimbabwe was then suspended from the councils of the Commonwealth. There it remained until the CHOGM in Nigeria in 2003, when the suspension was extended, prompting President Mugabe to withdraw his country from membership.

Looking back with hindsight on the way the Commonwealth handled the difficult Zimbabwe issue, it's interesting that as the drama unfolded, CMAG was actually able to be used as a tactical trade-off. Early on, Mugabe was enraged at the possibility that Zimbabwe might be placed on the CMAG agenda. In return for not doing so we were able to get his grudging consent to the troika and the visit of a group of eminent Commonwealth persons, which held meetings in the country.

In the end, neither CMAG nor CHOGMs were successful in the face of continuing hostility and intransigence from Mugabe, and Zimbabwe eventually walked out of the Commonwealth on 29 November 2003, with the President declaring that 'the Commonwealth has become a mere club'.

So the existence of CMAG didn't bring Zimbabwe to heel nor prevent it from pulling out of the Commonwealth. Did CMAG itself make a positive contribution to the way the Commonwealth dealt with Zimbabwe? Yes, I'm very sure it did.

In trying to evaluate the worth of the troika, one comes to the conclusion that it was a very neat way out of a highly charged political situation. The authority of the Commonwealth leadership of the troika was never in doubt and in fact beyond questioning by Mugabe's African friends. Its weakness lay in the troika's inability to maintain a constant, low-level contact with people in Harare, which would be normal if they were following a more conventional process. Although the troika expected me to remain engaged, it was Mugabe who decided I was equally complicit in the suspension and certainly not welcome in Harare.

If, however, the leaders had accepted the CMAG report at the Coolum CHOGM in March 2002 and not felt the need to intervene, the election observer mission may well have been cancelled or, if it had gone ahead and produced the very same report, the likelihood of getting a clean suspension would not have been as easy given the process that was required.

CMAG was continuing to mature and by May 2003 was holding its twenty-first meeting. It began with a pre-meeting dinner at my Hill Street residence in London, which I remember well because Yashwant Sinha, the new Indian foreign minister, was with a bunch of officials who really didn't want to let him out of their sight. The thought of him at a dinner for three hours discussing Pakistan without them seemed likely to cause them to have collective cardiac arrest.

The changing make-up of CMAG membership was a continuing focus of discussion, with a constant emphasis on the changing balance between the UK, the rest of the old Commonwealth, the Africans, the Caribbeans and so on. Most importantly, achieving the right balance between the developed and the developing world was critical, given the complex requirements of the two-term limit.

An example of the sort of tensions that could arise took place at the Abuja CHOGM in 2003, when I received a heavy demand from the Australian officials that Australia and the UK must be back on CMAG. I said I believed Canada was more entitled and was told in response that Canada was not tough enough. Australia came back to me when they heard in the corridor that Bangladesh would stay on. I said, 'No it won't, you'll just have to wait and see.'

What these officials seemed to miss was the perception by many that having a Secretary-General from a developed country like New Zealand, whose country thought similarly to Canada, Australia and the UK on many issues, was an extra voice for them on CMAG. I had not finished testing the Asians on my proposals, but I had always believed I adopted a fair position on all issues that reflected Commonwealth values. I could also sympathise with the perception of where I stood being a white kiwi.

So there it stood: no to Australia and the United Kingdom. One Australian official then confronted me in a most agitated state, demanding that Australia stay on. I told him they would have to just hope that Canada did the job. 'Well,' he remonstrated, 'they just aren't tough enough,' and off he went in a huff. Then John Howard came to see me to make sure I wouldn't be nominating Bangladesh for a third term. I said, 'No, you can relax, the Asians have it under control.'

And yet it's always been my view, one shared with many others, that the membership of CMAG is 70 per cent the person and 30 per cent the country. You have to have a sensible and active minister who retains the big picture, must know the subject better than his or her officials, listens to all sides and is prepared to cut deals. The minister must be able to see an issue from the point of view of the next-door neighbour, as well as the minister on the other side of the globe and thousands of kilometres away. Conversely, a minister representing a large and influential country who merely parrots an official line or reads blandly from a document, or a minister from a small country who's too terrified to speak, or an official trying to be a minister, all have little value and shouldn't be there.

An additional problem sometimes arises when a minister is replaced by another from within his or her own government but the replacement just does not fit into the group, the collective chemistry does not work. Another deficiency I saw a few times involved an enthusiastic official who replaced a minister, then decided to give the group a lecture on politics. The response from the ministers was usually a withering stare and silence. Or a new minister or his or her officials who had been too long steeped in UN culture might come to CMAG with a very different view of the world, and see the Commonwealth as a minor player. Finally, it was not unknown for a new person to view any issue from the automatic mindset that the large developed countries must pay the price for their terrible colonial behaviour. On CMAG we've seen them all.

About this time I suggested to ministers that we always have an agenda item labelled 'Other matters of interest to ministers'. There always seemed to be some issue somewhere that was bordering on being a violation of a Commonwealth principle. There was also a reluctance by some to talk about an issue in a member country if it wasn't on the agenda or known before-hand. It all became a little embarrassing and put the chair into a difficult position.

This new procedure enabled any minister, or even myself as the Secretary-General, to simply raise an issue. Whatever the subject, the understanding was that the discussion would not be part of the concluding statement. The ministers, I am glad to say, took full advantage of this. Of course, word of what was discussed would invariably get out via the diplomatic grapevine and a couple of times the offending country under discussion pulled back from its doubtful or questionable action rather than undergo greater scrutiny.

That to me was an excellent result, which really underlined the value of CMAG and the informality of its workings. There's no publicity if the crash doesn't happen, and CMAG can take credit for some crashes that didn't happen.

The 1999 CHOGM in Durban had decided that there was a need to have the Commonwealth speak at significant places such as the UN and that could only be done by a head of state. This was not something that Queen Elizabeth would wish for, hence the creation of the post of 'chair-in-office'. That chair would always be the head of government of the most recent CHOGM. Also, an extra member was added to the CMAG representing that country at the Australian 2002 meeting. Anyone examining the membership of CMAG over the years will be able to determine a reasonable pattern of membership through to changes made in 2009.

Britain's attitude to membership of CMAG remained an interesting one. When Sir Michael Jay at the Foreign and Commonwealth Office (FCO) made one of his regular plugs for CMAG membership at a meeting in May 2003, I told him bluntly that he had to demonstrate a firmer commitment to UK ministerial attendance at these meetings. I reminded him that the FCO had a secretary of state and three ministers in Whitehall. Then I told him of an instance when six Commonwealth ministers travelled to London for a meeting and not one British minister was available to walk across the park (St James's) to be there. On another occasion Peter Hain, then a FCO minister, left a CMAG meeting in New York to speak to diplomatic spouses.

'Your commitment and reputation need sharpening up,' I said. The point was taken. In all my discussions with Sir Michael Jay I never had the feeling he was a committed Commonwealth man. In fact, he was strongly criticised in the House of Lords in 2006 for making no mention of the Commonwealth in his annual report.

In December 2006 CMAG was once again galvanised into action by another coup in Fiji. This was effectively the fourth coup since

October 1987. All I could think of on hearing the news was, this is becoming a habit.

It wasn't completely unexpected, as for some time now the head of the armed forces, Commodore Bainimarama, had been criticising the government of Laisenia Qarase about corruption and leniency towards the leaders of the May 2000 coup led by George Speight. Many, including myself, tried to influence Bainimarama away from threats to take over the government, but with no success. On 5 December 2006, Commodore Bainimarama, as commander of the Royal Fiji Military Forces, took over the democratically elected government of Prime Minister Qarase.

For CMAG there was no option. It had to meet, and it would have been most unusual if suspension hadn't followed, given the illegal takeover of a democratically elected government and the precedents.

The big task was to ensure the minister from Papua New Guinea, a new CMAG member, could get to the meeting. A neighbouring country always has an important view of such an event, and Papua New Guinea was a member with Fiji of the Melanesian Spearhead Group. It played out as I anticipated, with CMAG following the Papua New Guinea lead of 'We must try to not hurt the poor people in the process of suspension.'

But now it was a matter of re-engaging with Fiji, and that wouldn't be easy. Over the course of the next twelve months I had many conversations and did meet with the commodore, but there was little if any progress. One of his heroes was President Musharraf in Pakistan, so I knew this wasn't going to resolve easily. Bainimarama had a single-minded view on what he had to do for Fiji. He wasn't going to deviate from his course despite pressure from the Commonwealth, the European Union and the US.

Our Papua New Guinea colleague was particularly incensed by the refusal of Bainimarama to meet with his Prime Minister, Sir Michael Somare. A top US State Department official referred to Bainimarama as 'defensive and paranoid'. Nevertheless, our engagement continued. The coup is discussed in more detail in Chapter 10.

At a CMAG dinner in New York late in my term as Secretary-General I was aware that there were some new ministers in our ranks. So in our private discussions I took the time to offer some thoughts about their role as CMAG ministers. These thoughts were gleaned from having been at every meeting of the group since 1995.

First, CMAG was, I said, a political body there to make political decisions. If the heads of government had wanted administrative decisions they would have put officials there.

Second, I told them, they'd give themselves a migraine if they started to unpick the successive Commonwealth declarations of Singapore, Harare, Millbrook and Latimer House[1] and try and link them together legally. Each was a stand-alone statement representing leaders' thinking at the time, building on previous statements in a political but not a legal sense.

Third, the role of CMAG ministers was to bring together their knowledge and history of the problem and apply the best collective leadership in order to bring the wavering state in question back to full Commonwealth membership.

As I look back on thirteen years of CMAG activity, I am prepared to give it high marks.

In the first instance, it represented a serious attempt by the Commonwealth to do *something*, to take positive action, when faced with massive democratic or human rights violations by a member state.

---

[1] The Latimer House Principles, agreed in the Abuja CHOGM, outline the independent yet interdependent roles of the executive, legislature and judiciary in member states.

Second, CMAG was put together by leaders who think politically about these things, and it continues to be refined by politically thinking ministers. This is one of its strengths.

Third, at a time when the Commonwealth has been constantly seeking to define what it stands for, it was logical that it would take the next step of creating a specific new organisation to respond to violations. This could only have happened when it was strongly needed, as with Nigeria.

Fourth, CMAG has established a level of credibility around its actions that puts it above criticism; it has created an environment in which countries actually have a genuine fear of being named or placed on the agenda.

In all the issues that it has had to deal with, CMAG may not have been the crucial factor that put a member state back on course, but it has always played an important part. One hears a lot of talk from people and organisations complaining about the loss of people's liberties (including from inside the Commonwealth), but it is the Commonwealth that follows it through month by month, even year by year. We were seen by some as pesky, a nuisance, interfering, high-handed and lacking in awareness – but we hung on just the same.

I believe we totally failed only once, and that was over Zimbabwe. Its leaders couldn't take the criticism, wouldn't engage and eventually left the Commonwealth (see Chapters 5 and 6). However, with Nigeria, Sierra Leone, The Gambia, Pakistan and Fiji, some useful things emerged. Engagement wasn't always easy, and not every initiative succeeded. But no country likes to be thrown out or suspended, or even chastised by members of an organisation they have willingly joined.

Partly due to these mechanisms it has become a seal of approval to belong to the Commonwealth. Many member states are particularly proud of that.

When most of the states listed above got over their yellow or red card punishment, they worked to get back into full membership. Presidents and prime ministers would be constantly reminded by their own citizens that they should get back to full membership, that's where they belonged. Losing access to the Commonwealth Games, missing out on valuable ministerial meetings and being ignored by the other members was for some like having a placard hanging from their neck advertising their deficiencies.

I do believe that if more international organisations other than the Commonwealth, and more recently the Pacific Islands Forum, had similar mechanisms, this world would be a safer place. In the end, nations are like people – they want to be in a group, they want to be respected, they want to participate and they want others to play by the rules.

So yes, CMAG has made that possible.

CHAPTER 4

Old Dominions with New Friends

It was an after-luncheon Retreat session at the 2005 Commonwealth Heads of Government Meeting (CHOGM) in Malta and the leaders had been arguing about an issue that was yet to be concluded. With a big smile on his face, Benjamin Mkapa, the President of Tanzania, looked round the room in a challenging way at the leaders, all seated in a large oval.

Pointing at Tony Blair, John Howard, Helen Clark and the Canadian Prime Minister's representative, he said, 'Look at the ABCs all sitting together, they're ganging up against us again.' This comment took most by surprise, but it did highlight a commonly held belief that the ABCs (shorthand for Australia, Britain, Canada and New Zealand) always settled on a position not always helpful to developing countries.

Later that day, I said to Mkapa, 'That was brave of you, especially as, with few exceptions, a group of West African leaders usually sits together, as do some Caribbeans and Pacific leaders in other groups.' He just laughed back and replied, 'Yes, but they [the ABCs] didn't notice that, did they?' And he was right.

From time to time developing country leaders would throw a barb at the ABCs for not really thinking about what was in the best interests of developing countries. As I saw it, there was some element of truth in this, but it was not a dominant feature.

As to groups? Well, surely, many leaders were just sitting with people they knew best?

Both within and outside the Commonwealth, those few old Commonwealth countries dominated by migrants from the UK always had a long association with that country, and less of a colonial relationship than many more recent members. After eight years of close involvement, my experiences left me with mixed views on the subject. The association was, of course, a mix of the old with the new, the old dominions working with the newly emerged democracies, the wealthy and the not-so-wealthy, the stable and the sometimes volatile – and with a perceived dominance by the UK over its former colonies.

The ABCs' history tended to underline and strengthen this perception. The former dominions enjoyed full self-government from the nineteenth century, and in the late 1950s and early 1960s were not entirely happy for emerging democracies to have a status equivalent to what they had with the UK. They saw themselves as a club within a club. The ABCs wanted exclusivity with the UK government and the monarch. They couldn't ignore the fact that most of their citizens had UK antecedents. They often took similar positions on contemporary issues, but I must say I never saw them aggressively and collectively pursue any result which really angered the other forty-seven or forty-eight developing countries of the membership.

The funding of the Commonwealth Secretariat, however, gave strength to the argument of undue influence. The UK, Australia, Canada and New Zealand together provided the Secretariat with £6 million, or about 61 per cent, of its budget and £17 million, or about 80 per cent, of its aid programme. So the taxpayers of those countries could well suggest, and often did suggest, that he who pays the piper calls the tune. Every year around budget preparation time, the big players tried very hard within the Secretariat to put in place those policies that suited them and their constituencies.

The mantra of the ABCs also never wavered: 'We want more

democracy, better governance, cleaner elections, reduced corruption, less nepotism, greater breadth of decision-making' – and so it went on. These were the lightest of sticks, but there always had to be some carrots: more aid, more technical expertise and so on. I don't ever remember hearing a threat that involved all stick and no carrot.

It might have been assumed that the 'old' Commonwealth, which had supported my initial candidacy, would have given me the greatest support during my stewardship, but that would have been a wrong assumption. If I had always marched to their drumbeat I would have permanently alienated the other fifty members. That would not have helped anybody. In fact, the way I responded to mandates from leaders or ministers often put me at odds with my own and other ABCs. That just went with the turf. Sometimes if the old guard did not like what leaders had agreed they would not hesitate to contest the issue on the basis of 'new information', expecting a Kiwi Secretary-General to be on their side. If these were my friends, I would not wish to meet my enemies.

It wasn't all antagonism, however. Canada, Australia and New Zealand were all founded on the basis that even if everyone was not born equal, they were at least entitled to equal opportunity, and that was a drumbeat that never ceased. Britain, on the other hand, possessing a society where class divisions were still reasonably evident, was not as demanding on the dismantling of hierarchical institutions so prevalent in the rest of the world.

Nevertheless, the UK, ever conscious that it was looked upon with great suspicion by most developing countries because of its former colonial status, soon learned that it had to be very careful with any new initiative. There was always the suspicion it was being done for all the wrong reasons. In some cases the British did galvanise themselves into a new position, obviously pushed by a minister, but often they got it horribly wrong. 'They didn't read the landscape,' I was fond of saying.

When a British official said what the Foreign Office wanted, he or she often had to be reminded it was actually the FCO, the Foreign *and Commonwealth* Office. At the end of one gruelling session, a sharp Commonwealth diplomat said to the British representative, 'If you take the C out of FCO you are left with FO, and I suggest you now do just that: F**k off.' It was a good thing that more people in the room laughed than grimaced.

In another part of the UK bailiwick were the British Overseas Territories, who occasionally did take advantage of their second-tier Commonwealth membership to try stretching their foreign policy boundaries. When they stepped outside the perimeter fence constructed by the UK for all its overseas territories, they would receive a schoolmasterly put-down reminiscent of *Tom Brown's School Days*.

These territories were not on their own in this respect. Australia often made it known to some Melanesian states, all of which had a large Australian aid programme, what response it hoped for on certain issues. This was particularly obvious with Papua New Guinea, which did not always assist ongoing relationships. And New Zealand was sometimes nervous if the Cook Islands or Niue asserted some independent thinking, but it never got near or close to a significant rift.

Canada, having strong commercial interests within the Caribbean, did try to influence a course of action there occasionally, but that never came to a rupture. Dominated by its relationship with the US and later by involvement in Afghanistan, Canada increasingly shifted its Caribbean connections to the outer reaches of government thinking.

Of interest was the role of India, a dominion for only two years, which had waxed and waned for many years over its Commonwealth membership. Prime Minister Nehru had been determined in 1949 that India should remain a member of the reconfigured Commonwealth, which was to include republics such as India and later Pakistan and Ceylon. But this soon gave way to a strong involvement in and significant leadership of the newly formed Non-Aligned Movement. This meant that India's representation at the Commonwealth summits from the 1960s was not often at head-of-government level.

It was pleasing to me that by the mid-1990s, under successive prime ministers including Narashima Rao, I. K. Gujral and A. B. Vajpayee, India was taking much more interest in the Commonwealth. This reached a high point in 2007 under Prime Minister Manmohan Singh when India successfully campaigned for Indian diplomat Kamalesh Sharma to become the Commonwealth Secretary-General to take over from me in 2008. However, it remained obvious to me that many Indian officials still deemed the Commonwealth to be the B team, preferring the A team action on the East River in mid-town Manhattan.

For me, it was most important that, with the Commonwealth's largest population, India played a positive role and made a solid financial contribution to our aid programme. The only downside I found was that India's second- and third-ranking London-based diplomats were still strongly influenced by the UN system of 'discuss and delay'. This did not always fit well with the Commonwealth's rapid-response attitude and consensus way of doing things. 'They had to be re-educated,' wryly noted one Canadian diplomat.

The countries that I have referred to were all major players. They were joined in that status from time to time by South Africa and Nigeria. South Africa did not make the most of its Commonwealth leadership, hankering at the time to get a place on the UN Security Council. Nigeria's President, Obasanjo, took a more active role, especially over Zimbabwe. If there was a downside with major players, with their bigger-than-usual staff numbers, it was that the junior staff members who were sent along to the executive committees started flexing their major-country muscles and naively digging into operational details, which often did more to delay proceedings than elicit useful information or change the course of action.

In my time I had quite severe run-ins with all the aforementioned countries, at head-of-mission level or with their second-tier diplomats. It felt to me that they often seemed to have time on their hands and wanted simply to meddle in operational matters. Sometimes they just demanded that I do something they believed should be done. So there were a few times when I found that it was a distinct advantage, having been a minister, to object and just stand firm. An experienced, well-trained diplomat will rarely get into a fight with a minister, or even a former minister.

Canada was the biggest regret in my period. With some sorrow I watched the cutting down of Jean Chrétien as Prime Minister by his colleagues and his replacement by the seemingly indecisive Paul Martin. Later, under a minority government, the Canadians practically disengaged. The officials in Ottawa and London wanted Canada to play a relevant role and be on significant committees, but they were rarely able to get a minister to come to a meeting. Thus their Commonwealth status slowly diminished.

Unfortunately, the minority Canadian government lasted for a long time, which didn't help Canada's relationships with other, smaller Commonwealth member countries. This was a huge change from more strongly committed previous prime ministers: John Diefenbaker, who led the opposition to apartheid; Lester Pearson, who campaigned for and secured the first Secretary-General job for a Canadian; and Pierre Trudeau, rightly given credit for inventing the leaders' Retreat. These were leaders who put considerable commitment, weight and energy into the organisation.

John Howard's coalition government in Australia was, through his strong leadership, a very firm Commonwealth believer, even if the officials didn't always see the organisation in quite the same way as the Prime Minister. In fact, Howard's thinking was probably closer to that of Sir Robert Menzies in previous decades. Officials complained about rising expenditure, but Howard would always wave it through, thinking of the greater good. When the pressure was on, Australia could be guaranteed to play a persuasive and constructive role.

New Zealand, being the smallest of all the dominions, tended to play a more low-key role, having a high profile only in the Pacific. Over the previous twenty years many Pacific leaders had had much close contact with successive New Zealand prime ministers, whom they often joined on the Royal New Zealand Air Force plane to travel to meetings around the world. That in itself smoothed over many troublesome issues that officials could not resolve. And it gave New Zealand a chance to influence the thinking of island leaders on issues prior to major meetings, an aspect never underestimated by officials.

Member countries that put effort into the organisation get back much more than just goodwill, and the old dominions are no exception. This is a relationship that can give you fifty-four global votes on any initiative you wish to pursue if it is done properly. Those that do it this way reap the benefits. Although all have treated the Commonwealth lightly from time to time, history shows the long-term benefits outweigh non-involvement. For this reason the recent standing back by the old dominions has a special and somewhat negative significance, and the rising influence of South Africa, Nigeria and India holds considerable promise.

Regrettably, the continuing divide of the old versus the new won't change much, but it would be an improvement if we saw evidence of Singapore and other Commonwealth countries with fast-rising GDPs joining the developed countries in doing more to help the poorer developing members as they have previously been helped.

CHAPTER 5

An Intense Involvement

In early 1993 I was transiting through Johannesburg on my way to strife-torn Somalia, where New Zealand troops were stationed. While dining in a restaurant in a Johannesburg hotel with one of my staff members and a local government official, I commented how incredibly knowledgeable our African waiter was. He looked us in the eye, he could discuss food options and wine varieties, and he was confident and very welcoming.

I remarked that he was a very good advertisement for South Africa just out of its apartheid years. 'Well, not really,' said my white South African host. 'He's from Zimbabwe, and they get a much better education than the black people of our country.' I've thought about that many times since then, about not only how liberating education is, but also how it can change an entire country.

President Robert Mugabe, as I was to realise, not only believed strongly in education but put it into practice, and there is much evidence that it paid off. Senior civil servants I met from Zimbabwe, many of whom had also received undergraduate and post-graduate education outside their country, could hold their own anywhere. And they did so with flair, panache and a dogged determination, all underpinned by huge confidence – which also meant, as time went on, that they were increasingly ready to challenge the control imposed by their President.

I did not make my first visit to Zimbabwe until 1999, when I was campaigning for the position of Secretary-General. By that time things were changing. President Mugabe was having trouble keeping the country's books in balance, pacifying his war veterans and keeping the growing opposition at bay. His status in the West as a leader in Africa was slowly diminishing.

In one of the Commonwealth Ministerial Action Group (CMAG) meetings prior to my becoming the Secretary-General, the chair of the group, Stan Mudenge, the foreign minister of Zimbabwe, went into a long tirade about how Zimbabwe was having major problems. 'We may have to take some extraordinary measures, but they will all be done within Zimbabwe law, even if Western countries disagree and think them to be illegal.'

That was a strong message, with a sharp edge: 'Don't even think of accusing us of violating Commonwealth principles – no matter what we do.' Of course, these comments came at a time when the worst excesses of Abacha's regime in Nigeria were still being played out – in that CMAG meeting and elsewhere.

It was around this time that my involvement with Zimbabwe became intense. It was fraught with difficulties and seemingly insurmountable challenges. But you cannot talk about Zimbabwe and these issues without looking back over the previous fifty to eighty years. In fact, maybe one should remind oneself that for perhaps a thousand years sophisticated African kingdoms occupied these fertile lands legally unchallenged – until Cecil Rhodes came on the scene a little over a century ago and the British South African Company (BSA) brought the first wave of white people into the country seeking gold and land.

Rhodesia, as it was known, never fell into the same governing category as neighbouring Zambia or Malawi, because of the large number of white settlers. The British were happy for them (meaning the white people) to run the country themselves. And so over a period of time, especially after each of the two world wars, more immigrants came from Europe, mostly from the United Kingdom, to take up farming on these most fertile lands. In the course of my engagement with black Zimbabweans it wasn't difficult to meet older people who had been forced off their ancestral lands to make way for more white farmers.

In 1962 the local white community expressed their dissatisfaction with the British, who would not give them carte blanche independence, by electing a hardline segregationist government led by Ian Smith of the Rhodesian Front Party. This provoked what developed into a long-running battle between the white minority, who received support from the apartheid regime in South Africa, and the black majority, who got political and other support from neighbouring countries. The UK was left, seemingly paralysed, in the middle. Conflict between the groups became the norm. There was no peace, and some 35,000 people on both sides were killed between 1964 and 1980, when full independence was imminent.

In 1965, by virtue of the 1930 Land Act and other measures, 3.5 million black people held rights to some 30 per cent of the arable land, which was mostly very poor. The white population of 250,000 held 51 per cent of the land, a large proportion of which was the most productive in the country. Black farmers were also restricted in whom they could sell their produce to.

Incensed that the British government appeared reluctant to act against Ian Smith, African leaders called an emergency meeting of Commonwealth leaders in Lagos, Nigeria, in 1966. Here enormous pressure was put on the United Kingdom's Prime Minister, Harold Wilson. Wilson was in a corner on this, even though his challengers were hardly themselves models of democracy. He simply wasn't prepared to use military force to oust Smith. This would in effect have set British soldiers against white soldiers in Rhodesia. He knew that the Second World War links were still far too strong and that his own servicemen were strongly opposed to such an action.

As we know, underground political movements developed. The Zimbabwe African National Union (ZANU), nominally aligned to Communist China, and the Zimbabwe African Peoples

Union (ZAPU), closer to the Soviet Union, were formed in the early 1960s to fight the colonial power. During the ensuing conflicts many of their leaders were killed or jailed. ZANU leader Robert Mugabe was locked up for eleven years. The two parties amalgamated in 1987 to form what is still the Zimbabwe African National Union, Patriotic Front (ZANU-PF).

Having seen Angola and Mozambique adopt majority rule, in the 1970s Smith pushed a pliant black Zimbabwean, Bishop Muzorewa, to the fore of what became a surrogate black government, reflecting 'an internal understanding' but with Smith still in control.

Exasperation still prevailed and so at the Commonwealth Heads of Government Meeting (CHOGM) in Lusaka, Zambia, in August 1979, Commonwealth leaders finally resolved to hold a constitutional conference on Rhodesia. This began a month later at Lancaster House in London. It had a three-phase objective: a ceasefire, the end of Smith's Unilateral Declaration of Independence (UDI) and full, free and fair elections.

The land issue was not satisfactorily resolved at Lancaster House, which left many unhappy. But convinced by President Machel of Mozambique, the Patriotic Front accepted a side proposal for the purchase back of land from white farmers. There was a firm undertaking from Britain, backed by the US, that this would take place, and the money was provided.

Elections were held in February 1980. Mugabe's ZANU party received fifty-seven out of eighty seats, Joshua Nkomo's ZAPU party, twenty, and Bishop Muzorewa, three. The Ian Smith party took all twenty seats reserved for white votes.

And so the new Zimbabwe was born – and it was clear who was the winner. But bloodshed was soon to follow after a falling out between Mugabe and Nkomo. This was more than a dispute between friends. Trained by North Koreans, Mugabe's forces soon hit the ZAPU party's followers, a tribally-based group of Ndebele people, who were crushed in Matabeleland. It is thought 10,000–30,000 people died in this conflict.

For a while there was peace, but Mugabe's supporters were crying out for land. A number of land purchases were made with the assistance of aid money. Some black farmers were installed, despite alleged corruption, but by the 1990s there were still more than 4,000 white farmers and they were still on the most productive land.

Very few white farmers and possibly fewer critics in London believed that the land would remain productive under black ownership and management. In a way they were right, because what had been created by the white colonists was a classic feudal-type society of white bosses (the owners) and black peasants (the workers). From what I saw on a number of visits, these were two groups as socially, educationally and economically separated as you could possibly get.

After apartheid was dismantled in South Africa, the torch of black leadership in Southern Africa passed almost invisibly from Robert Mugabe to Nelson Mandela. Losing some of his lustre in this way, Mugabe came under more pressure. While he may have put a lot of money into education, his not-so-well-educated war veterans were getting yet more restless for the land he had promised them.

Among black Zimbabweans there was intense jealousy between what was known as 'the book and the bush'. The former represented those who had gone off and become well-qualified at foreign universities; many did not physically fight against the colonial power or Ian Smith, but came back after independence and walked into many of the top jobs. The 'bush', of course, represented those who had fought in the guerrilla warfare, had seen much bloodshed and were awaiting the rewards or something in return.

During the Auckland CHOGM in 1995, Nigeria was suspended from Commonwealth membership. Immediately after the suspension, leaders created the Commonwealth Ministerial Action Group (CMAG), which I've described in detail in Chapter 3. CMAG was made up of eight Commonwealth foreign ministers, including myself, with the foreign minister of Zimbabwe, Stan Mudenge, elected chair of the group. And so began my intimate education about that country.

Following the 1997 United Kingdom elections and a change of government in that country, President Mugabe met with Prime Minister Tony Blair and Foreign Secretary Robin Cook at the CHOGM in Edinburgh. Mugabe told the new British leaders what had been agreed with the John Major government and expressed the hope that the current policy of land purchase would continue. In 1981 a land redistribution programme had been set up with funding from donors, principally Britain. It had started enthusiastically but had begun to falter when it was published in the British press that most of the farms redistributed went to ministers and their extended families.

At the Edinburgh CHOGM, Mugabe received a predictable UK response: 'We'll look into it.' But, in fact, a clear change in policy was taking place. Soon after, Clare Short, the new international development secretary (the aid programme section having been removed from the Foreign and Commonwealth Office), wrote to President Mugabe saying she would not be bound by British colonial legacies. There would be no more UK money paid as compensation to white farmers.

This was a bombshell and Mugabe detonated. If this was the position of the British government, he said, he would revert to the position of his Patriotic Front. The land had not been originally bought by the white farmers, so the Zimbabwe government would take it back. On second thoughts, he said it would pay, but only for the improvements made to the land.

Foreign Minister Mudenge was sent to London to remonstrate with Ms Short, but returned empty-handed. There would be no change in United Kingdom stance. For the Zimbabwe government this was humiliating, and Mugabe told many people that he could not believe a Labour government could be so bad. In comparison, Thatcher and Major now looked pretty good.

Britain had made it clear that it wanted out. Mugabe felt

diminished and angry, with his vengeance levels rising daily. He could not believe this was being done by a Labour government, which had always had more sympathy for his cause.

The war veterans demanded a better deal from Mugabe so he increased their pensions even though there was no budget for the policy change. A year later, probably realising how successful they were, they asked for more – and got it again. By now the internal accounts were heavily in deficit, inflation was increasing and spending power was diminishing. And to make matters worse, no one was listening to Mugabe any more – he was being overshadowed by Mandela.

The Mugabe message to the war veterans was now: 'If you want land, go and take it!' Of course, for international reasons Mugabe tried to sell the idea that this would be carefully managed through legislation and compensation for improvements, but in reality it was the beginning of a horrendous period of chaos and bloodshed that would last for over a decade.

One man's land grab is another's restoration of ownership. The British press saw it only one way. The white farmers had made Zimbabwe the bread basket of Africa, so they deserved nothing short of full compensation or full market value for the land. And if they didn't want to sell, they should have full protection under the law. As the land invasions started, there were calls for the Commonwealth to act against a country violating Commonwealth values.

Another catalyst for this uncertain environment was caused by the Zimbabwean government preparing a new draft constitution to replace the Lancaster House Agreement, and then putting the draft to a referendum. Among other things, it would allow the government to take designated land from the white farming community and have the British government pay the assessed compensation.

It was felt that this would easily pass, but with Mugabe becoming more unpopular and a legitimate opposition party, the Movement for Democratic Change (MDC), emerging, partisan and divisive politics meant the referendum was defeated in February 2000. This was a huge shock to the government, which was used to winning, and months later there were many who paid the price.

So how was the Commonwealth to respond? When I came into office on 1 April 2000 we were preparing to have a meeting of CMAG in May, and Australia, Barbados, the United Kingdom and Canada all wanted Zimbabwe on the agenda. Others in the group – Botswana, Bangladesh, Malaysia and Nigeria – aware that there had been an agreement between donors at a land conference back in 1998 where it was determined that black farmers would benefit from the government getting back 3 million hectares, were less prepared to discuss the issue. This land conference, which brought in a number of new substantial donors, had come up with a reasonable land acquisition solution. But Britain, not wishing to be told by others how to deal with Zimbabwe, was actively discouraging further financial contributions.

Some time in late 2000 I had a furious argument with British Foreign Secretary Robin Cook over the land issue. I was convinced you could not transfer these huge commercial farms directly into black ownership and continue with a similar feudal structure. You had to break up the properties into manageable sizes for rural families. He said he would not encourage peasant farming. I said at least the peasants would own the land, which would totally change their outlook. I believed natural development would then take place, with some selling to others and some staying on the land. He wouldn't agree, and there it rested.

Prior to the CMAG meeting, a group of four senior ministers from Zimbabwe came to London to have more meetings with the British government to see if a compensation package could be arranged. I asked to see them separately, but then I got a call from Cook who wanted me to join him for coffee with the ministers first, as he felt very exposed. I declined, as that was a purely bilateral issue.

I met with Foreign Minister Mudenge and outlined to him why CMAG ministers were likely to raise the Zimbabwean issue, even though it was not on the agenda. 'You just have to trust me to manage it,' I concluded, hoping it would settle him. But Mudenge was not happy and told me there would be no cooperation from Zimbabwe if CMAG discussed his country.

I had already spoken to Robert Mugabe twice on the phone, principally to ensure that he was fully informed on these discussions, and knowing it was a matter of pride for him that a number one talks only to another number one. In the current climate I was doubtful that he would talk to me. Until now he had been always courteous and friendly, but the caution was there.

The stakes were getting higher. The four visiting ministers did not get more than a cup of coffee with Cook and were then shuffled off to a junior minister. They could not get meetings with anyone else. They went home chastened, embarrassed and incredibly angry. They felt internationally humiliated. The issue was running hot in the UK, and in a BBC *HARDtalk* interview with Tim Sebastian I had to get quite rude about why the Commonwealth did not jump to the United Kingdom's wishes.

At the CMAG meeting in May 2000, the first since the 1999 CHOGM, a discussion on Zimbabwe developed under 'any other business' and so did break new ground for the organisation. At the end of a very productive discussion it was concluded that:

- Concerns were held about the violence, deaths, illegal land occupations and failure to uphold the rule of law.
- Support was expressed for an environment in which free and fair elections could be held.
- An apparent willingness for international observers to be present at elections was welcomed.
- The Secretary-General's decision to visit Zimbabwe to

convey these concerns and discuss the situation generally was also welcomed.

All the above may sound rather innocuous to an outsider. In fact, it wasn't the words but the fact that the discussion had taken place at all which would explode in Harare. It prompted Stan Mudenge, who had ceased to be on CMAG since 1999, to issue a three-page statement condemning CMAG for 'acting outside its procedures and not within its terms of reference', and so on.

It wasn't enough to stop my visit, but it would not make the visit at all easy. But the indications were that Mugabe was evidently still prepared to bend a little to maintain some evidence of cooperation.

Arriving in Harare early one morning from London via Johannesburg in May 2000, I still had no idea if there would be a meeting with the President. As the plane touched down on the long runway – longer than Heathrow, JFK or Charles de Gaulle airports – I noticed a huge crowd waiting. It looked ominous, and it was. This was not a state welcome.

For the first time ever the media was given total access to the foot of the steps coming down from the plane. Among this crowd of journalists, photographers and television cameras I could see two members of my advance party trying to position themselves to rescue me.

No luck. We shuffled towards the VIP lounge, me trying to half smile, saying I was there to listen. The cameras then followed me all the way, as I went in and out of the toilet and into the lounge. Then I told them there would be no press conference at that time.

And so to the proposed meeting with Mugabe. If it wasn't so serious, what happened next could be seen as an old-style movie comedy in which the characters go left and right and forwards and backwards, never quite knowing what was happening.

The meeting was on for midday, then advanced to 4 p.m., then back to 2 p.m., then the following morning, then the afternoon. Now, some governments have been known to push the most critical meeting right up against the visitor's known departure time, with obvious consequences. I sensed this was happening here, especially after the airport event with the press.

So we had to ensure that there were a number of alternatives. Despite the length of the Harare airport runway, this wasn't JFK with flights every minute. In fact, there were only three flights that could get me back to London in time for my first official meeting with Her Majesty the Queen at 11 a.m. on 17 May. I concluded that if that meeting, important as it was, had to be postponed then it would be. The meeting with Mugabe now had to take priority.

As a few of these conversations were no doubt picked up by the Zimbabwe security people we were soon asked, very suddenly, to get in the cars to go to the presidential palace. All was quiet when we arrived, to be greeted only by two stuffed lions either side of the main door. We waited and waited.

After about twenty minutes we heard sirens, then suddenly there were many vehicles, tyres screeching, bits of gravel flying, soldiers jumping out and surrounding the parking area – all to ensure that the principal occupant of the biggest car, President Robert Mugabe, was safe from whatever was about to threaten him. He leaped out of the car, smilingly shook my hand and we turned to face the cameras. He then firmly took my other hand (out of sight of the cameras, I was hoping) and we walked hand in hand into the meeting room. This was the third or fourth time I had met him. But it would be only our second – and last – really substantial meeting.

Two years before I had called on him as the New Zealand foreign minister campaigning for the job as Secretary-General. That was a relaxed meeting. He liked New Zealand and New Zealanders. We talked about cricket, of which he has a great deal of knowledge, and the benefits of the Commonwealth to countries like his. His only negative thought was that the number of Commonwealth scholarships had diminished and that was not good for developing countries. He was welcoming, appeared reasonable and seemed much aware of his status in Africa, even if to much of the world, the tide was going out.

This present meeting on 16 May 2000 was very important to me and, of course, for the Commonwealth's reputation generally. We now had somehow to get ahead of him and steer him away from actions that were violating Commonwealth principles and bringing him into conflict with many Commonwealth members.

I sat near him in a meeting room with a living-room-type setting. He had eight to ten officials; I had three or four. Then he started, and I've never seen such a fidgety person. My notes after the meeting record that he jiggled incessantly, hands flapping, head bobbing, elbows flexing and directing his comments everywhere: 'I've never seen such a level of nervous energy in one person. It's coming out of every pore of his skin.'

He said he knew why I had come, but I had to understand Zimbabwe politics:

We've had a history of bloodshed since we were invaded and since all wanted our independence.

I told Harold Wilson: you agree that Ian Smith is illegal then come and remove him, and he said he couldn't possibly use British soldiers to shoot at white settlers. We finally got our country back and got our independence, and Margaret Thatcher and then John Major were helping us buy back the land.

Now we have Tony Blair and his gay cabinet, a Labour government telling me there's no more money for land. My people must have land, they must have their own land back. It's in every Zimbabwean gene to need to own a piece of land. You see, Mr Secretary-General, the British government has reneged on a deal. The people are very agitated. This is not easy.

And so it went on, the Rhodesian/Zimbabwean difficult history. By now twenty minutes had gone by in this history lesson, and we were getting some repetition. I had heard the explanation behind the explanation, all the actions necessary for Zimbabwe integrity. But if I didn't get a word in soon I might as well not have been there. He had that particular habit of many politicians: if he thought I was about to interrupt his flow he would look at someone else.

'Mr President,' I began, 'I appreciate you've agreed to see me.' And away I went. 'Many Commonwealth members are concerned about the violence, the illegal occupation of land, the breaching of the rule of law and political intimidation. Zimbabwe is not on the CMAG agenda, but the group of foreign ministers tasked by leaders have discussed these issues and asked me to voice their concerns and to see if there is some way we can help.'

'Also,' I said very deliberately, 'some of your African colleagues are concerned that these issues will spill over into their countries. With your elections coming up it's important that these elections are free and fair and held in an atmosphere conducive for that to take place.'

'Of course,' he said. 'We always welcome observers. But I don't want any from Britain.'

'Well,' I said, 'Britain is still part of the Commonwealth group.'

He then cracked a joke about elections, which caused him to laugh uproariously – followed belatedly but equally enthusiastically by his civil servants. He then began talking about former UK Prime Minister Jim Callaghan, causing his own officials to look quite blank. Then it was back to the present.

'We are doing our best, Mr Secretary-General. I've had calls from Kofi Annan and Madeleine Albright recently, both wanting to send observers. We have no problem as long as they understand African politics, our laws on media access and the freedom to move,' he said forcefully.

I pointed out that the amount of time between announcing

an election and holding it was always a critical factor in relation to making preparations for observers. Then I reminded him that the Commonwealth election guidelines were agreed to by all Commonwealth leaders in Harare in 1991. Yes, of course he remembered that, and Zimbabwe would not be found wanting.

By now we had used up more than an hour, which was thirty minutes longer than we had expected. He was now more on the defensive, and he clearly wanted the meeting to end. The conversation was concluded by him saying, 'We'll now go out and you will tell the press what you have to tell them.' He laughed uproariously at his own joke, followed by the cheerleading squad.

I went out to meet the press with Foreign Minister Stan Mudenge, while the President, with his head down like a guerrilla soldier, slipped unnoticed round the back of the media scrum into his car and with a roar of engines and sirens the cavalcade was off.

First question: 'Was it possible to have free and fair elections in Zimbabwe?'

'Yes,' I said, 'it was possible.' I wasn't prepared to say probable. There were many things that had to happen, and then back and forwards the discussion went.

Then to Stan Mudenge, who got a much rougher time when he responded aggressively to the suggestion by a journalist that law and order could not prevail in the current climate. Of course, his answer created more and more questions. He left the platform not a happy man. Neither of us came out of it very well – me for having said it was possible to have free elections, which everybody agreed could only happen if many conditions were met, while the government felt the hostility of the international media.

Back at the hotel and in government offices there was now much we had to do, including many meetings with all who wanted to have a say: representatives of MDC, the election support network, war veterans, the commercial (white) farmers, democracy groups, women's groups and a mixture of others. It was a good sign that they wanted to see us knowing that all were critical of the government and more specifically of the ruling ZANU-PF.

We listened, we questioned, we cross-examined, but our message was the same to all. We were worried. We were concerned about the violence. We wanted to help. We wanted to assist with the elections. We wanted people working together. The Commonwealth had had a lot of experience in difficult situations all over the globe, and we were confident we could help.

But I left the country with mixed feelings. I was not at all confident we could achieve very much if key players really didn't want us there. Yet there was no doubt that many of those who came to see us, some in desperation, saw us as the only group that could get Mugabe and ZANU to change course.

The stark reality was that Robert Mugabe was in charge and he didn't want to lose an election. Losing the referendum had shaken his confidence and his war veterans were no longer controllable. I had listened patiently and left with him all our concerns, all recorded by his officials. Yes, he was listening, but I was not convinced there would be anything but a minor change in strategy, if any. If my conversation with the President had ended by talking about cricket or something light I would have been happier that we could come to some amicable agreement. He wasn't about to rebuff me, but his survival instincts were paramount. Everything else was secondary.

Some time later, one of my communication staffers said he thought he could 'sell Mugabe and his policies if he wasn't so belligerent'. In a way he was right. There certainly was a negative story of colonialism in Zimbabwe to be told. But it could have been better retailed, and we were now past that point. I had done what I had to do. There was nothing more I could have demanded, and if the level of antagonism had got higher we would have cut all communications. At this point I felt I could still get him on the phone.

Later in May I had my first formal meeting with Prime Minister Tony Blair and I told him that Mugabe loved having the United Kingdom as an enemy. 'He needs to accuse and attack someone, and with the British press constantly on the side of the white farmer, he's happy.' Blair knew things were spiralling out of control, but he didn't really know what to do.

Having got the green light to observe the elections, it was with some political sensitivity that we put together a team of election observers. There was no shortage of advice from Australia, New Zealand, Canada and the United Kingdom, but I didn't want to do anything that provided Mugabe with a reason for rejecting any Commonwealth findings – and that included the make-up of the observer group. After many calls and emails we ended up with thirty-three predominantly African or African-Caribbean observers. They were a mixture of political and electoral specialists and diplomats, and were headed up by the former President of Nigeria, General Abdulsalami Abubakar. This was the general who had taken control of the country after the sudden death in 1998 of the dictator General Abacha and brought that country rapidly back to democracy (see page 56).

The team worked well. Once on the ground they saw all the right people and organisations, with the exception of ZANU-PF, which was 'unavailable'. They listened carefully to reports from the MDC and other opposition parties about the targeted violence, the unresolved land crisis, the out-of-control war veterans and how the Commonwealth could assist alongside the national monitors. They heard that many meetings of the MDC had been broken up by thugs and that specific MDC candidates had been targeted.

The reports I was receiving from the assessment team who stayed behind in Harare after my visit, and from the advance observers, were to expect big problems. The war veterans were aggressive, the government was chastened by the loss of the referendum and ZANU was not used to losing, so nothing would be easy. Mugabe did not help by delaying important announcements relating to the election and not finalising the new electoral boundaries until five days before nominations closed. The rather hapless and under-funded Electoral Supervisory Commission could do little but indicate its concern at the level of violence and intimidation, while urging all, somewhat fruitlessly, to uphold the law.

Mugabe made sure he rejected any international observer groups he deemed would be unfriendly, which included the United Kingdom. The National Democratic Institute from Washington DC and even the UN walked out after they were told they would not be permitted to have a coordinating role with the government.

Although observers reported relative calm on the 25/26 June election day, up until then violence was breaking out everywhere. Their report stated they were concerned that the 'level of violence which disfigured the campaign was employed systematically as part of a strategy to diminish support for opposition parties'.

In Bulawayo one of our teams saw an MDC supporter beaten up by war veterans. Elsewhere, war veterans admitted to some of our observers that they had organised selective beatings. In some rural areas where the MDC had support, many voters were convinced by ZANU-PF people that however they voted, 'we [ZANU] will know'. Broadcasting on state radio and television was heavily biased, but the opposition made good use of the internet to inform its own supporters and the outside world what was going on.

When the results came out it was clear the MDC had done better than most expected, claiming fifty-nine but getting fifty-seven of the 120 seats being contested. However, with Mugabe being able to determine a further thirty seats, control of the legislature was never in doubt. In fact, even if the MDC had won 20 per cent more votes and ZANU 20 per cent fewer, the thirty presidential appointments would still have given Mugabe a majority.

Our observers wrote a very tough report, and I was pleased

that it was also unanimous. It was very unusual for words like violence and intimidation to appear in print in an election report, but it was all there along with about eleven positive recommendations, which if taken up would improve the way elections were run.

The task for me was to convince the government of Zimbabwe that such an election diminished the overall standing of the government and that by working with us along the lines of the recommendations there could be improvement. However, the sad fact was that no one in power in Zimbabwe, least of all the President, was ever going to risk losing control of the country – and certainly not through an election. We did get support for our views from the Southern African Development Community (SADC) Parliamentary Forum and the European Union, but there were too many governments, groups and individuals who were giving Zimbabwe the thumbs-up – mostly, I believe, to consign the matter to history as rapidly as possible. Very quickly the then deputy president of South Africa, Jacob Zuma, came to Harare and congratulated Mugabe on the ZANU victory. This set the tone for other observer groups and countries to accept that view and just move on.

Our best strategy for the Commonwealth was to continue to keep engaged, to keep out of the firing line of MDC electoral challenges and to try to see some improvement in the holding of a much more acceptable presidential election in 2002. To do so I needed the support of the neighbours, particularly Presidents Thabo Mbeki in South Africa, Sam Nujoma in Namibia, Festus Mogae in Botswana, Bakili Muluzi in Malawi and Joaquim Chissano in Mozambique. President Chiluba in Zambia was of little consequence given his own domestic political problems, including accusations of corruption. With the first two it was not going to be easy. Mogae and Muluzi would be cautiously staunch in the Commonwealth's favour, and Chissano had been President Mugabe's best man at his wedding to his second wife Grace just a few years before. Loyalty would be strained.

After many unreturned phone calls and messages via my offi-
cials I became very grumpy about the lack of response from
Mbeki (who was the chair of the Commonwealth) and the South
African government on a number of Commonwealth issues that
were bubbling along, such as Zimbabwe, Fiji and the Solomon
Islands, along with getting the High Level Review Group (HLRG)
off the ground and working. About the time I had almost given
up I got a message from the South African high commissioner in
London, Cheryl Carolus, that they wanted the Commonwealth
Secretariat to prepare background briefing papers for the HLRG
(something I wished they had requested two months before) and
that Mbeki wanted to see me in Lomé in Togo at the approaching African Summit.

My introduction to the Organisation of African Unity (OAU,
now the African Union/AU) in July 2000 in Lome, Togo, ensured
that nothing would ever surprise me again at future African summits. Despite our having sent an advance officer, there were no
hotel rooms for us on arrival. After much anguish, and veiled
threats from my African staffers, we got a new villa. But the paint
was still wet, there was no hot water, no food, no fridge and no
bedding for three out of the five of us. Somehow we made do.

President Gaddafi of Libya was clearly the majority share-
holder for this event, as there were more posters of him throughout
Lomé than there were of our host, President Eyadéma. Gaddafi
had brought a 200-car motorcade from Tripoli to Lomé via Accra
in Ghana. Within this motorcade were the longest Cadillac that's
ever been stretched and a van with a loaded rocket launcher on
the roof. I guess Gaddafi had to be ready for anything.

I finally got the meeting with President Mbeki, who said as
an opener that he was pleased about Zimbabwe and hoped that
Mugabe would give up office soon: 'The region has suffered
enough under his stewardship.' Well, I thought, that sounds
promising. We discussed the MDC challenges to the election

result and the elections generally, but I left the meeting surprised at his rather benign view of the country. Maybe he knew something that I did not.

The general view among the African leaders and ministers on Zimbabwe at the OAU summit was 'rough election, but time to move on' and 'we shouldn't rub his nose in the dirt any more'.

Parallel to these activities was the start of the formal meetings of the HLRG, whose role was to rethink the working of the Commonwealth, in particular the role of CMAG. The HLRG consisted of (at head of government level) South Africa (chair), Australia, Fiji, India, Malta, Tanzania, Trinidad and Tobago, the United Kingdom and Zimbabwe. For Zimbabwe and Tanzania there was a real determination to rein in CMAG, as well as to marginalise the role of the Secretary-General. For the others in the group, however, these issues were non-starters, so Zimbabwe and friends backed away, and no change was the result.

I was already aware that officials had their own ideas of where the Commonwealth should be heading, and that these did not always agree with the political views of the leaders. I was therefore insistent that the leaders met in the wings of the United Nations meetings in September in New York to ensure we got a firm political direction.

At the first of the New York meetings with officials in 2000 there was an early push by Tanzania and Zimbabwe to reduce the role of CMAG. Here I was lucky, because when the time came for the leaders to tick off these proposals, the chair President Mbeki rushed through the CMAG issues unchanged before President Mugabe arrived. I now knew that CMAG could and would stay with its original mandate, with reasonable powers to enquire about violations.

President Chissano of Mozambique came to see me at

Marlborough House in mid-December 2000. After we'd discussed a few Commonwealth/Mozambique issues, I asked him to do what he could to influence President Mugabe to take a much more conciliatory line. Since he and President Nujoma of Namibia were both planning to leave office, why could not their good friend Robert do the same? He said he would try.

As we moved into 2001, nothing was very settled in Zimbabwe. The violence continued and a newspaper office was fire-bombed. I tried ringing Mudenge three times towards the end of January to express our concerns, but never got through. He was always away at his ranch and out of mobile phone range. I issued a press release indicating that we were concerned, but it was really to let Harare know we were watching. And they certainly knew that the combative Zimbabwean high commissioner in London, Simbarashe Mumbengegwi, was angry because I did not talk to him first. Absolutely right, I thought – he would have spent all day disputing my comments.

In mid-March we had another meeting of the HLRG, and once again a very skilled Zimbabwe diplomat tried to convince his colleagues that CMAG should only come into play following an actual coup. This was clearly a kite being flown from Harare, but the wind was not behind it. This was especially evident in Britain, where a large section of the population continued to believe that the 4,000 white farmers controlling 75 per cent of the best land were somehow doing the country a favour. I personally believed the crisis was going to get worse before it got better, and until the land issue was resolved there would be little respect for the rule of law.

The Zimbabwe government was clearly worried about the MDC and its popularity, so thoughts were entertained on giving Morgan Tsvangirai a position in a government of national unity. Morgan was a most engaging, determined political trade unionist, who by now had a large following in favour of a change in government through his Movement for Democratic Change. Taking on the Mugabe/ZANU machine was clearly going to be a huge challenge, but he was a great soapbox orator and the crowds were getting in behind him. As a part-diversion, the government also intended to stir up problems in Matabeleland, which was the heartland of the MDC – although the ZANU-PF foot soldiers were told to try to keep killings to a minimum. Within ZANU, there was also internal strife between those military leaders who were benefiting from the Zimbabwe intervention in the mineral-rich Democratic Republic of the Congo and those who were not. So within the web of Zimbabwe there were many tangles.

I had breakfast in London with Foreign Minister Merafhe of Botswana and we discussed how we had to get ahead of this deteriorating situation. We might not resolve the issue, but at least we would be putting our stamp of concern firmly on the landscape. The best we could come up with was for a group of CMAG ministers to make a visit. This would have status and clout and would get attention, but for those very reasons would no doubt be turned down as too intrusive. The full ministerial group came to a lunch at my residence at Hill Street and all agreed that a firm line had to be taken. Foreign Minister Alexander Downer of Australia suggested an Eminent Persons Group, and I proposed the ministerial group I'd discussed with Merafhe.

The hardliners wanted to 'CMAG' Zimbabwe (yes, CMAG was moving from a title to a verb). This would mean the issue would sit firmly on the agenda, but the country wouldn't be suspended. But that did not get much support. As the debate evolved it was becoming obvious that a ministerial group led by Billie Miller, the foreign minister of Barbados, with Alexander Downer and Foreign Minister Sule Lamido of Nigeria, had the greatest support. The chair of CMAG, Merafhe, had taken a beating from the Zimbabweans over his previous chairman's statement, and as a border neighbour of Zimbabwe was better advised to keep his distance. But we never doubted his courage on these issues.

And so it was decided. We knew we were stepping into difficult territory. We knew there would be repercussions, but it had to be done. There was also the need to provide carrots with the sticks and to keep out of the Zimbabwe–United Kingdom crossfire.

Needless to say, within hours the decision was roundly rejected by Zimbabwe. They did not need Commonwealth ministers interfering in their affairs, and so on. After Easter everything got worse. Harare-based diplomats were being verbally attacked by Mudenge. Judges were being forced to resign.

Mugabe was defiant and refusing my phone calls. In only six months I had gone from being able to speak to Mugabe easily on the phone to now getting pushed down to Mudenge, then to a junior minister, then to an official. I said to my staff that by June they probably wouldn't let me speak to the office cleaner.

I also had to formally write to President Mugabe informing him of the outcome of the meeting and of CMAG's aspirations, 'all in the spirit of Commonwealth cooperation', and requesting that he receive a ministerial group 'to conduct consultations with your government'.

Whatever the eventual response to the letter from Harare, I felt there was a strong need to get someone into Mugabe's office to spell out exactly the Commonwealth's views. I had a suggestion for a senior Malaysian to make such a visit given that Dr Mahathir and Mugabe were quite close, but I preferred to consider Sir Shridath Ramphal, one of my predecessors. He had played a significant role during the Lancaster House talks on Zimbabwe independence and was still well regarded.

When Sir Shridath (or Sonny, as we all knew him) was back in England, we had a meeting on 2 May 2001 in which I gave him the updated background and our objectives. However, all his attempts to get through to Mugabe came to nought. Even Sonny on his private phone was unable to get past the gatekeepers. This told me that Mugabe was really circling the wagons and putting up the barricades.

I spent a few fruitless days again trying to get through by phone to Harare myself. In exasperation I wrote Mugabe a letter, then hand-delivered it to High Commissioner Simbarashe

Mumbengegwi, who, after being informed of what was expected of him, was speechless. 'A characteristic completely unknown to him,' said my aide Dr Victor Pungong. I told Victor there would be a one-in-ten chance of a reply. 'Too high,' said Victor.

Meanwhile, in what might have been seen by some as advantageous to us but certainly not of our making, Mugabe's key enforcer, Chenjerai 'Hitler' Hunzvi, had been killed in a road accident, and his belligerent mouthpiece Jonathan Moyo had resigned. On the downside, UN Secretary-General Kofi Annan told me he could not spend more time on Zimbabwe. It was producing no returns when there were so many other problems. By now, Sonny Ramphal had failed eight times to get through to President Mugabe on the phone. The situation was getting worse.

On another front, President Mbeki of South Africa was coming under pressure from the British press to do more about Zimbabwe, particularly because he was to receive a state visit in Britain with all the bells and whistles, including a stay at Buckingham Palace. So he developed his own initiative. This, he told me in a private meeting, would be a group of six Commonwealth foreign ministers, but not the three from CMAG. I would not be included either (conditions stipulated by Mugabe). I noted Mbeki was getting Mugabe's consent in advance. After a little thought, I suggested he should have a Caribbean minister, and at the dinner for the Queen the next evening Mbeki told me Mugabe had agreed to a Jamaican minister, who he regarded as friendly.

On another track, the Nigerians had also started an engagement with Zimbabwe following a meeting of Foreign Minister Lamido, former Nigerian President Babangida and Mugabe at another international conference in Jakarta. Now we had a clash as to whose event this was, and both African.

South Africa and Nigeria were crying out for the status. Having had so much bad press, Mbeki clearly wanted to remain in the driver's seat. But in Africa it's all about seniority and clout, and that was with President Obasanjo of Nigeria who could, when he felt like it, talk to Thabo Mbeki as he would a junior army officer. For the Commonwealth, the fact was that on this issue we needed both South Africa *and* Nigeria.

Jack Straw was the new British foreign secretary and I felt that on the British–Zimbabwe issue he would be better than Robin Cook, who was moved out to become the leader of the House of Commons and then moved to the back benches over the war in Iraq. He died suddenly in August 2005.

I was pleased Straw and I could have a chat about Zimbabwe when he came over to Marlborough House for lunch. We agreed that no one was making any progress with existing policies and there was a need to lower the temperature and megaphoning if any progress was to be made. This would not be easy when a journalist from the *Daily Telegraph* had just been arrested. As the 'three-minister mission' was dead in the water, the best hope was for the Nigerian mission to lead. Even though CMAG would take a back seat, it was still an all-Commonwealth approach.

Before Straw left I stressed that my job was also to keep the Commonwealth out of the bilateral UK–Zimbabwe crossfire. We shouldn't forget, I said, that Robert Mugabe still had many friends around the world. My notes from the meeting recall that we also reminisced about the Zimbabwe white farmers; the majority of those I met were not a very attractive group. They had not said much about the need for democracy when Mugabe took the trade unions head-on, or even when he clashed with the students. Their commitment to Zimbabwe seemed to be for the status quo, and many had the cushion of a British passport.

A CMAG meeting in early September 2001 focused on how best to make progress and on talking tough. Everyone's positions moved to the centre, with Australia and Nigeria taking the hardest and softest lines respectively. We all knew Sule Lamido, the Nigerian foreign minister, was on a high wire here given his role with the larger ministerial group.

Mompati Merafhe proved to be a most capable chair, pulling all the right strands together, settling down Jack Straw and Alex Downer, but remaining tough. Botswana, he told us, was suffering immensely due to the slow collapse of Zimbabwe. He then related the story of Mugabe ringing Botswanan President Festus Mogae and pleading for financial assistance, then after receiving a promise of a few million dollars he was abusing Botswana publicly for supporting 'the old Commonwealth'. 'He knows no shame,' said Mompati.

Musa Hitam of Malaysia amused us all by telling how he got chastised by Malaysian Prime Minister Dr Mahathir Mohamad for allowing CMAG to discuss human rights in Zimbabwe: a case of old friends sticking together.

On 5 September 2001 we left London for Abuja, Nigeria, and the birth of this new initiative. It was a mixed group, all Commonwealth but not designated as such: ministers, officials and a small support cast from the secretariat. At a breakfast the morning after our arrival, President Obasanjo immediately took command, expressing his exasperation before proceeding to speak in a tough, balanced and very succinct manner:

- Zimbabwe was a major problem, but we must not have an inquisition.
- The issue permeated Southern Africa.
- Land was only one issue. All issues relating to Zimbabwe politics and economy must be addressed.
- Obasanjo would himself go to Zimbabwe and carry the message. Mugabe had told him he was still 'the midwife'.
- There needed to be give and take.
- The Commonwealth could help. The world must see we were getting it right, and the role of the war veterans must diminish.

President Obasanjo said all the above in a twenty-minute speech without a note in his hand. The Zimbabwean representative was not there, but it gave the rest of us a guide.

Then to the first formal meeting of what became known as the 'Abuja Process', beginning with another tough opening statement by Nigerian Foreign Minister Sule Lamido. It was called a 'process' because Obasanjo didn't wish to predetermine the end. He sought a unanimously supported way of dealing with Zimbabwe's problematic land and governance issues that would get Mugabe to a face-saving position and take the whole debacle out of the international headlines, thereby achieving some satisfaction among Commonwealth members. The Western media headlines were the ones he wanted to kill off, as little about Zimbabwe featured in the African press. For an African problem the strategy was right, even if ultimately the results weren't achieved.

My own statement to the group referred to the anger, anguish and sorrow expressed by all Commonwealth countries. I said I had tried to keep the Commonwealth out of the firing line between the United Kingdom and Zimbabwe, and that I was continuously having to respond to a cynical and hostile British press for not doing enough.

I made it clear that 4,000 white farmers owning 80 per cent of the best land was unsustainable and had to end. I also referred to the New Zealand situation: disputes over land that had been expropriated more than a hundred years before were slowly being resolved within an agreed settlement process. Whether it was land, rule of law, human values or the media, we in this room could create change if everybody was willing.

When Zimbabwean Foreign Minister Stan Mudenge referred in his opening statement to 'the land crisis in Zimbabwe', I knew we had captured his mind. We were all familiar with the Zimbabwean defence, so their responses didn't take us far, but we all knew they could see dollar signs. It was obvious they were desperate for the money. On 7 September the Abuja Process was agreed. It was now up to the government of Zimbabwe to adhere to the document.

That should not have been difficult. The agreement recognised that land was at the centre of the crisis and that reforms must be made to benefit the people of Zimbabwe. Stress was placed on the need for reforms to be carried out recognising human rights, the rule of law, transparency and democratic principles. A commitment from the government of Zimbabwe agreed that there would be: no further land occupations; a speeded-up process for land delisting (that is, removing from a government list a parcel of land which the government had intended to appropriate); a commitment to restore the rule of law; and a recommitment to freedom of expression. It was all seemingly straightforward, but it was the implementation that would be crucial. We concluded by agreeing to meet in Harare on 27 and 28 October 2001.

At last we were holding the initiative. We were ahead of the play and were not just following as before. It was a lesson firmly learned, I noted at the time. Get in early before the problem really erupts; get to know the key players and the issues. Do your homework properly and you've got a better then even chance of preventing a bad situation getting worse.

Then came September 11, and the world stopped to watch the unbelievable in New York.

Everything was changing, and we had to do some hard talking to ensure that both Lamido from Nigeria and Downer from Australia remained engaged and were prepared to go to Harare and have a real face-to-face with Mugabe. I did not want to lose this Abuja initiative. It was all we had.

On 29 September I spoke to President Muluzi of Malawi, who had chaired a recent SADC meeting, and confirmed that the Abuja Process gave them all the backbone they needed to deliver Mugabe some straight talking. Bless them, I thought, it all helps. Each SADC leader had told Mugabe individually how his own country was being affected by the chaos and crisis in Zimbabwe: many were being overwhelmed with escaping

Zimbabweans; crime levels in the border areas were at epidemic level; there was evidence of very hungry people and no end in sight. Apparently, Mugabe looked very glum most of the time. The Zimbabwean war vets who attended were very demanding, but the commercial farmers, facing massive losses, turned out to be the most constructive. I was pleased this dialogue had taken place, as normally SADC kept well clear of political issues, so this showed high levels of concern among his neighbours – 'Let's hope the "Old Man" will change course.'

Finally, we got the green light from Mugabe. He couldn't resist the pressure from Obasanjo, and the issue had been taken 'out of the Commonwealth' even though I, at Obasanjo's insistence, was there. The Abuja Process ministerial group, initiated by President Obasanjo of Nigeria and now led by his foreign minister, took the overnight flight to Harare via Johannesburg on 25 October 2001. We landed at 8.30 a.m., and with no time for a shave, shower or breakfast were taken straight to State House to meet the 'Old Man'. We all felt a bit grubby.

It was so typical of Zimbabwean politics. We were given no time to put on a clean shirt, but still had to wait for more than half an hour until Mugabe arrived. This was the big test. Mugabe had removed Zimbabwe from CMAG surveillance, but he was now faced with his friend Obasanjo, a fellow African, bringing in a wider but still all-Commonwealth ministerial group, which included Zimbabwe itself and a supposed supporter in Jamaica.

From Mugabe we got the full nine-yard welcome and lecture. Two supportive vice-presidents, friendly handshakes, a cowering staff and the usual history, starting in the 1890s with Cecil Rhodes. We then moved through Rab Butler, Harold Wilson, Ian Smith, UDI, Peter Carrington, Margaret Thatcher and Tony Blair. He was emphatic: the government was not going to buy back the land stolen from them.

So it went on for more than thirty minutes. A few comments

were raised by the United Kingdom and Canada, which Mugabe batted away, and then I hopped in and pointed out how the Commonwealth observer group for the elections under former President Abdulsalami Abubakar of Nigeria had been critical of the recent election, particularly of distortions caused by the violence.

Mugabe threw back his head and laughed. Then all his officials followed in unison. When the laughter subsided Mugabe smiled at me and said: 'I see the Commonwealth has taken over this Nigerian mission.' And they all fell about laughing again. I sometimes think he deserved an Oscar for these performances.

We spent more than an hour with the President. It was necessary, markers were put down, but in substance it was unsatisfactory. We left State House with my telling the Zimbabwe officials we would want to see the President again before we left to report on our findings. They looked positively depressed at the thought of convincing the President of the proposal. So I raised it with Mudenge, who said it would be very difficult.

'Surely he wants to know what conclusions we've come to if he really supports the process?' I asked.

'Don,' he said grimly. 'It just won't work, he'll be out of Harare.'

Then after shaves, showers and clean clothes we began what was to become a series of very public meetings. It started with presentations from the lands minister on land reform, then regretfully descended into arguments about who we wanted to see while in the country.

It was finally agreed we would go to one farm nominated by the government, and one nominated by the commercial farmers. It was all rather acrimonious. Mudenge wasn't happy, but for the sake of peace he went along with it.

There were various presentations from many groups, but the most enlightened proposals came from the younger white farmers. Light-years away from their hard-line parents, this group had donated a million hectares for some trial settlements with black Zimbabwean farmers. They realised that their future could be achieved only by peaceful coexistence.

In their presentation, the older commercial farmers were intensely defensive, sitting rigid and unsmiling with their arms crossed. Their fear was that their forty to fifty years of hard work was about to simply disappear. They were obviously good farmers, and they knew how to get optimum productivity – but they were living in a privileged and almost feudal society. In many cases, they owned many farms; the well-known Oppenheimer family of De Beers fame, I was told, had more than 300,000 hectares. Their farm production was assisted by large quantities of cheap and uneducated labour.

White farmers often sent their kids to private schools. 'Is there any intermarriage?' I asked. I was told it was unheard of. For these people, time and events were moving too fast. 'We must have the rule of law,' they cried – which reverberated well with many British newspaper readers.

The war veterans were predictable in their need for land so long promised from their fighting in the bush, and were not all aggressive in their presentation to the group.

The next day the group was taken on helicopter rides to farms. The first farm, 250 kilometres south of Harare, was owned by a man who would not thank me to name him, who described himself as a cattle man whose family had come from South Africa in 1937. He now had twelve or fourteen farms, he couldn't quite remember. His farms had all been subject to the land invasions. He said he had little energy for a fight and just wanted one farm. His wife said he was near to a nervous breakdown.

Surrounded by many of his farm workers, I found the contrast was stark. They did not look healthy. Some had teeth missing, many wore hand-me-down clothes and they were small of stature. They did praise Mr Erasmus for the school he built. I asked where. They pointed to a red corrugated iron-covered shed. I said to the farmer quite innocently, 'Did your kids go there?' No, they hadn't: I think he said they went to school in Australia.

If these farm workers – who in reality were peasants – wanted anything, it was simply their own piece of land. Tragically, many were later to be thrown off the land along with their white owners, as the Zimbabwe political class moved in.

Then our delegation sat on benches in a large clearing and awaited the presentations. In front of us were 500 black farm workers sitting close together; round behind us, standing arms akimbo, were the many neighbouring white farmers, looking somewhat sullen. To one side were the many local dignitaries. There were many speeches, with everyone's point of view made strongly.

I got worried when the Canadian minister, the rather likeable lawyer David Kilgour, seemed to want to talk to the white farmers rather than listen to the speeches, which I didn't think was a good approach. I was right because there was soon a dispute between Kilgour and our chair, Lamido, on 'whether we are prepared to hear all the witnesses as you would do in a Nigerian court'. Lamido's reply was, 'This is not a court, David. We listen, we ask questions.' It wasn't a good display.

The leader of the war veterans then spoke. He raised tensions further, then lost the audience completely with obscure ramblings. His parting shot at the conclusion was that there were some war veterans 'who already have a piece of land and a posh car', and that was unfair. I wasn't sure if that meant none or all should have those assets.

Stan Mudenge opened his speech with a little dance and a ZANU-PF battle cry, and got the crowd stirred up. That was until his mobile phone rang and stalled his rhetoric. His speech was mostly in Shona, but his generosity shone through when he announced a decision that our host farm owner would have one of his farms delisted from acquisition.

Then the white farmers present gave out their written material to all the white members of the ministerial group but not the black members. I refused to receive it. When would they ever learn?

Now it was back into the helicopter to visit another farm, with a brief tourist stop at Masvingo to fuel up and visit the famous Great Zimbabwe ruins. This was the site of the ancient capital of the Kingdom of Zimbabwe and the home of the monarch. Built between the eleventh and fourteenth centuries, it was ultimately abandoned until rediscovered by Europeans in the late nineteenth century. It is a very important site which gave Zimbabwe its present name. We stalled there for about an hour for technical reasons, so I got into discussions with Mudenge as to the way forward. I didn't wish to alienate him on this process, as he was to be the carrier of all information to Mugabe. 'We can't go back to President Obasanjo with nothing,' I said. We agreed to round off a few sharp edges on the draft document, but there was still much to do on the big governance issues.

There was a strong academic side to Mudenge. He saw the need for major changes, but in an intellectual way, which did not suit the prevailing political climate. Mudenge had pointed out to me from the helicopter his own ancestral lands, 'owned by nice people who let us visit our family's burial site once a year'. It was another interesting angle on this perplexing land problem. It wasn't hard to meet Zimbabwean people who remembered being forced off their land during Prime Minister Smith's UDI years to allow the settlement of more white farmers.

The next farm (half an hour by helicopter from Harare) had been invaded, and two people had been killed there. Although this farm had been nominated by the commercial farmers' union for a visit, Mudenge said it wasn't a very safe place to go as black/white tensions would be high.

Once again the ministerial group sat on a length of timber supported by two boxes, constantly under the television cameras' surveillance. They heard from the white farmer about the plight of losing his farm because it was now completely surrounded by custom land, which is land held under cooperative tribal ownership and apparently maintained for the whole community, a fact that is challenged by some. This apparently curtailed the activities of our new host, and he was therefore prevented from carrying out proper farm management. He had trouble telling his story but was assisted by his very articulate wife.

Next, the police handed out a four-page statement on their role in the conflict. After others had had their say, a woman police officer rose to speak. Seeing that she was holding four closely-typed pages, I suggested to Lamido that as we had copies of the statement, could she just paraphrase? Lamido stopped the speaker with that suggestion, made in a very courteous way. But that made her angry and disappointed; she was going to read all four pages if it was the last thing she did. So in the end we saved no time; in fact, it took longer.

Three hours after the allocated time to hear submissions from the public the next day, we got under way and started to hear from many others. The MDC were good, but let themselves down when they incorrectly and unnecessarily denied they had received funds from the British-funded democracy-building organisation, the Westminster Foundation.

ZANU-PF were very articulate and declared that only they could deliver what the country needed. Then to the war veterans, who I asked whether they thought violence was the only way they could achieve their aims. In a roundabout way, the answer was yes.

Then the media. This meant the *Herald*, the government newspaper, versus the rest. From another paper, a determined and possibly courageous editor said the government were all liars and they covered up the truth. He asked rhetorically why the minister of lands' wife was on the Media Censorship Committee. That started some fireworks; it was probably the first time local ministers had to listen to criticism in silence.

The Law Society tabled a paper quite critical of the government. Then to the registrar general and minister of justice. I asked them if they had read the Commonwealth observers' report on the elections. They said they didn't know there was one, but they would get it and read it. My goodness, I thought, they were living in their own gated world, prepared to defend anything they did.

The day grew longer, with the government, represented by ministers and many officials, taking a beating and not liking it one bit. This was emphasised when one of our committee pointed out that their pamphlet on land included a statement that did not adhere to the Land Act. Well, that had the officials looking for someone to whom they could 'sheet home' the blame. But apparently he was not there.

When we started seriously drafting up a statement on the Saturday morning, our heads were swirling with faces, facts, figures, statements, actions, dramas and low-level conflict. It was stop-start. Canada and the United Kingdom, both represented by junior ministers, became very obstinate. Australia, represented by an official, said they would go with the flow and the rest, Nigeria, Jamaica, South Africa and Kenya, also represented by ministers, were reasonably productive.

We moved through draft and counter-draft and I was getting close to boiling point every time I heard David Kilgour tell us that he was a lawyer and we had to get it legally right, pointing out all the deficiencies of the Zimbabwean government. 'David,' I said, 'this is not a legal document. It is a political one, and this is but one stage of a long process.'

Many in Commonwealth Africa and beyond were watching our activities and awaiting a result, so we needed to conclude with a substantial document. We had to ensure that all who had come before us would see that they had been listened to and could read something of their thoughts in a final statement. There was a wide divide, remembering the young black farmers who would not talk to the more enlightened young white farmers 'because if we go to them we diminish ourselves'. The white farmers and the war veterans would never talk to each other. And then there were the highly educated ministers and officials – and their opposites, the semi-literate but very hard-working farm labourers. In this climate, satisfaction for all was not possible.

Back after lunch with the draft, I was asked to meet with the United Kingdom and Canadian senior officials out in the lobby. They could not live with the draft. 'OK,' I said, 'what's next?' 'Back to CMAG,' was their reply.

'That's fine,' I said. 'But don't forget that the Commonwealth would then be prevented from monitoring the presidential elections. Remember that CMAG means no cooperation from the Mugabe government. And remember that if Morgan Tsvangirai wanted one thing out of this process it was election monitoring – and you're about to throw that out the window. So what's your plan B?' Silence!

The meeting reopened with Kilgour saying he could not live with a statement that included all the things the Zimbabwe government claimed they had done. Mudenge said, 'OK, take them out.' But Kilgour was unaware of the trap he had set for himself.

When we got to the paragraph stating what the ministerial group had seen and heard and done, Mudenge said, 'Cross that out.' So after ten minutes of this there was only a skeleton left. The result, if left at that, would look as though we had caved in completely to the demands of the Zimbabwe government. That would not please Obasanjo, and would have a very negative impact on our mission.

It was then felt we might be able to have merely a 'chair statement'. I let the discussion go down this road just so ministers could see how unproductive it was. I then reminded them that the strongest statement was a unanimous communiqué; you then came down a peg to a communiqué by consensus (meaning not totally unanimous); and then a communiqué with some dissent noted; and then a 'barely supported' chairman's statement. This was the lowest, because everybody else could dissociate themselves from it.

So it was back to an attempt to agree on an unqualified communiqué. There was more wrangling over wording. When David Kilgour went outside for the third time to confer with his officials, Lamido erupted, asking Kilgour, 'Aren't you the minister? Can't you make up your own mind?'

We started again. 'Canada cannot live with this the way it is,' said Kilgour.

I took a big breath and exploded. 'There is only one reason we are here and that is because President Obasanjo got the green light to start this process. We have to report back to him. If all we've got is a chairman's statement he cannot go to Mugabe with any moral authority or weight of argument and the whole Abuja Process will be laughed off. If Abuja is to work you must have a unanimous communiqué. It should not be that difficult.'

I spoke quite forcefully, but at the same time I was thinking that Mudenge, clearly amused by these antics, was sure to report back to Mugabe on how divided we were.

So all the wording went back in, and Canada was told forcefully that not every paragraph had to conclude with the words 'according to the constitution and law of Zimbabwe'. This document was not going to end up in court. It was another milestone to keep us and the whole Abuja Process in play.

We had lost momentum through 9/11, but we ended up with a reasonable document which was nevertheless not appreciated by the government of Zimbabwe. But it would keep us close to the action, in play and close to the United Nations Development Programme (UNDP), which was pursuing similar objectives.

With different players we might have got a better result. There was only one foreign minister (Lamido), and three junior or deputy foreign ministers (the UK, Canada and Kenya). Then we had a labour minister (South Africa), an attorney general (Jamaica) and a senior official (Australia). All except Lamido would be aware that their respective senior minister, though not present, would be looking over their shoulders.

Inevitably, by early December 2001 the United Kingdom,

Australia and Canada were asking to have a CMAG meeting because it was believed that Mugabe was not living up to the Abuja Process commitments. This was something that would not go unnoticed in Harare. We decided on a teleconference, as I was in New Zealand. However, I did issue a warning to the group that it would be inappropriate to discuss the future of a Commonwealth member and possible status-downgrading within the Commonwealth over the phone. A teleconference would work only if the participants were likely to improve a country's status, leave it neutral or just exchange information. With that proviso, the conference was agreed to.

During the course of the phone conversation, however, it became apparent that Sule Lamido of Nigeria was not on the line. He had decided not to participate for fear it would show that CMAG had taken over the Abuja Process. With that information to hand, the Bangladeshis and Malaysians were cautious, being reluctant to antagonise either Nigeria or Zimbabwe, especially in the absence of the former. In the end, with Straw and Downer voicing their strong concerns that the situation had worsened, all finally agreed that CMAG would meet before the end of 2001, and that Zimbabwe would be discussed under 'any other business'. So it was not on the agenda, but it would be addressed, discussed and debated.

A new twist had occurred when I heard that Mugabe was again desperate for money. Earlier in the month, former President Shonekan of Nigeria had called into London after meeting Mugabe and said that Mugabe wanted to tie the acceptance of election observers to a financial commitment for land purchase from the United Kingdom. He went on to say that Mugabe would give a commitment, but the international community 'had to be resolute' – meaning an unequivocal commitment of money for farms. Well, I thought, that would go nowhere.

The CMAG meeting finally came together on 20 December 2001 with everyone conscious that there had been no real movement following the second and last Abuja Process visit. CMAG could no longer say nothing. Ministers were exasperated, and were talking tough.

Mompati Merafhe in the chair, in his reading of 'Harare' (the 1991 CHOGM declaration) and 'Millbrook' (the 1995 New Zealand CHOGM declaration), said there appeared to be a far too strict interpretation by some of Millbrook: 'In all my reading of both Harare and Millbrook, there are no explicit restrictions, there has been too narrow an interpretation, we must look at the principal values, from Singapore to Harare to Milbrook.' He went on to say, 'We have a strong position, we can move with confidence.' That statement from an African minister, followed by a very supportive and tough comment by Billie Miller of Barbados, gave ministers confidence to move determinedly in that direction.

Another African member went on to say that the least we could do was inscribe Zimbabwe on CMAG. 'They are an acute embarrassment to all in Southern Africa and dragging everyone down economically.' That was a definite sea change from our African colleagues, and reflected the acute embarrassment they all felt.

So it was a tough statement that came out of this CMAG meeting. It castigated the government, condemned the violence and criticised the way Zimbabwe had ignored protests from the UNDP, SADC and the Commonwealth.

In retrospect I know that the dialogue we had with Zimbabwe through the Abuja Process, the attempts to have Sonny Ramphal engaged, and proposed ministerial visits (limited though these were), would not have got to first base if Zimbabwe was already on the CMAG agenda. Obasanjo's authority had been paramount.

There were no surprises when in the first week of January 2002 the media reported chaos in Zimbabwe, continuous land invasions, partisan violence and random killings. Thoughts as to any commitment they had given within the Abuja Process had clearly been long forgotten. President Obasanjo, a good friend of President Mugabe, was now despairing and embarrassed. He had put in enormous personal time and effort, and it had come to naught. There were now worries in and out of Zimbabwe that high-profile opposition leaders would be killed. I didn't believe they would ever kill a senior MDC leader, but you couldn't be too sure.

We received an informal nod for observers to attend the forthcoming elections, so it was now time to ask our political division to get a list of proposed competent people together. I suggested we should now start applying for visas for those of our staff who would be going on the mission. But when one of my senior African advisers did just that he was roundly abused by the Zimbabwe high commissioner for having the tenacity to apply, and for breaching African solidarity. And anyway, the Commonwealth had not even been invited to observe. What it is to be an official caught in the line of fire.

Beyond all these minor diversions, we were only too aware that nothing in Zimbabwe was improving and nothing we had done had made the slightest difference. With nothing to lose, I wrote Mugabe a letter indicating all the issues we were concerned with. This letter was not going to change the world, but I had to get it on the record.

At the same time, Mugabe was losing friends rapidly. The relationship with the European Union was going downhill. President John Kufuor of Ghana was becoming openly angry that all the good he was doing in Ghana was being undermined by Mugabe's behaviour and colouring everybody's attitude to the rest of Africa. Mugabe's support from his long-time ally Sam Nujoma in Namibia had weakened. President Nujoma was doing a very good job of getting his people onto the land in conjunction with a German government land purchase programme, a good example for Mugabe to take note of.

Then at the end of January 2002 I received a not-very-surprising letter from President Thabo Mbeki, stating emphatically that

CMAG should not involve itself with Zimbabwe. It had no mandate and the HLRG gave it no direction to do so. It seemed to me that as the new chair of SADC, Mbeki had obviously convinced the others of the rightness of Zimbabwe's position with a push from Mugabe, but this letter from the chair of the Commonwealth was undermining all we were doing.

I rang Mbeki, telling him that if this letter got into the public domain, 'you as chairperson of the Commonwealth will be crucified'. His rather mild response was that he was only passing on the information, not owning it. I wasn't sure he could get out of it that easily, but I hoped he would think further about it.

Some time later I met with the chair of CMAG, Foreign Minister Merafhe of Botswana, and Foreign Minister Nkosazana Dlamini-Zuma of South Africa, and raised the issue of the letter. Dlamini-Zuma was surprised at not having seen this letter and said she would find out what caused it to be written. True to her word, some time later we got a letter retracting the original proposition. Well, that was a close-run thing, I thought; but it left me with less confidence in the office of President Mbeki.

With the continuing level of violence, the unpredictability and the recognition that Mugabe was not going to change course, the meeting of CMAG scheduled for late January 2002 was going to be a tough one, especially since it just preceded the CHOGM, now due to start in Coolum, Australia, in the first week of March.

This team of ministers was working well together, despite the hardliners and softliners pushing hard their respective positions. Australia and the United Kingdom were as usual the hardest, then Barbados, then Canada, Malaysia and Bangladesh, then Nigeria wanting a mild response so as not to undermine President Obasanjo's initiative. All knew that to suspend would have meant no observers at the Zimbabwe elections, so it was a matter of going right to the maximum – but not over.

Lamido reported that his President, along with former Nigerian President Shonekan, despite getting the full Zimbabwean welcome normally reserved for a state visit, had told Mugabe that Obasanjo's reputation was on the line and there had to be a change and a difference very soon.

And from another source we were told that the Mugabe/Mbeki letter asking us to keep CMAG out of Zimbabwe had not only been disowned, but was being blamed on an old friend, Abdul Minty, the acting head of foreign affairs in South Africa and long-time ANC activist. Poor old Abdul; failure's always an orphan, I thought.

Foreign Minister Merafhe, the chair of CMAG, pulled all the issues together at the meeting on 30 January, convincing his African colleagues that they had to go the full distance. So again, the continued violence was condemned, there was criticism of legislation that violated Commonwealth principles and another thanks was given that we were to be allowed to observe the presidential elections.

During this period Foreign Minister Lamido was talking to Obasanjo, who was talking to Mugabe. The result of not actually formally suspending Zimbabwe meant that Mugabe would allow six observers and three staff members as an advance team to be on the ground immediately. The Coolum CHOGM would be crunch-time for Zimbabwe. Neighbouring countries were frustrated that Mugabe's actions were affecting the way they were viewed by outsiders. That was not good for investment.

One piece of good news was once again getting former Nigerian President, General Abdulsalami Abubakar, to head up the observer mission. I noted at the time: 'The general is a cool customer, a confirmed democrat, always exudes confidence and is a very safe pair of hands. More importantly, he has the status that Mugabe cannot object to.' The rest of the team we brought together was dominated by African and African-Caribbeans, again to reduce unnecessary antagonism.

By the end of February 2002 we were all in the Australian town of Coolum for the postponed CHOGM. A few weeks after the 9/11 attacks in 2001, calls had come in from leaders expressing their doubts about getting to CHOGM the following November, but it was only a week in advance that it became clear the absences would make the meeting irrelevant. So after a discussion with the prospective host, Prime Minister John Howard, the plug was pulled.

Professor Ade Adefuye of Nigeria was now my point man in Africa and was keeping close to President Obasanjo over the Zimbabwe issue. This was when we started to develop some thoughts on an appropriate group of leaders to deal with the issue. The idea was to get some semblance of thinking from a small representative group on the direction leaders were best to pursue before the main leaders' sessions.

CMAG ministers began Zimbabwe discussions at a breakfast meeting, acknowledging that Commonwealth leaders recognised the right of CMAG to put Zimbabwe on the agenda. All ministers were prepared to hang tough, but we still had to pull Nigerian Foreign Minister Lamido along that path. The group was resolute in its statement, but not before chairman Merafhe had pointed out to Lamido that if the Commonwealth had not been tough on the Nigerian leadership he, Lamido, might still be in jail. So Lamido bowed to the heavier statement. The critical words were: 'endorse the decision by CMAG to keep Zimbabwe on its agenda, noting that the Millbrook Commonwealth Action Programme provides for a range of measures in such circumstances ranging from Commonwealth disapproval to suspension'.

However, by the time the executive session of leaders was about to start, Obasanjo, having heard from Adefuye what CMAG was recommending, including the use of the word 'suspension', told me he could not possibly go along with its recommendations. Why could we not have a troika of leaders to deal with Zimbabwe? It was an idea that had first emerged in the margins of a pre-CHOGM meeting of senior officials in London.

I was in conversation with President Ben Mkapa of Tanzania when President Obasanjo expressed this wish, and so I asked if he supported such a move. 'OK by me,' said Mkapa. I then moved a couple of metres and asked Prime Minister Howard if he would agree, recognising that this was a kick in the face for CMAG. Howard said he would talk to his foreign minister, Alexander Downer, who gave it a tentative yes, but asked where Mbeki stood.

Back to Obasanjo, who said he was about to ask him, and off he went, robes flowing behind him. I later heard that General Abubakar, my chief observer and friend of Obasanjo, had rung Obasanjo from Harare, very agitated by the lawlessness in Zimbabwe and seeking advice. Obasanjo said he should go and see Mugabe immediately, but first he would ring Mugabe himself to pave the way. 'You know, my friend President Mugabe, he doesn't appreciate criticism from anyone.'

Obasanjo then sought out Foreign Minister Mudenge, who was standing in for Mugabe, and really stripped him naked, saying that he, Obasanjo, was being humiliated given all the work he had put into this task and the Abuja Process. Stan Mudenge, a very lonely man at this CHOGM, looked totally chastened, head bowed in front of this senior President, and had nothing to say.

The discussions were strongly influenced by the fact that the presidential elections in Zimbabwe were to be about two weeks away, on 10 March. Many observers on the ground were reporting back very negative messages. Some talked too much. Before the debate started, Stan Mudenge, looking for any opportunity to win a point, sought me out and blasted me for the actions of a Commonwealth observer from Australia who on landing in Harare immediately condemned the elections, before they had even begun, to the local and international media.

'How,' said Stan Mudenge, 'can this man be an honest observer when he's made up his mind even before the elections are held?' 'Don't worry,' I said to Stan. 'I'll take care of it.'

I then sent a message to my senior staff officer in Harare to tell this person, whoever he or she was, to shut up. The observer concerned was prescient in his remarks, but not very diplomatic.

He turned out to have been Australian Labour Party opposition member Kevin Rudd, who later became Prime Minister.

When the debate started, the proposal to have a troika of leaders was already on the table and so acted as the focus. I will not breach the confidence of the Retreat, so I will convey only the general thinking.

Foreign Minister Mudenge of Zimbabwe was allowed the last comment, and opened on a light note by saying, 'Thank you, I knew you could not have *Hamlet* without the Prince of Denmark,' but the meeting was too highly charged for any-one to even think of chuckling. He then gave his defence of Mugabe's actions.

There was a very clear summarising from John Howard in the chair, noting that we had to await the upcoming election and the observer group report before deciding on future action. A sigh of relief echoed around the table of fifty-four leaders. Time had been bought and a line drawn. A clear way ahead had been set out, offering Zimbabwe another chance. And consensus had prevailed.

Mugabe would not have been happy with the report from his foreign minister. He had few die-hard supporters in that room, and those that were curtailed their speaking.

Nothing goes smoothly, and Mudenge took a second oppor-tunity to criticise me when Tony Blair, who said he was quoting one of the observers, stated the election campaign was being marred by violence. I pulled Blair aside. 'Tony,' I said. 'It's not good if the Zimbabwe government thinks the observers are reporting daily to the British government. It provides them with a reason to question their impartiality.' He took my point and didn't quote observers again, but you can never put that sort of comment back in the box.

The Zimbabwe issue coloured leaders' views on the worth of CHOGMs in the way it dominated the atmosphere of the confer-ence. It was the elephant in the room. A number of our leaders from small economies, especially small island states, felt that although the Zimbabwe question had to be tackled, it was taking precious time away from the economic, trade and social issues that were their bread and butter. 'We don't want to go through that marathon ever again,' said a prominent Caribbean leader.

Back in a very grey London, I was getting reports of heavy polling in Zimbabwe on 10 March 2002, but very long queues in Harare and Bulawayo, the MDC strongholds. Our observer team believed there were 40 per cent fewer polling booths in those areas. Jon Shepherd, my senior staff officer, who was back for his second election, told me that many people would not be able to vote, and brought this to the attention of the Registrar General. There was also evidence of much disenfranchisement of elderly white people, who had lived there all their lives. This even included former Prime Minister Garfield Todd. The noise in the international media and our representations worked, so it was pleasing to hear that the polls would remain open for another day.

The next day, 11 March, there was much reporting of violence, heavy-handed police actions and evidence that some polling places did not open the extra day because they received 'no official notification'. The polls finally closed, and word began coming back to London that our Commonwealth observers were not at all impressed.

All our observers had witnessed violence, so a consensus report would not be difficult to achieve. Several days later I heard that all was going well on the report until the observer from Namibia threatened to walk away. I was sorry to hear this, as the person concerned had proved to be a very good observer in Fiji. I did wonder if President Sam Nujoma, one of Mugabe's closest friends, was having an inappropriate influence.

On 15 March the preliminary report was released with no signature from the Namibian observer. It was a very critical report, and I was glad to hear that every negative statement could be backed up with facts.

In fact, the report was as tough and as condemnatory as any I had seen. The observers were highly impressed by the determination of the people, but were very disappointed by the levels of intimidation and violence. They referred to the intimidation meted out by 'youth trainees' and to the lack of police action against ZANU violence. The base electoral legislation was flawed, there were restrictions on civil society groups and thousands were disenfranchised. They concluded by stating that 'conditions did not adequately allow for a free expression of will by the electors'. In addition, they referred to the total lack of government action on the recommendations emerging from the May 2000 parliamentary elections.

The troika of Commonwealth leaders – Australia, Nigeria and South Africa, the present, future and past chairs in office – prepared to meet at Marlborough House amid an air of expectation. I proposed that there should be an informal discussion among the three and myself, in my office, to test the boundaries of thinking away from officials. Then we could go downstairs to one of the meeting rooms for a formal session. Not wishing to see leaders photographed against a background of eighteenth-century English leaders, I got our staff to change the artwork.

On 29 March Prime Minister Howard and Presidents Mbeki and Obasanjo arrived, so we had the obligatory photograph at the table in my office, and then when all others had left we took to the four easy chairs for the expected initial 20-minute off-the-record discussion. In the end we were there for more than two hours, and the officials downstairs were stamping their feet.

I quickly ran over the 2000 parliamentary election and how the government of Zimbabwe was clearly not prepared to consider implementing the recommendations from our observer group. I touched upon the tentative role played by CMAG so as not to alienate Zimbabwe; the determination of Zimbabwe to choose who the observers would be; the personal difficulties expressed to me by the heads of both observer teams, including the earlier one headed by former Nigerian President, General Abdulsalami Abubakar; and then the main points in the mission's recent report, concluding that the election was not free and fair and thus could not express the true wishes of the people.

President Mbeki said that he was getting alternative reports, but for the next hour and a half these three leaders worked their way towards a solution that only three senior political leaders could do, confident that this was the only game in town. Essentially, they trusted each other not to expose the other. The discussion ranged far and wide, but it always came back to, 'We have to satisfy the other fifty-one Commonwealth leaders and the people of Zimbabwe.'

There was concern that Zimbabwe had not responded positively to either the Abuja Process or to Obasanjo's interventions. The three leaders expressed anger at the manipulation of the country's Electoral Act, the Citizenship Act and the General Law Amendment Act. They noted that the Namibian observer had walked out and thus prevented unanimity, but at least there was no minority report.

There was a strong realisation that society in Zimbabwe was polarised, food shortages were a problem and no one needed another Matabeleland conflict. There had to be unity and reconciliation. Three and a half million Zimbabwe refugees in South Africa was enough, said Mbeki. At the same time, only Zimbabwe could mould its own future. They would not talk about the need for a government of national unity, but if one was created, perhaps Mugabe would then agree to leave the scene. All agreed that the treason charges against Tsvangirai, recently brought by the Mugabe government, could derail any reconciliation process – but if so, Robert Mugabe had assured his African colleagues that he could and would at any time suspend or commute such sentences.

The three leaders were also aware that with the troika containing two Africans and an Australian, and with a New Zealand Secretary-General, they had to work hard to prevent a split occurring on geographic or racial lines. At this point I was glad that I had ensured that the observer team was well over half dominated by Africans and African-Caribbeans.

As the discussion continued, it was becoming clear what the three could all give their support to. There had to be a penalty against the President and the government; there had to be encouragement for ZANU to reconcile with the MDC and have open debate about their differences; there had to be support from international players; and there had to be a cleaning up of bad practices.

After a couple of hours, with still no assistance from their respective officials, I brought in a couple of my staff members to help me draft a statement, with the three leaders helping as they chatted among themselves. I asked if they each wished to bring an official into the room. 'No,' said Obasanjo, 'we know what we've said, we'll suspend for twelve months, and we know what we want.'

Near the end of this marathon they suggested I bring all the Commonwealth high commissioners together and inform them of the troika's decisions. This would be programmed to take place just prior to the press conference, which they agreed needed only be the chair, John Howard, and myself.

Then there was a light-hearted discussion about who would ring President Mugabe. Back and forwards it went, until President Obasanjo agreed to be the one to tell Mugabe that Zimbabwe would be suspended from the councils of the Commonwealth for one year.

President Mbeki then thought it appropriate to ring Tony Blair, which he did.

Then my communications adviser, Joel Kibazo from Uganda, came into my room to say it would not be good for only John Howard and myself to be at the press conference. Two white faces on an African issue was not a good look. I suggested to Obasanjo and Mbeki that we should all be there, but that only John Howard would speak. Everyone was OK with that.

Obasanjo came back from his phone call to Mugabe still chuckling. 'I told President Mugabe he was suspended for twelve months. He thought I said "expelled". I said no, only "suspended", just like Sierra Leone. We're here to help.' His chuckling continued.

By now the high commissioners had gathered. As the Zimbabwean high commissioner was sitting by alphabet beside me at the end of the circle, I said to him quietly, 'Your country has been suspended for twelve months and President Mugabe's been informed,' but he remained quite impassive. I then read out the statement and after the phrase 'is suspended for twelve months' you could hear the oxygen getting sucked out of the room.

Then it was straight next door to the press conference and, as agreed, John Howard stepped up to the podium. The media representatives had that professional 'I am bored' look on their faces, even though they knew this was one of the biggest press conferences we had held in the Blenheim Saloon.

Once again everything stopped as the words 'suspended for twelve months' were uttered. There was a flurry of questions instantly directed towards President Obasanjo, but he and President Mbeki deflected them back to John Howard. John Howard handled it very well; he was measured and concerned, firm but compassionate. Then it was all over.

CHAPTER 6

Suspended from the Councils

A week later I thought about what had happened over Zimbabwe more in sorrow than in anger. Could we ever have saved Zimbabwe from that suspension?

Commonwealth leaders had taken a firm line, beginning with some exasperation at Coolum in March 2002. The Commonwealth Ministerial Action Group (CMAG) was under attack from Namibia and Tanzania, whose displeasure surfaced in Coolum and could not be ignored. The Commonwealth and its institutions had to be protected. Members were all aware of the Commonwealth values so very carefully codified from Singapore to Harare to Millbrook. The observer groups at the election were well aware that there was more international attention on them than on any other group because of their make-up. Obasanjo had real faith in General Abubakar, his fellow Nigerian, and took his views very seriously. They also knew that all comments by the observers were verifiable. There was concern about the likely reaction of Presidents Nujoma of Namibia, Mkapa of Tanzania, Mwanawasa of Zambia and Chissano of Mozambique, but everyone else hoped they would restrain their objections to decisive action regarding Zimbabwe.

Mugabe's arrogance had clearly got to Obasanjo, who otherwise could be a most generous person. Obasanjo was the only one who had equality with, if not seniority over Mugabe, and I believe he knew what the outcome would be before we started.

The troika process had worked well. Here were three prominent leaders, all with experience and maturity, who didn't have to answer to anyone other than their fellow leaders. They knew their subject, and did not need to seek the advice of officials. It was enough that they could just talk for a couple of hours, formulating their thoughts on a solution that would stand up to scrutiny. This offered a far greater buy-in than when one leader feels he's been outflanked by another leader's officials and only grumpily agrees.

Mugabe, on the other hand, I was later informed, was chastened, but also furious and vindictive. He had never believed his two fellow Africans would do anything more than congratulate him on the election win and tell him to get on with the job.

Nothing is ever final. The first demand came from my own Prime Minister, Helen Clark, insisting that Zimbabwe be prevented from participating in the Commonwealth Games scheduled for Manchester in the United Kingdom in 2002. It wasn't as though I or others wanted Zimbabwe in Manchester – it was just that Commonwealth leaders had authorised the troika to deal with all issues, and the last thing needed now was an 'old Commonwealth' country demanding more restrictions.

I hit the phones; Howard wasn't available, so I first raised Clark's objection with Prime Minister Jean Chrétien of Canada, to whom I was speaking on an unrelated subject, who said, 'Drop it, you won't help Mbeki or Obasanjo and it'll divide the Africans.' From Obasanjo and Mbeki: 'For God's sake, don't bring the Games into it now or it'll upset what we've already got!' So that was that.

In April I spoke on the phone to President Mbeki to obtain a report on discussions between the two Zimbabwe political parties in which South Africa and Nigeria were acting as midwives.

He said they were 'face to face, but they were talking past each other'. There was great anxiety over the agenda, but he stated rather optimistically, 'It's their country, they'll get there.' He went on to say, 'I don't want to encourage any more refugees from Zimbabwe to South Africa by expressing doomsday for Zimbabwe.' I remembered his comments in London that 3.5 million Zimbabweans in South Africa, out of a total of 12 million, was more than enough.

In late April I spoke again to Obasanjo, who said he was exasperated with Mugabe. 'He's frustrating me, he's becoming totally intransigent. I'll probably have to go there again.'

We needed a circuit-breaker. I decided to hold out the olive branch and invite the Zimbabwe high commissioner to lunch. Simbarashe Mumbengegwi and I went to the Landsdowne Club off Berkeley Square, where we talked for a long time. The high commissioner clearly still felt burned by the suspension and was angry about the 'very biased report' of the election observers, along with comments by me, Tony Blair and John Howard.

I, too, was angry, and told him how furious General Abubakar had been to read the rubbish written about him in the Zimbabwe papers. I told Mumbengegwi that Abubakar had told me and others that the situation on the ground was much worse than they had written about in their formal reports. I also said that Presidents Obasanjo and Mbeki were expecting real progress. Mumbengegwi was very senior in the Zimbabwe African National Union, Patriotic Front (ZANU-PF), so I knew my messages would get back to Mugabe. I was told by another Zimbabwe source that Mumbengegwi was getting very agitated in London; he was often not paid, and he was missing out on acquiring a farm or two for himself back home.

The lunch was supposed to bring about some useful dialogue. It might have got a message back to Harare, but it didn't achieve much else.

Early in June I was ambushed by the Southern African Development Community (SADC) high commissioners, who wished to 'talk about Zimbabwe'. The attack was launched against me because I had challenged a letter they'd sent to me telling me that CMAG had no right to do what it did. I reeled for a while under this onslaught, but I recognised that they had a right to speak for their governments.

Drawing breath, I then told them that they were challenging the consensus of the Commonwealth; that they were legally wrong; that the fact that three SADC members had not signed the letter was noted; and that CMAG – nine Commonwealth foreign ministers – were angry that such a group should challenge them.

That didn't impress them, and each high commissioner present made sure I heard the particular views of his or her country. It wasn't the toughest meeting I have attended, but it got my adrenalin going. It probably ended in a tie, but it was yet another example of Zimbabwe's determined diplomacy having orchestrated this ambush.

On a visit to East Africa, my discussion with President Muluzi of Malawi centred on the effect the collapsing Zimbabwe economy was having on his country. He had real concerns about the million-plus Malawians who had been in Zimbabwe for up to three generations working on farms, but who were now being disenfranchised by Mugabe. He said he knew we had to keep pressure on Mugabe. I hoped he was honest about the pressure, because he was actually the current SADC chair.

In late June I received a visit from Ali Bacher and colleagues representing the South African hosts of the upcoming cricket World Cup. Most games were to be played in South Africa, but some would be in Kenya and Zimbabwe. How would the latter be handled? I told them that Zimbabwe was suspended from the councils of the Commonwealth, but we would probably not make further decisions until March 2003 when the suspension expired.

However, I thought they should take on board the following matters that had emerged over the previous couple of years.

First, Mugabe was intent on taking over all white-owned farms; second, chaos would continue around land invasions and food shortages; third, Mugabe would make a big issue of 'Zimbabwe as normal' when entertaining international cricket teams. He did love cricket, as they knew, and maybe they should check with their insurers in case of losses due to game cancellations. Round and round the discussion went, and they left my office feeling rather gloomy. I regretted that they eventually decided in favour of holding the Zimbabwe fixtures.

At an Organisation of African Unity (OAU) summit in Durban in July 2002 I talked to Obasanjo, who after meeting Mugabe (who seemed to have been at his mildest) reported to me 'that the President declared he wanted dialogue with the white farmers. He would abide by the courts. Mugabe disliked Don McKinnon', he reported, 'and couldn't abide Morgan Tsvangirai, although he would most likely drop treason trial charges against Tsvangirai and could take some Movement for Democratic Change (MDC) members into the cabinet.' So much for the separation of powers, I thought.

I suggested to President Sam Nujoma of Namibia, who was always cheerful, that he might give his good friend Robert lessons on how to get money from a colonial power and thus see land redistributed among the indigenous people. He just laughed, knowing he was succeeding with the German government on land repatriation where Robert Mugabe was certainly not with the British.

It was inevitable I would run into Zimbabwe's foreign minister, Stan Mudenge, and I certainly would not have avoided him. Poor Stan looked exhausted. He was the international face of Zimbabwe and was under siege wherever he went, and limited where he could go. It was all taking a toll on him.

He totally rejected the suspension by the troika, and made it clear the government would challenge that decision.

Zimbabwe had no need to talk to the Secretary-General or to the Commonwealth – the President would talk only to the troika. He went on to say that despite the public comments of the commercial farmers, there would always be 3,000 white farmers in Zimbabwe. I then rather cheekily asked how much land the Oppenheimers still owned, knowing there had been extensive public comment about their alleged 'immunity' and they still held no less than 180,000 hectares. No one had witnessed any document listing their farms for seizure. But he let that one go past.

I now had a new head of the Political Affairs department in the Secretariat. Matthew Neuhaus was from Australia, a former high commissioner to Nigeria, a lawyer and a long-time student of Rhodesia/Zimbabwe history. Matthew had lived in East Africa as a child and spoke Swahili. He was to be very useful on the Zimbabwe issue.

We had decided there should be an interim meeting of the troika at the halfway mark of Zimbabwe's suspension. So on 21 September 2002 we were off to Abuja. But as I walked along the air bridge I got a call from Amitav Banerji, my chief of staff, to say the South Africans had just called to say Mugabe would not be there. It was very late in the day to hear that, especially since John Howard was now halfway across the world in transit. We later found out that Mugabe's no-show had been known to the Nigerians at least forty-eight hours before. Oh my, I thought, John Howard will really be spitting tacks.

We arrived at 4.30 a.m. and had a short rest, then went over to State House at Aso Rock and joined President Obasanjo and family for a church service in the chapel. Included in the service were cabinet ministers, defence chiefs, service chiefs, senators and others. It was a Baptist service, similar to what you'd see in the American South. I read a lesson, the President offered the last prayer, then I joined him and his family for lunch.

As I had predicted, John Howard was furious at Mugabe's

no-show. I suggested we could send a group of eminent citizens to report back, but Howard thought it would be better just to order an assessment in December by our officials. If it could be shown that there had been no improvement, he suggested, then we would move to full suspension. It wasn't difficult to agree with this – but would Obasanjo and Mbeki, the other two members of the troika, also agree? We would soon see.

I then found out that the no-show by Mugabe had not been a conspiracy between himself and Obasanjo, but a classic cock-up. Obasanjo had planned to have Mugabe in Abuja for a visit for a few days, then on the last day they would sit down and have a chat with Howard, Mbeki and myself. That way it wouldn't look like a kangaroo court. The trouble was that Obasanjo's people forgot to tell Howard the game plan. When Howard received notice of the meeting he told the Australian press that he and the others were meeting with Mugabe in Abuja and would ask him to explain himself. Naturally, Harare saw the Canberra statement and decided immediately that President Robert Mugabe was certainly not going to be subject to any inquisition, least of all in front of an Australian and a New Zealander. So he decided not to come.

Next morning the four of us (Obasanjo, Howard, Mbeki and myself) met to work through the next move, just as we had done in London. Obasanjo said that for Mugabe to come before a jury of his peers was just too much to swallow. He had tried to persuade him, but to no avail.

Once again we had to hang together for the Commonwealth. Thabo Mbeki still did not want a close involvement. His ANC party was supportive of Mugabe by a significant majority, and when I questioned the partiality of the Zimbabwe judiciary he was quick to defend them.

The conversation went round in circles, and we made little progress. There seemed little alternative to us simply waiting for another six months, in the meantime confirming that the suspension would continue.

John Howard left, saying to me, 'A waste of bloody time, Don – has no one any stomach for tough decisions? I know what Australia, Canada, the United Kingdom and New Zealand are thinking!' And off he went to his aircraft. The experience would colour his thinking at the end of the suspension period, I realised. Howard had played a very important role, listening carefully to the others. But, like the generation before me, he tended to see the Commonwealth through 'old Dominion eyes'.

An Abuja meeting involving Mugabe was never going to be easy to orchestrate, and this had simply been a waste of time. During one of the occasions when there was little else to talk about, I said to the three of them, 'If you think I've screwed up on this whole Zimbabwe thing, just say so, and I'll let it be known that I will not seek a second term as Secretary-General next November.'

'Forget that sort of talk,' I was told. 'We need you there.' Well, that was of some reassurance – at least for the time being. Even President Mbeki was supportive of my second term. And so it was back to London, with the Commonwealth at least on the moral high ground – for what that was worth.

Early in December 2002 I spoke to Mbeki about the MDC and ZANU talks, in which his own official was having difficulty keeping down the level of antagonism between the parties. He did not think much progress had been made, but: 'We have to be patient and only then can they get there.' I agreed with the latter point, but not with the former. I then said that the troika should be prepared to meet in March 2003, at the end of the twelve months, and I would obtain comments from other Commonwealth leaders in advance, along with an officials' report. Soon after, we set 29 March as the date for the troika to meet. Any other day would be criticised by Mugabe. I called President Obasanjo, who accepted the date and said that he and Mbeki would go to Zimbabwe before Christmas to make an assessment.

I did the rounds of a few Zimbabwe contacts and heard some depressing views. There were major food shortages, and supplies were being delivered only if cash was available. There had been more dramas around the land invasions, but interestingly enough, Mugabe was criticising those ministers who were trying to secure more than one farm. The government was still very sensitive about the Commonwealth suspension, and the message was that Zimbabwe diplomacy would go into overdrive in New York and other capitals to combat the negative image. This was something that we in the Commonwealth Secretariat would have to be ready to combat.

In early January 2003 the news out of Zimbabwe was as bad as ever, and South Africa and Nigeria seemed to have disengaged. It had all got to be very depressing for me, the mediator, with no indication of any change. In that role you do need some indication that things will change. If that wasn't happening, then it was understandable that the parties had simply lost interest.

Towards the end of January I wrote in my notes: 'Friends are now telling me that the Libyans are furious at the double-cross dealings of Zimbabwe officials who hike up the price of assets to pay for oil. Now Gaddafi has given up helping his fellow African and cut Mugabe off. So where does the oil come from now?'

In early February I got a ring from John Howard after he had received a call from Mbeki, effectively dumping on any possibility of another troika meeting. Mbeki and Obasanjo had spoken after the latter had been to Harare and Pretoria and decided that Mugabe had done enough.

'This,' I said, 'can only mean that Mugabe has told them what he may do in areas where he is perceived to have gone too far into non-democratic territory. They are getting ahead of the game. We have not done a review and any previous promise of Mugabe's has never been delivered.'

Howard was not happy. He took his role as chair of the troika seriously, and was doubly angry he had to take Mbeki's call in a phone box in Honolulu as he was in transit to Washington DC.

Howard had told the Australian press what President Mbeki had said, which of course infuriated Mbeki, who was always keen to keep others well away from Zimbabwe. This would take a while to settle, I thought, but we must stick to the plan.

On 11 February 2003, Judith Todd, daughter of the one-time and recently deceased Prime Minister of Southern Rhodesia, Garfield Todd, called into Marlborough House in advance of her father's memorial service in London two days later. I had not met her before. She was most engaging, and thoroughly committed to a vibrant Zimbabwe. She knew all the key players personally, and was able to talk about them. I said I wished I had met her father, but did recount going to a lecture he gave in Wellington that my own father had taken me to in the late 1940s. Our fathers were contemporaries at Otago University in New Zealand.

I had spoken to her father on the phone at his home in Bulawayo and she said he had always wished me well in my endeavours on the Zimbabwe issue. She commented how proud he had been, going to vote in the 2002 presidential elections, only to be told he was no longer on the roll. This was the man who as a missionary from New Zealand had set up a primary school in Zimbabwe at which a young Robert Mugabe was a teacher.

Next we received a bombshell of a letter from President Obasanjo to Prime Minister Howard, not only questioning Howard's ability to be an honest broker, but listing all Mugabe's pluses and therefore justifying a lifting of sanctions and suspension. It didn't feel to me that this was the writing of President Obasanjo, and I was right. It was, I was reliably told, written by two key officials who were both very anti-Commonwealth and it had somehow got through the system. It was an extraordinary way to destroy the troika, and did nothing for Obasanjo's credibility.

I went over to the Foreign and Commonwealth Office for a previously scheduled meeting with Baroness Amos and other FCO ministers. They were also horrified at the letter to Howard, which had obviously been very rapidly circulated by the Australians to their friends. I told them I would ring Obasanjo and tackle him head-on. I did this later in the afternoon, telling him we should not prejudge the issue as his letter did, but should await the review and obtain comment from other Commonwealth heads before our March meeting. His response was positive, which led me to believe he may not have fully read the letter that went to Howard. Things were not always as they seemed.

A message from Abuja left me in no doubt that Obasanjo expected the Zimbabwe suspension to remain until the Commonwealth Heads of Government Meeting (CHOGM) in Abuja in December 2003. He was still furious with Mugabe, but he would have to display himself publicly as pro-Zimbabwe and pro-Africa. He would not be unhappy if Mugabe did not turn up at the CHOGM. The battle lines were drawn, but there was a lot of fog on the battlefield.

On 13 February 2003 I spoke to Obasanjo about how infuriated Howard was at receiving the letter questioning his role as an honest broker. His response was 'I'll say it if I believe it.' I let that go, then said we still had to do a report and talk to other Commonwealth leaders. We could not have a division on this issue. The conversation went from tense to affable, and he repeated that 'he didn't want to steer me off any course'. He agreed I should test the temperature among Commonwealth leaders on this issue.

A week later I was in Malaysia at a Non-Aligned Movement (NAM) Conference, with my principal purpose now to get a feel from Commonwealth leaders of how they thought Zimbabwe should be dealt with. I met with a wide range of leaders, particularly from Africa and Asia. My meeting with Obasanjo was remarkable for his candour: 'I won't lose any tears if the suspension stays,' he asserted. The look of fury on the faces of some of his officials was amazing. Some could not even say hello to me. Obasanjo chatted a little and told me he had suggested to Mugabe that we talk. But no meeting took place, despite everyone's best efforts. Robert Mugabe was certainly not going to talk to Don McKinnon.

The divisions that were emerging among the Africans were not only important but also significant as African unity on a major issue started to weaken. Botswana, Lesotho, Kenya, Uganda, Ghana, Cameroon, Nigeria and Sierra Leone all agreed to roll over the suspension to the next CHOGM. Mozambique, Tanzania, The Gambia, Swaziland, Seychelles and Mauritius were all in the 'maybe' camp. An immediate lifting was supported only by South Africa, Namibia and Malawi, and, of course, Zimbabwe itself.

In Johannesburg a week later I had a chance for another meeting with Mbeki. He sighed deeply as I said the name Zimbabwe. 'We want to help them. We're selling them power. We're trying to make their power station work now, although it's held together with sticking plasters.'

I said I had talked to many leaders, and all had said the issue must not split the Commonwealth. He said there were too many Zimbabwe problems spilling over the border. 'I've got more than three million here and I don't want more!' But he intimated he could live with the suspension being rolled over to the CHOGM if that was what was needed to keep the Commonwealth together on the issue.

Having determined that a majority of Africans and most other Commonwealth leaders were supporting a continuation of the suspension until it could be addressed by leaders themselves as a whole at the upcoming CHOGM, it was time to talk again to John Howard, the Commonwealth Chair-in-Office. He was heartened by that information, so I went on to say he would get a report very soon, with Obasanjo and Mbeki receiving theirs the following day. By now I had been in contact with forty-three of the fifty-three leaders. Most, if not all, were reasonably up to date with recent events.

'Southern Africa and in fact all of Africa is becoming tainted by Mugabe's actions. It dries up foreign investment,' said Levy Mwanawasa of Zambia. He had just had enough. 'They're our neighbours, our brothers, but it's costing us.' It was President

Mwanawasa who, before his untimely death in 2008, referred to Zimbabwe's sinking as akin to that of the *Titanic*.

The Caribbean leaders had long been supporters of Mugabe and his front-line state credentials, but had now given up on him. Everybody was saying that this must not split the Commonwealth. No single leader wished to wield the sword, but all knew some retribution was required, and all would go with a consensus. The die was cast overwhelmingly in favour of sustaining the suspension so the wider group of CHOGM leaders could address the issue and bring it to a conclusion.

African politics was always fun to interpret, but this issue was no game. 'How,' I said to Mompati Merafhe on one occasion, 'can you reconcile Botswana's position within SADC calling for Zimbabwe's reinstatement in the Commonwealth and Botswana's position within the Commonwealth justifying the suspension?'

'Easy,' he said. 'One is African solidarity, the other is the Commonwealth.' Then he smiled and said, 'My deputy was at the SADC meeting and he just got blown along with the wind!'

On 15 March I spoke to Obasanjo and gave him the position of other Commonwealth leaders. He had just spoken to Mbeki. He accepted my analysis and 'would not lose sleep over the extended suspension'.

'But,' he went on to say, 'you'll have more difficulty with Thabo.'

I started calling President Mbeki at 6 a.m. when I was in Edinburgh. It was then 8 a.m. in Johannesburg. It was the usual 'He's busy', so I called back at 9 a.m. Then I called at noon. In the end I got him from my car after I left Heathrow Airport from the Edinburgh flight on the way to home in London.

I gave him a full synopsis of my findings. 'Sorry, Don, I haven't read the report.' But then, 'OK, if that's what you say I can go along with your proposal that the suspension holds until CHOGM.'

'That's fine,' I said. This was the green light. I would now move to release the decision immediately. After much drafting and redrafting, the statement was released on Sunday evening London time, thus hitting the Monday morning news in New Zealand and Australia. Having the statement go out under my name enabled each member of the troika to have a little wriggle room on their own interpretation.

By Monday afternoon there were a number of angry warnings from African high commissioners that this would mean blood on the floor. I said to my staff, 'I guess if these envoys want a fight, I am ready for a fight.' They knew I had done a lot of phoning, but their problem was they weren't quite sure what had been said to me by their leaders.

I arranged a meeting of high commissioners at Marlborough House and went through chapter and verse, concluding with the fact that I had spoken to Obasanjo and Mbeki on Saturday and Sunday morning. The South African number three was clearly not comfortable, and hesitatingly asked if John Howard had authorised me to talk to the other leaders. I said that the Secretary-General is entitled to talk to any leader direct at any time, and all three leaders of the troika knew every action I was taking.

Lesotho said I had not spoken to its government. 'Wrong,' I replied. 'I spoke to your Prime Minister at the NAM summit for twenty minutes.'

They had been outmanoeuvred, and now realised that some Southern African leaders had breached the solidarity on Zimbabwe with me privately. Those leaders did so because they knew it was the only way through a difficult situation; most agreed that if nothing in Zimbabwe was improving, there had to be some retribution. It was not a happy meeting, and I noted afterwards that I would need to patch up some relationships at a later date.

Now the counter-attack began, led by Zimbabwe with strong support from Swaziland and Malawi. But this, I knew, was sometimes a case of high commissioners taking a course of action in

London that did not always coincide with the policy position of their leaders.

There were more remonstrations by Southern African high commissioners, who simply could not accept that any of their leaders would have breached SADC solidarity. Most were still of the view that solidarity was more important than the issue itself. They've got a lot to learn about politics, I noted at the time, especially international politics.

Zimbabwe was throwing a lot of fuel on the fire and Obasanjo was now coming under much Pan-African pressure, so I said I would come to Abuja, then fly on to Pretoria to talk to Mbeki. I then spoke to Presidents Museveni (Uganda) and Chissano (Mozambique), and Prime Ministers Abdullah Badawi (Malaysia) and Patterson (Jamaica). All agreed this was a good idea, given the rumblings. This group was a useful sounding board for me outside the troika.

So in late March 2003, nearly twelve months after the suspension, it was back to Abuja, partly to convince Obasanjo of the actions taken, but more to convince his sceptical staffers. At a breakfast meeting, which was not going to be easy, I went straight onto the front foot with some of the facts that would play badly for Nigeria: the likelihood of some 'no-shows' at the CHOGM if Mugabe was there; how the cricket-loving Caribbeans had turned against Mugabe when he fired Henry Olonga from the Zimbabwean team for wearing a black armband; the embarrassment of some East African leaders; and how the chair of CMAG from Botswana himself was adamant about the suspension. Between me and my staff, we batted back most effectively every point they raised.

President Obasanjo then entered the debate, saying he would have to tell Mugabe that he must move on human rights. 'What else do I tell him?'

I said, 'Dialogue with the MDC, amend some pieces of very restrictive legislation, allow food aid to be widely spread and bring back the United Nations Development Programme

(UNDP) and us (the Secretariat) to assist with land redistribution.' It was then agreed that Obasanjo and maybe Mbeki would go to Harare and tell Mugabe what he had to do. This would be the price of Mugabe getting to the CHOGM. Then I would follow up by getting a group of eminent Commonwealth people in August to make an assessment and report progress to foreign ministers in New York in September.

We returned to State House a few hours later to be greeted by a smiling Adobe Obe, the President's special assistant. That told me we were in trouble. Yes, President Obasanjo had spoken to Mbeki, who declared he did not wish to hear the words 'troika' and 'suspension' ever again and would not countenance a foreign ministers' meeting in New York. But yes, an Eminent Persons Group could go ahead, and already we were thinking about Joe Clark, former Canadian Prime Minister, Kenneth Kaunda, former Prime Minister of Zambia, and one of my predecessors, Sonny Ramphal. So we stepped back from an 80 per cent gain to a 60 per cent gain.

Obasanjo was walking a political high wire. He was facing elections and as a key African leader he needed Western support for debt write-offs and big aid money. He was aware he was (wrongly) being tagged a lapdog to the West, and he truly wanted a successful CHOGM. It all revolved around his handling of Mugabe in Zimbabwe. He could not countenance the possibility of a no-show of key leaders if Mugabe was to be in the room.

At the end of March Mugabe struck back. French news agency AFP reported his reference to 'this racial high-handedness of John Howard, a racist Prime Minister, and his New Zealand neighbour Don McKinnon, who's single-handedly acting in a manner that threatens to wreck our Commonwealth'. Wow, I thought, that was rich.

Friends confirmed to me that the controversial Obasanjo letter to John Howard had been drafted by a Nigerian press officer and a senior diplomat in Zimbabwe Foreign Affairs.

It was also apparent that, in all of this, John Howard was
now seen as the enemy of Africa. Not a good start to the Abuja
2003 CHOGM.

The Zimbabwe issue permeated everything. In May 2003 there
was an attempt by the health minister of South Africa to have
Zimbabwe admitted to a meeting of Commonwealth health ministers at the World Health Organization HQ in Geneva. The
meeting was delayed as Zimbabwe's friends demanded to see the
actual legal instrument preventing Zimbabwe from participating.
I was lucky my senior and very effective deputy, Winston Cox
of Barbados, fully understood the issue and got it resolved. The
result: there was no Zimbabwe representation at the meeting.

Many of our discussions revolved around how we could get
a message to Mugabe through a third party. If we sent a high-
powered person, such as a serving or previous president, it would
look too obvious. But if we sent a skilled negotiator who was
not known in Harare, Mugabe wouldn't even open the door. We
just had to keep trying. Engage, engage, many African leaders
were urging us. But it's hard to do so if the other side doesn't
want to respond.

A lot of the speeches I was giving at this time, especially around
the United Kingdom, concluded with questions on Zimbabwe.
The view was generally held that Britain was 80 per cent in the
right. Why didn't Mbeki lean more heavily on Mugabe, and why
didn't the Commonwealth do more?

My response was that the Commonwealth was doing more
than the UN, the United Kingdom, the World Bank, the IMF, the
African Union (AU) and SADC, and it still came to naught. We
deserved an A+ for effort, but sure, you could give us a D– for
achievement. Mbeki didn't lean on Mugabe in the same way
that Britain would not always criticise France. New Zealanders
remember that when French agents blew up the vessel *Rainbow
Warrior* in Auckland harbour, this act of terrorism was not

criticised by the United Kingdom. That line of questioning would then end, with people wondering about the efficacy of diplomacy.

When the questions got onto the issue of land, I would point out that the government of Ian Smith had still been acquiring 'native land' without compensation right through to the end of UDI. So whose land was it really? These questions kept coming for my full eight years in the job, ad nauseam. I did allow myself to get a little tetchy from time to time.

In June I hosted a light lunch for the African high commissioners – against the advice of my staff, who thought I'd received enough punishment. I wanted to say to them directly just what I wanted them to know.

It was all very friendly for a while, until Tanzania opened up on the Zimbabwe issue, suggesting we, the Secretariat, could have done better and that I had manoeuvred the extension to the suspension. This diplomat, I knew, was 180 degrees away from his foreign minister on this issue, so I had to bite my tongue. Then it was all on. I sat back and let them all speak, including the Zimbabwe high commissioner.

As he moved into top gear I noticed that those high commissioners who actively supported the extended suspension – Ghana, Botswana, Sierra Leone, The Gambia, Seychelles – slowly and quietly left the room. Oh well, I thought, it's me versus them.

When all member countries had finished I very carefully gave them chapter and verse. First, their own leaders had concluded the Zimbabwe suspension should remain, even if it wasn't their country's official position. Africa did not have a single voice on this issue and anyone suggesting that these actions were racially based was spreading an untruth with malice.

'If any one of you thinks I have impugned the integrity of your leaders or have misrepresented your leaders you have a simple remedy. You can at the next CHOGM in Nigeria get a new Secretary-General.'

There was a stunned silence and they all left the room. Even my own staff looked a little shaken, but I felt pretty good.

I was due at an AU summit in Maputo in Mozambique on 9 July
2003. Yes, I was the only white face in the leaders lounge, but
I was never made to feel uncomfortable in this group, which
included non-Commonwealth leaders. At the official dinner I
was sitting a table away from Mugabe. Kofi Annan, who was
sitting beside Mugabe, suggested, 'Let's bring Don over here for
a little talk.' 'No!' Mugabe promptly said.

To return to Abuja, I hitched a ride on President Obasanjo's
aircraft, sitting in a very opulent cabin with some of his close
friends. Obasanjo never stops thinking about problems and strat-
egising solutions. He sat down and promptly said he had told
Mugabe he would not be invited to the forthcoming CHOGM.
And he would pull back from his direct involvement and recognise that Southern Africa was President Mbeki's patch. About
ten minutes of discussion, then off he went to the back of the
plane to talk to other staff.

When he came back later I tried to slow him down a little. It
was important, I said, that as the chair of CHOGM he was in full
command of the issue, for wider Commonwealth reasons. He
had to be able to give other Commonwealth leaders his personal
view of the situation and then to steer the Zimbabwe issue out
of the way on the first day. To have it hanging over the whole
conference for two and a half days would not be good and would
anger others, especially those who recalled its dominance at the
Coolum CHOGM.

He responded by saying he had told Mugabe that he was making life increasingly difficult for him and therefore no invitation
would be extended. Mugabe had then said, 'Please invite me and
I'll decline.' 'No, that would not work,' Obasanjo had replied.

Mbeki, he went on to say, believed the MDC wanted a deal
but because of divisions within the MDC between Tsvangirai
and his deputy, Welshman Ncube, nothing was happening.
Mugabe had told him he wanted to introduce a constitutional

change giving more power to the Prime Minister, who could then invite three or four MDC people to join a government of national unity. Mugabe himself would be part of the next parliamentary and presidential elections, but he would play less of an executive role. Obasanjo was playing it tough, which was good, but we both knew that Mugabe was constantly dropping promises on the floor and was capable of persuading others that he would deliver. Those people had more confidence in Mugabe than did Obasanjo and I.

I then requested my official, Professor Adefuye, to join us, and we went through it again. The minimum expected from Obasanjo would be: some constitutional change; the Zimbabwe Prime Minister would be appointed with the consent of the assembly; a government would be formed with three or four MDC ministers; and Mugabe's executive role would be diminished.

As I flew home to London from Abuja I surmised that only Obasanjo would be able to resolve the Zimbabwe issue. He was one of only two leaders in Africa whom Mugabe regarded as his superior – or at least as his equal – the other being Yoweri Museveni of Uganda. Both men had solid credentials as freedom fighters, both had been generals and they'd both been around as long as Mugabe. In Mugabe's view, all of the others in Commonwealth Africa were mere boys, not to be listened to. So far Obasanjo's dealings with Mugabe hadn't given him a lot of confidence, so I knew he would be tough. Obasanjo, I felt, was prepared to go the last mile for the sake of decency and African politics, and only if that failed could he show that no stone remained unturned and diminish any criticism from the G8. It was the G8 that were the key to getting some debt writedown in Nigeria, and Obasanjo had shown he was running a tight ship.

Another new British FCO minister, this time Chris Mullin from the left of the Labour Party, was now responsible for Africa and the Commonwealth. These ministers seemed to get rolled over every year or two, or even less. You just got to know them, build up their familiarity with the Commonwealth and then they went off to Education or somewhere. We had a good discussion and I could sense a practical-minded person – although what he really wanted me to do was help the UK get back onto membership of CMAG. He was clearly echoing the voice of his officials. I said it would be premature. I said I felt the FCO attitude towards Africa was dominated by Zimbabwe and Libya, and anyway the United Kingdom had been off CMAG for only two years. He disagreed that the United Kingdom had an obsession over Zimbabwe, but I thought, nonetheless, this is a minister with whom I could work.

In New York in July I heard that Zimbabwe was definitely out to get me by ensuring I did not get a second term. They had approached a senior African diplomat but had been rapidly told that an African would not be a credible candidate. They then went to a former UN senior official from Sri Lanka, whose CV read very well; they told him just how insensitive I was to cultural values, as well as being incompetent. This official then told his minister, Tyronne Fernando, who thought himself to be a respectable candidate but who would have preferred Kofi Annan's job (so he told me later).

My staff supporters wanted me to go out immediately and announce my intention to be available for a second term. But I preferred not to overreact and to await the endorsement of an approaching Pacific Islands Forum (PIF) Summit in Auckland, New Zealand. The prospect of a one-term Secretary-General became a new issue of some excitement around the Secretariat and some Commonwealth capitals, but I knew the Pacific leaders would be very unhappy if the first Secretary-General from the Pacific got rolled after only one term.

I wasn't, however, going to underestimate what Harare would

ABOVE Prime Minister Lawrence Gonzi of Malta was a champion of small states. He successfully initiated the Gozo Declaration for small states at the November 2005 Commonwealth Heads of Government Meeting (CHOGM) in Malta.

BELOW With HM The Queen.

ABOVE With former US Secretary of State Madeleine Albright, with whom I have had the pleasure to work closely.

BELOW LEFT This portrait of me by Richard McWhannell still hangs in Marlborough House.

BELOW RIGHT Every year on Commonwealth Day (in March) I visited schools to talk about the Commonwealth and what we did. Here I am at a primary school in south London showing the children just how widespread was the Commonwealth geographically.

ABOVE From UN Secretary-General Ban Ki-moon (pictured) and his predecessor Kofi Annan, I was given considerable assistance to promote many projects, along with a ready ear to discuss problems common to both our organisations.

BELOW LEFT New Zealand cartoonist Garrick Tremain had already decided my fate at the hands of Robert Mugabe in 2003.

BELOW RIGHT It was a tradition at CHOGM for the Queen to host a dinner. The Queen here was acknowledging the toast and clearly enjoying the evening.

ABOVE It was all smiles in early 2007 when I met President Mwai Kibaki, but regretfully he wasn't willing to make the appropriate changes to Kenya's Electoral Commission to neutralise the embedded partisanship.

BELOW Addressing a large group of schoolchildren on the work of the Commonwealth in November 2007.

ABOVE With Portia Simpson-Miller, Jamaica's first female Prime Minister and a leader who developed a great rapport with the people.

BELOW Exchanging the ANC handshake with President Thabo Mbeki of South Africa, whose presidency of Africa's wealthiest but socially most complex country was never going to be an easy run.

ABOVE After I addressed some 400 students at an all-girls' high school near Kampala in Uganda, some of the more enterprising ones decided they just had to get my autograph.

BELOW LEFT With a young Chagos Islands girl in Port Louis, Mauritius. The Chagos Islanders were forcibly removed from the islands by the British Government in the 1960s and settled in the Seychelles and Mauritius.

BELOW RIGHT An enjoyable moment with President Olusegun Obasanjo (third from left) of Nigeria, my wife Clare and Nigerian High Commissioner Christopher Kolade.

ABOVE For me, the challenges of Pakistan began during my time as New Zealand's foreign minister and continued through my full eight-year term as Secretary-General. This was one of many meetings over that period with President Pervez Musharraf.

BELOW With legendary former President Kenneth Kaunda of Zambia, who was of immense help to me in persuading King Mswati III of Swaziland to change the constitution and nurture new democratic institutions.

ABOVE Always a pleasure and rather humbling to receive an honorary doctorate. Here I am with the chancellor of Heriot-Watt University, Lord Mackay of Clashfern (second from left), and fellow honorees, having received the D.Litt in the city of Edinburgh, July 2005.

BELOW Would that all reports were so entertaining.

do. They would fight this one right up to the CHOGM, I felt, in many devious ways.

At the Auckland PIF Summit the first question I was asked by the New Zealand media was: would I get a second term? My response was that there were three requirements: first, that I wanted the job; second, that others wanted me; and third, that the New Zealand government supported me. My very supportive wife Clare, who was involved in a number of activities, including some charities, was really enjoying London and wasn't at all happy at the prospect of some unfriendly pro-Zimbabwe activists preventing me getting a second term.

The retreat of the Forum leaders, I was told, did not even bother discussing the second-term issue. There was unanimous support, and even the non-Commonwealth members of Palau, the Marshall Islands and the Federated States of Micronesia offered their votes! I left New Zealand with a warm feeling of support.

The CHOGM in Abuja was now just three months away and tensions were rising. Obasanjo admitted to me that he was under a lot of pressure from African colleagues to lift the Zimbabwe suspension. He said that Mugabe intended to have both the constitutional changes and a government of national unity in place very soon. I didn't believe it was possible; Obasanjo would have liked to think it was possible, but he had now been burnt too many times.

Mugabe, he said, had not at this stage been sent an invitation. I repeated that as chair of the Commonwealth meeting, Obasanjo could call the shots and still remain sensitive to SADC and AU thinking. Later, during a quiet moment away from officials, I raised my own candidacy with him; he said he thought my statement of 16 March 2003 (announcing the extension of Zimbabwe's suspension) had gone too far, but he expressed his total and unequivocal support for me.

In late August a war of words broke out between Australia and South Africa over Zimbabwe and the upcoming CHOGM. Australian Prime Minister John Howard was very gung-ho and was talking about taking responsibility for keeping Zimbabwe out of the CHOGM. South African President Thabo Mbeki was saying the Commonwealth must remain engaged, dialogue was important and help was needed.

The Zimbabwe papers took full advantage of this division, linking me to Howard, and Reuters even referred to me as an Australian. Always hard for a Kiwi to take!

I was also hearing from African friends about the frustration of those of their leaders who wanted to support Zimbabwe. From my notes at the time: 'They feel they are often cajoled into doing so, and are becoming embarrassed when they do so to have their loyalty questioned. They are all aware that nothing is working. They silently believe that Mugabe is working from the right motives to get the land back, but that he's made a real debacle of the implementation.' A fact unnoticed by Mugabe was that the new generation of African leaders, who had not been freedom fighters, respected their elders but their education at Western universities gave them a far more contemporary and global view of this issue. They were also more aware of the benefits of democracy and the need to keep onside with international banks.

No one could block out from their minds that Mugabe was a father figure for the liberation movement and a leader of the front-line states. It was more in sorrow than in anger that they were slowly leaving him to swing in the wind.

At a Commonwealth Parliamentary Conference in Uganda I seized a chance to talk to President Museveni about his desire to host the next CHOGM. 'General Obasanjo stole my CHOGM,' he said with a smile. Then he really cut loose on Zimbabwe: 'Mugabe's becoming Africa's enemy. He's anti-business and he's turning away investment from Africa.' He agreed to join a group to visit Mugabe after the CHOGM in Abuja, and he fully understood the need for the suspension to be sustained.

African loyalties run deep and can never be underestimated. It was only back in the 1990s that a summit meeting of the then Organisation of African Unity (OAU) tasked Presidents Mugabe and Museveni to go to Nigeria to meet the military dictator General Sani Abacha and to plead for former Presidents Obasanjo and Abiola to be released from prison. Abacha's alleged response was: 'If you want me to be a democrat I must treat everybody equally and so I must execute Obasanjo as I've executed the others!' Thank goodness he did not and Obasanjo was ultimately released, although not by Abacha. These stories cannot be ignored when African leaders talk and pay homage to each other.

Sir Nigel Scheinwald, the new foreign policy adviser at No. 10 Downing Street, was worried that Zimbabwe would just turn up at the Abuja CHOGM. He was more Europe- than Commonwealth-orientated; I doubted he could envisage a meeting such as the Retreat at the CHOGM where he would not be in the room sitting loyally and ready for anything behind his leader. Nigel has a bit to learn about the Commonwealth, I thought. But I told him, somewhat overconfidently, not to worry about Mugabe; Obasanjo had it well in hand, I said.

I received a visit from the Malawian London envoy Bright Msaka, who was clearly feeling bruised over our last Zimbabwe discussion. But he wanted me to know Malawi was supporting me 100 per cent for my re-election. Well, I thought, that's better than a kick – they're a small next-door neighbour, often beholden to Zimbabwe, and had been very pro-Mugabe. His further general comment reinforced my view that SADC was rethinking its position in the light of all the shenanigans, chaos and bloodshed going on in Zimbabwe.

Mugabe, he said, was furious. 'He'll pull down the pillars of the temple very soon. He just cannot believe he'll be excluded from a summit on the African continent.'

Now it was only a month out from the CHOGM. John Howard told me he was still worried that Mugabe would turn up. I hoped I'd allayed his fears. I called President Obasanjo, who had been to Harare the previous day. Mugabe, said Obasanjo, was continuing to say that he intended to be at the CHOGM and was entitled to be there. This was really upping the stakes.

Obasanjo was very sombre: 'I don't think Mugabe's done enough to warrant coming to the CHOGM.' He said he had tried to arrange a meeting between Mugabe and Tsvangirai after meeting the latter, but that was scuppered by Mugabe. Still, Obasanjo was the one African leader who would not be shy to embarrass Mugabe. If Mugabe thought he would get his way he was seriously miscalculating.

By the end of October 2003 there was nothing but bad news coming out of Zimbabwe on a wide range of fronts. That said, it now emerged that the Sri Lankan President, Mrs Chandrika Bandaranaike Kumaratunga, had hatched a deal with South Africa and Zimbabwe to support her former foreign minister, Lakshman Kadirgamar, for my job. 'We know Mr McKinnon will be at the end of his term,' was her message. So swords were indeed drawn.

Only a day later, however, on 26 November, there turned out to be a split between the Sri Lankan President and her Prime Minister over the Kadirgamar candidacy, and none of the three would be at the CHOGM. 'Hardly,' my notes say, 'a serious campaign move.' But despite the protestations of officials, or so they told me, the candidacy was not withdrawn.

The real push on the Secretary-General issue was coming from Zimbabwe, which was now working through a very willing South Africa. President Mbeki expressed to all he met his fury that I had allowed the suspension to continue when he had expected it to be lifted.

I also heard that Mbeki had told the Sri Lankans that he could deliver the African vote for their candidate. And I heard that British officials, who felt me a rather too independent-minded Secretary-General, had let the Sri Lankans know that they could support their candidate if it was all moving that way on the day. It's always nice to know who your friends are, but that's politics. I've seen that sort of behaviour too many times to be overly worried by it.

Before I left for Nigeria and the CHOGM, I paid a visit to No. 10 Downing Street to meet a very tired-looking Tony Blair. The Middle East conflicts were taking their toll. He wasn't particularly interested in Abuja, but he wanted to be satisfied that Mugabe would not be there. And he said he was totally frustrated with Mbeki. 'He's really an old-style Marxist,' he said. 'We are supporting you, though' – for which I thanked him. If he had heard the scuttlebutt about the Sri Lankan candidate he wasn't going to show it, especially if it came from the FCO.

And so it was time for Abuja and the CHOGM – time for much high drama and for a final resolution of the troubled relationship between Robert Mugabe's Zimbabwe and the Commonwealth.

On 2 December 2003 I started the day in Abuja with a breakfast meeting with Obasanjo, who was in a good mood and confident he could handle the Zimbabwe issue, even though Mugabe was becoming increasingly belligerent. I told him the media were now interested in only two things – Zimbabwe and the election of the Secretary-General – and said that with the assistance of Professor Adefuye we should get both out of the way early. Although the good professor was on my staff, he had been a strong and active supporter in the campaign to get Obasanjo elected as the UN Secretary-General some years before. So they knew each other very well.

We held a short council of war with key staff who wished to actively support my candidacy, and from them learned that South Africa and Namibia were pressuring all and sundry to vote for the Sri Lankan candidate.

On the job front, some friends were advising me that Kadirgamar would receive seven or eight votes. But the Zimbabweans, who of course were not at the conference but were camped out in various hotels around Abuja to spread their campaign team, were telling people it was all over for me.

On the evening of 4 December South Africa called all the Africans and Caribbeans to a meeting on the Secretary-General vote and on Zimbabwe. This was to be Mbeki's first strategic failure: the Caribbeans said they would all be supporting me, and would not let Zimbabwe off the hook. Worse still, we heard that a number of African leaders walked out of the meeting, highlighting their dislike for Mbeki's plan.

The next morning, 5 December, Obasanjo rang at 6.30 a.m. to ask me to meet him at 8.30 a.m. Adefuye reported on the failure of the Mbeki meeting. Obasanjo told me he wanted to deal with Zimbabwe early. He had spoken to Mugabe and had been told he had accepted the original twelve-month suspension. Zimbabwe had even reluctantly gone along with the additional nine months – but any more and Mugabe would walk out of the Commonwealth.

It was always a possibility, but after his government's behaviour in the past twelve months there was no possibility of him receiving united African support. So a major split in the Commonwealth was unlikely. We then discussed getting a small group of leaders to go off, look carefully and report back on the Zimbabwe issue. We soon agreed that Patterson of Jamaica would be a good chair and added to that South Africa, Mozambique, Australia, Canada and India. It was a good balance of Commonwealth heavyweights and friends of Zimbabwe.

For the formal start of the CHOGM we were greeting all the guest leaders as they arrived at two-minute intervals. Now all except Tony Blair were there. But then there was a little drama over whether Mr Blair would come before or after the Queen. He came after the Queen, with some bright spark announcing, 'But of course Tony comes after the Queen, he's the Emperor.'

At the first executive session President Obasanjo cut straight to the Zimbabwe issue by introducing his proposal for a small group of leaders to go away and bring back to the leaders a recommendation for a Commonwealth response to Zimbabwe.

After the members were announced, President Mbeki remonstrated that he should not be on due to his SADC role. It should be Tanzania. I quickly whispered to Obasanjo that Tanzania did not have a president here; they were represented by their foreign minister, and that would not look good.

Obasanjo then said that no, we could not have a foreign minister on such an important issue. With all the weight of his office and his seniority he declared, 'I expect President Mbeki will be the right person.'

So we had in the chair the long-serving Prime Minister of Jamaica, P. J. Patterson, who knew Mugabe well. He was a highly skilled lawyer, shared an African heritage and had everyone's confidence that he would do it right.

Prime Minister Howard of Australia, chair of the troika on Zimbabwe, which still had a standing mandate, would brook no nonsense. He believed Commonwealth values were what held us together and that flagrant breaches should not be ignored or hidden.

President Chissano of Mozambique, a long-time Mugabe supporter and best man at the last Mugabe wedding in 1996, also had very firm values, but he would be sympathetic to the old freedom fighter.

President Mbeki of South Africa had been caught in the headlights of the Western media for not doing enough. He knew Mugabe was breaching Commonwealth principles, but he also knew his own ANC were big Mugabe supporters.

Indian Prime Minister Atal Behari Vajpayee couldn't have been more remote from the issue, but as a very long-serving politician he had seen it all. His would be a balanced view, tinged with sympathy.

Prime Minister Jean Chrétien of Canada had spent enough

time with Commonwealth leaders to know what they would expect of any democratic leader. He would be tough, but he would also be sympathetic.

None of the group felt they had been done any favours by being selected. They left the room for their first meeting knowing what they had to do was not going to be easy. Whatever they came back with would not necessarily enjoy unanimous support.

The group had two reasonably productive meetings and all actively participated. All wanted Zimbabwe back. All knew there had been little or no progress in that country since the election. At a critical point, the chair noted that nobody in the group was asking to lift the suspension immediately. That was agreed. Slowly a set of words was put together that gave a reasonable reflection of all their views. However, there was as yet no conclusion on how to move towards lifting the suspension in the future.

Two forms of words were put into square brackets for the entirety of leaders to address. Option one revolved around the word 'unanimous', while option two was for 'consensus'. Note that this would involve only the individual leaders at the Retreat. There would be no officials except me, my note-taker and President Obasanjo's note-taker.

The Retreat debate opened with chair Patterson delivering a very good summary of the group's discussion. He took it step by step and said very carefully at a critical point of the meeting that he had asked three times if anyone felt the suspension should be immediately lifted and in each case the answer was no. The debate was one of the best I've heard, and it was possible only because the leaders were on their own. There were no officials who might use another leader's words against him or her later.

There was a general feeling among all leaders that the people of Zimbabwe were suffering and needed help; that people's aspirations must be allowed to be realised; that the issue of Zimbabwe must not divide the Commonwealth, and nor must the media; that the members must not let the house 'burn down'.

There was a small group that wanted the suspension lifted immediately. My notes show that the following phrases were used:

We must be unambiguous, the suspension must be lifted.
We sometimes expect democracy to mature too rapidly.
Mugabe will walk if the suspension is not lifted.
We've never heard the Zimbabwe side of the story.
Zimbabwe and Mugabe feel persecuted.
SADC says lift sanctions now.
We need dialogue, not suspension.

And from those advocating the suspension remain in place we heard the following:

We set our standards in Harare, we must stick to them.
We must be tough.
The reputation of the Commonwealth is on the line.
This is not the time to buckle.
We don't need to go as far as imposing sanctions, suspension
  is enough.
Decisive action is required.
We must be colour blind.

The debate lasted more than an hour and a half. It was summed up very cogently by Obasanjo, who realised full well that if the suspension was renewed for a second time then Mugabe would walk. In fact, he was already looking past that point, saying, 'We can still engage and help even if he does walk.'

Although SADC had a very firm collective line, there were a number of SADC leaders who did not feel obliged to stay with that, knowing as they did that Commonwealth values would mean nothing if the suspension was lifted now. The press were saying the same thing.

In the end, consensus, a long-used Commonwealth principle, won out over unanimity. It was a pity that Robert Mugabe wasn't there to hear the whole debate, that he didn't hear what his fellow leaders really thought instead of just assuming that his own supreme status, authority and seniority in Africa would carry the day.

Nevertheless, once the news got out there was a very angry response from Zimbabwe directed at its SADC colleagues. Zimbabwe demanded, with real threats, I was told, that no SADC leader had any right to accept a Commonwealth consensus on a continued suspension.

This was not helped by Tony Blair's early departure, when he announced to the waiting world media that Britain had scored a victory on the Zimbabwe issue. Obasanjo was furious, knowing how sensitive and precarious was the consensus. 'Tony must be told,' he said to my political director, 'that he can't behave like this.'

In a restricted executive session a few hours later, where there were also three to four officials per country, the dam looked as if it might crack. Prime Minister Mosisili of Lesotho, acting as chair of SADC political issues, stated that he was giving notice of SADC's disapproval of the decision.

President Obasanjo, clearly blindsided, asked, 'All of SADC?'

'All those that have signed,' was the response.

'Well, where do we go now?' asked Obasanjo, almost spitting out the words.

The officials, who had never witnessed such a challenge to Africa's most senior leader, were riveted to their seats. No one dared flicker an eyelid.

Others entered the debate. It was very obvious that between Zimbabwe and South Africa it had been decided that Lesotho would lead on this – and by the look on Prime Minister Mosisili's face he would have rather been anywhere but in this room.

'All right,' said Obasanjo. 'Let's note it and move on ... We can't go in this direction ... You must think again ... This is an attack on our consensus ... What you're suggesting is a breach of collective responsibility.'

Lesotho was now in full retreat from the prevailing consensus view, stating it was still not satisfied with the way the debate had gone. That was followed by a firm lecture from the chair: 'We all have domestic politics! We all have to sell it! This will not help!'

Then came a real tour de force from Prime Minister Patterson of Jamaica, whose admirable legal and political skills impressed the room. He said he had chaired the meeting painstakingly and regarded Mugabe as a friend. 'This isn't just a question of Commonwealth credibility, it also involves the integrity of the Nigerian President,' he said slowly and firmly. He then spent more than five minutes in that most attractive Caribbean accent going through all the points.

'We are dealing with two almost irreconcilable positions ... And we have got a consensus ... Certainly not everybody is happy ... But we must not show a split... As for the SADC,' he said forcefully, his eyes drilling in on key SADC leaders in the room, 'You should now state you'll be at the forefront of working with Zimbabwe in the future. And you should not refer publicly to what some individual members said in the Retreat.'

Nigeria had put in an enormous effort over the last few months, he said. 'We don't want to end up in a gulf of divisiveness. That's all I have to say.'

Such was the force of his argument and moral authority that you could have heard the proverbial pin drop. There was total silence for a minute or two, then chair Obasanjo said quietly, grimly and forcefully: 'I'll give SADC members ten minutes to reconsider their position.'

After twenty minutes the SADC members concluded their concerns, and returned to the room. The executive session resumed.

'We have decided,' said Prime Minister Mosisili from Lesotho, 'to tone down some of the language. And the separate SADC statement will be released from Lusaka rather than from here.'

From the chair Obasanjo: 'Thanks to all. The suspension of Zimbabwe remains according to the Retreat's recommendation. What's the next item on the agenda, Mr Secretary-General?'

That was the end of the beginning, because from that day on Zimbabwean diplomats began unleashing their fury on their fellow Africans for not supporting them – or at least for not preventing a consensus. Predictably, Robert Mugabe announced immediately from Harare that Zimbabwe would leave the Commonwealth.

This, I was told later by one of his ministers, was never a cabinet decision. 'The old man was so furious that he just acted alone, we never even had a discussion,' my friend said, adding with half a smile, 'not that it would have made much difference.'

In public, African leaders remained tight-lipped, knowing they had to let this hurricane of venom out of Harare blow itself out. One younger leader said to me that Mugabe would flail them over the day's events for some time, but it wouldn't destroy the Commonwealth as he would like it to. And Zimbabwe would come back some day.

Back in London, I wrote to the Queen informing her of the decision. I noted that our membership was now back to fifty-three, and that we would be lowering the Zimbabwean flag and removing the flagpole at the front of Marlborough House. One minor bonus – this wasn't a problem, because alphabetically it was at the end of the line.

On 29 November came a formal response from Mugabe: 'If our sovereignty is what we have to lose to be readmitted into the Commonwealth, well we will say goodbye to the Commonwealth, and perhaps the time has come to say so.'

The temperature rose more than a little on 7 December when, in response to the British media, Mugabe spat out, 'The Commonwealth is a mere club. It has become like *Animal Farm*, where some members are more equal than others. How can [PM Tony] Blair claim to regulate and direct events and still say all of us are equals?'

He was still clearly agitated six months later, in April 2004, when he said, 'We will never go back to the Commonwealth, we shall never go back to that evil organisation. We locked the door that we used to get out.'

I occasionally ran into prominent and still-friendly Zimbabweans in various places such as African airports or at summits or the UN who would smile and say, 'We'll be back when the old man's gone.' I, too, would smile, saying, 'That won't be a problem.'

Well, I hope so, but it's so regrettable that all the good Mugabe did in his early years, even up to 1997, has been so overshadowed by his reactionary, deplorable and quite irrational behaviour since that time. That so many people had to die, to a point where it was no longer even news, is just so painful for all. For millions of Africans he's still one of their saviours, but regrettably they do not have as much influence as those outside Africa, who expect better from him. Yes, I was the first Secretary-General to lose a country, but why should so many people continue to suffer while he's still in office? He probably correctly guessed that people would eventually get bored and just turn off news about Zimbabwe, and so ignore his continuing repression.

Meanwhile, the Commonwealth, despite all the pressures that might cause it to break, has stood united on principle and awaits the return of Zimbabwe when that country has arrived at the point where it can again subscribe to all Commonwealth values. The Commonwealth remains engaged where it can, particularly through its SADC members, and holds out the hand of reconciliation and support to Zimbabwe in its CHOGM communiqués. It has been a sad story, but the return of South Africa to the Commonwealth, after so many years on its own during the apartheid era, offers hope of what the future can bring.

CHAPTER 7

'Who Cares About the Commonwealth?'

In 2000 a very senior and patriotic Pakistani leader declared to me in a moment of frustration that he was angry with his own country as compared to India. 'Since 1947 they have had regular elections and have become a functioning democracy. We in Pakistan still can't get it right. We lurch from flawed elections to military coups and back again. It's embarrassing!'

The most recent of these events had been the year before, on 12 October 1999, when yet another military takeover of Pakistan had occurred. In the rest of the world there had been only mild surprise. In the country itself there had been joy in the streets, and little shooting or bloodshed.

Such events left some democrats bewildered. If one looked back over Pakistan's history one noted that military strong-men had ruled the country for more than half its life since independence. These leaders had often insisted that they were the only bulwark against communism, or that they were the only group that was truly patriotic and capable of safeguarding Pakistan's security and sovereignty against external threats. The military leaders also claimed to be better at governance and less corrupt – charges that Pakistani politicians were keen to demonstrate were wrong during the country's brief periods of democracy. From 1958 under Ayub Khan until the death of Zia-ul-Haq in 1988, the military had ruled the country intermittently for twenty-four years. So another coup came as no surprise.

Following its mandate, the Commonwealth immediately suspended Pakistan from the councils of the Commonwealth and dispatched a ministerial team under Canadian Foreign Minister Lloyd Axworthy (see page 58). As discussed in Chapter 3, following the suspension of Nigeria at the Auckland Commonwealth Heads of Government Meeting (CHOGM) in 1995, Commonwealth leaders had affirmed through the Millbrook Commonwealth Action Programme that any country in which a democratically elected government was overthrown would be suspended. No ifs, buts or maybes.

So a process had begun, including engagement with the coup leader General Pervez Musharraf, which was to last longer than most envisaged.

Not surprisingly, the new Pakistani government was not pleased to see the Axworthy-led group. There were some fairly tense meetings, which tended to conclude with the attitude on the part of the Pakistanis of 'Who cares about the Commonwealth?' This is the usual response of the government and the official media when any member is suspended. It seems to be a matter of national pride to be able to say: 'If they don't want us, well, we don't want them either!'

The Commonwealth Ministerial Action Group (CMAG) report to the Durban CHOGM in November 1999 noted that the people of Pakistan were fed up with the excesses of Nawaz Sharif's Pakistan Muslim League (N) government but were equally dissatisfied with the performance of the preceding Pakistan Peoples Party (PPP) government under Benazir Bhutto. The report also noted that even political parties welcomed the military coup in the hope that it would bring better governance and lead to a newly elected government that respected the rule of law and independence of the judiciary.

It was clearly very awkward for Lloyd Axworthy to inform Commonwealth leaders in Durban that the CMAG mission had returned from Pakistan with the impression that the coup was actually welcome in the country, not because Pakistanis had a liking for military rulers, but because they were utterly frustrated by the performance of the political parties. The report of the CMAG mission on Pakistan was therefore shelved and not made public.

That did not mean no action, however. The Commonwealth's experience around the suspension issue had been largely honed by its suspension of Nigeria in 1995 following the execution of a number of human rights activists by the military regime of General Abacha (see Chapter 3). The Durban CHOGM accordingly condemned the unconstitutional overthrow of the democratically elected government in Pakistan and called for the restoration of civilian democratic rule without delay. Leaders also endorsed CMAG's decision to suspend Pakistan from the councils of the Commonwealth pending the restoration of democracy. (This was the same CHOGM at which I was elected Secretary-General.)

It was now assumed that if a democratically elected Commonwealth government was overthrown there would be an automatic suspension. Nigeria's had been a full membership suspension; Pakistan's was from the councils of the Commonwealth. Full suspension would be the next step taken if the military regime failed to engage with CMAG or did not provide a road map of elections for the restoration of democracy.

After I took over as Secretary-General, the newly formed CMAG met on 2 May 2000 at Marlborough House. On Pakistan it concluded that we should remain engaged and pursue a definite commitment to a timetable to fully restore democracy, and that the Secretary-General should visit Pakistan.

In June 2000 another member country, Fiji, succumbed to martial law and the abrogation of its constitution by the military. CMAG suspended Fiji from the councils of the Commonwealth (see Chapter 10). So in addition to my other responsibilities as the new Secretary-General of the Commonwealth, I now had two suspended member countries to work with for the restoration of democracy and the rule of law. Knowing the sensitivity of political leaders when they are told by outsiders what to do, I knew these were not open and shut issues. It would have been misguided for me to believe that these were anything other than long-haul journeys that would require skilled relationship and confidence building before anything could happen.

Arriving in Islamabad on 25 August 2000, I and my two-person team were met by a distinctly unfriendly protocol officer, obviously ex-military (as were many in the public service), who told us what we would be doing. It wasn't very welcoming, but until I met General Musharraf we would just roll with the punches.

At the designated time we went in to meet him. He was elegantly dressed, with a perfectly trimmed moustache and highly polished boots. And, of course, he was in his general's uniform.

I didn't want to launch into a lecture. I knew we had to play this one long. I wanted to get to know him, not make him feel threatened by the Commonwealth, and I hoped that he would be prepared to see me again. So I let him talk. He was an ascetic individual, who strongly believed in his country. But for him and his military colleagues, he said, it had gone off the rails after independence with unbridled corruption followed by coups. He would like to give it a new start.

To me it seemed just a little naive to believe he could unilaterally change all the institutions and deliver democratic governance at the local, regional and national levels in two years. It would be well-nigh impossible. I did not believe he was taking into account that people have to be part of the process before they accept a solution. A military dictator prescribing what the organs of government should be is no different to a colonial power telling people what's good for them. To take just one example: to have a free and fair election he would have to ID card 80 million voters, many of whom were illiterate. The administrative effort alone would be enormous.

One thing that emerged from this long discussion with the

general was his obsession with – in fact, his hatred of – the feudal families that have dominated Pakistani politics for so long. The belief was that they were very corrupt, they were arrogant and greedy, and they were anything but democratic. In particular, he wanted to get back from these families and their banks all the ill-gotten wealth he believed they had stripped from the country and had hidden around the world. As for the army, he regarded them as a force for good and the only group of Pakistan citizens who truly represented the whole country.

After meeting the general, who now wanted to be called the chief executive, I met some of the judges who had taken an oath of allegiance to the chief executive in order to remain on the bench. A lot of questions are raised in your mind about judicial independence when you meet senior judges who not only have agreed to take this oath of allegiance, but also have no power to make an order against the chief executive. And it later emerged that they would support this rather dubious 'Doctrine of Necessity' for almost anything.

We then had a chance for dialogue with representatives of the political parties and civil society groups. What emerged from a day of listening and questioning was the profound feeling of distrust directed at the two major parties. The smaller groups were adamant there was a real role for the Commonwealth to get back what they believed were the stolen millions from the feudal and wealthy families (strenuously denied by them). Well, this wasn't the first time I'd heard that request and, of course, achieving that was easier said than done. While the Commonwealth may give technical assistance to a member country for that purpose, it was not until 2005 that President Obasanjo of Nigeria got the consent of leaders for the Secretariat to do work in this area – that is, actively assist governments to retrieve from foreign banks the ill-gotten gains of former corrupt leaders.

I left Pakistan with mixed thoughts. I had given General Musharraf the message of what the Commonwealth expected. I was confident I had left his office knowing he would not go

back to his officials and say: 'Don't ever let him near me again.'
He was not antagonistic towards the Commonwealth. He
felt we needed to understand his position, and we should
appreciate that he was doing much better than many African
leaders who had come to power in military coups. He felt he
had to stay on course. He knew the people of Pakistan liked
the Commonwealth and, of course, he understood the common
love of cricket. As a politician I never underestimate the value of
anything that brings people together, and sport is most definitely
in that category.

I was less than impressed by the judges. Many were weak and
just an extension of the military executive. I was not convinced
they really knew what democracy was, so there was a long way
to go.

To some extent the Commonwealth was on its own on the
Pakistan issue, because there were a number of foreign governments that took a rather benign view of the actions of General
Musharraf. Prime Minister Mori of Japan paid a visit to indicate
business as usual, the British resumed their arms sales and the
Americans kept up a positive dialogue. Many Muslim countries
did not regard this coup as particularly unusual, so for most, life
carried on. When you are expected to engage in such issues as I
was, you must always take seriously what the neighbouring governments are saying. You always need them to give you support,
however passive, and you must never forget they are permanent
fixtures while you are not.

We kept open the lines of communication and activities
resumed in New York in September 2000 when CMAG met with
Pakistan's foreign minister, Abdul Sattar, a career diplomat who
was immediately thrown off balance when the group's foreign
ministers displayed their political and not their diplomatic side.
That was why they were there, but in one instance the chair had
to intervene to prevent an argument boiling over between the UK

foreign secretary, Robin Cook, and Sattar, which had become too personal.

Sattar, on the other hand, was taking it all too lightly, and wasn't at all well prepared for the aggressive questioning. He had no idea of the logistics of enrolling 65–80 million people on the voters' register, for example. Strongly challenged by eight attacking ministers, he looked as if he felt like a defendant in the box, and he suddenly lost his cool. Strong messages were exchanged and some people realised for the first time that such meetings of Commonwealth ministers do not play by polite, politically correct UN rules.

We could not look forward to anything other than a long haul, certainly well beyond the two years stipulated by the CMAG guidelines.

I thought that having another meeting with Musharraf away from Islamabad would be useful to get a better feeling for his end game rather than us making unproductive demands. I was aware that not everybody wanted the Commonwealth to be strident, and that others thought he would do a good clean-up job. I knew the British were engaging positively with Musharraf because of Afghanistan and their belief that Pakistan was their ally in this area of high sensitivity. It wasn't unusual for a Commonwealth member to use the Commonwealth to beat up on a country, but then treat them as bosom buddies on certain bilateral issues. If I ever challenged a prime minister or a foreign minister on this I would usually receive a wry smile or 'Well, that's diplomacy.'

At the March 2001 meeting of CMAG in London, ministers heard presentations from representatives of Pakistan political parties and civil society organisations, including Commonwealth organisations. This was the second time CMAG had held consultations with political parties and NGOs from a suspended country, the first time being in July 1997 with Nigeria. By this time General Musharraf had organised the first round of local government elections in Pakistan on a non-party basis.

On 13 June 2001 I lunched with Foreign Minister Sattar

who, taking his cue from the unpleasant New York meeting the previous year, launched into me, saying the Commonwealth was not doing enough for Pakistan. This caught me a little off balance. 'Not correct,' I said, trying to look unfazed. 'We may not be doing specifically what you want, but do understand that we are offering to do what in our view is necessary for an election.' I told him that only by outlining a programme of activity with critical timelines by which progress could be measured could Pakistan be confident that leaders at the next CHOGM would not move towards full suspension.

A week later, General Musharraf appointed himself to the office of President, after President Rafiq Tarar's resignation. There was no doubt he did not want anyone questioning his authority or power, and as long as the President was senior to the Prime Minister this move was inevitable. Internationally it gave him more status, which was very important to him.

On 14 August 2001 President Musharraf announced his plans for the restoration of democracy, including the road map we had asked for, and said that he would hold parliamentary elections by October 2002.

A week later I left Uganda after attending a Commonwealth technology management conference and flew to Islamabad via Dubai. This was becoming a long week; I had some seventy hours of flying within a seven-day period, which forced me to draw heavily on my Protestant work ethic. Whether you are a New Zealand foreign minister or a secretary-general, travel and working away from your home base seems to take up about thirty per cent of your working year. And many of the flights aren't only three hours. You get sleep when you can.

The next day I was ready for my second meeting with President Musharraf, still very much a lone figure internationally. These meetings do not just happen – they need lots of planning. Many messages go back and forth before both sides are satisfied that there is likely to be an upside and very little downside. We all depend on our officials to keep the lines open, but in the end it's only a principal who can meet a principal. Keeping open the lines of communication around the Commonwealth was to me always fundamental to any success.

Officials said the meeting would last half an hour. In the end it went on for more than one hour. I received the official script for the first thirty minutes, then Musharraf loosened up, which I had really hoped for. He carefully, and without recourse to notes, went over what he wanted to achieve. He said he wanted to concentrate on three areas: accountability, grass roots democratisation and poverty alleviation.

On the first, he was determined to root out corruption at every level. Everyone had to explain how they got what they had. People needed to be more disciplined. On the second issue there was such nepotism and corruption in Pakistan politics that the only way to change it was to start from the ground up with new untainted people who would then progress through to national politics and so cleanse the system on the way up. On poverty alleviation, he wanted to widen the tax base, increase state-sponsored work and encourage small business start-ups.

Musharraf was unquestionably sincere. He knew this was what was required, but he knew that it could succeed only if the people believed in it and if he had a decade to see it through. It also reflected his political naivety – how can you change a people's political culture over a short period without them being part of the decision-making process?

Anyone knowing General Musharraf over these years would always comment on the sincerity of his beliefs. The trouble was that when his beliefs changed, so did the sincerity. He again underlined his complete disrespect for politicians and his faith only in the military to really achieve progress. I acknowledged the progress to date and reminded him that we would be swayed by deeds, not just by words. I left his presence feeling that he was opening up. He didn't see me as the enemy and I was one of the few people outside Pakistan who was talking to him.

I left Islamabad exhausted after a long trip, but satisfied

that I could engage with Musharraf. He understood me and we both knew what the other expected. It was only in the timing we disagreed.

Then the Twin Towers atrocity occurred in New York, and when the full meaning of 9/11 became apparent, the world changed. Suddenly President Musharraf became the centre of attention. For two years I had been one of the few people who had been talking with him. Now everyone wanted to take him home for dinner.

From the man who had been appealing to the West for understanding as to why a military coup was good for Pakistan, Musharraf became someone who everyone wanted to get alongside. Now we were fighting the war on terror in Afghanistan. Suddenly his often-reviled army was needed to fight the Taliban – with few realising that the Taliban were in fact a product of the earlier desire to chase the Russians out of Afghanistan, and were thus strongly supported in their endeavours by at least a third of the Pakistan Army.

So we entered 2002 as the unpopular and pesky Commonwealth, still urging that the Pakistan government needed to show the world that its democratic intentions were pure. On the other side, where there was a clear majority, the Western heavyweights, the Islamic community and South Asia were all giving Musharraf a lot of support – for different reasons. This not only made him feel better, it also strengthened his hand and enabled him to tighten his grip in critical areas.

In October 2000 a new envoy had taken up the role of Pakistan high commissioner in London. Abdul Kader Jaffer was a businessman from Karachi and a friend of the President. Having confided in me that he was a businessman and was never formally trained as a diplomat, Kader declared that we should get on very well.

We went on to have many one-on-one sessions. He never stuck to his own Foreign Office script, but told it in his own effective way. He saw me three or four times during 2002 and once came to remonstrate with me about a critical statement I had made about Musharraf's referendum, which asked the Pakistani people to endorse the President. I said OK, but the referendum was pathetic, and he was lucky I was not criticising him every day of the week for what his government was not doing.

He was able to smile through all of this, aware that there were certain games that had to be played. Diplomat or not, he was an energetic envoy for his country. In the world of diplomacy you soon get used to the double-speak. As a former foreign minister I often heard the comment, 'This is the way it has to be, even if I do not agree.' Needless to say, that would be said only by someone who knew it wouldn't be repeated publicly.

Now that the wars in both Iraq and Afghanistan were dominating the headlines there were many people in the British Foreign and Commonwealth Office (FCO) and in Downing Street who were quietly changing their tune. Having previously demanded the Commonwealth stand up for the principle of democracy, they now slowly sheathed their swords as Pakistan's involvement in the war against Al Qaeda became more salient and the military dictator in Pakistan became more useful.

At Commonwealth heads of government level, nonetheless, a tough line on Pakistan was maintained. The CHOGM in Coolum, near Brisbane in Australia, early in 2002 agreed that Pakistan should remain suspended from the councils of the Commonwealth and should be held to its commitment to hold elections by October 2002. The Secretary-General was to maintain an active role.

It was a fact that although the pressure from outside Pakistan had diminished, internally it was far from calm. Many groups, including bar associations, political parties and civil society groups, mounted petitions against the referendum, approving Musharraf as President.

Two of my officials (including a senior Pakistan national, Syed Sharfuddin), who were present in Pakistan at the time of the April 2002 referendum reported that certain conditions relating to the conduct of the referendum were not in keeping with the Commonwealth's best electoral practice. Official figures showed that Musharraf received over 98 per cent of the votes in a turn-out that was massively disputed. The controversial referendum gave President Musharraf a period of five years until October 2007 to continue his reform programme.

My own statement immediately criticised the Pakistan government, saying that 'I hope this action will not entrench any other form of undemocratic governance.' The CMAG meeting in Botswana in May 2002 displayed similar and frustrating concerns, calling the referendum 'a deviation from the road map to democracy'.

Around that time I was invited to lunch with a number of British Muslim peers at the House of Lords. Some were of Pakistani origin, and all were concerned that General Musharraf was becoming too dictatorial. I thought to myself, 'But isn't that what dictators are?' My assessment was that the Pakistan diaspora in the United Kingdom seemed evenly divided between the supporters of Bhutto, Nawaz Sharif and Musharraf.

The election planned for October was the big issue, however, so we sent a security consultant to Pakistan to assess the issues surrounding the October election. His response was very sombre. There would be negative attitudes towards 'white faces'. Each observer would need to be in a 4×4 vehicle with a well-trained crew and a guard, and followed by another 4×4 with a heavily armed team. The Commonwealth was not used to this. This was going to be costly and some candidates for this mission were already having cold feet.

But things did settle and we did adhere to some, if not all, of the consultant's recommendations. By late September 2002 we had assembled a group of twenty-two prominent Commonwealth citizens as observers, with nine staff members. Prior to their arrival in Pakistan, I recommended they meet for preliminary discussions in Dubai, where presumably their conversations would not be monitored, as they most certainly would be in Islamabad.

Generally, the elections went better than expected, but President Musharraf did not get the coalition of supporters into the Parliament that he had expected. The Commonwealth observer group concluded that the poll 'was well organised and mostly transparent', although 'the widespread use of government influence and resources to favour certain political parties and candidates did disadvantage others'. So there was some doubt as to whether there really was a level playing field.

At the next CMAG meeting, beginning on 31 October, members decided that Pakistan should remain suspended pending greater clarity and an assessment of the role and functions of democratic institutions. The Indian minister, who was still getting instructions from Delhi, said he could not live with the phrase 'welcome the Pakistan elections'. OK, I said, but I did suggest that as a CMAG minister he should lose his head office telephone number when he was at meetings. CMAG had to work for the collective Commonwealth good, not just advance the view of one's own country. He took my point.

In Pakistan the political situation was improving, even if Musharraf continued to pull all the strings. Assemblies were functioning, and a coalition now made up the government. The outstanding issue – and it continued to be so for a very long time – was whether Musharraf could be both army commander and president. This point divided everybody.

As time went by I had to change my view of Musharraf. He was becoming political with a small 'p' and applying those political skills very effectively. His intense belief in what Pakistan needed was paramount, and there was no hint of him salting away a fortune elsewhere in the world like many other dictators.

High Commissioner Kader came to see me in February 2003, trying to get a handle on how a CMAG meeting in May would treat Pakistan. He said compared to Zimbabwe, 'We should be back.' I did not give him much comfort, but two things kept coming to mind. I thought of Bangladesh, formerly East Pakistan, which had split with Pakistan years before, resulting in Pakistan staying out of the Commonwealth for seventeen years, which we did not wish to repeat. The other was that our African members expected our organisation to be as tough on Pakistan as we were on Zimbabwe.

On 17 May I had a long-awaited lunch with the new Pakistan foreign minister – the smiling, three-piece-suited, English-trained lawyer and strong anglophile Khurshid Kasuri. He told me that he was our best supporter. His ministry was against us and the President was agnostic. His fellow ministers regarded the Organisation of Islamic Cooperation (OIC) as more important than the Commonwealth. That to me was a very telling point as to their current foreign policy thinking.

In time I let it be known that I would like another meeting with President Musharraf. Unexpectedly, I received an invitation to the Lord Chancellor's dinner for the President on his visit to London. In my view the visit was not a good thing. It would not have happened to Fiji, Nigeria or Zimbabwe while they were suspended. It was an example of one policy for the Commonwealth and another policy for bilateral reasons.

A senior foreign affairs official was in President Musharraf's entourage. When he saw the guest list for the Lord Chancellor's dinner he realised that my status would put me close to the President at the top table. So he told a low-level Pakistan official that I had to be uninvited.

Then the FCO stumbled and bumbled into the debate, stating they were the inviters, but they would comply by putting me at a table out of sight of Musharraf. At which point I told them to go jump. I had no intention of being a pawn in their game.

The message my officials were receiving from the High Commission was that no way would a meeting take place.

A week later Pakistan High Commissioner Kader told me he
was very sorry I had not been able to meet with the President.
But then he dumped on me, blaming me because the President
was not able to meet the Queen. Thank goodness for that, I
thought. At the end of this brief visit, President Musharraf said
to the press that he looked forward to Pakistan rejoining the
Commonwealth. Photographs of the President meeting the
Queen would have been splashed across the Pakistan papers,
which would have pleased Musharraf but would have been a
country mile too far. So one step forward, one sideways and one
backwards – yet again.

I did attend a farewell function for High Commissioner Kader
at the English-Speaking Union, where he chided me in a good-
humoured way about keeping them out of the Commonwealth.
But overall he was a good envoy for his country and his president. He never got hung up on diplomatic niceties, was blunt
in his requests, accepted that no meant no and kept a sense of
humour. Not long after, he was replaced by the very experienced,
media-savvy Maleeha Lodhi; she brought a new and smiling
dimension into the relationship.

Organisations such as the English-Speaking Union and any
one of the eighty-five other organisations that are a formal part of
the Commonwealth family are useful for a raft of reasons. They
are often used as a conduit where other channels are blocked.
One can find there a level of expertise outside the mainstream
that is still part of the larger family and understands the way
things are done (see Chapter 12).

But nothing stays in balance. In late July I wished to address
the Commonwealth ambassadors at the United Nations in New
York. There were times when Commonwealth diplomats would
meet together for a specific purpose – as do the Africans, the
Caribbeans and the members of the OIC. There are different
configurations for different purposes.

So I was grateful when the Australians agreed to host such
a function. Unfortunately, they did not intend to invite the

Zimbabwean envoy because of that country's suspension. Yet they wanted the Pakistan ambassador, whose country was also suspended, at the gathering. I told Ambassador John Dauth that they both had to be either invited or not invited. Both countries were suspended from the councils of the Commonwealth, but this was not a council meeting (as ministerial meetings are). He said he would have to seek instructions. I decided this would become an obsession with the Australians and particularly with John Howard, and it was easier to go somewhere else. So we did.

In September 2003 we were back in New York. If you are a foreign minister and you don't go to the UN General Assembly when it opens in New York in September, you are not doing your job. Never will you have the chance to meet so many of your colleagues and be able to sort out some of those issues that have remained a problem all year or longer. I therefore took advantage of their presence to have a series of Commonwealth meetings, sometimes up to five or six over the week, which required the attendance of ministers.

The tension at the CMAG meeting on this occasion was a little higher. Many wanted Pakistan removed from the suspension list and many wanted the issue handcuffed to that of Zimbabwe. Asian and African diplomats were looking suspiciously at each other. And in both cases envy was never far away. In the face of some reluctance from India, CMAG gave further encouragement to normalising the role of the Pakistan executive and the legislature. Most importantly, CMAG tried to clarify the role of the President when he ceased to be the head of the army as well. President Musharraf was a soldier first and foremost and would clearly feel impotent without his military uniform. Opposing Pakistan political leaders knew this, and were continuing to whip their supporters into a frenzy on the issue of 'He must drop the uniform!'

A breakthrough came on Christmas Day 2003 when Musharraf confirmed that he would stand down as chief of the army on 31 December 2004. 'So,' I noted at the time, 'it's daylight at last.' I was hearing this while on vacation in New

Zealand in the southern summer. It was good news. Back in London I heard that India would not stand in the way of Pakistan being reinstated.

Foreign Minister Kasuri came to London and I invited him to dinner at my residence at Hill Street, having been told he didn't wish his officials to know he wanted to see me. For most of the dinner he remained rather coy, not wishing to show any enthusiasm. Despite this, his Oxbridge education, his three-piece suits and love of cricket were very much on display. He could never envisage a Pakistan permanently out of the Commonwealth.

I reflected that we were probably lucky that Kasuri, long versed in the ways of the Commonwealth, was inherently on our side. If there is one great benefit of developed countries offering scholarships and advanced education for other nationals it is that you build up a cadre of supporters for your way of life. In the English-speaking world the UK, Canada, Australia, New Zealand, now Singapore and, of course, the United States all understand this and reap the benefits.

At a pre-CMAG ministers' dinner in May 2004 the case I put to attendees was this: Pakistan had carried out elections which were deemed reasonable, they had functioning assemblies and they had legislated into statute all the legal framework orders. Moreover, those same assemblies had granted Musharraf the right to stay on as army chief until the end of December.

Most of the members were supportive of lifting the suspension, although Lesotho and India were hesitant and Sri Lanka was watching India to ensure Colombo wasn't exposed. There it rested for the evening. It hadn't been easy, but with more officials there than ministers there was a nervousness to commit, even in this private environment. So many had to go back to their capitals for instructions.

In the principals' meeting the next day an African minister whispered to me, 'Just sum up as you did last night and then none of us need to take a position in front of all the officials.' India, unfortunately, was represented by an acting high commissioner holding a sheaf of instructions. Seeing what was happening, with my summary only, he broke into a cold sweat and was unable to give a coherent message. There was then a suggestion by the foreign minister of Lesotho that we should hold out until the end of the year to make sure Musharraf kept his promise on the uniform. But the majority felt that since his commitment had now been legislatively endorsed, we should show some faith. So after four and a half years of suspension Pakistan was reinstated into the councils of the Commonwealth, though it remained on the CMAG agenda.

At the press conference that followed I was asked what would happen if President Musharraf didn't take off his uniform. I said his biggest problem, apart from the Commonwealth, was that it would put him in breach of his own constitution. What I could not have said was that with India on CMAG any window of opportunity for Indian support could close at any minute for any number of reasons.

By late June 2004 Musharraf was getting quite agitated in the face of expectations expressed by some cynics that he would break his promise and not shed his uniform at the end of the year. In fact, in one outburst he said he would not be dictated to by the Commonwealth. After a few more of these comments I took the opportunity to ask High Commissioner Lodhi to tell the President to stop beating up on me.

Then while I happened to be watching a test match at Lord's between New Zealand and England in July I received a call from Kasuri confirming the acceptance of my visit to Islamabad in October.

By early September, however, we had detected a strange push under way to keep Musharraf as head of the army. My notes at the time included this observation: 'As long as he keeps killing terrorists, the Americans and the British are relaxed about this position and his status. But one is left with the impression he just does not trust any of his own generals. If he can't find one to replace him, even though he had hand-picked all the current senior corps commanders, where will it all be in five years' time?'

You can never relax with the Pakistan media. This feeling was accentuated when I met the media in the press briefing room at the UN in New York on 23 September. All the questions came from the Pakistan media. And most of them were phrased in a way that invited me to praise the Pakistan President or condemn India. One has to follow the old political trick of unloading the loaded questions before one gives the yes or no answer. At the UN in New York one also learns to remember that the most apparently bored or even sleeping journalist is the one who's listening most intently. Another escape for me.

By now, all was arranged for the CMAG ministers to meet Kasuri informally in New York on Saturday morning, the day before the next CMAG meeting.

I arranged for a small meeting room along the corridor from the main conference area and had eight or nine chairs set in a fairly tight circle to maintain some intimacy. Before the meeting, Pakistan had support from Canada, Australia and Sri Lanka. The Africans were sceptical and Malta, Samoa and Bahamas were neutral. At my strong suggestion, Kasuri was to put his case for the complete normalisation of the Commonwealth–Pakistan relationship as succinctly as possible. He had asked for twenty minutes but that would have driven ministers insane; I said he could have ten. Unfortunately, he was wound up and overexcited and his mind was going at 100 mph. He overplayed his hand and didn't answer all the questions. Ministers were not impressed by his comparing A. Q. Khan, the man who sold nuclear secrets, to a sports star, so it all ended rather unsuccessfully after fifteen minutes.

Later, outside the meeting, Kasuri was still agitated about what he had said and how it had been received, and the questioning he had been subjected to. He was saying things like 'The visit of the Secretary-General will be called off.' 'National circumstances must prevail.' And 'Pakistan could always walk out!' To this, I said to my colleagues, 'We must not blink first.' We knew from this that he was in a corner and his President was in difficulty.

These were never easy meetings. We were like the optimistic angler trying to catch a 50 kg fish with a line that has a 5 kg breaking point. It's all about reading the politics, not the law. You are aware of precedents but you are not bound by them. So to go on the front foot and remind him that I was his friend, I rang Kasuri, had a good chat and suggested he invite some CMAG ministers to Pakistan.

So perhaps we were back to normal. I was reminded again that these issues are more often determined by human relationships than by anything else. When trouble strikes it will always come back to the need to build confidence and keep talking.

I flew to Islamabad on 21 October 2004 and my first call was on the President. I'd come to expect the visual security, the mirrors under the car, the scanners and the no-phone requirements (except for me), then it was into his office. The President entered looking a little nervous but smiling, and of course in uniform. After the pleasantries he seemed to follow a prepared text: 'We are pursuing democracy. We are not going to lose the ground we've gained. We have too many corrupt people, especially the feudal families, who've stripped the country of billions of dollars.'

He began to relax as we got into a dialogue about progress in which he acknowledged what the Commonwealth had done – and what it still had to do. We talked about the uniform issue and he was at pains to tell me that his tenure had a natural expiry date but that in fighting terrorism he needed room to move.

I asked whether he felt he was fighting with a hand tied behind his back. He said two hands.

I then asked for a private one-on-one. I told him I accepted his sincerity, but he was riding a tiger and there was no easy way to dismount. He had achieved a lot and he could use the Commonwealth to spread his story beyond the US and UK to Africa, the Pacific and the Caribbean. He took the point and said he would send Kasuri out more. I asked him when he thought the next level of leader would emerge who would not be corrupt. He said he had new corps commanders now moving up the ranks (ignoring anyone who could be described as a civilian, a telling point).

He once again came back to the feudal families. 'Many were worse than corrupt, they take money and buy judges.' He then said, 'You're the son of a general, you know how we think.' I followed with my message – you can't plant democracy and get the structure right unless you let the people be part of its design, growth, nurturing and protection. They have to see it as theirs, not as a gift from you similar to what the colonial power did.

He was smiling as I left and I knew I could get him on the phone when I needed to. It had all been extremely worthwhile. Maybe a step forward, I felt.

Prime Minister Shaukat Aziz was a most impressive ex-Citibank executive who was more a man from New York than from Islamabad. If they can get many like him to return, the country will do very well, I thought to myself. He did not appear to be the rubber stamp the opposition tried to label him as when he was finance minister. However, to go from the Senate into the House he needed to win a seat – which he did by standing in two seats for a by-election and winning both. There was some criticism of the voting procedures.

I also called on the very mild-mannered speaker of the Assembly, who had a whole new take on the functional – or dysfunctional – Parliament. As only graduates could be eligible for a parliamentary seat, many were elected as graduates of madrasas.

The trouble was that they had little empathy for Parliament's traditions or standing orders. When they were not satisfied with the speaker's ruling they would crowd round him, hurling abuse, threatening him physically, grabbing his microphone, tearing up his papers and bringing proceedings to a premature halt.

Well, 31 December 2004 came and went – and General Musharraf had not relinquished his general's uniform. To his credit, he openly conceded that he had gone back on his word. Meanwhile, the Asian tsunami had tragically swamped many countries in South and South-east Asia.

Pakistan's suspension had been lifted, but they were still on the CMAG agenda pending the separation of the offices of president and chief of army staff. The country had not left the Commonwealth, even though many senior Pakistan officials, those who leaned towards the OIC, clearly believed they should. We still had the 50 kg fish on a line with a 5 kg breaking point. Foreign Minister Kasuri was finally calling CMAG ministers personally for understanding. The politics finally ruled. On balance, I knew we would not have achieved unity on a re-suspension motion.

A Pakistan parliamentary delegation came to Marlborough House led by their speaker, who expected to talk about minor niceties while everyone else said nothing. I rapidly told them we were very disappointed in President Musharraf for breaking his promise and CMAG would have more to say. That broke up the unity of the group, who then started fighting and arguing among themselves.

The dinner before the next CMAG was held on the evening of 10 February 2005. I said I was really disappointed with Musharraf. We had to be tough with our statement – but, of course, what was finally said was up to the ministers.

It was a good, robust discussion, because everybody felt we had gone out on a limb to help. Canada was assertive. For the

Africans the issue was sensitive, because the African Union had just unilaterally suspended Togo following a botched takeover of the presidential office after the death of President Eyadéma. In the end the statement was as I had hoped: tough at the beginning to satisfy the most critical, and some crumbs at the end that Sri Lanka could highlight.

Then the press conference, which India wanted to avoid, so it was only the chairman from Nigeria, the deputy chair from Bahamas and myself. We had to eat some humble pie, but none of us got indigestion. One of the first lessons in politics is to be able to eat your own words and not get a stomach-ache in the morning.

No useful road is a smooth road. In a meeting with President Obasanjo of Nigeria some time later I asked about a statement of his that came out of the ABC network in Australia, to the effect that on the issue of Zimbabwe the Commonwealth had double standards. I said this was an unnecessary challenge to our unity and we argued accordingly (even though I did not feel he really meant it). What had caused this change of heart had been a meeting I had arranged between Obasanjo and Musharraf in New York. It was meant to be a tête-à-tête between Obasanjo and Musharraf, president to president, military leader to military leader. He agreed to do so. I believed it would be a good opportunity for President Obasanjo to impress upon President Musharraf that a competent and supported president, especially one with military experience, could retain control of the army even after formally giving up the post of army chief. There were a number of Commonwealth countries in which the civilian head of state was also the commander-in-chief of the armed forces.

Unfortunately, the meeting consisted of Musharraf lecturing Obasanjo on how he was on top of things. It turned out to be a bad call by me. It was also another example of an Asian leader being very reluctant to receive advice from an African counterpart. That feeling was often mutual, and one had to be sensitive about it. I can admit that within the Commonwealth Secretariat, personnel problems between peoples from Africa and Asia were more frequent than I had expected.

I received reports that Musharraf was under great strain from the earthquakes that devastated northern Pakistan in October 2005. I was told he was withdrawing into himself and depending on fewer and fewer people for advice. I heard from India that he wasn't trusting many people. This wasn't good news. It confirmed the tendency of dictators to reduce the number of people who have access to them and listen only to those who agree with them.

In February 2006 it was time to travel to India, Bangladesh and Pakistan, keeping up to date, keeping the pressure on both Pakistan and Bangladesh.

I had a useful meeting with Indian Prime Minister Manmohan Singh, who proved as graceful and gracious as ever. 'The more successful the Commonwealth is, the better for us,' he declared. On Pakistan he said he enjoyed working with Musharraf and believed him to be sincere. Of course, when you are in India as Secretary-General you always get asked about Pakistan. And no matter how careful you are with your replies, you are then attacked by the Pakistan media for discussing their country on Indian soil and your answers are presented in a way that creates a bigger problem. On this occasion, a Pakistan government information officer was prompted to retort that 'Pakistan will do what's best for Pakistan, not what Mr McKinnon wants!'

Then it was on to Islamabad and almost straight to Army House in Rawalpindi, where the President saw me the day before he was due to travel to China. I didn't want to waste time on pleasantries or even the earthquake, but went straight to the report he had received from Prime Minister Shaukat Aziz on the Malta CHOGM. 'They,' I said, referring to the other leaders, 'hope you will act in good faith.'

At this comment he visibly stiffened and pushed back into the corner of the couch. Then he said he wanted to talk about democracy. Once he got underway he began to relax and moved into the middle of the couch, and then we talked and argued for an hour and a half. At one point I had to defend many African leaders against the abuse he heaped on them for corruption and election-rigging as he challenged their commitment to democracy. He then back-pedalled, much to the relief of his officials.

I asked why, after six years and his intimate knowledge of all his corps commanders, there was not one he could trust to be army chief. This was not answered. Yes, he said the army should be subservient to the government, but not yet, thank you. A proposal that I had earlier canvassed with him – to be president and commander-in-chief of the armed forces without a uniform, as in most democracies – did not fall on fertile ground.

My notes from the time tell me that: 'He just does not believe anyone can do the job. He really has moved into that danger zone of being surrounded by "yes" men, and that will be his downfall. I am less confident now that he'll relinquish the army position before the 2007 elections, but at least his attitude towards me and the Commonwealth is much more positive.'

My summary on leaving Pakistan this time was that things were fragile but under control, and that Musharraf didn't really understand that although democracies don't always get it right, they know that they've got only themselves to blame and they try to do better next time. This is not at all the same as a dictator who insists he's responsible for everything.

'I've seen Musharraf grow as a politician,' my notes say. 'He's more adept at keeping many balls in the air, and Bhutto and Sharif won't easily take those balls from him. Despite what the others want, he still holds all the cards.'

In mid-2006 I called on ever-smiling Pakistan High Commissioner Lodhi and said I would like to send a small mission to Pakistan to study something about human rights, governance and electoral reforms, that sort of thing. I needed something that the CMAG ministers could study and chew over at the next meeting. She said she would try the idea out informally.

In early July we got a green light to send a junior-level mission. Well, it was better than nothing, and we were still the only organisation in play since the coup. I didn't want big gaps to appear between engagements. So, on 2 August, a small staff team including political, media, human rights and parliamentary officials would go. This was better than I expected and would definitely give our ministers something to cogitate on when in New York.

Meanwhile, I joined the gathering of the great, the good, the not-so-good and the bad in Havana, Cuba, for a Non-Aligned Movement meeting. It was always worth my while attending these meetings, given that most of the Commonwealth membership was there. I had a friendly meeting with President Musharraf, who looked genuinely pleased to see me. He was very proud of the recent long period of democratic rule in Pakistan that he had overseen, with stability achieved and more women enfranchised. He would go through to the 2007 elections, and he would keep his uniform on until then.

'Most people know what we're trying to achieve,' he told me. '2007 is the constitutional limit and I will stick to the constitution, but I have to tell you none of what I have achieved would have been possible without me being in uniform. Parliament allowed me to hold the two offices up to 2007. I will stick to that.' 'Very upbeat,' my notes say. 'Let's hope it can work.'

And then it was on to New York for CMAG. At the CMAG dinner I noted for ministers that there was continuing concern about the way the executive in Pakistan used ordinances when Parliament was not sitting, leaving little time properly to scrutinise legislation. But the functioning of the houses of Parliament was improving. The government was addressing the Hudood Ordinance, which would bring rape and adultery within the

penal code as opposed to regarding it as customary behaviour
where women were always held to be the guilty party. Civil
society, I reported, was being allowed more space and was functioning, but there was widespread scepticism over the integrity
of the judiciary. The media, though, had more freedom than
ever before.

In January 2007 there were complaints from the US and the
UK that Musharraf was not doing enough to fight terrorism,
and that he was just too focused on getting himself re-elected
President by an outgoing Parliament. It was an early sign that
these important friends that he touted so strongly might not be
sticking with him.

March was not Musharraf's month. What did he think he
was doing, I noted at the time, suspending the chief justice? This
was overstepping the mark. It was arrogant and seemed almost
to have been done as if he had just fired the man who cleaned
his shoes. His public thought similarly. They may not have
respected the judiciary but they did not expect to see a chief justice unceremoniously fired. Lawyers, of all people, joined street
demonstrations. It wasn't long before Musharraf began to look
like the emperor without half his clothes.

It was explained to me by someone close to the President that
this chief justice was not up to standard. He had made poor judg-
ments, his ego and level of self-importance were out of control,
and he had, I was told, persisted in commandeering government
helicopters to take him around the country on rather spurious
missions, some for merely family reasons. Maybe, I thought; I
did not have time to hear any other side to the story, but I suspected there was one.

By mid-May Musharraf was looking increasingly impotent.
Most of Pakistan's 16,000 lawyers should have been on his side,
but they were not. I surmised that maybe there was restlessness
because Musharraf was heading to beat the record in office of the

previous military ruler, Zia-ul-Haq, the last intimidating dictator. My notes say: 'Perhaps they feel he'll be there forever, and they didn't want that. He's vulnerable and they know it, so they're giving him a kick when he's down.'

Pakistan was descending into uncertainty. Bhutto and Sharif were now increasingly back in play, and the possibility that they might return was clearly creating fear within the leadership. Musharraf, ever the survivor, was now courting Bhutto in Dubai and in London, but no 'marriage' was ever likely to eventuate. I felt the balance was tipping. It seemed that when she wanted him, he didn't want her; when he needed her, she didn't need him.

When Bhutto visited me in July she claimed that the President was no longer in control. 'The chief justice is running rings around him,' she told me. 'And Musharraf may postpone the election.'

Meanwhile, the suspended chief justice was now on his own campaign all over the country, drawing large crowds and often creating mayhem. The violence in Karachi during his visit did the government a lot of damage. There was now increasing talk of a possible state of emergency as Musharraf's authority seemed to be breaking down everywhere.

By August both Bhutto and Sharif were clearly emboldened, and so we now had a three-way race, which was further emphasised when the court ruled that Nawaz Sharif could return. He set 10 September as his return date, which of course gave Musharraf plenty of time to organise an appropriate reception. The moment Sharif stepped from the plane they pushed him onto another. He was soon heading back to Saudi Arabia.

Shahbaz Sharif called into the Secretariat to keep us up to date on his brother Nawaz's plans. Shahbaz always visited my deputy, Mrs Florence Mugasha from Uganda. Nawaz Sharif could never bring himself, or lower himself, to come and see me as did Benazir Bhutto at least once a year. When he did want to see me, he invited me to meet him in the extremely opulent Dorchester Hotel around the corner from my residence. That was an image – me being summoned by him – that I did not want broadcast, so I said thanks, but no thanks. Nawaz never came to the Secretariat; Shahbaz, his brother, came just twice.

I received more calls from the energetic Pakistan high commissioner emphasising that the President's uniform was definitely coming off. Thanks, I thought, but we've heard it all before. We'll be very pleased to hear it first-hand – with photographic evidence.

And now to Islamabad in September 2007. On arrival it was straight to see a very chipper and smart Pervez Musharraf – the President and now the General – at Army House in Rawalpindi.

I was intrigued to hear him say: 'It was my lawyer who told the court I would remove the uniform when re-elected.' It felt to me as if he was about to announce his reneging on this commitment. But then he added, referring to the upcoming January (moved later to February) 2008 elections: 'I've got to give it up sometime and that time's as good as ever.' Good, I thought, we'd got past that one. I told the President that it was not easy to embrace his statement on shedding the uniform, as he had left me hung out to dry on his last broken promise. I said that Pakistan would most likely remain on the CMAG agenda at least through the elections. This was not well received, but he accepted it.

Foreign Minister Kasuri admitted the full frontal assault on Musharraf by the legal fraternity had been unexpected. 'We miscued and we now know we're not fully secure.' A meeting with Prime Minister Shaukat Aziz was equally illuminating. He seemed to work in parallel to the President rather than with him. He regaled me with all their successes and once again observed that the Retreat he attended at the Malta CHOGM in 2005 was the best international meeting he had ever attended.

However, in later discussions with a group of high commissioners I found them to be quite dismissive of Aziz. 'He's quite expendable and no longer influential,' observed one.

After the meeting, my senior staffer was told that when Aziz met Prime Minister Harper of Canada the latter could not get a word in. Harper is quiet, but not that quiet.

There was an amusing comment on my visit from a member of Nawaz Sharif's party who told me I was so popular in Pakistan I could win the presidency. This was on the basis that whenever I was there the government did just the right thing! Thanks, again, but no thanks.

On this visit I did not want any confusion in the media about what was said or done, so I did not speak to any media until just before my departure. For this I drafted a very tough statement on each of a number of points and gave them the full nine yards.

It was a very full press conference and I counted eighteen television cameras. I went through the statement point by point, saying that the next four months were critical. There must be adherence to the rule of law and the constitution, the Pakistan people must get beyond seeing the military as an alternative government and a good democracy means good economics.

In October 2007 Musharraf got himself re-elected by the outgoing assemblies. One hurdle over. Next the uniform, then the swearing-in.

By this time, Musharraf seemed to be planning his exit from politics. Events had determined him to be very much on the defensive in relation to Bhutto and Sharif. He now promulgated a National Reconciliation Ordnance (NRO), which granted immunity to Benazir Bhutto, her husband Asif Zardari, Nawaz Sharif and his brother Shahbaz Sharif. The NRO assured President Musharraf that in the event of the ruling PML (Q) party failing to keep its majority in the National Assembly (as indeed happened in the February 2008 elections), he would be able to coexist as President, assisted by the PPP leadership, which had little disagreement with his policies.

But nothing goes smoothly. On 5 November, an ominous date in British history for other reasons, Musharraf declared a State of

Emergency. Although there were still pleas of 'please understand us' to the US, the UK, the EU and the Commonwealth, this was nothing but martial law. I thought at the time, 'Now he's really lost it. He just won't trust the people.' In a democracy you can't get your own way on everything all the time. Now we had to bring CMAG together.

Pakistan High Commissioner Maleeha Lodhi called and I gave her both barrels: 'I am angry. We've stood with Pakistan for eight years. We've helped you over the bumps, explained the almost inexplicable, and defended you against many in the Commonwealth. Your President has fluffed this one. He's got it totally wrong. He's derailed his own process.

'This is a coup by General Musharraf against President Musharraf.'

She had only lame excuses. It's sometimes hard to be an envoy.

Two days later Kasuri phoned and I was still raging. This was no longer a uniform issue, I told him. Pakistan had also breached the Latimer House Principles. This was martial law. 'Your guy has called it wrong.'

'But I'm glad he rang,' my later notes say, 'as it indicates he's at least still sensitive to Commonwealth attitudes. At times such as these the danger is that you allow yourself to make a statement that severs forever your lines of communication.' With Kasuri, I knew this would not happen.

CMAG met on 12 November; the Pakistan media were predicting a demanding, volatile and lengthy meeting. In my introduction I said ministers could easily go within a centimetre of suspension, even though the sacking of all Musharraf's judges would alone justify it.

Canada and the UK proposed a tough line but pulled away from suspension, Malaysia also took a very tough line, while Sri Lanka tried to pull us back from the edge. Papua New Guinea said we should suspend. From Tanzania and St Lucia there was mild support for suspension.

The resulting outcome was as I'd predicted and was largely

determined by the fact that a pre-CHOGM CMAG meeting was to take place in Kampala in just ten days' time. Pakistan thus had ten days in which to respond to Commonwealth expectations.

I received a call from Kasuri's successor in the caretaker government that Musharraf had set up for the elections, Foreign Minister Inam-ul-Haq, who tried to explain all they had done and all they would do. All I could say was, 'The water has nearly all run out of the bath.' I had never had so many calls from folk in Islamabad displaying their sensitivity to possible Commonwealth actions.

On 22 November at the CHOGHM in Kampala, Uganda, we held a CMAG breakfast to keep ministers up to date. Their positions were as tough as expected, although they were not unanimous. The formal CMAG meeting began in the evening and it was a marathon.

I presented the overview: generally, Pakistan had not met CMAG expectations. I mentioned the sacking of the chief justice and some judges, that all rights were suspended and no court could question the government's actions; there was a media clamp-down; there could no longer be a guarantee on Musharraf's uniform issue, nor when elections would be held; and many people were under arrest and civilians could be tried in military courts. I concluded by stating that Commonwealth credibility was firmly on the line. After many hours of debate we held a straw poll: all advocated suspension except for Sri Lanka.

The chair pointed out that we were there not to review progress, but to establish whether Pakistan had fulfilled the conditions set out by CMAG ten days earlier.

Round and round we went, trying to convince Sri Lanka that there was no alternative. After three hours the chair and I had a private discussion with the Sri Lankan foreign minister. The outcome was that if we softened two paragraphs, suspension would be agreed.

The ministers all fronted up to the ensuing press conference, facing a very sceptical media. I then read out to the journalists

the paragraph in the press statement leading up to: 'so ministers are now suspending Pakistan from the councils of the
Commonwealth'. The news quickly and powerfully reverberated
out from Kampala. I felt the Commonwealth reputation had
been sustained.

But it wasn't quite all over yet. The executive session of
Commonwealth leaders on the opening day of the CHOGM
heard from Maltese Foreign Minister Michael Frendo, who
presented the CMAG report to the gathered presidents and
prime ministers.

There was an immediate response from Sri Lankan President
Mahinda Rajapaksa, who asked that the CMAG decision be
reversed. That hit a brick wall. After much debate Pakistan's
other ally, Malaysia, closed it down, with Prime Minister
Abdullah Badawi saying they were disappointed but would go
with consensus.

So having been suspended from 1999 until 2005, Pakistan
was now again suspended.

The reaction from Pakistan was muted. Everybody knew that
whichever party won the election would bring them back into
the Commonwealth. My chances of seeing them returned to the
fold before my departure in March 2008 receded rapidly, but
eventually they were readmitted in May 2008.

We decided to let the dust settle before seeking any mean-
ingful engagement with Pakistan. It was soon made known we
would not be welcome to observe the elections. I actually thought
it would more useful to get some CMAG ministers there after
the elections than to fight the observer issue. Against my advice,
the UK went overboard to get us there as observers and failed.

The world changed again when Benazir Bhutto was assassinated on 27 December 2007. It was all very sad, because I
think she had really had to think very hard about whether to
return to politics after many years on the outside living in peace
with her family. But she felt she could not ignore the pleas of her
people. It will be a long time before the Bhutto or Sharif names

are permanently erased from Pakistan politics. Feudalism and dynastic politics are a hindrance to true democracy – only equal education for all will make a difference. But in the early twenty-first century they remained a powerful element in Pakistan politics and society.

Next, Musharraf appointed former generals into key positions, one as a spokesperson and the other as head of the Interior Department. This is him just digging the hole deeper, I thought. Then he came to London on a visit, even though he was suspended from the Commonwealth. I can't believe the British would have allowed Mugabe to come to the UK in the same circumstances.

They say most politics ends in tears, and for Musharraf it did. He resigned in 2008 while facing impeachment, and three years later a court issued an arrest warrant for his alleged involvement in Bhutto's assassination. I understand that he currently lives in London and that he says he'll return to Pakistan in the near future.

Pervez Musharraf is basically a good person who believed sincerely in his own country, though he was grossly embarrassed by its history. He thought he knew what the country needed, and in many ways he achieved some very good changes. His weakness was that he never took the people with him. He could not bring himself to trust others and so he never learned the basic principle of democracy, which is that sometimes you just have to trust the people and do what they want.

Did the Commonwealth play a useful role? Yes, although it wasn't the paramount one. It did what it had to and deserves some credit, along with others, for what it achieved.

CHAPTER 8

Standing Up for Small States

My introduction to the Caribbean began in 1998/9 when I was campaigning there for the Secretary-General job. I found that the African-Caribbeans, who were the majority, were more confident and more comfortable in their own skin than were their United States counterparts. Both groups had descended from slaves, but the Caribbean groups were in the majority in their own countries, which clearly made a difference.

Another most attractive characteristic among many of their leadership was the strong evidence of an education in the classics. I so much enjoyed their speeches, always colourful and interspersed with appropriate quotes from Pericles, Plato, Shakespeare, the Bible or (one leader's favourite) the Third Law of Thermodynamics. By comparison with their Pacific counterparts, they were always larger than life and more widely educated. However, these characteristics alone do not a successful country make.

Early in my first term in June 2000, I had all the Caribbean high commissioners to a sandwich lunch at Marlborough House prior to me attending a leaders' summit in St Vincent and the Grenadines. This was an annual event in which the Commonwealth Caribbean leaders, plus the presidents of Suriname and occasionally Haiti, got together to discuss matters of regional interest. They also invited the secretaries-general of the UN, the Commonwealth and the Organisation of American States. So for me it was a good time to keep up with local issues, press for support for Commonwealth initiatives and keep up with other organisations in the region such as the Caribbean Development Bank.

The trip was an adventure. Having flown directly to Barbados, I met up with four prime ministers in the airport VIP lounge, who then prevented the flight to St Vincent leaving on time as they had to watch the end of a West Indies v. England cricket test. The West Indies needed to dismiss England for 188 to win the match. They did not, and soon we were airborne for Kingstown in St Vincent, then on to Canouan, a small island developed by an Italian company in the Grenadines group.

It was a good introduction to Caribbean politics, with debate about offshore banking, bananas, tourism, Official Development Assistance (ODA) and, of course, cricket. I soon developed much sympathy for these small states, who were simply too dependent on sugar and bananas for their income. They had all been told by World Bank economists to diversify.

That seemed sensible, but everywhere they turned they got knocked back. Their bananas had to compete with bananas produced by American interests in Ecuador, and their sugar got undercut by sugar beet subsidies in Europe. On top of all that there was much restlessness in major capitals over smaller countries such as those in the Caribbean allegedly sucking funds into their banks from European and American countries.

This latter issue came to the surface in September 2000 at a Commonwealth finance ministers' meeting when the OECD (Organisation for Economic Co-operation and Development) members, consisting of Australia, Canada, New Zealand and the United Kingdom, dumped a 'harmful tax initiative' on the table. They were reacting to a development in recent years in which many enterprising companies from developed countries had been setting up subsidiaries in smaller countries such as the

Caribbean for the most obvious of reasons – taxes there were very much lower.

OECD countries were most unhappy about this. They were losing tax income and did not appreciate countries in the Caribbean and the Pacific allowing this to happen. Competition is a great thing – as long as it does not harm me, as they say.

It wasn't long before there was a build-up of collective opposition to such initiatives, led by the OECD. But separating the illegal – such as money laundering and tax evasion – from the legal, which happened every day within the multinationals, was not easy. Much debate followed and the big hitters eventually got their way, ultimately wearing the smaller states down, convincing them there had to be a correction. The chairman of the OECD Fiscal Affairs Committee was the very competent and assertive Gabriel Makhlouf, a British Treasury official. He took no prisoners and made no friends among the small states.

This particular meeting concluded with OECD members stating that 'some form of sanctions might be necessary against those (states) considered to be non-cooperating'. This was a barely masked threat, of serious concern to a number of our smaller member countries. The OECD strategy had been to pick them off one by one. They would sit down with some of the island states' key officials and effectively threaten them if they did not change their tax regime.

Some states might have been involved in some illegal currency activities; for others, it was happening without their knowledge. But all I could see was that those with power and clout were in effect bullying the smaller countries into what they wanted them to do – to diminish or downsize their offshore banking centres, whether they were legal or illegal. I could see that unless someone stepped into the gap between the threatening OECD officials and the small states, the latter would just be crushed. If it was not the Commonwealth, who would it be? No one else who had any sort of clout was standing up for them.

Rather than take the OECD head-on, we agreed to promote

a meeting at Marlborough House to allow space for some dialogue and hopefully to look more coherently at the issue. We needed to ease the pressure on the small island states. We invited people from the World Bank, the IMF, OECD and regional organisations. Parallel to this, on the other side of the world, meetings organised by Japan, Australia and New Zealand led to similar discussions in the Pacific, also mandated by Commonwealth finance ministers. These two meetings ended with no one giving much ground, but so far no one was too angry. All agreed that a meeting in Barbados straight after New Year would be useful.

When you are living in Europe it doesn't take much encouragement to head for the Caribbean sun in January. If only the mood there had been as pleasant as the beaches. Talking among the delegates, I soon learned that: the OECD was hopelessly divided on this issue; the OECD ministers had expressed their displeasure at the way it was all going, but would support the officials; and some officials believed this would go the same way as had the Multinational Agreement on Investment (MAI), an initiative from the previous decade that was well thought out, but just did not fly. My opening speech was critical of the way the OECD was dumping on small states who were not part of, or members of, the OECD, and that the latter were aggressively using their economic leverage to get want they wanted.

None of this was easy and I'd already indirectly received a threat from the British that pushing too hard would not be seen by the UK as 'friendly'. The next message had come from another young, hapless British Treasury official asking me to 'tell Commonwealth leaders not to speak out on this issue before the meeting'. If this message came from the top, just what did these people think they were doing – still running an empire? Then the British Treasury breached the embargo by releasing statements of its own rather aggressive position two days before the meeting.

The debate went round in circles without achieving very

much, except that the OECD group now knew they were fighting uphill. Between myself and the small states there was a higher level of confidence. We felt we were standing on much firmer ground. Until the OECD could sort out what was legal or illegal in offshore banking, their position was unsustainable, held together only by Makhlouf's overly enthusiastic and rather aggressive Paris-based officials. The meeting broke up with all agreeing to meet in February 2001.

In late January the OECD countries wound up their level of aggressiveness. It seemed that the officials who had left Barbados in a more conciliatory mood had been then beaten up back home in Paris and told to toughen up. Out came another press release stating the need for 'unobliging states' to eliminate their banking deficiencies.

We then had the next meeting at Marlborough House. After only a few minutes, Prime Minister Owen Arthur of Barbados accused the OECD of not showing a willingness to understand the Commonwealth position. The Australian ambassador to the OECD in Paris was the co-chair, and proved to be strongly in support of the OECD position, which was not helpful to his country's Pacific neighbours. OECD members did not seem to see they had no mandate from the UN or an organisation of similar authority. It was all very nineteenth-century, like a city being run by wealthy merchants because they were the ones with the economic clout.

Then an internal OECD document came into our possession which laid out a strategy of reining in the Commonwealth, pulling Prime Minister Owen Arthur into line and getting states to sign up with them individually. This made me furious, as it was the opposite of what they said they would do.

Reuters also received the document and sought an interview. I gave the OECD a whack between the eyes, then released a statement stating we felt we were acting in good faith, whereas it wanted to be prosecutor, judge, jury and jailer. With no authority from anyone, OECD members had set themselves up as the world's financial policemen. The OECD intended to 'list' countries that it considered were uncooperative tax havens, without working with them to sift the legal from the illegal.

In a press conference held later, Owen Arthur said this was a case of 'the tyranny of the technocrats' and all most unfair to small states. He also added that the OECD couldn't even get some European states to comply. The Australians pulled their co-chair ambassador back to Australia. Most thought we had done a good job of kicking the OECD hard in the shins.

About a month later, in March 2001, I met with the Caribbean high commissioners. They were buzzing with congratulations on the position I had taken. They said I had finally earned my spurs in standing up for small states. It's always a fine line as to how far you can go without alienating yourself from your support base. But by the time I got to the next Caribbean summit in Nassau in the Bahamas, I was 'one of them'.

It was most interesting and amusing to see this drama come to an agreeable end, leaving egg all over the OECD officials, when the newly elected President George W. Bush appointed a new ambassador to the OECD. He immediately declared: 'What's wrong with low taxation?' With that the whole OECD case crumbled and was not to rise again.

It had been a very good example of officials receiving a mandate from ministers, but then driving blindly at full speed without any political radar to help them avoid obvious roadblocks. They were not able to acknowledge in their minds that any offshore banking can be a mix of legal and illegal. So instead of approaching countries asking how they could help them out of these problems, it was threats, attempts to divide and rule, beating them over the head and trying to win at any cost.

Our relationship with the OECD had now got so bad that I decided a peace offering was necessary. One afternoon I took two of my officials on the Eurostar to Paris and went to have a drink with OECD head Donald Johnson to try and mend some fences. Donald was still pretty angry and wasn't prepared to give much ground. But it did break the impasse, and after some months things got back to normal.

An interesting epilogue to this drama was to hear that in 2011 the lead OECD official, Gabriel Makhlouf, was appointed chief executive to the New Zealand Treasury. Well, no one asked me for a reference.

Going to Jamaica could be very depressing. It was a country that had once had the same population and per capita income as Singapore, but was now left a long way behind in income terms. The number of homicides was frightening, and Kingston was just not a safe town. Use of Jamaica by Colombian drug cartels to get their product into the US was destroying too much of what was good in the Jamaican people.

The leadership of P. J. Patterson in Jamaica was strong, with good ministers. But the insatiable appetite for drugs in the US was something they found hard to manage. It was made even more difficult when their countrymen were deported from the US and the UK after serving long prison sentences and would then set themselves up in Jamaican criminal activities with all the graduate training that American and British prisons could offer. How anyone can break this crime cycle in tough economic times has yet to be discovered. It cannot give much assurance to mothers of unemployed sons in low-income neighbourhoods that they will be looked after in their old age.

During my term in office, St Lucia and Dominica, like many other Caribbean islands, were facing a 30 per cent drop in revenue due not only to the impact of 9/11 on tourism but also to reductions in sugar and banana prices. It was no wonder that these small countries were moving into offshore banking. In early 2002 one group of Caribbean leaders were even enticed to go to Libya, where President Gaddafi made them many financial and oil promises for their salvation. In the end it all came to very little.

It was an interesting reflection of just how their relationships with the US had diminished from previous decades. I noticed more than once in meetings in Washington DC that officials responsible for the Americas never quite 'saw' the Caribbean, so dominated were they by Cuba, Venezuela, Bolivia and Mexico.

Trinidad and Tobago had got past some problematic elections, but there was still distrust among the political players. Having lost office, Basdeo Panday not only refused to leave office but also refused to take my calls. The love/hate relationship between the African- and Indo-Caribbean played itself out through the politics of Trinidad and Tobago, and also in Guyana. In fact, for me it had echoes of another country I was more familiar with – Fiji. It took a while to convince Panday he had lost the election, then Patrick Manning was once again able to become Prime Minister.

I found something similar happening in Guyana, when post-election demonstrations and violence in 2001 spilled out of control. Caribbean leaders were happy to support me and the Commonwealth with our involvement, but they were very reluctant to put themselves into a position of criticism. I was pleased, however, that the new Guyanese President, Bharrat Jagdeo, who had taken over from Janet Jagan, called me seeking assistance. He knew that such a volatile post-election period would be very difficult.

The Cooperative Republic of Guyana has tremendous potential. The problem is that people have been saying this for years, and it is still unnecessarily poor. Too many people are arguing over who is in control in Georgetown, there's too much governmental control of the economy and there are too many good Guyanese people in the US, Canada and the UK constantly proffering advice on what should happen.

On this particular occasion, I received a phone call from President Jagdeo asking for a Commonwealth envoy to bring about some peace between his party and that of Desmond Hoyte. I wanted to gauge his feeling on who could be useful. It was more a case of who he didn't want – not an Indo-Caribbean or an African-Caribbean, nor an African or an Indian, or an American, Canadian or a Brit. So I rang him back a few days later and asked if a Polynesian archbishop who had been involved in Fiji and had been governor general and thus de facto head of state in New Zealand would be of interest. Sir Paul Reeves was appointed by me on 28 August 2002 and was soon on his way. I told him I thought he should be able to solve most of the issues after three or four visits. In fact, it took thirteen or fourteen over five years, but with many ups and downs he finally got there.

One interesting down side to my relationship with the Caribbean leaders was an extraordinary period of success the New Zealand cricket team was having playing the West Indies (as their local cricketing team had always been known by) while touring the Caribbean.

'We'll have to send an armada to New Zealand,' said Ralph Gonsalves of St Vincent and the Grenadines.

'This is an assault on our sovereignty,' said Lester Bird of Antigua and Barbuda.

'This is a crisis for the Caribbean,' said Denzil Douglas of St Kitts and Nevis.

'Please treat us gently,' said Owen Arthur of Barbados.

Well, it doesn't happen often (at least not enough for New Zealand cricket enthusiasts), but it's a good feeling when your own team occasionally does well.

On 4 July 2002 we were all in Guyana for a CARICOM (Caribbean Community) summit, gathered at the residence of the US ambassador in Georgetown to celebrate that notable day in American history. Unfortunately, the Ambassador skipped the

pleasantries and launched into a lecture about what President Jagdeo should do to properly govern the country. It was very hectoring and embarrassing, especially as Jagdeo was standing beside him. I could just see a State Department official in Foggy Bottom in Washington DC drafting the words and cabling the Ambassador to deliver them on the day. I'm sure the US could have found a better way to criticise a head of government than to belittle him in front of guests.

The few days in Georgetown were very tense surrounding this annual CARICOM summit, so much so that when a hundred people stormed the President's office, two people were killed. I thought this would really escalate but, no, it barely raised headlines the next day.

My driver told me he was an Indo-Chinese Caribbean and he had married an African-Caribbean. Now neither family would talk to either of them. So deep are those racial divisions that probably two generations have to evolve before those attitudes diminish.

Opposition leader Desmond Hoyte mentioned to me that his grandfather and father told him constantly that Guyana had a lot of potential. And, he said with a chuckle, 'We're still saying it.' Then he went on to say that both major parties were Marxist, both believed in central control, protectionism and big debts – but now an Australian company owned even their bauxite mine. In his mind there was no immediate solution, stuck as they all were to outdated ideologies.

Late in October I had a phone conversation with President Jagdeo, hoping to push him harder on the question of parliamentary reforms. He said he was very happy with Sir Paul, just the right man, and would meet him anywhere, any time. He said he was sure things were moving in the right direction. Then I rang Hoyte, who had been very demanding of the Commonwealth, but to my dismay he wouldn't support Sir Paul's role. He wasn't opposed to it, but he wouldn't support it. I said that's not good enough, so I called him 'Mr President' a couple of times and he came round to being more supportive. One step forward and one sideways. You have to remain optimistic.

Between 17 and 22 November 2002, I was in St Vincent in the Caribbean for a Commonwealth justice ministers' conference. During the conference we learned of the death of Tim Hector in Antigua. With Rosie Douglas of Dominica dying eighteen months before and George Oldham of St Lucia most unwell, we were clearly nearing the end of an era dominated by those committed socialists who drove policy with their intellect and above all with their rhetoric. Few in the Caribbean in the years after independence were not moved by these powerful individuals. They were orators, poets and passionate people all. Their era had passed, and pragmatism was ruling.

In Grenada in late 2004 I witnessed the devastation of Hurricane Ivan, which had hit on 9 September. Ninety per cent of homes were wrecked; a wave 27 metres high and over 900 kilometres long had been recorded. State House was destroyed, crops were lost and much of the island was stripped of vegetation. The only plus seemed to be the option that now presented itself to plant new varieties of spice, the island's agricultural mainstay. The place looked awful, with UNICEF tents in rows and power lines strung from trees.

My recommendation to Prime Minister Keith Mitchell was to spend all day and all night on the phone personally asking heads of government everywhere for assistance. This was a strategy President Mandela had used – he would ring up another leader and ask for, say, 1,000 prefabricated school classrooms. Of course, everyone took a call from Mandela, and all said yes, even if it was at 4 a.m. and they were too sleepy to know what they agreed to. He certainly did. Regretfully it only partially worked for Grenada. In December that year the giant Indian Ocean Indonesian tsunami knocked every other national disaster out of the headlines, and many commitments to Grenada were simply forgotten.

The situation in Guyana continued to exercise me. A new personality was brought into the issue in the form of Sir Michael Davies, formerly clerk of the parliaments in the House of Lords. After a few months, his report in spring 2005 on the very dysfunctional Guyanese Parliament put the government and the President on the back foot. The report, which received much media attention, referred to Parliament being run by the executive as 'just another government department'. Parliament met at the whim of the executive, parliamentary committees were continually frustrated by the executive and the parliamentary order paper and questions went to the President's office first for approval. Similar thoughts had been highlighted by former US President Jimmy Carter, who had complained that the two sides just would not work together. It was a winner-take-all attitude, which polarised every aspect of life.

By early 2006 we were still scratching our collective heads on how to achieve momentum in Guyana. Sir Paul Reeves was to visit, and I knew he felt he was near the end of his engagement but wanted to see some productive milestones before the election. Many were saying more carrot than stick. Developing counties tend to push for the carrots and developed countries for the sticks. The question is always worth debating and considering – and knowing about the possibilities of the stick does concentrate the mind.

In May a Guyanese minister was assassinated, but in August elections were successfully held. On this occasion we succeeded in getting a Commonwealth observer group together. It happened rather carelessly, I thought in retrospect, as there seemed to be a majority of Africans or African-Caribbeans in the group, which would have been a problem if Jagdeo had lost. But he was far enough ahead to win comfortably. It was a reasonable election, with little corruption, and things settled down very quickly. Soon afterwards, I said to Paul Reeves that this was a good time to slip away if he wished. So after fourteen trips and reasonable progress over five years, he made his farewell calls. Was he effective? Yes. He didn't achieve all that we and he wanted, but in the absence of anyone else, he did prevent worse things happening. But accidents that don't happen do not make news.

The next year, 2007, I gave an address at the University of the West Indies in Jamaica. My speech was entitled 'Small States, Big Spirits'. I spoke to the gathering about vulnerabilities, cricket, reggae and what needed to be done, and suggested that all the challenges ahead told you one thing: TINA – There Is No Alternative. In dealing with the problems of Caribbean development there are no silver bullets, no fairy godmothers. I reminded them that forty years before, Singapore and Jamaica had the same per capita GDP. The value of good governance could never be underestimated.

I left Jamaica feeling quite positive about the various meetings I'd attended. That was, until I read a headline in the local paper, *The Gleaner*. It was 9 February and the headline was '182 murders since New Year'. That was only forty days, meaning four to five murders a day. What a horrible thought.

How do you possibly adjust to that? What do mothers think who are raising sons, as they see them grow into their teens, hanging around street corners? Do they wonder how long they will live? Do they remember cuddling them as four-year-olds? One distraught father was quoted as saying, 'He was a good boy, he didn't do no one no harm. It's not fair.'

It was chilling to read the next paragraph. Two men had burst into a gambling den, forced the four occupants to their knees and shot them all in the back of the head. It was all I could think of on my flight down to Barbados. Just where do you start to change this?

By late 2007 it was time to make some final calls. The Caribbean leaders had given me strong support ever since I came down firmly on their side over the offshore banking issue. Not to have done so would have had them categorise me as a South Pacific Brit who was protecting big banking interests.

So it was the usual rounds, with many more stories of Caribbean politics, of how they get ignored by the US as being too small (even though American troops did once invade Grenada). They will always be small players, but they know that when they work together they can achieve more. Many remember the West Indies Federation, which subsequently collapsed after many states left it. But like the Caribbean Court of Justice, those pan-regional initiatives will come to the fore again. Maybe even a federation will once again emerge.

You'll never take the politics or cricket out of the Caribbean. Politics and cricket – they go together, and long may it continue. As the noted Caribbean writer and cricket commentator C. L. R. James said, 'Cricket had plunged one into politics before I was aware of it. When I did turn to politics, I didn't have too much to learn.'

CHAPTER 9

Transforming the Political Culture

'Poverty, corruption, floods and two tenacious ladies,
and all before nine in the morning.'
Former Bangladesh Foreign Minister Morshed Khan (May 2002)

A visit to Bangladesh was at the top of my list after taking office
in April 2000, and I was there within the first month. One
reason, of course, was my hard-fought campaign for the position
of Secretary-General against Farooq Sobhan (see Chapter 1). It
was necessary for me to mend fences and ensure there was no
ill feeling. A number of Bangladeshi government officials had
been quick to tell me after my election in South Africa that it
had been a mistake for Bangladesh to field a candidate, but that
Mr Sobhan had got to Prime Minister Sheikh Hasina and sought
her support and commitment. Well, whether that was true or
not, I would probably soon find out.

I had met Sheikh Hasina in Durban, and was impressed by
her quiet but determined demeanour. She was the daughter of
the founding President, Sheikh Mujibur Rahman, and but for
her being in Germany on the night of 15 August 1975 she would
surely have been assassinated by disgruntled soldiers in Dhaka
along with her father, her mother, her three brothers and many
household staff.

With a population of about 130 million people, this nation,

which became independent from Pakistan in 1971, was the poorest of the poor. Such was its blood-stained and troubled start that an angry Pakistan, having lost what was then East Pakistan from its territory, stayed out of the Commonwealth for seventeen years.

On issues of governance, to quote Sheikh Hasina herself, Bangladesh has been a story of military interventions, phoney elections and fake votes in which the government machinery has been manipulated to stuff ballots and rig results. Bangladesh has a high rate of poverty and malnutrition. Traffic accidents are frequent due to poor health and safety checks. It also ranks high on the graph of natural disasters. No year seems to pass without a passenger ferry capsizing or a major flood hitting the country.

Bangladesh was also a committed Commonwealth member. Part of that enthusiasm arose from Pakistan being out of the Commonwealth for that long period. The Commonwealth had been prepared to take a stand on this, supporting the self-determination of the people of East Pakistan in their lengthy fight for independent status. It therefore meant a lot to Bangladesh to be in the Commonwealth when Pakistan was not.

My challenges on arriving in the country that first time on 19 April 2000, therefore, were many and varied. First, of course, I wanted to establish that there were no ill feelings following the Durban decision in my favour, and that Bangladesh would remain committed to the Commonwealth in all its forms. As a very fragile democracy, the country needed much support to grow and mature its democratic institutions, create more economic confidence and increase the per capita GDP. On a semi-related front, its national cricket team was beginning to challenge the bigger players, which was all good for a country's morale.

Although Bangladesh's candidate had failed to become Secretary-General, one element that helped raise the country's stature in the association was its membership of the Commonwealth Ministerial Action Group (CMAG). Bangladesh was important within CMAG because of Pakistan's suspension from the councils of the Commonwealth – CMAG would naturally give weight to Bangladesh's views on developments in Pakistan.

The first meeting I had was with Foreign Minister Alhaj Abdus Samad Azad, a seventy-four-year-old former freedom fighter who had also been foreign minister thirty years before. His life had been dominated by politics. He had been jailed by the British, the Pakistanis and, after the assassination of Mujibur Rahman, by the Bangladesh government. He had a wealth of knowledge, but was hard of hearing and not easy to understand; still, without any doubt, he had real status. He welcomed me as an old friend and nothing was too much trouble. He graciously hosted a pleasant dinner for me and said many nice things about me, so I knew we didn't have many fences to mend.

At the meeting with Prime Minister Sheikh Hasina I received the full story of her family's horrific history, which clearly had been seared into her mind. But it was only after I also met opposition leader Begum Khaleda Zia (who, unlike Sheikh Hasina but in common with many Muslim women, never shook the hand of a man) that I began to appreciate the antagonism these two women felt towards each other. Clearly they had inherited this from the previous leaders of their respective political parties – from Sheikh Mujibur Rahman in the case of his daughter, Sheikh Hasina, and from General Ziaur Rahman in the case of his wife, Begum Khaleda Zia.

Many political leaders acknowledged to me that the two women had reached the leadership by name and inheritance rather than by merit and hard graft. I believe this very much influenced their attitudes, relationships and decision-making processes. Most people rise in politics by learning how to climb the greasy pole, thus learning more from their mistakes than from their successes. Inherited leadership doesn't offer that useful apprenticeship; without it there will always be an element of insecurity. I have met many political leaders who have found themselves inheriting a position, and have often felt quite sorry for them. Most know they got there via a shortcut and thus often feel inadequate. Others may be totally arrogant. It unquestionably takes them a while to find their own feet and earn the genuine respect of others for their position on the presidential dais.

These two women were no exception. For a long time Bangladeshis were divided over the question of just who was the Father of the Nation. It depended on which political party you supported. The controversy was finally resolved in June 2009 when the High Court ruled that it was Bangabondhu Sheikh Mujibur Rahman and not General Ziaur Rahman who proclaimed independence from Pakistan in 1971.

Although it wasn't apparent at the time, this venom for each other was so deep-seated that there would be little we could achieve in this country – you would never get agreement from both women on anything. When I first met Begum Khaleda Zia while campaigning for the Secretary-General's job she said very little. It was all said by her party apparatchiks, seated on either side. She did warm up slowly in our conversations over the years, and on some issues was surprisingly not as hard-line as her officials.

Another unfortunate feature of Bangladeshi politics was that after every election it was winner-takes-all. This applied to not only the majority of parliamentary seats but also all the useful civil-servant positions, which changed as well. So no matter how clean or untainted the election process had been, the party that won (having first established its coalition partners) would push the losers firmly out beyond the sidelines, right out of the field of play. This is never a good thing in a developing country, in which people's identity with a political party can be very personal. Whether their party wins or loses an election can determine their personal future.

In an attempt to break the old mould of the government controlling everything about the election, the Commonwealth had, before my time as Secretary-General, appointed Sir Ninian Stephen in the role of a good Commonwealth citizen. This was a novel way of getting round what was becoming an endemic issue of political bias in the lead-up to an election. Sir Ninian was an Australian with a formidable career background: a Second World War veteran, highly respected constitutional lawyer, Queen's counsel, Supreme Court judge and for seven years governor general of his country.

Sir Ninian proposed the creation of a caretaker government in Bangladesh for a few months prior to each election, thus neutralising the political parties during that very sensitive period. It is a time when political parties everywhere always believe the incumbent party will use its authority to ensure it retains office – and there is much evidence to support such a view.

To me, the exercise was a very good example of the way the Commonwealth can draw upon someone with the experience, wisdom and gravitas of Sir Ninian. In Bangladesh it worked, giving all political parties something of an equal start to each campaign.

In most parliamentary democracies, the head of state symbolises the unity of the state and leaves politics to the head of government, who is also the head of the ruling party. The Bangladesh tradition was to have the prime minister and the president being loyal first to their party before serving the country. This applied not only to the ruling party (at that time the Bangladesh National Party) but also to the opposition – because when they won the elections they behaved in exactly the same fashion.

I thought it would take years before this cycle was broken to allow the true spirit of democracy to filter through the Bangladesh governance structures. It seemed to me that an obviously neutral Commonwealth could assist the ongoing development of more mature democratic institutions in order to give people more faith in the political process. In retrospect, maybe this was naive, but we had enough evidence that if you could break down old barriers, few if any states would go back to the old ways.

Bangladesh was in the grip of electoral violence for most of 2001. In June a bomb in the Awami League office in Dhaka killed twenty-two people. In September eight people were killed and hundreds were injured in two bomb explosions at election rallies. Nothing looked at all promising except for the fact that Sheikh Hasina completed her full term of office as Prime Minister in July 2001 and stepped down to allow a caretaker administration to conduct the general election in accordance with the constitution. At that time it appeared that Bangladesh had graduated from the politics of instability and violence to a level where the transfer of political power could take place through peaceful elections and adherence to the rule of law.

The elections brought to power Begum Khaleda Zia's Bangladesh National Party (BNP) and its three coalition partners, much to the surprise and distress of Sheikh Hasina and the Awami League. Begum Khaleda Zia thus became Prime Minister and Morshed Khan, a wealthy businessman from Chittagong, took over as foreign minister. A more enthusiastic minister with such excellent international business contacts would be hard to find. He could also articulate Bangladesh's foreign policy more effectively than career diplomats.

The assessment that Bangladesh had crossed the bridge and was on its way to becoming a mature democracy unfortunately proved incorrect. Sheikh Hasina's party had been very confident of being re-elected, and after the results she cried foul. Meanwhile, after forming her government, Begum Khaleda Zia started to undermine the role of the opposition by denying them time even during parliamentary debates. In June 2002 Begum Khaleda Zia accused President Badruddoza Chowdhury, a senior BNP leader and a supporter of her late husband, of breaching party discipline. His sin was not following tradition and visiting the grave of her late husband President Ziaur Rahman on the anniversary of the latter's death. This break from party solidarity, and insult to Begum Khaleda Zia, was followed by a resolution of BNP parliamentarians calling for him to resign. Chowdhury then found himself a lonely voice in the party and had no choice but to quit his office.

The brief from my officials on my second visit to Bangladesh, from 25–27 August 2002, was that the government needed to develop a post-election democratic culture, which took into account a responsible opposition and a ruling party willing to take constructive criticism and include the opposition in the political process. During the two-day visit, I met Khaleda Zia and Sheikh Hasina in their reversed roles as Prime Minister and leader of the opposition and heard the same stories from each.

Sheikh Hasina was still convinced that she had been robbed of the election. But before I could discuss this in detail, out came the album of photos of alleged Awami League people who had been assaulted, raped or killed. Here was the bloody evidence: limbless people, males with genitalia removed, half of people's heads blown off, page after page, accompanied by a diatribe against the BNP and against those who assassinated her family. It was all very graphic indeed.

The one message I tried to leave with Sheikh Hasina was: 'Don't be like the BNP and boycott Parliament.' I reiterated to her that Parliament is designed to give the opposition a voice and a forum to challenge the government. Moreover, governments don't need Parliament if the opposition is not there. She nodded in agreement, but I knew my message was not going to overturn more than thirty years of parliamentary walkouts by both parties. I relayed the same message through the local media, stating that the defeated party must be a formidable opposition, not a government in exile.

I was impressed with the perseverance of a Bangladesh university professor, Muhammad Yunus, who had started a bank for the poor in the early 1980s after being denied a small loan by a commercial bank. The Grameen Bank, which he founded in Bangladesh in 1983, grew in the rural areas in a short period of time, and Yunus became known all over the world as the father of the microcredit scheme for the poor. I met Yunus in

Bangladesh in 2002 and decided to invite him to deliver the prestigious Commonwealth Lecture in London in 2003 on the subject of 'Halving Poverty by 2015: The Role of the Commonwealth'.

Announcing the choice of Professor Yunus on 11 March 2003, I said: 'Like most great ideas, the concept behind Grameen Bank is extremely simple: trust poor people, extend credit and they will take themselves out of poverty. Grameen Bank is the living proof that with original ideas and a strong will, poverty can be beaten.' I was glad to get him for the lecture, and he joined the company of such esteemed people as Nelson Mandela, Jim Wolfensohn, Kofi Annan and Mary Robinson at that annual forum. We were also able to assist in transporting the Grameen Bank model to other Commonwealth countries to great effect.

In 2003 I found another opportunity to visit Bangladesh when I addressed the opening of the 49th Commonwealth Parliamentary Conference, which was held in Dhaka from 4–12 October. Once again my ambition was to advance the country's snail-like democratic progress. Sheikh Hasina was adamant that the Awami League would boycott the conference and thus embarrass the ruling party in the presence of parliamentarians from all over the Commonwealth. I later learned that the Awami League was justified in its protest because the speaker of the People's Assembly, barrister Jamiruddin Sircar, had maintained an overly partisan attitude and almost excluded the opposition from consultations in the preparations for the conference.

As I often did when making such visits, I asked if I could attend Parliament, where I knew I would be publicly introduced. After only twenty minutes in the chamber it was all very obvious. The way in which Parliament was being used by both government and opposition members was a recipe to make everybody very angry. Added to that was a clearly biased speaker. It was an intensely dysfunctional body.

Having been a parliamentarian, a house leader and a whip, you just know instinctively what works and what doesn't in parliaments anywhere. Two examples from this visit: a minister

in response to a question talked at great length about everything other than the subject of the question; and on a point of
order Sheikh Hasina spoke for twenty-five minutes on the death
of her family. Nothing that resembled a contemporary legislature was working. It was going to be a long haul to create a
workable Parliament.

The Commonwealth Parliamentary Association (CPA) meeting opened in Dhaka on 4 October 2003 without any Awami
League parliamentarian in the delegation of the host Parliament.
The absence of the leader of the opposition was also conspicuous,
and said volumes about what needed to be done in Bangladesh
towards restoring healthy parliamentary processes.

At a meeting at her Dhanmondi residence, I urged Hasina
to return to the meetings and to take the extra step of showing
the government that if the ruling party was behaving badly, the
opposition was prepared to go the extra mile for the sake of
the dignity of the country at this major parliamentary event.
Although I could see that our reasoning was fully understood
by Sheikh Hasina, her hawkish advisers, notably Awami League
Secretary-General Abdul Jalil and Awami League presidium
member Kazi Zafrullah, were not prepared to see their leader
undo the decision at the last minute. No amount of pleading
would make her change her mind.

Returning to my hotel I reflected that being a leader means
having the ability to challenge the opinions of your officials
or even colleagues on important occasions, not to let crucial decisions be influenced by petty agendas and not to miss
unique opportunities.

On the other side of the road, of course, the BNP people
were also not prepared to admit that they made mistakes. The
BNP side kept mumbling about administration problems. That
evening I vented my spleen to both Saifur Rahman and Morshed
Kahn over these intransigent attitudes. Both agreed that little
could be achieved while these two women were in power and
opposition, with each wishing to strangle the other.

With fifty-three countries in the Commonwealth and a high proportion seeking assistance, there is only so much time you can spend trying to change the habits of those who do not wish to be changed. It's not only in Bangladesh but in a number of Commonwealth countries that you see dynastic politics, dysfunctional parliaments, ineffective political processes and outdated rules and procedures gripped strongly by those who never wish to lose power.

As all Bangladesh parliamentarians were members of the Commonwealth Parliamentary Association, I decided that I would try to find in other Commonwealth countries two or three former senior MPs well versed in the role, the management and the running of Parliament to come for a couple of weeks and see if they could, by persuasion, affect changes that might produce a more smooth-running Bangladeshi Parliament. Of course, I was told, 'You can't tell us anything about democracy.' But despite this misplaced confidence I still went to the leaders.

Prime Minister Begum Khaleda Zia was supportive. Sheikh Hasina was supportive. And both thought the former deputy prime minister of Malaysia, Tun Musa Hitam, a fine former parliamentarian, would be the right person to lead the mission. That was until Khaleda Zia heard that Hasina was in favour, at which point she promptly withdrew her support. So that initiative died before it could draw breath. The CPA was also concerned about the dysfunctional parliamentary practices and planned a goodwill mission to try to change that. This, too, was rejected.

On 21 May 2004 Britain's high commissioner to Bangladesh, Anwaruzzaman Chowdhury, escaped a terrorist attempt on his life in Sylhet. In August a grenade attack on an opposition Awami League rally killed twenty-two people. Sheikh Hasina survived the attack, but her adviser Ivy Rahman and some other party workers were killed. Three years before, the BNP-led Parliament had repealed a law granting life-long security to Sheikh Hasina

and her sister Sheikh Rehana. The Awami League leader was convinced that the BNP and its coalition partners, especially Jamaat, were secretly planning to get her killed – like her father and other relatives.

I rang Sheikh Hasina in sympathy and suggested that a level of public reconciliation between her and Khaleda Zia might quieten down some of their most zealous supporters. But things got no better when no arrests were made. There were no witnesses, and no member of the Awami League was appointed to the Commission of Inquiry. I was left with the thought that only time and new personalities could ever make a difference.

The frenzy of violence continued throughout 2005, making the Awami League even more resolute in its belief that the BNP government had to go before its full term was up. In January 2005 a prominent Awami League leader and a key contributor to the Awami League's election manifesto, Shah A. M. S. Kibria, was killed in a grenade attack at a political rally. The Awami League called a nationwide strike to mourn his death.

And so it continued. In August 2005, in an amazingly well-orchestrated and clandestine operation, about 350 bombs went off on the same day in small towns and cities across Bangladesh. Fortunately, the death toll was low, but this had to be one of the most well-planned and effectively executed terrorist attacks ever known. Bangladesh security agencies were criticised for not only failing to apprehend terrorists but also committing gross human rights violations in the form of torture and extra-judicial killings of civilians.

As there had to be an election within twelve months – by January 2007 – it was important for me to visit Bangladesh once again to offer assistance and to voice Commonwealth concerns about the deteriorating situation. The upsurge in violence and the growing international criticism had caught the government by surprise. It immediately cracked down on members of the banned militant group Jamaat-ul-Mujahideen, but all of that seemed too little, too late. There were attacks on the courts, and a suicide bomber killed many in a Dhaka marketplace.

When I arrived in Dhaka on my fifth visit I had a meeting with Morshed Khan, as ebullient as ever. Before I went to see his Prime Minister, Khaleda Zia, he told me to 'give her a strong message'. Was he too scared to tell her that himself? He laughed and said, 'We all are!'

At my meeting with Begum Zia she spent much of the time making asides in Bengali – these, however, were understood by both my officials. She then asked for an observer mission for the upcoming elections. So far, so good. I then asked for a one-on-one meeting with her alone. I put it to her that many Commonwealth leaders wanted her and Hasina to bring the temperature down and reduce the antagonism. It was creating distrust at lower levels and sparking the violence, especially since it was an election year. She took it in good spirit and said she felt she had moved towards Hasina, but the latter had to move too. It was not an entirely engaging response.

I then went to see Sheikh Hasina in her heavily fortified enclave in Dhanmondi. She said she was convinced that they were out to kill her, and that the government was about to extend the tenure of the most senior judge, meaning he would retire not at sixty-five but at sixty-seven – to ensure they got him as the chief adviser before the elections. It seemed a valid point. It was time to leave Dhaka again, with little achieved.

In May 2006 it was decided informally among the European Union, ourselves, the United Kingdom and the United States that the opposing camps simply must be brought together. Of course, this was easier said than done.

Meanwhile, in August, voter registrations for upcoming elections got underway. An earlier understanding with the Bangladesh Election Commission to have a Secretariat team observe the registration process was suddenly shut down. It was perceived they would be too intrusive. Where were our allies now? Morshed Khan and Saifur Rahman seemed to have disappeared from the scene and our messages were falling on deaf ears. These were the warning signs that nothing would run smoothly.

I took the opportunity to call the President about this state of affairs, but his response, by the way he spoke to me, was clearly written in front of him, no doubt by Foreign Affairs. He continued to read the answers, seemingly unaware that they did not answer my questions; he was going to read me all five answers anyway. This did not augur well for the coming months.

On 28 October 2006, Khaleda Zia stepped down after completing her five-year term as Prime Minister. Three cheers for Bangladesh? Not so, because she had left a mess behind in the form of an uncertain caretaker arrangement. The next day, President Iajuddin Ahmed was sworn in as the head of the caretaker government. It was an improvisation on the existing arrangement to get the opposition alongside. The Awami League gave President Ahmed a deadline of 30 November to implement a number of proposals to prove his impartiality. These included the removal of a large number of civil servants and election officers in the districts, as well as consultations with the Awami League for selecting other caretaker advisers.

Soon after Khaleda Zia stepped down, the Bangladesh High Commission sent word to us that the Commonwealth election assessment mission to Dhaka could go ahead. So a two-person team from the Secretariat visited Dhaka to assess the situation. They met the Chief Election Commissioner and the leaders of major political parties, and concluded that the Awami League and its fourteen allied parties were not prepared to accept the conduct and outcome of the elections under the present caretaker set-up. There would be more violence if changes were not made in the administration of elections and proven politically-orientated personalities were not excluded from the caretaker government.

A great deal of uncertainty over the entire governmental system now prevailed. The Election Commission announced an election date of 22 January 2007, but the opposition alliance declared it would boycott the poll and began a three-day transport blockade of Dhaka. Much of the country was paralysed. Then, on 11 January, President Iajuddin Ahmed declared a state of emergency and postponed the elections indefinitely.

A day before the proclamation of the state of emergency I had said in a press statement in London: 'Bangladesh is at the crossroads. It is incumbent upon all political parties and stake-holders in the election process to work towards a solution to avert a major political crisis and keep the interests of the nation uppermost in mind. Dialogue at the highest political levels in Bangladesh is the need of the hour. This is a real test of leadership and political will.'

So who was in charge? The new chief adviser Dr Fakhruddin Ahmed was a very mild-mannered former economist, but it was the military behind him who were calling the shots. It was a military coup through the back door. Many people were arrested and the Awami League and BNP leadership were floundering.

Should the issue have been addressed by the Commonwealth Ministerial Action Group (CMAG) in an extraordinary session, as had happened when democratically-elected governments were overthrown in Sierra Leone, Fiji, Solomon Islands and Pakistan? Probably so, but we would have spent six months writing letters back and forth as required, and would probably not have achieved unanimity even then. I decided that the issue was sufficiently serious that I should write to the CMAG ministers apprising them of this most undemocratic situation. We would just have to put up with any objections from the caretaker administration in Dhaka. There was nothing in the rules that said whether I should or should not do this. To me, this was not a time to sit on our hands and say there was no provision for such an unusual action.

Of course, the true international democrats who normally beat loudly on the drum for first principles were mute, and started bending like reeds. Australia, the United Kingdom and Canada all thought this was a good way to have a clean-up to start again, and so suppressed any criticism. When I asked them if this was their best response to a military coup, they all smiled. To top it all, there was a statement from the Pakistan high commissioner that of course his government would support the Bangladesh Army! Frankly, I thought it was the height of naivety for these diplomats to believe you could achieve positive political change this way, through a military coup.

In March 2007 I visited Bangladesh again, to get a first-hand account of who was running the country and keep the pressure on. I attended a luncheon that included ten of the advisers that made up the new caretaker government. They all seemed rather pleased with themselves to be in such influential positions. At the end of the lunch I was asked to say a few words. I stressed the onerous responsibility that had fallen on their shoulders. Their principal task now was to deliver an election as soon as possible. I said that people might congratulate them now for the wonderful job they were doing, but people might also get very angry if they were continually denied their rights.

In another part of Dhaka I asked two former generals who were now in charge of government departments: 'Is this not a military coup?' They both said yes. You did not need to be told the army was firmly on one side.

I could easily see that the leadership of the two parties was largely responsible for the current situation. The antagonism between the two women had not diminished. Sheikh Hasina was in the US, but our meeting with Begum Khaleda Zia was calm, friendly and using more English. She asked that the Commonwealth continue to monitor human rights violations in Bangladesh, but at no stage did she stamp her feet about the close civilian-military leadership of the interim government. Well, it was pleasing to know the Commonwealth was still considered credible and in demand. Often those out of power plead for our involvement, but when they are in power and don't wish to lose we are sometimes seen as a nuisance. In cricketing parlance, you've just got to keep playing a straight bat.

When leaving the country I ensured that my views were also aired through the media so that everyone in Bangladesh knew what the Commonwealth expected from the interim government and political parties to ensure the return of democracy. At a crowded press conference in Dhaka on 21 March 2007, I highlighted four key points: (1) the government should announce as early as possible a road map of its programmes, policy objectives and schedule of elections with clear timelines; (2) it should respect human rights, the rule of law and due processes while pursuing its clean-up operations; (3) it should lift the current state of emergency and suspension of political activity without delay and restore the fundamental rights of citizens; and (4) it should finalise a new voters' register, introduce internal democracy in political parties and review parliamentary rules and standing orders to restore the primacy of elected and accountable constitutional authority.

In response to a question about the Bangladesh issue being dealt with by CMAG, I said that if the situation in Bangladesh did not change soon, CMAG could discuss it formally. I sensed that the media did not know much about CMAG mechanisms, but they had grabbed the bait. No government likes to consider the possibility of being on the CMAG agenda. I exited through the kitchen and headed straight to the airport.

When I mentioned this de facto military coup later in London, I was chastised by the Bangladesh High Commission. My response was that I wouldn't be quiet, and I might even name the generals who concurred with me.

On 31 August 2007 the Election Commission indicated that it would begin a dialogue with political parties on holding the elections. At the same time the government announced that it would ease the ban on political parties for indoor political activities.

I thought this was a good beginning, but not enough to satisfy political parties and the people about the process.

In a press statement issued from London I said: 'I am concerned about the very large number of political detainees, reportedly over 100,000, who have yet to be brought to trial. It is crucial for the caretaker government to respect the human rights of all its citizens and to ensure that the rule of law and due process are respected. The judicial processes should deal with detainees swiftly, fairly and transparently.'

After I left Marlborough House on 31 March 2008 on completion of my term of office, the interim government took another six months to stabilise the situation before it called general elections on 18 December 2008. A Commonwealth observer group visited Bangladesh in 2008, concluding that the elections had been freely held and that the results reflected accurately the will of the people of Bangladesh. The Awami League captured more than a two-thirds majority in the People's Assembly and Sheikh Hasina became Prime Minister.

One hopes that Bangladesh political parties have learnt the lesson that unless the political culture is fundamentally transformed to meet the requirements of representative democracy, to allow separation of powers and to respect the rule of law, the mere ritual of holding periodic elections is not enough to guarantee peace and stability. The Commonwealth and other respectable organisations must remain engaged and keep prodding and encouraging a better level of performance.

Sometimes you just have to wait for events to change the landscape and create possibilities for more substantial and sustainable change.

CHAPTER 10

Friends, Coups and Suspensions

If there was an area of the Commonwealth I knew better than most, it was the Pacific. My first serious visit to the region had been in the late 1980s, when I had joined a New Zealand government minister on a flight sponsored by the New Zealand government. We were passengers travelling with a small technical team whose role was to calibrate the coordinates of airports throughout the Pacific.

We were welcomed in Norfolk Island, the Cook Islands, Samoa, Tonga and even Tahiti, and I had a good chance to talk to local political and community leaders. I enjoyed the generous hospitality, lovely warm weather and great swimming and snorkelling, but I also developed a new appreciation of where New Zealand fitted into this vast area of Polynesia.

The next time I went, as foreign minister, to Fiji some four years after the coups of 1987. The feeling among the local people was still very tense, and my meeting with former Prime Minister and the giant of Pacific politics, Ratu Sir Kamisese Mara, was difficult to say the least. That tour came to an abrupt halt when the first Gulf War broke out and New Zealand wanted to play its part, so we immediately returned to Wellington.

Taking note of what I had seen and heard from these visits, I considered it most important that not only the New Zealand government but also New Zealand members of Parliament should have good relationships in the Pacific. So I started a series of annual tours of at least five or six Pacific countries, courtesy again of the Royal New Zealand Air Force and their Boeing 727, to develop an appreciation of just how the strength, breadth and depth of the relationship could be developed and sustained. The programme was launched, with the first group consisting of seven or eight backbench MPs and their spouses or partners, four or five NGO representatives, two defence-force personnel and four high-school students. With my own Foreign Affairs staff and others from the Ministry of Foreign Affairs and Trade, we usually filled nearly half the plane.

At every stop, each of the separate groups went off in a different direction – the students went to schools and were locally billeted, NGOs visited organisations they were supporting, MPs went everywhere and I had my bilateral meetings with presidents, prime ministers and foreign ministers.

The whole exercise increased immensely the understanding of the Palagi (European) and Maori New Zealanders of that immense region. So I was pleased to hear that all my successors as foreign ministers continued the tradition. From Papua New Guinea in the west to Kiribati in the north and to French Polynesia across to the east, all were visited from time to time.

When I became Secretary-General in 2000, having got, I believe, one hundred per cent support from the Commonwealth Pacific members, I did not believe there were onerous problems to address. The Solomon Islands were in the most difficulty, with clashes between island groups and a weak government. Tonga was still very much a feudal monarchy, with a restless population but little sign of democratic change. Fiji had slowly come out of its isolation and rejoined the Commonwealth at the 1997 Commonwealth Heads of Government Meeting (CHOGM) in Edinburgh. The Pacific Islands Forum (PIF) was playing an even more useful role through its membership and secretariat. And Australia and New Zealand, the big players with their large financial contributions, were trying hard not to apply undue influence on too many decisions.

It therefore came as the proverbial bolt from the blue to hear there had been another coup in Fiji on 19 May 2000. No one saw this coming, even though there had been low-level agitation about the very abrasive and strong-minded first elected Indo-Fijian Prime Minister, Mahendra Chaudhry.

I heard the news early in the morning in London and went to the office at 7 a.m. in order to keep abreast of the drama, as there would be immediate questions asked of my office and the Secretariat. Being only the second person to get to the office that morning prompted me to upbraid the senior political staff about their very casual response. 'If there is a coup in a Commonwealth country, I expect you to get to the office immediately – you don't cruise in at the usual time – after 9.30 a.m.!'

We soon got to know George Speight, the coup leader (see Chapter 3). He was an Australian-educated Fijian and known to be a failed businessman who was opposed to the country's Indo-Fijian leadership. Not only did he manage to secure support from some dissident members of the Republic of Fiji Military Force (RFMF) who were heavily armed, plus some former cabinet ministers, but he had also taken hostage thirty-five members of Parliament, locking them up in the debating chamber.

I made telephone calls to former coup leader and former Prime Minister, Sitiveni Rabuka, and to President Ratu Sir Kamisese Mara, who was at the time the Pacific's senior statesman. Both were perplexed, angry and defiant. 'Who does he think he is?' was their attitude towards Speight. It was amazing that no one knew anything about George Speight. He was on no one's address list, no one's watch list; he just came from nowhere. What he did have, however, was a highly developed sense of his own self-importance.

As I've outlined in Chapter 3, after discussions with various people in the region and with Kofi Annan, the UN Secretary-General in New York, it was agreed that with Annan's envoy in East Timor, Sergio de Mello (an extremely experienced UN diplomat from Brazil, who was later killed in Iraq) and I would go to Fiji to talk to Speight. We would hopefully come up with some solutions.

De Mello's aircraft picked up me and one of my senior political advisers, Adefuye, from Honiara and flew us to Suva on 25 May 2000. Even though de Mello's experience was wide (he spoke four languages and was well-versed in international law), this, he admitted, would be a challenge. I was glad that I knew many individuals inside and outside the Fiji government. Professor Adefuye was my principal African adviser and had been my predecessor's envoy, assisting former Prime Minister Rabuka to bring an end to ethnic clashes in the Solomons. He had been through coups in Nigeria, and he was an obvious choice to take with me to Fiji.

On arrival in Suva we were met by Nik Kiddle, a senior New Zealand diplomat, who would help us manoeuvre around Suva and try to avoid the media. The Fiji officials who met us were quite uncertain as to their role, nervously looking over their shoulders. It was all rather chaotic.

I found President Mara very tired and drawn, and looking much older. His voice was not strong. The coup had caught him by surprise, and his daughter Adi Koila, who was married to the speaker of Parliament, Ratu Epeli Nailatikau, was one of the hostages. It was, he said, 'an attack on the constitution and the leadership'.

Next, I said we had to see the hostages. We didn't wish to leave the country until we had seen them all alive.

In order to avoid the constant pressure and demands of the media – the BBC, CNN, ABC, and TVNZ, plus many newspapers and radio – we sequestered ourselves at the New Zealand High Commission residence. Many came to see us, and the most worried and perplexed were former senior politicians. None of them had any idea what Speight wanted, where he had come from or why it started.

I had known from following Fiji politics for more than a decade that Prime Minister Chaudhry was an ambitious, smart and assertive individual with a background of extensive involvement in the trade union and sugar politics in Fiji. He was clearly determined to do as much as he could as rapidly as he could, at any cost. He seemed especially out to challenge those who ensured that his racial group were always second-class, especially remembering the overthrow of Timoci Bavadra by Rabuka in 1987. The fact that he knew Fiji politics very well suggested to me that his premiership was all about payback. Even President Ratu Mara disclosed to me that he advised Chaudhry to slow down because he was antagonising too many people. He needed to be more cautious when dealing with land issues.

In the late afternoon we went to meet Speight. From here on the situation would have seemed almost comical if it hadn't been so serious. Speight had said we had to see him before he would let us see the hostages. So we walked into the compound of Parliament, all sealed off by Speight's people. Standing around were a number of gun-wielding young men who, I thought, could easily let off a round without realising it. I thought, if I get killed here it'll be more by accident than intent. But also in the compound were the media, with seemingly unlimited freedom. Speight told me later, 'Oh, we feed all the media three times a day!' Well, I thought, so much for the free, independent and 'we can't be bought off' media.

The UN were clearly worried about de Mello's security (I wasn't considered to be valuable) so he was pleased that in the chaos around the entry point, his well-armed Egyptian protection officer got into the compound with him. Jamal even got his high-powered pistol through Speight's security, so sloppy were they in their procedures. He then told me with professional pride that he could have killed five of them before any one of them could respond. He had nothing but contempt for what he saw as a bunch of amateurs.

So now we were surrounded by several hundred of Speight's

supporters and thirty media, with only a vague idea of what was coming next. After a few false turns, we ended up in a room to wait. Speight arrived like a media star, in a freshly ironed shirt and neat tie and surrounded by enthusiastic, fast-stepping rebel soldiers shoving people every which way.

He kept repeating 'I'm only going to tell you one thing', 'I want you to remember just one thing' and 'There's just one thing I want you to take away', six or eight times. He was well spoken and the message was: 'This country belongs to the Fijians, and we don't need to put up with what the British bequeathed us in terms of Indians or Western ideas.'

And as an afterthought: 'We couldn't care less about the international community.' He was high on either drugs or adrenalin. But it was all bumper-sticker stuff, nothing very profound.

We didn't wish to antagonise him, because he had more guns than we did, so we talked about possible ways to proceed and expressed the view that the issues in Fiji were not singular to Fiji alone. But he wasn't listening. My colleague de Mello then talked of the challenges of indigenous peoples, but before he had even made his argument he was jumped on by Berenado Vunibobo, a former Mara and Rabuka minister, for comparing Brazil to Fiji. Round and round we went, and so it ended, with no resolution. Vunibobo was later appointed Fiji's ambassador to the UN in 2008, only to be recalled before his three-year term ended.

It seemed to be more Keystone Cops than a serious coup against a sovereign government, as we waited in a small office while Speight prepared himself for the next move. He chatted with us as if this was the most normal thing in the world.

We were finally led into the vast debating chamber of Parliament. It had been darkened, so at first it was hard to see anybody. The first hostage to recognise me was Tupeni Baba, then deputy prime minister, whom I greeted warmly. 'What's happening?' the hostages asked. They had not been given any outside news.

As I went round greeting them and hugging some, I told them

why we were there. The international community was very concerned at what was happening. We had told Speight he should
give up this venture. We could not release them, but we wanted
to report on their health. Some of the women were now crying.
Yes, they had food and access to toilets, but they had no idea
what would happen to them. They'd been ten days in captiv-
ity, amid great uncertainty. Some had expected to be killed at
any moment.

After twenty minutes with the Fijian group we were taken to
another room, where the Indo-Fijian hostages were held. Most of
them were lying on mattresses. Prime Minister Chaudhry was the
first to recognise me. We greeted them all, with more hugs, and
explained what we were trying to do, hopefully leaving them with
some hope. We felt helpless that we could do so little for them.

Then we held a press conference. Our message was clear and
simple: yes, the hostages were in good health, but that was no
substitute for freedom. Speight had no international support; he
should give up or release the hostages; more international pressure would be brought to bear on Fiji.

It wasn't easy. We obviously didn't want to antagonise Speight
or make life worse for the hostages. It was the Fijian leadership
who had to get this sorted out.

Shortly before 1 a.m. former Prime Minister Rabuka came to
see me. I've never seen anyone so sad and depressed – the polar
opposite to the very confident soldier who had taken over the
country by means of a coup in 1987. He didn't know what had
happened; he would have to leave the country; could I get him
New Zealand residency? He could be a taxi driver in Auckland,
he said, in a most resigned way. He really thought he had done
a good job of developing a new constitution, 'and now look
what's happened'. We talked until about 3 a.m. but could see no
easy solution.

In the weeks that followed, I reflected on what had gone wrong.

Rabuka, with the help of the traditional Fijian leadership and a cross-section of the community, helped considerably by the Indo-Fijian lawyer and political leader Jai Ram Reddy, had seen a new constitution legislated and signed into law on 25 July 1997. This third constitution for Fiji had, with one amendment, been endorsed by both the lower and upper houses, and by the Great Council of Chiefs. As New Zealand minister some years before, I had asked our country's former governor general, Sir Paul Reeves, to help draft that new constitution, with Mr Tomasi Vakatora and Professor Brij Lal representing the two major races. That worked well, then it was Rabuka and Reddy who, apart from campaigning in unison, had also agreed to work together after the 1999 general election to form a multi-party cabinet.

But Rabuka and Reddy seriously miscalculated the strength of ethnicity in Fijian politics. A complicated voting system didn't help. So both were shocked when their respective political parties were soundly defeated in the elections. The two main ethnic groups may well have seen this collaboration between the two leaders as a sell-out of their respective interests. Also, Chaudhry's Fiji Labour Party (FLP), which secured the support of the Indo-Fijians, had won the elections overwhelmingly by outmanoeuvring them through this rather complex voting system. That antagonised many Fijians, who thought they had lost political control of their country again.

It may have begun merely with whispers around a kava bowl, but Speight and his colleagues had decided to move. It just shouldn't have happened, and slowly, in a very Pacific way, it was wound back.

At a special meeting of CMAG on 6 June at which I was able to report on my mission, the ministers forthwith suspended Fiji from the councils of the Commonwealth.

Now it was the military commander Voreqe (Frank) Bainimarama who took control. He had become head of the armed forces after the previous commander, Brigadier Ratu Epeli Ganilau, left for politics. It was Bainimarama who appointed Laisenia Qarase, a Fiji businessman, as an interim leader and Prime Minister, after Speight and his fellow coup leaders had agreed to release the hostages.

The release of the hostages on 13 July 2000 after the fifty-eight-day crisis followed the Muanikau Accord, which also granted Speight and his followers immunity from prosecution. Bainimarama then reneged on the conditions of the accord, claiming that Speight's followers were refusing to give up their weapons. After the hostage release, Speight and others were arrested. Speight is still, at time of writing, serving a life sentence in prison for treason.

A Commonwealth meeting scheduled to be held in Fiji in 2000 was moved to Samoa. This was where I first met Samoan diplomat Albert Mariner, who was soon to join the Commonwealth Secretariat and become my Pacific expert. He later proved a very influential interlocutor among the key players in the region.

And now the Commonwealth Ministerial Action Group (CMAG) was involved, I succeeded in dispatching Justice Pius Langa of South Africa in December 2000 to get alongside the key people in Fiji to promote change and return to a reasonable semblance of democracy (see Chapter 3). By the middle of June 2001, Langa was mildly optimistic about the forthcoming elections.

About this time, I received an invitation to be a guest at the August PIF meeting, to be held on Nauru. For a time a financially and phosphate-rich country, Nauru was now very poor. There was little phosphate left to mine, and many of the country's investments had just disappeared. Yet they obviously felt they had to keep up appearances. On arrival each leader and I were presented with three island shirts, two calculators, two briefcases and a bottle of Johnnie Walker Blue Label Scotch whisky. I guess the government felt it necessary to be generous, but we would all have understood if there were no gifts.

Despite the best efforts of the René Harris government, Naura had got itself into more strife by becoming something of a tax haven. I had seen too many examples of poor small island states having been encouraged to diversify and to set up (or allow to be set up) financial institutions for anyone outside the country to use. In many cases, these new banks were created to allow people to pay less tax somewhere else – or to launder funds to destroy or confuse any knowledge as to their source. In some cases, governments knew exactly what they were buying into, and in many other cases they had no idea.

In one case, a businessman from Panama set up a financial structure on a Pacific island that was in effect the office of some 150 companies, all having funds moving in and out. The government had no idea what was going on, as it just received a set fee from the Panamanian through the company's registration. Needless to say, others in leading Western capitals knew exactly what was going on, and started beating up on these island states. Or they supported the OECD (Organisation for Economic Co-operation and Development) pressure to clamp down on these so-called tax havens. Our engagement with island states and the OECD was designed to sift the legal from the illegal. Too many island states were getting chastised as much for the legal as the illegal. I cover this in more detail in Chapter 8.

By 2006 we had to recognise that Nauru simply had no money. We had to declare the country a special member (from 2007 it was renamed 'Member in arrears') with no status within the organisation. This meant that it could not attend CHOGMs or ministerial meetings. It was all very sad because it is these small countries that benefit the most from seeing how others face problems and overcome their difficulties. We did leave Naura's flag flying in front of Marlborough House.

I had watched the travails of Nauru over a long period.

The country had been rich, but now the people were poor and scratching out the last of the phosphate. It was very sad that they had so little to show for the long history of phosphate mining and the large royalties received over many years.

They were becoming a burden to Australia, which didn't find the issue easy to deal with. There were times when I thought that to give all 9,000–10,000 Nauruans an Australian passport might be the cheapest way out, followed by a reduction in the amount of direct aid to the island. The movement of people between Australia and the island would stabilise at a level where only those who could afford to live on the island or accept subsistence living would do so, but I wouldn't be too sure of overall acceptance in Australia of such a proposal.

Meanwhile, between 25 August and 1 September 2001, elections were held in Fiji. Deposed Prime Minister Chaudhry was refusing to be quiet and wasn't making life easy for anyone. But a Commonwealth observer group led by Sir Henry Forde QC from Barbados awarded a B-plus for the elections, and Qarase's party won thirty-two seats, or 48 per cent, of the vote. With twenty-seven seats for the FLP, but only six seats for the George Speight party, the latter's influence was now, thank goodness, much diminished.

We all crossed our fingers as Qarase was sworn in as Prime Minister, but when he put together his cabinet, it didn't include any FLP representatives. Chaudhry declared he had accepted an offer from Qarase to include an FLP member, but Qarase then said that including the FLP would make it all 'unworkable'. Chaudhry replied that he would see him in court.

Fiji remained suspended from the Commonwealth's councils. But the Commonwealth high commissioners in London were divided on what should happen next. India and the United Kingdom were taking a hard line, Australia and New Zealand a softer one, and Malaysia and Papua New Guinea regarded the current impasse as basically being back to normal. Finally, in December the suspension was lifted, with strong opposition from Mahendra Chaudhry, who continued to protest because the lifting of the suspension in effect confirmed he no longer had a claim to the prime ministership.

Some time later I revisited Suva, and at a social function, talked to a number of the Fijian MPs who had been held by Speight, including many that I had met during that period. Two MPs told me they still had nightmares about the ordeal, and one said to see me brought back those memories. I apologised I was having that effect on her, and thank goodness she was able to show a small, quick smile.

'Was Fiji making progress on racial issues?' I asked a group. I was told there were more Fijians going to the Indian schools because they were now improved; maybe 5 per cent of marriages were now interracial, up from zero; and more Fijians were going into business, previously the preserve of the Indo-Fijian population. Well, I thought, it's a start – but we've a long, long way to go.

Another Commonwealth Pacific issue that required my attention was the Solomon Islands, east of Papua New Guinea, a Commonwealth country consisting of nearly a thousand islands. Here it was very depressing that, frankly, nothing seemed to be working.

No one liked the phrase 'recolonise', but it seemed to be the case that the only way to get things moving again was to invite non-Solomon Islanders with the appropriate experience to fill a scattering of positions in the middle and upper rankings of the civil service. Running a justice department, a treasury or a land title office required people who could start retraining programmes all over again to bring Solomon Islanders through into more positions of responsibility.

Some people argued that the Solomons were independent,

and thus now on their own – so let them rebuild their country themselves. Yes, this was a very good argument. The trouble was that there was too much lawlessness, corruption and intimidation by militants, who were still heavily armed. There were even indiscriminate killings. And a lot of the money running the state was coming from foreign donors.

Once again, the daily lives of the people of the Solomons were being influenced by outsiders. Many people actually regarded this as beneficial, given the extra money that flowed in; the older ones remembered the bloodshed of the battlegrounds of Guadalcanal in the Second World War, and more recently through the last three years of the 1990s the bloody clashes between the local Guadalcanalese and the neighbouring Malaitans. Further, the community in Honiara had been harbouring dissidents from Bougainville, whom they regarded as brothers, during the civil insurrection against the Papua New Guinea government. This also created sporadic bloodshed. For the people, security and a job were more important than hostility to foreign faces in government offices.

But how to encourage something that would not make the anti-colonial UN people apoplectic? There was also a call to consider replacing the current provincial government with a federal state system. A proposed federal system of government had been one of the key features of the Townsville Peace Agreement of October 2000 between the Malaitans and the Guadalcanalese. While this was strongly opposed by both Australia and New Zealand, I agreed as a conflict prevention measure that the Commonwealth Secretariat would send in a constitutional law expert to start looking at options and work with the local government officials.

A draft bill was subsequently prepared, and is probably now collecting dust due to the lack of support from the key donors and general opposition, especially from Malaita.

I paid a flying visit to Kiribati, one of those Pacific atoll states that are members of the Commonwealth. To be honest, I despair a little when visiting these countries. Sea levels are rising, there is no land more than 2 metres above sea level and there seems little future for young people.

Kiribati was well governed by the very experienced President, Anote Tong, but I wish Australia and New Zealand would adopt a more liberal immigration policy to help relieve some of the pressure. Unfortunately, the alternative will be inevitable panic when increasing numbers of people have to be taken off if they can no longer grow their own food due to increasing saline levels. Of course, if they ran out of food a hundred years ago, they would just push out their canoes and find another island. That's not possible now.

Another problem is rubbish: old cans, old refrigerators, deep freezers. Where do you put these things – you can't dig holes, you can't dump them out at sea (although if you did drop them into the Marianas Trench, the deepest piece of ocean in the world, I'm sure the effect would be zero). So the population increases, inorganic garbage accumulates and there are more and more problems with unemployed testosterone-filled young males.

Managing Commonwealth ministerial meetings in the Pacific provided its own challenges partly due to their lack of frequency. All ministerials (finance, sports, youth, etc.) are very different, but ministers for women's affairs were most demanding on the Secretariat.

I noted over the years that officials who work for women's affairs ministers are often zealously and even recklessly ahead of their ministers on many issues. At one meeting of Commonwealth women's affairs ministers in Fiji, the ministers were feeling so marginalised by their own officials that they decided to meet on their own – which of course exasperated their staff. Nothing seemed to be going right, and some officials were becoming more and more belligerent as to *their* 'rights'.

Later at this meeting I had to get quite tough with some of these officials, who were standing in for ministers and demanding excessive attention, over 'their rights'. They seemed not to know they did not have the ranking of a minister. 'Ministers,' I said, 'always take priority over everybody else. It's not appropriate for officials to hold out if there is otherwise a consensus among the ministers present.' The unwritten message was that if an official's country didn't deem this meeting important enough for a minister to attend, then their representatives did not have the right to block progress.

Once people got used to the ways of the Commonwealth and put aside the habits they had learned at the UN, the system worked very well. UN conferences, wherever they were held, always recognised whoever was sitting behind their country's flag, regardless of whether this person was the president or a third secretary. This wasn't the case in Commonwealth meetings; the elected politicians and especially ministers always had priority speaking rights over bureaucrats. This reminder needed to be pointed out at the beginning of every meeting, which protected the chair from unnecessary challenges.

The vexing question of political change in the island kingdom of Tonga continued to demand our attention. The country was refusing to move with the times, and most people agreed that little real change seemed possible as long as King Taufa'ahau Tupou remained alive. In the meantime, Tonga remained an old-fashioned kingdom with little democracy evident. Could the Commonwealth be the circuit-breaker to get things started?

In 2003 I hosted a lunch for Crown Prince Tupouto'a of Tonga in London, at which he described most of his cabinet ministers as 'having the IQ of ants'. Others, including his cousin, he insisted, 'believed anything could be fixed with a prayer'. I noted after the meeting: 'Never short of a colourful phrase but there's still some way to go.'

A very tough media bill proposing many press restrictions had been introduced in the Tongan Parliament. I didn't want to go public on this just yet, so I rang Prince Lavaka, the Prime Minister, in June, and asked him to look very carefully at the judicial implications. His response was rather cute: 'Tonga has never been a democracy, and doesn't pretend to be one. This is where we have to clarify the rights of the executive before the rights of the judiciary are defined! We still believe in the independence of the judiciary!' Yes, I said, but under Commonwealth principles, signed onto by successive Tongan prime ministers, there is expected to be an adherence to the independence of the judiciary. And so on.

After a few more minutes of discussion, the Prime Minister said, 'Thank you for your call, Secretary-General. I'm glad to have heard from you, but the killing of people in Africa is surely more important than what's happening in Tonga.' Sometimes it happens: you take one step forward and two backwards.

Meanwhile, many Tongans were becoming restless. There were reports of 4,000-plus people marching against electricity price rises, while another group were protesting against an extra tax on farmers. 'This is putting the Tongan government under great pressure,' I wrote in my notes at the time, 'but with the King ill, they don't know which way to turn, or how to respond.'

Finally, Prince Tu'ipelehake, a pro-democracy nephew of the King, arranged for me to receive an invitation to visit Tonga from Princess Pilolevu, the King's elder daughter, acting as the Princess Regent. So, after many stops and starts, I did get to Tonga at the end of August 2005. It was a tense time. Half of the public service was on strike, the pressure for political reform was set for a showdown and the Prime Minister's office had made it clear I was anything but welcome. 'Not a convenient time to visit', I was informed.

Of course, I could not decline an invitation from the Princess Regent, who clearly outranked the Prime Minister, her brother. I received full protocol facilities on arrival, and within half an hour was in a meeting with a quite distressed Princess Regent. The first thing I told her was that I had not come to solve the strike, unless the government and the strikers both wanted Commonwealth assistance. I had come to talk about the larger issues and was pleased she had with her the foreign minister and the lands minister, both supportive of reforms, plus a handful of officials.

I said I wanted them to know some things, as during the preliminary niceties they themselves had raised the issue of political reform. If they didn't like what I said they could ask me to leave and that would be that. 'No, no,' said the Princess, 'we value our membership of the Commonwealth.'

So I went through the menu:

First, for too long the royal family and the government had been resisting real change.

Second, I realised Tonga had never been a democracy, but as a Commonwealth member the country had signed up to the Harare Declaration, which required some democratic forward movement.

Third, their neighbours (Somare of Papua New Guinea, Tuilaepa of Samoa and Nailatikau of Fiji) all wanted to see Tonga change in the interests of Pacific stability, but they would not megaphone the message. I wanted to point out that they supported my visit and my message.

Fourth, the per capita income in Tonga used to be higher than that of Samoa, but now in Tonga it was US$2,400 and in Samoa US$5,600. This point really hit home with the Princess and the ministers.

Last, of the six monarchies in the Commonwealth (they were always interested in the British monarchy) Tonga was the one most resisting change. I added that even the 900-year-old House of Lords was undergoing change. The important issue was to give people hope that change would happen. It didn't need to be fast, but a start needed to be made.

They took it well. No, they wouldn't ask me to leave the

country immediately. They knew change would have to begin and the Princess was certainly aware of the professional neutrality of the Commonwealth. That's where we left it – any further discussion in front of a member of the royal family would have become embarrassing.

I noticed behaviour among many Tongans that was similar to that which I found among Libyans. Many people were fearful of making decisions in case they offended someone further up the ladder. So you got a collective inertia. No one wanted to initiate anything, so no one could be blamed for doing nothing. To an outsider it was exasperating.

At a dinner in the evening, I stressed to the key players that there was a fire burning for reform and if someone threw a bucket of jet fuel onto it, there would be no senior leadership left in the country, including many at the dinner. They all had a responsibility to start the move towards change slowly and to manage it carefully. And it was vital that they kept the people informed.

It was a terrible shock when Prince Tu'ipelehake and his wife were killed in a car crash in California on 6 July 2006. It was a blow to much more than just his family; this son of royalty had been pulling hard to bring the islands into a modern democracy. He was the enthusiastic patron of the Human Rights and Democracy Movement. California was the last leg of his consultations with the ex-pat Tongan community on political reform.

Shortly after, in September 2006, came the expected death of King Taufa'ahau Tupou. With the Crown Prince becoming King George Tupou V, the stage was set. Political change was now inevitable.

On 5 December 2006, after almost daily reports reaching us in London of ongoing clashes between the Fijian military commander Frank Bainimarama and Prime Minister Laisenia Qarase, Bainimarama made his move and executed the fourth coup against an elected Fiji government.

The Commonwealth took the only action it could and suspended Fiji once again from the councils of the Commonwealth. Former Prime Minister Mahendra Chaudhry became finance minister, a rather bizarre appointment given his earlier aggressive attitude to the previous coup. It was getting more like Gilbert and Sullivan by the day. The Melanesian Spearhead Group, a loose regional grouping, became a little defensive, but Prime Minister Somare of Papua New Guinea was very angry. Shortly after, I noted that so far there had been no bloodshed, but there was much uncertainty and no one had any real idea what Bainimarama's plan really was. As with previous suspensions, Fiji and the Commonwealth stopped speaking at official level.

In March 2007 an old friend from my primary school days in Wellington, Dr Ngatata Love (a leading civil servant and academic), came to see me when I was in Auckland. He knew Fiji, and he knew Mahendra Chaudhry. After a long discussion we agreed that if the new government in Fiji would accept help from New Zealand on voter registration, it would be a positive step forward. I particularly wanted to get my head of human rights into Fiji to make a report, so Ngatata said he would speak to both Chaudhry and Bainimarama with these objectives. Essentially, if we could start with these and develop an understanding, we could make some progress. I was pleased that the regime did accept my human rights officer, Rabab Fatima from Bangladesh. They opened all the doors for her and she wrote a very fine and very critical report, which was made available to the ministers on CMAG. Regretfully, we did not get a green light for the voter registration.

As my last PIF meeting was shortly to take place in Tonga, I wanted to host a dinner for the leaders to say thanks for all the support they had given me over the previous ten years, and before that as New Zealand's foreign minister. I knew I would have to invite Bainimarama, as he was an accepted Pacific leader at the Forum. If I had not, a large number of the Island leaders would have been offended and might not have turned up.

However, my own Prime Minister, Helen Clark, got very

tetchy, asking how I could possibly ask to dinner a man whose country was suspended. I said that was the politics of the Pacific – he'd been accepted at the Forum in Tonga as Fiji's leader whether we liked it or not. She and Alexander Downer, Australia's foreign minister, then decided they could not attend. Bainimarama, on the other hand, decided not to attend if Clark and Downer were there. So in the end none of the three turned up. Otherwise, it was a very warm and chatty occasion, concluding with some very complimentary remarks from Somare to me.

At the opening ceremony next day the crowd of onlookers and participants managed polite and warm applause for all leaders as they arrived, but when Bainimarama's car pulled up at the dais the crowd just roared their heads off in endless approval. This was the Pacific's way of showing Australia and New Zealand that 'we'll do it our way'.

During the Forum I succeeded in steering Frank Bainimarama into a side room, where we had a very long talk. There were, I said, a lot of things the Commonwealth could assist him with to bring the country back to where it was, including new elections. 'Would the Commonwealth expel Fiji?' he asked. I said it was a possibility, especially if he refused to have elections. Overall, this conversation lasted one hour, just him and me, and he said he would be prepared to see Sir Paul Reeves.

Regretfully, although Sir Paul made a number of visits to Fiji as the special Commonwealth envoy and was reappointed to the role of special envoy by my successor Kamalesh Sharma, little progress was made in the years that followed. It was going to be a long, slow journey, I noted as I left office only a few weeks after the Tongan meeting. It is by no means certain there will be elections in Fiji in 2014 or any time soon. At the time of writing, Bainimarama has recently announced the much-awaited constitutional process and the composition of the commission. Voter registration will soon commence and any former politician will be able to contest the election.

Fiji has changed – the Methodist church and the great Council of Chiefs have lost their political clout and there's less money, but there's no sign of popular uprising, nor much hope among the people for change. For their part, Australian and New Zealand tourists still flock to Nadi and the offshore islands for the southern hemisphere winter, thereby keeping the economy somewhat in balance.

Looking back, if there was one action I would not repeat it would be not to condemn Bainimarama's earlier idea of a 'people's charter' to prevent abuse of the constitution. Perhaps I should have been more prepared to work with him to help get the people behind it. Would it have made a difference? I am not sure. These are always hard decisions. I witnessed Musharraf in Pakistan create some very valuable democratic structures, only to lose all when he went too far by not ever trusting his people to play their part.

Will Bainimarama succeed? It's too early to say. The country remains suspended from the councils of the Commonwealth but the Pacific ministers, particularly those of New Zealand and Australia, remain fully engaged.

CHAPTER 11

A Royal Challenge

'Uneasy lies the head that wears a crown'
William Shakespeare, *Henry IV, Part II*

Swaziland is one of six monarchies in the Commonwealth, and probably the one in which the monarch enjoys the greatest authority. It is a small and interesting by-product of the old Empire and one whose current governing practices have been far from democratic. Many people who have heard of Swaziland are aware of a king who not only has many wives but who chooses a new one each year from the annual 'dance of the virgins'. Photographs of these events often make the overseas papers, but that is where outsiders' knowledge of the country largely ends. Others may know that it is a small landlocked country surrounded by South Africa and Mozambique and that it depends economically on donors, agriculture and tourism. As Swaziland only possesses small airports, to fly to and from the country most travellers usually go from Johannesburg. Many would say the country is politically insignificant, but not for us in the Commonwealth.

Early in my term I became aware that there was considerable unrest taking place in the country for a variety of reasons, reflected in marches and demonstrations against the government. This caused the government to issue yet another decree, with heavy penalties for those who transgressed. Not least of all the objections was that the government tended to be an extension of the royal family and was therefore quite autocratic in its behaviour. Nobody in authority, it seemed to me, had a name other than Dlamini, the name of the royal family.

A number of fruitless meetings with Swaziland senior ministers or officials involving myself and my senior staffers in New York and London had produced nothing which could be considered a productive response. We had to talk to the King, and so began a dialogue and an involvement that over the course of the next four years produced a new constitution, diminished the King's authority by half and set the country on a new and challenging journey.

I heard King Mswati III would be transiting London after attending an Aids conference in New York, and so I decided we had to have a get-together. I met His Majesty in late June 2001 at the Dorchester Hotel, just around the corner from my house. He was then about thirty-three, very affable and friendly. His English was very good because he had been at secondary school in England, and he had been on the throne since 1986. Although his handful of officials sat there stony-faced, it was a good meeting.

How to open a discussion that will contain some criticisms is never straightforward with such a person. I had to acknowledge his very prominent authority and recognise the fact that in his country, a big majority of the population, whether they were wealthy and privileged or poor, admired and respected the office, especially in the person of the present King who was in front of me now.

I had no desire to win early points but sought merely to gain a level of acceptance that would be useful in a long game. But I also knew that through the media a number of his people knew what was going on in other countries, so some issues could not be suppressed for ever. If they weren't dealt with soon they could become more costly later.

I also agreed that Swaziland was a very traditional society, with a strong culture, whose people had pride in their independence. But that didn't mean that changes were impossible. I pointed out that a recent decree taking away citizens' rights was a dangerous and provocative move, especially at a time when he himself was supporting a review of the constitution.

He readily accepted there were challenges and problems. He said he did want to get it right; and without being specific, he referred to many around him who did not want change. Their view was that they were doing fine, so why change anything?

To avoid getting into a difficult discussion at this point, I asked if he and I could have a private meeting. He readily agreed and all the officials left. I then pointed out that change did have to occur, that we in the Commonwealth could help him and that if it was done properly, he would still be on the throne in fifty years. Nobody would be saying that Swaziland was undemocratic. I made reference to Queen Elizabeth II living not 400 metres away, with little independent executive authority but still held in very high esteem.

We debated these issues for another half-hour, while outside, my principal African adviser, Professor Ade Adefuye, was telling the Swazi officials that I would be telling the King that Swaziland under its present policies would soon be on the Commonwealth Ministerial Action Group (CMAG) agenda. It was a little strong, but it was a point well made.

In my concluding comments to His Majesty I stressed that every country had a different form of democracy, that there were many examples in the Commonwealth where the traditional was blended with the contemporary and that the same could be done in his kingdom.

I invited him to think carefully about the path ahead, to ensure he did not alienate his fellow Commonwealth leaders and to work towards a democratic structure that was supported and defended by the Swazi people.

He left saying he had enjoyed the discussion and wanted me

to keep in touch with him. He also agreed that Professor Adefuye could come to the capital, Manzini, in a few weeks and advance the discussions. Subsequently, I lost count of the number of times Adefuye went to Swaziland, and we agreed that he would never leave the country without making a courtesy call on the King. This was to ensure that there could be no doubts spread by others in the country about the nature of his mission.

In August 2001, I decided it was timely for me to visit and see if we could introduce a plan to move ahead in a way that people could support.

Of course, Commonwealth links with Swaziland were not all about governance or the lack of it. We had mining, poverty reduction and debt management programmes in place in the country, and we had trained over 350 Swazi nationals in a variety of fields. As in most Commonwealth countries, this was nothing unusual. It wasn't as if they'd never seen us before.

My meeting with the King was very productive and we soon moved to a one-on-one discussion. I acknowledged that the changes required would be difficult and would give him problems, but he had to look ten, twenty or thirty years ahead. I acknowledged that his biggest objectors would be current ministers, officials and his own family members.

I said there was a need to begin afresh. To help him begin a new constitutional review I would nominate two senior Commonwealth lawyers who were familiar with constitutions, would come from developing countries and would have experience of dealing with royalty. These latter two points visibly relaxed him, as obviously advice from alien sources in the past had been something he had resisted.

In January 2002, after canvassing widely, I brought together Dr S. K. B. Asante, chief of the Asante royal family of Ghana and former solicitor general of Ghana, and Hon. David Tupou, former minister of justice and attorney general of Tonga and a man very close to the Tongan royal family. Regrettably, due to personal circumstances we had to replace Dr Asante with

Professor E. V. O. Dankwa, who was also from the Asante Kingdom in Ghana.

It was a very successful move. They were not only accepted by the King but also spent hours and days with key Swazi people and with a special group headed up by one of the King's relations, a man who proved to be an absolute stalwart in the process, one Prince David Dlamini. Very soon Prince David was splitting his time between being ambassador to Denmark and beginning work on the new draft constitution. He was sensibly later given full ministerial rank and dropped his ambassadorial role, which ensured a high level of momentum.

Keeping up with the genealogy of senior Swazi people was often not easy. Prince David was the King's half-brother, and it had been assumed by many that he would become the King rather than Mswati. He was well educated, with a PhD in engineering, and he had wide diplomatic experience. When some of the family later wanted Prince David to be Prime Minister, another faction vetoed it, causing tensions among the wives and offspring of the previous king. In this society, this was apparently not unusual.

In March 2002 at the Commonwealth Heads of Government Meeting (CHOGM) in Coolum, Australia, I had another opportunity to discuss progress with King Mswati. He expressed his pleasure at the way the Commonwealth worked and was pleased with the two special envoys. 'They already understand us very well,' he told me. 'Can Professor Adefuye come back soon?' I said most certainly, and I would make sure he started softening up the 'old guard'.

With Hon. David Tupou of Tonga, Adefuye visited Swaziland in June 2002 and laid out a broad prescription for change, which was agreed to by the King at a marathon session. The sensitivity of political parties and gender issues was acknowledged, and there was a side agreement that the Commonwealth would help renew the membership of the Swazi Supreme Court. The Professor had to emphasise strongly the acceptance of the need for an independent judiciary.

A month later, in July 2002, I was due to go back to Swaziland. My officials had done a sterling job of preparing my brief and I was well prepared. Everything I had to say to the King was agreed among us: the good progress on constitutional drafting; the maintenance of Swazi culture in the document; and our declared willingness to walk alongside the King for as long as it took. There was likely to be one small negative moment when I had to criticise the parallel process of an internal security bill, provisions of which were restrictive and not in keeping with the aims of the constitution.

My meeting with the King went well and contained no surprises. The sensitivities were still all there, but they had not stalled the process. Prince David had taken over as chair of the Constitutional Drafting Committee, which was a very good appointment.

Then we met with the Commission and, on Prince David's advice, gave them a very frank series of messages. This project was not for them, I said, but for their children's children. The constitution they were drafting must be for ever. What was more, the public demanded involvement – this was not the eighteenth century, when people like Jefferson and Adams could get together and write the American Constitution without a lot of public input. People would only defend a constitution, I said, if they'd been part of its development.

After I'd returned to London, Adefuye had gone back to Swaziland to calm a crisis between the police and the judiciary over a girl allegedly abducted by the King's people. The King then got into a public conflict with the judges over this, at which point one resigned. Adefuye used all his diplomatic skills and the King retracted and apologised to the judges, which was a real political advancement. I was very pleased when the chief justice of South Africa, Pius Langa, congratulated the Commonwealth on this peace-making initiative and calm slowly prevailed.

Sometimes we found that after giving undertakings to Adefuye, the King would be pressured by family members to resist a change. I was told by a member of the family that the King's mother and other princes kept telling him that Adefuye and I were trying to make an 'England' out of Swaziland. It was an indication of the continuing significance of divisions within the royal family.

Then in December 2002 there was a direct challenge to the judiciary by none other than the Prime Minister. A positive effect was that this angered the public, putting them fully in favour of the judges' independence. It was most unfortunate that at the time Swaziland became independent it had inherited a supreme court of five white South African judges, all very capable, but all now over seventy-five years old. They simply didn't fit the local landscape any more.

By early 2003 much work had been done. Villages around the country had held discussions, and the citizens had made their views known. They wanted democracy but they still revered their King. They wanted a say, but they didn't want to reduce his authority.

I went to Swaziland in March 2003 and was driven straight to meet with the Prime Minister, a very dour individual who clearly hoped he could have the job for life. In two minutes he thanked me for everything, then said we should meet the press. I said there were a few things I wanted him to note first. So I started talking constitution. The document wouldn't please everybody, I said. Some would say it had gone too far, others would say not far enough. Merging the traditional and the contemporary was possible; the country couldn't remain cocooned forever; his principal aid donors were watching this very closely. After twenty minutes of discussion and some argument he had agreed to all I said – but judging by his body language, I was not convinced he was for change.

Then to the King's palace, which was less like the hut setting where he met many of his subjects and more like a five-star hotel, where we found him, resplendent in his robes, with Prince David. In our now usual one-on-one I told him that so far, all was going well. 'But what you say at the public launch of the draft constitution will be very important and will have a huge bearing on the debate that follows.' I emphasised that his Commonwealth neighbours and his aid donors would be analysing every word. 'The marching in the streets over the last few days is a sign of restlessness that could overturn the throne,' I said, 'but the right words from their leader about the future could settle things down. They need to feel they have an involvement in the future. You will', I concluded, 'lose some authority, but you will gain influence.'

He took it all in calmly, not unaware that it was a huge leap forward. He said his people were very keen, meaning his top officials and family, but this was not said with any firmness. I left the country feeling that we could not have done more to ensure the draft constitution got to first base.

In May 2003 I met the King again in London during one of his transit stops. I again raised the question of the ageing, white senior judges. 'I'll help you start some changes,' was the comment I left him with. Later I sent a note to our legal division asking them to talk to the Commonwealth Magistrates and Judges Association to help find suitable candidates.

Nothing will ever go smoothly, as I found when Prince David called through London the following year and told me that the conservative forces in the country, who wanted no change, had teamed up with the Queen Mother to work in concert against the constitution. He was worried that the King would buckle under family pressure. On the plus side, he reported that two of the judges had said they would resign once things had settled, which was good news.

'Well, we're all in the tunnel now,' I noted at the time, 'and there can't be any backing out.'

Unfortunately, the only press the King was getting was about collecting or choosing another wife or buying a new Maybach car. The country's aid donors were not impressed. It would not be easy for me to discuss this with the King, so I knew I would have to find someone appropriate to broach the issue.

It was most prescient that during my attendance at the inauguration of President Guebuza of Mozambique on 2 February
2005, I spoke to former Presidents Chissano of Mozambique and
Kaunda of Zambia. Both fully understood the negative media
Swaziland was getting, and why, and we all agreed that someone
else had to talk to the King about these issues. It didn't take long
to decide that the one person who could talk to the King was
former President Kenneth Kaunda of Zambia.

So at the Namibian inauguration of President Pohamba
on 21 March 2005, I asked the King if I could bring Kenneth
Kaunda with me for a private chat. 'Of course,' he said. KK,
as we all knew him, was actually the King's godfather, and had
readily agreed to participate.

KK opened the discussion by apologising to the King for not
being a good godfather, also referring to the fact that the King's
own father was KK's godfather. Then he carefully laid out the
issues. The King had to get closer to the people and back on-side
with the donors. 'These wives of yours are all very costly. Look
at all those houses and cars, all the things they buy. Get an old
Land-Rover. Put a few goats in the back every time you go to a
village. Give away the goats, talk with the people and they'll love
you forever. You need the Western press to see your positive side.
You have to get away from the negative news.'

And so it went on for an hour, while I just listened. The King
received this advice from the elderly statesman very positively,
so it all concluded most amicably.

By and large the politics of Swaziland were running very
smoothly through 2005, but I was getting a little anxious that
I did not see an early time slot on the parliamentary agenda for
the new constitution to be passed. We always had to take into
account that the King went 'into seclusion' from time to time.
Known as Incwala, this religious/political ritual observed by the
kingdom was expected to be a period of prayer and renewal
and was deemed to be unifying for the nation. However, short
of a major cataclysmic event, no one saw the King for nearly a

month, thus taking him out of the equation for signing bills from Parliament. I was told that it would all happen in January 2006.

Then came the unexpected, when in January 2006 I received word that there had been some people arrested for treason under the 1973 decree. I challenged Swazi officials, stating that this could have been overridden on a de facto basis by the provisions of the new constitution if there was the political will to do so, and thank goodness this was later confirmed by the Prime Minister.

We finally heard, shortly after this, that the constitution would be implemented very soon. Could I come to Swaziland in early February for the opening of Parliament on the 10th? I agreed, as long as the 1973 decree was repealed by that date. That condition was on the advice of Adefuye, who was fearful of some backsliding.

The opening was a solemn occasion, with speeches from the King and the President of the Assembly. Next came a private lunch with the King and Kaunda, and then a most amusing semi-cultural event in which there were various skits by politicians making fools of each other. It wasn't something you normally see in Africa.

It was a masterstroke, even better than I expected, having KK there. He was the godfather, elder-statesman and mentor, an authoritative individual who gave real substance to the Commonwealth's involvement and commitment and endorsed all the changes. I also had to concede that my earlier misgivings about the King's fortitude under pressure were unfounded. Despite the protestations of family members, especially from his mother, the King did not bend under their relentless demands.

Swaziland now slowly slipped off our agenda, until I heard later in the year that the University of Swaziland had conferred on me in my absence an honorary degree. Well, that was fine, if a little unusual. Later I heard that the announcement was incorrect; they intended to confer the degree when I went there in December 2006 to reinforce what had been achieved. This would then be part of a Southern African tour of Namibia, Botswana, South Africa and Lesotho.

There was still some agitation from the 'progressives', who were needling the government and the King to allow political parties. In my meeting with them (and they represented perhaps only 10–15 per cent of the vote) I explained that on these issues you never start with a clean sheet of paper. Most societies have centuries of history they wish to be reflected in a new constitution. No society could swallow too many changes at once. Surely if political parties could be deferred for five years that should not be a big problem? I told them I was sure they could see that the glass was more than half full.

At the University of Swaziland I was told that they did intend to confer an honorary degree – but actually they weren't able to do so there and then, as the King wished to be present, and he was still in seclusion.

So now to June 2007 for the degree conferment and my last official visit. It was a very impressive gathering – a full convocation of 300–400 academics and students, with an amazing array of practical and other talents. My acceptance speech was all about the Commonwealth's continuing commitment to Swaziland and the need for the younger people, meaning the students, to continue the forward movement for the benefit of subsequent generations. The King was duly reported as referring to me as 'a brilliant ambassador'. It was nice to see it in print.

I remained convinced that we had helped the Swazi government and the King to pull back from a precipice. If they had continued to govern by decree they could well have ended up facing a revolution. Our way had been a long, slow process, but eventually most people came to believe it was the only way forward. The people's contemporary aspirations couldn't be divorced from their traditional and cultural history. The long and involved discussions that had taken place throughout the Swazi community had meant that the people had a say and that there was a greater buy-in.

Admittedly, this was not a constitution you would write if you began with a blank sheet of paper. But you have to begin where you are, not where you would like to be. In the end, the fact that His Majesty lost nearly 50 per cent of his authority was no small change. Anyone thinking the King could have been forced to lose 90–100 per cent without bloodshed was in dreamland.

Changing a constitution is the easier part; it's the changing of people's attitudes that takes longer, sometimes two generations. But it's better to carry out these big changes step by step, always making gains and avoiding the backsliding.

No, Swaziland doesn't have the most perfect constitution that could have emerged from the legal/academic world. But it is owned by the people of Swaziland, and that's more important. The constitution will change again, and I hope it will allow political parties and so reposition itself within the local landscape which is the Kingdom of Swaziland. I remain proud of the Commonwealth's contribution.

A couple of years later, well after my stewardship, a Swazi ambassador giving testimony to a United States Senate committee was describing how the Commonwealth-inspired constitution was as we had left it. It is still the bible for the conduct of Swazi government business. The cabinet still has a majority of elected people and the Judicial Services Commission is in place to appoint and discipline judges. Nor has the new electoral system changed, despite the desire of some to do so at an earlier stage.

Not the time to walk away, just continue to walk quietly alongside.

CHAPTER 12

Fine-tuning an International Organisation

As a New Zealander, I came to the Secretary-General role from a country that had been going through massive economic and structural changes, not only within the government but also throughout the country. To many, therefore, I was a feared change manager. Many people, especially Secretariat staff, feared a massive upheaval that would be particularly detrimental to existing staff. Many staff members raised their concerns with their high commissioners. They hoped that this revolution would be stopped in its tracks.

I had no intention of starting a revolution. For my part, I wanted to know what material and human resources were needed to ensure the Secretariat carried out its work expeditiously and competently. That is something never easy to measure from the outside, and I was not short of advice from the United Kingdom, Australia, Canada, India, South Africa and New Zealand.

My initial impression on entering the Secretariat was that it was low on energy, or was just waiting for a new direction. Everyone seemed to be working in individual silos, without regard for what others down the corridor were doing.

We employed people in the Secretariat from all fifty-four member countries, even though at any one time probably only forty-five countries were represented. I soon learnt that most staff wanted to be firmly padlocked to the organisation with only them, the employees, holding the key. Many staff members who had come from developing countries, especially in Africa or Asia, had of course moved their families to London. Having got their kids into English schools, they would do almost anything to ensure they stayed with the Secretariat indefinitely. This was understandable. Ensuring their kids got an education that many at home could only dream about was not a minor matter. They were certainly not going to allow this new Secretary-General from New Zealand to shake up these conditions of employment to their disadvantage.

To me, the working environment was not conducive to the good management of an international organisation. I also soon found that officials at the various London Commonwealth High Commissions watched very carefully who the Secretary-General employed, and insisted that whatever number their country had within the staff should never be reduced.

We had an interesting division within the Commonwealth membership in that four developed countries (the UK, Canada, Australia and New Zealand) wanted to see concentration on the good governance area: improved elections, corruption-free societies, the rule of law, an independent judiciary, a free press and so on. Developing countries, on the other hand, were not always so focused on these particular requirements as long as they received their development spending. This developing group would occasionally use their greater numbers to reduce the pace of the good governance issues – although they were always aware that to jeopardise the Commonwealth's development funding, most of which came from about six countries, would not be a very smart move.

When I first began seeking advice from a variety of Commonwealth watchers about the organisation and the task I was taking on, I heard phrases such as: 'it needs to respond more rapidly to crises'; 'needs to speak out louder'; 'must stand up to other organisations, especially the OECD [Organisation for Economic Co-operation and Development]'; 'needs more staff turnover to refresh the organisation'; 'needs to build bridges'; and 'meetings are producing shrinking returns'.

I was now more than ever determined that if I was to meet my objectives of achieving credibility and relevance in the organisation, there had to be a shake-up. But this could only be achieved if it was carefully planned, fully explained and executed with determination.

There were, however, some surprises in store. The first was in the financial area, where I had great difficulty getting from the senior finance staff answers to some very basic questions. Our auditors had for some years had reason to tag the accounts for various perceived deficiencies. This was not at all a satisfactory situation; it was, in fact, embarrassing for a chief executive. For me, it was a challenge.

Another dark cloud appeared on the horizon when I looked at the pension arrangements for staff, all of which were based on final salary compensation. This was a policy that was now not only out of date but also totally unsustainable. I convinced management that this had to be closed to any new members, which was a good decision, but by the time the decision came into effect the fund was to decline even further. New staff members were given options of other superannuation schemes to join.

By the beginning of 2002, having finally got to the bottom of understanding our finances, I was faced with the glaringly obvious. In simple terms our salary and related expenses were increasing by 6 per cent per year, but our revenue was only increasing by 1–1.5 per cent. The only way to manage this would be to permanently drop six or seven people every year from the payroll. Therefore, unless we wanted a continually diminishing staff, we had to have a strategy to align revenue with expenses. Continuing as we were meant there would be no relevant staff left in ten to fifteen years.

Discussing this situation with some senior staff, I was surprised at those who could naively suggest we just ask governments for more money. I knew what the answer would be, given all that had been said prior to my taking up the post. To placate the agitated staff, a request for more funding was put to the governing board, which made all the major policy decisions, in four different ways and at least four times – and the response was four emphatic negatives.

To get it all rectified, workable and sustainable, we had to restructure salaries and terms and conditions of service to equate with income: no easy task. Up until now this component had taken up two-thirds of the central account, so we would also have to keep the future salary structure within this two-thirds band. We could no longer bring in new officers at the bottom of a grade, progress them year by year to the top of the grade and in addition give them a cost-of-living adjustment. We would just have to set a salary for a job and only occasionally make provision for such an adjustment. Of course, one of our problems was that with little staff turnover, a high proportion of staff were at the top of the salary grade, so average staff costs were well above the middle line.

An equally difficult and demanding challenge was my desire to achieve a greater turnover of staff by placing time limits on all in the so-called professional or diplomatic grades, which amounted to nearly half of the total staff working at Marlborough House. So for the senior staff, consisting of three grades below deputy secretary-general, there would be a maximum of two three-year terms; for the next three grades, there would be a maximum of three three-year terms.

I wanted this international organisation to have a transparent and balanced budget. I did not want more staff reductions. I did not want the auditors to continue to tag the accounts. We had to draw a line under the old pension scheme. We had to see a greater level of rotation among senior staff to stimulate greater rejuvenation, energy and innovation. I also concluded that having three deputy secretaries-general was unnecessary and that two would be enough, with myself taking a line position of responsibility for three of the divisions.

This brought me into conflict with the very able permanent under-secretary of the Foreign and Commonwealth Office Sir John (now Lord) Kerr, a straight talker. John came to see me to insist that his government should always hold a deputy secretary-general position. No, he would not accept a holiday from that position. No, he would not accept an assistant secretary-general position. No, he would not accept the head of administration.

I said to John, you want me to tighten the place up, achieve greater efficiencies. We don't need all three and with only two positions you can't have one held by the United Kingdom, the Secretary-General from New Zealand and only one other position for either Africa, Asia or the Caribbean.

He said, 'Don, that's your problem.'

'I agree, John, it's my problem and you're not getting the position. Treat it as a rest period, as is your membership of CMAG [Commonwealth Ministerial Action Group], you can't stay there permanently either.'

I then made him grimace when I repeated to him what his boss, Foreign and Commonwealth Secretary Robin Cook, had told me in 1999: 'Don, we're supporting you because you look like us!'

I had now opened up a number of difficult fronts. They were not quite battle lines, but careful management was needed. Too many battles, advised my senior staff. Yes, true, I thought, but better than a piecemeal approach. However, changes are never possible if you've got everybody working against you. Now the task was to get key people on-side and slowly build that group.

I invited to a breakfast meeting at the Hill Street residence the key officials from the High Commissions who monitored our activities through their membership of the Finance Committee. This was the group that met regularly to help set policy, budgets and the interpretation of mandates.

My message was as simple as possible. We had a systemic financial problem. The cost of salaries and other directly related costs had to equate with income. We couldn't continue having those costs increasing at 6 per cent p.a. and income by only 1 per cent p.a. It would require a new salary structure without built-in escalations. To achieve that, we had to rotate regularly all senior staff on a six- or nine-year rotation. I needed the immediate and unequivocal support of all the Commonwealth governments to set this in place. In the end, we got there: all would support.

I then began a series of meetings with the directors, and then with the all-important staff association. I also talked to the staff, in small meetings of eight to ten people.

It's worth noting here that the pressure from prime ministers, presidents and senior ministers to take some of their nationals into the Secretariat never abated. Regrettably, more often than not they offered someone who was well over the retirement age, or someone they just wanted out of the country. My response was often, 'That's fine, we'd be happy to help out. But first help me and take back home someone who's been at the Secretariat for more than fifteen years.' A long silence usually followed.

Slowly the tide turned, but in the process I was censured by the Commonwealth Secretariat Staff Association (CSSA) at a meeting in October 2002. The big issue for them was management withholding a 1 per cent salary uplift to compensate for inflation. How could we, I asked staff, in all conscience pay this out given our financial situation?

After the censure motion there was a view in some quarters that I would feel pressured to come to some agreement after private talks with the association executive. 'No,' I said, 'governments have been saying for years we must learn to live within our income. You've publicly censured me. You've taken the gloves off. Well, I'm ready for a public fight – and you are going to lose.' This was not what they expected.

I asked the retiring head of finance how he ever could know what funds he had. He didn't, was his answer. All moneys went into a bucket and we took it out as we needed it. There was always wastage. We were also soon to find that extensive extra budgeted funds were sitting idle because the purpose for which they had been sent to the Secretariat was no longer relevant, or a programme had not used all the funds allocated.

Then we found that some staff were still being paid an allowance for their dependent children even though the kids had long since left home and were no longer in education. Around the same time, I announced that membership of the staff union should be optional, not mandatory. Freedom of association was a view held in a majority of Commonwealth countries.

A letter came from the CSSA, which was probably libellous of me and the two deputies. The letter included a call by the staff association to be involved in all management decisions. It was not the first time they had indicated they wanted to participate in all recruiting, including shortlisting and final decision-making. Most of the time my deputies and I got on very well with staff association executive members, but sometimes their herd mentality took over. This latest proposal was a desire to adopt a Soviet collective-farm mentality in which everybody took part in the decision-making, but no one took responsibility for the outcomes. All bad decisions would fall back on the Secretary-General, who would have become a minor functionary with little authority. In the end we just let that one go and stuck with our objectives.

We finally got a new salary structure sorted out after making some amendments, taking the sharp edges off and listening to many people, but it would still be 2003 before we could implement it.

In March 2004 I brought all the CSSA into my office for lunch and realised the message of paying people for what they do, not for time served, was getting through. Also, rotation was now terminating the employment of some of the longest-serving officers, who were now the most unhappy of the unhappy. They were being replaced by new people, with new ideas and energy, who willingly accepted the new conditions of service.

We had also concluded changes in the governing structures. There was now a board of governors representing each member country. This in turn nominated an executive committee, which oversaw the management of the Secretariat. This executive committee (Excom) of twelve represented the six biggest financial contributors and regularly rotated six other places on a regional basis. The new committee was supposed to take a more mature management role and to cover all the Secretariat's finances. But for the first few meetings little seemed to have changed. Third secretaries would be sent along with formal prepared statements drafted back in their home capitals. They'd simply read them out and sit back and wait!

In the Excom of May 2004 my safety valve blew out: 'These practices of reading and not thinking are simply not good enough. Your governments need to be more actively involved and willing to contribute towards decisions. If you're to come to this meeting you must know the subject intimately and be ready to debate the issue constructively. You must be prepared to help develop a collective view and cut deals where necessary. If you can't do that, then send more senior people to the meeting who can.'

Then there was the pension problem. All our staff pension money was tied up in a UK plc, Equitable Life, which along with most other pension firms was suffering financially. So by 2005 the UK's pension situation, which was showing very low returns, had got so bad that I actually had no alternative but to go to governments and ask for more money to top up the fund, now sorely diminished. I also took the opportunity to remind them of their misguided commitment some years before to underwrite the scheme if required. There was much grumbling and groaning, with some London high commissioners declaring quite reasonably that there was no money at home. But in the end we got there, although some of the funds had to come from our own budget. A few more projects for needy people in poor countries were then cancelled.

I was keen to create a greater role for foreign ministers in the running of the Commonwealth. As the Commonwealth had evolved through Heads of Government Meetings (CHOGM), many other meetings had also developed at the same time. We had regular conferences of different ministers representing finance, education, health, environment, youth, women's affairs and sport – but never foreign ministers. It was also clear that leaders' agendas were becoming more complex, and that they did not need to address issues that could be more sensibly dealt with by their foreign ministers.

So, starting with a two-hour meeting of all Commonwealth foreign ministers at the United Nations in New York in September 2002 when everyone was there for the annual General Assembly meetings, we slowly built among the ministers an interest in Commonwealth activities. This was important to me, because up until now it had been the foreign ministries – the officials, not the actual ministers – who had been calling the shots on Commonwealth policy.

Meeting in New York was somewhat novel for the Commonwealth, but it was supported and it worked. I also decided that we had to develop a positive engagement with the United States. You can't do anything internationally without bumping into American business, aid programmes or diplomacy.

So I went from New York to Washington DC every September and discovered very rapidly that the American view of the Commonwealth was still rooted somewhere back in the 1960s. I tried to use all the contacts I had made as a foreign minister to bring their thinking up to date. I found in meetings with Vice-President Cheney, former Secretaries of State James Baker, Warren Christopher and the still hard-working Madeleine Albright, as well as with Senator Richard Lugar and World Bank heads Jim Wolfensohn and Robert Zoellick, that the doors were all open. We were soon having regular meetings at the State Department, the White House, the National Security Council and with the Democrat and Republican Party organisations. It wasn't just talking; much was translated into cooperation in parts of the world where we were all promoting more democracy.

And now to the Secretary-General position itself.

Such positions are never advertised. You won't find any reference to them in the pages of the *Economist* and you'll only hear mutterings about the positions from governments – ultimately it's a few key people who decide, and the world is then informed. Of course, I include here the Secretary-General of the Commonwealth, but I've noted the same procedure is used in many other political organisations: the Pacific Islands Forum, the African Union, the Caribbean Community, the Islamic Conference and the European Union.

Choosing such a chief executive can be a Byzantine affair. It is likely to be 99 per cent politics, and mostly international politics, and there's little reason to believe it will change. Before you think about the individual with the so-called right credentials, you have to decide on the country he or she represents, or the region or the ethnic or even the religious grouping.

It's obvious that the role of diplomats is very important. Often their advice to their political bosses can have a strong impact. It's easy to see that when those veto-wielding countries in the UN are assessing a future Secretary-General, it'll be the view of the senior diplomats that will prevail. A former president or prime minister will often not succeed because they will be seen as too senior for the diplomats to handle. I've frequently noticed that the most senior of diplomats anywhere, steeped as they are in the art of serving and getting along, can never easily bring themselves to call a present or even a former political leader by their first name.

The Commonwealth with which I am familiar is no different. All five secretaries-general have been the product of political horse-trading prior to the decision being made by government leaders.

Arnold Smith of Canada, an experienced diplomat, was the preferred choice at the beginning in 1965, and set high standards. Sir Shridath Ramphal was a very eloquent lawyer, and the former

justice minister of Guyana earned the support of the Caribbean
and South Asia. When he was to be replaced in 1989 the tussle
between Malcolm Fraser, the former Prime Minister of Australia,
and Chief Emeka Anyaoku of Nigeria, a diplomat, Secretariat
employee and briefly foreign minister, came down in the latter's
favour partly because Africa wanted him and they had the numbers. Australia represented the old Commonwealth, as did Smith,
and it was too soon after a Canadian had held the position.

It was also said that Margaret Thatcher couldn't stand the
possibility of Fraser ringing her up and telling her what to do.

Before declaring myself as a candidate, I tested the support
I could get, then marketed myself as an Asia/Pacific candidate.
One possible Asian candidate fell away, and only a former for-
eign secretary from Bangladesh and I were left to contest (see
Chapter 1).

In my case, if there had been a candidate qualified in diplomacy or international law with a doctorate in politics and
economics you would have said that person was better qualified,
but that was not the way it worked. That person would probably always get a position in an international organisation, but
without the political connections, never above the deputy level.
Politicians such as myself, though not necessarily qualified in all
those categories noted above, do often provide a useful bridge
between the professionals and the political leaders.

A very important factor in my case was that having been a
nine-year foreign minister and a six-year deputy prime minister,
I was familiar enough to address any leader informally and, with
a couple of exceptions, get them any time on the phone.

So does the system work? In most cases, yes, unless it is
dumbed down to a too-low common denominator, as can so
easily happen.

Diplomacy is about ensuring that you keep control of the way
you are seen by outsiders and that you seek to change people's

opinions to your advantage. So how often do member countries wish to use the Commonwealth to extend their interests abroad? The answer, confirmed by many Commonwealth watchers, is 'sometimes, but usually not enough'.

Part of the answer goes back to the fact that, unlike the hard-diplomacy capacity of the European Union or NATO, the Commonwealth will only have a 'soft' diplomacy capability. Still, in my eight years, the countries that made the greatest continuous use of the Commonwealth networks were the smaller or economically weaker ones. For a Caribbean island wishing to extend its influence into Africa or a Pacific island into Asia, the Commonwealth network was a clearly signposted path to follow. It could produce results.

I experienced the value of this network when campaigning as a foreign minister for a New Zealand seat on the UN Security Council. On meeting my principal competitor, Sweden's foreign minister, while lobbying for votes at a Non-Aligned Movement summit in Jakarta, it came to me forcefully that I had these tremendous Commonwealth links into Africa and Asia whereas the Swedes had few multi-country connections outside the Nordic group. In this particular case it worked for us, and losing the vote nearly brought down the Swedish government.

I soon found there was a lot of experience within developing countries of getting all they could from an aid programme while at the same time being rather tardy about instigating the governmental reforms that were usually part of the package.

The pressure underneath all of this engagement, and the bigger half of the true role of the Commonwealth, was to create more and better democracies. These should not be democracies modelled on some liberal Western template, but they should be democracies where all adult people have a say about who governs them and are able to exercise some influence over the policies devised by the governing body.

'My people cannot eat democracy,' was a phrase I heard far too often. 'We need more development.' Well, that was not a problem, because it was evident to all that the more democracy you have, the more development you will get. It is all about the confidence that emerges from predictability and the spread of decision-making. Nevertheless, selling democracy was markedly helped by the carrot of aid money. And, further, once people had achieved some say over their future they didn't easily let it go. Equally important in this mix were the Commonwealth's formal stated values: the Singapore Declaration, followed by the Harare Declaration, followed by the Millbrook Commonwealth Action Programme and the Latimer House guidelines. These were all resolutions signed up to by Commonwealth leaders, which committed them to that difficult path to a true democracy.

Information and publicity were important. Early on I had been reading much about the Secretariat's work and wondered why the Commonwealth family of citizens didn't know more about these activities. I thought we were hiding our light under a bushel. This organisation was carrying out lots of good-sized projects all around the world, but few people knew about them. These were projects that really did benefit the lives of people, especially young people, and they were something we could be proud of. On examining the situation further I found that sometimes we did not even get the credit when the project was completed. Further questioning discovered that although approved in London at the Secretariat, many projects were often implemented by third parties and consultants who, when the job was concluded, just packed their suitcases and left the country.

How could the Commonwealth Secretariat possibly expect continued support when no one knew what we had done?

So one of my early goals was that we had to achieve lots of local publicity – at the start of a project, during it and when we finished. Even that was not easy because all our media people were in London. They had somehow to link up with newspapers in, say, Ghana to ensure the right information came out at the right time and, of course, where possible with a photograph. I found it unfortunate that many of the consultants who implemented the projects were not interested in advertising their results.

Of even greater interest was the range of projects that was undertaken by the Secretariat and the constant lobbying by the ABCs (Australia, Britain and Canada, plus New Zealand), who always demanded that every project had to have a strong governance element. The developing countries were happy to go along with these governance projects because that ensured other development projects would be supported. Governance programmes included reconfiguring a justice department, anti-corruption measures, restructuring an electoral commission, seminars for parliamentarians, voter registration, lectures on managing transparent public accounts and so on.

Of course, the developing countries usually preferred projects aimed at improving agriculture, fishing, tourism or forestry, because you could see the physical result. A new airport or highway was a real bonus – and it would inevitably carry the name of the leader in preparation for the next election.

From the time I arrived, the persistent mantra of the ABCs, particularly the Canadians, concerned the need for more money to be spent on governance and less on development projects. It was always good to debate these issues, but each new official who came to these executive meetings from the ABC group would take this line with fresh fervour. While you can never draw hard and fast lines, I could see my role was to protect a reasonable portion of the budget for development but at the same time ensure that the governance projects were seen in a positive light – that they weren't just a trade-off.

Criticism also came from the big payers about the relevance of some of the development work. 'Was it supply- or demand-driven?' I was constantly asked. The answer was both. Countries putting forward their individual needs meant that it was obviously demand-driven, but they had to fit in with the overall strategic plan. This wasn't really a major problem as long as all were subject to the same scrutiny.

However, it did emerge in my wanderings around the Secretariat that certain supply-driven projects were also part of our toolbox of aid. This might come about when one of our senior development staff or an outside consultant, noticing a downturn in his or her future work, would make it known to a certain friendly government that he or she was available. So far, so good. But then what followed was a message to someone in that friendly government to send a request to the Secretariat indicating the need for a certain programme – and could the Commonwealth Secretariat supply such a person?

Not long after my arrival at Marlborough House I became aware of the many institutions, organisations and professional groups that carried the name Commonwealth in their title. It was a surprise to me to find out there were more than sixty of these organisations, and what a rich, diverse and valuable group they were.

The oldest had been around in various forms since 1901. This was the Commonwealth Telecommunications Organisation (CTO). Of course, the modern Commonwealth also inherited the Royal Commonwealth Society, which had begun its life as far back as 1868. The newest at the time was the Commonwealth branch of Amnesty International.

Alongside us in Marlborough House was our sister organisation the Commonwealth Foundation, set up in the 1960s to engage with civil society, encourage the growth of professional organisations and foster the 'de-anglicisation' of those organisations. It has now a very broad mandate for engagement generally.

The obvious benefit for a Secretary-General was a huge hinterland of expertise within what turned out to be nearly ninety organisations covering an enormous range of activity, which could be harnessed for the greater good of Commonwealth citizens.

It did strike me, however, that although some had a large

membership – there was the 16,000-plus of the Common-wealth Parliamentary Association and the very high-profile Commonwealth Games – there were also organisations that seemed to be not much more than one person and a word processor.

None of these organisations had any direct line of responsi-bility to the Secretary-General, but to get a better handle on the situation I suggested to leaders that we could have a look at what was there. And so we did.

Letters went out to all the groups that made up the Commonwealth civil society, asking about their purpose, membership and financial status, and whether they were truly pan-Commonwealth. We now had eighty-six organ-isations that all had a relevant purpose in life and had broad Commonwealth membership.

I now had the perfect database to benefit us all. If I wanted judges, I could call on the Commonwealth Magistrates' and Judges' Association. If I sought forestry expertise there was the Commonwealth Forestry Association. Observers for elec-tions could be drawn from the Commonwealth Parliamentary Association. And so on.

I realised that all this was critical to understanding the enduring strength of the Commonwealth. Why did all these people get together in like-minded organisations under a Commonwealth banner? I guess it goes back to that factor of all speaking the same language – and I don't only mean the English language. I mean we all understand the general language of our very similar institutions: parliamentary systems, judicial structures, education and health ministries, not ignoring an understanding of the laws of cricket! We willingly group together with those who have similar interests and whom we easily understand.

Which of course takes me back to when I was campaigning for New Zealand to get a seat on the UN Security Council. What a huge network I had compared with my Swedish competitor. So when Dr Boutros Boutros-Ghali asked me how he could develop similar organisations within or under the La Francophonie umbrella, of which he was then the Secretary-General, I pointed out that the first of our eighty-six organisations began in 1868. It wasn't an easy template to replicate. It was a unique international grouping of enormous breadth and depth, and it was truly global.

One of my first tasks on returning to New Zealand was to officiate at the annual Commonwealth Writers' Prize ceremony in Auckland. I was amused to hear one of the winning authors say how proud he was to win such an important global competition because, he added, with a big grin on his face, the famous Man Booker Prize was merely a regional competition.

I continued to be very aware of the vulnerability of small states. There are thirty-two of them in the Commonwealth. If a hurricane hits Florida, people may be killed and houses damaged, but the overall effect on the United States is minimal. The same hurricane hitting a Caribbean or Pacific state can wipe out 80–90 per cent of the country's assets.

In addition to the dangers of disasters such as this, small states very easily lose their best people to other higher-paying countries. Small states also do not have a big audience when they raise vital issues. They have little leverage in the WTO or the United Nations and they have a harder job convincing global bankers that they constitute a financially viable investment opportunity.

They do, however, know that by grouping with others they can gain extra leverage. They learn ways round blockages, but they still know they just cannot grow into big states. They are price takers, not price makers. As one island entrepreneur said to me, 'Everything we sell is wholesale and everything we buy is retail.' That rather sums up the narrow gap of wealth creation.

Yet I cannot help noting that Singapore and Malta are two Commonwealth members who have no natural resources except their people and are good examples of what you can do with the right policies. Not all of our thirty-two small states have achieved a similar transition. Some are restricted by their history, by their governing structures or by their culture. But that is no reason for the Commonwealth not to help them move ahead and create more opportunities for their citizens.

You cannot mention the vulnerability of small states without mentioning the issue of climate change and rising sea levels. Most cities in the world are at sea level or not much above, but they've also got the ability to manage the threat and provide protection for their people. If the level of the sea rises, then you move to higher ground. That's fine, but moving a whole town or a small country is more difficult.

The bigger problem concerns those countries – or more specifically those islands – whose total land area is not more than a couple of metres above sea level. A number of these are members of the Commonwealth – the Maldives, Kiribati and Tuvalu are three examples. Where do approximately 500,000 people go when their whole island becomes uninhabitable or threatens to disappear under water? Some very good work has been done on the vulnerability of small states, notably involving the Maltese and the Maldivians, with many others making significant and experienced contributions. I was delighted during one meeting with the then president of the World Bank, Jim Wolfensohn, that he was prepared to break with Bank traditions and agree to put small states into a special category for assistance. That gave a worthwhile boost to all those slaving away for recognition for many years.

However, even in New Zealand and Australia I am not confident there is a policy in place ready to respond to the needs of the 110,000 people of Tuvalu and Kiribati if both those countries become uninhabitable due to rising sea levels.

CHAPTER 13

The Non-Political Mandates

The issues that make headlines worldwide tend to be the disaster at the bottom of the cliff. Building fences at the top of the cliff is all about preventing those disasters. For the Commonwealth, that includes building stable, democratic institutions, about which more below.

Economic

Doha, the capital of Qatar, was not the most well-known city in the Middle East, let alone in the world. But in late 2001 everyone who was engaged in or had an interest in international trade was repeating the name almost daily. For this was the city where a new round of multilateral negotiations to free up international trade was launched.

Within developing countries such as those in the Commonwealth there was a growing level of optimism that finally the world would give them – and particularly their agricultural products – a chance to compete on a level playing field. Would the participants succeed in collectively freeing up international trade to make the world a better place by creating a greater spread of wealth? Or, once again, would hopes be dashed against the wall of protection so effectively built by the wealthy few?

There had been the Kennedy Round, the Tokyo Round and the Uruguay Round, all of which had made trade advances. But there was still a long way to go, especially in agriculture, which remained set in stone, principally because of France, Germany, the United States and Japan.

The Doha Round was launched in the year 2001 and I was amused to hear my economic officials tell me that the round would be concluded within three years. I had been a foreign and trade minister during most of the Uruguay Round, which was also to have taken three years but in the end took more than seven. I was not optimistic.

For the bulk of the developing countries of the Commonwealth their chance to influence such negotiations is very minimal. But you can't do nothing, and so many requests came into the Secretariat for assistance. Small states just do not have the necessary expertise in international trade, and in fact many do not even have a department within their government to provide the right advice.

Sometimes small groupings of countries, such as those in the Caribbean, the Pacific or even Africa, can work collectively, thus spreading the cost of the exercise among them.

At the Secretariat we saw this as an area that needed our support. But this was not universally accepted among our developed members, who saw it working against their own interests. There were very strong objections from my own country, New Zealand, for example. 'Bring it on,' was the message I insisted got back to them. Even New Zealand would not wish publicly to object to small states getting vital economic assistance at this critical time.

After the financial crises of the late 1990s, I felt there had never been a better time, or a greater need, for developing countries to obtain access to the markets of the European Union, the United States and Japan.

There was no shortage of optimism at the beginning of the Doha Round – even though it was to stall in July 2009 and shows little likelihood of a restart before the end of 2012. The fact is that multilateral trade negotiations are the only way trade barriers can be removed. You have to use every opportunity to understand what's going on, even if you are only a receiver of decisions, not a maker of them.

It was soon established that the needs of developing countries, especially the small ones, were beyond the level of our Secretariat budget at the time. So I was immensely pleased that one of my senior officials, who knew all the back corridors of the European Union, was soon to hear them announce a grant of €15 million to us at the Commonwealth to help developing countries build up their trade capacity and know-how. It still amuses me that this grant was made to help small states fight against the interests of the European Union. As if they say: 'I'll pay you to punch me in the face.' But never look a gift horse in the mouth, and we did not.

With that money and working with L'Agence Intergouvernementale de la Francophonie via a Memorandum of Understanding (MOU) on 7 November 2003, we set up six hubs in the Caribbean, East, West and Central Africa, the Pacific and South Africa. There were six trade policy advisers and twenty-nine analysts spread throughout. These teams of well-qualified, often quite young people were the saviours for those countries, which otherwise simply did not know what was going on.

World politics and trade politics get daily more complicated. So while we were getting countries up to the mark on Doha issues, the European Union, not wishing to deal with island states as a collective, was expecting each Caribbean or Pacific state to enter into a unilateral economic partnership agreement. This was more for the benefit of the European Union than the small states. It was a real David and Goliath situation, so we stepped in to help the Davids – which did achieve some good results when you consider the alternative.

To add some intellectual grunt to our arguments, we commissioned Economics Nobel Laureate Joseph Stiglitz to produce a report on the current situation. It was entitled 'An Agenda for the Development Round of Trade Negotiations in the Aftermath of Cancun', after the Mexican city in which the talks had stalled. Stiglitz's thesis was: 'If it's not a round to benefit developing countries, it's not worth having.'

Since at the time of writing little of what we were hoping for has been achieved, did we do the right thing? The alternative would have been to ignore our membership's needs at a time when they could well have got a worse deal. We could not have contemplated that. Many of our people received a lot of up-to-date information and education about the twenty-first-century trading world, and that was very useful.

An indication of the need for Commonwealth members to be educated was provided by Finance Minister Tutoatasi Fakafanua of Tonga, who amused one meeting during my time when he said: 'When I leave my country, out goes 50 per cent of our economic intelligence.' It was a telling illustration of the resource problems of small, developing states.

Many other issues rose to the top of the in-tray and had to be dealt with to help our poorer membership: how to address the special needs of the small vulnerable states that made up the majority of Commonwealth members? How to attract more direct foreign investment in emerging markets through reducing the costs of doing so? How to combat money laundering? How to strengthen the negotiating capacity of small, poor, vulnerable states in global climate-change negotiations? How to build up the resources in our regional development banks? How to pursue debt elimination or reduction in highly indebted countries? Addressing the last issue began as an initiative in a Commonwealth finance ministers' meeting and was later accepted by the full membership of the World Bank and IMF.

I was particularly keen for our experts to develop best-practice models for making Commonwealth countries' public accounts more accessible, transparent and understandable. People understand very easily if you can show where the money comes from and where it goes. Most countries' treasurers have made their public accounts into voluminous, obtuse documents that most people struggle to comprehend. As a senior minister in New Zealand, I used to value the newspaper the day after a budget was released. Its version of the budget was much simplified and understandable.

Public sector reform and training

As discussed in Chapter 12, there was among the staff of the Commonwealth Secretariat a fear that the new Secretary-General from New Zealand would turn the place upside down in an attempt to reform this public sector institution. Certainly, the traumatic period of reform New Zealand had gone through in the late 1980s and 1990s presented a high-profile example of reform policies which had led to the public service being reduced and many long-serving public servants losing their jobs and entitlements.

What was ironic was that there was a key group of people within the Secretariat who, as a result of various Commonwealth Heads of Government Meeting (CHOGM) and ministerial edicts, were now preaching and advocating public sector reform all around the Commonwealth – but not for them, no thanks.

Despite the fact that to some people New Zealand was tainted with an anti-public service mentality, a university in Wellington was able to partner with the Secretariat to offer a twelve-week course of study in public sector reform. I was pleased to note that senior civil servants had come from all over the Commonwealth to do this course, which happily enhanced New Zealand's name in the process. Following the 1997 CHOGM, the Commonwealth Association for Corporate Governance (CACG) devised a set of Principles for Corporate Governance in the Commonwealth. Then the Commonwealth Business Council (CBC), situated along the road from us, brought together the various business associations within the Commonwealth and established its own fifteen-point guidelines for 'good corporate governance'. Although it was initially only voluntary, leaders adopted this CBC proposal at the Abuja CHOGM in 2003.

The guidelines for business, governments and joint business/ government included elections for directors, transparency of accounts and regular shareholders' meetings. They became core Commonwealth values to aspire to – or, alternatively, an impediment to those who wished to bypass them.

In 2005 I was asked by newly-elected President Guebuza of Mozambique to run two weeks of seminars for his whole cabinet, most of whom were new. 'They're so new they don't know what to do,' he told me. 'Could you find some experienced people to educate them?'

It was a most interesting challenge and one I just had to say yes to, so I immediately sought out a training team. And what a powerful team they turned out to be: Sir Lloyd Sandiford, former Prime Minister of Barbados; Sir Nicholas Montagu, former chair of the United Kingdom Inland Revenue Authority; Neil Walter, former chief executive of the New Zealand Ministry of Foreign Affairs; Noelle Alexander, former minister of admin and manpower from the Seychelles; and Geraldine Fraser-Moleketi, South African minister of public service.

The reports that came back from the ministers, the executive trainers and the President were all positive. Later I thought, there aren't many places where you can get a cabinet of new ministers to sit still for a couple of weeks and have a bunch of public sector foreigners tell them what they should do and how to do it. It was an example of a new Commonwealth country being more committed to the Commonwealth than many of the older ones.

Later we were asked to send a similar team to Botswana. Then a less political team went back to Mozambique to make sure the senior officials within that new government got the same message. It was also a reasonable example of how the Commonwealth can move rapidly; from request to delivery would not have taken more than three weeks.

A sidebar to all this activity was the volunteer aid programme we called Commonwealth Services Abroad (CWSA). This programme brings in retired or even mid-career civil servants and deploys them in the public sector of another country where there is a need or just a weakness to be plugged. It's not a big programme, as only thirty people are deployed per year, but they are all much appreciated by their hosts.

Through various schemes in my time we trained some 6,000 public officials.

Youth – half the Commonwealth

At the CHOGM in Ottawa in 1973, the Commonwealth took the significant step of setting up a youth division within the Secretariat. In 1979 the leaders gave this a huge push by committing not less than £1 million to the project (otherwise many other projects would have been placed in jeopardy). Thus began a programme of training youth leaders, promoting the involvement of young people and broadening the understanding of the Commonwealth among young people. Four regional youth offices were established.

Soon these youth activities were well embedded within the Commonwealth system. I was told frequently that only the Commonwealth had a dedicated programme for youth, and many were surprised that it survived. Of course, it's never easy to measure the success or otherwise of such organisations. How does leadership training add to the economic well-being of a country? It's hard to say. For me, to keep young people occupied and to give them a platform on which to talk and do things is better than the alternatives.

I was impressed by one programme developed by the Commonwealth Youth Programme (CYP) that recruited HIV-infected young people to talk to their peers about the dangers of becoming infected, how it can be avoided and, if you are infected, how to live with it. I saw these young people telling remarkable and persuasive stories that had an impact far beyond that which could have been given by a sixty-two-year-old, white, male, suited Secretary-General. I knew this was a programme that deserved maximum support.

While it's easy to be sceptical about the many ideas that fall easily from articulate adults onto the table and are expected to be implemented, I decided you had to see all these through the eyes of a young person in a developing country. They probably had only a limited education, which drastically limited their horizons, and probably only a vague or restricted idea as to where to go next. For those people to advance themselves, these programmes had to be good. The young people had to see some immediate benefit, so it wasn't always productive to look too critically through a cost/benefits lens.

In fact, some 700–800 youth-orientated Commonwealth businesses began over a ten-year period.

While all these programmes moved at different speeds, our revenue streams were becoming uncertain. The voluntary contributions of governments began to drift down during my time, though not dramatically, just various governments finding reasons to reduce their payments. Sometimes we suffered because a youth minister did not have the clout at the cabinet table to get what he or she wanted.

I decided a new strategy was needed. It would be based around those leaders who were strongly committed to the programme. From them I obtained a commitment to a new funding model, essentially increasing their levies, which was then taken to the full leaders' meeting at the Kampala CHOGM in 2007. It worked.

The child soldiers captured by the notorious Joseph Kony of the Lord's Resistance Army of Uganda galvanised us into renewed activity. To meet young people barely out of their teens who had knowingly killed people, including members of their own family, left us feeling chilled. Nevertheless, we set up a facility in northern Uganda to help de-traumatise some of these kids. It was not easy and it was not always successful. Seeing how kids can be so easily kidnapped and destroyed in this way so early in their life makes you feel angry and depressed.

Should the Commonwealth spend its time on youth issues?

In my view the answer is yes, but we shouldn't expect the results to be easily measurable. You try things out; if they work you go looking for other funders, and you always give dispossessed youth the message that you're prepared to try anything that will help.

The Kampala CHOGM found the leaders re-energised on the youth issue. We succeeded in getting a four-paragraph statement into the Kampala communiqué that recognised the benefits of our youth programme, reaffirmed members' commitment to it and called on all Commonwealth countries to step up their voluntary contributions. I left office feeling that youth would now be on a smoother track.

Human rights

When I arrived at Marlborough House I was told: 'We have a lawyer working in the legal division who's responsible for human rights issues.' Well, I thought, that's interesting – but burying your principal in another department is not really the way to show that you take the issue seriously. I had already been told by many staff members that 'we leave human rights issues to the United Nations'. Not any more, we don't, I thought to myself.

After a few months and some quiet discussions I outlined a plan to the senior staff to build up a separate unit, but in a way that wasn't going to frighten the horses. With a study into the human rights work of the Secretariat by Dr Chaloka Beyani of the London School of Economics providing some pointers, I tackled the organisational role and status of the team. After an abortive attempt to recruit someone from outside in early 2001, I proposed to an existing staff member that he take the job.

So it was that in January 2002 a South African lawyer of Asian descent stepped up to do the job. Hanif Vally was a quietly spoken officer who was reliable and dedicated. This was exactly what I wanted, someone who could assiduously build up the unit to a level of independent credibility.

Soon Hanif was being invited to go and make speeches in

New York and in various capitals about our values and our work. Other rights organisations came to visit the Secretariat. Papers were written, and soon the staff level within the unit expanded. By 2004/5 the Secretariat had a credible unit with a mandate which included promoting programmes that integrated civil, political, economic and social rights; publishing human rights materials; working with other key agencies (including NGOs and the UN); providing the Secretary-General with advice in relation to Commonwealth Ministerial Action Group (CMAG) deliberations; and taking the lead on mainstreaming rights work across the organisation. When Hanif left he was replaced by an experienced Bangladeshi diplomat, Rabab Fatima, and when she left another woman of Asian descent, Dr Purna Sen, took over. Momentum continued to the satisfaction of all.

The unit received healthy impetus from ministers and governments generally. Those who were in disagreement with such initiatives said very little. Soon publications were going out for school use. There was much collaboration with other international human rights groups. CMAG ministers began to ask for reports and advice on how the unit measured the human rights in specified countries.

In 2006 we embarked on a campaign to encourage a number of Commonwealth countries to ratify the two major human rights conventions that had been adopted by the UN from 1948 onwards. It was amazing that there were still a dozen or so countries that found reasons not to ratify these most fundamental, globally-supported human rights instruments. We were also asked to help establish in The Gambia the African Court for Human Rights. We worked with a coalition of civil society organisations in Africa, the Centre for Human Rights at Pretoria University and the government of Kenya to host a conference on the establishment of the court.

Papers on best-practice guidelines were sent all around the Commonwealth, and within the Secretariat we insisted that all staff decisions had to take human rights into account.

By 2007 we were able to help each country develop a human rights model that most suited its own political landscape. Most members had constitutions that guaranteed rights to their people, and they had signed up to international standards through ratifications of various treaties. Many sought support from the Secretariat in realising these commitments. Our Human Rights Unit was offering capacity-building through training and publications, including on human trafficking, freedom of association, the treatment of victims of crime, and a special focus on young people and rights.

When I left office the unit consisted of five people, all of whom were very successful at encouraging change where it was needed and discouraging those practices, not just customary ones, that people everywhere regarded as repugnant. We were now where we should be, and there were no member countries demanding we desist. This set a positive foundation for the future development of human rights work in the Commonwealth.

Gender issues

Issues of gender did not just creep up on us, they were always there. I found there was a strong feeling among Secretariat staff who carefully followed the deliberations of ministerial meetings devoted to women's issues that we had to do more. Within the Secretariat, as the employer we reaffirmed our commitment to have equal treatment of all, regardless of gender. This was given a strong push by the women staff gathering in the Blenheim Saloon (the beautiful room just inside the door of Marlborough House, named after the Battle of Blenheim in 1704). They made sure the male staff, some distinctly unreconstructed, knew what side to be on.

A conference in Mauritius in 2003 brought together women from both government and the wider community and committed to working harder to combat violence against women. This set the scene for much of our work.

We participated actively in the Commonwealth Business

Women's Network and were told by World Bank officials that it was the best example of gender promotions and implementation they had seen. 'Always nice to get praise, no matter who from,' I noted at the time.

New initiatives to involve women in peacemaking emerged from war-torn Sierra Leone, similar to the initiatives I started as a New Zealand foreign minister on the Papua New Guinea island of Bougainville after the civil war there eight years before.

By 2005 the trend of highlighting indigenous women's rights had moved to centre stage, and a strong plan of action to carry through to 2010 was agreed to. This included: gender democracy within peace and conflict, within human rights and law, within poverty eradication, and education about HIV and Aids.

On this issue, I felt that we were by now in the right place. We could spotlight problem areas, we had good advocacy for change and among our unit of officials in London we had real intellectual horsepower.

Health

The area of health is as deep as it is wide, and in every country there's an insatiable demand for more and more spending. Every government in the world knows it must deliver a service to its people, but how much it can provide is very much determined by the money available.

Within our Secretariat, then as now, the health team was very small, so we had to be careful in picking our targets. The HIV/Aids pandemic was self-selecting, but we searched for things our group could do that the WHO or sovereign governments could not. We came up with a proposal which began in 1993 with the creation of 'Youth Ambassadors for Positive Living' – getting young people who were themselves HIV positive to spread the message about this virus was a great idea (see page 286). It was very obvious that the messages and chats between the young people were most successful.

One perennial problem in developing counties was the

constant loss of health workers to developed countries. We set up
a document in 2003, which became the 'Commonwealth Code of
Practice for the International Recruitment of Health Workers'. It
wasn't perfect, but it did make governments in developed countries hesitate before actively recruiting in the poorer states. Still,
you could never stop a medically qualified person wanting to go
to Canada or Australia to better themselves and their families.

Conferences of health ministers were usually held in advance
of the WHO annual meetings in Geneva. This was good for our
developing country ministers, who got two bites at some issues.
However, such meetings tended to produce obvious results with
which few would disagree: concern about health worker migration; the need for a multi-sectored and multifaceted approach
to HIV/Aids; the problem of infant and maternal mortality; the
need to educate more midwives; and of course poverty, which
then and now remains the principal obstacle.

I felt we were doing the right thing on Aids, and working with
a Commonwealth organisation, 'Para 55', gave us extra reach.
Our professionals came up with a good idea on the maternal and
infant mortality issue. They produced eight short movies, which
were copied many times and shown on TV and laptops everywhere. They were educational, easy to understand and became
the perfect teaching tool.

We had narrowed our focus down to three issues: reduce
maternal mortality; reduce infant mortality among the under-
fives; combat HIV/Aids and malaria.

The issue of malaria had got under my skin, as it were, years
before when I'd noticed how prevalent and deadly this disease
was in the Pacific. I'd become incensed at the global ban on DDT.
Rachel Carson's book *Silent Spring* had helped bring about the
ban. My view was that this was fine for developed countries, but
in parts of the developing world, which included some poorer
Commonwealth countries, it wasn't so simple. Banning DDT
there was preventing serious attempts to eradicate the disease. I
had staff members who had lost children to malaria, and half of

my senior staff were permanent carriers due to previous exposures. Finally, the WHO relented on the issue, and it was with some pleasure that I witnessed a positive debate getting under way to actively promote a return to a measured and careful use of DDT.

I am pleased that the WHO finally agreed to change its views on the subject. Obviously, we won't return to the wholesale use of DDT as was carried out in the 1950s and 60s, but a more judicious and controlled application, along with other means, is the sensible way to tackle malaria. With 850,000 deaths from the disease in 2008, it cannot be ignored.

Looking back and asking myself how, as an organisation with a tiny budget compared with the United Nations and other large agencies, we responded to the infant and maternal mortality and HIV/Aids issues, I conclude that we found a niche and we made it work.

Education

Nothing can change people's lives, especially those of young people, as fast as education. If I came across a tribe of people who had access to food and not much else and I had to bring them to a more healthy civilised state, the three priorities would be: access to fresh water, a suitable way of getting rid of waste water, then education.

When I joined the Secretariat I could see we took education very seriously, but I felt we were placing far too much emphasis on getting more graduates in countries where there were still limitless demands for primary education. If there are 100 million young people in the world who will never see the inside of a classroom, probably over 60 million of them are in the Commonwealth. That seemed to me to be a priority.

I had read through a number of CHOGM communiqués and ministerial requests, and couldn't disagree with the general approach. But the list never changed much: improve access and equity; enhance capacity for more resource materials; low-cost books; and more teacher training. I felt we needed to examine ways to get more kids into primary education within existing funding levels.

My first education ministers' conference was in Halifax, Canada, with the theme 'Education empowers the poor'. But then I found that in addition to debating these issues, the education ministers were actually placing more and more education-related demands on the table for our officials to implement. How does this work, I thought?

I asked my head of education later: 'What do we do with all these requests?' 'Oh,' he said. 'Quite easy. We carry out the ones we think we can.'

Well, for me that was most unsatisfactory. So by the next education ministers' meeting I had ensured that the meeting understood that every request for action had to be accompanied by a funding proposal from a member government, the Secretariat or another acceptable source. The last thing I needed was angry ministers who felt their requests had not been rejected, but had been ignored.

One area I became acutely aware of was the constant loss of trained teachers to developed counties (see also pages 291–2, Health). There was a blatant grab taking place to lure away people trained at high cost in developing countries. Globally, of course, it remains a huge issue. Most people want to better themselves; most will be prepared to live in another country if they can improve the lot of themselves and their children. As a result, many smaller countries simply cannot keep up with meeting their own need for trained teachers and health professionals.

One does have to accept that professionally trained people will shift to another country to improve themselves, but my targets were the governments of developed countries, who were setting up massive recruiting campaigns to lure these people away from where they were most needed. It turned out to be a challenge that took up a lot of time, and it created a lot of grumpiness among officials in the United Kingdom, in particular.

But in 2004 we achieved the signing of a document called 'The Commonwealth Teachers Recruitment Proposal', which I am pleased to say has since been picked up by a number of non-Commonwealth countries.

The document required any government that wished to recruit to sit down with the target country's government and put its cards on the table. This brought the issue into the open, where it needed to be. It wasn't perfect. It didn't stop individuals responding to overseas advertisements and it didn't stop private-sector recruiting firms. But some countries were able to extract concessions for their losses. Overall it was a small gain, but it was still significant.

I often wondered about the dollar value of the long hours spent on this issue by our professionals, of the seminars, the travel to international conferences, the trees cut down for the paper required – might it not have been better spent on just getting more kids into primary schools?

There was never any serious disagreement among the Secretariat and member countries over the reports on these issues that were produced every year. The messages were constant: no one size of programme fits all; the need to acknowledge religion, gender, ethnicity and resource availability; planning must include an analysis of wastage; supporting children with special needs is always a challenge; there must be rigid standards to prevent gender violence; teacher qualifications should be truly international; there is a need for pan-Commonwealth qualifications for education leadership; and so on.

The challenge for an international organisation such as the Commonwealth Secretariat is to carve out an area in which expertise can be developed, the results can be proven and more outside funding can be attracted. Requests coming in from ministers or ministries of education are sometimes best diverted to other organisations. The strap-line sticker to glue to the top of every computer screen of an international educational professional should be: '100 million kids didn't go to school today'.

Epilogue

In my early days living in London, constantly thinking about the job I was elected to do, I would take my young son for a walk to Grosvenor Square, about three blocks north of our official residence in Mayfair. There was plenty of room for a two-year-old to run round, a few but not too many dogs, people to watch. It was very pleasant on a sunny day, with old leafy trees for shade and an ornamental pool, ideal for trailing little hands. Many a time young James would climb round the child-friendly Franklin Delano Roosevelt Memorial, and I often found myself thinking about the freedoms that were written in stone on that memorial: freedom of speech, of worship, from want and from fear. The more I thought about these, the more I realised that they said it all. It was Roosevelt's State of the Union speech on 6 January 1941 in which these freedoms, derived no doubt from the US Declaration of Independence, were first enunciated in this form. It was these same freedoms that were behind the United Nations Declaration of Human Rights less than ten years later.

It was not difficult for me, therefore, to keep in mind these simple, critically important rights; those who enjoy them worry only about the smaller problems of life, while those who live without these freedoms never achieve their full human potential. The Commonwealth first formally declared its own values in Singapore in 1971 and expressed the UN's aspirations in even greater detail. It did so to help member countries to more easily work towards those goals and lift the lives of their peoples. The

Commonwealth's values were later incorporated in the Harare and Millbrook principles and the Latimer House guidelines.

In my time as Secretary-General we were challenged by a few member states prepared to violate Commonwealth principles. A very few tried to rewrite those values, but failed to diminish our common cause. Usually their failed efforts came after they took oppressive action against their people and then objected to being challenged by other Commonwealth nations. We stood firm and unwavering.

The question remains, and the answer is always the same – if everyone on the planet had those four freedoms, would the world be a better place? The answer has to be, yes.

Having existed in one form or another since the 1870s, the Commonwealth remains committed to improving people's lives. It is axiomatic that it should be judged for what it achieves, but with fifty-four countries and some 2.26 billion people (2012), the work will never be completed. With a small budget compared to many other international organisations, it must choose its projects carefully. If a programme can improve the lives of a million people, wonderful. If it can improve the lives of only a few, is that not still an important outcome?

The test of the relevance of any organisation must include these questions – is it doing what is expected of it, is it fulfilling its mandate? How to measure this is difficult – bear in mind that much of what it does will changes lives, but not generate headlines, in a world where success is often measured in terms of column inches or television sound bites.

When I look at the Commonwealth in 2012 and see no one-party states, only one military dictatorship and a lot more free trade, I know that hundreds of millions of people are better off than they were twelve years ago. I know my work and that of my predecessors has contributed to a better life for many people.

Whether these people would be as well off without Commonwealth membership is not easy to judge, but I somehow doubt it. Sure, some of the slack might have been taken up by other organisations if the Commonwealth had cut back or ceased to exist, but none of the member states would be willing to take that gamble.

The crude fact is that there is much more to do before 7 billion people around the globe all enjoy the four underlying freedoms we espouse.

As long as the Commonwealth 'sticks to its knitting' it will be able to take credit (silently or not) for what it does. In a 2003 report I commissioned from a Commonwealth Eminent Persons Group (headed up by current Indian Prime Minister Manmohan Singh) it was made clear that citizens of countries that have democracy, believe in democracy and make it work have better lives than those in countries which don't. The report's bumper sticker says it all: 'The more democracy you have the more development you'll get.'

The important thing is never to give up. Sometimes, you can pause for breath, take stock and even decide to set some problems aside temporarily, but the Commonwealth's credibility will be sustained only if the 'have nots' believe you continue to work in their best interests.

Referring back to the four basic freedoms, I asked myself all the time – do these people live reduced lives because of their religious beliefs; are they able to feed and clothe themselves; do they live in fear of terrorism or their fellow citizen; are they free to speak out on any issue? Until these issues are resolved, the Commonwealth's work must continue.

Despite the fact that our good work was not 'sexy' in media terms, I pushed hard throughout my stewardship of the Commonwealth to let people know what we were up to in our huge range of activities. After all, the Commonwealth's programmes are funded by taxpayers throughout the Commonwealth, and ministers of foreign affairs and finance must each year justify continued contribution to the Commonwealth in a climate where domestic spending is constrained. Keeping up good media coverage helps to take some pressure off ministers struggling to justify the expenditure.

Good news is no news, so I sometimes had to use stealth to get any attention for the Commonwealth. I found the British press would always prick up their ears if we mentioned Zimbabwe, so it became a guise to use Zimbabwe as the means to get other points across. Sometimes issues involving Pakistan or Swaziland, two countries that also absorbed the attention of the British press, provided a mechanism for broader coverage. Our media people worked long and often late at night, across many time zones, to get the good news stories out, hoping for some return for the effort involved.

Piggybacking on the United Nations, the European Union and other regional organisations to magnify the message was another way of breaking through that news barrier – though we had to be careful we owned our stories and were not marginalised by organisations with greater resources.

The key to assessing press releases is not how many flew electronically out of Marlborough House every day, but how many ended up in newspapers or news bulletins and were actually read or seen by our constituents. I came to a view very early in my political life that if you are regularly in the news, you at least appear to be doing something useful. It's a rather cynical view, but one that fits the sound-bite world in which we work.

I would have liked in this book to talk about the work we did in Sierra Leone among the members of the Revolutionary United Front (RUF), who perpetuated barbaric cruelty under the influence of Foday Sankoh and Charles Taylor. Our work was important in rehabilitating the so-called 'war veterans', but we were not the main players in resolving this ghastly mess. In the newly stable and democratic Ghana we assisted with a new primary school curriculum; in Papua New Guinea we provided a new configuration of the Defence Force; we addressed governance issues in the Caribbean, and ran youth programmes based in Lusaka, Honiara, Chandigarh and Georgetown. We helped redesign the electoral system in Lesotho, helped establish fishing agreements in the Pacific in partnership with Iceland and observed elections in many Commonwealth countries.

Each of these is an engrossing story, all are about enhancing people's lives and most will never make the news, let alone front pages. The Secretariat's library of publications alone is an enormous resource to anybody interested in development and the betterment of people's lives.

I have already in this book addressed the help we gave to Swaziland with its constitution, and we were able to do the same for the Maldives. I can't think of any other international organisation that can call upon good people within its diverse organisations to help with equally diverse issues. These range from foresters to magistrates, judges, journalists, architects and university administrators, all belonging to the nearly ninety organisations of the great Commonwealth family.

By a circuitous route, I hope I have now answered the question: will the Commonwealth still be of use to countries in fifty years' time? My answer is yes, but with qualifications.

First, the Commonwealth must continue to aspire to the great ambition of all people having those central personal freedoms, with all countries finally ratifying and adhering to the UN Declaration of Human Rights and the Conventions on Social, Civil and Political Rights.

Second, the Secretary-General and the Commonwealth chairperson must not hesitate to speak out on issues that are clearly in violation of Commonwealth values. Megaphone diplomacy is a measure of last resort, but it does have a place.

Third, it must continue to refine the ability of the Commonwealth Ministerial Action Group (CMAG) to deal with those states that persistently violate these principles. Changes within CMAG may always be incremental, but it is important that unscrupulous nations don't get away with actions that are not necessarily circumscribed by CMAG.

Fourthly, the Commonwealth must show through all of its aid programmes that people are receiving real benefits and that standards of living are being enhanced. It must ensure that the small states can continue to magnify their voices and add weight to their concerns by joining with others for collective impact.

Also, the commitment of a nation's leader to ensuring that he or she is not just allowing, but actively encouraging, democratic development in the country is critically important. Leaders must understand that people want a say in their future, and only democracy can do that.

And finally back at Marlborough House, to ensure the Secretariat is full of competent, energetic people, the Secretary-General needs to keep bringing in new people, new faces and new talents. Each new person brings a fresh desire to succeed, enthusiasm, new ideas and renewed energy. Staff who work there and then return to their country take home a wealth of ideas and energy.

So I conclude where I started back in 1999. Despite all its history, colourful characters and life-changing achievements, the Commonwealth can never rest on its laurels. As with selling yourself politically, it's not about how wonderful you were yesterday; Commonwealth citizens will quite rightly continue to ask 'But what are you doing for me tomorrow?' Hence the Commonwealth will (and should) always be measured by its actions and intentions. Relevance and credibility are what it's all about.

As long as just one of our Commonwealth citizens lives in fear, suffers for belonging to the 'wrong' faith, is scared to speak out or feels threatened by others, there is work to be done.

I started these reflections with a quote from Nelson Mandela. I will end with another from him: 'Let there be justice for all. Let there be peace for all. Let there be work, bread, water and salt for all.'

Afterword

by Olusegun Obasanjo, President of Nigeria 1999–2007

In the Ring gives fresh insight into the workings of a very important, though under-valued, international organisation. The Commonwealth, which I personally regard as one of the few positive effects of colonialism, has, in recent times, distinguished itself as a force for good in many ways.

Don was gracious enough to involve me in a number of issues that he had to deal with during his tenure as Secretary-General. Zimbabwe was, of course, his greatest challenge. It was a difficult issue, but the Commonwealth won international respect for its stand on the issues of democracy, human rights and the rule of law.

I appreciated the manner in which Don delicately balanced the competing demands of the old and new Commonwealth members. The UK, Canada, Australia and New Zealand wanted to see the organisation concentrating on good governance, improved elections, corruption-free societies, the rule of law, an independent judiciary and a free press. Good and important as these are, the developing countries also wanted focus on economic and social development as well. Don admirably balanced these competing attitudes.

In the Ring will be of tremendous use to experts and students of international organisations as well as to the general reader. I recommend it to all those who believe in democracy, human rights, rule of law, peace, international cooperation and sustainable development.

Olusegun Obasanjo
July 2012

Index

NEW WORLDS FOR OLD

DUNCAN LUNAN
NEW WORLDS FOR OLD

WESTBRIDGE BOOKS

A Division of David & Charles

441064558 PA

00064451

British Library Cataloguing in Publication Data
Lunan, Duncan
  New worlds for old.
  1. Solar system 2. Interplanetary voyages
  3. Astronomy – History – 20th century
  I. Title
  521'.54   QB501

  ISBN 0–7153–7772–8

© Duncan Lunan 1979

All rights reserved. No part of this
publication may be reproduced, stored
in retrieval system, or transmitted, in
any form or by any means, electronic,
mechanical, photocopying, recording or
otherwise, without the prior permission
of Westbridge Books

Set by Trade Linotype Limited
and printed in Great Britain
by Redwood Burn, Trowbridge and Esher
for Westbridge Books (A Division of David & Charles)
Brunel House Newton Abbot Devon

To Hermann Oberth
pioneer of astronautics Honorary Member of ASTRA

with thanks

from Oscar Schwiglhofer and the other ASTRA members

Contents

Preface

Like its predecessor, *Man and the Stars* (published in the US as *Interstellar Contact*), *New Worlds for Old* is based on an extended series of lectures and discussions held at ASTRA, the Association in Scotland to Research into Astronautics. This volume presents the 'new look' of the Solar System built up by space exploration to date; a later book, provisionally entitled *Man and the Planets*, will discuss the possible future of exploration and development. Thanks are due to Professor T. R. Nonweiler, Professor A. E. Roy, A. F. Nimmo, John Macvey, Oscar Schwiglhofer and Anthony Lawton for the lectures around which the project took shape; Dr Roy, Mr Nimmo, Mr Macvey and Mr Lawton appear in their own words as guest contributors. The contributions of other ASTRA members will be found in the text – James Campbell, Billy Ramsay, Robert Shaw, Chris Boyce, Robbie Chalmers, John Kelk, Mel Adam, John Braithwaite, Pat McNally, Joyce Mains, Tony Thomson, Linda Lunan, Bill Barr, Bob Cochrane, Margaret Schwiglhofer . . . and of course Ed Buckley and Gavin Roberts, who took an active part in the discussions as well as creating the artwork. In addition we have to thank Professor Nonweiler and Glasgow University Faculty of Engineering for providing the facilities for a one-day seminar at the midpoint of the project.

Our thanks are also due to the Jet Propulsion Laboratory (hereinafter referred to as JPL) of California Institute of Technology for their generous supply of Mariner 9, Mariner 10 and Viking photographs to ASTRA; likewise to NASA's Ames Research Centre for Pioneer 10 and 11 photographs and for news releases; and to Ms Jeri Bell and Mr Bill Slattery of NASA for their hospitality to ASTRA members at Kennedy Space Centre in July 1975. NASA reports listed in the Bibliography were lent by the British Interplanetary Society, and Mr Len Carter's help is gratefully acknowledged. Lastly (as promised), special thanks to the Inter-Library Loans Department of Glasgow University Library, who are probably dreading the start of our next project. ("May I have three dozen application forms, please . . . ?")

DL

PART I
Background and methods

1 Exploring the Solar System

"What, quite unmann'd in folly?"

Reply to critics of NASA's priorities (with thanks
to William Shakespeare)

It would be wrong to give the impression that knowledge of the planetary
system we live in was static before the "space age" began in 1957. Only
a hundred years ago, one of the most telling arguments against Darwinian
evolution was that the Sun, generating its heat by a steady progress of
shrinking, could not have given birth to the Earth more than a few thousand
years ago. In the Foreword to the 1909 edition of *The Earth's Beginning*,
first published in 1901, Sir Robert Ball declares that "The discovery of
radium, and the wonderful phenomena associated therewith, has pointed
out a possible escape from one of the gravest difficulties in science".[1] The
curtain had risen: nuclear physics had the Sun's basic principles resolved
by mid-century. With developing understanding of the Sun and of the true
age of the Solar System there came increasing insight into Earth's origins
and history: hypotheses such as continental drift, once dismissed as wildly
improbable, advanced steadily towards general acceptance.

In his next paragraph, Sir Robert wrote: "The most notable fact which
emerges from the modern study of the structure of the heavens is the ever-
increasing significance and importance of the spiral nebulae." That remark
proved so prophetic that for most of the following decades professional
astronomers directed their attention beyond the Solar System and beyond
the Milky Way, too enthralled by the deeps of space and time to regard
the planets as really important. It is instructive to leaf through popular books
on astronomy and space travel from the 1950s and see how old the accompanying photographs are. Amateur astronomers watched the Moon and
the planets, steadily improving on the existing maps, but any new phenomena they reported – the gegenschein, "Moon-glows", the "Ashen Light"
on Venus, the fourth ring of Saturn – were transitory or highly elusive and
could easily be put down to eyestrain or imagination. The basic questions
of planetary astronomy remained unchanged for fifty years. Were lunar
craters formed by meteorites or volcanoes? Was Venus a dust bowl, a vast
swamp, or covered in ocean? Was there life on Mars, were the canals real,
and if so were they the work of intelligence? Were the asteroids debris of a
planet which disintegrated, or leftovers from the original formation of the
System? Was the Red Spot on Jupiter an island floating in a sea of gas,
or a storm over a mountain on a huge solid world below the clouds? With

HARRIS PUBLIC LIBRARY PRESTON

little to work on except visual observations from the bottom of Earth's turbulent atmosphere, the astronomers weren't getting enough new facts even to vary the questions.

With the beginning of physical exploration by spacecraft, new and previously unsuspected facts came pouring in. Explorer 1 found that the Earth was sheathed in belts of trapped radiation. Luna 2 indicated that the Moon has no intrinsic magnetic field. Luna 3 photographed the Moon's far side, never before seen by Man, and silenced those who said it would be just like the side we could see. Mariner 2 discovered the Solar Wind, disposing forever of the "emptiness" of space, before going on to scan a Venus stranger than anyone had foreseen. Mariner 4 took a strip of photographs across a cratered Mars and removed all notions of a flat, eroded desert, strewn only with sand dunes.

Curiously enough, and for reasons which could stand deeper analysis, most of the new discoveries were presented to the public as bad news. Earth's radiation belts would make manned spaceflight impossible; and if the Moon had no protective magnetic field, the hazard of solar flares would make lunar bases or colonies impossible. The "New Look of Venus" was greeted not as a challenge but as a death-blow. No fish-men! No dinosaurs! No more flights to *that* place! As for Mars – in the opening paragraph of his book, *Search the Solar System*, James Strong wrote: "In the summer of 1965, the United States interplanetary probe, Mariner 4, flew past Mars, and soon after began to radio back photographs of the planetary surface. It is no exaggeration to say that public opinion was dismayed as, frame after frame, the cameras revealed a scene of endless desolation, a cratered ruin . . . and it was idle to pretend that the glamour of space travel had not also diminished".[2] Later in his book, Strong describes the findings of the Mariner 9 Mars orbiter with equal lack of enthusiasm.

With all respect to Strong's technical knowledge in his field, some protest has to be raised. I don't know of any branch of the media in which the Mariner 4 pictures were available "frame after frame" for study. The first, third and middle photos of the sequence were printed in some newspapers, in the blurred versions released before computer enhancement had brought up the details hidden by lack of contrast. Personally, I was thrilled when the first shots revealed that Mars had a true landscape instead of the traditional expanse of dunes. Lunar-type scenery in colour, overlaid with an atmosphere and clouds, with the stars even brighter in daytime than had been imagined . . . now there was a new world to conjure with! I hunted in vain for a full set of the photographs, a demand not met until publication of Richardson's *Mars* months later.[3] As regards signs of life, one had to be more patient – Earth's surface would appear lifeless to Mariner 4's cameras. Mariner 9's revelations made life on Mars seem much more probable, with discoveries totally unexpected on the "old" or "new" Mars. (Hence the title of Chapter 6.) During *that* mission, the photos were not reaching the public through the media at all; yet at a sports day in Hamilton, Lanarkshire, at a display of Mariner 9 pictures supplied by JPL, it took six ASTRA members three full hours to answer questions from 250 members of the "not interested" public.

There is no conspiracy to conceal space research findings from the public, although to the enthusiast it can easily seem that way. But in the higher levels of the media there is sometimes an attitude (which one well-known broadcaster expressed to me in so many words) which goes: "I am not interested in this, therefore no one is interested in this, therefore there shall be no coverage of it"; and takes root at junior levels in the form: "It's absolutely fascinating, but of course nobody *out there* wants to know." These are self-fulfilling prophecies. When the news is put across, sparks fly; ASTRA's sports ground experience is typical. Douglas Arnold, a lecturer giving "space presentations" using films and still photography, reports, "Time and time again I have been asked 'Why haven't we been able to see this material before? We had no idea it existed.' . . . To talk about people being blasé when they have not a chance to see the superb photographic and other images returned to Earth is ludicrous . . . How many people have had the chance of seeing the official NASA mission films on TV . . . ?"[4]

Once upon a time, public antipathy to space was blamed upon horror fiction. If so, reaction to TV and political sensitivity are both greater than generally supposed; but as a child, keenly sensitive to adult disapproval, I was in no doubt that Britain's lack of a space programme stemmed directly from the dramatic success of the Quatermass serials. More recently, we have seen the absurdity of deducing it from, and attributing it to, the fact that not everyone wanted to see every last pebble lifted off the lunar surface. As Robert Robinson witheringly pointed out in the BBC's "Points of View" program, when men are risking their lives to extend the frontiers of knowledge it seems hard to compare their efforts directly, as entertainment, with pop stars and detective stories. Science is not a spectator sport and the fascination of research lies in doing it, or in studying the results. The cancellation of Apollo seems to be the first (and let us hope the last) example of a major decision affecting the future of the human race taken on the basis of TV viewing figures alone.

In reality, I believe, the supposed lack of interest in space rests on lack of knowledge, plus poor presentation of what coverage there has been. The planetary pictures ignored by the press; individual Surveyor frames of the lunar surface (universally described as dull) but not the dramatic mosaics they made up; the first blurred photos on the TV News, but never the enhanced final versions; the photos and films brought back from the Moon and Skylab hardly seen, however much better than live coverage; extended coverage of spacecraft recovery (welcome, but slow), but years since a broadcast stayed with a liftoff long enough to let us know whether the astronauts made it into orbit. Chapters 2 and 4 contain some head-hunting – without naming names, since the broadcast word cannot be called back.

ASTRA's discussion project on the exploration of the Solar System has its origin in an exciting lecture by Ed Buckley late in 1971 on "The Artist's View of the Solar System". Apollo 15 was safely back from Hadley Rille, the first surprises from Mariner 9 were turning up in yellow JPL envelopes and somewhere during the evening the phrase, "the 'new' Solar System", embedded itself in ASTRA's vocabulary as Ed showed a series of contrasting

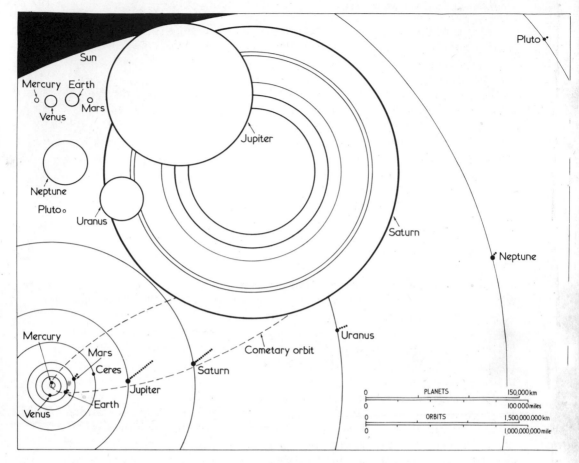

Sun
Mercury   Earth
Venus   Mars
Jupiter
Neptune
Pluto
Uranus
Saturn
Pluto
Neptune
Uranus

Mercury
Mars
Ceres
Venus   Earth   Jupiter   Saturn
Cometary orbit

	PLANETS	
0		150,000 km
0		100,000 miles
	ORBITS	
0		1,500,000,000 km
0		1,000,000,000 mile

[Fig 1]

drawings, emphasizing how different the Moon, Venus and (already) the outer planets were from the traditional artists' impressions. Two years later, Ed produced an outline of a discussion project for ASTRA to take up after completion of our first book, *Man and the Stars*.

As first envisaged, the Interplanetary Project would have led to a book called *Man and the Planets* presenting the "new" Solar System in text and artwork and explaining, by contrast with the old beliefs about the planets, why it was far more interesting and more challenging than even ASTRA had expected. The second main objective was to assess the meaning of the new System for mankind: the resources it had to offer, the potential for human life outside the Earth, and the options presented to space-faring civilization over the next 200 years. Following *Man and the Stars*, which examined the long-term future of interstellar travel and communication, the book would be an obvious step towards a third volume, *Man and the Earth*, which would show the immediate relevance of space technology to human survival.

We had underestimated the scale of the new Solar System, however. While the project was in progress, it had to cope with the quantum jumps suggested for hypothetical planets still further out than Pluto. Here too the possibilities are more complex and far-reaching than one might suppose.

Next in order of mass below the planets come their satellites, individually or in groups, seven of them (including Earth's Moon) large enough to be considered true planets (like Mercury) had they orbited the Sun alone. The lesser members of the System are the asteroids and comets, both reducing to the fragments we call meteoroids: the latter by an evolutionary progress, the former by decreasing order of size. Below them comes the dust cloud of the Zodiacal Light, now known to fill the inner System "like a thick fog" relative to the clarity of interstellar space; lastly (in order of size) the outward-coursing nuclei and elementary particles of the Solar Wind, with dense streams from sunspots and flares, shockwaves around planets, and high-energy belts of trapped particles around Earth and Jupiter. Although it becomes increasingly turbulent with increasing distance from the Sun, the Solar Wind has now been traced by Pioneer 10 to well beyond the orbit of Saturn; and although the Pioneer probes have detected interstellar gases flowing into the Solar System, the definite boundary of the Solar Wind has still to be located. When Jupiter passed between Pioneer 10 and the Sun Solar Wind readings were briefly cut off, indicating that Jupiter's magnetic "tail" maintains a clear zone in the Solar Wind extending to beyond Saturn's orbit; Earth's "tail" may likewise extend for millions of km. Last of all, out beyond the Sun's distant envelope of comets, on out to where the Sun is not distinguished even by brightness from the other stars, extends a vast realm of space which in terms of density might seem purest void; yet, as shown in Chapter 12, it is far from empty.

All but the last two members of the list have been known constituents of the Solar System for more than a century, although the extent of the Zodiacal Light was not suspected until Pioneer 10's flight to Jupiter in 1972–73. But our ideas about all these bodies have been changing radically ever since Explorer 1 discovered Earth's radiation belts (named after Dr James Van Allen) early in 1958. With the completion of the Viking missions, we have reached a good point to take stock. We have extensive data on the Moon, particularly from six manned landings, but no more big surprises are expected until NASA's unmanned satellite is placed in polar orbit to extend the Apollo surveys of the lunar equator. The Soviet Union has landed several probes on Venus, the last two carrying cameras, and placed two probes in Venus orbit; NASA has probed the atmosphere and has an orbiter on station, but they are expected to add to our knowledge rather than revise it as drastically as did Mariners 2 and 10, or Veneras 7–10. Mercury has been photographed three times by Mariner 10, over the same hemi-spere each time, and while the other side may have shocks for us no missions are planned for the next few years. The USA has had three Mars orbiters and two highly successful landers: Soviet missions are not likely to produce sensational results in the next couple of years, unless they can land in terrain quite different from the Viking panoramas. Jupiter and its moons doubtless have many surprises still in store, but these may emerge from the proposed orbiter missions of the 1980s rather than from the Voyager flybys of 1979. Mariner Jupiter–Uranus still lies years in the future,

TABLE I

Planet	Diameter (Equator) km	Mean Distance from Sun km	Number of Moons Known (1979)	Composition
Mercury	4,875	57,896,640	None	Metal core, rocky crust
Venus	12,188	108,181,100	None	Metal core? rocky crust
Earth	12,756	149,566,200	1	Metal core, rocky crust
Mars	6,782	227,893,900	2	Rock/metal crust, small core
Jupiter	142,718	778,297,400	14	Gaseous, mostly hydrogen/helium; possible helium core
Saturn	120,836	1,432,978,000	10	Gaseous; core unknown
Uranus	46,661	2,859,226,000	5	Gaseous; core unknown
Neptune	45,052	4,504,290,000	2	Gaseous; core unknown
Pluto	unknown	5,879,940,000	1	Unknown

NB: During the 1960s and 1970s, space probe missions and radar studies of planets continually refined the accepted values for the distances and diameters of the planets. As a first result, slight but significant differences are found at present between one reference work and another and no one wanting exact figures should take a general work like this as Gospel.

in our knowledge provided by Pioneer 10, Pioneer 11, Skylab, Kohoutek's Comet, Mariner 10, Venera 9, Venera 10, and ultimately Vikings 1 and 2 – not to mention better and better data from NASA's high-altitude flying observatories and increasingly detailed radar mapping of the planets at Arecibo. It was like trying to write an encyclopedia of the ancient world with a Columbus or a Marco Polo reporting home every seven or eight weeks. In the end it became clear that there would have to be two books: *New Worlds for Old*, presenting the new Solar System, and *Man and the Planets* considering it – all of it – as Man's future home. But ASTRA never drops its "sales pitch for the future": in their contributions to *New Worlds for Old*, A. F. Nimmo and A. T. Lawton offer some deliberately provocative speculation on the nearest and most distant resources available to mankind.

First we have to map out the territory which has come to seem so new and strange. There is no easy way to express the vastness of the Solar System on a single sheet of paper; fig. 1 shows, by visual grouping, the relationships between the known bodies which make up that great moving array. But for our purposes the Solar System is defined as the volume of space within which matter is subject to the gravitational pull of the Sun, and, A. T. Lawton shows in Chapter 12, that volume is spectacularly larger than casual assumptions would suggest. Its primary occupants are the planets, in order outwards Mercury, Venus, Earth, Mars, Jupiter, Saturn, Uranus, Neptune and Pluto. The name "Vulcan" has been reserved for over a century for a planet nearer to the Sun than is Mercury, should one be found; more recently the names "Poseidon" and "Persephone" have been difficulties of releasing lander payloads on approach to the planet rather than from orbit, but even with Viking there were multiple risks: any medium-sized boulder could smash the spacecraft and both landing sites had plenty of such hazards, despite the attempt to land Viking 2 on sand. Had the spacecraft landed on permafrost, which may be common on Mars, the heat generated by its radioactive-isotope power source would have caused it to sink; if it landed on rock, its scoop could not pick up soil samples for analysis. Luckily both spacecraft landed on firm soil, but Viking 2 came down with one foot on a rock and ended up with a pronounced tilt. Most telling of all, however, was the first comment from a geologist after the thrill of the Viking 1 panorama died down a little: "I want to know what's over that horizon . . ."

Mention of the Viking scoop raises the question of the quality of results. Viking's hydrazine fuel had to be subjected to extra processing before the mission to protect any life nearby from one of its normal by-products – cyanide! With that problem solved, it remained possible that Martian micro-organisms existed just below the surface, protected by a thin cover of soil, and died of exposure to solar ultraviolet radiation in the time between the disturbance of the landing and the first taking of samples. Alternatively Martian life might be a feather-light coating on the surface and itself be blown away.

With unmanned soft-landers, the problem of surface contamination is almost inescapable, and the samples obtained are virtually taken at random. The Luna probes have returned only grams of material, from within reach of their drills, contaminated at least on the surface by rocket exhausts, as compared with the hundreds of kg returned by the Apollo astronauts – almost every sample documented, photographed *in situ* with a colour chart and gnomon, and with the site photographed again after removal. Above all, they were intelligently selected from "geological stations" spread out for kilometres around the touchdown sites. Yet an astronomy student who visited ASTRA declared, with supreme confidence, "You can't deny that the scientific results from Luna and Lunokhod are far superior to those from Apollo." The resulting storm of protest may partly explain why he didn't come back. Lunokhod has mobility, true: but the total terrain covered by Lunokhod 1 is comparable with that covered on foot by the Apollo 14 astronauts, dragging a cart. For it to do even that tied up a team of five controllers for months, as Lunokhod crawled about the surface – partly because the controllers had to have time to avoid hazards, despite the three-second timelag on signals to and from the Earth, but mostly because the TV "eyes" were so near the ground. The Moon is a small world (even for a standing man, the horizon is only 3km away) and Lunokhod's horizon was very close. Although the limitation was obvious – e.g., from pictures of the return to the parent vehicle – it seems to pass without comment. Lunokhod could pass within metres of a potentially important find, like Apollo 17's "orange soil", without being aware of it; a sample like the "Genesis rock", which had fallen by chance on a large boulder, would probably be out of sight as well as out of reach. Lastly, it's worth noting that the colour band of Cernan and Schmitt's orange soil was too narrow for the Lunar Rover's TV system : had the Rover been an unmanned vehicle like Lunokhod, the deposit would probably have passed unnoticed. The human eye and the discriminating brain are still an unbeatable combination : Gordon Cooper's observations in Earth orbit were so detailed that Mission Control thought he might be hallucinating, and, although the Moon had been surveyed by unmanned Lunar Orbiters, it was Al Worden, in the Apollo 15 Command Module, who picked out the apparent evidence of volcanism which took Apollo 17 to Taurus-Littrow.

When Brian Aldiss wrote his classic short story, "Who Can Replace a Man?"[6] he was thinking of decision-taking capability. There are plans in both USA and USSR for "Mars Rovers" which would negotiate obstacles like mechanical mice in a maze;[7] the US versions may have "hands". But such complexity requires major developments in computer technology, and difficult problems would still have to be relayed to Earth. On a Viking-type mission, such a situation would immobilize the rover for 40 minutes; on one of the moons of Saturn, the delay would be fully two hours. And unless communications relays are used, as James Strong suggests,[2] then the further Earth moves from the Sun in the sky, the shorter will be the useful working day . . .

James Campbell suggested at ASTRA that decision-taking computers may look much more effective after, say, twenty years of designing computers to work in high vacuum. Nevertheless, picture a machine capable of running the Apollo 17 mission and one hears echoes of that sad voice from *2001*: "Some of my decisions haven't been too good lately . . ." The problem of brawn still remains. John W. Campbell pointed out some years ago that, in any attempt to build a manlike machine, the materials used must be compromises between performance and weight.[8] To have the strength and the resilience of bone and muscle, the components must be either very light (therefore fragile) or heavy (therefore vulnerable to falls, etc.) and, no matter what they are made of, they won't repair themselves however long they rest. Another part of the machine, or another machine altogether, must put Humpty together again.

Consider the requirements for a machine to match the performance of the Apollo astronauts on the Moon. It must have one set of eyes near the ground to guide its feet, and another about 2m in the air. For stability, no doubt it will be squat : but the stalk for the upper eyes must be flexible enough to withstand starting and stopping, yet rigid enough not to sway when travelling at speed. The whole unit must be able to get near enough to samples to study them and pick them up, yet still be stable with a 2m stalk; it must be able to keep its balance on a slope, right itself after a tumble, and clean itself of dust (a recurring problem with Lunar Rover). It must be able to range about for kilometres without having to stay in line-of-sight of the parent vehicle. If it breaks a mudguard, it must be able (without instructions) to mend itself with maps and sticky tape . . . How cheap and lightweight is it *now*, compared to a man and his life-support equipment?

Next consider deploying an emergency parasol and freeing a trapped solar sail, as in the Skylab repair job . . .

To sum up, the supposed superiority of the Soviet missions lies only in the attitude that anything done by a machine must be more effective than anything done by a man. It is the superiority of the first Orbiting Astronomical Observatory, a total loss which could have been fixed by any repairman with a spanner. NASA's remote-control experts have done wonderful things, like bringing the SERT 2 ion-drive experiment back to life after several years out of action, but there is no substitute for that final Apollo instruction, "If all else fails, apply space boot." (When BBC commentators were calling Lunokhod "a slap in the face to America's whole Apollo programme", there was a joke going around ASTRA that Scott and Irwin would be retargeted to Mare Imbrium because the Soviets had requested a wheel-change.) Vikings 1 and 2 both had their sample arms coaxed back into action after jamming, but the Viking 1 seismometer remained stolidly out of the game. There was no cross-check for the curious lack of seismic activity reported by Viking 2. Q.E.D.

The attitude, "Where possible we should send a machine instead of a man", is some way down the line from the one attacked in *Man and the Stars* – "Interstellar communication by radio is philosophically more satisfying than physical space travel" – but its end-point is the same. Both propositions stand near the head of a line of argument which concludes: "It is better to lie than to sit, better to die than to live, and best of all is not to be born at all." It stems from fear of meeting the unknown, fear of risk, fear of struggle. In the last analysis, from the viewpoint of the human race, it is anti-survival – and there, until *Man and the Planets*, we rest our case.

Despite all protests, therefore, ASTRA supports NASA in its current order of priorities. Visiting Cape Canaveral for the last Apollo mission, the Apollo–Soyuz rendezvous, was worth it just to meet so many people who shared that view. The future of mankind lies with Man in Space, and NASA has had to sacrifice almost everything to keep that initiative alive. ASTRA hardly groaned as the Grand Tour probes were dropped, taking out the great objective of a mission to every planet in the 1970s and the Self Testing and Repair computer, a new generation of electronic wizardry. We stood firm, bleeding only slightly, as Mariner 9 ran out of fuel unnecessarily for a saving of $30,000,[9] and Mariner 10 and Viking 1 results were lost for lack of tracking facilities.[10, 11] We said little, although boiling inwardly, as the last two Moon landings were cancelled for savings smaller than the cost of the B–52s lost in the Christmas bombing of Hanoi. We practised smiling sadly as lack of funds forced out the "Wet" space laboratories, the 1986 Mars landing, the Nuclear Shuttle (and with it the lunar space station and lunar base), the Space Tug (and with it all 1980s Moon landings), Saturn V itself (and with it the permanent Space Station), and even the second Skylab was relegated to the Smithsonian Air and Space Museum. We were able to take those losses because the projects were based on early 1960s technology and there are better things to come. But the unkindest cut of all, from the NASA viewpoint, must have been the sacrifice of 300,000 skilled employees in the Space Agency and supporting industries.[12] Even the launch crew who put the Apollo–Soyuz mission into orbit were fired *the same day*, to save every possible dollar. Yet the space-program workers blame the government, not the program's priorities: contacted about possible work on the Space Shuttle, 80% of the personnel laid off by North American Rockwell's Space Division said they would like to rejoin the company.[13] When ASTRA members were given a private tour of the Kennedy Space Centre, two days after the Apollo–Soyuz liftoff, work was already beginning in the *other* control room. The sign on the door said: "Firing Control Room, Space Shuttle Operations. Target Launch Date, July 1979."

The Space Shuttle is far more than a toehold maintained on the skills of manned spaceflight. As first envisaged, it was to have been a two-stage vehicle with each stage winged, manned, and fully reusable. Now it will ride into space on a huge expendable fuel tank, flanked by two solid-fuel boosters which can be refurbished and reused a fair number of times if recovered successfully from the Atlantic (fig. 2). Its flexibility has been reduced in other ways: it can no longer fly around the USA on its own jet engines, but must ride piggy-back on a Boeing 747. But the Shuttle Orbiter is still essentially what it was: a winged vehicle, carrying up to 29 tonnes of cargo, capable of carrying up to seven people into Earth orbit. Each vehicle will be able to fly up to 500 missions and at least one Shuttle launch can be expected every fortnight throughout the 1980s. The Shuttle

[Fig 2]

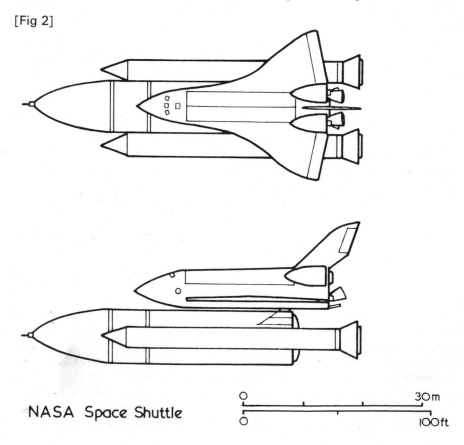

NASA Space Shuttle

is the first of a generation of spacecraft which will make the throwaway boosters we are used to seem as wasteful as scuttling ocean liners after every voyage.

Shuttle operations will concentrate, for obvious reasons, on studies directly beneficial to Earthbound humanity. The European Spacelab, the research module which will ride in the cargo bay on many missions, will be extensively used for research into manufacturing in space, orbital surveys of Earth's resources, developments in weather, communications and navigational satellites, medical studies, and in general setting space technology to work actively for mankind instead of by casual "spin-off". On the pure research side, NASA and the European Space Agency are developing Space Telescope, a Shuttle-launched instrument which will be of tremendous value to deep-space and planetary astronomy. Even a 36cm-diameter telescope in space would show more planetary detail than any telescope on Earth,[14] and Space Telescope designs go up to 240cm.[15]

But the development of the Shuttle has a more subtle aspect, of which its allies are very well aware. Artificial satellites are already big business: in 1976, 15 out of 19 NASA launches were for "cash customers" – other nations, other government agencies, and commercial firms.[16] There were also a significant number of military launches. All that business will now be coming to the Shuttle, and will mean the phasing out of all expendable boosters except the low-cost, low-payload Scout. Goodbye to Titan III, farewell Atlas, farewell Thor (you served us well, baby). Most of Kennedy Space Centre will go back to the wildlife reserve and the action will be concentrated on the Vehicle Assembly Building, the Crawlerway, Pads 39A and B – and the only new element, the Space Shuttle runway, where for the first time in the history of the Cape the Big Birds will come back, to fly once more.

Originally there was to have been a manned Space Tug, to take payloads out from close-Earth orbit to more distant ones, especially to the "stationary" 24-hours' orbit 35,000km out. Now that job will have to be done by expendable upper stages, so we may not have heard the last of Agena, Delta and the others which have been mated so successfully to Atlas and Thor in the past. Certainly we have not heard the last of Centaur, the liquid oxygen/liquid hydrogen upper stage which, with the help of Atlas, sent off the Mariners and Pioneers to capture "the new look of the Solar System" for us. If there are to be any scientific missions to the planets in the 1980s, they will be taken up into orbit by Shuttle and taken out by Centaur from there. Their payloads will be bigger than Atlas–Centaur or even Titan III could lift, and this opens up a dizzying range of possibilities: Mars rover, Mars sample return, Phobos or Deimos sample return, Venus orbiter, Venus radar mapper, Venus atmosphere "buoyant station", Venus lander, Mercury orbiter, Mariner Jupiter orbiter, another Pioneer–Jupiter, Ganymede orbiter/lander, Mariner Saturn orbiter, Pioneer Saturn–Uranus, Mariner Uranus–Neptune, asteroid rendezvous, Comet Encke flyby, Comet Encke rendezvous, Comet Halley flyby. All these are missions which *could* be launched, using Shuttle, by 1990.[17]

How many of them we will get, bearing in mind that NASA doesn't yet have funds for the Mariner Jupiter–Uranus mission in 1981, remains to be seen. But one colossal victory is now within NASA's grasp: to continue their activities in space, the military, commercial and scientific worlds of the West will have to accept that manned Shuttles will take their payloads up there, and men will dispatch them, refurbish them or bring them back where appropriate. The situation is likely to be permanent because the balance of terror between East and West is now maintained by solid-fuelled missiles (Polaris, Poseidon and Minuteman) with virtually no application to space missions and none whatever to interplanetary exploration. If the instruments of terror alter, it will probably be towards sea power and air-breathing missiles and away from rockets altogether. There seems no chance of another development race with liquid-fuelled missiles, like the one which put Thor, Atlas and Titan (and before them Jupiter and Redstone) at the disposal of the scientific and commercial communities. The Space Shuttle gives men and women a permanent role in Earth orbit, and in energy terms, in the words of Robert A. Heinlein, if you can get into Earth orbit you are half way to anywhere.[18]

2 How We Got Here

The last and greatest frontier of them all lies just 17 miles from your front door – straight up.

Aerospace scientist, late 1950s

Early in January 1969, when our heads were ringing with the return of Apollo 8 from the Moon, a friend and I repaired to the Full Moon in Taunton, Somerset. We had resolved, by way of rehearsal for the Moon landing, to drink to every historical figure who deserved some credit for the achievement. (John had the history of astronomy at his fingertips, and at that time I could name every astronaut and cosmonaut who had flown in space.) A crowd soon gathered to watch these two mad men knocking back a succession of toasts, each more bizarre than the last – "Zeno, for the paradox" for example (a digression, admittedly, but irresistible – we had already drunk to the *other* Xeno.)

The project went well enough, up to about the Renaissance. By then it was clear that the roll of honour was going to turn into a race with closing time. In fact, we did reach "Lovell, Borman and Anders!" as "time" was called for the last time, but it was done only by bracketing the astronautical toasts into larger and larger groups: Tsiolkovsky, Oberth and Goddard were taken together, all German experimenters except Max Valier likewise, Project Mercury and Project Gemini were taken in two swallows, and apart from the Apollo 8 team themselves, the only astronauts named were Grissom, White and Chaffee, the victims of the Apollo 204 fire, and Komarov, killed in Soyuz 1.

For whatever reasons, this sequence closely parallels the average chapter or TV program covering the history of space flight. Nine times out of ten, the viewer gets an exposition of the intellectual stepladder from the Earth-centred Ptolemaic conception of the Universe, up rung by rung with Copernicus, Tycho Brahe, Kepler, Galileo, Newton, Herschel and Hubble to present-day appreciation of the vastness of the cosmos, followed by that much-used film of the Saturn V staging and a voice off saying: ". . . and now, Man has landed on the Moon!" If the history of space flight *alone* is more rigidly adhered to, it tends to begin with Lucian of Samos in 45AD, and proceed steadily *via* Domingo Gonzales and his swans, Cyrano de Bergerac and his bottles of dew, Jules Verne's space-gun and H. G. Wells' Cavorite, followed by the enunciation of the true theory of astronautics by Tsiolkovsky, duplicated and applied by Oberth and Goddard. That leaves time for a slide of the V2, a clip of Gagarin and Kruschev waving in Red

Square, and back to the Saturn V staging just in time for the signature tune.

The object is not to denigrate the pioneers of astronomy and astronautics, nor to mock the writers and broadcasters who've listed them. But the story has been told so often that no reader should have trouble seeking it out.

The approach of this chapter, by contrast, is to present a short history of the *idea* of space travel, mainly in terms of visual images – necessarily a short history, because there couldn't be an evolving image of space flight until there were real "space rockets" to build it around.

It has been said that "the biggest trouble with the space age is that prophesy gets to be history before it becomes current fact". The process can be disorienting : I sometimes find myself wondering what on Earth happened to the spaceships I dreamed of in my childhood. The process of change can be traced clearly through the files of the *Daily Express*, following the *Jeff Hawke* strip which disappeared in 1974 after 21 entertaining years (it was briefly reborn in the *Scottish Daily News*). In the early stories multi-engined boosters push graceful winged rockets into orbit, or rendezvous with chemically fuelled deep-space ships with clustered fuel tanks and spherical cabins. As the 1960s progress, the spacecraft become capsules, the boosters cylindrical with fewer, bigger engines; the deep-space vessels lose their big tanks and acquire nuclear engines, moving the cabins for'ard on long booms and sprouting heat-radiating panels. In the early 1970s, the ferry rockets become lifting bodies, and in the last *Daily Express* story the Space Shuttle makes its appearance (and crashes, *absit omen*). Only the wheel-type space station remains constant throughout.*

The first clear set of space-travel images evolved in the early '50s. There had been a pioneering study of a solid-fuelled Moon rocket by the British Interplanetary Society before World War Two, but that failed completely to establish itself as a symbol of "space travel". After the war, the situation was very different. Paintings and drawings illustrating space travel were appearing on both sides of the Atlantic, culminating in the near-simultaneous appearance of two outstanding books : *The Conquest of Space* by Willy Ley, with paintings by Chesley Bonestell,[1] and *The Exploration of Space* by Arthur C. Clarke, artwork by R. A. Smith.[2]

Smith's work featured astronautical concepts worked out with H. E. Ross; a fuller set appeared in *Space Travel* by Gatland and Kunesch in 1952,[3] and in 1954 an entire book was devoted to them.[4] Meantime, in the USA, Ley and Bonestell were participating in major symposia, organized by *Collier's Magazine*, on the space station[5] and on flight to the Moon,[6] evolving images which became fixed in the public mind for many years.

I've already remarked that before Sputnik 1 it was tough being a child interested in space travel. But the situation held some elements of magic which the modern generation can't possibly share. The hardware which

---

*The evolution of the aircraft in the strip would make an equally fascinating study. Around 1956, Hawke flies the first Vickers Valiant to Australia; ten years or so later, "I was talking to an old codger the other day who once flew a *Vulcan* . . ."

[Fig 3]

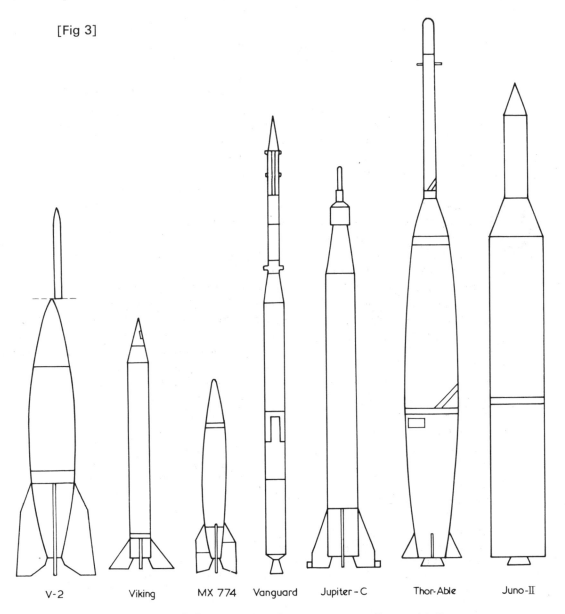

| V-2 | Viking | MX 774 | Vanguard | Jupiter-C | Thor-Able | Juno-II |

had given shape and form to the abstract concept "spaceship" was associated with two place-names I never hear, even now, without a jolt of excitement: White Sands Proving Ground, New Mexico, and Edwards Air Force Base, Mojave Desert, California.

At the end of the war, Western experts who fully appreciated the potential of the long-range rocket as a weapon engaged in a mighty effort to snatch as much German hardware and expertise as possible from areas soon to fall under Soviet control. In this they were helped considerably by the desire of the scientific brains behind the V2 *not* to disappear behind the Iron Curtain. (Folklore persistently applies the name "Operation Paperclip" to the operation, although the original name was "Overcast".[7]) A large number of V2s and other rockets were delivered to the USA, along with their creators, and divided up between the three armed services for evaluation and further development.

Initially, all three operations were centred at White Sands. In the early days conditions were primitive and a highly idiosyncratic attitude developed, compounded of toughness and total dedication to the rockets. J. Gordon Vaeth recalls personnel scattering under a falling V2/WAC Corporal "Bumper" (fig. 3), none of them really knowing where to run.[8] When a heavily armoured blockhouse was provided, much closer to the launch point than today's control centres, it was still common practice for personnel to rush outside to watch as soon as the rocket cleared the pad. The practice was ended after workers on the MX–774 had to rush back in, because it was falling on top of them.[9] At the South Uist rocket range, back in 1958, I was told by a British army officer that, in the development of the Firestone Corporal at White Sands, the impact point of each missile had been pinpointed by observers *sitting on the target*.

A more serious problem in the early days was the lack of means to *stop* a missile, after it was clear of the launch pad. In 1947 the problem came to a head when a V2 crossed the border into Mexico and fell in the cemetery of Juaraz.[10] Fortunately a fiesta was in progress, with fireworks, and local complaints were moderate. Nevertheless, a radio command receiver was devised to shut off the fuel of erring rockets, and the fateful word "cut-off" ended many a record bid thereafter. (More recently, the command has been replaced by the Range Safety Officer's still more chilling "destruct", since at Kennedy Space Centre and Vandenburg explosives are used to stop misbehaving rockets.*)

The first major advance undertaken using the V2 was the US Army's "Project Bumper", the first US two-stage rocket. In the fifth shot of the series, the WAC Corporal upper stage reached an altitude of 400km, in February 1949;[13] from 1950 firings in the series were made from Patrick Air Force Base, Cape Canaveral, for maximum horizontal range.[14] (Bumpers 7 and 8 were the first firings from the site, which wasn't to become well known to the public until the artificial satellite programme of the International Geophysical Year.)

Perhaps the most difficult thing to imagine, for today's space-mad kids, is not the isolation of being interested in space before 1957, but how *slowly* everything moved at that time. When space first caught my attention at the age of seven, the Bumper altitude record was already more than three years old and it was to stand unbroken for four more years; the single-stage record of 250km, set by Viking 11 in 1954, was to stand for even longer.† V2, Bumper and Viking, being relatively free from security restrictions on photographs, were the dominant images of space research in book and magazine illustrations for fully eight years. When the altitude record *was*

---

*This did not prevent the disappearance of a Snark pilotless bomber into the Brazilian jungle[11] or the killing of a Cuban cow (later buried with full state honours) by Transit 3–A.[12]

†Reference 14 gives 158 miles (253km) as a single-stage altitude record established by an Aerobee-Hi, but Aerobee-Hi was a two-stage sounding rocket.

broken in 1956, by a Jupiter–C nosecone which reached 640km at the peak of its trajectory, nobody knew exactly what it looked like, and besides, there was much more interest in the horizontal distance covered, 4,800km. (Although Jupiter–C was a research rocket, the coming era of the ICBM – Intercontinental Ballistic Missile – was all too clearly visible.) A vertical launch to 1,080km[14] attracted still less attention, until there was a sudden need after Sputnik 1 to show that the USA was doing *something* in space.

From the V2 and Project Bumper, the US Army line of development produced the Redstone missile and Jupiter–C research vehicle, of which Redstone was the first stage. These developments were out of the public eye and attention focussed entirely on Viking, the US Navy's research project. There were two models of Viking, seven of each being launched, and the second configuration represented space research to a whole generation. The major design advance, pioneered by the Air Force MX–774 and in Viking, was the gimballed rocket motor, gyroscopically controlled, for steering and attitude control. Although it gave tremendous trouble in the early stages this development became a standard feature of liquid-fuelled rockets, replacing the graphite vanes in the exhaust by which the V2 and Redstone were guided. However, R. A. Smith had shown rockets with exhaust vanes in his paintings[4] and the image continued to appear in artwork and science fiction. (To refer to *Jeff Hawke* again, there was a story in which Hawke had to go out of his ship in dangerous circumstances to free a jammed vane.)

The Viking Rocket Story was excitingly told from first hand by Milton W. Rosen.[15] It contains a step-by-step history of developments which now seem commonplace, to the extent that no US astronaut and no known cosmonaut has yet been killed by a launch vehicle; yet twenty years ago practical engineers were reacting with horror to the idea of clustering Viking engines, much less putting human beings on top of them.[16] The Viking development was certainly packed with incident – Viking 4 was launched at *sea*, from the USS *Norton Sound*.* Viking 6 lost its fins in flight and "performed violent manoeuvres"; Viking 8 ripped itself out of the stand on a static firing and made a two-minute unscheduled flight ending with an unpredictable bang. Viking 9 was the first successful flight of the new airframe; Viking 10 was something else again.

It has to be explained that Viking was built like a V2, in the sense that it was rigid in all axes. Modern rockets are built to withstand considerably narrower ranges of stress: I once saw a film of an Atlas looping the loop (as Viking 6 did), and the lecturer explained that the disaster showed the structure was still too heavy – since rockets aren't meant to do aerobatics, there's no reason for them to be stressed to withstand them. The Russian launch vehicles are still solid, by the way; Western experts watched in amazement as one was hoisted sideways into position at the Paris Air Show by a cable attached at only two points, guided by a man standing between

---

*The trick had been done with a V2, off the USS *Midway*, and the Peenemunde team had proposed to launch V2s *underwater* during the War, but never tried it.[17] As far as I know it's never been done since with a liquid-fuelled rocket, at least not in the West.

them! Atlas, Titan and Saturn all require internal pressure bracing just to stand upright under their own weight, and they're just not stressed to be swung about like that under a crane. Viking wasn't in that category: it was even moved about by a 'Barr cart', consisting of a nose-wheel and two wheels attached to fins.

Viking 10 was set up for static firing, successfully, only to have the motor explode at the launch attempt. Automated hoses on the pad quenched the main fire, but one small flame wasn't covered – alcohol was bleeding from the propellant tank onto the hot tail assembly. Unable to resist the temptation, the personnel left the blockhouse and put out the flame by hand. (By modern standards, the blockhouse was only a stone's throw from the launch pad.) However, alcohol continued to drain from the tank and a vacuum formed in the upper half. If air pressure crushed it, the propellant would cascade into the hot tail section and the whole issue would blow to pieces. In *The Viking Rocket Story* there is actually a photograph of three men discussing this on the pad with the caption, "Look at that tank – the *bottom* is starting to dimple." (My italics.) So, of course, they shot a hole in it to let the air in.

Before the Viking program, there had been three White Sands firings of the Air Force MX–774, which became the prototype of the Atlas. Unlike Viking, it was held together by internal pressure bracing, but nevertheless the first one survived a (less violent) explosion on the pad. There was then a threat that mounting pressure in the liquid oxygen tank would split the rocket, exactly the opposite of the Viking problem, and a Navy guard offered to shoot a hole in the rocket.[9] I have always wondered if those two incidents were connected. When the problem recurred in a later test, owing to the valve's freezing shut, the Test Conductor climbed up the rocket and pounded on the valve until it opened. (Neither program had a monopoly of toughness, dedication or insanity.)

The manned rocket flight program at Edwards Air Force Base was scarcely dull, meantime. The Air Force Bell X–1 team (fig. 4) had moved out to Edwards in 1946, to begin a program of rocket takeoffs, air-launches from the bomb-bay of a modified B–29, and "dead-stick" landings on the kilometres of dry lake bed around Edwards. The same air-launch technique was used with all subsequent rocket aircraft: three X–1s, X–1A, B, D and E (the latter a rebuilt X–1); the Douglas Skyrocket, and the Bell X–2 (fig. 5). In later tests an uprated B–29, the B–50, was the "mother ship".

1 and 2: The new look of the Moon. *Above,* before the Apollo landings it was supposed that lunar mountains were steep and jagged, that rilles and chasms were sheer and sharp-edged, that even the smallest craters had sharp, raised rims, and that bright stars filled the sky. But in reality *(below)* lunar outlines are soft, and no stars are visible in sunlight. This painting shows the Apollo 15 crew at Hadley Rille. Note the striations on the mountains in the background. *(Paintings by Ed Buckley.)*

[Fig 4]

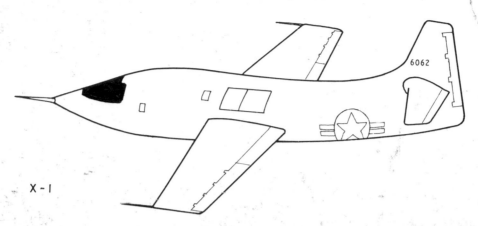

X - 1

Probably no single image of that era means "space research" more vividly than the burst of light in the pilot's eyes as the rocket aircraft slid backwards out of the bomber; the plume from the liquid oxygen tank cutting off; the rocket chambers firing; and the experimental ship coming suddenly to life, pushing forward under the bomber, then tipping the nose up and climbing towards the fringe of space. The X–15, the ultimate vehicle of that program, performed the same manoeuvres except that the pilot had a far lonelier ride, isolated under the wing of a B–52, and couldn't jump clear as Everest did when the X–1D exploded and was jettisoned from the bomb-bay of a B–50.[18] (On the other hand, the X–15 pilot could eject at any time if trouble developed: the X–1 had no escape system of any kind, and more than once the pilot had to jettison the rocket propellant and oxidant, before gliding home.)

On the first X–1 powered flight, in August 1947, Captain 'Chuck' Yeager rolled the aircraft, dived with the engine off and climbed again under power, exceeding the permitted g–pull for that stage of the program.[19] In October he took the X–1 through the Sound Barrier, the first time Mach 1 had been exceeded, with two broken ribs which he had concealed from the flight doctors. (In his novel *Fallen Star*, wanting to indicate that a prototype is particularly unsafe, James Blish has a character say: "Chuck Yeager wouldn't fly that 'plane.") Scott Crossfield later flew the X–1 with three broken ribs, but he had an elevator to get him from the bomb-bay to the door in the side of the X–1 cockpit, whereas Yeager had to climb down a ladder into the slipstream.[16]

3 and 4: The old Mars and the old Venus. "Mars Expedition over Deimos" *(above)*, painting dating from 1964, shows the "old" Mars as flat and smooth, the moons as light-coloured (Phobos is in transit across the planet). *Below,* the one-time popular conception of Venus as a world of swamps, roamed by monsters akin to Earth's prehistoric reptiles. *(Paintings by Ed Buckley.)*

The history of the rocket aircraft is a succession of aborted flights, interspersed with explosions and fires before drop, in flight and on the ground.
Accidental drops sometimes occurred, as when a Naval pilot decided to
abort and said: "Secure the drop." Unfortunately the Air Force bomber
crew thought this meant he was ready to go, so out he went – another case
of jettisoned propellant and a long glide to the dry lake. Abandoned missions
occurred most commonly because the multi-chambered rocket engines would
lose pressure somewhere in the plumbing, usually after hours of preparation
and a tedious climb to the bomber's maximum altitude. In the classic case,
the first air launch of the Douglas Skyrocket, a communications problem
kept the B–29 pilot from hearing Bridgeman's order to abort the mission.
Hastily switching everything back on, Bridgeman was launched with a
shout of: "Don't drop me, George . . ." After a brief internal debate, he
decided to fire the ailing rocket engine, and got an ignition six full seconds
later. Climbing past the B–29, he remarked, "Goddam it, George, I *told*
you not to drop me."

"You got keen friends, Bridgeman," the chase aircraft remarked.[20]

Another aspect of the rocket flights, not emphasized to the public, was
that the aircraft were attaining heights and speeds for which the designers
of the time could not adequately prepare them. Stability problems beset all
the programs: Bridgeman spun the Skyrocket for over 2,000m, and later
encountered nightmarish roll problems in the all-rocket version of the
aircraft. Yeager, flying the X–1A, broke the cockpit canopy with his head
during a "tumble" from which it took over 15,500m to recover. And
finally Mel Apt, only seconds after becoming the first man to reach Mach 3,
lost control of the X–2 and tried to escape by blowing off the nose of the
aircraft. Years before, when Bridgeman was introduced to a similar escape
system in the Skyrocket, he was told: "So far, nobody's tried it." The
system did not work for Apt, and several documentaries since have included
the harrowing cockpit film of the pilot being thrown about, with the Sun

[Fig 5]

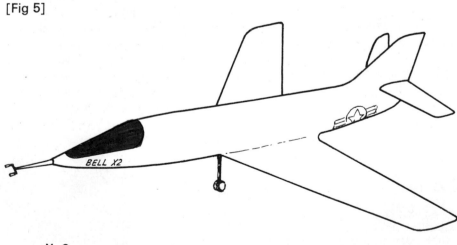

BELL X2

X–2

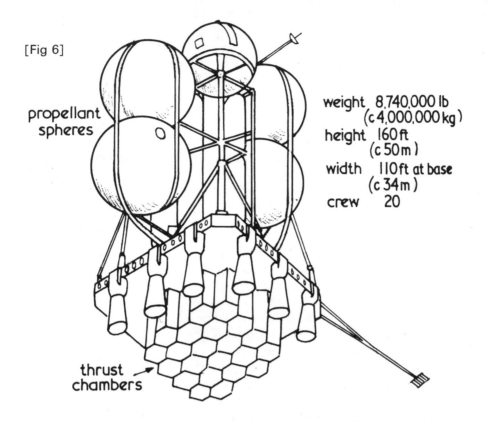

[Fig 6]

propellant
spheres

weight 8,740,000 lb
        (c 4,000,000 kg)
height 160 ft
        (c 50 m)
width   110 ft at base
        (c 34 m)
crew   20

thrust
chambers

Von Braun Moonship (c 1953)

flashing in and out of the spinning capsule, all the way to the ground. This was the only death of a rocket pilot in one of the early ships, although Ziegler had been killed beside an X–2 which exploded in its B–50 bomb bay. As a curious kind of tribute, Hollywood produced a film called *Brink of Hell*, using stock shots from the X–2 program, in which the characters corresponding to the two X–2 victims were allowed to survive their respective accidents.

Based on the work at Edwards and White Sands, it was possible for writers and artists to build up a set of futuristic images and sell them as propaganda for a US space programme. Arthur C. Clarke has written of this process: "In the early 1950s, more and more attention began to be focussed on artificial satellites, and the useful abbreviation ESV (Earth Satellite Vehicle) came into general use. The advocates of ESVs fell into two distinct camps; one contained Dr Wernher von Braun, while the other contained practically everyone else. This was not quite so unequal a division as it might seem at first sight, and with the assistance of *Collier's Magazine* Dr von Braun was able to make a large fraction of the United States extremely satellite-conscious in early 1952 . . ."[11]

The means was the project already mentioned, "Across the Space Frontier".[5] The target set and discussed by that symposium was the creation of a wheel-type space station, 250ft (76.2m) across, at an altitude of 1,075 miles (1,720km). (At the time, the existence of the Van Allen radiation belts was unknown.) The project envolved three-stage launch vehicles, weighing

7,000 tons at launch, with 51 engines in the first stage. The wheel-type station, with its double-skin "meteor bumper" and mercury boiler trough around the upper rim, was a standard feature of space art for years thereafter. The second *Collier's* symposium, a year later, considered a three-ship expedition to reach the Moon from the space station, and again set the standard image of the Moon-rocket for years to come (fig. 6).[6]

The historical ironies of what followed seem like pure science fiction, of the early Heinlein era, but more elaborate than anything in "The Man Who Sold the Moon". Jonathon Norton Leonard was one of the few commentators to note than von Braun was deeply tied up with the US Army Redstone Arsenal at Huntsville, Alabama, and for security reasons couldn't be talking about the current state of US rocket development.[10] The true facts were that the Redstone missile was about to enter service with US forces, and the engines developed by Rocketdyne for the Air Force Navaho project, applied in Redstone,[21] were already being modified for the Army's Jupiter IRBM (Intermediate Range Ballistic Missile).[22] In short, von Braun knew that the USA already had the technical capability to orbit satellites, launch moonprobes and, with further development, put a man on the Moon – all that was lacking was public interest, and that was generated by the *Collier's* symposia.

Criticism and debate all served the purpose, and rocket experts took the bait without hesitation. L. R. Shepherd and A. V. Cleaver of the British Interplanetary Society publicly attacked the deliberately over-optimistic parts of the space station project.[23] Dr Rosen of the Viking project was equally appalled,[10] as well he might be : the Moon rockets used engines of 13,800kg thrust, not too great an uprating of the 10-ton Viking motor output, but they were to be clustered in groups of thirty. The first-stage launcher motors had 279,400kg thrust *each*, and there were 51 in all ! (In 1950 the National Advisory Committee for Aeronautics sat, hard, for fear of ridicule, on a proposal to launch a modified X–2 on a booster with *five* Viking engines.[16] 1952 was the year of the Viking 8 breakaway, and two years prior to the Viking 10 explosion.)

But the first effect of the argument was to increase official confidence in the Viking system. By 1956, von Braun had the ability to launch artificial satellites with Redstone, using solid-fuel upper stages (Project Orbiter).[11] Instead the official go-ahead was given to the Navy, to develop Viking into a satellite launcher (Vanguard) for the International Geophysical Year. (Vikings 13 and 14 were fired from Cape Canaveral, carrying Vanguard upper stages.)[11, 13] The reasoning was that Viking had been a pure research vehicle, whereas Redstone was a weapon of war : researching Project Vanguard for *The Making of a Moon*, Arthur C. Clarke was repeatedly told, "*Don't* call it a missile, it's a vehicle."

The Russians had no such qualms. They had no intention of revealing their launch vehicle in any case, because it was the T–1 IRBM, initially developed from the V2s they had captured along with German engineers (rather than scientists) after the war. But those engineers had been returned to the West, after years of isolation from the Russian space effort to prevent the West's learning much from their experiences.[24] As a result, the Russians were able to keep Western experts guessing for many years about the rapid upward leaps, from one mission to the next, in the capability of the Soviet launch vehicles.

The answer was in fact revealed in a book called *Sputnik into Space*, which came into English *via* Italian.[25] It showed a design for a "freighter rocket to transport material to the space station", which produced hearty laughs because it was a crude modification of a colour plate from *Across the Space Frontier*. It wasn't until the Vostok launcher was revealed at the Paris Air Show, ten years later, that Western experts learned that the USSR had actually developed reliable, low-thrust motors clustered in large numbers (32, counting steering motors, in the Vostok first stage) instead of uprating their motors to the huge thrusts being mastered in the West. Still more blatantly, two stamps issued by Czechoslovakia in 1961 showed the Soviet launcher configuration quite accurately, but among so many stylized and imaginary designs they passed unnoticed.

These were minor jokes, however, compared with the master-stroke of 4 October 1957, when Sputnik 1 went into orbit weighing about ten times as much as the biggest Vanguard planned. The timing was impeccable: marking the anniversary of the Russian revolution and the Tsiolkovsky centenary, it also wholly eclipsed the US Project Farside, which was intended to send a rocket 6,400km into space a few days later.[13] (A previous attempt had been aborted by a transmitter failure.[14]) The historical consequences are well known: Vanguard suddenly became a political matter, resulting in total ignominy when the first 3-stage shot rose 1m, lost thrust, struck the rim of the pad and exploded. The von Braun team, who had been ready all along, had by now been given the go-ahead and placed Explorer 1 in orbit at the first attempt, in January 1958.[26] After some discreditable shouting about the relative merits of the two space programs (leading to the world-wide but false myth of "Russia's Germans are better than America's Germans") the USA finally began to take space research seriously in political terms, and the military research teams were integrated with the civilian NACA under the new heading "National Aeronautics and Space Administration" (NASA). One of its first commitments was the US man-in-space objective, Project Mercury.

Meantime, however, another game was being played, in which history repeated itself almost perfectly. Within five months of receiving the go-ahead in January 1958[21] the US Air Force had been ready to launch the world's first Moon probe with the Thor–Able booster, in which the Thor missile (developed from Navaho, like Redstone and Jupiter) was mated with the Able second stage of Vanguard (fig. 3). The project was an ambitious one, intended to place a TV camera and other instruments in orbit around the Moon. These were the first Pioneer probes, to be followed by less complex Army payloads launched by Juno II, which had a Jupiter first stage and solid-fuelled upper stages from Jupiter–C.* The first three

*To avoid confusion, it had been decided that the Redstone-based research vehicle would be known as Juno I, while the Jupiter-based one would be known as Juno II. Chaos was the only result. However, the exchanges of technology between the Navaho-Redstone-Jupiter-Thor-Vanguard-Juno programs go some way to answer the charge that inter-service rivalry held the USA back in the "space race" with Russia.

Air Force orbiter attempts failed, likewise the first Army attempt at a lunar flyby. The feat was then accomplished by the Russian Mechta probe, later designated Luna 1.

Although Jupiter–C did represent satellite launchers in the public mind to some extent, the phase was brief. The early Vanguard failures, and the total concealment of the Russian launch vehicles, caused a massive public identification of the Thor–Able with the concept of space travel. Although none of the Thor–Able Pioneers reached the Moon (Pioneer 1, the "Glorious Failure", did best with a peak altitude of 115,800km), the identification wasn't foolish because the Thor, with various upper stages and clip-on boosters, has been the "work-horse" of unmanned satellite launches ever since. For years Thor–Able launches were used to illustrate anything to do with spaceflight, appropriate or not: on the one hand a serious British television production, about an astronaut refusing to trigger a biological warfare payload on the Moon; on the other *The Man in the Moon*, with Kenneth More, *The Road to Hong Kong*, with Bob Hope and Bing Crosby, a Scottish Television production, *Pathfinders to Venus*, in which a Thor–Able represented a *Russian* spacecraft taking off . . . and even the LP of John Glenn's flight has the launch of Pioneer 1 on the cover.[27]

The unmanned space probes, however, were not the focus of public attention for long. (After the first three Soviet missions, and the Pioneer 4 flyby, nobody got near the Moon successfully for years.) The man-in-space program, and particularly the animal experiments leading up to it, made the headlines: the Soviet space program using dogs, the US preferring chimpanzees. Although Laika in Sputnik 2 was the only victim not *intended* to survive, a wave of public protest built up and finally broke, retreating exhausted, after two dogs were killed in Spaceship 3. In all, about a dozen animals flew into space during the development of the Vostok and Mercury spacecraft, and only Spaceship 3 failed to return to Earth. The occupants became the symbol of the anti-vivisection movement – with which there was precious little parallel – and impassioned writers declared that no cost in human life would be worth the suffering of animals in space.

In the real world, meantime, human volunteers continued the punishing, dangerous investigation of the anticipated stresses of space flight. Test subjects were exposed to high *g*–loads in centrifuges, starved of oxygen, baked, frozen, tumbled in simulators to overload their senses and kept in solitary confinement to study sensory and social deprivation. Peak *g*–loads were studied by rocket sled riders, particularly by Colonel John Stapp; balloon pilots spent more than a day 27–30km up, evaluating the unknown dangers of cosmic radiation and the "breakoff" phenomenon of psychological isola-tion from the Earth;[28] parachute jumps were conducted from those altitudes, to test pressure suits and extend the study of weightlessness (the pilot fell for kilometres through the stratosphere before significant air resistance built up). All these elements of "space medicine" had caught the public eye in the 1950s, but in the outcry over a dozen animal flights they were effectively forgotten.

The rocket aircraft program was continuing with the X–15, which had been delivered to Edwards in 1958 (fig. 7). Its design had a profound effect

[Fig 7]

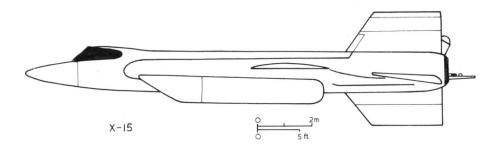

X-15

on space art: hypersonic research had shown that the needle nose and tapered wings of the early 1950s designs could not absorb or disperse the temperatures of atmospheric entry; and, moreover, the ship was black, not white or silver, to radiate away as much heat as possible. Looking back, however, the X–15 seems much nearer to the 1950s concepts than to the Shuttle designs of the present day – particularly with its ventral fin, which had to be blown clear before landing. Asked what would happen if it failed to separate, spokesmen replied that it would become the world's fastest plough.[16]

Owing to production difficulties, the first two X–15s were originally fitted with X–1 type rocket engines, giving them eight thrust chambers in all. Despite the experience gained over the years, history repeated itself as the peroxide turbines burned out before launch; number 2 aircraft had a peroxide explosion after a ground test and an alcohol fire after the first powered flight; on a later mission the same aircraft had an explosion and fire in flight, and broke in half on touchdown. When the number 3 X–15 was delivered in 1960 with the big, single-chambered XLR–99 engine, it blew up on the ground, hurling the nose section with Scott Crossfield at the controls for 6m.

Around this time the fickle attention of the world began to switch to Project Mercury, and later achievements of the X–15 with its big engine drew relatively little notice in the press. The X–15 was to reach altitudes up to 108km, gaining astronauts' wings for several pilots (the limiting altitude for this purpose is 50 miles (80km), above which aerodynamic controls are ineffective), and speeds up to 7,272kph (with extra tanks). 199 missions were flown, ending in 1968 less than two months before the Apollo 8 mission.[29] In that time there was only one fatal accident, when a mistake by the pilot, Michael J. Adams, caused the ship to break up during re-entry. Nevertheless, as experience was gained, no more was heard of plans to send the X–15 to its maximum attainable altitude of 227km; a proposal to send it up to 14,400km, using a Navaho booster, had been turned down long before.

An X–15B orbiter, with an Atlas missile sustainer engine and three Navahos as boosters, likewise never got off the drawing board;[16] a later form of this proposal would have used a Titan missile as launch vehicle. An Air Force plan was taken up instead, for a vehicle called Dyna-Soar (the first of the great space puns). Dyna-Soar (fig. 8), eventually classified X–20, would have been built by Boeing and placed in orbit by Titan 2 (see below). The project was dropped before the first flight tests at Edwards, because it was ahead of its time; but the re-entry principle it incorporated, using the flat underside of the vehicle as a braking and heat-radiating surface, was correctly taken up by space artists as "the look of the future" and has now emerged, more than ten years later, as the common factor in all suggested configurations for the Space Shuttle.

[Fig 8]

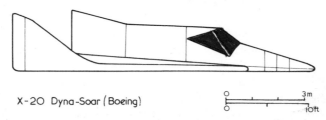

X-20 Dyna-Soar (Boeing)

From 1960 on, the image of spaceflight had shifted completely from winged spacecraft to capsules. A major turning point in the process was the flight test of a Project Mercury Redstone, launching a chimpanzee named Ham downrange in a Mercury capsule from Cape Canaveral.[30] Two similar sub-orbital shots were to be made by Shepard and Grissom before the Mercury capsule was put into orbit. Although the USSR scored a tremendous propaganda triumph by placing Yuri Gagarin in orbit, in April 1961, that and subsequent Soviet flights had little impact on the *idea* of space flight because nobody knew what the Russian spacecraft looked like. Films released at the time were obvious fakes, showing cannon shells being jerked upwards on wires, and misleading models and sketches added to the confusion. A detailed, fascinating attempt to resolve the contradictions produced a Vostok "design" which proved, in due course, to be quite wrong.[31] For the public, however, the prevailing images of the Russian space program were faces, uniforms and parades.

Although there were only two manned Mercury–Redstone flights they made their mark, primarily because they took so long to get off (fig. 9). The Redstone was now known to rocket engineers as "Old Reliable", but in these days when Apollos take off on time to the second it's amazing to recollect how many times the MR flights were postponed. The second flight had a special impact because the capsule escape hatch blew out after splash-down, and Grissom was nearly drowned by the downwash from the heli-copter trying to save him. Afterwards, he described closing the neck dam of his suit as "the best thing I did all day".[32]

By the end of 1961 the confused forward groping of the US space program had straightened up towards a firm set of objectives, ending with the Moon landing. As recently as 1960, commentators complained that NASA had no firm public commitment beyond Project Mercury.[33] (Exactly the same problem was to throw the program, after the Moon landing, into the disorder from which it hasn't yet fully recovered.) But in May 1961 President Kennedy stated explicitly: "I believe this nation should commit itself to achieving the goal, before this decade is out, of landing a man on the Moon and returning him safely to the Earth."[34] Project Apollo, which had been moving slowly since its creation in 1959, acquired a firm schedule, and Project Gemini was initiated to build up space experience meantime, bridging the gap between Mercury and Apollo.[35]

The launch vehicles for these projects continued (and concluded, as far as one can see at present) the lines of development begun with the captured V2s after the war. The Atlas missile had been developed by Convair, for the Air Force, from the MX–774 test vehicle of the 1940s – a rocket which had used V2 fins, to take advantage of existing wind tunnel data, although the shape had originally been chosen to fit German railway tunnels. Martin had developed, from the Viking and Vanguard projects, the Air Force's second liquid-fuelled ICBM, Titan 1.[22] Titan 2, with an uprated second stage, had been the proposed launcher for the X–15B and the Dyna-Soar, and now became the launcher for the two-man Gemini spacecraft. Saturn 1 (also first intended as a Dyna-Soar booster[35]) was produced by von Braun's former Army team, now re-designated as NASA's George C. Marshall Spaceflight Centre,[34] using clustered tanks and engines developed directly from the Redstone and Jupiter programs.

[Fig 9]

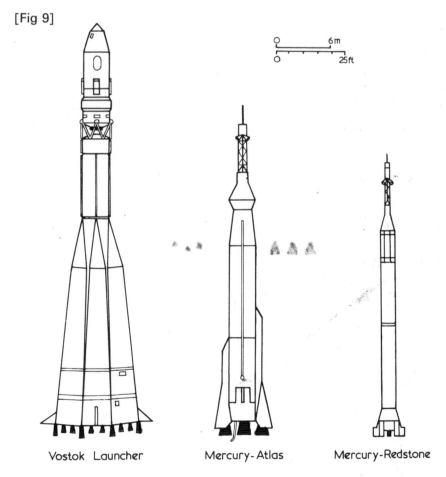

Vostok Launcher   Mercury-Atlas   Mercury-Redstone

With the commitment to reach the Moon before 1970, NASA dropped
the long-term Nova project, an enormous booster intended to land an
Apollo directly on the Moon and bring it straight back;[36] instead, final plans
involved Lunar Orbit Rendezvous, allowing lunar return missions with
Saturn V[34] – itself a massive development. (Each of its five F–1 engines –
Nova would have had eight – developed 680,000kg of thrust, equal to the
combined output of Saturn 1's eight motors (fig. 10). Nevertheless, the
achievement and the time-scale were well within the technical reach of the
USA at the start of the 1960s; had Kennedy survived and remained in
office, one wonders how much higher today's targets would be set.)

[Fig 10]

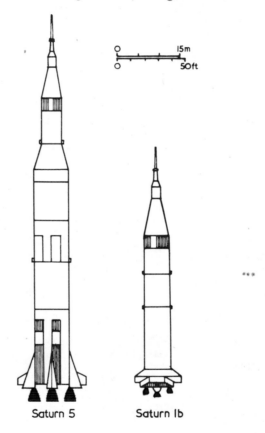

Saturn 5   Saturn Ib

How soon Project Mercury was forgotten by the people who said space
flights were boring! On Glenn's second orbit, a faulty warning light indicated that the shock-absorbing "landing bag" might have deployed,
displacing his heat-shield. That gave us our first real experience of the break
in capsule communications during re-entry, wondering whether the spacecraft will be heard again in a few minutes or come down in a rain of
fragments. For Glenn, the other side of the situation had a special fascination as he watched fragments of his retro-rockets (not jettisoned after firing,
just in case the shield *was* loose) go flying past, and wondered if the shield
was breaking up. On Scott Carpenter's mission, the nightmare came half-
way true when nothing was heard, even long after the capsule must have

touched down if it had survived at all. It turned out that Carpenter had over-used his attitude control jets and run out of steam (literally) at the critical time, with the result that he overshot the splashdown target by 400km. He had an even prettier view than Glenn's on the way down – a green glow where the top was burning off his capsule.[32] On the final Mercury flight, Cooper had a full-scale autopilot failure to contend with after 24 hours in space, and had to make retrofire and entry on manual control. Seven years later, people were taking Moon landings for granted.

Although John Glenn's liftoff in the Mercury–Atlas was used quite a bit in advertisements, the Gemini–Titan combination was much the stronger image of spaceflight in the 1960s (fig. 11). Even now, to some extent, Gemini still represents "man in space". This may have been partly due to cleaner

[Fig 11]

Gemini –Titan 2

lines (Titan didn't have the flared booster engine "skirt" of the Atlas, and couldn't take the aerodynamic loads of an escape tower above the capsule), and also due to live TV coverage of liftoff and splashdown, but to a large extent it must be because Gemini was the first spacecraft to be photographed from outside, close up, in flight.[37] At any rate, Gemini liftoffs and in-flight simulations were extensively used in the Bond films and their imitators. Another factor "fixing" the Gemini image was that, owing to its shape, a high proportion of the space photographs taken with hand-held cameras included the nose of the spacecraft.[34]

The Gemini program had its fair share of excitement and danger, although at times it projected a less romantic image than the Mercury and Apollo programs. (The first manned flight, GT–3, was named "The Unsinkable Molly Brown" by Grissom, hoping not to repeat the sinking of his Mercury capsule; the other Geminis were known only by numbers.) From Gemini 4, Ed White made the first US "space-walk": the achievement was already credited to Leonov in Voshkod 2, but McDivitt's colour pictures of White floating on his umbilical cord with the Earth behind him are still the best known of their kind.[38] White also carried on the tradition of *enjoying* the experience (when ordered to descend from 30km up in the Man High balloon projects, Kittinger had radioed: "Come and get me . . ."[28]). Mission Control's plaintive "Please, Ed, get back in the spaceship" has always seemed to me to mark the end of an era.

One of the many Gemini objectives was rendezvous and docking in space. The USSR had twice put two spacecraft into space at the same time, but neither pair had closed to within a kilometer. Gemini rendezvous were to be with unmanned Agena target vehicles, launched by Atlas boosters: the first attempt was to be made with Gemini 6, but the Agena exploded before making orbit. To avoid delaying the program, NASA launched Gemini 7, then sent Gemini 6 up to join it – after a delay of three days caused by a loose electrical plug in the launch vehicle. (The first attempt to launch Gemini 6 is still, in my opinion, the most frightening piece of film to come out of spaceflight to date. Although the "escape tower" rockets, to lift a capsule clear of a crippled spacecraft, have been extensively tested for Mercury and Apollo – using "Little Joe" 1 and 2 solid-fuel rockets – they have never had to be used in earnest. Remembering the nose pod of the Skyrocket and X–2, and the death of Captain Apt, I for one would be delighted to see it relegated to the history books unused. As noted, however, the Gemini–Titan combination had no escape tower; instead, *very* high-power ejector seats were to be used if a mission had to be aborted in the lower atmosphere. Tests had shown that the astronauts could get clear of an exploding Titan, even on the launch pad, but obviously the system was far more dangerous than being lifted off, capsule and all, by an escape tower. The Gemini 6 electrical failure occurred at T minus 2.2 seconds, so on film the flame comes welling out under the rocket, then disappears again as the computers detect the fault and shut down the motors. Conditioned by – for example – the explosion of the big X–15 engine, my brain tells me that the unscheduled disappearance of a rocket flame is followed by an explosion, and every time I see that film my heart stops.)

Gemini 6 and 7 achieved a successful rendezvous. The first docking was achieved by Armstrong and Scott in Gemini 8, but, after their link-up with the docking target, a thruster jammed on and threw the linked spacecraft into wild gyrations. The Gemini broke free and made an emergency return to Earth. Gemini 9 fared little better, since the Agena shrouds jammed over the docking target (Thomas Stafford called it "an angry alligator"), and it was left to Gemini 10 to achieve the first full rendezvous and docking.

After Gemini 12, Apollo was expected to begin the program leading to lunar landing almost at once. Three whole years remained for meeting President Kennedy's target, but on the other hand a USSR Moon landing was more than half predicted for October, the fiftieth anniversary of the Russian

Revolution. Undoubtedly the Russians knew that Soyuz would *not* be ready so soon, but the USA didn't. It will be interesting, in a few decades' time, to see whether historians blame the fatalities of early 1967 on the USA's attempt to catch up on the imagined Soviet lead and the USSR's determination to hold onto a lead already very short, poised on a base of technology and space experience much narrower than the US program. Russia had already put three men into space, for example, but they had been jammed without pressure suits into a stripped-down Vostok renamed "Voshkod" – a propaganda exercise which held back their main program for a full year.[39]

Whatever the underlying pressures, Grissom, White and Chaffee died in the Apollo fire of January 1967, and Komarov (previously the Voshkod 1 Commander) died on the first Soyuz mission when his parachute failed to open, less than three months later. For years commentators had speculated about the effect of deaths in space on public opinion;[33] the question has still to be answered, since the subsequent Soyuz[11] tragedy was again on re-entry, and in all fatalities to date the bodies have been recovered and honourably interred. Undoubtedly the 1967 accidents had a profound impact : naturally the Russian investigation was not made public, but the Apollo one was, and bad design and bad workmanship were blamed.[34]* "Overconfidence" was given as a possible reason, although the successes of the Gemini program hadn't been exactly effortless. But Komarov's death so soon afterwards clearly suggested that the two programs were being rushed by pressures from outside, and led, in my opinion, to a strong public reaction against the whole idea of a "space race". It's not unreasonable to suggest that the Soviet leaders recognised the shift in outside world opinion at an early stage, and shifted the priorities of their space program from the prestige/scientific race to the Moon to practical studies in Earth-orbit.

The redesign and rebuilding of the Apollo Command Module took eighteen months. The first manned mission to orbit, Apollo 7, was not without misgivings : the astronauts objected strongly to a request to mend some broken wiring, and Mission Commander Schirra remarked, "Broken wires are what we're all afraid of up here." Nevertheless, the mission was a

---

*Relatively little was said about bad management *per se*, but one major point arises which I've never seen mentioned in accounts of the Apollo 204 fire. It's a commonplace of television series like *Star Trek* or *Voyage to the Bottom of the Sea* that, when a new system is given its first operational test, all personnel except the stars are removed "because they aren't necessary"; the infallible automatic system then runs amok and kills people. In real life, rehearsals are supposed to have *more* safety precautions than normal operations, because you're trying to find out what can go wrong – particularly what you haven't anticipated. The Apollo was pressurized with pure oxygen at *above normal air pressure* (three times the pure oxygen pressure in orbit); presumably the hatch was designed not to open easily when under pressure from inside, but it took 90 seconds to open at the best of times (to save astronauts from death by water, which Grissom had so narrowly escaped). The idea of oxygen fire in the spacecraft shouldn't have been unthinkable – there had been enough misgivings about short-circuits during Cooper's Mercury flight – but in any case fire-fighting and other safety personnel should have been on the gantry just because, in a countdown simulation, the regular personnel were to leave it. Instead the rehearsal wasn't considered "hazardous" because the rocket wasn't fuelled, and no emergency teams were provided.[34] It seemed extraordinary to me even before I took management studies, and still seems an amazing lapse in management thinking.

success and, in what seemed a remarkable surge of confidence, NASA
scheduled the next mission – the first manned launch of Saturn V – to
spend 20 hours in orbit around the Moon. Apollo 8 made a major impression : mainly by supplying Man's first personal close-up of another planet,
but also because live TV from space, showing the astronauts making full
use of the space within the capsule in zero–g, brought home to the public
just how far we had come from the "shoehorn-small" Mercury capsule and
the "telephone box" Gemini.

[Fig 12]

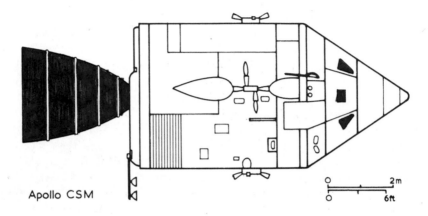

Apollo CSM

2 m
6 ft

For the last few years, the Apollo Command and Service Module/Lunar
Module combination has been the prevailing image of space research (figs.
12 and 13). It's interesting, however, that the Lunar Module is often
visualized in *Earth* orbit, because the photographs of the first flight test are
still among the most-reproduced images of space, available as colour posters,
postcards and slides. Another point was that the Apollo 9 CSM/LM were
the first spaceships with names since Grissom's Gemini, and more people
could probably name "Spider" and "Gumdrop" than any other vehicles in
the Apollo program – possibly second to "Eagle", with "Snoopy" in
third place, but a long way ahead of "Challenger", "Yankee Clipper",
"Endeavour" and the rest.

Undoubtedly the Lunar Module on the Moon, especially with the Lunar
Rover, has established images which will last for many years. Skylab hasn't
had the same impact, perhaps because even after that incredible repair
job ("Skylab Two – we fix anything !") the space station looked lopsided
and makeshift, seen from outside (fig. 14). Saturn V seems to be used
increasingly as an advertising symbol, now that its rôle is over – and of
course it's invariably used in *Star Trek* and *The Six Million Dollar Man.*
But in general the rôle of the big throwaway booster in manned flight
ended for the West with the Apollo–Soyuz rendezvous in 1975. Since the
Soviet launch vehicles have never made much impression on films, advertising, space art, etc., we can expect the whole public image of space research

to swing increasingly towards the Space Shuttle as the 1970s end. When the Shuttle becomes operational the throwaway booster will be phased out of *unmanned* space launches. It's a strange thought that in 1985 the whole image of the giant cylindrical rocket will seem more archaic than Mercury–Atlas seems now, or Viking seemed in 1965, or the V2 ten years after the war.

[Fig 13]

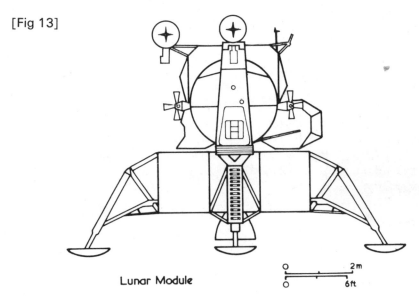

Lunar Module

[Fig 14]

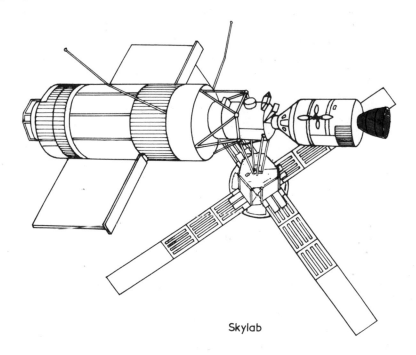

Skylab

After the Thor–Able Moon probes, unmanned launches drew relatively little attention and made no great impact in visual terms. After the US Army's Moon launches the Thor returned as the basic booster for the deep-space Pioneers 5, 6, 7, 8 and 9 – the last four of which were still operational late in 1976. For lunar and planetary missions Atlas became the workhorse, initially as Atlas–Able, then Atlas–Agena (Mariners 2, 4 and 5, and the Ranger Moonprobes), lastly Atlas–Centaur (Surveyor lunar landers, Mariners 6, 7, 9 and 10). After the launch of Pioneer 9 in 1968 Thor had one last bow, placing Radio Astronomy Explorer in orbit around the Moon in 1973, but otherwise left the field beyond Earth orbit entirely to Atlas payloads. The first and probably last challenges to that supremacy were the two Viking and Voyager launches using Titan III – a booster glimpsed briefly in the film *Marooned* but otherwise so limited to military launches that it hasn't affected the image of space flight at all.

The achievements of the unmanned lunar probes will be touched on in Chapter 4, although Part 2 of this book concentrates heavily on Apollo. When it comes to our new knowledge of the planets, however, we have only robot explorers to thank.

5 and 6: Mars in fiction and in reality. *Above,* Ray Bradbury's Mars, with fragile cities on the canals of a dead or dying civilization. *Below,* the Viking lander view—rock-strewn desert, with a permanent dust haze making the sky pink, dust that is occasionally whipped up into violent storms. There is, however, something strange about that distant hillside . . . *(Paintings by Ed Buckley.)*

3 Interplanetary Navigation

A. E. Roy, FRAS, FBIS,
Professor of Astronomy, University of Glasgow

Schirra : 5, 4, 3, 2, 1, fire !
Glenn : Roger, retros are firing.
Schirra : Yeah, they be.
Glenn : Are they ever ! It feels like I'm going back towards Hawaii.
Schirra : Don't do that. You want to go to the east coast.

Retrofire, Friendship 7, 20th February 1962

Interplanetary navigation is concerned with ways and means of getting there – and back. It is an extension of traditional skills acquired and exercized by Man from his earliest days on planet Earth. When he wanted to cross a deep river he used a log to support himself and the current or a crude paddle to propel him. Later, more ambitiously and ingeniously, he built canoes, raised masts and sails in even bigger boats, and voyaged over immense distances, ultimately from continent to continent. Finally his ships became self-propelled as he mastered power-sources.

As navigational aids he enrolled the stars, the Sun and the Moon and drew maps, plotting on them not only coastlines and dangerous reefs but also currents that could aid or hinder his progress. He invented compass and sextant and chronometer; more recently the tremendous progress in electronics has provided him with highly sophisticated shore- or satellite-based navigational aids.

In all navigational situations there are good ways and bad ways of tackling the problems involved. At best, bad ways produce delay, frustration, failure; at worst, death is the penalty exacted by nature. This latter

7: The new look of Mars. Orbital photographs from Mariner 9 and the Viking probes showed that Mars was spectacular and colourful. Nix Olympica and the other three largest volcanoes stand at the upper end of the great equatorial rift, Valles Marineris. The approaching spacecraft is a "Waverider" atmosphere entry probe, designed by Professor T. R. Nonweiler. *(Painting by Gavin Roberts.)*

was so when the field of operations comprized the oceans and deserts of Earth; it is certainly the case when Man navigates in the vaster field of the Solar System, where the ports themselves make ocean voyages and the currents of gravity are everchanging. Nevertheless, there are compensations, as we shall see. Astronomy has provided us with highly reliable maps and schedules; electronics, radar and computer technology have supplied navigational aids; rocket technology gives means of propulsion adequate even today to explore the inner Solar System by manned spacecraft and the outer reaches by instrumental probes.

The nine major planets move in almost circular, almost coplanar orbits about the Sun. There is a one-way traffic rule; looking down on the Solar System from far above the Earth's north pole, all traffic moves anticlockwise about the Sun. To a high degree of approximation the planets obey Kepler's three laws:

1   Each planet's orbit is an ellipse with the Sun at one focus;
2   The radius vector joining planet to Sun sweeps out equal areas in equal times;
3   The square of the period of revolution of each planet about the Sun is proportional to the cube of its average distance from the Sun.

[Fig 15]

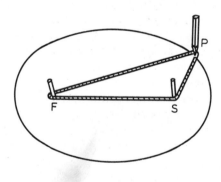

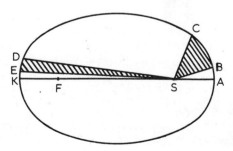

The gardener lays out an elliptical flower-bed by sticking two pegs S and F into the ground; he then throws a loop of cord over them and, keeping the loop taut by means of a third stick P, makes the third stick trace out a curve (fig. 15). The nearer the two fixed pegs are, the closer the ellipse becomes to a circle. The positions of the two pegs are the foci. Kepler's first law states that the Sun is at one of the foci, say S, and the planet traces out an elliptical orbit.

Kepler's second law describes the way in which the planet moves in its orbit. When the planet is at A it is nearest to the Sun and is said to be at *perihelion*; when it is at K it is furthest away, at *aphelion*. Now, for Kepler's second law to hold, if the radius vectors SB, SC, SD and SE giving four positions of the planet are such that the area SBC is equal to the area SDE, then the time the planet spends between B and C has to be equal to the time spent by the planet between D and E. But the lines SB and SC are shorter than SD and SE so that for the two areas to be equal, the arc BC must be longer than the arc DE. The speed of the planet in its orbit between B and C is therefore greater than between D and E. So the planet must move fastest at perihelion and slowest at aphelion. For example, Mars has a perihelion velocity of 26.39km per second and an aphelion velocity of 21.88km per second.

Kepler's third law relates the times it takes planets to move once round the Sun (their *periods of revolution*) to their average distances from the Sun (their *semimajor axes*). The bigger the orbit, the longer the time. Earth takes one year, for example, while Pluto's period of revolution is almost 248 years.

Knowing these facts, an interplanetary timetable can be set up, giving the positions of all the planets at suitable intervals of a day or so with respect to some convenient reference system. The reference system often used is the plane of the Earth's orbit about the Sun (the *plane of the ecliptic*) and a particular direction in this plane measured from the Sun's centre. The angular distance of the planet from this direction (towards the *vernal equinox*), measured along the ecliptic, is the planet's *celestial longitude*; its angular distance above or below the ecliptic is its *celestial latitude*; its distance from the Sun is its *radius vector*. Values of these quantities for each planet are tabulated in the national nautical almanacs, such as the British *Astronomical Ephemeris*, for each day of the year.

The problem is complicated, however, by the fact that all the planets disturb each others' orbits by means of their mutual gravitational attractions. The orbits change gradually with time, tilting slightly, precessing, wobbling, stretching and compressing like plasticine rings under the spectral fingers of gravitation. The planets themselves are sometimes running a little early or late compared to the positions they would have occupied if they did not mutually disturb one another. But these complications are second-order effects, accurately computed by the methods of celestial mechanics and allowed for in the almanacs.

So we have at any time an accurate map of the Solar System even although the ports of call themselves move. Distances are known with high precision; for example, the Earth–Moon distance is known at any time to an accuracy of plus or minus 30cm while the tens of millions of kilometres distances to Venus and Mars are probably subject to errors of no more than a kilometre or so! We will see later that to use the ingenious dodge of a planetary encounter to provide a powerful boost to the rocket without excessive fuel expenditure requires such accurate knowledge of inter-planetary distances.

Dr Walter Hohmann was one of the pioneers in studying the orbits best suited for interplanetary travel. As long ago as 1925 he demonstrated that the most economical use of fuel resulted if the rocket engine were fired either along or in the opposite direction to the orbit of departure or destination. Thus, if we wish to leave the inner orbit of radius a and proceed into the outer orbit of radius b, an elliptic transfer orbit tangential to both is preferable (fig. 16). The rocket motor is fired for a few minutes at A to add sufficient speed to the rocket to insert it into the transfer orbit. Thereafter the motor is shut down – apart from very momentary mid-course correction burns – and the rocket coasts under the attraction of the Sun's gravitational field until it nears B. Here a second impulse is required given by a second major use of the rocket motor to give the vehicle the extra velocity to enter the outer orbit. If the second impulse did not take place, then the vehicle would simply fall back towards the Sun, coasting along the other half of the transfer ellipse until it began a new outward transfer from A.

[Fig 16]

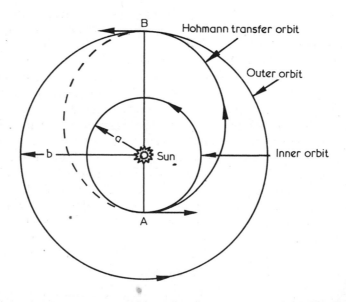

The full name for such an orbit is a *Hohmann co-tangential two-impulse elliptic transfer*. Obviously the simple picture sketched above is not the whole story. In the real case – for example, a transfer from Earth to Mars – the two orbits, outer and inner, are occupied by planets, whose time-tables have to be taken into account. It is therefore not possible to set off at any time into the wild blue yonder. Mars and the rocket should approach B together. For transfer between any pair of planets, therefore, there exists a set of dates, the so-called launch windows, within which missions can begin. If a round trip is required, a waiting period at the planet of destination is inevitable, adding to the total mission time. In Table II we see transfer times, waiting times and round-trip times for journeys by Hohmann elliptic transfer orbits from Earth to the other planets in the Solar System.

TABLE II

Planet	Transfer Time t_T (years)	Minimum Waiting Time t_W (years)	Total Round Trip Time $T\ 2t_T\ t_W$	First Velocity Change Required to Earth's Orbital Velocity of 29.77 kps
Mercury	0.289	0.183	0.76	−7.53
Venus	0.400	1.278	2.08	−2.49
Mars	0.709	1.242	2.66	2.93
Jupiter	2.731	0.588	6.05	8.80
Saturn	6.048	0.936	13.03	10.29
Uranus	16.04	0.932	33.01	11.30
Neptune	30.62	0.766	62.01	11.67
Pluto	45.47	0.061	91.00	11.83

The mission times for Venusian, Martian and Mercury round trips are not impossible to contemplate for manned voyages, the interesting fact emerging that the Mercury mission lasts only about a third and a quarter as long respectively as the Venusian and Martian missions. The important factor in these cases is the long waiting time at Mars and Venus before the return journey can be begun. For all other journeys, however, manned voyages by Hohmann transfers are obviously out of the question.

In the final column of the table we see the change in velocity required by the spacecraft when it enters the Hohmann transfer orbit on leaving Earth. If it left the vicinity of Earth with little or no velocity relative to our planet it would have the Earth's orbital velocity about the Sun of 29.8km per second. In order to enter the required transfer orbit that will carry it to the planet of destination it must add to its speed the value given in the last column of the table. The negative values for trips to Mercury and Venus follow from the fact that they move in orbits nearer the Sun than Earth does: some of the Earth's orbital velocity imparted to the vehicle must therefore be killed so that it will fall towards the Sun. For a Mercury transfer, for example, the vehicle must leave the Earth's neighbourhood with a speed of 7.53km per second relative to the Earth and in the opposite direction to that in which the Earth is travelling so that the spacecraft's speed relative to the Sun is 29.8 − 7.53 = 22.27km per second in the forward direction.

Comparable velocity changes are required at the other end of the transfer to give the vehicle essentially the orbital velocity of the planet of destination. Adding the two impulse velocities together gives the velocity budget for the trip. When the facts that the planetary orbits are neither circular nor coplanar are taken into account, the budget for a particular mission has to be modified by only a few per cent. Adding a few per cent again for mid-course corrections gives the final total required.

Even for Hohmann orbits, however, the picture must be examined more closely. The Sun's gravitational field is dominant over 90% of the journey but, near a planet, the planetary gravitational field is in control. The concept of the *sphere of influence*, a roughly spherical region centred at the planet, is useful here. Within it the vehicle's planetocentric orbit is only slightly modified by the Sun's pull.

In Table III the sizes of the planets' spheres of influence are given. It is perhaps surprising that Jupiter's domain is not the largest – less extensive than those of Saturn, Uranus and Neptune, which are far less massive planets. This is because in the outer Solar System the Sun's gravitational field is weaker and the planets there can grab more territory! The third column, however, gives a better way of expressing matters, namely the radius of the sphere of influence as a fraction of the planet's distance from the Sun. There it is seen that Jupiter possesses the most powerful gravitational "fishing-net", as evidenced by its extensive system of fourteen moons and its observed influence, sometimes drastic, on the orbits of comets that venture too near the giant planet.

Navigating a spacecraft from Earth to Mars is readily understood now using the concept of the sphere of influence. Usually the vehicle, after lift-off, is injected into a circum-Earth parking orbit about 240km above the surface for systems check-out purposes. At the right moment, its motor is fired to increase its velocity beyond escape velocity from the Earth's sphere of influence. The vehicle now coasts out of the Earth's sphere of influence on a hyperbolic escape trajectory. The time at which the motor is fired depends essentially upon whether it is desired to add (*firing position B*) or subtract (*firing position A*) velocity from the Earth's orbital velocity when the vehicle leaves the sphere of influnce and enters interplanetary space (fig. 17).

[Fig 17]

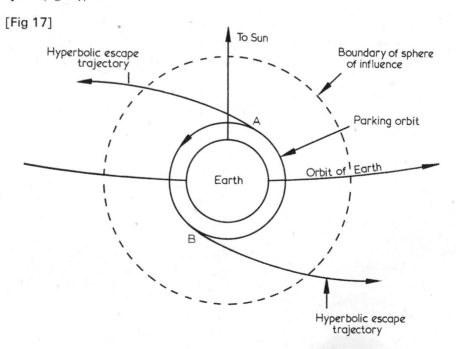

The spacecraft's velocity and position relative to the Sun no~
its subsequent Hohmann transfer orbit in interplanetary space.
orbit is free of error or has been adjusted by one or more mid-co~
corrections, it will in due course enter the sphere of influence of the plane
of destination, say Mars. Unless the motor is fired again, the spacecraft
will pass through the Martian sphere of influence on a hyperbolic encounter
path, escaping once more into interplanetary space after reaching a
minimum height above the planet's surface (fig. 18).

TABLE III
Radius of Sphere of Influence

Planet	Millions of kilometres	Fraction of planet's distance from Sun	Astronomical units
Mercury	0.113	0.0019	0.00075
Venus	0.615	0.0057	0.0041
Earth	0.925	0.0062	0.0062
Mars	0.579	0.0025	0.0039
Jupiter	48.119	0.0619	0.322
Saturn	54.545	0.0382	0.365
Uranus	51.971	0.0181	0.348
Neptune	86.886	0.0193	0.581
Pluto	33.950	0.0057	0.227

The early Mariner missions to Mars and Venus did just that, collecting
their harvest of pictures and other information during the few hours they
dipped deeply within those planets' spheres of influence. Mariner 9, however, was injected into an elliptic capture orbit about Mars by firing its
rocket motor near the planet, decreasing its hyperbolic velocity to below
escape velocity. With a longer burn and further fuel expenditure, the velocity

[Fig 18]

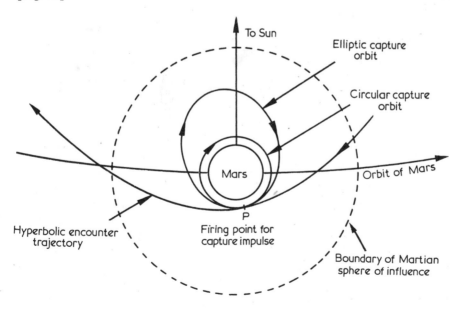

could have been reduced to circular velocity but this would have been a needless waste of payload, the scientific mission being perfectly compatible with an elliptic orbit.

A planetary encounter without capture can produce drastic changes in the subsequent interplanetary orbit of a spacecraft. Mariner 10's flypast of Venus so changed its orbit that it dipped in towards the Sun, making three flypasts of Mercury at six-monthly intervals and providing the first ever close-up pictures of the innermost planet's moon-like surface. Pioneer 10, the first probe to Jupiter, penetrated its system in December 1973. The giant planet's powerful gravitational field ejected it finally from its sphere of influence with such velocity that it is now on its way into interstellar space. Because this long voyage was planned for, the payload carried mankind's famous gold-plated visiting card bearing information and designs it is hoped will lead any intelligent species finding it back to Earth. Pioneer 11, which flew past Jupiter in December 1974, also utilized Jupiter's gravitational field to place itself on a new interplanetary transfer scheduled to produce the first flypast of Saturn in 1979.

Hohmann's pioneer study of transfer orbits showed that a fuel-economical orbit is time-consuming. Journeys to Mars and Venus no longer are made by Hohmann transfer; the rockets of the 1970s are powerful enough to use faster transfers that intersect these planetary orbits at an angle, not only cutting down transfer times but allowing larger payloads, a wider choice of transfer orbit and consequently a welcome stretching of launch-windows. But, if it were not for the use of planetary encounters that use the planets' gravitational fields as velocity amplifiers, Mercury and the planets beyond Jupiter would still require essentially Hohmann transfers.

The question of error-sensitivity is important here. Slight errors in position and/or velocity at a given time accumulate dramatically given the time to do so. Hohmann transfers are slow and are particularly prone to such processes. Thus the effect of an error in the impulse that places the vehicle into its hyperbolic escape orbit within the planet's sphere of influence leads to errors in the position and velocity it has when it leaves the sphere of influence and enters interplanetary space. The heliocentric transfer orbit is slightly changed as a consequence and the vehicle arrives (if it does arrive!) at the sphere of influence of the planet of destination at a changed point. The time is different – also the arrival velocity – so that the new planetocentric hyperbolic encounter orbit requires a new capture orbit firing program with a probably excessive expenditure of fuel.

Some examples show how error-sensitive such orbits are. Suppose a Mars mission leaves a circum-Earth parking orbit (height 459km) with a velocity error of only 0.3m per second. Calculations show that, if uncorrected, the vehicle will have a position error of 40,000km by the time it reaches the Martian orbit. The same tiny velocity error for a Jovian mission results in a position error of the order of 120,700km. It is obvious, then, that essential ingredients of interplanetary navigation are the ability to measure quickly and accurately the spacecraft's position and velocity at any time, the fast calculation of the necessary corrected schedule so that corrections can be made as quickly as possible (the longer the delay the more fuel spent). To carry out these tasks there must be provided ground-based or on-board navigational aids – the space equivalent of sextant, chronometer and Loran beacon –, fast electronic computers, long-range communication systems and an adequate fuel supply for course adjustment.

There are a number of navigational aids available. As time passes, some will be improved, others will become obsolete and be discarded. New methods will be developed. Some aids are Earth-based; some are vehicle-based. The choice depends not only upon the mission and payload mass available for navigational equipment but also on the phase of the mission – and also on whether it is an unmanned or manned project. Thus a number of methods may well enter into the navigational armoury for a single mission. The most practical are based upon optical tracking, radar tracking and the use of inertial equipment (comprizing stabilized platforms and accelerometers). In addition, fast electronic computers, ship· or ground-based, are required.

Optical tracking of a ship by Earth-based instruments is restricted to a few million km. Beyond this distance any ship of reasonable size would be below the limit of visibility. For example, at a distance of 80,000,000km a sphere of 275m diameter and 100% reflecting power would be well beyond the capabilities of even Baker–Nunn cameras – specially developed for tracking Earth satellites. For ships near Earth, however, optical tracking is feasible. And from the ship itself, such methods may be used when near a planet or moon, only light and compact equipment being required.

Radar tracking can be either Earth- or ship-based, although equipment of only moderate power and range can be carried on a ship. Radar can be passive or active. In the former case, a radiotelescope on Earth can send out a short and powerful burst of radio waves and detect the weak echo reflected from the target. Radar astronomy utilizes the largest installations, such as the 305m dish at Arecibo, Puerto Rico, to measure the distances of planets such as Venus, Jupiter and Saturn. By this means, it has produced highly accurate maps of the Solar System. In the process it has also gathered other information – for example, knowledge of the atmosphere-enshrouded surface of Venus and the nature of the rings of Saturn. But planetary targets are large. No ship would produce a radar echo capable of being detected at such distances.

Active radar tracking employs a transponder in the spacecraft. This device, by directional antenna, accepts the radar pulse from the distant radio telescope, gives the attenuated signal a boost in strength, changes its frequency by a known amount and returns it after a known delay. This electronic wash-and-scrub-and-brush-up achieves a signal that, although unbelievably weak when it returns to Earth, is still capable of being detected by Earth stations. The range of present-day equipment of this nature extends to well beyond the orbit of Saturn.

The data supplied by such systems are highly accurate range and range-rate measurements as well as directions. The range (line of sight distance) is obtained essentially from a knowledge of the velocity of electromagnetic radiation such as radio and light through space and the time between transmission and reception. The range-rate (line of sight speed) is found from the measurement of the frequency shift between transmitted and received radiation (allowing, of course, for the transponder's deliberate shift) caused by the Doppler effect. (This is the name given to the well-known increase or decrease in the frequency of sound or electromagnetic waves caused by the speed of approach or recession of the source relative to the observer. A simple formula enables the velocity in terms of the speed of light to be found from the fractional change in the frequency.)

The radiotelescopes and computers of the Deep Space Instrumentation Facility stations provide present and future positions and velocities of the vehicle. The computers compare the spacecraft's orbit with the planned one and compute the mid-course fine adjustment burns required to put the ship into a new orbit. This is not necessarily the initially desired orbit since the present "erroneous" position of the ship may make it less fuel-consuming to change to a new orbit which also achieves the mission's goal than to attempt a correction putting the ship on to the originally planned course.

Ship-based radar becomes important when the interplanetary spacecraft approaches the planet of destination; it is also important in rendezvous manoeuvres. It has been improved from the early days when Gemini two-man craft practised rendezvous with Agena rockets in Earth satellite orbits by means of onboard radar and computer.

Stabilized platforms and accelerometers of very high standards are now available. Such systems provide attitude reference even if the spacecraft tumbles and can provide coordinates of position and velocity at the end of a powered phase of the mission. In the Gemini capsule the stabilized platform was only 25 x 20cm and weighed about 58kg.

The stabilized platform-accelerometer method of inertial navigation provides an inertial attitude reference system by utilizing well tried principles. Gyroscopes are used – in general, one single-degree-of-freedom gyro being necessary for each of the three mutually perpendicular axes. The acceleration of the vehicle in a given direction is measured by an accelerometer. As with the gyros, an accelerometer is required on the platform for each of the three perpendicular axes to provide the necessary data for an inertial navigation system.

Before launching the vehicle or just prior to a powered phase, the platform is locked on to the desired reference system. During firing, the computer accepts the accelerometer readings, integrating them twice to obtain the components of velocity and position at any instant. In particular, at the end of the powered phase, the characteristics of elements of the spacecraft's orbit can be computed. Comparison with the desired orbit can then be made and the first mid-course correction program can be calculated. The inertial guidance system can then be used to control the manoeuvre.

Space-sextants for measuring the angles between stars and members of the Solar System visible from the ship have been designed and used in the Apollo program. The stars, at an effectively infinite distance from the ship, form a useful reference system of points of known coordinates. Standard procedures exist that lead from sets of such angle measurements to a knowledge of the ship's position and velocity at a given time. In addition, such a position- and velocity-finding method enables a check to be made on the stabilized inertial platform system. Once this calibration is made, the inertial navigation system can be used to control the application of the mid-course correction thrust.

It would therefore appear that, when Man voyages into the depths of the Solar System, science and technology will be able to provide him with a versatile armoury of navigational methods. At any time, even when he is out of touch with Earth, he will be capable of measuring position and velocity and will know what course to take to bring him back safely to the blue-and-green planet that gave him birth.

PART II

Manned exploration:
the new Moon in the old Moon's arms

4 The Exploration of the Moon

Soviet space experts announced today that they had 'lassoed the Moon' with their Zond 5 spacecraft, and brought it back through a six-mile window in the atmosphere to a perfect splashdown in the Indian Ocean.

Press report, September 1968

The night of the first Moon landing was a unique occasion in ASTRA's history. The tension during the approach was quite fantastic: we were expecting the Lunar Module to hover before touching down, as NASA publications had assured us it would do, and there they were 30m up and still travelling forward at 2.75m per second. At 23m up forward speed was 1.8m per second and I was just thinking it would cancel out nicely when we thought we heard:

HOUSTON: "Sixty seconds".

EAGLE: "Lights on; down 2½. Forward, forward forty feet [12.2m], down 2½ [0.76m], picking up some dust . . ."[1]

At that point, although we didn't know it until after the touchdown, Armstrong had already found himself descending into a crater and had taken over manual control to fly on over it, extending the descent track a few hundred metres. The "forty feet" figure was altitude, not forward velocity, at this stage. From the appalled looks that shot round our group, however, at least three of us suspected that the computer, which had given overload warnings earlier in the approach, had now lost control of the ship in the pitch axis. Even if the astronauts straightened it up manually, if the ship touched the ground with 50kph forward velocity it would surely turn right over. I had been muttering "Kill that horizontal component" under my breath for the last few seconds anyway and, when it apparently shot up from 1.8m per second to 12.2 my reaction was: "Dear God, he's lost it." Instead, of course, the supposed forward speed dropped equally suddenly to 1.2m per second, and the LM came down like the helicopters in which the crew had practiced. There was an agonizing pause, followed by: "Houston, Tranquillity Base here. The Eagle has landed."

Ed Buckley's 1962 drawing (fig. 19), based on the first publicly revealed mockup of the Lunar Module (still called Lunar Excursion Module in those days), captures the spirit of anticipation which had been building for so many years. I was still at school when Ed passed that drawing round, as part of a set he had prepared for a lecture on "Lunar Colonization". At the point when the scene with the flag came true, I had been an Honours graduate for a year in spite of changing faculties. "We did it, we did it . . ." Amazingly, complaints about the US flag on the Moon began to march hand-in-hand with complaints about the expense, as if a nation which had spent so much "in peace for all mankind" wasn't entitled to show its symbols. It took a surprisingly long time, with me, for the full significance of "The Eagle has landed" to sink in. The American Eagle, yes . . . but behind it stands the Roman Eagle, among others – Tolkien's "The Eagles are coming!" and Titov's triumphant, "I am Eagle!" We haven't seen the last of that image, by a long way.

Perhaps one of the most disappointing revelations, taking something away from the idea that the Moon landing belonged to everyone and not just to the USA, was the Soviet attempt to return samples from the Moon at the same time using Luna 15. It was probably the first time since Project West Ford that one could say of any spacecraft, "I'm glad that failed." There had been considerable speculation at ASTRA, as elsewhere, about Luna 15's rôle: in the last few hours before the LM touchdown John Braithwaite suggested that we find out what odds we could get, at that point, that the Russians would still land first. Eventually we agreed that to

[Fig 19]

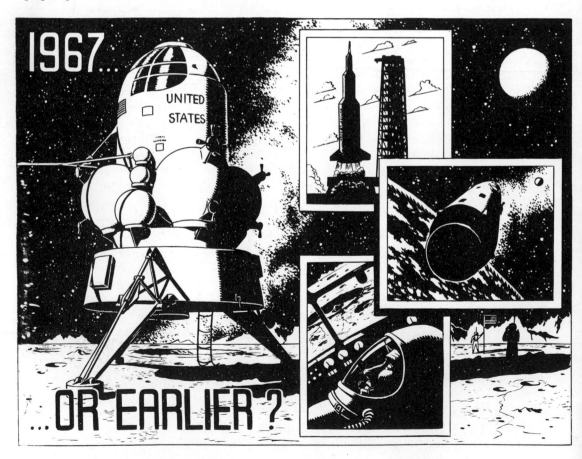

impose radio silence on a manned lunar spacecraft would be far too risky, and concluded that the USSR could only have put up three things entitling it to a share of the Apollo glory: a remote-controlled "lifeboat" capable of lifting Armstrong and Aldrin to rendezvous orbit if the LM failed; a "tanker" with enough fuel to allow the Command Module to reach the LM, if it became trapped in an orbit too low or too high for the scheduled rendezvous; a "Moon house" with sufficient supplies to keep the astronauts alive until rescued, if for any reason they couldn't take off.

But two hours before the LM liftoff Luna 15 began descent manoeuvres and crashed in Mare Crisium: eventually it became clear that the flight had been an attempt to belittle the American achievement by returning a small, random sample with an unmanned craft. Luckily for future cooperation the attempt did fail, and when Lunas 16, 20 and 24 returned samples there were exchanges for material from the Apollo sites. It should again be noted that, whereas Armstrong was able to avoid rough ground on the first manned landing, Lunas 18, 22 and 23 failed to return samples to Earth just because they could not.

The Apollo 11 touchdown was about 6.5km from the intended landing point, but that didn't matter because the chosen region, in the Sea of Tranquillity, was one of the flattest and most uniform places on the Moon. The lunar "seas" (*maria*) are geologically more recent and much smoother than the "highlands". At that stage samples from *anywhere* on the Moon represented a gigantic step forward, in scientific terms – especially because they were intelligently selected, not just happening to lie under a drill or within reach of a grab, and because they were complemented by the solar wind collection experiment which indicated the conditions to which the samples had been exposed for so many years. Likewise the seismometer and other instruments deployed and left were of great value, because discrimination was exercized in picking their exact spots, and they were broadcasting from a site whose general characteristics were known. But the main object of the first landing was just to show that it could be done: the first full flight test of the Lunar Module, including landing and takeoff, and proof that landing on another world did nothing extraordinary to Man – biologically or mentally. It's worth noting that at one time up to 15 practice flights were thought necessary before a landing could be attempted.[2]

For the maximum scientific return, the first series of landings should visit as many sites as possible, as different from one another as possible. Pinpoint landings were going to be needed, firstly to put men and equipment within reach of particular geological features (e.g., Hadley Rille) and secondly because in the lunar highlands and mountains there wouldn't be kilometres of flat "lurain" out of which any landing spot would serve, as long as it wasn't in a crater. The LM would have to be able to find a preselected valley or plateau to get down in one piece.

Logically, then, Apollo 12 had to show whether such landings were possible by attempting an accurate touchdown, although for safety another flat region had to surround the target. For scientific purposes the landing should be in another lunar "sea", not Mare Tranquillitatis again: the mission selected was a landing in Oceanus Procellarum alongside the

Surveyor 3 spacecraft, which had been on the lunar surface for $2\frac{1}{2}$ years. As well as examining the effects of 950 days on the Moon, the mission allowed direct comparison of a human viewpoint with one previously obtained by a machine.

There turned out to be little comparison, despite the failure of the Apollo 12 TV camera when it was accidentally pointed at the Sun. Bean and Conrad bounced around on the Moon with great enthusiasm (as indeed anyone would, after being struck by lightning during takeoff from Earth and spotting the Surveyor from the LM window during approach) and their multiple, human-eye-level views of the scene between the LM and the Surveyor put the unmanned craft's pictures wholly in the shade. The comparison isn't entirely fair, because when the Surveyor pictures were built up into mosaics they gave a better idea of the look of the Moon; but the big composite pictures never made the press. After the panoramas obtained by the relatively unsophisticated Luna 9, coverage had been limited to isolated Surveyor frames showing close-ups of individual rocks, the marks made by spacecraft footpads and entrenching tools, and shots of the spacecraft shadow and distant hills at sunset. In compiling material for this book, I had a real jolt when I opened a 1966 *National Geographic* and found myself looking through a Surveyor 1 mosaic, as through a window, on to the lunar surface whose general appearance has since become so familiar.[3] Surveyor 3 mosaics could be found only in official publications, and it was even stranger to find in them the strewn angular blocks and crater slopes of the Apollo 12 site.[4] Press concentration on individual Surveyor frames must surely be at least partly responsible for the public impression that the Moon is boring.

Little if anything said by the astronauts supports that impression. The surface of the Moon has turned out to be completely different from the early ideas of astronomers, writers and artists. It was generally supposed that in the absence of atmosphere all lunar surfaces would be shear and jagged, as indeed the larger features seem to be when studied from Earth. The mistake was that in vacuum, since light travels in straight lines and the Sun isn't a large-diameter light source, *any* shape on the Moon will throw a sharp shadow and look jagged from here. The classic representations of the Moon, models built by Naismith and Carpenter from telescopic drawings, show even the smallest craters with raised, jagged rims and needle-like rock pinnacles.[5] Another false belief was that, in one-sixth gravity, mountains and slopes generally would be steeper than on Earth; the misconception appears even in Berry's recent *The Next Ten Thousand Years*,[6] and is very evident in artwork – particularly artists' impressions of lunar exploration – at least until the late 1960s. However, as Arthur C. Clarke pointed out in 1951, the angle of a naturally forming slope is determined by geometry, not by the prevailing gravity field, and is the same on the Moon as on the Earth.[7] Even Clarke supposed that without atmosphere the rocks might be sharp and jagged; and I remember Sandy Glover, then President of ASTRA, leafing through *The Conquest of Space* and Pesek's *The Moon and the Planets*[8] muttering, "There's far too much erosion. What's supposed to have caused all this weathering?" As it turned out, even those artists had underestimated the effects of temperature during the great age of the Moon: most crater rims were barely perceptible, and on major features like Mount Hadley and Hadley Rille there wasn't a sharp edge to be seen (Plate 2).

The sharp divisions of light and shade apply down to the smallest lunar pebble. The result is that the visual character of the surface changes completely with the angle of view relative to the Sun: Armstrong and Aldrin noticed the effect even before leaving the LM. "It's gray and it's very white as you look into the zero phase line. And it's considerably darker gray, more like an ashen gray, as you look out 90° to the Sun . . ."[1] Up-Sun, as pictures round the back of the LM showed, the ground appears darker still because it's full of shadows, and when the Sun is higher the lunar soil looks brown.[9] On Earth such effects are much less noticeable because all shadows are softened by light diffused or refracted by the atmosphere, but on the Moon the whole appearance of the landscape changes as the observer moves about.[10] Dave Scott reported that the ground underfoot was always white or grey, but in the distance all round him it became "golden tan".

All Moon landings so far have been made soon after sunrise, when shadows threw the ground into relief and temperatures were low; although any surface exposed perpendicular to the sunlight became very hot, of course. Scott and Irwin on Apollo 15 noticed temperatures rising by their third Earth day on the Moon, and also a marked change in the landscape: as Hadley Rille lost its shadows and became less spectacular, the mountains became dazzling in full sunlight.[11] Matched photographs taken three days apart by the Apollo 17 crew, from the LM window, show the effect clearly.[12] Before complaining about the "sameness" of the Moon, it's worth remembering that all the Apollo landings were made in similar latitudes, and in the same slot of the slow-moving lunar day.

Clarke had pointed out, back in 1951, that on the Moon in sunlight one wouldn't be able to see the stars because the eyes would adjust fully to the glare from the surface.[7] Gemini experiments showed that illumination in space was generally 20% above Earth-surface level,[13] and, although the Moon reflects only 7% of the sunlight falling on it, it can still wash all but the brightest stars out of the sky down here. "The Moon doth with delight, Look round her when the heavens are bare . . ." – and her own skies are bare indeed. Everyone knew that the artists' impressions were wrong, with stars clear down to the horizon, but I don't know if anyone really expected that total blackness in which the Earth, although twelve times the size of the Moon seen from here, seemed so incredibly far away. Repeatedly the remote-control operator of the Rover TV camera would track up the axis of the S–band antenna until he found the Earth again, as if to reassure himself that it hadn't been swallowed by a passing Chinese dragon. Yet none of the astronauts have been lonely or frightened under that sky: Conrad specifically denied it after Apollo 12,[14] and Irwin found his clarity of vision and thought reached the intensity of a religious experience. The lunar sky is bare but not empty: as C. S. Lewis predicted in *Out of the Silent Planet*, space is full of life and energy.[15]

Because of the absolute light and shade of the lunar surface, an observer has only to shade his eyes from sunlight and the ground to bring the stars into view. The statement is made by all the experts and comes up repeatedly in science fiction: in a recent story by Hal Clement a character does it on his first time "outside", just to get his bearings (wrongly, since the Moon's polo star is Zeta Draconis, not Polaris).[16] Interestingly enough, in spite of the deep shadow of the LM available in all those sunrise landings, as far as I know none of the astronauts tried it. Star clusters and other objects were studied in the ultraviolet from the shadow of the Apollo 16 LM,[17] but apparently nobody allocated enough EVA minutes to let the eyes adjust and get an idea of lunar night.

The complaints about lack of colour on the Moon should be answered at night, when we are able to put men there for extended visits – at least on the side of the Moon facing the blue–green Earth. Earth itself will be almost fixed in the sky, while the stars behind it drift slowly from East to West: by the following sunrise Earth will have turned fourteen times on its axis, but it's unlikely that continents can be distinguished under the cloud cover without a telescope, except perhaps for the distinctive brown patch of the Sahara. It used to be said that, in theory, the Great Wall of China could be seen from the Moon; in future generations one feels that may be a very rare event, combining perfect eyesight and perfect conditions, rather like seeing the moons of Jupiter from Earth. Seen from the Moon, Earth is four times the diameter of the Moon seen from here, twelve times the area and at least 60 times as bright. Normal Earthlight will be bright enough to read by; the full Earth will be dazzling and to watch, say, the Moon's shadow crossing it during the terrestrial eclipse of the Sun, dark glasses or visors will be required.

Consequently one will have to find shade from the Earthlight, even in the lunar night, to see the stars properly. Again they will be there, in full glory, to the fully shaded and adjusted eye. But, notwithstanding the predicted loneliness out of sight of Earth, night on the lunar Farside may be sought just for the stars: darkened filters can be dispensed with safely and the eyes can be allowed hours to adjust, without the daytime risk of blindness incurred in a moment of carelessness. So far, nobody on the Moon has had the chance to stand and think, even for five minutes – we don't have any idea of the poems and symphonies to come. As for the paintings – well, so far Ed Buckley and Gavin Roberts are working from only photographs and imagination.

In the later stages of the Surveyor program the spacecraft undertook to photograph some of these events: the changing phases of the Earth, the mysterious afterglow of lunar sunset, the bright specks of laser beams shining on Surveyor 7 across 400,000km. Surveyor 3 had the opportunity to capture an event imagined by successive artists since 1874[5] when in the late morning of its first lunar day the Sun was eclipsed by the Earth. From Earth the event would be seen as an eclipse of the Moon, in which the Moon turns a distinctive blood-red as longer wavelengths are trapped by our atmosphere (that's why our sky is blue). As expected, the Surveyor pictures showed a red ring surrounding the black disc of Earth's nightside as it passed across the Sun; but the cloud cover proved more significant than expected, with gaps between the clouds showing as "beads",[4] somewhat analogous to the

"Bailly's Beads" seen between the lunar mountains at the end of an eclipse of the Sun seen from here.

In one 1920s painting, the artist got the colour effects completely wrong and showed the full Earth in red![18] To see the Moon's rocks lit in red, instead of white sunlight or blue earthlight, future explorers will have to wait for eclipses. Now that we have recording instruments on the Moon, eclipses are of great scientific interest, because the temperature drops far more sharply than at lunar sunset, when the Sun takes an hour to go down. Eclipse studies have revealed several interesting spots where heat is escaping faster than average from the interior of the Moon.[19]

Since Surveyor 1 had survived fourteen days of lunar night, it wasn't surprising that Surveyor 3 stayed operational during the relatively brief temperature changes of the eclipse. By the time of the Apollo 12 landing, of course, the Surveyor had been inert for many months and there was great interest in its condition: as well as the temperature changes of 35 lunar months, the spacecraft had been subjected to the light but ultra-fast bombardment of micrometeors and for half that time to the sub-atomic bombardment of the solar wind. At that time, moreover, although no organic matter had been found in the Apollo 11 samples, the astronauts were still being quarantined on return from the Moon in case they brought back any life-forms dangerous to terrestrial life. Had anything "colonized" the Surveyor?

All the questions had interesting answers. The pinpoint landing was achieved, with a touchdown just over 83m from the Surveyor and less than 0.6m off target.[20] On their second EVA (Extra-Vehicular Activity) Bean and Conrad approached the Surveyor and found its white paint had turned yellow or brown, while its glass panels had been broken. The spacecraft had bounced on its original landing and photographs of the marks showed little difference if any from Surveyor's own pictures at the time; nor could any significant meteoroid damage be found on the TV camera and other parts removed from the Surveyor and brought back to Earth. There were a large number of minute white craters where the discoloured paint had been sandblasted by the dust storm of the LM touchdown[21] – but it seemed the meteor danger to lunar installations was greatly exaggerated. 33 swabs were taken from the TV camera, back on Earth, and introduced into nutrient solutions;[22] only one showed a reaction, a growth of Streptococcus mitis bacteria.[23] Clearly this was not a lunar lifeform, and it was suggested that the bacterium had survived pre-flight sterilization, flight to the Moon and 950 days on the Moon itself; but while it had come from a piece of foam, which might have protected it, it was the only sample (even from the foam) to show a reaction and might have been accidentally contaminated in the laboratory, although precautions had of course been taken.[22]

One aim of the Apollo program was to establish a series of automatic research stations in different parts of the Moon, in precisely chosen locations, to extend the scientific study of each site far beyond the few days of the visits. The first such scientific station was deployed by the Apollo 11 astronauts, but was battery powered; only the laser reflector experiment, intended for very accurate study of the Moon's distance and motion, will remain operational more or less indefinitely, since it is a passive system. Once Apollo 11 had proved the program was practicable, however, more sophisticated systems were sent to the Moon. The Apollo 12 ALSEP (Apollo Lunar Surface Experiments Package) was set up and then fuelled with Plutonium–238, carefully transferred from a storage point in the LM Descent Stage: as of November 1973 the nuclear generator was still fully operational after four years, as were the other four placed by later expeditions.[24] It later passed the five-year mark, its full design lifetime, plus three more years, during which the Apollo 14 unit briefly fell silent. It had been established that moonquakes were concentrated at apogee and perigee, and that Fra Mauro was above an apogee quake centre. In January 1976 the Apollo 14 ALSEP "died", but returned to life in February with one experiment problem "cured"; but at the end of 1977 funding was withdrawn and all the stations were shut down.

Once again the LM Ascent Stage operated perfectly and brought the Moon explorers safely back to the orbiting Apollo. The rendezvous and docking were shown live on television, and a certain commentator was carried away with excitement on glimpsing the astronauts' helmets through the LM windows. "We can see into the spacecraft," he cried, "and they're in there!"

Unless you really know what you're looking at, however, a docking isn't visually very exciting, and certainly didn't make up for the loss of TV pictures from the lunar surface. There was a nice takeoff of the disappointment in *The Rolf Harris Show*, in which the cameras supposedly failed during a Young Generation dance routine and Harris filled in with verbal commentary and simulations. It's usually said that the turn-down in public interest came immediately after Apollo 11, but my impression was that trying to cover 12 without pictures had a great deal more to do with it. We watched the liftoff of Apollo 13 at the home of an ASTRA member, who refused to have the set back on later to find out whether the Trans-Lunar Injection (the rocket burn from parking orbit to Moonbound trajectory) had gone well; it was just too boring to be tolerable.

Two days later I put on my radio for the morning headlines and was shaken by an item beginning: "The trouble with Apollo 13: all plans for a lunar landing have been abandoned and the survival of the astronauts is very much in doubt . . ." The worst thing was that the item assumed, only four hours after the event, that anyone switching on at 8am already knew what had happened. The general consensus at the office was that the spacecraft had probably been struck by a meteor, although it seemed desperately bad luck that such a million-to-one event should occur so early in the history of manned spaceflight.

In fact, a liquid oxygen tank in the Service Module had exploded. The Apollo Service Module, which decelerated the ship into orbit around the Moon and later returned it to Earth, carried LO_2 (liquid oxygen) and liquid hydrogen (LH_2) to power the fuel cells which generate the spacecraft's electricity; in addition, the oxygen tanks supplied the cabin pressurization. All the LO_2 and LH_2 tanks were concentrated with the fuel cells in Sector 4 of the Service Module, an arrangement which proved highly vulnerable.[25]

Since oxygen has to be supplied to the fuel cells (and to the astronauts!) in gaseous form, the tanks contained heater elements which had been damaged, in one Apollo 13 tank, during prelaunch tests. Failing to switch off, the elements reached a temperature at which their insulation charred away; the bare wires then triggered a full-scale fire.[26] The vent valve on that tank had been passed as within acceptable tolerances, although it had not evacuated the tank according to specifications in ground tests; it certainly was not able to cope with the sudden increase in pressure as fire broke out in the tank. Technically, the experts continue to call the Apollo 13 event a "fire" rather than an explosion, because the tank was disrupted by the physical result of liquid oxygen turning into gas rather than by direct release of chemical energy. There may be some similarly precise description of what happened to the tank itself ("non-optimal maintenance of structural integrity" was suggested at ASTRA), but it came apart with "a pretty large bang" which was eventually discovered to have taken the side off the Service Module.

The crew had just finished a TV broadcast to Earth at the time, and so far the flight had been routine: film shows the Mission Control personnel casually sitting at their consoles, and all the eyes coming up together, all the heads turning, as Lovell announces from the spacecraft, "Houston, we've had a problem." Specifically, the ship had undergone "a Main Bus B under-volt", which was a precise way of saying that electrical power from the fuel cells was dropping away to nothing. In addition the instruments showed that life-support oxygen supplies were diminishing rapidly: the astronauts could see gas escaping from the Service Module, and the cloud of gas and ice crystals developing around the spacecraft was seen by two observers on Earth.[27] Remaining oxygen and power would last only 15 minutes, and two hours after the explosion the Command Module was without power, with hardly any drinking water left, and rapidly becoming uninhabitable owing to the build-up of carbon dioxide.

By that time the Lunar Module had been fully powered up and was acting as a lifeboat. It was, however, a lifeboat which had to stay attached to its ship, because the LM could not survive entry into the Earth's atmosphere. Since the LM on its own has a 'velocity budget' of at least 2.57km per second, it came as no surprise that it could shift the locked spacecraft into Earth-return trajectory: what really surprised me was that anything so fragile could push the combined mass of the Command and Service Modules (still almost fully fuelled) without crumpling. But NASA had in fact considered the possible rôle of the LM as a lifeboat, and providentially the original Lunar Module Pilot had been replaced by Jack Swigert, who had made a specialized study of just that possibility.

Lovell, Swigert and Haise improvised an air-purifying system, using the lunar spacesuit hoses to pass used air through lithium hydroxide in the Command Module, and the Apollo was rotated ("barbecue mode") to keep the CM controls from freezing, while cooling water was passed through to the LM in plastic bags.[28]

Round about 1955, faced with a particularly difficult manoeuvre, one of Jeff Hawke's imaginary colleagues remarked: "Just to make it really easy,

I'll come in backwards." The Apollo 13 return was very much in that category: a particularly fiendish touch was that, since the Apollo was already on its modified trajectory for the Fra Mauro landing site (and now had to be modified *back*), the S–IVB upper stage was causing radio interference as it made its own way towards the Moon, to provide a bigger impact for the seismometers there – the impact of the Apollo 12 Ascent Stage had provided results nobody could quite believe (see later).

Apollo 13's return to Earth generated amazing scenes. I found myself in a public bar, packed to the doors; in absolute silence everybody in the place was watching the small screen up above the bar itself – and on the screen was the Apollo 13 Command Module with all three 'chutes open. There was time, as the horizon came up behind it, to think that few images could have meant more in the circumstances – and that neither a football match nor the Miss World contest has generated that kind of attention, in total silence, in any Glasgow pub I've ever been in.

In all, we were to get back to the Moon four more times, in the first round. First, however, there was a pause of more than a year for thorough investigations and action. An extra oxygen tank for life-support was mounted in Sector 1 of the Service Module; extra battery power was provided, enough to bring back the CSM without fuel cells even if the LM were disabled as well; and additional water supplies were also built in – quite apart from the precautions taken to prevent another oxygen tank explosion.[29] Perhaps, in the circumstances, it was inevitable that Apollo 14 should seem an anticlimax, despite the difficulties of the first landing in the lunar highlands. Alan Shepard's triumphant return to space after ten years attracted very little attention. The TV cameras had been modified to survive an accidental glimpse of the Sun; unfortunately, while the S–band antenna deployed by the Apollo 12 crew should have allowed good pictures of the walk to the Surveyor, the Apollo 14 camera could give us nothing but a long, long look into the Sun along the tracks of the astronauts, wheeling their Modular Equipment Transporter (in ordinary terms, a hand-cart) towards Cone Crater, 305m across and about 1.6km away.

Despite the remarkable efforts of Shepard and Mitchell, negotiating such difficult terrain in pressure suits while manhandling the MET, one has to suspect that this mission lost the Moon landings some public support. The camera was looking into the Sun (coming back, the astronauts complained about difficulty moving in their own shadows[30]) and could not be moved by remote control: the pattern of solar reflections across the lens stayed virtually put throughout, moreover, owing to the slow rotation of the Moon. Shepard and Mitchell eventually abandoned their struggle only 23m, as it turned out, from the crater rim – lacking the navigational aids of later missions, and with their view blocked by boulders, they could not judge their position with sufficient accuracy. As a result, despite valuable geological sampling on the outside of Cone Crater, no studies were made on the inside of the largest crater to be approached during the Moon landings and no photos of it were obtained – much less of the ambitious plan to roll boulders down the inner wall. Landings in much bigger craters – Tycho and/or Alphonsus – were then in the program, but never materialized.

It had now been shown, however, that the LM's capability for specified landing sites – demonstrated in theory by Apollo 12 – could be used in practice for a series of research landings in "interesting" locations. By analogy with the old Chinese curse, "May you live in interesting times!", such locations were by definition difficult places to land, rimmed by mountains, chasms and other features on which geologists and pilots would have precisely opposing views. Apollo 15's target was certainly interesting enough: a bend in Hadley Rille (a feature comparable to the Grand Canyon) overlooked by Mount Hadley, 4,600m high but comparable to Everest in its relation to its surroundings.[9] Apart from the Rille itself, the main object was to sample the edge of Mare Imbrium for original material of the lunar crust: Fra Mauro had provided material ejected during the colossal impact which formed Imbrium itself.[31]

Apollo 15 added a new dimension to lunar exploration with the first use of the Lunar Rover, a vehicle which has been described as an 8-million-dollar beach buggy,[11] a spacecraft on wheels,[32] and whose unpacking Harrison Schmitt described as "no small chore when the luggage includes your automobile".[12] Although LRV operations were confined to a 5km radius, to make sure that the astronauts could walk back if the vehicle broke down, there was a spectacular improvement in mobility and coverage – including the first live shots of takeoff from the Moon, during which Al Worden in the Command Module couldn't resist playing "Off we go, into the wild blue yonder" on tape. Unfortunately the camera didn't keep working long enough to capture a subsequent eclipse in colour. Since the Rover camera was remote-controlled, it allowed later viewers to look over the shoulders of the Apollo 16 and 17 crews (seen in amazing clarity owing to computer clean-up of the incoming pictures) during their EVAs at Descartes and Taurus-Littrow, except when their geological enthusiasm took them out of sight behind huge boulders: on one such occasion, Mission Control was heard to remark, "And as our crew sinks slowly in the West ..."

The scientific content of the Apollo program rose sharply from one mission to the next, with inevitable drops in viewing figures at each stage – but it seems heartbreaking that the program should have been abandoned apparently *because* results were materializing in this way.

The first question, and the hardest of all to answer, is "Where did the Moon come from?" It's far from obvious why Earth has a satellite which seems to belong in the retinue of the giant planets, or alternatively be a planet in its own right like Mercury. Mars, which is half the diameter of the Earth, has two minute moons apparently captured from the Asteroid Belt; Venus, nearly the same size as Earth, has no moon at all – indeed, it has been suggested that Mercury may once have been a companion of Venus but was wrenched to freedom. The main astronomical notions are: that the Moon was once physically part of the Earth; or that it was originally an independent world, either forming as a companion to the Earth or being captured by it – perhaps only a few hundred million years ago.[33] Again, the major features of the Moon's face might be recent – warmth radiating from the Imbrium lava flows might have caused Earth's Tertiary

Period, mere tens of millions of years ago[34] – but the majority view was that the lunar surface would carry a record of the earliest days of the Solar System.

Fascinatingly, that turned out to be true without answering the original question. First indications were that the Apollo 11 samples were around 3,500 million years old,[35] while Oceanus Procellarum was 1,000 million years younger[36]; but with the further data obtained from Taurus-Littrow and Hadley, Luna 16 samples, and more detailed analysis, it seems that the formation of the maria took place between 3,200 and 3,800 million years ago.[37] By contrast, Earth's ocean basins are less than 300 million years old and hardly any parts of Earth's present surface are as old as 3,000 million years, due to volcanic activity and the continuous action of the atmosphere. Yet the lunar "seas" are the most *recent* features of the Moon's surface: great lava flows which followed the major period of crater formation, flooding many older formations which now appear as bright peaks isolated in the maria (Pico in Mare Imbrium is a famous example), as "ghost rings" visible at certain angles of illumination, and as scallops on the mare edges – Sinus Iridum, the Bay of Rainbows, being one.

At the two highland sites visited, Fra Mauro and Descartes, extensive breccias (broken rock) indicated heavy bombardment of the lunar surface 3,800–4,000 million years ago. So complete was the shattering and melting that hardly any moonrocks are as old as 4,600 million years (not even Apollo 15's famous "Genesis Rock"), and the hope of finding original Solar System material has not been realized. Indeed it now seems that the planetary surfaces have all been blasted and melted over and over again during the first few hundred million years of their histories, and to obtain original material we should look at the remaining free-flying material in the Solar System – the asteroids, the nuclei of the comets, and perhaps the extraordinary moons of Mars.

The influence of impacts on the lunar surface was obvious even in the mare landings: one of the first revelations of the Apollo 11 EVA was that there are large amounts of glass in the rock (natural glass is very rare on Earth, found only as obsidian). Buzz Aldrin had said in jest that he expected to find a purple rock on the Moon, but in fact he did find tinted glass.[38] When an Apollo 11 sample was displayed in Glasgow, in a rotating plastic globe, its surface showed pinpoint flashes as the glass microspheres embedded in it caught the museum lights. Very few people seemed to look at the rock long enough to notice that it wasn't just a gray pebble.

There will be a book to be written, some day, about the travels and adventures of the moonrock around the world. So far, under 10% of the Apollo samples has had detailed analysis[37] – not too surprising, since the work is very slow, very painstaking and (on a day-to-day basis) not very exciting. After all, we could hardly expect to continue at the level of the BBC *Tomorrow's World* programme when a phalanx of Securicor men straight from Heathrow lined the studio to guard all the moonrock *en route* to British researchers in the first division of Apollo 11 samples.

In 1968, even after the photographic coverage of the Moon from Lunar Orbiter, and photography up to impact by Rangers 7, 8 and 9, it was still possible for a distinguished scientist to say: "I see no evidence for lava flows on the Moon."[39] Until Ranger 7, the first successful shot in the program, it had been possible to maintain that the maria were deep basins of dust into which spacecraft would sink – a view directly opposed to the one that there would be little erosion on the Moon. Rangers 7, 8 and 9 took detailed pictures up to impact in Mare Nubium, Mare Tranquillitatis and the crater Alphonsus; small craters were detected down to 25cm across, proving that the "seas" were not deep dust; the next step, taken by Luna and Surveyor probes, was to learn whether they were firm enough to support spacecraft.

(Although the seas are not deep dust beds, the general idea of dust movement from the lunar mountains may nevertheless be correct. It has been suggested that the "Moon glows" reported by amateur astronomers may be dust movements, possibly electrostatic, rather than the volcanic events usually surmised.[40])

Inevitably the first landings opened up a further range of possibilities. The Lunar Orbiters had discovered "mascons", concentrations of high-density material underneath the maria. Were they the remains of giant meteorites which had created the maria? If, as began to be believed, they were upwellings of denser material from below, then had the "Imbrium event" and the rest been impacts or volcanic? Strong cases for the volcanic origins of lunar features had been made in the past,[34] and appeared to be strengthened by the relative scarcity of maria on the Farside of the Moon – whatever the origin of the lava flows, tidal forces imposed by the Earth seemed to be involved.

After Apollo 14's sampling of the breccia south of Mare Imbrium, it came to be accepted that big impacts, in the later stages of cooling of the Moon, had been followed later by lava flows which filled the maria. Immediately two further questions arose. Had the Moon ever been molten right through, or was its early formation a relatively gentle accretion of cold particles, with only the surface layers melting under bombardment as the Solar System was swept clear? Or was there still volcanic activity on the Moon after all? The professional astronomers had solidly maintained for decades that the Moon was completely dead, cold right through, a world without activity apart from the occasional meteor strike. Amateur astronomers had doggedly continued to report mists and glows on the lunar surface, particularly in the larger craters, and in 1959 Kozyrev had obtained a spectrogram of an apparent carbon dioxide outbreak in Alphonsus.[41]

Apollo 15's landing at Hadley Rille was intended to look into those questions. The lunar rilles were unexplained features, and it was possible that volcanic forces were involved in their origin: Scott and Irwin thought the Rille was a geological rift, formed by lateral movement of the lunar crust (the Straight Wall in Mare Nubium is an example of vertical movement) but the majority scientific opinion is that the Rille is a collapsed lava tube. A remarkable feature of the site was that the marked striations in the walls of the Rille, enhancing its resemblance to the Grand Canyon, were matched by extraordinary parallel strata sweeping diagonally across the face of Mount Hadley.[9] (Scott was so impressed by the regularity of those bands that the Flying Saucer movement now maintains he was describing an artificial structure.[42]) Those observations ended ideas that the Moon's battered crust would be homogenous.

As well as the Lunar Rover, Apollo 15 had a major innovation in the form of the SIM (Scientific Instrument Module) bay built into Sector 1 of the Apollo Service Module, below the new tanks added after Apollo 13. While Scott and Irwin were on the Moon, Worden in the CSM was carrying out a major program of orbital studies, during which he reported apparently volcanic domes and cinder cones in the valley of Taurus-Littrow. Taurus-Littrow become the site of the Apollo 17 landing, and there was great excitement when "orange soil" was discovered at Shorty crater, in dark rim material which looked like a volcanic vent. Alas, the orange colour proved to be due to coloured glass,[12] like Aldrin's "purple rock". Later the crew were heard announcing what appeared to be volcanic dikes in the boulders they were studying, but that doesn't seem to have been confirmed yet.

Meanwhile, the interior of the Moon was turning out "curiouser and curiouser". It was known, of course, that the Moon's overall density was lower than the Earth's, and no one was very surprised when Luna 2 established in 1959 that there was no planetary magnetic field like the Earth's. In the absence of an electrically conducting core, no such field would be expected. But there were reports that the seismometer left behind by Apollo 11 was picking up only surface tremors, with no waves coming from deeper within the Moon.[43] "Instrument malfunction" was suspected. But when the Apollo 12 Ascent Stage was deliberately crashed back into the Moon near the newly deployed ALSEP, the selenologists were amazed to find that even this minor blow set the Moon "ringing like a bell" – reverberations continued for 55 minutes, more than ten times longer than expected. Perhaps the Moon was unstable, and the impact had triggered a cascade of minor avalanches, crater wall slumping and crustal fractures?[44] It seemed unlikely, since meteorite impacts must occur *fairly* often; but it raised uneasy thoughts about crevasses opening under Lunar Modules, or rolling landslides, if there were to be meteor strikes while crews were on the Moon. The other explanation put forward, with a nervous laugh, was that of course the Moon just might be hollow . . .

That wild notion attracted some attention at ASTRA. Early in 1969 John Braithwaite had calculated that, with a sufficiently compressed form of molecular storage, all the information in the Universe could theoretically be encoded on the inside of a hollow sphere the size of the Earth, to be read out by a central scanning unit – although, as Robert Sheckley has pointed out, there might be some difficulty in framing apposite questions.[45] At that time there were still some grounds for suggesting, as I. S. Shlovskii had done, that the inner moon of Mars might be a hollow metal sphere – the next intuitive leap would be that possibly, just possibly, someone had placed a Galactic Library where we could reach it when we were ready to use it.

But if the *Moon* were hollow . . . Maybe there isn't as much information in the Universe as we thought, or indeterminacy limits the amount which can be set down. And there is the continuing, nagging problem that the

Moon seems to be too big to be a natural companion of the Earth. Fantastic as it would be if we had evolved in the shadow of the Universal Library, "everybody's got to be somewhere". As it was announced that the Apollo 13 S–IVB stage would be deliberately crashed into the Moon (reverberations lasted four hours that time), and some scientists speculated about an exception to the Test Ban Treaty, Just this Once,[28] the question arose, "If it is the Universal Library, how hard do we have to hit it to interrogate it?" The mere thought of a dump of all the recordable knowledge in the Universe, across only 400,000km, is enough to give anyone a headache.

The eventual conclusion was that the Moon's crust was remarkably rigid and so the reverberations took much longer to die out than they would in the Earth's crust. After all, the crust had to be unusually rigid to support the mascons, and those high-density lumps embedded in it might be involved in the unusual seismic processes. But if the Moon had an unusual crust, were we still certain that all was dead and inert underneath? Sure enough, the Apollo 12 magnetometer reported that there *was* a magnetic field in Oceanus Procellarum. Until more magnetometers were positioned, it wouldn't be possible to say whether the field was on the surface or from below – it might emanate from the mascons, for instance. (It turned out to be in the surface rocks.[39]) But, either way, it seemed that the Moon had had a magnetic field in the past. Perhaps the Moon was formed hot, with a molten core which soon cooled down.

Part of the Apollo 15 scientific objectives now assumed great importance. Scott and Irwin were to obtain geological core samples from depths to 3m, but in addition two 3m holes were to accommodate a series of thermometers, connected to the ALSEP transmitter, to monitor the flow of heat from the interior of the Moon. The ground at Hadley Base proved surprisingly resistant, to the extent that Scott told Mission Control he hoped fooling around with the drill was more important than studying the geology of the area. Indeed, it turned out to be important: far from indicating the cooldown of a once-hot Moon, the Heat Flow Experiment strongly suggested that the lunar interior was still active. The Moon's centre must be considerably more radioactive than the meteorites which had formed the basis of previous Earth and Moon conceptual models.[46] Confirmation of the heat-flow value was urgently needed, but, alas, in deploying the Apollo 16 ALSEP John Young caught his foot in the Heat Flow Experiment cable. For the first time the three seconds' time-lag to and from the Moon became critical and Mission Control could only watch in despair as Young turned, in the usual lunar slow-motion, and tore the cable out of the apparatus. A repair attempt inside the LM was considered, but dismissed owing to lack of time;[47] instead another Heat Flow Experiment (not originally planned) was added to the Apollo 17 ALSEP and was the first package to be deployed.[48] By chance, BBC radio coverage picked up what I consider the best line spoken on the Moon, as Eugene Cernan belligerently declared: "Okay, nobody touch my Heat Flow Experiment!"

The Taurus-Littrow readings apparently confirmed the Hadley Base data: the Moon was losing heat, overall, half as fast as the Earth – meaning that, by unit of volume, the lunar interior generated twice as much heat as the Earth's core.[39] Evidence for radioactive materials on the Moon, in relative abundance, was building up from the orbital gamma-ray experiments carried by the Apollo SIM bay: a band across Mare Imbrium from north of Fra Mauro to west of Hadley Rille is twenty times richer in uranium and thorium than any other mountain or mare region.[37] The Apollo 15 orbital alpha-particle spectrometer detected radon, produced by radioactive decay, emanating from the crater Aristarchus;[19] similar emissions were found in Grimaldi.[39] By 1977 the heat-flow estimates had been reduced by one third, but the core material was still more active than Earth's.

Another Apollo 15 task was seen as still more important: its ALSEP seismometer readings could be triangulated with those from the Apollo 12 and 14 instruments to pinpoint the origins of "moonquakes". The jackpot came on 13 May 1972, when a meteorite about 1.8m in diameter struck the Moon 141km north of Fra Mauro, creating a new crater 90m across.[49] Such major events on the Moon are probably years apart on average, and the scientific community was delighted to have one when no less than four ALSEP seismometers (12, 14, 15 and 16) were operating.[50] Better still, on 17 July a mass of at least a tonne fell on the far side of the Moon.[39]

Under Fra Mauro, from analysis of the shockwaves, the lunar crust appeared to be twice as thick as under Earth's continents. The seismic waves indicated that, below the broken rock/soil layer ("regolith") which covers the entire Moon, the mountains were solid rock: the findings tied in with the stratification observed in Mount Hadley, and the analysis of the Luna 20 mountain samples, which were 50–60% anorthosite like the "Genesis Rock".[51] But far more important was the absence of shear waves passing through the heart of the Moon: data from both impacts indicated that the Moon had a liquid core 965km down, extending 772km from the centre.

Continued monitoring revealed many small "moonquakes" occurring at the boundary layer, apparently produced by tidal stresses (all the Apollo 12 seismometer events occurred within three days of perigee, when the Moon is nearest to the Earth,[43] and the Apollo 14 ALSEP's month of silence was another demonstration). Stranger still, it has been shown that the Moon's centre of mass is displaced 3.2km towards Earth from the actual centre of the Moon; one of the first major results of the SIM bay laser altimeter was to pin down the discrepancy.[52] As yet there's no adequate explanation for this peculiarity of the lunar core – the core that nobody thought could exist.

What, then, of that other great question – how did the Moon get there in the first place? The three main alternatives are that the Moon separated from the Earth, perhaps from the bed of what is now the Pacific Ocean; that the Moon formed as a companion to the Earth, at the same time that Earth itself took shape; and that the Moon was a completely independent body, a planet in its own right, which was captured by the Earth and now shares its orbit around the Sun. (The Moon's path, as seen from the Sun, is not a set of overlapping circles but a smooth succession of scallop-shaped curves, weaving back and forth across the orbit of the Earth.)

The classic view, of birth from the Earth, has always been subject to crippling problems: for example, there are clearly defined mathematical limits, called Roche Limits, to the minimum distances which must exist between one heavenly body and another if the smaller is not to be torn apart by tidal stresses imposed by the larger. Saturn's rings are within the planet's Roche Limit, and clearly show that no large solid body can exist there. If the Moon broke free from the Earth it should have disintegrated at once, and all the king's horses and all the king's men would have had trouble reassembling it. (The same applies, with all the forces involved magnified immensely, to Immanuel Velikovsky's idea that Venus was "born" out of Jupiter.)

Another objection, voiced before the first Moon landing, was that if Earth's continental material (generally called SiAl or SiNaK from the chemical symbols of the predominant elements) were originally a crust covering the whole planet, then the departing Moon should have taken fully three-quarters of it to give the present distribution. The bulge separating from Earth would thus have to have a larger surface area than Earth itself, a hypothesis which C. W. Wolfe of Boston University politely called "mechanically unattractive".[53] Moreover, by that time partial chemical analysis, by the alpha-particle scattering experiment on Surveyors 5 and 6, indicated that the best terrestrial match for moonrock was basalt, the material of the ocean basins.[54] The general view now is that moonrock is chemically so different from terrestrial materials that the two bodies probably formed separately:[37] even the preliminary analysis of the Apollo 11 samples revealed a major difference, a higher proportion of titanium than in any terrestrial rocks.[55] In general, moonrock is richer in elements which form refractory compounds at 1600–1800 K – i.e., the Moon seems to have formed out of a hotter cloud than the one indicated by Earth's crustal materials.[37] (The major consequence, as regards future plans for the Moon, is that there is no water bound up in moonrock. Minute traces of rusty iron were found in two Apollo 14 samples, but they may have been hydrated after return to Earth.)

The separation hypothesis is not dead yet, however. O'Keefe has pointed out that some tektites, mysterious glassy fragments found in large numbers in various, widely separated parts of the Earth, resemble terrestrial rocks much more closely than the known moonrocks. Yet there is no evidence of the huge impacts which would have been needed to throw so much matter out of Earth's atmosphere; nor, even if there had been such impacts, would the returning fragments have travelled fast enough to be ablated as they are in the Australian tektite field.[56] (Chapman has argued that the tektites are mostly debris from the impact which formed the lunar crater Tycho; two particularly large fragments striking Germany and Ghana produced the Czechoslovakian and Ivory Coast tektite fields, which *are* terrestrial secondary fragments.[57]) O'Keefe's suggestion is that deep within the Moon there may be a layer identical to the Earth's crust[56] (and therefore, presumably, a moonlike layer within the Earth). Having dispensed with the idea that the Moon might be hollow, we now have to consider that it may be inside-out!

The idea that Earth and Moon formed separately, but as companions, is likewise still in circulation. Reid has suggested, as an addition, that initially the Moon may have had satellites of its own; the combined tidal action of the Earth and Moon would have caused such bodies' orbits to decay. After break-up within the Moon's Roche Limit, the biggest fragments would take about another thousand years to crash onto the Moon, perhaps forming Mare Crisium and Mare Serenitatis.[59]

An attractive alternative to the conventional ideas has been advanced independently by Smith and Mitler, the latter extending calculations by Opik.[58] They suggest that a number of "proto-moonlets" formed between 0.8 and 1.2 Astronomical Units from the Sun. (Earth's orbital distance, about 150 million km, is 1AU, by definition.) These bodies formed hot and differentiated into core and mantle structures like the Earth's. One by one, however, they passed Earth between the Roche Limits for rock and iron and broke up, the dense core material flying on while the crustal matter was trapped in orbit around the Earth and coalesced into the present Moon. In the final stage of sweeping up the loose matter in the System some core fragments might strike the Moon, releasing the lava flows which formed the mascons and the maria.

It's at this point, having summarized some of the big question-and-answer situations in the exploration of the Moon, that the story of detection comes to an abrupt halt. Once upon a time the Moon landings were to go up to Apollo 20 : Fra Mauro was to have been the Apollo 13 target, and, in addition to Hadley, Descartes and the vicinity of Littrow, there were to be landings in Censorinus, Copernicus, Tycho and the Marius Hills.[60] Apart from the last, which like Taurus-Littrow was an apparently volcanic region, all the sites not reached were craters. The way things turned out, indeed, the biggest crater approached was Cone, at Fra Mauro, and the astronauts didn't manage to see into it. Notice how the landings would have continued the lines of enquiry presented above : Marius might have provided the conclusive evidence of volcanism not found at Taurus-Littrow; Copernicus and Tycho are both relatively late, major craters, surrounded by extensive "ray" systems of light-coloured crustal material hurled out by the impacts, and both have been reported to generate "mists" which may be gases escaping from the interior of the Moon; Alphonsus, another suggested target, was the crater in which Kozyrev reported a carbon dioxide outbreak, and had been photographed up to impact by Ranger 9, as well as by Lunar Orbiter IV – outcrops in the 1,800m walls might be ancient highland rocks; crustal rocks from great depths may be found in the central peak; the central ridge of the crater may be formed of extruded volcanic rock, and dark-haloed craters, possibly volcanic, lie along the faults in the crater floor where the Kozyrev outbreak was observed.[61]

Tycho could have settled the tektite question, at least in part; the floors of Tycho and Copernicus are not flooded with lava, and so should have provided data on the lunar crust, the material below it *and* the material which struck it. Dr Leon T. Silver said, "If you had only two missions left to make, you'd send one of them to Tycho."[28] If Tycho samples *had* matched terrestrial rocks in composition, the origin of the Moon might have been established; but at all events, if the question is answered now it will be by long and thorough detective work which might have been avoided had the program taken its course.

For sheer visual spectacle, the crater landings should also have been outstanding – less so on the ground, perhaps, unless made near the walls or the central peaks, because the nearness of the lunar horizon would hide most of the scenery from an observer out on the crater floor; but on approach – well, the Lunar Orbiter oblique shot of Copernicus has been dubbed "the picture of the century".[62]

In concluding the defense of the Moon landings, something should be said about the attempts which have been made, in the media, to belittle the astronauts themselves. When Ed Mitchell of Apollo 14 was in the UK, assisting BBC coverage of lunar missions, he was repeatedly asked a blanket question which went: "Borman has taken up religion, Irwin says he found God on the Moon, you yourself have become involved in ESP, the Apollo 15 crew were involved in a scandal over stamps, Aldrin has had a nervous breakdown and several of the astronauts are divorced – doesn't all this prove that the strains of spaceflight are too much for man to cope with?" To this Captain Mitchell would reply politely, each time, that he couldn't speak for the personal experiences and problems of the other astronauts; but that he hadn't undergone any unbearable stress in space, and his interest in psychic phenomena dated back many years – his experiments during his own flight had been organized with the help of the Rhine Foundation for Research on the Nature of Man, and of the American Society for Psychical Research.[63]

A similar reply could in fact be made concerning the religious commitments of Borman and Irwin. Borman was already a lay reader at his episcopal church before he went to the Moon;[64] Irwin reveals in his autobiography that he had experienced deep religious feelings before, and the effect of the lunar mission was to make those feelings permanent.[11] Speaking as a non-believer, I have to say that I find the astronauts' displays of religion embarrassing; although not more so, certainly, that Kruschev's inanity about Gagarin and Titov failing to see God in space, to which Grissom and others made stereotyped replies at the time.[65] I think it's fair to ask why the Apollo 8 crew had to read the Book of Genesis at Christmas, rather than the New Testament, and what influence they had on the California Board of Education, which has yielded to fundamentalist pressure and now requires Genesis to be taught as a valid alternative to the known history of the Earth.[66] (In case any reader thinks that's a minor backward step, let us recall that certain Catholic colleges taught the revolution of the Earth around the Sun as a convenient *but false* hypothesis until well into the 19th century, and the Church continued to claim – though not exercise – the right of Inquisition until still more recently.)

Nevertheless, the astronauts are entitled to their beliefs and one can only deplore a militant atheist attempt, in 1970, to obtain a Supreme Court injunction against public prayers in space.[28] With reference to the supposed crack-ups of the astronauts involved, one has to point out that there are still some sections of society where preaching the Christian faith is not regarded as discreditable, nor yet as indicating *ipso facto* that a man has lost his wits. Victorian science writers would have expected a space traveller's religious convictions to be strengthened; they would be amazed to find so few probing interviewers asking whether Irwin's experience might conceivably be genuine.

The so-called "stamp scandal" seems a clear instance of grasping any stick to beat the space program. Stamp collecting is a virtuous hobby, which small boys are encouraged to take up for vaguely character-building reasons. It takes real imagination to relate it to the solemn tones in which we were told Scott and Irwin took stamps to the Moon, as if it had been raw heroin to be cut with moondust. Even stranger, we recalled from the TV coverage (and from the NASA film) stamps being cancelled quite openly at Hadley Base, while now we were assured stamps had been carried in secret. A British newspaper published an exposé of misconduct by astronauts since the outset. It was alleged that Scott Carpenter had been dismissed from the space program for disobedience and irresponsibility in orbit, leading to the near-destruction of the Mercury capsule during re-entry (if so, it's odd that he should be trusted in the no-less-responsible aquanaut program). More seriously, it was said that Grissom's near-drowning was because his suit was weighted down with coins and souvenirs. Grissom, of course, was safely dead in the Apollo fire and unable to reply, but that in itself suggests a contradiction. In view of the reason given for Carpenter's alleged dismissal, how had Grissom come to be trusted with the proving flights of both Gemini and Apollo?

In due course the results of NASA's investigation were published. In addition to 243 authorized postal covers carried by the astronauts, a further 398 had been carried without permission. "These covers were not listed as being in Scott's preference kit; had they been so listed, they would probably have been routinely approved for inclusion in a preference kit as had the 243 authorized covers noted above."[67] For taking the covers without prior permission, the astronauts' military Efficiency Reports were endorsed with a finding of lack of judgment; for the intention to profit from the sale of the covers (unlike the authorized ones), they received formal reprimands.

It would be interesting, although perhaps not pleasant, to meet the genius who decided the astronauts shouldn't profit from their efforts even *via* such a harmless activity as philately. I visualize it as a committee effort – "These rules won't do, Mr Chairman, they'd let them take *stamps* to the Moon" (gasps of horror all round). It's striking that the media point, quite rightly, to astronauts' broken marriages and nervous breakdowns as indications of the demands made on them, in training and still more in subsequent publicity,[38] but simultaneously accept without question the policy that the men concerned shall receive no direct return for those personal sacrifices. It's nice (as well as helpful to other authors) that one by one they are reaping an indirect reward by writing books. Meanwhile, the Apollo 15 investigation concludes: ". . . the Department of Justice is investigating whether any criminal statutes have been violated and also whether any civil action on behalf of the Government is warranted. The Department of Justice has requested that NASA issue no further statement on this matter until the Department has completed its review."

In this chapter, I've tried to show how much was achieved in the Moon landings, and why ASTRA's view is that the cost and effort involved were worthwhile. In the process it has become much clearer to me, and hopefully to the reader as well, how much was lost by halting the endeavour in full flight. When the last two landings were cancelled, even scientists opposed to manned spaceflight were moved to protest: after the massive initial investment had been made, the full scientific return should surely have been realized – the saving on the last two missions was miniscule by comparison. Dr Thomas Gold described it as "like buying a Rolls-Royce and then not using it because you claim you can't afford the gas".[28]

The Radio Astronomy Explorer satellite, placed in orbit around the Moon in June 1973, uses the Moon as a shield from the radio noise of the Earth and Sun but is not engaged in studies of the Moon itself. Consequently the only scientific investigations of the Moon now under way are the analyses of the returned moonrock. More than 360kg were returned in all: only 80% have had even cursory examination so far, 5% have been distributed to investigators and 3% have been fully analysed.[68] NASA hopes to launch a polar orbiting lunar satellite, carrying gamma- and X-ray spectrometers to map the geochemical profile of the entire lunar surface. (This was another of the Apollo missions which might have been, extending SIM studies to the whole Moon.) The scientific importance of the mission should be obvious. But for our purposes it should be doubly welcomed, because it will allow more detailed assessment of the resources of the Moon and their possible use to mankind. It seems highly likely that Man's return to the Moon will have practical objectives, beyond the resumption of scientific exploration, and the spectrometer satellite will help bring those objectives into focus.

5 The Colonization of the Moon

A. F. Nimmo
President, European Space Association

> Man might as well project a voyage to the Moon, as attempt to employ
> steam navigation across the stormy North Atlantic ocean.
>> Dr Dionysius Lardner to the British Association, 1838

In 1967, at the Dallas Symposium on the Commercial Uses of Space,
Barron Hilton proposed that an orbital hotel could be made a viable
economic proposition. I'm sure it would be, and that the Lunar Hilton
will be even more so. It will probably be booked up for decades in advance.

Provided there was a regular reliable transport system to and from the
Moon, and that it wasn't too expensive, most people would probably like to
go there. All human beings are by definition involved in mankind's never-
ending search for adventure but, equally, nobody is going to spend the
vast sums which would be required to set up a lunar colony unless they
can persuade themselves that there are more practical reasons for doing
so than simple adventure. The questions as to whether or not the Moon
will ever be colonized and as to what kind of colony it will be if we do
build one, will depend entirely on what kind of motivation we have for
doing so, so we must first ask ourselves the question: "Why go to the Moon?"
The answer most commonly given by scientists to this question can be
summed up in one word, "knowledge". This is natural, as the increase of
human knowledge is the business of science. Here are ten possible reasons
which might be put forward, but there would no doubt be many more:

(1) To study the subject of gravity in ways in which it cannot be studied
from this planet alone.

(2) To study the effects on human and on other life of gravity when it
is only one sixth of that on Earth. It has even been suggested that a cure
for cancer may be found in a lunar medical laboratory.

(3) To study time.

(4) To study the effects of the extremes of lunar temperatures upon the
various chemical combinations present, coupled with both the low gravity
and high vacuum.

(5) To study new compounds which may be found or manufactured there.

(6) A large number of the experiments which could be done in artificial satellites could be done just as easily on the Moon, and probably with more comfort. In the cases where gravity was required there would be no need to simulate this artificially as in a satellite; and if a scientific colony were going to the Moon anyway for other purposes it could possibly be more economic to include a couple of, say, vacuum technologists and their equipment than to build and launch an artificial satellite specifically for their purposes. It might even become possible that some of their equipment could be built on the spot with material from lunar sources.

(7) By studying solar phenomena from the Moon and their effects on the weather on both the Moon and the Earth, meteorologists might greatly increase their knowledge.

(8) To search for evidence which may be available on the Moon which could help in the study of the origins and history of the Solar System.

(9) To take advantage of the Moon's comparatively low gravitational field by using it as a stepping stone towards the exploration and exploitation of space and other parts of the Solar System.

(10) To build larger or better telescopes than can be built here on Earth for X-ray, radio and optical astronomy. X-ray telescopes, for example, could be used to pinpoint quasars with much greater accuracy from the Moon than from here on Earth; if you built a 90m reflector telescope on the Moon you could resolve a planet of approximately Jupiter's size orbiting Alpha Centauri. It has been claimed that, by making use of modern computer enhancement and other electronic techniques, it might be possible to extend the search out to eight parsecs or thereabouts and to resolve much smaller planets around the nearer stars. Such a telescope just could not be built here on Earth with our present techniques, and, while a new process at present under investigation might enable us to do so, we would still have the fuzziness of the Earth's atmosphere to contend with. If used to focus solar radiation, such a reflector on the Moon might also be a very handy power source – apart altogether from what it might do to cosmology.

Unfortunately, irrespective of how useful much of this new knowledge might prove to the human race, it is unlikely that many of our politicians would be impressed by it and, even if they were, it would be well-nigh impossible to put these kinds of ideas over to the general public with sufficient impact to persuade them to shell out the tremendous amounts of money which would be required to set up a lunar colony. If the expense could be reduced this difficulty could be partially avoided.

So long as the cost of space exploration remains as high as it is at present, and so long as the reasons for going there remain as uninteresting (and in some cases unintelligible) to the public as many of those at present being put forward, it will remain most unlikely that any serious attempt will be made to set up a lunar colony. In order to determine whether or not it would really be worth our while to set up a permanent base or colony there, let us therefore look at the problem of cost and see if this can be brought down to more reasonable levels, and then consider whether the Moon has any potential (other than that of adding to our store of pure knowledge) which could be used on a practical basis to help solve problems with which we are already faced, or which can be seen clearly arising in our near future.

The modern Moon rocket consists of several gigantic fuel tanks, vast quantities of fuel, a collection of mighty engines, guidance systems, and a tiny capsule containing men and their equipment. The vast majority of its mass is the mass of the engines and of the fuel to lift them and itself. If it had to carry up less fuel it could have smaller, less massive and less costly engines, or carry up more men and equipment. In either case the cost per man of transport to the Moon and back would be less. A rough breakdown of the purposes for which all this fuel is required at present shows that fuel is needed not only for each surface-to-orbit transition and for Earth-orbit-to-lunar-orbit transfer, but also to carry engines, fuel, tanks and structure for each later stage of the mission.

The Americans have developed a shuttle vehicle which is capable of going up to orbit and then coming back down and landing on Earth under its own power. Even such a vehicle will not cut down on any of the above requirements, as all of these objects and fuel to power the various stages will still have to be taken up. Should it be possible, however, to refuel on the Moon itself, a lot of this take-off mass would immediately be removed. Even better, if fuel could be placed in lunar orbit from the Moon, refuelling could be done there. A lunar station capable of launching fuel into lunar orbit could launch it into Earth orbit. In fact, due to the Moon's lower gravity we could find it much cheaper in such circumstances to do all Earth-orbit refuelling with fuel from the Moon.

Further, with orbital refuel capabilities and a shuttle service we should be able to construct and launch reusable inter-orbit vehicles between Earth and Moon and institute a lunar shuttle service as well. It might well work out cheaper to refuel future more advanced shuttles in Earth orbit, to carry down from orbit the fuel to power flight back up again. With this system the Earth would not be required to provide any fuel whatsoever for space flight, and all the hardware would be much cheaper to build; in the case of the purely space-going vehicles, it would probably last virtually forever. Space journeys could become cheaper than aeroplane flights.

The most common element in our Universe, hydrogen, is first-class fuel for rocket propulsion, in its liquid form (LH_2) or in chemical combination. In their article "The Carbon Chemistry of the Moon" in *Scientific American* for October 1972, Geoffrey Eglinton, James R. Maxwell and Colin T. Pillinger describe a pyrolysis of lunar fines brought back by Apollo 11. "As the temperature was raised our spectrometer showed abundant hydrogen, then small amounts of methane, other hydrocarbons of low molecular weight and the noble gases." They later go to to say: "Hydrogen, carbon and nitrogen are concentrated at the surface of the grains of the lunar fines," and that there was "superabundance of oxygen from silicates and other lunar sources". There have also been several other reports confirming the discovery of hydrogen on the Moon as a result of other analyses of rock and soil brought back by Apollo 11 and the other manned lunar missions.

It would appear from this that all one had to do was to heat the lunar soil to obtain an abundance of hydrogen. Unfortunately, the hydrogen compounds are at the *surfaces* of lunar grains and were most probably deposited by the Solar Wind. The absence of water in lunar samples studied so far suggests that hydrogen may not be available from moonrock in significant quantities. However (all of this is very tentative), it is suspected that infall material containing such hydrogen may go down to depths of several hundred metres in places. Fresh pressure from meteoritic bombardment could even have created veins of water, which would thereafter solidify to ice, sixty to a hundred metres below ground level in some areas. This creates the possibility of a lunar ice-mining industry, but such veins of ice are very unlikely. Even if they are there, mining them might not be worthwhile, since use of lunar oxygen alone in LH_2/LO_2 rockets would still increase the payload of lunar landers by 60%. A process has been developed for extraction of oxygen from lunar rock, by chemical combination with hydrogen brought from Earth. If the water so formed is electrolysed to release free oxygen, the hydrogen can be reused. (For the water supplies a lunar colony would require, it has been suggested that a superconducting ion scoop could collect thousands of tons of hydrogen per year from the Solar Wind.)

In order to make lunar colonization economic we must therefore first build a fuel-manufacturing chemical plant on the Moon. If in addition we were to set up Arthur Clarke's lunatron concept, a version of which has now been renamed the "mass driver", we could probably reduce the costs of our space flights even further. This concept uses a solar-powered linear motor to launch objects, even spaceships, electromagnetically from a slightly rising ramp on the Moon. According to theory this could be achieved by solar power using a few kilometres of track. Acceleration might be too strong to launch humans this way, but it would be suitable for freight. If this was used in conjunction with our chemical plant, large numbers of fuel tanks could be placed very cleaply in lunar orbit, just waiting for the Earth ships to dock with them, with the use of only a little of their fuel for orbit circularization. Similar fuel tanks could be launched from the Moon into Earth orbit.

Without much further advance on our present technology we could set up this chemical plant, including mining machines to dig up and deliver the right kinds of rock to it, and the lunatron system, on an almost completely automatic basis. The cost of producing rocket fuel on the Moon and of delivering it to both lunar and Earth orbits, with neither labour nor energy expenses to speak of, should work out to a very small fraction of its cost here on Earth, taking into account that due to the almost total lack of weather as we know it in space and on the Moon there will be hardly any depreciation costs. When the day comes – as it probably will – when even the fuel tanks, engines and shuttles for the initial lift-off from Earth are stamped "Made in Luna City", it may well become as cheap (if not cheaper) to go to the Moon as to fly the Atlantic.

Setting the whole thing up, of course, would still be enormously expensive. The question, "Why go to the Moon?" is still valid, but we are all familiar with the fact that we have an energy crisis. The Moon is a powerhouse in the sky! Might there not be some way in which we could use the energy we could tap up there to our advantage here on Earth?

Instead of asking "Why go to the Moon?" let us ask: "In what way would a lunar colony benefit humanity or the nation which put it there in such a way as to be obviously a necessity rather than an expensive luxury?" Looking at the problem from this slightly different angle might help us decide whether or not we will go and what kind of colony it might be. Or how about this: "Why should a politician want a lunar colony?" Here are ten more suggestions:

(1)   Energy. We have mentioned this before but on the Moon as in space there is solar power galore. Many writers have suggested that we should use mirror collectors (although personally I prefer the term reflector collectors), as a method of harnessing this. At ASTRA, Robert Shaw has suggested thermocouples using metal rods, one end of which would be in shadow while the other was in lunar sunshine. Many other interesting concepts have been produced by others, but suffice it to say that devizing automatic electricity generators to provide cheap or even free power on the Moon should provide little difficulty, beyond that of the initial set-up expense, to our modern society and technology. The problem still remains, however, as to what good this will do us here on Earth.

The Americans have already experimented with satellite solar power stations (SSPS) using microwaves to beam the power down to Earth. The problem with this has been one of expense: they reckon it would be about ten to twenty times more expensive than oil-powered electricity generation. This process could be improved, of course, and in the kind of situation we are envisaging on the Moon the beaming might not prove so expensive anyway; also, as the oil runs out and inflation here on Earth takes its usual toll, the expense may not appear nearly as great. In the meantime it would probably be better to use power on the Moon for other purposes which might bring us other benefits.

(2)   There is another possible way in which energy might be beamed down to Earth from the Moon: by laser (in fact, we have already beamed weak laser beams up to the Moon from the Earth). Laser technology is still in its infancy. If we could develop it to the stage where giant lasers could send down powerful beams to our planet from the Moon this would obviously be of tremendous benefit.

Every invention has its snags, however, and the problem with immensely powerful lasers on the Moon is that they could be used as weapons. With the addition of some artificial satellites to the system, such machines might be used to melt nuclear missiles in flight anywhere on Earth at any time of day or night. This would clearly make nuclear war obsolete but nobody could really heave any sighs of relief or sleep any sounder on that account, for these same beams could also boil you in your bed. The idea of death-rays from the sky, it appears, will just not lie down and die!

(3)   A better use for lunar power would probably be to power industry on the spot. If most of our industry were removed from the Earth to the Moon most of our chemical and nuclear pollution would go with it and the Earth might well become a much greener and healthier place to live on. It is unlikely that this reason would excite our politicians as much as the last one.

(4)   Most industrial processes would be considerably altered if placed in a gravitational field one-sixth of our own, but many of these alterations could be beneficial. For instance, Arthur Clarke has pointed out that the 200-inch (5m) reflector telescope on Mount Palomar has a mass of 500 tonnes: on the Moon such a telescope could be made with a mass of only 60 tonnes due to the fact that it would not have to contend with either gravity or weather. With a mass of 60 tonnes on the Moon its actual lunar *weight* would be only 10 tonnes. This kind of argument would apply equally to many other kinds of heavy industry. High-vacuum technology for industrial purposes like electronics would also gain tremendously if situated on the Moon. Coupled with a cheap transport system for freight from the Moon to the Earth some of these ideas begin to look not only practicable but profitable.

(5)   Many completely new technologies would be possible on the Moon, technologies just not possible at all here on Earth. What these will be we can only surmise at present, as we cannot know definitely until we have a lunar colony up there carrying out experiments; but we do know that the different relationship of natural forces should produce differences in the results of their application. Many areas for this have already been postulated. We may be able to manufacture new alloys or other materials which might make our plastics industry on Earth green with envy; or, what happens to drinks when fermentation takes place at one-sixth of our gravity? Who knows, in a few years' time Lunar Whisky may be all the rage?

(6)   Again, with a cheap transport system to Earth, not only our politicians might be interested in mining ventures on the Moon. This would obviously be especially so if some rich veins of valuable minerals were to be found. The Moon has a surface area somewhat larger than that of Africa: even though this does not prove it will turn out to be as rich as Africa in minerals there is no evidence to the contrary either, and, in view of the fact that we seem to be running out of everything down here, it might well be a good idea to send up some prospectors for a more thorough investigation.

(7)   Another of Arthur Clarke's suggestions is that a study of the lunar surface might indicate why metallic ores are distributed and concentrated as they are. This information would be very useful here on Earth.

(8)   Whoever owns Luna City Television Station should be able to hold the whole Earth captive almost every night at some point during peak viewing times; and, sending from the Moon, half the time is peak viewing time somewhere down here. Think of all that advertising revenue – and all of it at peak prices! Computer-enhancement might have problems at first, but I'm sure that they would be solved, and all nations would receive the service.

(9) Another point that has been demonstrated about the lunar soil brought back by the American astronauts is that, with the addition of some air, fresh lunar soil is every bit as good as, if not better than, terrestrial soil for the purposes of growing plants. In the light of this discovery, wouldn't it be wise to cover over a small crater or two with some transparent material which would let in the lunar sunlight without melting or cracking with its temperature, fill the gap between with soil and cover with some suitable concoction of available gases, then start a few experiments with the growing of our seeds on the Moon? Once we've developed an edible plant to the state that it will flourish on the Moon after a fashion, we could start expanding to use other craters, improving our strain all the time. When we find we've used up all the smaller craters we could progress to the larger ones, and when we've used them all up we could start on the plains. How about vast lunar food farms and a colony of farmers on the Moon? On a world the size of Africa, with virgin soil and 14 days' solid sunlight every month followed by 14 days' darkness, even if we managed to regulate the temperatures in our craters the food we developed would be very different from anything we know now. Nonetheless, coupled with a cheap transport system to Earth, it would certainly stave off a lot of starvation here.

(10) Population. Very few people think that our going to the Moon is a possible part-solution to this problem, but nobody has come up with any reason for this except that we haven't the capability to build spaceships able to carry hundreds of millions of people at a time. Not only is this somewhat reminiscent of the idea that heavier than air machines could never fly, but like that idea it is just not true. Schemes for doing very nearly this have already been proposed. In particular, Gerard O'Neill's proposals, which have received wide circulation, show how, commencing with our present technological know-how *alone*, we could build space habitats capable of supporting 10,000,000 by the year 2008, and we could have a smaller version up there supporting a mere 10,000 by as soon as 1998! While this may seem fantastic, how many of our present achievements would have seemed fantastic if published in 1879? Surely, any scientist in 1879 who proposed that several men would have been to the Moon and back within a hundred years would have been thought fit only for the lunatic asylum. If the kind of lunar-fuelled Earth–Moon transport system outlined earlier were to be set up it is easily conceivable that millions would avail themselves of it, and lunar and even interplanetary tourism would flourish. Let us not, therefore, dismiss without careful consideration the concept of spaceships big enough to carry millions at a time.

The basic problem is not a question of technology but of motivation. Even given the terrifying prospect of billions starving to death here on Earth due to overpopulation, many people are even more terrified of the prospect of going out to space, possibly to live and work there and never to return. In the technologically more civilized countries of the West, probably the only countries really capable of leading humanity out into space, the starvation happens in a far country and a brief glimpse of a starving child on a television screen is all we see of it. This will not always be so, unfortunately, if we wait until mass starvation hits us also; we may already have left it too late, for colonization projects take prodigious quantities of time.

In the event that we do not develop extraterrestrial locales for farming purposes, we are going to face insurmountable problems in the feeding of our population here on Earth. At the time of writing there is a margin of only 3% of world agricultural yield over demand. The weather alone can cause as much as a 10% drop in any one year. The Canadian Government's "Environment Canada" research group says: "It is quite feasible that global temperatures could change by 1° within 50 years, but what are to be feared most are not the direct effects of this thermal change on agricultural production, but the regional change in rainfall and perhaps the more frequent occurrence of frosts than would be expected from the thermal change." In the Sahel region of Africa we have already seen some of the most devastating effects of changes in rainfall patterns as millions suffered when the Sahara desert moved southwards, but the danger-points are not always as obvious as this.

Approximately 40% of India is powered by hydroelectricity. Recently this has been badly affected by droughts. The demand for power in the area is increasing by about 12% per annum, so the outlook is bleak. The wheat crops of the Punjab and Haryana rely on electric water pumps, so they have suffered not only from lack of water to grow the wheat but from lack of power for the pumps. In addition, the power shortage has interfered with the operation of fertilizer factories; the resulting shortage of fertilizers has caused even more damage to the agricultural production.

A 10% drop in the US wheat crop could cause a reduction in their wheat exports of about 4,000,000 tonnes, which if it coincided with a bad year for Russian wheat would cause a really terrible famine in many parts of the world. Present estimates suggest that there is a 29% chance of such a drought happening in the USA within the next three years. Obviously we are all relying too much on too few sources. Agricultural production as a whole is also bound to be affected by the repeating series of economic crises we are going through, each one worse than the previous one.

"Why worry," some say. "If we develop all the land and water available, from the tops of the mountains to the bottom of the oceans, this planet can support 36 billions. By the end of this century we may have 7 or 8 billions. It'll take ages before we get to 36 billion. Why worry?"

Throughout much of the history of Man the rate of increase of population has itself been continually rising. At present, approximately 2.5 babies are born for every hundred people of the world population every year. If we could arrest the increase in the rate of increase so that the population continued to rise at this rate only, we would still reach a total world population of over 36 billion in about 90 years.

This means that we could reach the 36 billion figure within the lifetime of your grandchildren, probably within that of your children, and possibly even within your own lifetime. It will take less than 30 years longer to double that population to 72 billion, and, if the increase in the rate is not arrested, presuming that we could work miracles and feed our ever increasing population without going out to space, we could come to the situation described in Table V. Here are the annual birth and death rates underlying this table :

TABLE IV

	Developed World			Developing World		
	Births*	Deaths*	Increase*	Births*	Deaths*	Increase*
1960-1970	20	9	11	41	17	24
1970-1980	17	7	10	40	15	25
1980-1990	13	6	7	42	13	29
1990-2000	10	4	6	42	10	32
2000-2010	8	3	5	41	7	34
2010-2020	5	2	3	41	5	36
2020-2030	3	2	1	41	3	38
2030-2040	2	2	0	43	2	41
2040-2050	2	2	0	40	2	38
2050-2060	2	3	-1	41	2	39
2060-2070	2	4	-2	41	1	40
2070-2080	2	6	-4	39	2	37
2080-2090	1	10	-9	42	1	41
2090-2100	0	15	-15	41	1	40

*per 1,000 population per annum.

It is assumed here that trends continue more or less as they are going at present. The birth rates of the people of the Developed World continue to fall until they just die out. The birth rate in the developing World remains more or less as at present while their death rate falls away with the proliferation of medical facilities and advances.

TABLE V
World Population 1970-2100

1970	3,631,798,000	2020	13,289,334,821	2060	56,007,720,534
1980	4,457,702,165	2030	18,639,220,340	2070	82,261,526,846
1990	5,620,191,916	2040	27,113,244,896	2080	117,460,352,413
2000	**7,302,480,748**	**2048**	**36,017,160,010**	2090	174,735,586,477
2010	9,727,603,442	2050	38,690,158,176	2100	257,857,595,167

At the present rate of 2.5% per annum, in 70 years we would find our population rising by 1,000 million each year, so if we wait until then before deciding to go to space we will certainly have left things far too late. Even at present, with our relatively small population, we are adding approximately 80 million extra people a year. As our chances of arresting this increase and remaining human (let alone humane) seem unlikely, we are either going to have to develop enough spaceships to deport vast numbers of our population off-planet before 70 years is up or terraform enough planets and build enough spaceships to bring food from them in addition to fully developing the Earth. Or we could permit vast numbers to starve unnecessarily. The future will probably hold a mixture of these solutions. Some will go off-planet, some food will be brought in, more development will take place here and also, unfortunately, many will undoubtedly starve.

Rafael M. Salas, Executive Director of the United Nations Fund for Population Activities, said in his address to the Second Asian Population Conference in Tokyo, Japan, on 1 November 1972 : "Changes in fertility behaviour are more likely to occur as an integral part of an overall process of social and economic change which is, generally speaking, not yet occurring on a sufficiently broad scale in most developing countries." Later he continued : "Whatever success is achieved through current efforts to reduce fertility, the population of the developing regions will almost certainly double within the next twenty-five to thirty years. Population growth of this magnitude can seriously jeopardize hopes for any substantial improvement in living standards in the coming decades. The situation is such that urgent consideration must now be given to the need for alternative development strategies on the one hand and fundamental changes in the relations between the rich and poor countries on the other."

Spaceflight must be regarded as not only one of but the most important of these alternative strategies for development to help feed our starving population. Without it there may be little future left for any other development.

Just because we don't have large space-liners now doesn't mean we won't ever have them. Our population expansion is being caused mainly by the fact that advances in medical research tend to be put to use more for death control than for birth control, particularly in the developing world. Mahmoud Mamdani's work, to cite but one study, shows that this is primarily because poor agricultural workers need and therefore want more children, and to solve this we must help their society develop until this need no longer exists.

Several of the possible medical advances (e.g., availability of cloned organs for transplant without rejection problems) which appear to be in the pipeline may aggravate our population problem still further, particularly in the developing world where an acceleration in the fall of the death rate with a static birth rate could help to bring about mass starvation – and, by increasing the number of poor, might trigger still further increases rather than decreases in the birth rate.

Another aspect of population growth which we have not yet considered is the possible effects of a grossly overpopulated environment on our psychology and sociology. US scientist John B. Calhoun has carried out some experiments to determine these.

In his first experiment he fenced off a quarter-acre (0.1 hectare) enclosure into which he placed plenty of food and a number of carefully selected disease-free Norway rats. After approximately twenty-seven months the population stabilized at about 150. From the numbers which he had already placed in the enclosure and from the known normal breeding habits of Norway rats, 5,000 might have been expected. The population increase was apparently so low because stress from social interaction disrupted the maternal behaviour in such a way that very few young survived.

He then carried out another six experiments indoors under carefully controlled circumstances. The structure of the food hoppers in the first three experiments was such as to cause the rats to have to spend some time to obtain a satisfactory quantity of food, thus increasing the chances of meeting other rats while doing so. Naturally this had the effect of turning eating into a social event in the rats' daily lives.

In each case the period of observation was 16 months and in each case the population was permitted to reach approximately twice the numbers which experience indicated could occupy the space available with only a moderate amount of stress from spatial interaction. In the first three experiments each population commenced with a total of 32 rats, and in the second three with a total of 56 rats. At the start of each experiment the rats were evenly divided between males and females. Only rats which had just passed their weaning stages were used in the experiments at the initial stages. Eight rats, four male and four female – in the second three experiments, fourteen rats, seven male and seven female – were placed in each of four pens.

By the twelfth month each population had reached about eighty. After this the removal of infants surviving weaning held the population steady. Groups of about sixty out of the eighty would congregate to eat together in what Calhoun called "behavioural sinks" during the first three experiments, ruining most other social behaviour. With these sinks the overall mortality rate for infants was as high as 96% – even without them, in the last three experiments, it was as high as 80%.

Many females were unable to carry pregnancy to full term or, if they did, to survive delivery. Spontaneous abortions were rife. In the behavioural sinks a great number fell short on their maternal duties. The males became sexual deviates, frenetically overactive or pathologically withdrawn, and only going out to eat and drink when the others were asleep.

Mortality rates increased throughout the experiments right up to the sixteenth month, but even so the number of young surviving was always enough to offset this and to increase the size of the population had they not been removed. Evidence indicated, however, that in time the population would have died out. The four healthiest males and the four healthiest females at the end of the first experiment were six months old and in the prime of rat life. Even although they no longer lived in over-populated conditions they produced fewer litters than normal and none of the infants born survived to maturity.

The situation with regard to humanity is not quite the same as with Calhoun's rats. Unlike them, we have to struggle for a living, and we don't know quite how much of their exotic behaviour was brought about by the sheer boredom of having virtually unlimited food, drink, etc., laid on. Some groups showed behaviour parallel with our own teenage cults, a fair amount of which seems to be caused by boredom in our richer societies.

Perhaps the most fearsome point in Calhoun's experiments was that, due to fewer litters being had by rats accustomed to overpopulation and to the low survival ability of the offspring, it looked as if in time the population would in fact die out completely. In the human case we have an advanced medical science which might increase the chances of survival of our infants in similar circumstances, but there are some uneasy parallels here. Spontaneous abortions are already commonplace in several parts of the developing world and even in the UK, where the spontaneous variety are still rare, the number of deliberate abortions is now higher than the number of births per annum.

While the behaviour of Calhoun's rats cannot be taken as a direct parallel of anticipated human behaviour in the years to come, it must be taken as a warning that, irrespective of how many people we manage to feed, clothe and house in our expanding population, overcrowding will itself cause major social and probably political unrest which could destroy our civilization. If, as it seems, there are already one or two parallels evident, how much more like the rat population will we be in the middle of the next century when our numbers are at several times their present level?

If humanity is to survive in the long term we will have no option but to develop the kind of giant spaceships necessary to carry billions to interstellar destinations. As we have no idea how long this development will take we should commence now. Otherwise all the indications we do have are that we will be too late. We may already be too late.

In 1474 Toscanelli, the librarian at Florence, told his friend Columbus that the world was round. It said so in one of the books of the Apocrypha. Later Columbus borrowed a copy from a clerical friend in Spain and there it was, in the first book of Esdras. It is quite interesting to note that this book appears to have been translated from Aramaic Hebrew at the great library at Alexandria during the second century BC, for the head of this library during the second half of the third century BC and the first few years of the second was none other than Eratosthenes, the man who first measured the curvature of the Earth. He was also a philologist of repute, and a good friend of Archimedes, in turn a pupil of Aristarchus: according to Aristarchus, the Earth was round, it went around the Sun, and the stars were very distant.

When Columbus sailed across the Atlantic a young man of 19 was studying the ancient Greek scholars. In 1530, when he was 57, and the whole world had been set to thinking that the world must indeed be round, Copernicus published his ideas. Within a hundred years we had Tycho Brahe, Kepler and Galileo, and within the next fifty they were followed by Newton and Leibnitz. Science got back under way. It took less than 480 years from the date of Columbus' sailing to Neil Armstrong's "giant leap for mankind" on the Moon.

If humanity had listened to Aristarchus and Eratosthenes instead of waiting for Columbus, the first man might have walked on the Moon around 280AD. We would by now have had about 1,700 years of space-flight. Our present population would already be spread not only around our own Solar System but quite possibly around several others as well. Science might now be so far in advance of our present level that none of today's scientists could recognize it at all. It is highly unlikely that we would have had any population or world food problems either.

Taking all the foregoing into account it should now be clear to all that overpopulation can indeed be a motive for colonization not only of the Moon but of all other planetary and satellite bodies which can be colonized in our systems, and later of others beyond it. It is my own personal belief that it will not only be one of the motives but that it will be the major motive for several centuries to come.

While backing the UN and its associated organizations to the hilt in all their plans to develop the Earth's resources to the full benefit of humanity and to minimize the population explosion as much as possible within the limits posed by the necessity of the continued development of a healthy society, it is my contention that the kind of stability with regard to population growth which many optimistic researchers foresee is in fact a physical impossibility. A study of the cosmos will lead many intelligent people to the somewhat intriguing conclusion that life itself, particularly intelligent life, is the opposing force in the Universe to entropy. If this is the case, then the only possibilities which are open to any civilization are either progression or regression; stability is just not possible except in the shortest of terms.

It is my view that humanity must be permitted to continue to expand, and to enable us to do so we must continue to expand territorially. It does not matter that we can't at present produce spaceships to move hundreds of millions to planets where at present they couldn't breathe anyway. What *does* matter is that the research necessary for continued exploration of our Solar System in the first instance be continued, that as a matter of urgency permanent bases be set up on as many non-terrestrial bodies as possible, and that the idea that we can rely on the resources of only one small planet for future human progress be shown to all to be totally fallacious.

The psychological benefits from that last procedure would be enormous. In the ensuing general change of attitudes the correct climate of thought would arise to produce the inventions enabling us to transport goods economically from planet to planet and from solar system to solar system.

The colonization of the Moon will probably commence with the setting up of the chemical plant and lunatron launch system described earlier, plus an array of solar power reflector collectors. A medical research centre will soon expand into a major hospital, and an experimental lunar farm project will probably follow fairly quickly. It won't be long before industry adds its own research centres, which in turn will probably be closely followed by the first lunar hotel. This will soon be followed by many more. As soon as fuel stores are established in orbit around both Moon and Earth and a fleet of Earth–Moon shuttles and lunar landing shuttles is in operation, our whole Solar System will be opened up very quickly. Within a century we may have almost as many separate communities off Earth as we now have members of the UN.

I believe that most people deep down in their hearts nurture a fellow feeling for the human race as a whole, and that few are really selfish in the sense of not caring for others or for their children and their children's children. I believe that almost all of us at one time or another fleetingly wonder at what the world will be like in the time of our children's children's children. This being so, I believe that if all the people on our planet were to understand how important the earliest possible colonization of the Moon will be to all those children, people in many parts of the world might even *want* to pay extra taxes to support a project to that end. Upon this colonization lies all possible hope for a happy and progressive future for our race. It is the next logical step in human evolution and without it there will be nothing but misery and ultimate extinction for all human kind.

PART III
Unmanned exploration:
the new look of the planets

6 There are __What__ on Mars?

. . . but to say truth, with some small qualification, they have one and the self-same opinion about the essence and matter of the heavens; that it is not hard and impenetrable, as Peripatetics hold, transparent, of a *quinta essentia* [fifth essence], "but that it is as penetrable and soft as the air itself is, and that the planets move in it, as birds in the air, fishes in the sea" . . . as Mars among the rest, which sometimes, as Kepler confirms by his own and Tycho's accurate observations, comes nearer the Earth than the Sun, and is again eftsoons aloft in Jupiter's orb; and other sufficient reasons, far above the Moon . . . If the heavens then be penetrable, and no lets, it were not amiss in this aerial progress to make wings and fly up, which that Turk in Busbequius made his fellow-citizens in Constantinople believe he would perform; and some newfangled wits, methinks, should some time or other find out; or if that may not be, yet with a Galileo's glass, or Icaromenippus' wings in Lucian, command the spheres and heavens, and see what is done amongst them.

Robert Burton,
The Anatomy of Melancholy, 1651

The *True History* and *Icaromenippus* of Lucian of Samos are 1,500 years older than the first interplanetary tales of our own culture. The main reason for the gap is that it had become an article of faith that Earth was encased in concentric, solid shells bearing the planets. Arthur Koestler has written of it, "The Babylonian oyster-world, which lay three or four thousand years back, was full of dynamism and imagination compared with this pedantically graded Universe, wrapped in cellophane spheres, and kept by God in the deep-freeze locker to hide its eternal shame."[1] By observation and calculation it was shown that comets' paths pierced the supposed celestial spheres; but were comets solid or mere apparitions? Early in the 17th century, however, the first telescopes were producing evidence that the planets were solid worlds, not perfect reflecting globes; and, using observations compiled by Tycho Brahe, Kepler showed that the orbit of Mars was not merely a circle with the Sun as its centre, as Copernicus maintained, but was an ellipse with the Sun at one focus. The impenetrable barriers went down and, as Burton reported with delight, the way into space was open.

In the public mind, the association of Mars with interplanetary travel has continued ever since. Some years ago, there was an eastern European joke about a bookseller arrested because, although the bestsellers on display were officially approved, the titles ran *We Want to Live, Far from Moscow, In the Shadow of the Skyscrapers, Under a Foreign Flag.* Read in the same way, the popular books about Mars spell out a fanfare – *Guide to Mars, The Green and Red Planet, There IS Life on Mars, Mars, Mars and the Mind of Man!* Yet supposedly, as soon as the first close-up pictures of the planet were obtained, public interest waned so sharply that the Mariner 9 findings weren't even worth reporting. The opening paragraphs of James Strong's *Search the Solar System* have already been quoted (Chapter 1); in a recent article in *Analog* it was suggested that, if Viking failed to find life on Mars in 1976, public support for the space program might be withdrawn altogether.[2]

It's not easy to see, however, what was so wonderful about the "old" Mars compared to what we know now. Early in the 20th century the world had been stimulated by Percival Lowell's concept of a Martian civilization constructing vast canals to irrigate a few narrow strips of a dying world; but by the 1950s the firm consensus of scientific thought was that there was no breathable atmosphere, virtually no water, and no form of life higher than lichens – or possibly mosses at the equator. Whether there had been denser air, water and advanced life in the past was a pure guess, but now Mars was "a clock which had run down": even the hills had been worn down by erosion, until the planet-wide sand-dunes were broken only by plateaux 1km or so high. Patrick Moore thought in 1955 that there might be higher ground, prophetically giving Nix Olympica as an example; but nothing over about 3,000m.[3]

Mars has always been notoriously difficult to observe, and worse still to photograph – partly because of its small image, even in the most powerful telescopes, and partly because of the combined blurring effect of its atmosphere and the Earth's. In ideal conditions, and especially in rare moments of perfect seeing, it was reported that the dark markings of the planet (especially the "canals") were resolved into much finer detail, usually blurred again before it could be recorded or memorized. Artists' impressions of the planet, and scientific expectations of the first space-probe photos, showed firmer outlines around the dark areas and blurred, fainter, natural-looking streaks for canals, but all as flush with the surface as the colours in a glass marble.

On 15 July 1965 Mariner 4 flew past Mars, taking 19 photographs at slant ranges between 11,250 and 16,900km. A few days later, the UK journal *New Scientist* had a dramatic cover showing the first three shots superimposed on a segment of the planetary grid. One feature instantly caught the attention: it was obvious that Mars had craters.

It had always been supposed that, being nearer the Asteroid Belt, Mars would be bombarded more than the Earth. But it was thought that Mars's atmosphere was dense enough to protect the surface as well as Earth's does against all but the largest projectiles; and that erosion would wear down and fill in the craters, as it has done almost everywhere on Earth. However, Clyde Tombaugh had suggested that the "oases" where canals met might be big impact craters, from which radiated cracks in the surface giving shelter to life;[3] in particular, a dark spot called Trivium Charontis, which seemed unaffected by seasonal changes, might be depressed several thousand metres below the surrounding desert.

More than sixty craters appeared in the Mariner 4 pictures, which covered about 1% of the planet's surface. On that basis, there might be as many as 6,000 craters altogether on Mars: the landscape might be repetitive, but it certainly wasn't flat. Nor was the scenery more than superficially like the Moon's: photo number 11, almost the only one to appear in the press after the first three, showed extensive weathering of the crater rims. On the question of retaining interest, it's unfortunate that the first three missions took black-and-white pictures only, and that Mariner 9's colour system broke down after only a few shots had been obtained.[4] According to the Soviet Mars 4 and 5 probes, in 1974, the Martian plains are orange, the upper mountain slopes blue, and the craters bluish-green;[5] while Viking Orbiter pictures showed a pink and purple planet, and the surface reds are more vivid than any artist imagined.

Summarizing the first analysis of the Mariner 4 pictures, Robert S. Richardson wrote: "The principal topographic features . . . are not of the type that would be produced by stress and deformation originating within the planet, as is the case with Earth. Earth is internally dynamic, creating mountains and continents, but Mars has evidently long been inactive. Lack of internal activity is consistent with the negative outcome of the magnetometer experiment, which failed to detect a Martian magnetic field* . . . None of the pictures show any trace of the canals."[6] (Richardson was not surprised, since the canals would be diffuse bands and, in southern hemisphere midwinter, would contrast poorly with the terrain.)

But the following year, addressing an ASTRA meeting, A. E. Roy produced a version of photo number 11 which had been computer-processed ("cleaned up") to remove noise in the incoming signal and enhance contrast. Many more craters could be seen; but, still more fascinating, across the large crater filling most of the frame ran two converging lines, which seemed to pierce the crater wall and continue, less conspicuously, on the rough terrain outside. Its 48km or so diameter was equivalent, supposedly, to a medium-sized canal, but in appearance it resembled a double geological fault, with subsidence. Could it be evidence of internal geological activity, and would all the canals be similar? Small craters could be seen within the "canal", right on the edge of detectability; and on the north-east corner of the crater appeared a three-dimensional feature which might be a lava field, or possibly a dust cloud. At that ASTRA meeting, we anticipated the Mariner 9 revelations by six years; but, interestingly enough, that cleaned-up photo was scarcely discussed in print elsewhere.

As Mariner 4 passed behind Mars, its signals were muffled by the atmosphere before being cut off by the planet. The results of the occultation experiment were a blow, as far as life on Mars was concerned – either indigenous, or emigrating from Earth. The Martian atmosphere had only 1% or 2% of the density of Earth's at sea level: it had been thought that

*But see later.

air pressure would be equivalent to that on the summit of Everest, but it was nearer to Earth's air pressure at a height of over 32km. The sky on Mars would be black, not royal or navy blue as had been thought, and the surface would be subjected to high levels of solar ultraviolet radiation. Conventional aircraft would not be usable, and parachutes (unless enormous) of very limited use. The "conventional" Mars base, with its flexible transparent dome held up by internal pressurization, became too flimsy; and we had to drop the notion that people could go about on Mars in warm clothing and oxygen masks – pressure suits will be needed after all.

But there were mysteries here – mysteries of astronomical literature in the first instance, apart from the puzzles of Mars. Before the space probes, no account of Mars was complete without a reference to the "Violet Layer", located 13–19km above the surface and strongly scattering blue and violet light, making the atmosphere almost opaque at those wavelengths. Its effect on uv radiation couldn't be determined, of course, because uv photography was blanked out by absorption in the Earth's atmosphere. But it was asserted that in 1941, during one of the rare clearings of the Violet Layer, the development of the dark areas during the Martian spring was halted until the Layer reformed. Some experts didn't hesitate to call the event proof that the dark areas were vegetation, and that the Violet Layer shielded the ground from ultraviolet radiation.[3]

After Mariner 9 and Viking it seems that the "seasonal" changes on Mars are due to redistribution of dark and light dust, with a cyclic pattern brought about by regular shifts in the prevailing winds.[7] The "Wave of Darkening", spreading from the poles to the equator each spring, has been explained by the changes in wind pattern beginning at the poles, when the caps begin to evaporate (although some experts now think there is no such progression in the change[8]). It had been suggested that the Violet Layer was fine dust, in suspension, and that now seems likely: the clearings of the Layer would indicate temporary calms, in which the redistribution of surface dust would of course halt. But in normal conditions the atmosphere of Mars is virtually transparent to uv (Mariner 9 assessed surface relief using an ultraviolet spectrometer), yet Martian dust in quantity is opaque to it, so the question is not fully settled yet. Perhaps the most remarkable thing, however, is the detective work I had to do for the last three sentences: the "Wave of Darkening" and the "Violet Layer", once so prominent in descriptions of Mars, have scarcely been mentioned in the last few years.

Nothing was found in the Mariner 4 pictures suggesting the work of intelligence – nor indeed was it likely, at that resolution, that such work would be recognizable unless it were as big as Lowell's canal system. So much emphasis was placed on the lack of canals, however, in some quarters, that *Analog* brought out a set of V2 photographs, giving much better resolution of the southern USA than Mariner 4 did of Mars, but "proving" there was no life on Earth, much less intelligence. In particular, only one crater could be found (Meteor Crater in Arizona) of the type so essential to the Martian ecology.[9]

Only Mariner 5 (Venus flyby) and Mariner 10, the recent Venus/Mercury probe, were planned as single-spacecraft missions. Mariner 2 was successfully sent to Venus only after Mariner 1 had to be destroyed in flight, and history repeated itself with Mars and the failure of Mariner 3. Mariner 9's mission had to be changed to encompass as much as possible of the program it was to have shared with Mariner 8. The Mariner 6 and 7 Mars flyby was the only successful two-probe mission in the program; and even that was a near thing, because on final approach to the planet contact with Mariner 7 was lost for more than seven hours.[10] The spacecraft had lost its lock on Earth and the reference star Canopus, and when it was contacted and re-aligned it was found that 20 of its 90 telemetry channels were unusable. Reports at the time attributed the accident to a meteoroid, but more recently it has been called a battery explosion.[7]

Nevertheless, both spacecraft transmitted pictures of the Martian disc, the "far encounter" pictures, and Mariner 6 photographed a large equatorial region in close-up while Mariner 7 scanned the south pole. It took nearly two years for all the pictures to be computer-enhanced and detailed maps to be prepared, and the experience gained allowed the Mariner 9 pictures to be processed very much more rapidly.[11]

On the whole, the far-encounter pictures were disappointing – at the time. With the disk of Mars nearly full, much as it always looks from Earth, they showed few craters (no shadows to throw them into relief) and, being in black-and-white, resembled the first pictures of the Moon's Farside (Luna 3, 1959) rather than the clear views of Mars the enthusiasts had anticipated. But Mariner 7 found two previously unseen features. Nix Olympica, the "strange" region Moore had suspected of being "elevated above the general level", appeared as a bright double ring, identified as a crater 3–500km across with another crater at its centre.[12] Strange bright streaks lay around it in the Tharsis region, one of them curving away from it like a shock-wave (in retrospect). To the south-east, curving away around the planet parallel to the equator, was a dark, jagged band identified with the Agathadaemon canal.[10]

The photographs showing Agathadaemon could be received only with mixed feelings. For seventy years or more argument had raged as to whether the "*canali*" first reported by Schiaperelli were actual linear features or due to mental joining-up of unrelated detail at the limit of visibility. A famous experiment with schoolchildren merely exacerbated the argument, and a modern, better educated class failed to produce "canals" when the experiment was repeated.[3] Nevertheless, I can testify to the "joining-up' effect because I experienced it while watching a speeded-up film of the rotation of Mars – a regular pattern of fine lines flashed into view for about a second, near the shadowed edge of the disk. Now here was at least one canal definitely shown to be a roughly linear feature, but obviously natural. Carl Sagan was to remark later: "There is no question that the straightness of the lines is due to intelligence. The only question concerns which side of the telescope the intelligence is on."[7] But, in retrospect, given that these pictures (particularly Mariner 7 far-encounter shots 73 and 74[10]) are dominated by Nix Olympica and Agathadaemon, the most remarkable thing about them was the *lack* of speculation they aroused.

The near-encounter views confirmed the conclusions suggested by the

Mariner 4 photos. "A dull uninteresting landscape," said a scientist quoted by the *National Geographic Magazine*. "Everything in the Mariner pictures indicates very gentle slopes on Mars. There are no mountain ranges, no great faults, no extensive volcanic fields, in fact no evidence of volcanic activity. You could stand in a crater on Mars and never know it – even one that appears sharp and clear in the pictures."[13]

Even so, there were some interesting features. "Chaotic terrain" was found, with great crater-free expanses of rough ground patterned with ridges – perhaps due to subterranean collapse, it was suggested, although that seemed to imply volcanic activity or permafrost. On the other hand, the Hellas region was absolutely clear of all detail: even the faint smudges visible in the pictures could be traced to TV faults. "A powerful erasing process" was blamed, although it might be asked why the whole surface wasn't similarly affected. Near the south pole a double crater was dubbed "the giant's footprint" because of the effect of fore-shortening; they shared a common wall, very much broken down, where in similar lunar formations one crater usually impinges sharply on the other. In Deucalionis Regio, near the equator, Mariner 6 found a double-walled crater very similar to the Orientale Basin on the Moon. The crater floor had not filled with darker material from below, but dark-floored craters were found around Sinus Meridiani on the lines of supposed "canals", proving the "joining-up" process did occur. "The Mariner pictures . . . spell the end of the Martian canals. They show conclusively that they are not continuous narrow lines . . ." wrote one expert, mentally fragmenting the quite clear far-encounter shot of Agathadaemon at the start of his article.

The south polar cap on Mars is smaller than the northern one, and in many southern hemisphere summers it had seemed to disappear altogether. The Mariner 7 pictures were taken when the cap had diminished a great deal and gave an odd effect of reversed illumination, since the sunlit slopes of craters and ridges were clear of ice and looked dark. It was generally agreed that the cap was frozen carbon dioxide; drifts still lying in shadow were obviously many metres deep, and water ice in the sunlight couldn't have evaporated so rapidly.[11] But, in the region where the cap survives longest, an intriguing structure of curved concentric ridges was revealed. It was suggested that these might be scarps along the edge of a permanent or semipermanent ice field, but the idea didn't make much impression and the general view was that the caps were carbon dioxide, mixed with a very little water ice. The prospect of life on Mars, now or in the past, seemed very remote: if there had ever been large amounts of water (unlikely, in the absence of volcanic activity), it could not have existed in liquid form on the surface, nor have been retained in the thin atmosphere.

In November 1971, Mariner 9 was successfully placed in orbit around Mars. As already noted, Mariner 8 (intended to go into relatively close orbit) had been destroyed during launch, and Mariner 9 was therefore placed in an orbit similar to the ellipse intended for Mariner 8, but approaching still closer to the planet.

NASA's Jet Propulsion Laboratory very kindly supplied ASTRA with batches of Mariner 9 photos until the mission ended, nearly a year later.

The effect was that we were looking over the experts' shoulders during a long and dramatic multiple re-write of everything which had previously been said or thought about the planet. We felt particularly privileged because none of the discoveries were coming out in the news media. Journals like *New Scientist*, of course, reported what was going on, but in this instance seeing was believing and we had literally dozens of photos to study, far more than *New Scientist* could print. A large number of the shots appeared in *Spaceflight*, but there was a delay of two or three months before any given picture appeared. In addition, more details could be seen in the original prints than in the journals; and every print had JPL's description and initial evaluation printed on the back. It was the next best thing to being at JPL, watching computer enhancement bring out the details – a process vividly described by Carl Sagan in *The Cosmic Connection*.[14]

The first two photos we received were taken on approach to the planet, showing it roughly in half phase. Even by comparison with the Mariner 6 and 7 far-encounter pictures, they might at first be described as disappointing: astronomers had been reporting for some time that a major dust storm was covering most of the planet. In the first of the two pictures, the south polar cap could be seen dimly and at first glance that was all. A longer look began to reveal craters, however, right on the limit of visibility – once the first few were spotted, hundreds could be traced from minimum visual clues. The second shot showed a definite marking: Nix Olympica had come round into daylight and appeared as a large dark spot. On the back of the photo, it was noted that radar studies indicated Nix Olympica was one of the highest spots on Mars; perhaps, although ring-shaped, it might be a mountain or plateau showing above the dust. (An earlier photograph in the series, taken as Nix Olympica emerged from the terminator, added three more similar spots in a straight line, some distance to the east.)

A further set of pictures was taken on the final stage of the approach, before Mariner 9 made orbit. One we received showed a large crater in Arsia Silva, poking up through the dust – blurred, but recognisable. Streaks more than 1,000km long led away from it, either atmospheric turbulence patterns or dunes, according to the caption. If dunes, they were as extensive as the longest in the Sahara or in Peru. In *Spaceflight* for February 1972 there appeared a mosaic of final-approach pictures of the area, showing that Arsia Silva was the southernmost of the three dark spots east of Nix Olympica;[15] because of their appearance during the storm the three objects were temporarily designated North Spot, Middle Spot and South Spot.

In the mosaic, however, it was obvious that the streaks were atmospheric patterns. Obviously the dust storm was thick, for even after computer enhancement few other details were showing. Even if the Martian dust were very fine, the length of the eddies suggested wind speeds of hundreds of km per hour. A photograph of the south polar cap, one of the few other features visible on the planet, showed complex overlapping vortices of dust swirling around it. Wind speeds of 300–600kph were estimated, and another prediction – "The winds of Mars might buffet a man unmercifully without his being aware of it" – went out of the window. But nobody was giving much thought to how high the dust might go – we were still conditioned to thinking Mars was flat.

Since it alone could be seen clearly, the south polar cap became the first photographic target. The central region with the curved ridges or scarps now showed as a much more pronounced cap, through which the ridges ran for all the world like veins. Continuing photography during November 1972 showed the linear markings becoming more pronounced, so rapidly that the disappearing frost could only be carbon dioxide; even so, the exposed undersurfaces must be very smooth. By the end of the month, "underlying low relief of distinctive character" seemed to be emerging along the sides of the dark bands.

By that time Mariner 9 had company in orbit around the planet. Two Soviet probes, Mars 2 and 3, had achieved orbit around Mars after releasing landing capsules. The Mars 2 lander crashed, and was declared to have successfully planted the pennant which is the first Soviet objective with regard to any heavenly body. Mars 3 landed between Electris and Phaethontis, in smooth terrain; its TV camera began transmitting after 90 seconds, but 20 seconds later all contact was lost. No detail was visible in the small part of one frame received on Earth, and that was the end of that. Considering the conditions in which the attempt was made, it was amazing that the spacecraft had touched down softly – that its parachute had remained open, that its rocket thrust had remained vertical. Once it was down, however, the 110 seconds' further transmission was almost certainly the time it took the dust to penetrate the probe or cover it (Martian dust contains large quantities of iron oxide – more exotic explanations of its colour, such as planet-wide nitrogen-dominated chemistry[6] or carbon suboxide polymers,[13] have now been ruled out – and would stop radio signals quite effectively).

Two other objects orbit Mars, the moons Phobos and Deimos, both natural – or were they? A great deal of mystery surrounded the moons of Mars, beginning with Swift's announcement in *Gulliver's Travels*, Book 3, that the astronomers of Laputa had discovered two satellites of Mars, long before they *were* found in 1877. The orbital elements given by Swift were well wide of the mark and can be ascribed to coincidence.[6] But the coincidence is remarkable because Swift did indicate the two strange things about the respective orbits: Phobos is the only known natural satellite in the System with a period shorter than its planet's day, while Deimos' period is so close to synchronous orbit that it takes three days to drift across the Martian sky between rising and setting. In 1959, I. S. Shlovskii had calculated from the estimated density of the Martian atmosphere and the apparent acceleration of Phobos, presumably due to atmospheric drag, that Phobos must be hollow – although, if it were a space station, it was a very large one.

As Ed Buckley pointed out in his lecture on "the new look of the Solar System", artists had conventionally assumed that Phobos and Deimos would be made of the same materials as Mars itself, and perhaps even be lighter in tone than the planet. To demonstrate, he produced a drawing of "Old Mars", with green "seas" of vegetation, canals like railway tracks and a near-white, shining Phobos in the foreground. But Mariner 6 had obtained a distant view of Phobos silhouetted against the planet, at such a distance that nothing much could be seen – except that Phobos was dark, and not spherical. A better shot, although still distant, was taken by Mariner 9 in the final stages of approach: it showed Phobos was about 22.5km by 16, appreciably bigger than expected, and its size had been underestimated because it was much darker than had been assumed. Indeed, it was the darkest object yet photographed in the Solar System, and silhouetted against the planet it looked as black as Egypt's night. The idea that Phobos might be artificial had been dropped after Mariner 4: the Martian air was too thin to cause significant drag on Phobos, and the acceleration, confirmed by Mariner 9, was due to tidal drag.

Late in November, both moons were photographed in relative close-up from Mars orbit. At once the idea that they were fragile, pumice-like objects vanished, and any suggestion that they were low density artificial objects could be forgotten. (At that point Ed theatrically removed the light Phobos from his drawing to reveal a darker one underneath.) Both moons turned out to be very rough objects, heavily battered by meteor impacts, and therefore of high enough density to withstand complete fragmentation. From one angle, Phobos resembled a neolithic hand-axe and probably was produced by the same process – chipping along fracture lines.[14] An early suggestion was that the moons might be nickel-iron fragments from the core of a planet which disrupted to form the Asteroid Belt. (Current ideas suppose several planetesimals rather than a single planet.) More recently basalt (like the lunar maria) or carbonaceous chondrite material (found in a significant proportion of meteorites) has been suggested.[16] The latter case, especially, might mean that Phobos and Deimos are among the oldest objects in the Solar System and would provide scientific samples of great importance.

Early in December, the dust storm on Mars began to settle. The first objects to clear were the dark spots – Nix Olympica and its three neighbours. The results were startling. All four objects were craters, very obviously volcanic: Nix Olympica and North Spot, now tentatively placed "near Ascraeus Lacus", were multiple, overlapping shallow-floored craters which just couldn't be impact features. Middle Spot, "near Pavonis Lacus" was a single crater, but it too looked more like a terrestrial volcanic caldera than anything previously seen on the Moon or Mars. South Spot, "near Nodus Gordii", showed multiple concentric fractures on the western rim, strongly suggesting a caldera or volcanic collapse crater.

In retrospect, the information given on the backs of the photos seems amusingly conservative. It is noted each time that the craters and their immediate surroundings are high ground, "emerging island-like from a sea of wind-blown dust". The great swirls in the blur round each crater "are probably atmospheric". In South Spot, "whether the pictures show a smooth crater floor or obscuring wind-blown dust remains to be seen". The obscuration around the craters caused one major confusion which has still to be resolved: South Spot, formerly associated with Arsia Silva, was now "near Nodus Gordii". Comparison with pre-Mariner maps shows that the first identification was correct – Richardson's *Mars* is very helpful because in plate 27 it shows the famous "W-shaped cloud" of 1926 superimposed on the Mars map, and one arm of the W lies over the three volcanoes.[6] The *National Geographic* Mars map (February 1973) correctly identifies Arsia Silva, but *Mars*, the atlas compiled by Moore and Cross,[8] follows JPL and calls it Nodus Gordii, which actually lies several hundred km to the west.

The next shot of Nix Olympica was a gem. As the dust storm continued to subside surrounding terrain was becoming visible. On the crater complex shot, taken on 27 November, the JPL caption had mentioned that the outer ring noted in Mariner 6 and 7 shots was still hidden by dust. Now we received two overhead views, taken on the same pass by Mariner 9's wide-angle and telephoto lenses. "The complex of craters . . . appears to sit on top of a broad plateau, the lobate edge of which is seen at right centre. The narrow-angle picture shows intricate surface detail not seen in previous Mariner pictures. The feathery texture and the very small intersecting lobes suggest flowage of material downslope and away from the central crater complex . . ."

This was the first high-resolution photo we had received, apart from the close-ups of the south polar cap. Now the dust had settled, things were getting really exciting. The first wide-angle pictures had been startling enough – volcanoes on Mars, good heavens! The suspense was killing. Sure enough, the Martian volcanoes still had their Sunday punch to deliver, and it hit us at the beginning of February 1972.

JPL P–12834, on which Gavin Roberts based Plate 9, was a mosaic of Nix Olympica pictures taken in late January as the dust really *did* subside. It turned out that, when the "plateau" picture was obtained, the dust was still floating at heights of several thousand metres. Looking back at it, yes, the picture did become steadily more blurred towards the edges – that lava flow was "down-slope" with a vengeance! Nix Olympica was suddenly revealed to be not a double crater, not a plateau, but a towering shield-like volcano geologically similar to Mauna Loa (Hawaii) although more than twice as wide across the base (some 500km in all). "If you want to know what it looks like," my sister suggested, "stand on the floor of the Pacific and look up . . ." But Ed Buckley made a few rough calculations and suggested that just the cliffs around the base might be nearly 1,000m high. A preliminary pressure mapping by the Mariner 9 uv spectrometer suggested that, just part-way up the slope, the altitude was about 6,000m (no height estimates could be made until the dust settled, because it reflected ultraviolet radiation very effectively); the summit might be relatively as high as Mauna Loa's, which is over 9,000m above the sea floor. Take the Liathach ridge from Scotland, put Everest on top, add the crater of Vesuvius, and stand well back to see it . . . but even then you'd have to scale it up. When the uv scanning was completed Nix Olympica was the highest mountain known to man, some 25.75km tall.

It's difficult to convey the full impact of that discovery. A string of quotations from well-known authors ("There are no mountains on Mars . . .", "Mars is not a hilly world . . .") would be repetitive, as well as unkind. Suffice it to say that, from being a flat, dead world, Mars had suddenly become very dynamic indeed. Close-ups of Pavonis Lacus in January showed that "Middle Spot's" summit crater had, like South Spot's, been formed by subsidence: it too had a smooth floor, probably a former lava lake, and its walls were deeply scored where loose material had slid downslope and then been carried away by the storm. "Just as on Earth," said JPL in another poetic flash, "the relentless forces of nature attack and wear down all objects exposed to them." And indeed we knew now how powerful those forces must be, to hide even the summit of Nix Olympica when the storm was raging; so to maintain such mountains in spite of them, Mars must have been very active, so recently that fresh eruptions would be no surprise.*

And what was that about cliffs around Nix Olympica? The other three giant volcanoes – and other cones, elsewhere on the planet – merge smoothly into the terrain. Towards the edge of the Nix Olympica lava flows the ground is rough, but immediately around the cliffs the plain is smooth and almost featureless – and the base of Nix Olympica is 300–600m below those of North, South and Middle Spots.[8] Could it be, by any chance, after all those years knocking Edgar Rice Burroughs' dead sea-bottoms of Mars . . . ?

Yes, it just could be. By the beginning of February 1972 there was mounting evidence that there had been liquid water on Mars, in the relatively recent past. As soon as the ground began to show through the storm it emerged that Mariners 4, 6 and 7 had all photographed similar strips of cratered terrain, mainly the "dark areas" visible from Earth, and a great deal of the surface was quite different. One of the first features to show in December 1971 was Phoenicis Lacus, $5\frac{1}{2}$km above the mean surface, which was young terrain with few impact craters; volcanic deposits, broken into a mosaic by fault valleys 2.5km across. In early January, extensive canyonlands similar in scale to the US Grand Canyon were found in Noctis Lacus, with fluted walls indicating partial shaping by wind erosion. Wind could also have carved out "extraordinary pits and hollows" in the south polar region, but the lack of interior terracing implied that the initial hollows had not been formed by subsidence. "Provocative questions" were posed: could the structures have been formed by "the thawing of large accumulations of ground ice"? The rapid disappearance of the south polar cap had stopped and, by early February, the height of southern-hemisphere summer, the overall appearance of the cap had changed little further. The idea that the main cap was water ice was right back in circulation.

In late January a further Noctis Lacus picture was released, showing "an intricate network of branching chasms", "dramatic evidence of erosional processes at work on the fractured volcanic table lands". The network "appears to hang like a giant chandelier from the Martian equator" and became known informally as "the Chandelier". But right next to it to the

---

*Incidentally, plate 9 shows that the artist still has a major rôle in expounding astronomical discoveries. When the Nix Olympica mosaic was "cleaned up" to remove overlap between plates, etc., it suffered a marked loss of contrast and became less dramatic – compare the print in *Mars and the Mind of Man*[7] and others with the original, reproduced in *Mars* (Moore and Cross).[8]

east, continuing the jagged line photographed by Mariner 7, was "a vast chasm", with extensive tributaries along its north and south walls – and each of these small branches was as large as the Grand Canyon on Earth. Photographs of the same region (Tithonius Lacus), released in late February, showed that one small part of the system was nearly twice as deep as the Grand Canyon and nearly six times as wide. It was suggested that the appearance of water action was illusory – some of the canyons were completely enclosed. An example over 300km long and 3–5km deep appears in *Mars and the Mind of Man*,[7] but in the editor's view the picture shows conventional drainage is not necessarily involved in canyon formation – not that it rules out the action of water.

More was to come. When an equatorial photomosaic was released in May, extending from 30° north to 30° south and for 130° in longitude, the Chandelier and the Tithonius Lacus rifts were shown to be part of an enormous break in the Martian surface: 4,000km long, 120km wide and some 6,000m deep. "On Earth, the Mars feature would extend from Los Angeles to New York, with Los Angeles and San Diego on opposite rims." Walter Sullivan has put forward a striking possible explanation: the great rift valley may be a Martian equivalent of the process (plate tectonics) spreading apart the ocean floors on Earth. On Earth the feature would be an incipient ocean, if there were water to fill it, and, where the rift is doubled, we should regard it not as two parallel chasms but as a widening one with a rising central ridge.[7]

"But wouldn't that imply that Mars is differentiated, and has a molten core?" one is inescapably led to ask. Sure enough, a suggestion has arisen that Mars is partially differentiated, with a core taking up about half the planet's radius and becoming denser as iron drains from the mantle.[17] (Mariner 9 found that Mars has a large equatorial bulge, previously unknown, and is gravitationally "rough" – perhaps because of mascons.[15])

Before long a whole book will doubtless be written about the great rift, its features and its formation. A point worth mentioning is Dr Conway Leovy's suggestion that, when one end is sunlit and the other is in shadow, the temperature differentials will cause mighty winds to blow through the chasm. Perhaps the effect can be seen in the fluting of the canyon walls and the carving out of the tributaries:[4] certainly there is evidence of extensive landslide movement from the plateau into the canyon.[7] But, Ed Buckley was moved to ask, what about the sound of those winds at morning and evening, as they play across the mouths of the branching chasms like so many vast organ pipes? Could a man hear it and stay sane?

A minor point, taking us back to the psychology of Martian experts, is that everybody still says: "There are no canals." Yet a glance at the old maps shows the rift as a canal – Moore's *Guide to Mars* shows it as Agathadaemon, running from Phoenicis Lacus to Aurorae Sinus, although that doesn't match the description in the Appendices.[3] That was the identification given from the Mariner 7 pictures,[10] although in fact the system begins in Tharsis, north of Phoenicis Lacus. Three different maps in Richardson's *Mars* divide up and name the feature three different ways, with combinations of Tithonius Lacus, Melas Lacus, Coprates and Agathadaemon, all but the last of which appear in Moore and Cross's *Mars* as sections of the rift, running west to east. Taken separately or together they don't form the more spectacular canals, but they are beyond doubt a linear feature along the equator of Mars, identified as a canal – a visual cue around which the observers may have built their imagined networks. The only sense in which no canals exist is in Lowell's use of the term for great artificial waterways; even the shade of Schiaperelli can insist that at least one of his *canali* exists, for *canali* means "channels". C. S. Lewis had suggested in fiction, and Tombaugh and others in all seriousness, that the canals might be huge chasms and cracks in the planet's surface. At any rate, when I took JPL P–12732 (a 500km stretch of Tithonius Lacus) into ASTRA and said, "How about that for a Martian canal, then?" everyone was willing to accept that Mariner 9 had found at least one.

From the original calm world, our idea of Mars suddenly had to include violent storms; from being flat, it changed to include towering mountains and enormous chasms; far from being run down, it proved to be dynamic; and, instead of evolving faster than Earth and long since having run its course, it seemed to be still in the throes of the changes Earth completed at the dawn of its history. Almost the only aspect of the "old Mars" still to be discounted was that the planet was dry.

As to the evidence of the great rift, opinions differed. Some said the rift had been produced by faulting and subsidence, some by the separation of two great plate systems; some said there had been water erosion, some that wind alone was responsible. But if the great volcanoes had spewed up water vapour and carbon dioxide in sufficient quantities for liquid water to form, even temporarily, it would have run downhill through the rift until it reached the outlet in Chryse, unless it evaporated *en route*.[8] Even now, white clouds, presumably ice crystals, are often reported over Nix Olympica – hence its name – and in 1926, when a great W-shaped cloud formed in the region, two of its arms stretched south from Ascraeus Lacus into the rift system. For flash floods, all that was needed was more water and denser air.

More striking indications were already at hand. On 2 February, two photographs were released showing sinuous valleys – "an unexpected feature on the Martian surface" (although with the mountains, the chasms and now apparent riverbeds appearing on successive days, the word "unexpected" was rapidly losing all meaning). There were only two known geological features to which the valleys could be compared: riverbeds on Earth and canyons like Hadley Rille on the Moon. But none of the lunar rilles showed the branching tributaries of these channels – and, although the uv spectrometer showed very little water vapour in the Martian air, the south polar cap looked as if it was there for keeps: by that time of year, frozen carbon dioxide should have been long gone.

At the end of February, a photo was obtained of an oval tableland near the south pole, ringed with contour lines. It was suggested that the lines were dust or volcanic ash, laid down by carbon dioxide or water ice. Further photography of the polar regions, reproduced in *Mars and the Mind of Man*, showed extensive stretches of this "laminated terrain" surrounding the icecap, the "low relief of distinctive character" which had begun to appear earlier. But the concentric rings of the oval tableland were specially interesting, very strongly suggesting "massive amounts of water ice trapped below the surface". The notion was supported by the appearance, from *beneath* the deposits, of older unlayered terrain "deeply etched with jagged pits and grooves" – the same "extraordinary pits and hollows" photographed in early January, with the suggestion of large-scale ice melting, 500 metres deep. An extensive transition region of this kind was shown to surround the pole.[8]

If water existed, what about life? Early in January, photos had been obtained showing "dark splotches" in Phaethontis and Hellespontus, not visible in Mariner 7 pictures from 1969. Similar changes, some of them on a very large scale, had been advanced at one time as evidence for plant life.[18] A high-resolution photograph of the Hellespontus region, however, showed that the blotches there were fields of dark dunes tens of km long and about 1.6km apart. It might have been a relief to find *some* dunes, at least, after all those years believing the entire planet was sown with them, except that nobody had predicted the Martian dunes would be in elliptical patches picked up by violent storms from one place and set down in another; nor, indeed, that they would be dark instead of light. Extensive systems of dark and light trails were found leading out of craters, clearly pointing out the direction of the wind when it died and allowing large parts of the planetary air circulation to be charted. In Tharsis, in the vicinity of the giant volcanoes and the higher end of the great rift, long bright streaks were found unconnected with craters; but craters need not be the only sources of dust.[19]

On 2 March, a photo was released showing "a striking geometric pattern" near the Martian south pole, resembling "the ruins of an ancient metropolis". JPL considered that the ridges were resistant material which had filled cross-cutting channels, then been exposed by wind erosion (but they had taken nearly a month to think about it). "Filling of faults by intruded molten rock or filling of crevasses in an ancient ice mass by wind-blown dust are two possible mechanisms"; no evidence for life yet, but ice was coming to seem "a less dramatic explanation"!

Throughout the mission to date, all latitudes above 45°N had been covered by cloud and virtually nothing could be seen. On 2 March a photo reached us showing Mare Acidalium, near the north pole: a single crater showed through the haze, rimmed with frost and generating wave clouds which continued for hundreds of kilometres downwind. Infrared measure-

8: The new look of Phobos. Before the Mariner missions the moons of Mars were thought to be low-density bright objects. Mariner 9 showed them to be dark battered fragments, perhaps among the oldest material in the Solar System. The spacecraft in the foreground is the cancelled NERVA manned Mars mission; perhaps one day . . . *(Painting by Gavin Roberts.)*

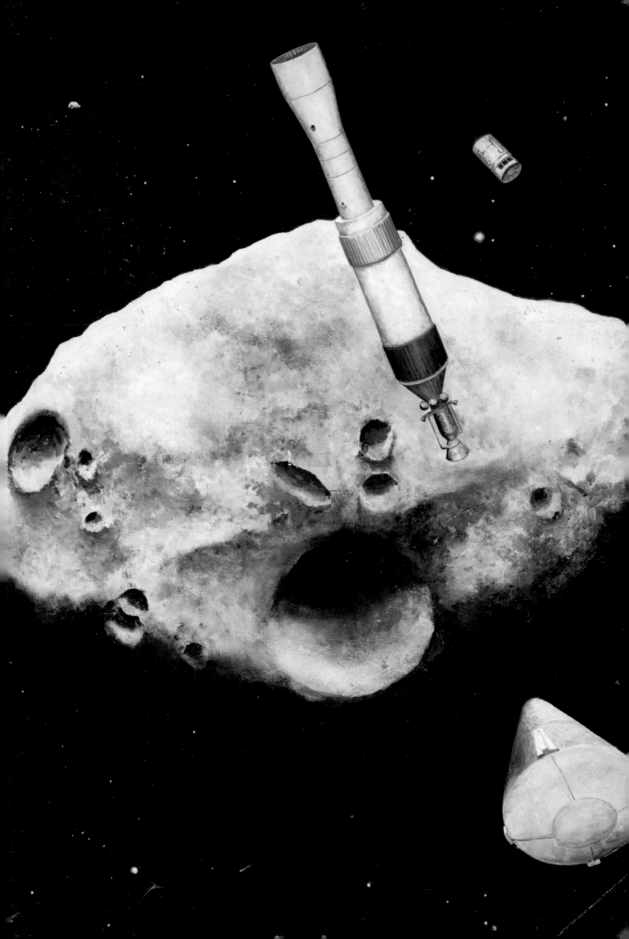

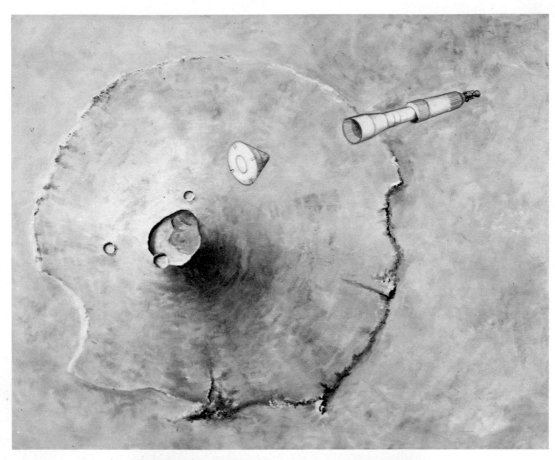

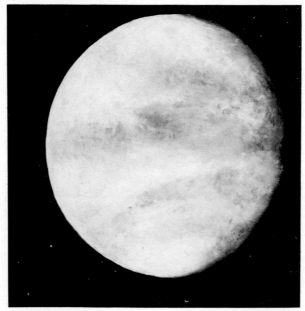

ments indicated that the clouds were cold enough to be frozen carbon dioxide. On 2 April, Mariner 9 was powered down because its orbit was entering Mars's shadow, and when it was reactivated on 4 June spring had come in the northern hemisphere and the clouds had dispersed.

The northern cap proved to resemble the southern one, even to sporting a set of spiral ridges, but was very much larger – 1,000km across at its minimum extent, in the second week of October. Oblique photographs of the polar region showed "circular landforms" like those near the south pole and now believed to be "the edges of layered rocks . . . like a stack of saucers that overlie, and are younger than, the ancient cratered terrain that surrounds the polar region". Tilting might indicate "depression of the Martian crust in the polar region by the overlying ice". We had come some way from the idea of carbon dioxide frost, at most a few metres thick!

In the second week of October, the cap had reached its minimum extent and, as at the south pole, the spiral markings had proved to be the sunward-facing edges of layered terrain; in conjunction with an eroded channel penetrating deep into the cap, they gave it a convoluted appearance very like a human brain. In fact, the JPL print also gave a high-resolution view of two "owl-like" craters – eyes! – in the collar of rough, dark terrain.

In the meantime, evidence of surface-water action continued to accumulate. One of the later pictures in March had shown an intricate network of "braided channels" sweeping past a crater, signs of fluid erosion of some kind; a system of numerous small channels was found in cratered terrain early in June. As Carl Sagan remarked, the channels were concentrated near the Martian equator – evidence that they were temperature-related – and didn't start or end in craters.[7] "Undoubtedly" there was subsurface permafrost; an article in *The Glasgow Herald* suggested that permafrost might be melted by big meteorite impacts, providing temporary water flows which soon evaporated. Other theorists still maintained that the "channels" were probably caused by volcanic subsidence;[20] temporary atmospheres and released permafrost had been invoked to explain radial channels around some lunar craters, once upon a time. But ultraviolet spectrometer results now suggested, from the amount of free hydrogen in the atmosphere, that Mars was losing 450,000 litres of water *per day* into space; probably it was outgassing from the volcanoes – white clouds had been reported often enough – but how great were the water resources being tapped?

On 27 October Mariner 9 was switched off altogether because its nitrogen

9 and 10: *Above,* NERVA over Nix Olympica. The largest volcano and highest known mountain in the Solar System, this is some 26km high, 500km across at the base, and ringed by cliffs suggesting water action. Until Mariner 9 Mars was thought to be flat, dry and without volcanoes. *Below,* the new look of Venus, as photographed by Mariner 10. The clouds of Venus rotate much faster than the planet retrograde; they form a distinctive "Y" when they strike the permanent high-pressure area at the subsolar point.
(Paintings by Gavin Roberts.)

gas supplies, used for attitude control, were exhausted. The last 15 pictures – of the little covered northern regions – were not transmitted to Earth – infuriatingly: for a further $30,000 Mariner could have been equipped before launch to switch the residual fuel in the propellant tanks into the attitude control system, thereby gaining not just those 15 pictures, but another whole operational year in Mars orbit. As Sagan remarks, there is now no way in which we can obtain those views of northern hemisphere summer, 1972 – whose value we have no way of knowing – unless we send men to Mars within fifty years to collect them.[14]

But unless the channels are volcanic, or temporary permafrost outflows after impacts, it seemed that in the relatively recent past – in view of the wind erosion working to conceal the evidence – there was liquid water on the surface of Mars, and the atmosphere all over the planet must have been dense enough to permit it. The big question then arises, where has it all gone? The situation is very different from the classical picture of a Martian atmosphere leaking away into space over geological ages. It wasn't long, however, before Carl Sagan came up with a possible explanation.[21]

We began this chapter with the fact that the orbit of Mars is an ellipse – as are all the planetary orbits, although Mars' is more elliptical than most – and Kepler's proof of it opened up the first possibility of true inter-planetary travel. (Willy Ley has remarked that if Kepler had chosen instead to determine the orbit of Venus, which is very close to a circle, history might have taken a different course.[22]) The Earth's orbit is also somewhat elliptical, and the tilt of Earth's axis is such that the southern hemisphere points sunwards near perihelion (nearest point of the orbit to the Sun). As a result, temperatures in the southern hemisphere are generally higher than in the north.

Mars, too, has a pronounced axial tilt; but the effect on seasonal temperatures is enhanced because the orbit is more elliptical. When Mars is at aphelion (furthest from the Sun) the northern hemisphere is in summer, but remains considerably colder than the southern hemisphere summer at perihelion. The situation is not permanent, however. Like Earth's, the axis of Mars precesses, with a period of about 50,000 years, and now that we know Mars has an equatorial bulge like Earth's the precession is not surprising (precession of the Earth's axis – often called "precession of the Equinoxes" – is caused by the pull of the Sun and Moon on the Earth's equatorial bulge). Consequently, over 50,000 years, Mars may undergo a cycle of changes making Earth's ice ages seem trivial.[14] As one polar cap or the other swings way from the Sun, it could become a "cold trap" in which more and more water and carbon dioxide ice is deposited and retained. As surface pressure drops, the threshold altitude below which liquid water can exist is reduced – solar ultraviolet radiation strikes deeper into the atmosphere each year, until eventually all water vapour not frozen at the poles has been disassociated into hydrogen and oxygen; the hydrogen escapes at once and the oxygen does the same or is locked up in chemical combination with other elements at ground level. The dynamics of the atmosphere change until the great dust storms become possible, and Mars settles into the ice age in which we see it today.

But, as the poles continue their slow movement in the sky, the Sun comes to bear on the frozen hemisphere near perihelion. The cap begins to lose more ice in summer than it regains in winter – carbon dioxide re-enters the atmosphere first, raising the surface pressure and also the temperature by "greenhouse effect"; eventually conditions allow water to escape from the cap without being disassociated and lost, and then, as Mel Adam put it at ASTRA, "It *does* rain on Mars – once every 25,000 years . . ." There is a true "Martian spring" in which rivers flow, lakes and even seas form; but, as the poles move on, the opposite cap is now turning away from the Sun and starting to grow . . .

If that were all the story, Mars would have lost all its water by now, just as astronomers imagined earlier this century, except that the process would have been cyclic instead of continuous. But, since we know that there are volcanoes on Mars, recently active, and even now suspected of giving off ice clouds, it seemed obvious how the annual losses were made good. In February 1974 the Russian Mars 5 probe was placed in orbit around the planet and produced evidence that there is even more water vapour in the atmosphere now than had been estimated – and the losses had been estimated at 450,000 litres per day, remember. Further support for the presence of water was provided by a photometer which detected traces of ozone:[23] the Mariner 9 estimate of a water loss had been based on uv spectrometer observations of hydrogen in the atmosphere. If the hydrogen came from water disassociating, it could be predicted that in the thin atmosphere, under solar uv bombardment, the oxygen released would form ozone – and that would rapidly combine with other elements, or escape.

No fewer than four Soviet spacecraft had been dispatched to Mars in 1973. Mars 4, the first to arrive, did not fire its braking engine but obtained TV pictures during the flyby. Mars 5 successfully entered orbit and began returning pictures. Mars 6 released a landing capsule which successfully entered the atmosphere; during the parachute descent it made the first direct measurements conducted in the Martian atmosphere. Only twenty seconds before touchdown, all contact with the spacecraft was lost. One important datum had already been broadcast, however: 20–30% of the atmosphere might consist of inert gas, probably argon. Such a high proportion of such a rare element would support the notion that 99% of the Martian atmosphere is currently in frozen form at the poles.[24]

No pictures had yet been obtained from the Martian surface. A fourth attempt was made with Mars 7, which reached the planet in March 1974; but the landing capsule separated prematurely from the spacecraft and missed the planet by 1,300km. Further Soviet attempts were predicted for 1976, but did not materialize – leaving the stage clear for the commemoration of the US bicentennial with the most ambitious unmanned spacecraft to date, the inelegant but sophisticated Vikings 1 and 2.

Viking mission planning went to great lengths to avoid the pitfalls of previous Mars ventures. The frustrations of previous oppositions, particularly the close ones of 1956 and 1971, had led to the suggestion that the most violent Martian dust storms occurred when Earth passed between Mars and the Sun. The influence of the Earth, if any, had still to be explained: it seems the great storms begin a little like hurricanes on Earth, with a build-up of floating dust over one of the raised "continents" in the Martian southern hemisphere. Terrestrial hurricanes are seemingly born over the Sahara, growing in size and violence when the dry wind-patterns move out to sea. On Mars the driving energy comes not from water vapour but from solar heat soaked up by the suspended dust. Less than 0.025mm across,[4] easily raised by "dust-devils", the particles trap energy which is normally lost into space during the Martian night; after two weeks or so, a positive feedback mechanism expands the storm to cover the whole planet in 5–6 weeks.[25] A planet-wide storm can rage for 10–25 weeks, with wind speeds up to 650km per hour; moving dust drifts at the summit of Pavonis Mons, photographed by Mariner 9, showed that the winds were blowing at half the local speed of sound.[16]

In the circumstances, the "death" of Mars 3 was hardly surprising. At the height of the storm, not far from Hellas (probably the least healthy spot on the planet at the time), its successful landing is more surprizing than its short life thereafter. Mars 6 was a stranger case, since there was no storm at the time – but, in general, landings near opposition seemed to be dangerous. The Viking landings were therefore planned to occur when Mars was nearly as far from Earth as it could get, with a timelag of twenty minutes each way for radio signals instead of only two minutes at opposition. In November 1976, only three months after the Viking 2 touchdown, scientists would have a month to take stock of findings to date while Mars was screened from communications behind the Sun.[26]

Obviously such a timetable (taking the spacecraft beyond the orbit of Mars for a significant part of the trajectory) was much more demanding than the minimum-energy transfers described by Professor Roy in Chapter 3, giving planetary encounters near opposition. But the powerful launch combination of a Titan IIIC booster and a Centaur upper stage allowed Viking enough mass for further precautions. Although the spacecraft followed Soviet practice in splitting into two units, an Orbiter and a Lander, the separations would not occur until *after* the Orbiters had been success-fully captured by the planet. There was therefore no risk of missing the planet, like the Mars 7 lander, and atmosphere entry velocity would be lower than in the Soviet attempts. Better still, however, the Vikings could wait up to fifty days in orbit for any unexpected storms to die down, and were expected to spend twenty to thirty days on "site evaluation" before going down. Lastly, Viking was designed to touch down safely in wind speeds of up to nearly 250km per hour.[27]

"The primary objective of the mission," Carl Sagan wrote, "is to search for life on Mars."[26] That objective was subject to a great deal of hostile discussion, both for and against the probability that life did in fact exist. Many scientists objected strongly to the risk that Viking might contaminate the planet with terrestrial bacteria, ruining its own results and compromising future programs. NASA went to great lengths to minimize the danger: the Vikings were thoroughly sterilized after being sealed into the atmo-sphere-entry aeroshells. Other objectors, convinced that Mars was lifeless and demanding more emphasis on physical exploration, called Viking's priorities "a last tribute to Lowell's Mars". A third group, accepting the ice-age model of Mars's climate, maintained that any Martian life would be far below the surface in hibernation and that public disappointment at a negative result might bring the space program to a halt.[2] At the other end of the scale, there was a tendency for science writers to be hypnotized by Viking's biological experiments, reeling off detailed technical descriptions like mystical incantations.

Along the line, the philosophical importance of the search tended to be lost. It went far beyond the merely factual question of what was to be found on Mars; like the discovery of planetary systems orbiting other stars, a positive result would profoundly affect the status of Man and the human mind. For much of the 20th century, it was believed that the Solar System had been created by an amazing chance, the close encounter of two stars: it was possible to argue that the added odds against the appearance of life, and the evolution of the questioning mind of Man, were far too great for any of the process to have been an accident. There is no need to detail the dangers we have created for ourselves in the belief that Earth was made for us, and that we have some great destiny which ensures that we are protected from the consequences of our folly. If the story of life is being played on other stages, we can stop deluding ourselves that we're something special. On the other hand, many people who *are* aware of the dangers we face need to be assured that life on Earth isn't *just* an accident, that terrestrial life is "natural" and not a unique aberration, and that we may hope to seek out active minds elsewhere and communicate with them. As Philip Morrison of Massachusetts Institute of Technology put it, finding life on one other planet would "transfer the origin of life from a miracle to a statistic".[28] Set in such a context, Viking itself seems a remarkably modest instrument: in the late 20th century, for the first time, we have been able to seek the answer to such questions in a metal and plastic box, 29 x 34 x 27cm, 350 million km away.

After the long build-up to the Viking project, and with only one twin-probe success to date after four attempts, there was an inevitable nagging feeling that at least one of the Mars landers might not get away from Earth. There were troubles in the final stages of preparation, and Viking B was exchanged for Viking A on the pad and so became Viking 1 after launch. But both boosters performed well, and the outward journeys to Mars were almost without incident. The only technical trouble to develop *en route*, on both spacecraft, was in the miniature ovens to be used for baking samples of Martian soil. The backup ovens remained operational, however, and despite some sensational reports that the spacecraft had fallen victim to "the Great Galactic Ghoul" – a super-gremlin supposedly inhabiting the region where Mariner 7 ran into trouble – Viking 1 was decelerated into orbit around Mars on 20 June 1976. Despite the delays before launch, there was still a good chance of a landing on 4 July, the bicentennial of American independence.

Photographic coverage had already begun on the approach to the planet. From 560,000km out the four great volcanoes were plainly visible, with the impact basin of Argyre far to the north.[29] (A spectacular colour print in

Sky & Telescope, showing the volcanoes and part of the Great Rift[30] – now termed Valles Marineris – made it necessary for Gavin Roberts to produce a second, brighter, version of plate 7.) A 38-minute engine burn, the longest so far attempted in deep space, brought the probe into elliptical orbit with a period of 42.6 hours; a second burn the following day lowered the period to 24.6 hours. Each Martian day, at its closest approach to the planet, the Viking Orbiter would be over the prime landing site in Chryse Planitia.

The Viking landing sites had been selected after intensive study of Mariner 9's photographic coverage. With a whole planet to range, it was difficult to pick out two sites of prime scientific interest, but the startling "new" geology of Mars had simplified the task a great deal. Viking 1 was intended to land in Chryse, 4,900m below mean surface level, where the downhill end of the Great Rift opens out into a complex of branching channels. Even if no water had drained out lately on to the plains there could be extensive deposits below the surface, and whatever minerals might support Martian life should have been laid down in bulk. Viking 2's planned target was in some ways even more promising – Cydonia, a region of Mare Acidalium in the northern hemisphere of the planet. Surface atmospheric pressure on Mars is equivalent to that 30,500m above sea level on Earth, but in Cydonia, 5,500m below the mean surface, it should be possible in theory for liquid water to form in some seasons. The chances seem particularly favourable because for much of the year Cydonia lies under the North Polar Hood, the cloud cover which initially hid the northern latitudes from Mariner 9. There are few lower spots on Mars and the lowest of them all, the Hellas basin, showed so few features because it is usually filled with dust. Soviet scientists had suggested, indeed, that most of the dust which covers the planet in the great storms comes out of pockets such as Hellas.[31] Though Hellas is 9,500m deep, it is not promising for landings, water or life!

Objections had been raised to the Cydonia landing; one was the risk mentioned in Chapter 1, that if Viking touched down on permafrost the heat from its radioactive power source would cause it to thaw the ground and sink. A more serious one still was that, unlike Chryse, Cydonia was too far north to be studied by radar from Arecibo and might be too rough to permit a landing. Moreover, the decision would have to be taken before Viking 2 went into orbit around Mars, and therefore before the biology experiments on Viking 1 had been completed.[26] Earth-based radar's assessment of Chryse proved inadequate, however: photos from Viking 1 Orbiter showed *plenty* of evidence of water action, far too many channels, boulders and changes in surface level for a safe landing. The second target site, further west, was better but still unacceptable. Even Viking 1's angle of view was quite good enough to rule out Cydonia altogether, and Viking 2's second target in Alba Patera later proved to be a nightmare of crisscrossing faults! By 28 June the Viking 1 cameras were searching for new sites.

On 7 July the western part of Chryse was picked out, after three other sites had been rejected. The necessary changes in orbit were made two days later, and on 20 July the lander separated from the orbiter on the descending leg of the ellipse. Because of the signal timelag from Earth the release took place far out from the planet, and $3\frac{1}{2}$ hours passed before the landing. The parachute descent and release from the aeroshell were completely successful and, after descending the last 1,200m on its rocket motors, Viking touched down at 4.30 in the Martian afternoon. After all the precautions against the worst of Martian weather, conditions at the landing site had turned out to be virtually perfect.

The only remaining fear had been that the lander would land on a boulder and smash itself, overturn, or settle at too great an angle for the experiments to be performed. Almost from the first, as photographs reached Earth 19 minutes later, it was obvious that this was no idle worry. Following Surveyor practice on the Moon, the first shots were of the ground immediately around the spacecraft, but as panoramas and high-resolution frames were built up big boulders were found strewn around the landscape, ranging up to 4m across.[32] The sunrise panorama, taken on 3 August, threw into sharp relief a 3m boulder close at hand.[33] For all the sophistication of Viking's unmanned landing techniques, in the last second or two of descent its survival had remained a matter of blind chance.

Studying the photographs on the first day, in black and white, more than one observer remarked on the Earthlike qualities of the scene – particularly if compared to the deserts of Arizona and New Mexico. Only the skyline seemed to suggest otherwise, with two noticeable dips which could be crater rims. Some at least of the surrounding rocks might be impact debris, thrown up from well below the surface. How frustrating not to be able to sample the crater rims and floors to find out! Three distinct types of rock showed in the photos: rough-textured igneous rocks, apparently produced by slow cooling; fine-textured, rapidly cooled rocks; and very smooth light-coloured ones which might have been transported (e.g., by dust storms) from some distance away.[34] Hollowed rocks tended to support the suggestion that the surface was primarily basalt, overlaid with thin soil and partly exposed by wind.[32] Wind action was shown by streaks of dust deposited behind rocks, by undercutting of some boulders, and by a small field of sand dunes (clearly seen in the sunrise panorama) which had been moving across the landscape. Wind speeds at landing had been only 24kph, and in successive pictures it seemed that all was still – but Viking might last long enough to capture some action later in the Martian season. One more day would be long enough for the next Viking achievement, however: the first automated three-colour photography on the surface of another heavenly body.

"Old Mars" paintings had shown the dangers of prophesy: in *The Splendour of the Heavens*, published in the 1920s,[35] and in the *Conquest of Space* paintings of the 1940s,[36] Mars has flat vegetation patchworks, flimsy dust storms and canals like railways. In *The Exploration of Mars* (1956) the landscapes are more convincing, but yellow, flat and eroded, under a deep blue sky – although one painting illustrates the hypothesis that the canals are great chasms, filled occasionally with cloud.[22] One of Ludek Pesek's Mars paintings for *The National Geographic Magazine* in 1970 was captioned "a dull uninteresting landscape", with the sky deeper blue than ever.[13]

"Of the Viking pictures," I wrote some years ago in the first draft of this chapter, "only two predictions can safely be made. First, they will be denounced as boring in some quarters before the prints are dry; secondly, they will turn out to be quite unlike what most of us expected." The first prediction was duly fulfilled by a Scots women's page editor who said she could find prettier pebbles on Largs beach. The second hit us right in the eye with the first colour shots: Mars was more red, much more vivid than had been imagined, and even the sky was pink! Even in the currently gentle weather conditions, a fine haze of dust covered the sky. Some early prints showed the sky as a pale, Earthlike blue,[34] but when all the data had been evaluated and the colours definitely established the pink sky was the correct version (plate 6). To the best of my knowledge, not a single author or artist had predicted anything of the kind. The nearest hint to it had been the Mars 4 and 5 indications that the plains of Mars were orange;[5] interestingly enough, many of the rocks in the middle distance from Viking did have the blue-green tint which the Soviet probes had ascribed to the craters.[33]

With the photographic milestones passed, Viking's scientific experiments came to the fore. The principal objects were to study the composition and movement of the atmosphere, to monitor seismic activity, and (before determining the composition of the soil in detail) to test it for the presence of life. The atmosphere studies began during the descent from space, and immediately produced two important results. The high concentrations of argon suggested by Soviet scientists did not exist, although small amounts of argon were present. The case for most of the atmosphere being frozen at the poles was weakened, and with it the hypothesis that Mars has Earth-like conditions in 25,000-year cycles, though the relative abundance of isotopes did suggest a denser atmosphere at *some* time in the past. Indeed, there turned out to be nitrogen in Mars' atmosphere after all – enough to suggest an Earthlike atmosphere in the remote geological past. Even today, Mars could be supplying more usable nitrogen to surface life than Earth does.[34] The questions were, had life appeared in that early era and had it adapted to changing conditions since?

It seemed for a while that we might suffer total frustration on the biology experiments, because the sample-gathering arm was jammed. With the ingenuity we now take almost for granted, JPL engineers duplicated the problem and solved it on Earth, then repeated the operation on Mars by remote control. The seismometer package could not be helped in the same way, however: its sensing elements had been "caged" to prevent damage during landing, and they remained locked and useless. There were recurring fights with the sample arm, but eventually the biology experiments all had material to work with.

In one test, the "gas-exchange" experiment, the Martian soil was soaked in a nutrient solution and the atmosphere in the experiment chamber was monitored for changes. Even if Martian life wasn't nourished by the compounds our microbes appreciate, it could be expected to react by the Sagans' recipe: "Just add water." There were immediate results: a dramatically large flow of oxygen was detected, tailing off after 24 hours. In an adjacent chamber, "the labelled release experiment", the nutrient added was "tagged" with carbon-14, a radioactive isotope. Here too there was activity: radioactive carbon dioxide was given off, but ceased after 70 hours. With Earth soil, bearing life, a similar gas flow might have been spread over 10 days.[37] The last test, the "pyrolytic release experiment", incubated its sample in an atmosphere of "tagged" carbon dioxide and monoxide, then cooked it at 600°C to drive off any gases which had been incorporated into organic compounds. This time the results were strangely inconclusive. The level of activity resembled that of near-sterile Antarctic soil, and suggested that the other results were at least partly due to chemical reactions, not to the biochemical action of life.

As more elaborate tests were performed, the findings became more ambiguous. The labelled-release experiment was given a second dose of nutrient, but after an initial surge of activity the tagged carbon dioxide level *decreased*. Had organic compounds absorbed it, or was the apparatus leaking? As monitoring continued, the tagged CO_2 level began to rise again; but it was too late to stop Viking from dropping the sample to begin again with a fresh one.[38] The next phase was to repeat the labelled release and pyrolytic release experiments with sterilized samples, cooked at 160°C for three hours. Nothing happened – the strongest indication yet that the previous activity was biological, not simply chemical.[39] Similar results on Earth would have been taken to indicate the presence of life, but were they conclusive for Mars?[40] One really serious problem was developing in the Gas Chromatograph/Mass Spectrometer experiment, where other samples were being vaporized and analyzed in detail. The analyses were not finding anything recognizably similar to terrestrial organic compounds, and seemed to imply that if there *were* life in the Martian soil it must be quite unlike our own.

Now came the real bite of the limitations on Viking's funding. As Sagan had pointed out more than a year before, NASA did not have and could not afford the tracking facilities to operate both Viking landers on the surface at the same time. A large part of the potential benefit of sending two probes to Mars would be thrown away if there could be no synoptic coverage, with observations made simultaneously at two points on the Martian surface.[26] As it happened, the failure of Viking 1's seismometer had removed much of that potential in any case and the meteorology experiments were kept in direct contact with Earth; but now the tests on Viking 1's samples had to stop, leaving samples incubating in the chambers for (hopefully) resumed testing three months later.[41]

As already mentioned, Viking 2's primary and secondary targets were ruled out by photography from orbit. As well as trying to minimize the danger of a crash there was a good case for landing in a different type of terrain, and the region selected was Utopia Planitia, a plain apparently covered with sand dunes and windblown sediment. Although craters could be discerned in it their outlines were softened and rocky ground would be less likely to endanger the spacecraft. During the descent a temporary power failure occurred on the Orbiter, but the system was flexible enough to store the approach data which might have been lost. Viking 2 landed on 3

September : right at the outset, from the first photographs obtained, it was obvious that Mars had sprung another surprise. Instead of dunes the landing site was spread with rocks, even more thickly than the Viking 1 site; the spacecraft had settled at an 8° angle, presumably because one footpad was resting on a rock.

Utopia was too far north for radar scanning from Earth, but after the disqualification of the prime Viking 1 site that consideration was perhaps a little less important. Despite the "forest of rocks", indeed, the Viking 2 panoramas showed a noticeably flatter skyline than Viking 1's. At 48°N, the site matched at least one of Cydonia's original selection criteria – it is covered annually by the North Polar Hood, and in some seasons at least there might possibly be liquid water. On the extreme left of the first panorama there appeared a sinuous line, weaving between the stones towards the lander like the bed of a dried-up stream. Light streaks, possibly salts leached from the soil, could be seen in it at its nearest, and were within reach of the sample arm (after it too had been cured of mechanical troubles); but preliminary analysis turned up no differences from other samples.[42]

Viking 2's seismometer was successfully activated, but it was reported on BBC–TV's *The Sky at Night* that it was recording only activity within the spacecraft itself. The negative results might be due to the way the spacecraft is lying, but with no Viking 1 readings for comparison (much less synoptic coverage) it is impossible to say. The point is far from minor. Rangers 3, 4 and 5 had tried unsuccessfully to land seismometer payloads on the Moon in the early 1960s, and when an instrument was hand-placed by the Apollo 11 crew its results proved to be quite unexpected (page 82). The questions posed by the Moon's complex interior are still not resolved. Likewise with Mars, the state of the planet's evolution depends very much on conditions within the core. Mars is known to be "lumpy", particularly in the young volcanic regions, which would imply considerable internal stress. Early Mariner results, including the lack of a detectable magnetic field, led to the suggestion that Mars had no Earth-type core. But Mars 2 and 3 indic-ated a weak planetary magnetic field,[23] Mars 5 supported them,[24] and Mars 6 results were still more definite – field strength was estimated at 7–10 times that in interplanetary space.[43] During atmosphere entry the Viking landers detected a possible magnetic field shockwave. The Great Rift may be an embryonic ocean, the line of the great volcanoes may show the movement of an underground heat source, dust plumes emanating·from craters may imply continuing volcanism – but we need seismic data to find out what's really going on inside the planet. Even the likelihood of life is affected : if Mars is undifferentiated, with no separation of heavier elements into a core, then the crust may be too poor in light elements to form organic compounds in quantity. The volcanoes are important partly because they indicate internal activity, partly because the first amino acids on Earth may have been synthesized from volcanic gases.[44] When were the volcanoes active, what is the state of the interior, is Mars evolving slowly or "frozen" at an earlier stage than the Earth?

Viking soil analysis can provide only part of the story. In fact, the samples suggest that the crust has not undergone extensive differentiation: iron is particularly plentiful, making up no less than 14% of the soil.[45] The red colour is indeed due to iron oxide, as had been suspected for so long. Calcium, silicon, titanium and aluminium are the other main constituents. Even the Viking 1 samples contained a "surprizing" amount of water, confirming high-altitude aircraft observations – it seems that there are mineral hydrates on large areas of the Martian surface, and Carl Sagan has suggested that, to a lifeform which could separate water from rock, the "deserts" of Mars would seem veritable oceans.[19]

In the search for life itself, Viking 2 took up where Viking 1 left off. Great ingenuity went into experiments aimed at producing a definite answer. In the pyrolytic release experiment samples were incubated in the dark, instead of under simulated sunlight; nothing happened.[46] That might suggest that previous positive results were due to biological photosynthesis. In the labelled release experiment the sample was heated for three hours at 50°C, hopefully to damage microorganisms but not enough to alter the soil chemistry. The reaction rate altered but there was still no conclusive answer – and with Viking 2, as with the first lander, detailed soil analysis failed to find organic compounds. "All the signs suggest that life exists on Mars," said Gerald Soffen, the Viking Project's chief scientist, "but we can't find any bodies!"

Still another hypothesis was that there might be life under the rocks, sheltering from the solar ultraviolet radiation. The rocket landings might have disturbed the soil enough to kill off near-surface life in the open. The first experiment on that idea turned up a fresh puzzle, as an ordinary-looking rock refused to shift for the sample arm. Perhaps there was more of the stone beneath the surface, or perhaps it was glued to the surface in some way – a useful skill for Martian life to develop . . . In a second attempt a sample of shaded soil was scooped up successfully, though after three days' exposure to sunlight, and on analysis was found to contain acetone – an organic conpound itself, and a solvent for other organics. What did that indicate? With fresh samples taken aboard, contact ceased as Mars went behind the Sun. Both probes were successfully reactivated a month later. But long incubation periods have not produced clearer answers from the soil samples – the biology experiments ended at the onset of Martian winter without having provided any definite answers.

When Viking 1 was partly deactivated, its orbiter had been freed to take a "science walk" around the planet, moving the lowest point of its orbit away from the landing site. Detailed photographic coverage accumulated faster than the science team could react to it.[47] From the very outset, the orbiters had been sending pictures which made the Mariner 9 images seem crude by comparison. For example, part of the trouble with the original landing site in Chryse was that the water channels had cut deeper into the landscape than anticipated. Ares Vallis, the largest of the apparent rivers, contained huge islands carved out by erosion: seven distinct layers of rock were visible on their flanks, providing the first evidence of stratification in the Martian crust.[29] It wasn't unexpected, but it was nice to know it was there. At higher resolution, the channel floors proved to be *very* rough.[33]

The higher the resolution, the more evidence for water action was revealed. In Lunae Planum, west of Chryse, a crater adjacent to the Kasei Vallis "river bed" had dropped ejecta into the channel, showing clearly that at least some craters were younger than water flows.[48] In an Orbiter 1 photo, a crater with a large central peak (Arandas) was surrounded by contrast with material which had flowed outwards from the impact, instead of being thrown. "The general pattern of the ejected material is reminiscent of those which occur with experimental craters in waterlogged ground." (Waterlogged ground? Mars?) In Capri, originally designated as a "supersafe" landing area for Viking 2, there were great depressions apparently created by melting of subsurface ice, with scoured-out channels leading away downhill. Northwest of the original Viking 1 site, faults and ridges had broken up lava flows, to be cut in turn by sinuous channels gouged by pent-up water. That entire frame, 240 by 190km, had been swept by water – a scene nobody would have believed before 1972.

At present the main erosion forces on Mars are the joint product of wind and sand. JPL provided two spectacular prints showing their effect: Gangis Chasma, one of the side branches of the Great Rift, is apparently growing by a continuing process of slumping and wind excavation. Landslides lined the valley floor, and one huge avalanche had rolled half-way across it, about 30km. Near it, a 50km-long field of dunes was moving up the valley. In the accompanying high-resolution view, it was obvious that when the wind dropped the leading dunes had been climbing the rock wall into the higher part of the canyon; in the next storm, if they get past the big landslide, no doubt they will eventually escape from Gangis Chasma altogether and move on to bury some other region. When we go to Mars, we will have to site our ground bases with some care : the individual dunes in that moving field are nearly 500m across!

Many of those features appeared in a mosaic of part of Valles Marineris, the Great Rift itself.[48] Great aprons of debris had fallen some two kilometres to the canyon floor, and the fluting effect of the wind could be seen on the walls, which had bitten into a crater on the mesa above. The exposed strata showed a tough upper layer, possibly lava flows, overlying softer material which could be ash or dust. At the foot of the canyon rim the harder material had remained as huge boulders, while the softer debris spread out across the floor. Between the landslide aprons, linear streaks showed the prevailing wind direction; and, most interesting of all, in view of the "embryo ocean" hypothesis about the Great Rift, the canyon floor showed clusters of volcanic conical hills.

There were spectacular shots of the great volcanoes, of course : one showed Nix Olympica's caldera projecting, not from a dust storm this time, but from a sea of clouds.[45] Apparently the clouds were water ice, condensed and frozen as the air moved 19km up the slopes of the volcano. Beyond it, wave cloud trains stretched for hundreds of km, and still higher stratified hazes showed beyond. The latter showed more clearly in an oblique view across Argyre, which proved to be a relatively smooth plain surrounded by heavily cratered country; the haze layers were 24 to 40km up, presumably carbon dioxide crystals.[48]

Another orbiter discovery, one more part of the new pattern, was that enough water vapour was deposited in the Martian night to form fog in the valleys at dawn. Viking 1 had reported temperatures lowest just before dawn, highest at 3pm, in a temperature profile much like terrestrial deserts – but colder! The gentle winds in Chryse, repeating themselves over a twenty-day pattern, gave no hints of violence to come as the Martian year progressed, but there was one ominous warning sign: air pressure was dropping steadily overall. The southern hemisphere was controlling weather in the northern, as carbon dioxide froze out at the south polar cap. On approach Viking 1 had spotted a huge deposit of frost (probably CO_2) in Hellas, the lowest region on Mars.[49] Somewhere around the end of 1976, the trend would start to turn; dust storms were photographed in Argyre in February 1977, and in the Great Rift by March, building up to a global obscuration;[58] but by September there had been no major storms over the landers, and water ice had formed around Viking 2 under a whiter sky.[59]

By then most of the complex experiments had failed due to leaks or voltage surges, and apart from the seismometer, the meteorological sensors, and an occasional picture or test for wind-blown dust, all Viking 2's power was going to the heaters as temperatures fell towards $-123°C$.[60] The orbiters were no longer tied to their daily low pass over the landers, but after the dust cleared the Viking 1 orbiter and lander collaborated, timing a solar eclipse by Phobos, to fix the lander's position to within 200m.[58]

About a third of the present atmosphere freezes out annually at one or other of the polar caps.[50] But as the orbiters mapped the water vapour profiles of the atmosphere, concentrating on the north polar cap so briefly surveyed by Mariner 9, evidence began to mount that Mars was less like the pre-Mariner model than even Carl Sagan had guessed when he put forward his controversial 50,000-year cycle. From a thin crust of carbon dioxide, at most half a metre thick, the north polar cap had come to be imagined as a huge deposit of water and carbon dioxide containing 90% of the "true" atmosphere of Mars, as dense (in its gaseous phase) as Earth's. The water was there, all right, hanging as vapour over the pole; but both the cap and the atmosphere over it were too warm for carbon dioxide to remain frozen, and the cap was stable. Since the surrounding craters were filled with smooth ice (crater Korolev was casually described in *New Scientist* as a 90km-diameter ice rink), the ice might be hundreds of metres thick – and all water. The cyclic ice-age model of Mars was in trouble, not for lack of water, but because Viking couldn't find the carbon dioxide!

The highest concentrations of water vapour were found over the dark band surrounding the polar cap, around latitude 70–80°N. About 25% of all the water vapour in the atmosphere was in those latitudes, especially in the lower regions such as Utopia and Arcadia, so Viking 2 was well placed in that respect. Mid-latitude permafrost regions were the major source of the annual changes, it seemed. The new model of Mars took on the character of "old Venus", except that the water was frozen: Mars might be a water planet, a shell of ice surrounding a rocky core, pierced by volcanoes and overlaid with lava flows. Not far below the surface there could be huge ice deposits. Dr Farmer, leader of the water-vapour mapping team, described the north polar cap as "the tip of an iceberg floating in a sea of rock, which is rather different from the geologists' view of Mars". Even in a book studded with memorable understatements, that one is hard to top.

Detailed photography of the North polar region was producing more mysteries. In September 1976 Viking 2 obtained an oblique view of the dark polar ridges and it was suggested that they might somehow be caused by winds spiralling outwards from the pole. But the spiral pattern continued into a vast sea of dark dunes surrounding the polar region, breaking up into a variety of other forms on its southern edge.[61] Craters were buried in it and in places it smothered the "layered terrain" below the polar ice. The dunes showed no fresh craters, so were either recent or mobile. Could all that material have come from the dark ridges of the polar cap? Or was it related to the moving fields of dark dunes found by Mariner 9 – was it migrating north on to the polar cap?

Here follows an original suggestion of my own. Mars shows clear evidence of a liquid water epoch, yet the CO_2 (presumably) which made up the denser atmosphere is now missing. When the CO_2 was thought to be locked up in the North polar cap, it was suggested that a carbonaceous chondrite asteroid (see Chapter 8) might be disintegrated over the pole to darken the cap and make it absorb more sunlight, to release the CO_2 and make Mars more earthlike.[62] And the laminated terrain of the polar cap shows "uncomformable contacts" implying at least one erosional interruption in the seasonal pattern of deposition.[61]

Suppose then that a natural carbonaceous impact injected a great quantity of dark dust into the Martian atmosphere. Phobos and Deimos, which are dark and may be captured asteroids, are spiralling inexorably towards Mars due to tidal action;[63] and a similar explanation now seems most likely for the mid-air explosion of the 1908 Tunguska meteorite, which released a great deal of dust into Earth's atmosphere.[64] If enough dust were transported to the poles Mars might have bloomed for a time, with rivers, seas and life; life which, as on Earth, drew carbon dioxide from the atmosphere and released free oxygen. But free oxygen on Mars would escape into space, and, as the "Long Winter" returned, and the winds reversed and blew the dust clear of the pole, there would not be enough CO_2 to be laid down for the next precessional Spring. Life on Mars might have known many cycles, but burned itself out in an unseasonal warm spell; or, as Shakespeare so chillingly says in *Richard III*, "Short summers lightly have a forward spring."

What, then, about the great search for life? If ever Mars had an Earthlike atmosphere and oceans, it may have been at the outset of its history. If life appeared then it could survive only by permanent adaptation to the present hostile conditions, rather than *via* suspended animation for 25,000 years at a time. If there is water underground, in the volcanic regions, that would be the first refuge. Has there been time enough since to evolve and reclaim the surface? Life on Earth still needs technology to occupy the South Pole – evolution alone was not enough.

Robert L. Staehle has put forward a convincing case for a polar-ice sample return mission as a still higher priority than rock sample retrieval.[49] A deep core taken from a Martian polar cap could provide detailed information on the weather pattern, changes in atmospheric composition, the history of volcanic activity, presence of airborne microorganisms, etc. The Viking results confirm the value of such samples: a core deep enough to go back 25,000 years or more could rule out the cyclic model of the Martian atmosphere – or confirm it after all, confounding us once more! If the main liquid water phase was billions of years ago, however, the cores may have to go down a long way to confirm it, perhaps to tell us that there was life on Mars, long ago and less lucky than life on Earth. To go so deep we may have to send men to Mars, after all.

At the start of the 1970s, NASA had every intention of doing so. By the mid-1980s, using the Space Shuttle and the heavy lift capability of Saturn V, there might have been big space stations orbiting Earth, a smaller one circling the Moon, a lunar base, and a 12-man Mars mission ready for launch. The Mars ships were to be based on space-station core modules and propelled by clusters of the standard Earth–Moon Nuclear Shuttles. Not only was that program halted for lack of funds, it was taken apart, causing massive redundancies in the US aerospace industry. Project NERVA, the nuclear rocket program, was abandoned; production of Saturn V was stopped and the production lines were dismantled. The Mars mission is hardly even a footnote in history, surviving only in artists' impressions like plates 7 and 8. To resurrect it would cost more than to start again from scratch.

There is good reason to think that we shall get to Mars, some day. ASTRA is not downhearted because the 1986 NERVA mission was based on the technology of the early 1960s, and there are better things on the drawing board. There are designs for a Heavy Lift Vehicle based on the Space Shuttle, and for an up-rated Shuttle which, used as a piggyback booster, could orbit a payload comparable with Saturn V's. Such launchers will be needed to put up the parts of nuclear rockets. The job could be done with chemical propellants and hundreds of Shuttle launches, but, as Dr Roy showed in Chapter 3, minimum-energy missions between planets are slow and chancy affairs. Even the NERVA Mars missions were criticized by Dr Krafft Ehricke and others as "marginal".[51] To go to Mars in style we may eventually use engines like those of the British Interplanetary Society "Project Daedalus". Daedalus is supposed to be an interstellar probe, using a pulsed nuclear fusion drive to accelerate for years at 0.1 to 1.0g.[52] It has been estimated that, starting now, a mission to Barnard's Star at the end of the century could be assembled for about the cost of the Vietnam War. But pulsed nuclear fusion is under intensive study as a possible solution to the energy crisis; and, applied to spaceship propulsion, it could take us to Mars in a matter of days. "Within the Solar System," said one member of the study team, "Daedalus is pure Flash Gordon in its potential . . ." Meantime however, there are clues to suggest that the USSR may be planning a three-year Mars mission – on Hohmann orbits, and presumably chemically fuelled.

In Arthur C. Clarke's 1951 novel *The Sands of Mars* nuclear-powered ships transit between Earth and Mars, landing on low-gravity Phobos to transfer passengers and cargo to winged shuttles for the planet below. The winged shuttles are less likely now (although not entirely ruled out), but otherwise the prediction may be valid. Landings on Phobos are virtually guaranteed, in any case; there may even be unmanned sample return missions in the 1980s if NASA can raise the funds so soon.

Although overshadowed by the changing views of Mars, our ideas about Phobos have altered more radically than for any other body in the Solar System. From bright, flimsy satellites of pumice, Phobos and Deimos became first dense lumps of nickel-iron, then battered carbonaceous chondrite, perhaps the primal material of the Solar System. Because of their small size, they might never have been internally heated and could still be undifferentiated.[53] Deimos showed signs of a dark covering of dust,[54] but there was disagreement about whether Phobos had been "sputtered clean" by meteoroids.

Viking 1 orbiter successfully photographed the hitherto unseen side of Phobos, finding nothing dramatic apart from another large crater. Viking 2, however, passed Phobos at 877km and photographed the same side as Mariner 9, resolving features down to 40 metres across.[47] There was a crater with a central peak, and crater chains parallel to the equator.[55] What were such features – especially the chains, produced by secondary impacts – doing on so small a body as Phobos? Even stranger, the surface (including the floors of the larger craters) was striped by parallel lines, inclined about 30° to the equator. At least sixty of them could be seen in a single photograph. Perhaps they were the strata of some ancient body from which Phobos and Deimos fragmented. Was Phobos a crustal fragment of primordial Solar System rock, stratified from north to south and "with its name going right through it"?

Coverage of the markings improved as the Vikings moved in closer. From 120km, in February 1977, they proved to be not strata but grooves, 100–200m wide, following contours and breaking through the walls of medium-sized craters, but not visible on the inner slopes.[65] If they were hidden by regolith, it must after all be very deep. Smaller craters were almost obliterated by the grooves, as if some very heavy object had been rolling around; and from 500km out Orbiter 1 had spotted hummocks or boulder-sized objects resting on the surface. The grooves were concentric with Phobos, and gathered around the North of the satellite, and it was suggested that they might be due to tidal stresses as Phobos spiralled inwards. If so, Deimos should show few grooves if any at its greater distance.[66] None were found, indeed, in a close pass at 23km which revealed

11 and 12: *Above,* the new look of Mercury, as photographed by Mariner 10. The "maria" of Mercury are thinner than the Moon's, and curved scarps hundreds of kilometres long suggest that the planet contracted after the crust solidified. *(Painting by Gavin Roberts.) Below,* the "old" Jupiter with the nuclear-powered "dumb-bell" spaceship design of the 1950's in the foreground. *(Painting by Ed Buckley.)*

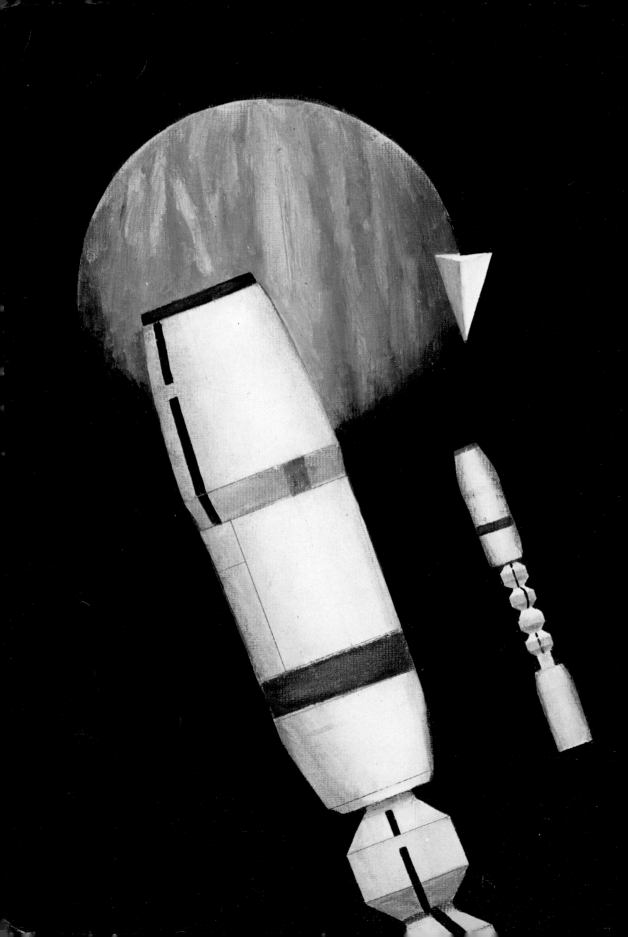

a deep layer of regolith; but nevertheless the Phobos grooves are now thought to be too old to be tidal.[67] They may instead be associated with the formation of a large crater called Stickney; or, then again, perhaps not.

There will be geologists on Phobos, it seems, before much longer. Tiny though it is, that little world is hinting at challenges to science fully as great as those of the planet itself.

13: The "new" Jupiter is much hotter and more turbulent than was imagined. *(Painting by Gavin Roberts.)*

7 Mariner Missions and Venera Ventures

Very different conditions obtain on our neighbour planet, which is closer both to the Sun, and to ourselves, the radiant Venus . . . The humidity is probably about six times the average of that on Earth, or three times that in Congo . . . We must therefore conclude that everything on Venus is dripping wet.

Svante Arrhenius, The Destinies of the Stars, 1915[1]

Venus was the first planet where spacecraft study produced really dramatic results; the final chapter of *Mariner: Mission to Venus*, produced by JPL in 1963, is entitled *The New Look of Venus*.[2] At that time both US and Soviet spacecraft had flown past the Moon, and in addition Luna 2 and Luna 3 had, respectively, struck the Moon and photographed its far side, but the only real "news" was that the Moon had no magnetic field like the Earth's, and maria were relatively rarer on the Farside. Venus and (presumably) Mars had been passed at close range by Soviet probes, but in both cases radio contact had been lost *en route*. The first US Venus probe, Mariner 1, had to be destroyed by the Range Safety Officer because of an error in the guidance program. In addition, Mariners 1 and 2 were improvized spacecraft, just over one-third the weight of the Mariner A spacecraft which was to have been launched to Venus by Atlas-Centaur. (Centaur, the first LH_2/LO_2 upper stage, provided massive technical problems and became operational years behind the original schedule.) It would be fair to say that few of us expected Mariner 2 to make it – although, if the art were ever to be mastered, sooner or later there had to be a success.

It is remarkable that both the US and USSR chose to begin their interplanetary programs with Venus. Commentators who relate everything in the space program to public interest might bear in mind that Mars was not the first target, for all its association with "space travel". The reasons for the choice were practical: Venus at its nearest comes within 42 million km of the Earth, while Mars's nearest is 56 million km. Moreover, because of its elliptical orbit Mars is much closer at some oppositions than others, and the dawning interplanetary capability in the early 1960s fell right between the close oppositions of 1956 and 1971. Venus' orbit is much closer to a circle, and so the planet became a prime target as soon as interplanetary launchers became available.

For the most part, our knowledge of Mars came from direct visual observation – an occupation increasingly relegated to amateurs as professional astronomers and big instruments concentrated on stars and galaxies. The division of labour wasn't unreasonable because, with two atmospheres to interfere with seeing, very little was gained by pointing big telescopes at Mars, except in the most perfect conditions. As for Venus, there was virtually nothing to see. It had long been established that Venus was covered by dense clouds, and nothing could be seen of the surface – unless, as some astronomers maintained, mountains up to 43km high could be detected.[3] The features which were persistently reported – shadowy markings, bright polar "caps", the "Ashen Light" on the night side of the planet – were as controversial as Martian canals, but even more fleeting if they were real at all.

Yet the first telescopic observations of Venus were explosive in their implications; no less so than Kepler's deduction that Mars moved in an ellipse. The Venus shock came from the observations of Galileo, so dramatic that he chose to announce them first in a cryptogram: *"Haec immatura a me iam frustra leguntur o.y."*, an anagram of *"Cynthias figuras aemulatur mater amorum"* ("The mother of loves [Venus] emulates the shapes of Cynthia [the Moon]").* If Venus could be seen in crescent phase from Earth, then it had to revolve around the Sun and not around the Earth itself. From there it was relatively easy to surmize, since the telescope showed moons like ours going round Jupiter, that Earth, too, might be a planet and go around the Sun as Copernicus had suggested.

Issac Asimov has speculated that, since the Moon seems to have evolved away from the Earth, it might conceivably have become the partner of Venus instead of the Earth (although there are some grounds to suspect that neither Venus nor Mercury can retain a large satellite in stable orbit[4]). If so, it would have been clearly visible from here, and its motion around Venus would be obvious – even more striking than the Moon's motion around the Earth, seen from Mars. It would then have been obvious from the outset that the "Morning Star(s)" and "Evening Star(s)" were the same, and moved around the Sun just as the fainter "star" moved around the bright one.[5] Now it took well under 400 years to get from acceptance of the Copernican Hypothesis to the first Moon landing. Asimov has asked elsewhere just how far we would have come by now if the Greeks has listened to Aristarchus in 300BC when he taught that all the planets went around the Sun;[6] but if the major clues had been visible to the naked eye throughout history, how much more might have been achieved by now !

As the centuries of observation piled up, speculation grew about the

*Kepler, who was not initially in Galileo's confidence, was forced to attempt his own solutions to the cryptograms announcing the phases of Venus and the triple nature of Saturn – Galileo's telescope could not resolve the rings and made it appear that Saturn was flanked by two other spheres. Kepler 'decoded' them as 'Hail, burning twin, offspring of Mars' – i.e. Mars has two satellites, and 'There is a red spot in Jupiter which rotates mathematically'. Struggling astronomy students have been heard to remark that Kepler should have stuck to cryptograms and left planetary motions alone.

clouds and what lay beneath them. The first suggestion was that, since Venus was not much smaller than the Earth, its atmosphere was basically like the Earth's and the clouds were water vapour. After all, a great deal of Earth's surface is hidden by cloud on any particular day.[7] Perhaps the entire surface of Venus was covered by water; however, spectroscopic examination showed nothing conclusive except the presence of carbon dioxide. Patrick Moore remarked that seas on Venus would be oceans of soda-water, but space-travellers were unlikely to find anything to mix with it.[8] A slightly different surface layout might provide vast, low-lying steamy swamps; pursuing the argument that Mars was further from the Sun and older or more evolved than the Earth (untrue, as we now know), it was often suggested that Venus might be in a phase similar to the Carboniferous period on Earth, 200 million years ago, when the great coal beds were laid down. Better still, perhaps evolution might be a few tens of millions of years further along and Venus might have real live dinosaurs. Everything in children's fantasy has to be the biggest, fiercest and most spectacular, so my generation grew up with the monsters fighting in the misty swamps, with other astronomical models of Venus as pale and unwanted alternatives.

Adult science fiction rapidly moved on to more subtle possibilities. Ray Bradbury[9] and John Wyndham[10] both portrayed Venus as a soaking, miserable place, claimed mainly by plant life, but most writers supposed that reptilian evolution on Venus had advanced far enough to produce intelligence – thereby providing a range of ethical problems to be explored, assuming human landings and colonization.[11] The theme was so thoroughly explored that it became a cliché. Henry Kuttner stands out as a writer who created a different Venus, without intelligent life but with plants and animals so voracious that human settlers were confined to "keeps" on the sea bed.[12]

The idea that Venus might be a gigantic dustbowl, with the clouds a yellow-white pall whipped up by continuous winds, attracted very little attention; if you wanted deserts for a story, Mars had them in plenty. Nor did Fred Hoyle's suggestion, that Venus might be awash with oil and stoking the clouds with hydrocarbons, arouse as much interest as a breathable atmosphere, plus swamps and reptiles. (The most outrageous suggestion, from the TV series *Pathfinders to Venus*, was that the clouds were mostly carbon dioxide buoyed up on a lighter layer of oxygen below, like a jet of water in a shooting gallery! I think that was when childhood ended and I gave up the dinosaurs for more cerebral SF.)

When Mariner 2 took off, nobody knew whether Venus was smooth or hilly, or how long its day was. The composition of the atmosphere was unknown, apart from the carbon dioxide; the planet's mass and density could only be guessed at, the surface temperature was a source of controversy. There were measurements indicating very high temperatures – or were the emissions produced by a hyperactive ionosphere? We had already had the frustration of losing the Russian Venus 1 when it was on course to pass Venus at a distance of a mere 96,500km. Mariner 2 had a tremendously elaborate series of operations to perform, as it seemed in those days: after deploying its solar panels and high-gain antenna, the spacecraft had to hunt for the Sun and lock on to it, then hunt for Earth in another axis and lock on to that (starting again on command from Earth, if it found the Moon by mistake); it had to take up a quite different attitude for mid-course correction, make the correct rocket burn, then find Sun and Earth all over again; passing Venus it had to take up a third orientation, and activate the scanning radiometers on schedule; finally it had to find Sun and Earth *again*, in order to return the data. Nothing like it had worked before and, besides, the spacecraft was a rush job.

Well, there is a first time for everything. Mariner 2 successfully performed the entire sequence, with a little help from its friends – e.g., the Venus encounter mode had to be set up by direct command from Earth, when the on-board computer missed its cue. Two pieces of information were quickly made public, from a "quick-look" scan of the data: the first, a major revelation, was that Venus had no magnetic field detectable at 34,751km. The second, which later proved to be wrong, was that surface temperatures were low (On BBC TV's *That Was the Week That Was,* David Frost announced that men had been wrong all down the ages. "Venus isn't nearly as hot as she's cracked up to be, and has no magnetic attraction at all.") But it soon emerged, from detailed analysis of the microwave and infrared radiometer data, that the surface temperature was 430° C. If there was to be any liquid on the surface, it would have to be molten metal, not water.[2] The energetic ionosphere, which might have accounted for the high-temperature indications seen from Earth, was not to be found.

What a sensation! It was the first of its kind, since the Mars revelations were still in the future and the first Moon landing still seven years away. The Flying Saucer movement, which had long maintained that the Venusians were just like us (only more advanced), issued statements that Mariner 2 had been captured by the Venusians, who were feeding it false information. Since the probe was still being tracked, now well past Venus and drawing Sunwards towards perihelion, the explanation found little scientific favour. Even in 1973, several Flying Saucer speakers at the Sunderland "Beyond this Horizon" festival asserted that there are Earth-surface conditions on Venus. When Colin Ronan tried to make the true facts known, he was "refuted" with Sputnik 2's failure to detect oxygen in the Earth's atmosphere in 1957. Alas, however, in three successful Venus flybys and thirteen penetrations of the atmosphere (including six soft landings), the high temperatures have been absolutely confirmed; the swamps, the reptiles and the golden-haired Saucerians have all had their day.

Apart from the high temperatures, relatively little was learned from Mariner 2 about the mysterious world beneath the clouds. A cold spot was found on the terminator ("cold" being 11C° below the surroundings) and it was suggested that it might be caused by a high plateau (but see later). A high cloud was more likely, however, since the plateau or mountain would have to be *very* high. Perhaps it was just as well Mars had not been photographed at the time, since more recent radar studies indicate that Venus is in fact very flat, relative to the Earth and Moon. There were still suggestions that Venus might have polar icecaps, but the radiometer data indicated that surface temperatures were very even – as was to be expected, if the 430° figure was due to the "greenhouse effect" of a dense carbon dioxide atmosphere. In 1961 Carl Sagan had predicted that the temperature difference from equator to poles was 100° or less, too hot everywhere for terrestrial organic compounds to survive.[13] The alternative was that the apparent polar temperatures were illusory (the electrical discharge model again), but in 1967 Sagan and Pollock considered that notion was incompatible with the Mariner 2 data overall.

How long was the day on Venus? The even temperatures extended right across the terminator into the night side of the planet – a result that was to appear even stranger when the true rotation of Venus was determined (see below). It had seemed the rotation had to be relatively rapid to keep the dark side from cooling down significantly – Sagan's 1961 summary gave a period of 5–30 Earth days[13] – but now estimates were grouped around 230 days, longer than the planet's year.[14] And what were the clouds? Initially news releases suggested a "smog of condensed hydrocarbons", seeming to confirm the Hoyle hypothesis, although the surface itself would be too hot for the seas of oil. The hydrocarbon identification was later withdrawn, however, and water ice became the favoured candidate.[15] It was popular with spaceflight fans because it would allow Carl Sagan's plan to "terraform" Venus, making it habitable for Man, by seeding the clouds with blue-green algae.[13]

One of the most important Mariner 2 discoveries, however, concerned the interplanetary medium – which could no longer be termed mere "space". Clues such as comet-tail behaviour had suggested a "wind" of plasma continuously flowing out from the Sun, compressing Earth's magnetic field on the sunward side: Mariner 2 confirmed its existence, averaging 0.6–1.2 protons and electrons per cm^3 and moving at 320–800km per second – equivalent to a temperature of a 550,000C.[2] Continuing investigation up to Pioneer 11 has charted the Solar Wind to the orbit of Saturn and beyond – the outer boundary will soon be determined. But in a sense the inner planets and their satellites are immersed in the outer atmosphere of the Sun – space is no longer empty.

A pause ensued. Soviet attempts to probe Venus continued and, despite a number of failures to leave parking orbit, two Venera spacecraft were again placed on trajectory in 1965.* Venera 2 passed the planet at 24,000km but returned no data; Venera 3 hit the atmosphere but again no new information was obtained.

1967 was a good year for Venus flights. As already remarked, there were great expectations of a Soviet Moon flight in October, on the 50th

---

*After some years of confusion, it's now more or less settled that Soviet probes to Venus will be called "Venera", so avoiding the difficulties of the last chapter – where some sentences had to be deliberately ambiguous, to avoid writing "the Soviet Mars Mars probes".

anniversary of the Russian Revolution and the 10th anniversary of Sputnik 1. Instead, Venera 4 made a successful entry into the Venus atmosphere on 18 October and transmitted data during a 94-minute parachute descent. The results were particularly valuable because they were obtained only a day before the successful Venus flyby of Mariner 5 at 3,990km. NASA was very pleased with that success because it was achieved at low cost with another improvized spacecraft – Mariner 5 was built mostly out of backup components for Mariner 4, and useful comparisons could be made because Mariner 4 continued transmitting until it ran out of attitude-control gas on 14 December 1967, three years after launch. In August the two spacecraft were almost in a straight line with the Sun and in September they lay close to the spiral lines of the solar magnetic field; no major solar flares occurred during the period but nevertheless the two spacecraft together were able to extend the mapping of the Solar Wind.[16]

Mariner 5 and Venera 4 together verified the Mariner 2 findings and supplied enough extra information for the pieces to start falling into place. There was still no detectable magnetic field, and Mariner showed that on the edge of the atmosphere the Solar Wind formed a bow shock, with a corresponding cavity behind the planet, instead of being deflected into radiation belts. Tests early in the Venera parachute descent gave the atmospheric composition as 90% carbon dioxide, plus or minus 10; two alternative models were constructed in due course to explain the overall readings, one giving 85% carbon dioxide and the other 99%. At first it was thought that the Venera had reached the surface, but comparison with the Mariner results showed that the radar altimeter readings had been misinterpreted – the probe was twice as high as at first thought. Readings had ended at about 19km altitude, but by extrapolation surface pressure was estimated to be very high. (When surface measurements *were* made 90 atmospheres' pressure at least was reported.) The very high mountains were suggested again, but radar scanning indicated no high ground within hundreds of km – and nothing near that height in any case.

The first radar scans of surface relief had been made in 1962, and six features had been plotted with enough certainty over later Earth-Venus conjunctions for the rotation period *and direction* to be determined. The rotation was retrograde: in relation to every other body in the Solar System (although with Uranus it's a question of semantics – see Chapter 10), Venus rotates backwards, turning clockwise as seen from above the north pole. First estimates of around 230 days had suggested that, unlike Mercury, which was thought to keep the same face always turned to the Sun, Venus was *star*-locked – a relationship so bizarre that it surely must be a coincidence, and a particularly curious one since the stars could never be seen from the surface of the planet. (Mariner 2's three scans had found no breaks in the clouds, nor did the later Venera orbiters.)

But the more accurate estimates available by the late 1960s gave a period of 243.1 days – appreciably longer than the planet's year of 224.7 days. In fact it appeared that Venus was *Earth*-locked – its day was just one-fifth of the synodic period (mean time between conjunction). Almost at once, radar profiles of Mercury indicated that it was in the same condition: at each conjunction the same features pointed towards Earth, fooling visual observers into thinking Mercury was locked to the Sun.

Unfortunately, it now seems that there is no subtle resonance which has locked the rotations of Venus and Mercury to the movements of the Earth. The news is disappointing, because Sagan thought such an effect might allow habitable planets to orbit the numerous faint red stars in the Galaxy.[17] For example, Barnard's Star is known to have a planetary system, but any world close enough to the star to support life would have its rotation trapped by tidal forces, leaving only a narrow twilight zone with bearable temperatures. The apparent "Earth-lock" of Venus and Mercury made the red class M stars seem much more likely to support life. But still more accurate measurements indicate a Venus "day" of 242.98 Earth days, *not* in lock with the Earth;[18] and it seems that Mercury, which has a markedly eliptical orbit, *is* in Sun-lock at perihelion and the apparent Earth-lock is a coincidence.[19]

A pretty problem: for an observer on the surface of Venus, how does the Sun move? From noon to noon, it seems, takes 116.77 days: the effect of retrograde rotation, longer than the year, is to give a noon-to-noon period totally different from the planet's sidereal "day" – not that the stars can be seen in any case. But the Sun could be seen all the time, in theory, if the atmosphere were clear enough – because the dense carbon dioxide is super-refractive, one could see round and round the planet. Wherever he stood on the surface, the observer would find himself at the foot of an apparent bowl extending up to infinity with the entire surface spread out on it, more magnified with each repetition and more distorted – with a sufficiently powerful telescope with a Newtonian focus, he could see multiple images of himself outdoing any fairground hall of mirrors . . . Luckily or unluckily, depending on one's sense of adventure, visibility at the surface of Venus is limited and future astronauts will not be told, "When you get out, don't over-refract!"

In James Strong's *Search the Solar System*, the effect is represented by alternating bands of day-light and darkness on the sides of the theoretical "bowl".[20] But, as Gavin Roberts pointed out, part of the effect would be that the Sun would always be visible, wherever the observer was located; the band of night would be slightly darker, owing to the longer path sunlight follows to reach the ground, but the whole illusion rests on an imagined transparent atmosphere so the effect would be virtually undetectable. Although I haven't seen the suggestion anywhere, it seems to me that super-refraction must have *some* bearing on the even temperatures of day and night, even although the accepted mechanism of heat storage and transport in the atmosphere accounts for most of it. Now we see, however, that Mariner 2 was actually scanning the sun*rise* terminator, not the sunset one, and the equatorial cold spot, 11° below the surroundings, may have been the coolest place on the planet, coming out of night.[21]

Instead of seeing the Sun course across the sky from west to east, unnaturally fast as well as going the wrong way, the observer would see it stay put above the bowl and grow dim and then bright over a 116-day cycle. He might conclude that the Sun was a long-period variable except that, in this imaginary situation, he could see the bands of dimness moving down the bowl towards him. It would be an attractive effect if the descending bands were in sunset colours. Even so, he might find it very hard to determine the true state of affairs; the atmosphere is super-refractive to radio waves as well as light.[16] Even beings who "saw" by radio (very large beings, probably fixed) would require a Copernicus of outstanding genius to give them a true picture of the Solar System. For practical purposes, however, it gives outsiders like us the advantage that we can communicate with a spacecraft or ground base on Venus all year round, whether or not it's facing towards us: we don't need Earth-locked rotation after all!

Veneras 5 and 6 entered the planet's atmosphere in May 1969, lasting 53 and 51 minutes respectively from the start of parachute descent. Both probes were crushed by pressures of 27 atmospheres before reaching the surface, somewhat shaking a 1968 estimate of 20 atmospheres' maximum.[14] Estimates of carbon dioxide content were now 93–97%, with some nitrogen, not more than 0.4% oxygen, and very little water vapour.[22] Each penetration was extending the survival of Soviet probes in the Venusian atmosphere, as conditions became better known and design experience was gained. Sooner or later there had to be a landing – it was now generally accepted that Venera 4 hadn't hit a mountaintop, as radar scanning continued to build up a picture of a relatively low-relief surface. There was always the possibility that a landing couldn't be established; e.g., if the probes were descending towards oceans of liquid metal. But, in December 1970, Venera 7 concluded a 35-minute descent successfully and sent data from the surface for 23 minutes. Surface temperature was $475\,^{\circ}C \pm 20$, pressure 90 atmospheres ± 15.[23]

For Venera 8, the descent capsule was extensively redesigned, now that the requirements could be properly defined.[24] As a result, in July 1972 the spacecraft was able to last 50 minutes on the surface and more sophisticated measurements could be made on the ground and during the descent. It was established that the cloud formations' base was fully 35km above the surface, and there was enough light at ground level to allow photography on future missions.[25] Wind effects were encountered during the descent, but sideways drift at touchdown was only 2 metres per second. Surface radioactivity was detected, indicating that the rock at the landing site contained 4% potassium, 0.0002% uranium and 0.00065% thorium; the ratio of the elements resembled that in Earth rocks "that have been subjected to secondary changes [atmospheric effects] after melting out of the Earth's core",[26] but the actual percentages were higher than in terrestrial basalts.[27]

Now the biggest single mystery was the composition of the clouds. Near the base of the cloud layer Venera 8 found less than 1% of water vapour; Veneras 5 and 6 had found that there was more water vapour in Venus's atmosphere than in Earth's,[19] although if it all could be precipitated on to the surface, the average depth would be under half a metre,[28] far less than there is in Earth's oceans and atmosphere combined. It seemed unlikely that water ice could account for a cloud layer 24km thick. The mystery was aggravated by the discovery that the cloud layer pulsates, varying synchronously all over the disc by about a kilometre in altitude with a period of four days. A great deal of energy would be required to shift the cloud-top level in this way: "It is difficult to see where it can come from on a slowly revolving planet with low and spatially uniform absorption of solar radiation."[29]

There were other indications of a four-day periodicity in the Venusian atmosphere. Elusive "dark markings" reported by astronomers over the years had proved to be more conspicuous in the ultraviolet, and, although some features seemed to recur in a constant relationship to the subsolar point and the terminator,[13] others were alleged to have a rotation period of four days – 60 times as fast as the planet's rotation, and indicating wind speeds of 100 metres/second in the upper cloud layers.[19] Not all experts accepted these observations: ". . . these motions of the Venus atmosphere have not yielded any incisive results about the planetary circulation – which, being almost free of Coriolis force, will be significant for theoretical meteorology when it is observed."[14] (The same argument had been fought some years before. In 1957 Dr M. W. Ovenden wrote of the spectroscopic method of determining planetary rotation: "The reason it fails on Venus is that we do not see the surface of Venus at all. The whole planet is covered with dense white cloud . . ." To this Patrick Moore replied: "In fact, an atmosphere will in the main rotate with the solid body of a planet . . ."[3])

In February 1974, the first photographic Venus flyby was conducted by Mariner 10. Like Mariner 5 this was a single-spacecraft mission, and there were grave doubts about the outcome when temperature problems developed in the cameras soon after launch. Test pictures of the Earth and Moon were received successfully, however, as the probe moved out into space, including photos from some 1.6 million km out – the first time Earth had been photographed from beyond the orbit of the Moon (it looks much the same). During the Venus flyby an extended series of ultraviolet pictures were obtained over several days, the closest approach to the planet being 5,790km; the results were discussed in detail by Dr Garry Hunt on Patrick Moore's "Sky at Night" program a month later, and JPL subsequently supplied a representative set of the pictures to ASTRA for the *Man and the Planets* project.

The evidence of high-speed rotation was obvious from the outset, and collation of the pictures verified the four-day period for the upper atmosphere. (A "creaky film" of Mariner frames covering several days was shown in a BBC-2 documentary in 1975.) One of the major features was a huge eye-like cloud permanently facing the Sun, while the rest of the cloud layer rotates backwards past it at hundreds of km per hour. The clouds come over the terminator from the nightside in parallel streams; impinging on the high-pressure area at the sub-solar point, the equatorial streams form a shockwave which corresponds to the Y-shaped ultraviolet feature sometimes observed from Earth. The parallel streams in the northern and southern hemispheres are then forced upwards into still faster spirals around the poles, explaining the "bright caps" so often reported, and providing the biggest demonstration of Coriolis force with which the Universe had yet obliged us.

Detailed pictures of the dark belt of the "Y" feature showed rising and falling currents, typical of convection in Earth's atmosphere. The polar spirals, however, appeared virtually free of storms in spite of the very high velocities, and photographs of the limb of the planet, showing layers of haze like terrestrial smog, confirmed that the clouds are not like water-vapour formations over Earth. The atmosphere circulation is rapid enough to keep temperatures even, regardless of latitude and time of day; and spectroscopic studies confirmed the opinion of Carl Sagan, in 1973[28], that the clouds are made up of fine droplets of sulphuric acid (H_2SO_4).

By now virtually all the superlatives and the synonyms for "surprise" are used up. Suffice it to say that, as far as I know, no science-fiction writer had ever provoked the scientific community by giving Venus an atmosphere of sulphuric acid, much less an *upper* atmosphere. Even now it sounds like a schoolboy's fantasy. In that very month, the *Journal* of the British Interplanetary Society noted the publication of a symposium on Solar System chemistry, predicting that Venus would be "essentially sulphur-free".[30]

It was now calculated that, at the time of Venus' formation, its surface, at that distance from the Sun, would have been too hot for oceans to form, thus there was no opportunity for carbon dioxide to be dissolved, forming carbonic acid, and then attack calcium and magnesium silicates to form huge chalk beds – as happened on Earth.[31] In the documentary mentioned above, it was suggested that, if Earth had formed only about 6 million km nearer the Sun, it too could have a Venus-type atmosphere.

Because of the atmospheric composition, the early Venus would have suffered a "greenhouse effect", forcing up the temperatures still further. Much of the water would react with other constituents to form the sulphuric acid clouds; most of the remainder would be dissociated by solar ultraviolet radiation, and the liberated hydrogen would be lost into space. However, Mariner 10 detected about twice as much free hydrogen as expected. It was suggested that the source might have been a recent impact by the nucleus of a comet. If so, however, the atmospheric hydrogen should contain a significant proportion of deuterium, which was not detected. More probably, the Venusian atmosphere has a steady inflow of hydrogen from the Solar Wind; since deuterium fuses more readily than "ordinary" hydrogen, the Sun's supplies of it should have been used up long ago, and since Venus has no magnetic field the Solar Wind impinges directly on the atmosphere instead of being diverted into radiation belts like Earth's.[21] Another significant result was the detection of helium in the atmosphere; an accurate estimate of the quantity will reveal the amount of radioactive decay occurring at the planet's surface. It will be interesting to see how the figure relates to the Venera 8 measurements.

Nevertheless, the idea that Venus may have sustained a big impact recently shouldn't be forgotten entirely. JPL radar studies initiated in 1970 began with a resolution of 50km, but by 1973 had produced a map of an area of 1,450 x 890km with 10km resolution. A dozen craters were found ranging up to 160km in diameter, plus smaller ones 40–96.5km across. On the Earth, Moon and Mars, all craters of such sizes appear to be impact features. But the area surveyed was very flat, with a maximum height variation of 914m;[32] since it was already known that the planet was pretty flat overall, it seemed possible that the winds reach down to the surface and it has been scoured down, as Mars was once thought to be. If so, perhaps the craters are relatively recent.

But, after the Mariner 2 mission, there were speculations that the magnetic field of Venus might be undetectable because it was reversing its polarity – as Earth's field does, at apparently random intervals, every 100,000 to ten million years.[33] It has been suggested more recently that the reversals may have been precipitated by big impacts, about once every 170,000 years on average.[34] Big impacts have also been blamed for the "megadeaths" in Earth's history, when many different species were wiped out simultaneously. Other explanations have been put forward, such as radiation from a nearby supernova or solar "hiccups", but they don't explain the simultaneous deaths of marine species. Three-quarters of Earth's surface is ocean, however, and the effects of a giant sea impact are even more cataclysmic than a corresponding event on land.[35] Furthermore, the marine megadeaths seem to be associated with reversals of the magnetic field.[28]

Now, all this is just a correlation of my own, lining up a set of hypotheses which seem to dovetail neatly into the idea that Venus has taken one or more severe blows recently. On the other hand, it has been suggested very plausibly that Venus simply rotates too slowly for a dynamo process to bring a magnetic field into being.[21] But another hypothesis tending to support impact can be thrown into the melting pot: the present composition of the atmosphere may be very recent indeed, perhaps only a few hundred years old and not destined to last.[36] (Please note, however, that we are still talking about Venus conditions maintained by solar heat and "greenhouse effect", *not* about Immanuel Velikovsky's notion that Venus itself is only about 2,500 years old.) It has also been suggested that surface studies on Venus and Mercury may show temperature drops contemporary with Earth's ice ages, indicating "cosmic factors" in Earth's climatic conditions; and other surface studies, especially in the outer Solar System, might confirm the supernova hypothesis concerning Earth's "megadeaths".[37] An emerging Venus magnetic field, and evidence that the craters are recent, would strongly support the impact suggestion.

Veneras 9 and 10 reached Venus in late October 1975, becoming the first spacecraft to go into orbit around the planet, with a period of two days. It was announced that the orbiters' scanning had confirmed the four-day rotation of the upper cloud layers. Both spacecraft successfully set down landers on the surface and sent back panoramic photographs; Venera 9 survived for 53 minutes and Venera 10 for 65. The pictures were a surprise in many ways: the level of illumination was said to be "equivalent to Moscow noon on a cloudy day" and there was so much contrast that some thought the frames must be flash pictures. Floodlights were in fact carried, but not used.[38] Super-refraction was not evident, perhaps because the horizon was too close at 2–300m: the panoramas made the landscape seem *convex* rather than concave, the effect of a "fish-eye" lens.[39] Both views showed a clear horizon, but since the clouds are obviously fairly bright on the underside one would want to be sure the spacecraft were both on flat surfaces before accepting that as evidence against super-refraction.

The nature of the surface was the biggest surprise: both landscapes were strewn with boulders and it was said on BBC's "The Sky at Night" that there were no signs of a dust-cloud on touchdown, at 24kph. In particular the stones in the Venera 9 shots were sharp-edged and apparently recent in origin – interestingly enough, one suggestion was debris from a recent big impact. The Venera 10 boulders were smoother, possibly part of an old volcanic mountain, according to *New Scientist*.[40] But, in general, there were no signs of the strong surface winds and high erosion previously expected; indeed, it was suggested that the dense atmosphere protects the surface, which may be less eroded than those of Mercury, the Moon, Earth or Mars. The very flat character of Venus' surface would then become a real puzzle. The contrast visible in the photographs was very striking, in view of the diffuse light – so much so that some experts wonder whether the dark undersides of the rocks *are* actually shadows.

After the Mariner 9 experience, no one can be in a hurry to say whether those two spots on the Venus surface are typical. On "The Sky at Night" Dr Garry Hunt was moved to regret that Pioneer–Venus had no planned picture-taking capability. "Well, I'm sure the Russians will take some more," Patrick Moore replied.

As of January 1976 the Venera orbiters were still operational, and had confirmed (but not explained) the occasional "Ashen Light" over the dark side of the planet.[41] Volcanic activity on Venus was confirmed in 1976 by radar scans from Goldstone and Arecibo: there was a rift valley 1500km long, a lava field as large as Hudson's Bay with long parallel ridges, and a volcano 400km across, with an 80km crater, but only 1km high.[69, 70] If the winds don't reach the surface, why is everything so *flat*?

The next US missions were flown with Pioneer spacecraft; the Mariner–Venus era is over for the present. Two Pioneers were sent to Venus in 1978, one to be placed in orbit and transmit data for a full Venus year. It arrived five days before Pioneer–Venus 2, the Multiprobe, which separated 11 million km out into five components.[42] The "bus" vehicle, which had no heat-shield, sent upper atmosphere readings until it burned out: the main Sounder with three sub-probes,[43] called Day, Night and North after their target areas, made a parachute descent to 47km. Although protected by titanium pressure shells and diamond radiometer windows (on which customs duty had been refunded after "shipping out of the country"), the sounders were then allowed to fall freely to make sure they reached the ground before failing. In the event, all four succeeded and one sub-probe survived the 43kpm impact to continue sending for a further hour. The atmosphere sounding technique was an extension of the Viking aeroshell measurements, and a prelude to the Pioneer–Jupiter entry probe (see Chapter 9). The first major result was that the atmosphere is rich in Argon–36, a rare gas isotope which was thought to have been flushed out of the Solar System very early in its history.

Veneras 11 and 12 landed at Christmas 1978, lasting 110 minutes and 95 minutes respectively, but no results were announced immediately. Meanwhile, Pioneer–Venus 1 had begun its photographic, upper atmosphere sounding, and radar mapping programme. An entire hemisphere of Venus has never been scanned from Earth, because of the near Earth-lock of the rotation, so there may be surprises ahead: after all, the Earth, Moon, Mars and Mercury all have one hemisphere markedly different from the other.

James Strong had suggested that detailed radar mapping of the surface would be the major contribution of a Venus orbiter. There were suggestions that the entry craft should attempt to come to rest during the descent, to float under a hydrogen balloon in temperatures of 20°C. Unfortunately, however, that layer of the atmosphere is about 58km up, in the clouds, so photography would be useless unless there are breaks in the lower cloud strata.[20] Joint Soviet and French plans have discussed a still higher operational altitude, about 61km, assuming a temperature of 0°C.[44] Balloon probes are now being considered for Shuttle-launched missions in the 1980s. Their rôle again seems to be largely confined to radar studies. One Soviet idea was that smaller probes might be dropped in various locations as the probe was carried along by the winds; they would have to be monitored by an orbiter, however, since the balloon would be carried round the north or south polar spiral and wouldn't pass over the same spot again. Even if the path of the airstream were identical with the previous circuit, the planet would have rotated below it.

The concept of a floating atmosphere station brings us to a final highly speculative idea advanced by Robbie Chalmers at ASTRA. What if the atmosphere of Venus, like that of Earth, is the product of living organisms – not the end-product of runaway atmospheric pollution, as it would be for us, but optimum conditions for whatever lives there? Isaac Asimov has suggested that Venus might support a fluorocarbon life form, using sulphur as a solvent.[45] Certainly, we know there's sulphur there now. But Robbie wondered if the sulphuric acid might be 'the water of life' for the dominant Venus form – a creature made of what we would consider inorganic materials, "fed" by natural electrical cells, with a smog of sulphuric acid droplets as electrolyte. N. W. Pirie has suggested that germanium might be able to operate as a biochemical analogue to carbon;[46] could our electrical "life" grow its own transistors and begin to evolve into a planet-wide computer? Such a creature would like an inert atmosphere, 99% carbon dioxide, and would be quite glad not to have a planetary magnetic field. Since there is no adequate explanation yet for the rapid rotation of the Venus atmosphere, Robbie suggested that it was deliberately shifted by his "creature" to maintain even temperatures all over. Such a creature would think of itself as the planet, or the thinking part of it – its attitude to the environment would be that of the brain to the body.

In Stanislaw Lem's novel *Solaris* the confusingly named "space station" hovered over a gigantic "ocean" which was a vast, planet-wide lifeform, able to communicate with the human observers only through their emotions.[47] Chalmers' notion might put future Venus explorers in a similar situation. Let us reflect that, after "occupying" the interior of a suitably shaped crater, the creature has only to hit upon a natural wave-guide and, in principle, it has a sense which will reveal the outside Universe. Super-refractivity shouldn't affect signals coming straight down, and by trial and error the creature can bring the radio "sky" into focus. According to Sagan ("Controversy", BBC-2, 6 March 1975), a radio-telescope the size of the converted valley at Arecibo can talk to an equivalent telescope, with a bandpass of one hertz and an information flow of one bit per second, anywhere in the Galaxy. In human terms a conversation with intelligence at the furthest reach of the Milky Way, taking 134,000 years for question and answer, would be intolerably slow (so far, we don't even have a listening watch for near neighbours), but to a fixed immortal lifeform, what does time matter? With any luck at all, its first conversations would be with entities much nearer than the furthest point of the Galaxy. Once it had found another enquiring mind to converse with, it could keep one "eye" open for that conversation and look about with the others for more distant contacts. Eventually, it could be handling as many conversations as a telephone exchange – it's often estimated that there could be a million or more communicative civilizations in the Galaxy.

F. J. Dyson has suggested a way in which the rotation of a planet could be altered, by magnetic interaction of conducting bands parallel to the equator and solar-powered artificial satellites.[48] Of course, Venus couldn't achieve that without outside advice on the type of objects to be "grown" for launch, and couldn't launch them unless by laser system propulsion from the bottom of the atmosphere (a super-refracted light beam, building up intensity round and round the planet by constructive interference?). But it's hard to see how orbit could be achieved without a second impulse, and even in fun I'd baulk at Venus "growing" solid-fuel rockets at those temperatures. In any case the rotation *hasn't* been artificially slowed to turn off the magnetic field; presumably there would be a residual field, if the planet has a large iron core. But, as regards the *exact* speed of rotation – aren't you glad that Venus isn't locked to the stars, as they thought in 1962, nor to the Earth, as they thought in 1967?

The Mariner 10 mission was the first to turn the "gravitational slingshot" technique to serious use. As recently as 1967, a Jupiter flyby expelling the probe from the Solar System had been considered "not feasible with the present state of the art";[49] by 1974 that slingshot had been achieved by Pioneer 10, and NASA was ready for an attempt, *via* Venus, to send Mariner 10 to Mercury.

Of all the planets visible to the naked eye, and therefore known since antiquity, Mercury was the most enigmatic. Only 58 million kilometres from the Sun (on average) and circling it every 88 days, Mercury makes fleeting appearances in Earth's morning or evening sky and retreats almost at once towards the glare of the Sun. It was estimated that only one person in forty saw Mercury in a lifetime (Copernicus, it is said, never saw it at all); in an age of street lighting, probably even fewer do. There was no planet, not even Venus, of which less was learned after the invention of the telescope. Midway in size between the Moon and Mars but much further away than either, and never seen in a completely dark sky, Mercury revealed a disc with phases and surface markings, but very little more could be said.

The rest of our knowledge of Mercury came from its relationship with the Sun. When in transit across the face of the Sun, Mercury had no surrounding halo of atmospheric refraction; in particular, there was no "black drop" effect when the planet was at the edge of the solar disc. Any atmosphere must therefore be very tenuous; some observers reported mists and even clouds, but spectroscopic and other measurements were at the extreme limit of accuracy and weren't conclusive. Kozyrev, who made the controversial report of a gas outbreak in Alphonsus (page 79), was unable to detect any trace of a Hermian atmosphere in 1961.[50] Beyond doubt, therefore, Mercury must be a world of extreme temperatures; there would be no protection for anything exposed to the glare of the Sun, no warmth carried by convection into the shadows, and no atmospheric blanket to slow down the loss of heat into space after nightfall. But it was soon reported that conditions must be even more extreme: Schiaparelli announced late in the 19th century that Mercury's "day" was 88 days, equal to its year. Mercury would therefore keep the same face to the Sun from one year to another, as the Moon does month by month to the Earth.

The consequences would be dramatic. Since Mercury's orbit is a pronounced ellipse, an observer in the middle of the sunlit face would find the Sun on the meridian only at perihelion and at aphelion, when it would look considerably smaller. As it grew and shrank in size, the Sun would rock slowly first to one side of the meridian, then the other. Meantime, it would be rising or setting in the "twilight zones" along the terminator, the only places on the planet where temperatures would vary significantly during a "day". At the terminator there might be "mountains of eternal day" like the Moon's, but the backs of the peaks would be in permanent shadow like the foothills – and they could be in any latitude, not just at the poles. The dark side of the planet might, paradoxically, be the coldest place in the Solar System, since it was *never* exposed to sunlight.

The notion of trapped rotation has had a marked influence on SF writers. The classic Mercury story was Alan E. Nourse's "Brightside Crossing", about a surface journey across the sunlit hemisphere at perihelion.[51] (As far as I know, nobody portrayed the bitter dark side, although it would have a beauty of its own with the full Venus, and the blue-green Earth with its white companion, bright enough to cast shadows as they looped among the steadily shifting stars.) In *Jack of Shadows*, Roger Zelazny portrayed an Earthlike world with a trapped rotation, with science and technology dominant on the sunlit face and a nightside ruled by magic.[52] One of the memorable images is of a sphinx-like figure, Morningstar, doomed to watch just beyond the terminator for the sunrise that never comes. A still stranger world appears in Arthur C. Clarke's "The Wall of Darkness":[53] it keeps the same face always to its sun, and a great wall rings it at the terminator. Eventually a man scales the wall, only to return to his starting point – there is no far side to the wall, or to the planet, because at the terminator space folds back on itself like a Mobius strip . . .

By 1965, radar techniques had improved enough for attempts to map the surface of Mercury. The immediate revelation was that Mercury's day, relative to the stars, is 58.6 Earth days, not 88. But often when seen from Earth in a given phase, roughly the same features were visible – hence the supposition that the rotation was in simple Sun-lock. (This must be one of Nature's best jokes on science to date.) At first it was suspected that Mercury might actually be Earth-locked, as Venus was then thought to be: although the cause of such a lock was mysterious, it seemed striking that *both* planets apparently had it. Two mechanisms have since been put forward to explain Mercury's rotation in terms of Sun-lock. The planet's *solar* day (not its day relative to the stars) is exactly *twice* the year, a lock which can be explained by tidal forces;[54] but it has also been suggested that the rotation is in simple Sun-lock during perihelion passage, and out of it for the rest of the Hermian year.[19] It seems unlikely that the orbital eccentricity and therefore the length of the year, should have the unique value which would allow both explanations to be correct.

By the first explanation an observer experiencing midday at perihelion in a given year would be at midnight the following year and back at midday the year after. The second would mean that the Sun would be at rest in the sky when at its largest and hottest. Either way, the apparent movement of the Sun is complex. Between aphelion and perihelion, the Sun comes slowly up the sky in the west; after perihelion passage, it continues slowly towards the east (even though the planet's rotation is not retrograde, like Venus). If the effects of orbital motion and rotation cancel out at perihelion, the Sun will come to rest for a while before moving on; but if the one-day/two-year lock is the true account, near perihelion the Sun will move *back* in the sky from east to west, growing larger as it does so. An ill-prepared explorer, thinking himself safe after sunset, might get a nasty surprise when the Sun came back over the same horizon larger and fiercer than before.

Surface radar scanning continued, with steady improvements in resolution. In 1971, studies of the equatorial region showed less height variation than the surface of Mars or even Venus, although the surface itself was rougher than Mars' or Venus'. "Anomalous reflections features" had previously been reported in higher latitudes, but these lay outside the 1971 scan region.[55] Scanning in 1972, studying the equator again but with much higher resolution, revealed craters averaging 50km across and a "promontory" about 1,300m in height.[56] There were some indications of craters up to 500km across, but these were treated "with some reserve"; and it seemed that some parts of the surface were covered with fine detail, while others were relatively bland.

Altogether, the developing picture was that Mercury's surface was much like the Moon's – as had long been predicted from the two bodies' similarity in size and albedo. But still this was a very general picture, and detailed photography by Mariner 10 was an exciting prospect. To reach Mercury without a Venus slingshot, either a Saturn V launch vehicle or an ion-drive probe would be required;[57] and, since the next Venus missions would be the Pioneer impact/orbiter combination, Mariner 10 might be the only Mercury mission of the decade. Still more exciting, if the first flyby were a success, the probe's orbit could be aligned to pass Mercury a second time and possibly even a third. Initial reports of camera temperature problems were discouraging, but after the success of the Venus flyby the Mercury prospects seemed much improved.

The first images, the far-encounter shots, showed Mercury in crescent phase and revealed little detail except for mysterious white blotches.[58] These were later found to be bright craters with surrounding ray systems, like Tycho on the Moon; the most prominent was named "Kuiper" after the distinguished planetary astronomer and Mariner team member who had died during the mission.

An important part of the Mariner mission was to search, in the ultraviolet, for small satellites of Venus and Mercury. The Venus search was negative but first press reports announced that a small moon of Mercury had been discovered. Alas, it was soon realised that the uv source was actually 31 Crater, a star, glimpsed beyond the planet. But a mystery remained: the first "sighting" of the supposed moon had been *against the background of the planet*, on the night side.[59] It was thought that the observation might be related to auroral activity; but after the flyby, when the occultation of spacecraft signals by the planet had been studied, no evidence was found for any atmosphere over the night side.[60]

During the close encounter phase, which lasted twelve hours, the spacecraft passed within 5,950km of the planet. The photographic coverage has been described as "an information explosion", by contrast with the vague sketches and blurred photos obtainable from Earth. Comparison of the pre- and post-encounter pictures showed that Mercury, like the Moon, has two distinct hemispheres – one heavily cratered, the other with prominent maria. Radar had already revealed craters on Mercury, so the extensive evidence of bombardment wasn't a complete surprise; but it was very interesting, since Mercury is so far from the Asteroid Belt, and shed more light on the history of the inner planets.* Crater

---

*Robert Shaw had predicted at ASTRA before the flyby that Mercury would be relatively lightly cratered, with a range of crater ages, indicating the amount of loose material present in the Solar System.

chains like the Moon's were found, and small craters impinging on larger ones, but never vice versa, just as on the Moon. But for some reason it has become fashionable to describe the Mercury terrain as *exactly* like the Moon's when there are in fact striking differences.

Firstly, many of the maria were thinner than the Moon's, submerging less of the older highland topography. Crater floors were likewise less filled by lava; in one case a crater had been partly "invaded", leaving a lobate scarp across the older floor material as if the advancing lava had been frozen in its tracks.[60] In general craters were shallower than the Moon's with well developed central peaks and ring structures and less extensive surrounding blankets of debris. Secondary craters were likewise closer to their primary impacts; all those differences could be attributed to Mercury's surface gravity, which is similar to that on Mars. Mercury's density indicates a large metallic core, taking up 70–80% of its radius;[58] and, to everyone's surprise, after negative results with Venus and the very low fields of the Moon and Mars, Mercury was found to have a magnetic field (also residual, perhaps) with about 0.007 of the Earth's field intensity at the planetary surface.[60] In consequence Mercury also has a Solar Wind shockwave, similarly unexpected; it wasn't clear whether the planet had true radiation belts (see later).

With an internal composition so different from the Moon's, major differences in surface features could be expected. Most conspicuous were extensive curved scarps ranging up to 3.2km in height and running for hundreds of km across the surface; the second flyby, in September 1974, showed that the scarps were a major feature of the planet, sometimes cutting right through craters.[61] In the Caloris Basin, a gigantic impact feature like the Moon's Mare Orientale or Imbrium, there is an extensive system of ridges and cracks indicating subsidence or sub-surface movement. ("Weird terrain", with hills and ridges cutting across craters, is found at the point antipodal to Caloris – as it is on the Moon, antipodal to Imbrium and Orientale. Shockwaves from the impacts, concentrated at the antipodes, may have produced violent upheavals there.) From the interacting scarps and faults, including a cliff 2,300m high, it has been suggested that during the final bombardment phase Mercury *contracted*, due to compression of the iron-rich core.[61] Thus the faults would be quite different from the seabed chasms of Earth, the Great Rift on Mars and the Alpine Valley on the Moon, all of which are apparently produced by the spreading apart of surface features.

The highest-resolution pictures showed that in some areas, at least, surface features were eroded in patterns unlike the Moon's. One picture supplied to ASTRA by JPL (P-14466) showed "a heavily cratered surface with many low hills" which might almost have been part of Mars, with crater walls broken by many parallel, non-radial smooth-floored valleys as if by wind erosion. Temperature gradients over the surface indicate that Mercury is covered by a dust layer like lunar regolith;[62] but the maximum temperature on the daylit hemisphere during the first flyby was 460 K – cooler than the surface of Venus! Traces were found of a very thin atmosphere on the day side of the planet, below 10^{-11} of

Earth-surface pressure (too thin to be detected by occultation of space-craft signals), and containing helium, presumably generated by radioactive decay of uranium and thorium.[60] Alas, pressures were far too low to permit a notion of V. A. Firsoff's that, on Dollfus' estimate of atmospheric pressure, Mercury could have ice caps down to a limiting latitude of 80° 22′.[63] In any case, close-ups of the south pole in the second flyby showed that a polar cap was lacking.[61]

For the second flyby, there had been a choice between a dayside pass, extending coverage of the surface from 25% to 37%, and a night-side pass for study of the magnetic field. The photography option was taken. (Since 176 days had passed the same side of Mercury was facing the Sun, so the ultraviolet mystery on the dark side remains a mystery.) The third flyby was now scheduled for February 1975, but there were grave doubts as to whether the attitude control gas would last long enough. Once again, as with Mariner 4 and Mariner 9, the spacecraft had out-performed expectations and its operations were to be curtailed by its simply running out of gas.

Much of the gas consumption had been due to passing dust specks. Shining brilliantly, so near the Sun, they had confused the spacecraft's Canopus sensor and caused it to track the dust before returning to the correct orientation.[61] After the second flyby, Mariner 10 was placed in a slow 60-hour roll and oriented by sunlight pressure on the solar panels and high-gain antenna, with the star tracker and attitude control jets idle.[64] But at the critical moment, when the roll was stopped in preparation for the third flyby, a dust particle was picked up by the tracker and the spacecraft lost contact with Earth entirely. The JPL antenna at Gold-stone failed to get through to Mariner and a tracking station had to be "borrowed" from another program, the Helios deep-space probe, to order the spacecraft back into the correct attitude.

The main objective in the third encounter was investigation of the magnetic field. The second pass had been over the sunward side and the south pole, for maximum photographic coverage, and outside the Solar Wind "bow shock". This time Mariner flew through the magnetic "tail" behind the planet and over the northern hemisphere, confirming that the magnetic field was intrinsic to the planet and not generated by induction from the Solar Wind, as some experts had suggested.[60] The question now is whether the field is residual, in surface rocks, or maintained by an active dynamo mechanism in a fluid core, like the Earth's. JPL experts favour the latter, although it leaves many questions to be answered: until the Mariner mission, it would have been thought that Mercury's rotation was too slow for such effects. (After all, it is 58.6 times longer than Earth's and more than one-fifth of Venus'.) But one question was definitely settled: on the sunward side the Solar Wind compresses the magnetic field lines down towards the planet, leaving no room for radiation belts to form.[64]

Technical problems at the Canberra and Goldstone receiving stations caused much of the photographic coverage to be lost, and some of the high-resolution pictures were of poor quality. But the cracks in the Caloris

Basin and the masses of jumbled blocks antipodal to it were photo-graphed with higher resolution than before : some of the Caloris cracks may be collapsed lava tubes, as Hadley Rille on the Moon is believed to be, rather than fractures caused by overall subsidence. The "weird terrain" proved to be almost free of secondary impact craters, raising a suspicion that it may have been shaped by heat rather than focussed shockwaves from the Caloris impact. Because of Mercury's strange rotation, the "weird terrain" takes turns with Caloris to receive the full noonday force of the Sun at perihelion.

Another very interesting discovery was of very old, smooth terrain apparently formed after the initial accretion of the planet. No such areas were found on the Moon because of the intensity of the subsequent bombardment, which melted the entire original surface. Its preservation on Mercury is due to the higher surface gravity, which made the impact effects more localized. When manned spacecraft reach Mercury, sample collection in those areas will be a high scientific priority.

On the other hand, the photographs support infrared studies made from Earth, against a rather frightening hypothesis put forward by Gold after the Apollo 12 mission. Gold suggested that glazed rocks found in Oceanus Procellarum might have been melted on one side by a 10–100 second solar flare-up, to around 100 times its normal intensity, not more than 30,000 years ago.[65] The suggestion was the basis of a powerful story by Larry Niven, "Inconstant Moon", in which the Moon grows much brighter one night and it is thought at first that the Sun, round on the other side of the world, has gone nova.[66] But at Mercury's present distance from the Sun such an outburst would melt and glaze an entire hemisphere; and while Mercury *might* have been more distant from the Sun 30,000 years ago, there's no reason to believe so. Other possible explanations – e.g., that the surface has been roughened in the last 30,000 years – are ruled out by the Mariner photos, and it's much more likely that the lunar glazed rocks have a different explanation.

It is possible that Mercury was further from the Sun in the *remote* past. Because of the ellipticity of its orbit, and the general relationship of sizes, it has been suggested more than once that Mercury may be an escaped moon of Venus. Now that we know Mercury has one side more heavily cratered than the other, like the Moon, the idea comes forward that it may once have been partly shielded by trapped rotation around Venus.[67] If so, however, the present Sun-locked rotation shows that Mercury's escape (by solar tidal interaction) would have been a long time in the past, much longer than 30,000 years. (Mercury's asymmetrical distribution of craters may therefore be still another count against Velikovsky.) It's interesting that Mercury and Venus may therefore have formed a double planet in the past, like Earth and Moon, and, if they had stayed together, might have given terrestrial cosmology the boost imagined by Isaac Asimov[5] (see page 139).

But, if so, the relative histories of the two pairs of bodies must be different. We know the Moon's material formed in a hotter cloud than Earth's, probably nearer to the Sun, and may have coalesced finally in orbit around the Earth from the crustal fragments of the original planetesimal bodies. Mercury, however, has a large metallic core and would either have been formed independently of Venus, captured intact, then lost again; *or* would have formed intact in orbit around Venus. If the latter, it's strange that Venus' rotation is retrograde, and so much slower than Mercury's is even now. There *is* a hypothesis that Venus formed at a different time of the Galactic Year, perhaps 200 million years earlier or later than the other planets (see Chapter 10),* although it lacks mathematical justification; altogether, Mercury's structure and history are a long way from being a carbon copy of the Moon's.

For the moment, further Mercury insights must come from Earth-based studies or continuing detective work on the Mariner 10 material. For example, analysis of the Doppler shifts during the third encounter may allow some mapping of the interior structure of the planet.[64] But, unless the Soviet Union undertakes a Mercury mission, there are not likely to be any more flights until the 1980s. 1980, 1985 and 1986 all offer launch windows for Venus-Mercury missions; using the Space Shuffle to carry probe and Centaur LH_2/LO_2 upper stage into orbit, midcourse burns would allow the payload to be placed in orbit around Mercury.[57] Because of the relative positions of the planets, if a 1983 launch were required the probe would have to make *three* Venus flybys to be placed in a Mercury encounter trajectory; two Venus flybys are required for a 1988 launch.

James Strong has suggested that a Mercury orbiter should be a "clamshell" vehicle, closed up into a reflecting sphere when in sunlight and opening big radiative panels to shed heat when in the shadow of the planet.[20] An orbiter would allow more detailed mapping of Mercury's interior, just as the Lunar Orbiters revealed the mascons and the Moon's offset centre of mass (Chapter 4). Another rôle for such a craft might be to relay signals to and from a surface-roving vehicle, which would have to average only 3.7kph to stay near the terminator in relatively bearable temperatures. But since the horizon is close, such a vehicle would be very liable to get trapped (and doomed to roast) before a command from Earth could make it swerve out of danger. Surface exploration of Mercury may demand Man's presence, at least in orbit overhead.

The Solar System is not known to have any members permanently closer to the Sun than Mercury. The particles of the Solar Wind stream constantly outwards; dust particles drift slowly inwards, due to the "Poynting-Robertson effect";† some comets pass close to the face of the Sun, and the elliptical orbit of the asteroid Icarus takes it so close that at perihelion it grows red-hot; but there are no bodies known to stay permanently

*But *not* only centuries ago, as Velikovsky maintains.

†The Poynting-Robertson effect is a subtle one, applying significantly only to very small dust particles. It rests on the phenomenon of aberration, which – for instance – makes raindrops falling vertically appear to come from in front of a moving vehicle. There is a slight forward displacement of sunlight striking a body orbiting the Sun, and the shift of radiative pressure is enough to cause dust to spiral very slowly sunwards.

within Mercury's orbit. Yet in the 19th century there were several reports of small objects near the Sun or passing in front of it, and the hypothetical inner planet was named "Vulcan". Interest in the possibility waned after Einstein's General Theory of Relativity was able to provide a full description of Mercury's orbital motion, which had seemed to be perturbed by some unknown body.

ASTRA, however, usually gives an interesting notion a shake or two before dropping it. Robert Shaw suggested that Vulcan might be virtually in synchronous orbit over the Sun, so that it would normally be taken for a sunspot when observed against the face of the Sun. The suggestion would give Vulcan a year of 25.38 Earth days, and its orbital radius would be 25,147,000km (0.169 Astronomical Units); the result doesn't appear odd, relative to the spacing of the other planets, although it can't be expressed in terms of the "Bode's Law" progression (which roughly delineates all the planetary orbits out to Uranus) because Mercury's orbit is the first term of the series.

It might be worth mentioning, *en passant*, that in the 19th century Le Verrier calculated Vulcan's orbital radius as 21,000,000km, and its synodic period (i.e., time taken to circle the Sun, relative to the Earth) as 19¾ days.[68] Vulcan failed to reappear at the time predicted, and the fact is generally supposed to invalidate the observations of Vulcan reported by Lescarbault. Relativistic effects on Vulcan's motion would be greater than those on Mercury's, and would not have been taken into account in 1860; it would be interesting to find out whether they could be large enough to change the date and time of transit predicted by Le Verrier.

Shaw's suggestion would make a bigger difference. There have been some recent searches for Vulcan near the Sun during eclipses, and even reports of a 800km body at 0.1 AU, so it would be worth scanning at 0.169 AU, if only to eliminate the possibility.

8 The Barren Rocks

Inter Jovem et Martem planetam interposui. [Between Jupiter and Mars I have put a planet.]

Johannes Kepler

Kepler's third law of planetary motion allowed an estimate of the scale of the Solar System, relative to the "Astronomical Unit" – Earth's mean distance from the Sun. At once it seemed, intuitively, that the gap between Mars and Jupiter spoiled a general symmetry of the System – not the even spacing of ripples on a pond, but increasing separation of the orbits with increasing distance from the Sun. "Bode's Law" eventually expressed the relationship arithmetically, but it doesn't yet have any dynamical explanation – and it seems to break down in the outer System, failing with the mean distances of Neptune and Pluto. It agrees well, however, with the distances of Ceres, Pallas, Juno, Vesta and the thousands of other bodies less than 1,000km in diameter, orbiting the Sun between Mars and Jupiter, mostly between 2.1 and 3.3 AU and all unknown until the invention of the telescope.

The detailed structure and composition of the Asteroid Belt are still far from fully known. For every object tracked long enough for its orbit to be calculated (over 1,650 by 1964[1]), perhaps five times as many are sighted and lost. The smaller the diameter, the more asteroids are observed; if the progression continues all the way down to dust particles, it has been estimated that there could be 40-50,000 objects about 1,000m in diameter, two and a half million around 100m across, 125 million 10m in diameter . . . Whether such large numbers of particles really exist depends on the processes of formation: at one time it was supposed that collisions between asteroids would create large numbers of small fragments, replenishing the dust swept inwards by the Poynting-Robertson effect.[2] Recently, however, it has been argued that collision between major asteroids should be very rare indeed;[3] and, to emphasize the point, it has been calculated that, if there were 460,000 asteroids large enough to make significant space mission targets, all circling the Sun in circular coplanar orbits within the Belt, the average separation between them would be 1,200,000km.[4] Since the Asteroid Belt is actually about 80,000,000km thick, the mean separation between major members will be much greater.

The main Asteroid Belt is structured, like the rings of Saturn, by the gravitational pulls of neighbouring bodies – principally Jupiter. There are three main bands within the Belt, separated by "Kirkwood gaps" where the orbital periods would be in resonance with Jupiter's year, and the orbits therefore unstable. The precise number of "zones of avoidance" is uncertain : Kirkwood himself calculated that there should be three gaps,[1] and some estimates put the total as high as seven, one of them due to Mars.[5] Passing through the Belt from July 1972 to February 1973, Pioneer 10 found that collisions with particles 0.01–0.1mm in diameter remained constant throughout, but 0.1–1.0mm collisions increased three-fold towards the centres of the three main bands.[6]

However, the Asteroid Belt doesn't contain all the small objects orbiting the Sun. "Earth-grazing" asteroids such as Apollo are found in highly elliptical orbits bringing them sunwards to within Earth's orbit; Icarus goes well within the orbit of Mercury. In the opposite direction, Hidalgo swings far out toward the orbit of Saturn. There is good reason to think that the outer moons of Jupiter, which have retrograde, highly inclined orbits, and Phoebe, the retrograde outer moon of Saturn, may be captured asteroids. There are two groups of "Trojan" asteroids sharing Jupiter's orbit, wandering considerably in longitude but maintaining a general relationship with the Sun–Jupiter Equilateral points (corresponding dynamically to the Earth–Moon Equilaterals suggested for O'Neill colonies).* And, although they occupy near-circular equatorial orbits in the normal direction, it has been suggested that the moons of Mars may have been free-flying asteroids in the past.

The simplest apparent explanation for the origin of all these little worlds would be that once they were a single planet, orbiting in the predicted Bode's Law position between Mars and Jupiter. Collision with another body (perhaps a sister to our Moon) might have shattered it; or internal stresses (perhaps aggravated by Jupiter's pull) might have torn it apart, but no suitable energy source has been suggested. The name "Phaeton" has been suggested for the hypothetical world, after the improvident youth who borrowed the Sun's chariot and had to be felled with a thunderbolt. "Aztex" has been suggested as an alternative (with the official recognition of "Hun Kal" as a feature on Mercury, astronomy seems to be breaking out of Greek and Roman mythology at last).

Professor Michael Ovenden, a member of the British Interplanetary Society Scottish branch (which was to become ASTRA), has suggested that the existing distribution of the planets requires a body 90 times the mass of the Earth, between Mars and Jupiter, up to 16 million years ago. Objectors reply that there is at most 0.1 of the mass of Earth in the entire Asteroid Belt;[7] some sources put the figure as low as 0.01 or

*There is no general solution for the "3-body problem" of a body's movement under the gravitational pulls of two others. Five special solutions were determined, by the mathematician Lagrange, for points where the third body could hold a stable relationship with the other two. For the Earth and Moon, for example, the Legrange points would be : (1), between the Earth and Moon, closer to the Moon; (2), beyond the Moon, further from it than the L_1 point; (3), on the far side of the Earth from the Moon, at the same distance; (4) and (5), ahead of and behind the Moon in its orbit, equidistant from the Moon and the Earth. The Trojan asteroids are trapped in the Sun–Jupiter L_4 and L_5 positions.

even as low as 0.001.[5] A long-standing objection to the "disruption hypothesis" was that the asteroid orbits are grouped into "families"; each family could have a common origin, but the families themselves cannot be traced back mathematically to a single parent body.

Apart from the Moon (very recently), asteroids may be the only heavenly bodies from which we have solid samples for study in the laboratory. Meteorites have been landing on the Earth and accumulating in museums throughout history: the ancient Egyptians knew iron only from meteorite falls, and as I write a search is being organized for a stone which fell from the sky and raised a "pillar of cloud" in 1646. Science consigned all such reports to folklore until late in the 19th century; the French Academy of Sciences declared: "Stones do not fall from the sky, because there are no stones in the sky"; but solid lumps of stone and metal stubbornly fell nevertheless, and eventually became a major field of scientific study.

The meteors which streak across the night sky are almost all specks of dust, and may all originate from comets. Dust outbreaks have been observed during comets' passage around the Sun, and "meteor showers" are observed where certain comets' paths cross the orbit of the Earth. Some faint comets have dispersed altogether into meteor swarms during a century or so of observation. Pioneer 10 made the important discovery that the dust causing the Zodiacal Light, the glow which extends to east and west of the Sun along the plane of the Solar System, is not a local cloud around the Earth or even around the Sun; it extends at least as far as the Asteroid Belt, making the inner system "a dense fog bank" compared with the clarity of interstellar space. Likewise the gegenschein, a glow directly opposite the Sun in the sky, was found to move out with the spacecraft. (It is amusing to recall that its existence, too, was doubted until recently by many astronomers.) Speaking at Glasgow Astronomical Society in 1974, Dr David Clarke said that such large quantities of dust must be replenished steadily from somewhere – perhaps from comets. Another possible source, perhaps also responsible for the dust deposits in the comets, is suggested by Anthony Lawton in Chapter 12.

It has been suggested that the "Earth-grazing" asteroids are the nuclei of larger short-period comets, from which all gases have been driven off by solar radiation. At least two reports of "star-like objects" in a comet nucleus support the hypothesis.[5] If so, the Earth-grazing asteroids will presumably be quite different from the main Belt; although there *is* a hypothesis that comets form in the inner Solar System and contain "ordinary" meteoritic matter,[8] the general view is that comets are the outermost members of the system and only chance perturbations bring them sunwards. There are good grounds for the suggestion that cometary materials are very light and porous; but some of the nickel-iron chunks which have landed on Earth seem to have formed within relatively dense, massive bodies, presumably the original protoplanets of the Asteroid Belt. Internal evidence suggests that there were several such bodies, with different masses and compositions – a major argument against the existence of Phaeton.

A very important part of the argument turns on the existence of a class of meteorites called carbonaceous chondrites – objects so loosely structured, in some cases, that initially there was doubt that they were meteorites at all. The particles first made the headlines when organic compounds were found in them; there were even marks which might have been evidence of microscopic life-forms. There was a great deal of argument about contamination of the samples by terrestial compounds, pollen, etc.; but with discoveries of organic compounds of increasing complexity in comets, in interstellar space and in the atmosphere of Jupiter, and serious suggestions that the outer system may be rich in organic compounds dating from its early history, the analyses of carbonaceous chondrites are no longer controversial. It seems clear, however, that the compounds were formed "naturally", not by the action of life.

F. L. Whipple suggested that carbonaceous chondrites might be the solid matter of comets.[9] Their basic composition corresponds to the Sun's, apart from the most volatile substances such as the rare gases; and they have clearly been subject to very little heating since their formation. There is growing agreement that chondrites as a class may be the primeval matter of the Solar System;[10] one of the most recent suggestions is that, in the Asteroid Belt, Jupiter's influence gave the protoplanetoids such large relative velocities that the larger bodies were shattered by collisions instead of accreting into a fifth planet.[11] On this hypothesis, the carbonaceous chondrite material would have formed the outer crusts of primal bodies in the Belt beyond 2.3 AU; nearer the Sun, the asteroids would form with crusts of basaltic achondrites.* Iron cores, surrounded by "ordinary" chondrites, would form in both cases as melting and differentiation continued, although the melting process has still to be explained. (Residual magnetism may be a clue;[5] and there is a suggestion that the protoplanet material might have been melted by interaction with the magnetic field of the young Sun. The supposition is that the Sun was then a rapidly rotating "T Tauri" type star, not yet evolved into the stable yellow dwarf we know today.[12]) Whatever it was, not all asteroids seem to have been similarly affected: both Ceres and Pallas reflect light like carbonaceous chondrites,[13] but Ceres may be undifferentiated, while Pallas has a sizable core and only a thin carbonaceous crust left.[11]

Thus the wide variation in composition of meteorites, and in the surface spectra of asteroids, would be explained in terms of multiple collisions and crustal fragmentation early in the history of the Belt. Vesta, for example, may be a relatively intact sample of the protoplanets nearer the Sun, still retaining its basalt crust; a large number of asteroids 100–200km across may represent cores of similar bodies, while Toro (see later) could be a large fragment of a shattered mantle. Stony-iron meteorites would come from the outer cores of such differentiated objects; brecciated meteorites (mixed, broken rock), on the other hand, have been exposed to the Solar Wind on asteroid surfaces for some time before being expelled

---

*Chondrites are meteorites containing small, fused spheres of silicates and other materials; all meteorites from which these "marbles" are absent are therefore achondrites.

into space. About twenty of the asteroids are known to have rock/dust "regoliths" like the Moon's; Icarus is an interesting case, because apparently it hasn't been sputtered clean in spite of its close approaches to the Sun.[14] But the existing dust layers are apparently too thin to account for the proportion of brecciated meteorites: it appears that the breccias were created by bombardment *after* the asteroids were formed (like the bombardment sustained by the Moon and Mercury), and dispelled into space by a few major collisions about ten million years ago.[11]

To evaluate the conflicting hypotheses, space probes and manned missions will ultimately be required. In the first instance, much useful information will be gained from simple photography, to try to determine the surface compositions – e.g., are "Earth-grazers" dead cometary nuclei, different from "true" asteroids?[9] Accurate evaluation of the diameter, shape, rotation, mass and therefore density of asteroids can be obtained from flyby missions; orbiter probes will be required to determine the internal structures. Because of the relatively low masses of the asteroids, the effects of mascons and the like will be more prominent. On the other hand, orbiting any but the largest asteroids will be a precarious business: from fluctuations in their brightness, it is known that many asteroids are irregular in shape and have inconvenient rotations. Eros, for example, is roughly elliptical, but spins about the short axis of the ellipse. Since orbital velocity around such a small body will be very low, a spacecraft will easily be perturbed into collision with some projection.

The first missions to asteroids will presumably be to "Earth-grazers" because of their relative accessibility. As long ago as 1964 Cole and Cox proposed setting such a target for Project Apollo, on the grounds that the Russians might either land on the Moon first, or go for an asteroid in order to achieve the first landing on a heavenly body.[1] Had their suggestion been adopted the project name might have become literal – an Apollo mission to an Apollo-class asteroid. The suggested target was 1949 III, listed in reference works as Comet Wilson-Harrington because in two photographs it appeared to have a slight gaseous tail. It might, perhaps, be a cometary nucleus shedding its last traces of ice. Technically, Wilson-Harrington was an "Amor-class" asteroid because it did not cross the Earth's orbit. A return mission to Wilson-Harrington would require much less expenditure of energy than a Moon landing and return; mission time would be over six weeks, however, so Apollo's life-support facilities would have needed considerable stretching.

Wilson-Harrington has not been relocated since 1949, but in 1976 the Earth was passed by an asteroid designated 1976 AA, described as "the easiest object to reach after the Moon".[15] The Earth-grazer Geographos offers another easy target in energy terms, although that would be a long-drawn-out mission including a Venus flyby in order to change orbital plane.[1] 1976 AA will not make another close pass until the 1990s, however, and the next Geographos close encounter will be in the mid-1980s. Most asteroid mission studies have therefore concentrated on Eros, which although harder to reach is one of the most studied asteroids and has "launch windows" at roughly two-year intervals.[16]

Eros is roughly 37km long by 16km across, and it rotates around its short axis in 5.27 hours – fast enough to make effective gravity significantly higher at the poles than on the very high "mountains" of the equator. Surface gravity is estimated to be one-thousandth or less of Earth's, so there is a very real danger that a probe will bounce back into space. James Strong suggests that the probe should anchor itself to a point near one of the poles and winch itself down;[17] the anchor point will have to be as near the pole as possible, however, or else conservation of angular momentum will tend to dash the spacecraft against the rock. (In a story of my own I suggested anchoring by explosive pitons fired out on cables, but that won't work on the regolith with which most asteroids are covered, and Eros is dusty, at least.[18]) The landing point of an unmanned probe demands sunlight, for power generation, and line-of-sight communications with Earth. In 1978, which offered the most favourable encounter (in energy terms) for sixteen years, a polar landing could have been made in late July: the Sun would have been 18° above the horizon and Earth 21°,[19] just far enough from the Sun for clear communications.[16]

The horizon would be very close, however; conventional roving vehicles would be out of the question; and the spacecraft would have to stay put for up to a year (depending on the propulsion system) before taking off to return samples. The various problems led Robert Shaw to suggest a "thistledown" spacecraft, or better still a mesh ball or series of loops like the Lunar Rover wheel, which could flatten itself against the asteroid surface, and use adhesives to glue itself to protruding ledges and rocks. It might be even more effective to let the probe bounce around freely on the surface, perhaps firing a laser at interesting surface features to obtain spectroscopic analyses.

Another possible target would be the asteroid Toro, whose intricate orbit confuses even the experts.[20] Piecing together various reports, it seems that Toro has an orbital period of 1.6 years; thus it completes five revolutions around the Sun in eight Earth years.[21] But its orbit ranges from near that of Venus to near that of Mars, and its period may well be locked with *their* years as well as ours. Thus there would be a recurring pattern of close approaches to Earth, Venus and Mars, coming to within 0.13AU of each.[22] But the relationship to Earth is particularly complex: Toro passed us in February 1968, again in August 1972, again in January–February 1976, August 1980, and so on. Successive passes are therefore in front of the Earth, behind it, in front, behind . . . It would be very interesting to discover whether Toro is a dead cometary nucleus, added relatively recently to the inner Solar System, or is by any chance a primal fragment from the creation of the inner planets. If so it might be unique and of incalculable scientific value, preserved by its orbit from the general "sweeping up" which occurred about four billion years ago.

"Sweeping up" still continues, however – on a lesser scale, but quite enough to cause serious concern. The dust which falls daily into Earth's atmosphere is no problem – on the contrary, it is an important part of the atmospheric processes precipitating rainfall. Even the meteors which streak across the night sky are usually no larger than grains of sand. Objects big enough to reach the Earth's surface are too rare to bother the insurance companies – there is one known case where a woman was bruised on the leg, and but one recorded fatality to date. Yet in the volume of space swept out by the Earth as it circles the Sun year by year, century by century, rarity becomes purely relative.

Isaac Asimov has classified objects weighing a few dozen tons as "city-busters" – equivalent generally to nuclear weapons in the amount of energy they release on impact, with the effects of penetrating the surface thrown in.[23] Two such objects have struck the Earth so far *this century*, both of them in what is now the USSR, both miraculously in uninhabited regions. The first of them, in 1908, was precisely on the latitude of Leningrad. The explosion was at least in the megaton range and was accompanied by a searing heat flash, a mushroom cloud, and a shock-wave which devastated surrounding forests and was detected all over the world. Evidence at the site suggests that the object exploded in the air, and the (somewhat shaky) scientific explanation is that it was a fragment of cometary ice. Speaking at Glasgow University Astronomical Society, Dr David Hughes argued that such a body would disintegrate when its altitude equalled its diameter and the pressure wave of its supersonic boom was trapped between it and the ground. Knowing the recalcitrant nature of terrestrial ice, however, and given that cometary ice may be of higher density, it seemed that a great many fragments should have torn into the ground below.

A more speculative idea is that it was a nuclear-powered spacecraft; and there was a short-lived suggestion that it might have been a micro-scopic "black hole" passing right through the Earth (that one was obviously wrong because there was no shockwave radiating from where the object supposedly emerged). Most recently, Ian Ridpath has suggested that the object was a carbonaceous chondrite which shattered completely into dust at the critical altitude.[29] The explanation is almost certainly correct because a great deal of dust was released into the atmosphere and traces of it were found at the site; and fireball network studies have shown that there are far more massive, fragile meteors disintegrating in the atmosphere than anyone previously suspected. The brightest fireball recorded (Sumava 1974) was evidently a 200-tonne boulder, too fragile to stand up under its own weight on Earth.[30] But the reader is invited to pause for a moment and think of the most likely explanation, if it happens *now*, to be put upon a heat flash, mushroom cloud and blast occurring anywhere in the Soviet Union, the Middle East, Europe, China or the USA – and what is likely to happen next.

From that point of view, probably the most terrifying photos of the decade appear in *Sky and Telescope* for July 1974. They show a meteorite, whose mass may have been as high as several thousand metric tons, passing through the Earth's atmosphere without striking the ground. It passed within 58km of the surface at 15km/sec, causing sonic booms; its flight was from Utah, over Montana and out into space again over Alberta. The Flying Saucer movement claims it for a spaceship; would that it *had* been anything so innocuous. In a very low-key assessment of what could have happened, Luigi G. Jacchia wrote: "It seemed strange not to have any report of impact . . . A body capable of producing a fireball having the observed brilliance would have impacted with the energy of an atomic bomb, and seismic disturbances should have been recorded."[24] Military and political ones, too, I fear.

Coming in for impact, objects weighing thousands of tons are scarcely slowed down by the atmosphere.[5] Beginning his novel *Rendezvous with Rama* with an imagined 1,000-tonne impact in Italy, Arthur C. Clarke writes: "It was as if a great war had been fought and lost in a single morning."[25] No impacts on such a scale have taken place during recorded history, yet we know they do occur: Barringer Crater in the USA and Chubb Crater in Canada are only two of the impact features which Earth's dynamic surface has not yet erased. Still larger collisions take place, it is estimated, at intervals of about 170,000 years; in Chapter 7 we discussed the possibility that they bring about reversals in the Earth's magnetic field. The Vredevort Ring in South Africa was formed by a 35-billion-tonne impact, smaller than any of the known Earth-grazing asteroids. Such an impact on land would virtually sterilize the continent affected;[26] in the sea (three-quarters of the target area) it would devastate an entire hemisphere of the planet, sweep clear all but the mountains of the other hemisphere, and raise enough dust into the stratosphere to cut off the sunlight for years.[27] In 1951, only seven Earth-grazing asteroids were known; the total is rising steadily, and at least four have been added in the last two years – one of them "spotted" within 1,600,000km of the Earth.

In *Man and the Stars* there was brief mention of a possible "Politics of Survival" – a program of action spread over about three centuries, aimed at guaranteeing the survival of the human race. The threats to be countered were stated under eight headings – five of them man made, three of them external. One of those three was "giant meteor impact", and I make no apology whatever for repeating the point here. In pursuing "deterrence" based on nuclear weapons, one of the craziest aspects of a crazy philosophy is that we have reduced the impact mass needed to bring about our annihilation by about nine orders of magnitude.

The only ways to kill the killer asteroids will involve manned space-flight. An asteroid a kilometre or more across is not going to vanish obligingly if struck by a nuclear warhead, even if it is detected in time, a big booster is available, and guidance is good enough to meet it head-on. Such threats will have to be pinpointed well in advance by a radar watch covering the inner Solar System, and men will have to reach the ones which threaten us. If they arrive early enough, they can perhaps deflect the asteroids back out of Earth's orbital track; failing that, the only hope seems to be to sink shafts and try to shatter the deadly little worlds by internal resonance.

Cole and Cox,[1] Stine[28] and other writers have looked at the resources of the asteroids and their economic and social possibilities. The topic proves to be extremely important. At a high enough level, such technology could more than handle any dangers presented by wandering small fry like Eros or Icarus. But, whereas most of the development of the Solar System can be presented on a take-it-or-leave-it-basis (with a grim future for Earth if we leave it), the reach for the asteroids is ultimately a matter of unadorned survival. If we do not wipe ourselves out, no other outside forces intervene, and yet we do not claim the little worlds, then eventually one of them will claim us.

9 Jupiter — The Big Issues

The Solar System consists of Jupiter plus debris.

Isaac Asimov

Jupiter is more massive than all the other planets and their moons put together. One of the newer games with which astronomers frighten themselves to sleep is calculating just how close we came to having two suns instead of a planetary system at all. As it is, Jupiter may well have shone by its own light during the final stages of contraction; some authorities argue that it may briefly have sustained fusion reactions and burned like a star; and it seems that Jupiter's mass was enough to prevent the material of the asteroids from coalescing into planets. At 20–30 times its actual mass, Jupiter could easily qualify as a star; some would call it a star at only five times its mass.[1] Had Jupiter managed to capture so much mass from the condensing primal nebula, it is far from certain that there would be any other planets, habitable or otherwise.

Before 1920, when its thermal flux was first measured, Jupiter was actually assumed to be uncooled, a molten primal world. *Return to Mars*, the second of Captain W. E. John's juvenile space novels, had a spaceship plunging dramatically towards a flaming Jupiter; but when that was written (in the 1950s) it had long been known that the planet's outer atmosphere was very cold, more than $100C°$ below freezing. It was assumed that the cold went down all the way to the surface (if there was one), and the Wildt model of Jupiter gave it a metallic core and a rock crust overlaid with thousands of km of ice, overlaid with still more thousands of km of atmosphere. The atmosphere obviously *was* thick because it was divided into bright strips and dark bands rotating at different speeds in different latitudes. Perhaps, then, there was no rock/metal core and the atmosphere became liquid at great depth; still further down, hydrogen would be compressed into a lattice with metallic properties. Methane and ammonia were detected in the atmosphere and helium was expected, but not free hydrogen or oxygen.[2]

As befitted the largest planet, Jupiter had a great retinue of moons. The four major ones, almost visible to the naked eye, were discovered by Galileo and demolished the notion that all the heavenly bodies "must" go around the Earth. More and more moons were detected as time went by, and as of 1978 the total stands at 14. There have been suggestions in the past that Jupiter has a ring of orbiting particles, like Saturn's,[3] and that it may have an asteroid belt of its own between Io and the innermost moon, named Amalthea.[4] Neither hypothesis was confirmed by the Pioneer 10 and 11 probes, but the Galilean moons have proved to be highly exotic in their own right.

The situation among the moons of Jupiter is as confused as compass directions on the Moon were before Project Apollo. (South was always at the top of the map, but east and west were a mirror-image of Earth's – so the Sun rose in the west, despite the Moon's direct rotation.) The four "Galilean" moons were officially named, and numbered outwards from the planet, but then Amalthea was found, within the orbit of Io, and numbered V. The fainter moons then continued to be numbered in order of discovery, and like Amalthea's their unofficial names were never officially ratified (fig. 20, p. 176–7). It looked as if the history of the Moon maps would be repeated and NASA would sweep the nonsense aside when space missions became a reality, but instead still another set of names was put up to the International Astronomical Union,[5] and adopted. (Table VI, p. 175.)

The new names were chosen on the basis that names ending in "a" would indicate direct revolution around the planet, while names ending in "e" would be retrograde – except, of course for Ganymede . . .

Of all Jupiter's features, none has caught the public imagination like the Great Red Spot. Larger in surface area than Earth itself, it glows like an angry wound below the planet's equatorial zone, forcing the faster-moving "System 1" of the equator and its belts to curve around it at hundreds of kilometres per hour. First observed in 1664, although Kepler's false solution of Galileo's anagram had "predicted" it even earlier, it had faded a great deal this century and in a small telescope it now seems gray, although larger instruments and close-ups bring out its distinctive and suggestive hue. At one time it was thought to be the mouth of a colossal volcano; but it was seen to vary its position when pulled by the South Tropical Disturbance, a forty-year-old storm nearly as conspicuous as the Spot itself. V. A. Firsoff thought that it might be a failed satellite, buoyed up on the denser layers of the planet;[6] a raft of different forms of ice was another possibility;[7] in *Man and the Stars* I suggested (as mere speculation) that it might have been dropped deliberately by some visitors trying to encourage evolution, to give life on Jupiter a land surface to conquer. The more mundane explanation was that it was a "Taylor column", a huge atmospheric whirlpool over a mountain (towering a whole kilometre, despite Jupiter's gravity[7]) on a solid core 3,000km below. If so, its rotation – several minutes different from any other atmospheric feature – would presumably mark the true "day" of the planet.

Things began to move in 1955, when bursts of radio noise were detected from Jupiter, in patterns coinciding roughly with the rotation of the planet yet not associated with any striking surface features. Colossal lightning discharges were put forward as an explanation, but the effect was quite unlike terrestrial lightning. In 1960, F. Graham Smith wrote that the position of a radio source might be located by occultation, as one of the Galilean moons passed in front of the planet.[8] When the correlation was made an unexpected result emerged: the radio outbursts were associated with the movements of Io, apparently focussed towards Earth by the moon when it was at right angles to the line of sight.[9] Since Earth's Van Allen Belts had now been mapped by spacecraft, it was soon suggested that Jupiter had a powerful magnetic field and huge radiation belts, which were perturbed by Io, and perhaps by Amalthea and Europa. There were also signs of another disturbing influence, perhaps an undetected satellite[9] – but it was located between Amalthea and Io, where Alfvén had suggested Jupiter might have its own asteroid belt.

First radio observations of Jupiter confirmed the low temperatures of the visible clouds.[8] But as observations were made at other wavelengths, penetrating deeper into the atmosphere, warmer layers were found. Early in the 1960s, Carl Sagan had suggested that the "greenhouse effect" might trap solar energy, as on Venus, and raise the temperature of the layers below – perhaps enough to permit the existence of liquid water.[10] Continuing studies showed, however, that Jupiter emits $2\frac{1}{2}$ times as much heat as it receives from the Sun. Some estimates put the core temperature as high as $500,000°$ K,[9] and Krafft Ehricke classified the interior of Jupiter as "pyro-abyssal".[11] Star occultations by Jupiter showed that, below the troposphere, temperature increased steadily with depth.[12] Gravitational contraction was the most likely heat source, although, if so, any solid core would have to be much smaller than had been supposed – and the 27,000km of overlying ice predicted by Wildt was now ruled out, beyond question. Now it seemed certain that there would be a Jovian layer with Earth-surface temperatures. If there was water there, would there be life? All the necessary conditions existed for the synthesis of complex organic compounds – in fact, the Red Spot had just the colour of the amino acids synthesized in laboratory experiments with "primal atmospheres". (See Chapter 13.)

There were therefore great expectations as Pioneer 10 closed with Jupiter in November 1973, after successfully negotiating the Asteroid Belt. The vast scale of the Jovian system was shown by the fact that, when Pioneer crossed the orbit of the outermost moon, Hades, it was still 23,650,000km from the planet with 26 days to go to flyby.[13] There is in fact a gap of 7,900,000km between the outer, retrograde moons – almost certainly captured asteroids – and the ones with direct rotation which apparently "belong" to the planet. (Jupiter 13, reported in September 1974 and confirmed in October, was the outermost of the direct satellites, at 12,390,000km.[14]) The flyby itself took place on 3 December 1973, at a velocity of 132,000kph passing 130,000km above the visible surface (202,000km from the planet's centre!). The radiation belts were traversed safely, despite misgivings: since their intensity was unknown, one scientist at least was perfectly prepared for the spacecraft to "drop dead". In fact, the instruments were 90% saturated and, if Pioneer 10 had passed 105,000km closer to the planet, it would probably have been silenced.[15]

On 26 November the spacecraft had reached the boundary of Jupiter's magnetic field, 6,919,000km out; much further than expected, yet within the orbits of Hades, Poseidon, Pan, Andastrea, Jupiter 13 and 14, Demeter, Hera and Hestia — i.e., only the Galileans and Amalthea are enveloped in the magnetic field. On 30 November, however, 3,862,000km from Jupiter, Solar Wind readings began again and continued for eleven hollrs before the spacecraft re-entered the magnetic field 3.2 million kilometres from the planet. Data from Pioneer 11, by then half way through the Asteroid Belt, confirmed that Jupiter's magnetic field had been compressed (to half its former radius, in the sunward direction) by a surge in the Solar Wind. This was the first indication of the "wobbliness" of Jupiter's magnetosphere, which has since been compared to a huge jellyfish.

The magnetic field has two components. A dipole field like Earth's, but inclined at 11° to the planet's axis of rotation and opposite to Earth's — i.e., with magnetic north near the geographic south pole — is eight times as strong as ours; but the outer field is stronger still, and stretches out for millions of kilometres along a disk which is warped northwards on the sunward side, southwards on the other. The magnetic field contains the radiation belts, of trapped protons and electrons, respectively 3,000 and 10,000 times the peak levels in Earth orbit;[13] Jupiter's magnetic "tail" stretches to beyond the orbit of Saturn, and Pioneer 10 passed through it in 1976, $2\frac{1}{2}$ years after Jupiter flyby, 692,000,000km "down-Sun" from the planet.

The Pioneer picture-taking system was not a TV camera, as with the Mariner spacecraft, but an imaging polarimeter scanning the planet in red and blue light. The instrument scanned the planet in strips as Pioneer spun, and the resulting pictures had to be rectified as well as edited by computer to produce the final versions. One effect of the process was that the pictures were first produced by mirror-image pairs.[16] Confusion still results: the BBC-2 documentary already mentioned showed a series of photos combined into a Pioneer 10 approach film, but the planet was left-to-right inverted throughout; the same applies to a photo in *New Science in the Solar System*,[15] although that may be a printer's error. A possible contributory factor was that NASA information but a study of the pictures released by the Ames Research Centre, with the terminator on the left throughout the imaging sequence, made it seem that the spacecraft passed in front of Jupiter, to sunward.

The pictures released by Ames come in three forms: red-light images, blue images of the same views, and colour prints made by computer combination of the two. In many cases the monochrome prints show details not visible in the colour combinations, and in still more they show contrasting details owing to different penetrations into the atmosphere, different reflecting properties of cloud layers, etc. In general, the pictures showed great amounts of detail not visible from Earth. One major surprise, when they were related to infrared and ultraviolet scanner data, was that the bright bands of Jupiter are high-altitude ammonia clouds. But for them, the whole disk would be the dark brown of the low-lying strips between the clouds. Conditioned by years of reference to the dark strips as "cloud belts", I had always assumed — for instance, in a short story called "The Galilean Problem"[17] – that they would be higher than the golden-white bands which take up most of the disk; in fact, they are a terrifying 20km deep.[13]

The whole planet is in convection, with bright regions rising, dark ones falling, and lateral winds caused by Coriolis force blowing in opposite directions, parallel to the equator. As was to be expected, there is extensive turbulence at the boundaries between the bright "zones" with different rotation speeds: in the northern hemisphere, turbulence is shown by S-shaped clouds and waves, in the south by "arcing structures" thousands of km long and by long, dark filaments.

The southern hemisphere also showed "white ovals" which had been seen from Earth. These proved to be cloud cells, up to half the diameter of the Earth, with dark halos – rising cloud columns, apparently, emphasizing the huge scale of the atmospheric circulation systems. The equatorial zone showed a huge nucleus of this kind, with a plume trailing for 64,000km behind it – more than five times the diameter of the Earth. An even longer plume, without a nucleus, preceded it around the planet; all features in the equatorial zone were greatly elongated, indicating jetstreams whose relative speeds approached 400kph – comparable to the relative velocities of the major rotation systems; e.g., of the "equatorial current" passing the Great Red Spot.

The Spot itself was doubtless the feature most eagerly awaited. Thanks to Jupiter's rapid rotation, it came out of the darkness early in the encounter (before the bright equatorial nuclei) and had come round again several times by the time the planet was a crescent, with the spacecraft drawing away. (Jupiter had never been seen with significant phases before.) The first views released, before computer processing, showed features which were presumably illusory, since they don't appear in later prints: a white spot in the centre of the Red Spot, and huge dark swirls impinging on it.

A connection with storms was suggested by major turbulence along most of the terminator as the Spot came into view, preceded on one appearance by the shadow of Io. Due north of the Spot, at the corresponding latitude in the northern hemisphere, was a circular storm almost as large as the Spot itself. Its details were more obvious in red light than blue, and it was associated with a smaller, sharper storm in the bright zone above. A colour photograph (A73–9224) from the Spot's previous transit across the daylit hemisphere shows another equally large storm following the first; close-ups of the North Temperate Region some days later showed a complex structure of swirling cloud formations, indicating extensive north-south motion in that part of Jupiter's atmosphere.

The lack of permanent Jovian features (apart from the Red Spot, so far) makes it difficult to describe the atmospheric phenomena. Until recently there was an accepted classification by latitude – Equatorial Zone, North Equatorial Belt, North Tropical Zone, and so on – in which the Red Spot lay in a conspicuous hollow in the southern edge of the South Equatorial Belt. An Equatorial Band, dividing the Zone into two, had occasionally been noted as an "elusive feature". But in recent years a dark equatorial belt has become extremely prominent; not by up-welling, as at first thought, but by a downdraught or general clearing of the high, bright clouds. The shading spread over most of the northern half of the former Equatorial Zone, while the bright southern half moved further south, until the Red Spot lay in a slight hollow in the *north* edge of a Belt. Fascinatingly, in the Pioneer 10 photos the former South Equatorial Belt can still be seen, although very faintly (it can be traced right round the planet in NASA's high-quality prints, but not in most reproductions), and the original classification of markings is still in use (e.g., in ref. 15), although it no longer matches the prominent features of the planet.

In the colour photo cited above (A73–9224), the former "hollow" north of the Spot can still be traced in the form of a shockwave upwind of the Spot. In blue light two Spot transits later, when Pioneer was 872,000km closer, the stream can be seen splitting into two beyond the Spot, with the lower branch continuing on the line of the former Belt (photo A73–9190–B). The corresponding red-light image (A73–9190–R) shows four enormous whirlwinds taking up almost the whole area of the Spot, the smallest one superimposed on two of the big ones, and one or possibly two circular patterns of similar size downwind of the Spot, interacting with the converging gas streams to produce a series of colossal ripples; while back upwind, back towards the terminator, the Spot casts an obvious shadow. It is in fact 8km higher than the surrounding cloud deck.[15]

At first glance, the details could support either the circular storm or the floating solid mass as an explanation of the Spot. But, during its detailed coverage of the Equatorial and North Tropical Zones, Pioneer photographed a Little Red Spot, first sighted from Earth only six months before. It had the form of two interlocked spirals (not discernible in the colour print, A73–9204) and its importance was that theoreticians were forced to consider red spots as phenomena which could arise and disappear again in various locations. The Little Spot had in fact disappeared by the time of the Pioneer 11 flyby, in November 1974. Whether or not the Great Spot is a Taylor column, therefore, red spots apparently don't have to be generated by permanent surface features below. If anything sub-tends a spot, then, it might be a raft of various ices, eventually broken up by the action of winds above and currents below; but mathematical models are emerging to suggest that the spots are a class of storms so violent that even Jupiter can sustain only one at a time. Competitors can only grow so far before they are dispersed.

There were stronger indications that Jupiter has no solid surface near enough to the top of the atmosphere to affect it. The heat flow from Jupiter was confirmed to be more than twice the incoming solar energy; a continuing gravitational contraction of only 1mm per year would supply the energy required.[15] Any rocky core would therefore have to be very small, and at a temperature of 30,000° C it certainly would not be covered with ice![13] From 24,000km down to the centre Jupiter must consist mostly of hydrogen in its metallic high-pressure form, although one suggested mechanism for contraction is the condensation of a helium core, now 10% of the total mass of the planet.[18] (Helium was identified in Jupiter's atmosphere for the first time during the Pioneer 10 flyby.[15]) Heat is carried out from the core by convection: the hydrogen currents rise 2,400km per year, taking 10 to 100 years to reach the surface.[13] Hydrogen is, after all, the major constituent of the planet; it is much more like a failed star than the cold methane-ammonia planet we supposed.

As already mentioned, significant Jupiter phases cannot be seen from Earth; Pioneer 10's pictures of the crescent after flyby "stir the imagination of astronomers", according to Dr Tom Gehrels, and give information about light-scattering in the atmosphere (stratosphere dust, absorbing sunlight and raising temperature, was implied by the radio occultation experiment when Pioneer went behind the planet[19]). There was a joke at ASTRA that Jupiter might surprise everyone and be equally bright all the way round; it turned out that in the infrared, because of the heat flowing out from the planet, the statement is perfectly true!

The recent evolution of the Equatorial Band goes a long way to discount the supposed glimpses of a Jupiter ring system like Saturn's. Pioneer 10 did find that the dust density near the planet was 300 times that of interplanetary space,[19] but no indications have been published suggesting rings. Going in to 130,000km, Pioneer 10 should have confirmed the supposed Jovian asteroid belt at 254,209km;[5] but neither Pioneer 10 or 11 figures indicating increased dust impacts in that region have been published. It remains to be seen whether a fifteenth satellite has to be there, after all.

It was confirmed that the radiation belts are attenuated by the Galilean moons, which absorb protons and electrons impinging on them. The Galileans, large enough to be considered worlds in their own right, were scheduled for special attention from both Pioneers. There were clear indications that all four had extensive deposits of the volatile compounds so conspicuously missing from the Moon. Soviet radio studies of the outer Galilean, Callisto, indicated that it was covered with brilliantly reflecting

TABLE VI The Renamed Moons of Jupiter

No. outwards from Planet	Astronomical Number	Unofficial Name	Official or New Name
1	V	Amalthea	Amalthea
2	I	—	Io
3	II	—	Europa
4	III	—	Ganymede
5	IV	—	Callisto
6	XIII	—	Leda
7	VI	Hestia	Himalia
8	X	Demeter	Lysithea
9	VII	Hera	Elara
10	XII	Adastrea or Andastrea	Ananke
11	XI	Pan	Carme
12	VIII	Poseidon	Pasiphae
13	IX	Hades	Sinope

(Jupiter XIV data not available.)

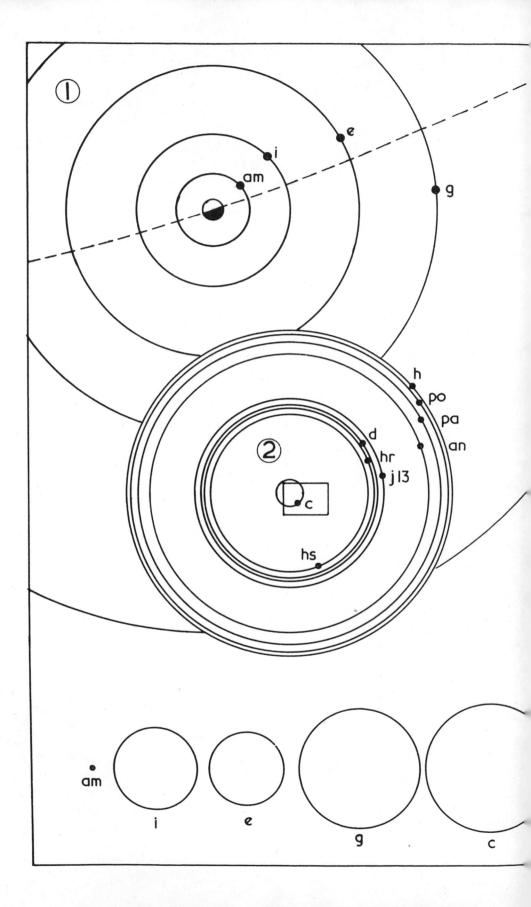

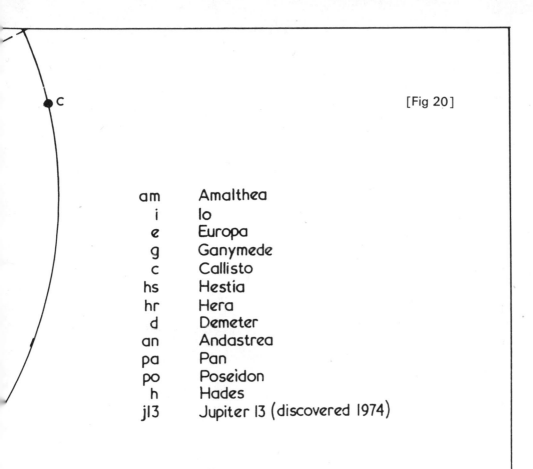

●c

[Fig 20]

am	Amalthea
i	Io
e	Europa
g	Ganymede
c	Callisto
hs	Hestia
hr	Hera
d	Demeter
an	Andastrea
pa	Pan
po	Poseidon
h	Hades
j13	Jupiter 13 (discovered 1974)

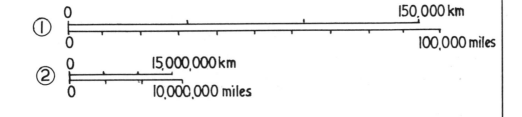

① 0 ————————————————— 150,000 km
  0 ————————————————— 100,000 miles

② 0 ——— 15,000,000 km
  0 ——— 10,000,000 miles

?
●●●●●●● ●
hr d an pa po h j13

ice;[20] light-polarization curves, however, suggest that, while Ganymede, Europa and Io are ice-covered, Callisto has a dusty regolith like the Moon's on its leading face (i.e., its western hemisphere) and bare rock on the other.[21] Pioneer 11 provided a partial reconciliation of the conflicting results: Callisto has a small but well-defined south polar cap.[22]

Red and blue Pioneer 10 views of Ganymede were supplied to us by Ames Research Centre, and a colour print uniting them appeared in *Sky and Telescope*, January 1975.[23] At least one expert had predicted that the moons of Jupiter should be free of craters, compared to the Moon and Mars, apart from the occasional impact of a stray asteroid.[24] Even from 751,000km, however, with a resolution of 770km, the Pioneer pictures revealed extensive cratering and at least two dark maria like the Moon's implying very big impacts (Ganymede is 10% larger than Mercury in diameter). On the eastern limb, indeed, is a dark "bite" so large and conspicuous that it looks like the start of an eclipse. Other parts of the disk were very bright and may well be the water ice detected in spectroscopic studies from Earth. (Methane and ammonia may also be present.) In our prints more detail can be seen near the centre of the disk in red light, but the opposite is true in the small-scale reproductions in *Sky and Telescope*.[23] Whether the differences are due to atmosphere remains to be seen: an atmosphere with a surface pressure one millionth that of Earth's has been inferred from star occultations.[25] In addition, the Galileans have been reported to have "hot shadows" – i.e., temperatures within the shadows, as they cross the planet, are higher than on the rest of Jupiter's disk.[3] A similar effect in the shadow of the rings of Saturn has been attributed to a greenhouse effect of a thin water-vapour atmosphere, driven off from the ring particles by collisions.[26]

Io, the innermost of the Galilean moons, was already known to be in a different class from the others. After eclipse by the planet it was reported sometimes to be distinctly brighter when it emerged from shadow, as if an atmosphere had been partly or wholly frozen, to be restored by sublimation in sunlight. Pioneer 10 signals, occulted by the moon, indicated an atmosphere 110km deep and 20,000 times thinner than Earth's (but much denser than star occultations had suggested[25]). Io and Europa are roughly twice as dense as Ganymede and Callisto, and may have an appreciable metallic content (Io's density lies midway between Mars' and the Moon's[19]). The picture became much more complicated when Pioneer 10 revealed that Io's atmosphere extends around Jupiter for 60° in either direction (i.e., to the Jupiter–Io Equilateral points) in a segment of a torus-shaped ring.[15]* Atomic hydrogen was identified, and Pioneer 11, studying Jupiter's shadow on the cloud, showed that it is not self-luminous and extends for less than a Jupiter diameter out of the orbital plane[27] – far enough, however, to envelop the planet! But Earth-based observations established that Io's distinctive orange colour is due

*In my childhood there was a novel around, by E. C. Eliott, called *Kemlo and the Zones of Silence*. It was set on a group of asteroids, in a permanent linear relationship, within a common belt of atmosphere. Everyone knew the set-up was dynamically impossible. If there are "Trojan" asteroids in the Jupiter–Io Equilaterals, however . . .

at least partly to the presence of atomic sodium,[28] in a cloud up to an altitude of 16,000km. Pioneer 10 detected hydrogen, nitrogen and sodium in Io's atmosphere, and a long-distance view confirmed that Io's disk is bright orange.

A possible explanation is that Io's surface has deposits of ammonia snow, with dissolved sodium and potassium. Ammonia in the atmosphere would be dissociated by sunlight into nitrogen and hydrogen, which would escape from Io to be trapped in its orbit, temporarily, by Jupiter's gravitational field. In the presence of sodium, the upper atmosphere could be intensely heated during auroral activity, and nitrogen, sodium and other elements could escape into the torus.[29] The prediction that Io and Ganymede would have ionospheres was confirmed by Pioneer 10, but so far only hydrogen has been found in the torus and a similar, predicted, Ganymede torus has not been confirmed. (Nor has one been found around Callisto.[27]) The latest suggestion is that Jupiter's radio emission may, after all, be due to lightning – but megaton-energy lightning bolts, striking through the ionized plasma of the torus, all the way from Io to the clouds of Jupiter itself.

Alternatively Io's surface might have extended salt beds, perhaps deposited by evaporation of water from below ground in the past. If so, Europa and Ganymede might still have sub-surface "oceans" – see later. (Both Ganymede and Europa seem to have *surface* water ice.[13]) Proton bombardment at the poles, where the effect of the radiation belt is most intense, would explain the "sputtering" of sodium into space and Io's dark polar caps. It is also possible, in view of A. T. Lawton's hypothesis and its development (Chapter 12), that sodium and other elements are entering Io's atmosphere from *outside*, by infall from the outer Solar System. And part of Io's colouring might conceivably be due to a surface layer of organic compounds; such layers may be common on the surfaces of the outer planets' moons,[30] but in particular the colour of Titan (Saturn's largest moon) resembles those of laboratory "primal atmospheres" after formation of complex organic compounds. Given a suitable heat-source – e.g., volcanic activity – and transport of complex compounds by the shifting ammonia snows into chasms shielded from the merciless radiation bombardment, there might conceivably be life on Io.

The prospects for life in Jupiter itself continue to improve. More and more of the compounds "predicted" by laboratory photochemical experiments have been found in the spectrum of the planet – first ethane and acetylene, then ethylene and phosphene.[31] Pioneer observations indicate these compounds are in a haze layer, above an inversion layer 225km down.[13] A still more important discovery was announced by Ames Research Centre in February 1975: a 91cm infrared telescope, flown in a NASA C–141 Airborne Infrared Observatory, had located water vapour in Jupiter's atmosphere – at room temperature, and 20 atmospheres' pressure. Given an infall of organic compounds from the upper atmosphere – particularly, perhaps, from the dissolution of features like the Little Red Spot – there is a very good chance that life may exist in a huge layer within the planet.

The currently favoured atmosphere model involves a layer of water vapour droplets, with dissolved ammonia, below a layer of ice crystals and immediately above the level where hydrogen becomes liquid 960km down.[13] The likelihood of life, and the Taylor column hypothesis concerning the Great Red Spot, would then be very much affected by one theoretical core model which involves incomplete hydrogen/helium mixing, with solid hydrogen and dissolved helium floating on a liquid hydrogen layer with a higher proportion of helium.[53] If the great vortex reaches down far enough to cool the water below, perhaps a water iceberg forms on the hydrogen crust . . . in which case the Spot would be self-sustaining. The disappearance of the Little Spot might be explained if crosswinds disrupted the vortex and the iceberg melted before it was re-established. A permanent stable ice continent under the Great Red Spot would give life a solid surface to conquer, in due course. As it is, any Jupiter-based life is "planetogenic", sustaining itself on chemical energy extracted from the environment,[11] and presumably could not pass the unicellular level of evolution until it had literally eaten the world (although Sagan and others have imagined upper atmosphere life subsisting on solar energy and predators, perhaps kilometres across, feeding on simpler forms brought down by convection).[54] Unfortunately, there does not seem to be enough oxygen available to turn the whole of Jupiter int carbon dioxide and water . . . but, if there were an ice continent below the Red Spot with a steady rain of organic compounds from above, Jovian evolution might be able to branch away from the terrestrial model altogether. The possibilities will have to be checked before plans to industrialize Jupiter are put into effect.

Pioneer 11 was launched in April 1973, and reached Jupiter in December 1974. The fluctuations of the outer magnetic field were dramatically confirmed on the approach – Pioneer ran into the wavering bow shock wave no less than three times, at different distances from the planet.[27] Closest approach was 42,000km above the cloud tops, moving so rapidly (172,000kph) that picture-taking had to be halted. The flight path crossed Jupiter's equator from the south at a 54° angle and went out over the north pole. Pioneer 10 data had indicated that such a brief exposure ("through the dragon's mouth") to the most intense part of the radiation belts, the flat sheet north of the equator, would not destroy the spacecraft's electronics, and it was therefore possible to redirect it by gravitational slingshot for an encounter with Saturn in 1979. *En route*, it also becomes the first spacecraft to make observations out of the plane of the Ecliptic. Pioneer 10 was accelerated in its flyby to well over Solar System escape velocity and will fly out into interstellar space in the general direction of Aldebaran, going back along the Sun's track around the Galaxy; after its Saturn flyby Pioneer 11 could be sent "up-Sun", towards the Apex of the Sun's Way near Vega. Both spacecraft carry plaques giving basic data on Man and the Solar System in case they are found by other intelligent beings, millions of years from now.

Jupiter had changed significantly since Pioneer 10's pass. The Little Red Spot had disappeared; the bright zone surrounding the Great one had moved south still further, leaving the Spot clear of the dark band below. But south-east of the Spot a white upwelling oval had approached, with a dark low-lying ellipse south-east of that; and a close-up from 402,000km showed that the bright patch impinged on the dark band far enough to be caught by upper-atmosphere turbulence around the Spot. A great bridge of bright cloud had been drawn across the dark lane into the converging jetstreams to the east of the Spot. Within the Spot itself huge vortices could again be seen, and faint blue clouds showed along its northern edge.[27] Even looking at the photos, it takes an effort to realize that the features can be compared in size to the planet Earth itself.

The most dramatic Pioneer 11 shots, however, were of the north pole. After the views of Jupiter in crescent phase caught by Pioneer 10, the next target vista, unattainable from Earth, had to be one of the polar regions. Partly because of Jupiter's polar flattening and partly because of the sheer size of the planet, Pioneer 10's view of the far north had been too foreshortened to show significant detail, apart from a long dark streak — presumably of unusual depth — on the fringe of the polar cap. *Sky and Telescope* printed two Pioneer 11 views of the northern hemisphere with the Red Spot just visible to the south, and a close-up — before computer editing and processing to remove distortion — of finely detailed structures in the boundary layers of the polar region. After processing, that view was considered so important that Ames Research Centre sent ASTRA three copies of it: a first print, a second with sharper contrast, and a magnified view of the most convoluted section.

The North Temperate region and its boundary with the polar cap proved to be full of scallops and swirls in shear areas between belts of the planet rotating at different speeds — enough detail to keep planetary meteorologists busy for years. Small white spots, up to a few hundred km in diameter, appeared to be convective storms like terrestrial hurricanes. There was good reason to think, in fact, that the rising gas columns contained water vapour as well as ammonia. In the shear areas relative jetstream velocities reached 500kph.

The dynamics of the polar region are not yet understood properly because there is virtually no solar heating and the planet's internal heat becomes dominant. In addition, Coriolis forces are much greater around it than at the equator (where "centrifugal force" reduces the effective gravity, owing to Jupiter's rapid rotation). There was an ASTRA speculation that the polar region, which is calm, might be *hotter* than the equator, since it is closer to the hot interior. (Polar flattening is even greater than is apparent to the eye.[19]) In fact, internal heat loses the contest, but only just: the north pole is only 2.8C° colder than the equator. The relatively stagnant polar regions may be the best place to search for life, because elsewhere organic materials would be dragged down by convection into regions of great heat.[32]

After the Pioneer flybys the Galilean moons continued to be

studied intensively. JPL radar studies showed Ganymede as rougher than the Moon, Mars, Mercury or anything to date except the asteroid Toro; there may be a great deal of rubble embedded in the ice, making the surface rougher to radar than it is in fact.[43] The densities of the moons decrease with distance from the planet, as if due to heat emitted during its formation;[44] and an explanation emerged at last for the decametric radio bursts linked to the motions of Io. Apparently the sodium cloud permits the formation of a "flux tube" linking Io's poles to the Jovian ionosphere. Io's core must be electrically conducting, because as it orbits within Jupiter's magnetic field it builds up a charge which arcs to Jupiter and back, with the energy of several H-bombs, twice during Io's 42-hour "month".[45]

But for absorption by the moons, Jupiter's radiation belts would be 100 times more intense (they are equivalent to a high-altitude nuclear explosion as it is), and once every 13 months, when Earth and Jupiter are connected by lines of the interplanetary magnetic field, high-energy electrons escaping from the magnetosphere are channelled to Earth.[46] As well as reaching out beyond Saturn with its magnetic "tail", and swinging the Sun itself around with its gravity, Jupiter can reach inwards as far as Mercury with its electron bursts. One wonders just how important our relations with Jupiter will ultimately prove to be.

In 1977 two spacecraft were launched on a mission previously designated Mariner Jupiter–Saturn.[33] Whereas Pioneer spacecraft are best suited to environmental studies, especially in the interplanetary medium, being spin-stabilized, Mariners provide fixed platforms for planetary studies.[34] Instead of visual plaques both spacecraft carried gramophone records, to tell any finders millions of years hence about "The Sounds of Earth".[47] A Bach extract was included in a gesture to Lewis Thomas, who had suggested Bach for interstellar communication, "though that would be boasting".

The greatest joke, however, was that at liftoff both spacecraft were renamed Voyager. Voyager was to have been a Mars and Venus soft-lander/orbiter combination, launched by Saturn boosters, to take over planetary exploration from the Mariner series in the mid-1960s.[48] With reduced funds and smaller boosters the Mariner series had to be extended, until as Viking it became sophisticated enough to fulfil the original Voyager objectives. Now Mariners were bound for Saturn and beyond, and Voyager was to be their new name!

At Jupiter, the Voyagers will have 100 times the data transmission capability of the Pioneer probes, including true TV, and will be able to send a picture in 42 seconds instead of 78 minutes.[33] (But the cancelled Grand Tour missions would have had more bit-rate capability at *Neptune* than the Pioneers had at Jupiter.) Voyager 1 will fly through the Io flux tube and photograph the south pole of Io from 22,000km, and obtain the first photos of Amalthea, but will stay more than four times as far from the planet as Pioneer 11's "Dragon's Mouth" pass. (The "Grand Tour" planetary configuration makes the Saturn redirection much easier now.) Voyager 2 will be twice as far out again, to preserve the Uranus option after the Saturn flyby, but will be closer to Ganymede and Europa; Voyager 1 will take close-ups of Callisto on the way out. *All* the satellites will be photographed in greater detail than can be seen from Earth. At the moment of writing both spacecraft are in flight; Voyager 1 has had receiver problems but they have been overcome.

Like all the Mariner series, the Voyager spacecraft were produced by the highly successful JPL management and construction team who had begun work on the Ranger moonprobes in 1960.[48] For the first time there were no new projects in the pipeline: in 1976 Congress had again refused funds for a Pioneer Jupiter Orbiter or a Mariner Jupiter–Uranus.[49] In 1977 start-funding for Pioneer was authorized by the appropriate House and Senate Committees, only to be opposed in Congress by a Representative who called for a vote with only two days' notice. Luckily the vote was delayed four more days and in that time NASA, JPL, the L5 Society, the American Astronomical Society and other groups raised enough public support to have the amendment defeated.[50] The JOP mission remains in the program and it looks as if the political tide may have turned at last. In 1978, NASA announced that Pioneer Jupiter Orbiter had been named Galileo.

The Jupiter Orbiter will use Pioneer 10/11 backup hardware (as Mariner 5 was based on Mariner 4 spares) and be launched in 1981.[35] The mission can't be flown sooner because Jupiter will be out of the Ecliptic meantime, and a more powerful launch vehicle would be required. Galileo will be launched from Earth orbit by a Centaur upper stage, having been taken up in the Space Shuttle, and will have a prolonged flight time of 1,000 days. Part of the extra payload will have to be allocated to a braking rocket, however, because slingshot capture is not possible even using the Galilean moons. Ganymede gives the biggest braking effect during a flyby,[36] but capture using Jupiter's pull alone is best suited to a Callisto encounter.[37] Either way, rocket braking will also be needed, but nevertheless an atmosphere entry capsule will be added to the payload for release before retrofire.[51]

A Ganymede flyby is scheduled later, and could put the probe into an inclined orbit, for more effective mapping of the planet's magnetic field. (Such an orbit may be necessary in any case, to reduce exposure to the radiation belts.) It has also been suggested that while Jupiter's dust cloud (300 times the dust density in interplanetary space) poses no threat to flyby missions, it might reduce the operational lifetime of an orbiter.[19] But in one respect a Jupiter orbiter will be easier to plan than one circling the Moon or Mars: Pioneers 10 and 11 found that Jupiter's density increases evenly to the centre, and no mascons were detected, so the only perturbing effect from the planet will be the pull of its equatorial bulge. In future orbiter missions perturbations from the moons may be deliberately sought: using the attractively named techniques of "orbit pumping", "orbit cranking" and "resonance hopping", a spacecraft could explore the Jupiter system thoroughly in a prolonged game of celestial billiards.[38]

As regards atmosphere entry the position is (of course) complex. For example, a TOPS probe (cancelled for lack of funds) might have relayed data from an entry probe down at 300 atmospheres' pressure within the planet; but a Pioneer-type flyby would allow tracking for only $1\frac{1}{2}$ hours, down to 73 atmospheres' pressure, before losing contact owing to the rapid rotation of the planet.[39] Grand Tour missions (also cancelled) would have allowed penetration to 100 atmospheres at most, even with two-part spacecraft separating within the atmosphere. The Galileo entry vehicle will return data for only 30 minutes, after a $300g$ deceleration from a 47km/sec atmosphere entry.[51] On future missions extended tracking and deep penetration will require either close orbit, at around the distance of Amalthea, or the use of relay satellites in "Trojan" positions with the Galilean moons. James Strong has suggested the same technique for extended contact with a lander on one of the Galileans,[9] so atmosphere entry probes may accompany, say, the proposed Ganymede lander in 1990,[40] rather than later Jupiter Orbiters.

Landings on the Galilean moons might discover complex surface chemistries. It has been suggested that the outer planet moons may have surface deposits of "natural" organic compounds, like those in comets and meteorites.[39] At ASTRA, Robert Shaw suggested that life might be evolved following the passage of a comet through the Jovian system: now that we know comets have immense hydrogen haloes, we might expect that when one interacts with the thin atmospheres of the Galileans it generates powerful electric storms, perhaps synthesizing complex molecules as lightning may have done on the primeval Earth. (It would be gentler than the 400kv bolts of the flux tube, presumably.) With the storms, and the successive freezing and thawing of the atmosphere during eclipses, such compounds might find their way into liquid reservoirs below ground — or interact more slowly in the snow. Any life which comes into being has to survive the radiation belts, however; if sheltered by a crevice, it must have some energy source such as volcanism to take the place of sunlight.

A. T. Lawton's hypothesis in Chapter 12 offers another possible basis for Galilean life. Lawton confines his argument to dust clouds between the Sun and the nearer stars, but in discussion he has suggested that there might be a ring of dust surrounding the Solar System, steadily draining into it (Chapter 12 Appendix). In that way the Galilean moons could have been subjected, over a long period, to an infall of interstellar dust rich in heavier elements from supernova explosions. Such surface dust might well give the Galileans complex chemistries. Everything then depends, again, on whether storms transfer such compounds into crevices — to shelter from the radiation, perhaps to trickle downward into warmer regions.

Underground water would greatly increase the chances that life might evolve. In a liquid medium, the required chemical interactions are far more likely to occur and primitive organisms have better chances to spread, survive and evolve. There is water ice on Ganymede and Callisto, at least; their densities are low; is it too speculative to imagine internal heat and subterranean lakes, even seas?

On 4 May 1976 Ames Research Centre sent us the most staggering release to date. Ganymede, it seems, may be almost *all* water – a single droplet larger than Mercury, encased in rock and ice. Imagine looking out of a window at that, orbiting it. landing on it – 272 billion km³ of water, 8,000km in diameter, comparable with the ocean Jupiter might have had on the combined Wildt–Sagan model.[10] Imagine penetrating the crust, sending the first bathyscaph down . . . Will the water be clear or cloudy? How far will the lights carry? Could there be life in that unimaginable blackness, clinging to pockets of radioactive heat on the underside of that extraordinary shell?

To reach Ganymede, or any of the Galileans except Callisto, we ourselves have to pass the hazard of the radiation belts. Pioneer 10 sustained a near-sterilizing flux during its flyby, enough to kill 99.9% of spore-forming bacteria and "supralethal" for all other forms of life; many writers, including even Ben Bova[41] and Jerry Pournelle,[42] have been sufficiently daunted to say that Jupiter's riches are out of our reach – but don't believe it. There are ironies here. The situation is not the same as with the discovery of Earth's Van Allen Belts, when journalists rushed to assure us that now Man could never reach the Moon: it will take more than sheer speed to get us through Jupiter's belts, but it can be done.

Earth orbit is no longer quite "half-way to anywhere", in Pournelle's favourite phrase, but once terrestrial industry is established in Earth orbit, there are only three intermediate steps and probably not more than a hundred years to pass before there are marine biologists on Ganymede.

10 The Stations Further Out

It was shift, boys, shift!
There wasn't the slightest doubt,
It was time to make a shift
For the stations further out . . .

Traditional Australian song

Pioneer 10 crossed the orbit of Saturn in February 1976, telling us that the Solar Wind does, after all, reach out to that distance. Its subsequent encounter with Jupiter's magnetic "tail" shows that Saturn, too, must pass through it every twenty years. Apart from that, our knowledge of the four outer planets and their moons rests on Earth-based observations, and will stay that way until Pioneer 11 reaches Saturn in 1979. Even now, however, the "old" outer System is being demolished by new observational techniques and more dynamic, more challenging environments are being pieced together to replace it. Saturn, Uranus, Neptune and their moons – particularly Titan – are not what we thought they were; Pluto remains an enigma, but it may be the key to great things.

Visually, the rings of Saturn are the major feature distinguishing the planet from Jupiter. The impact of first seeing the rings through a telescope is comparable only to first sight of the craters of the Moon. Even a "picture-book astronomer" like myself can feel that he's advanced the field a little when another layman exclaims: "Good grief! it really *has* got a ring around it . . ."

The planet is not just a carbon copy of Jupiter, however, despite its great size and its composition of hydrogen, methane, ammonia and (presumably) helium. To begin with, Saturn is not massive enough to form metallic hydrogen in the depths and therefore might not have a magnetic field and radiation belts.[1] Confounding prediction, Radio Astronomy Explorer 2 has found from lunar orbit that Saturn is a radio source with a $10\frac{1}{2}$ hour period: a magnetic field at least three times Earth's, with associated radiation belts, is strongly indicated.[2] Saturn is much less dense than Jupiter, and is in fact less dense than water (it is sometimes fancifully drawn floating, rings and all, in a boundless ocean – like the one in which swims the turtle on whose shell stands the elephant on whose back rests the Earth, according to Indian mythology). If Jupiter has differentiated to the extent of forming a helium core, Saturn may in fact have a solid core, a notion which is supported by Soviet mathematical studies.[3] Mitton (ref. 1) supposes that this might be a rock and metal core, overlaid with ices as in early models of Jupiter; radio observations indicate, however, that like the "new" Jupiter Saturn is hotter than expected below the clouds[4] and high temperatures may therefore exist in the depths. Because of Saturn's lower mass, it may not have sustained fusion reactions during contraction and the environment may be less "contaminated" by heavy hydrogen than Jupiter's – leading to the speculation that Saturn might be an even better prospect for life than Jupiter. As regards availability of organic compounds, the entire equatorial zone of Saturn is reported to have a reddish tint.[5]

The rings stand a good chance of retaining their mystery until Pioneer 11's flyby, at least. It is now well over three hundred years since Christian Huygens solved the first part of the puzzle, announcing in a famous anagram that Saturn was surrounded by a flat ring, nowhere touching the planet, and therefore was not a triple world (as Galileo had supposed), nor one equipped with handles, as some observers had reported in astonishment. In 1857 James Clerk Maxwell demonstrated mathematically that the rings could only be composed of myriads of particles circling Saturn in independent orbits; in 1867 the divisions in the rings were explained in terms of "Kirkwood gaps", like those of the asteroid belt, produced by the perturbing influences of the moons; in 1895 spectroscopic observations confirmed that the velocity of rotation fell off with distance from the planet, whereas, had the rings been solid, the outer rim would be moving much faster than the inner one. Thus the rings had to be made up of individual particles. But particles of what? and how did they get into that amazing configuration? The possible answers are contradictory, and the whole picture is still vague enough to allow startling suggestions.

The stunning perfection of the rings could be achieved only in a system of colossal size. The diameter of the ring system to the outer edge of ring A, assumed until recently to be the boundary of the whole system, is 272,400km. The three major rings (A, B and C) fit neatly within Saturn's Roche Limit and it was assumed for many years that they were the debris of a satellite which had been torn apart by tidal forces. The problem was to explain how such a satellite could have been made to enter the Roche Limit, when it must originally have had a safe orbit beyond it. Perhaps the rings were primary Solar System material prevented from coalescing by Saturn's disturbing proximity; but, if so, why shouldn't all the planets – especially the giant ones – have rings? (See later.)

A particularly attractive suggestion is that one or more satellites were disrupted when the Roche Limit moved *out*, due to continued growth of the planet by accretion early in the history of the Solar System.[6] It has been argued that, when molecular cohesion is taken into account, no body smaller than 200km in diameter would be disrupted by Saturn, even if constructed entirely of ice; the rings' thickness is only 3–4km, from extensive observations in 1966.[7] Thus the Roche Limit alone cannot account for the present make-up of the rings; but multiple collisions, after the break-up of a big satellite, might perhaps have reduced the ring particles to their present size.

The picture is complicated, however, by the confirmation in 1967 of a
D ring outside ring A, more than doubling the true diameter of the ring
system.[7] For many years observers had been reporting this ring's existence,
as a dusky band like the "Crepe Ring", ring C, but the generally accepted
view was that any such effects could be explained by particles outside
the plane of the known rings; the outer ring was described as "a sort of
'Loch Ness monster' of Saturn".[8] Not only does it exist, however, but it
envelops Janus, a tenth satellite of Saturn discovered in the same year
only about three Earth radii (19,000km) from the outer edge of ring A.
(The two discoveries spoil the previous happy situation – compared with
the Jupiter system – whereby the rings were numbered inwards and the
moons were numbered outwards. Worse still, ring D is now defined as
between ring C and the planetary atmosphere, and what was ring D is
now ring E.[54] But at least all Saturn's moons have official names.) Janus's
diameter is estimated at 350km,[9] so, had it formed (briefly) just a few
thousand km closer to Saturn, the rings might have been even more
spectacular. As it is, Janus may be one of the most dangerous objects
in the Solar System to visit by spacecraft, even on a polar approach.

So what are the ring particles – what are they made of? how large
are they? and what shape? First results suggested that particles in rings
A and B could be kilometres across, and a great deal of SF has been
written about rock or ice mining in the rings. But they reflect radar like
rocks about 12cm across, or possibly metallic particles a metre or more
in diameter. These results may be due to multiple scattering, because
infrared observations suggest diameters of about one centimetre.[10] The
particles in ring A are certainly less than about 200m in diameter,
because stars don't flicker as they pass behind them,[8] and other radar
work suggests a mean diameter of 50cm for ring B particles.[11] (We
might hope for small sizes, to prevent commercial plundering of the rings
in the future.) The radar results suggest that the ring particles are rough
rock,[10] and the phase curves of the rings at different angles of illumination
resemble those of the Moon and Callisto,[7] suggesting extensive surface
pitting in multiple collisions. The rings' albedo is much higher than the
Moon's or Callisto's, however, and gives good reason to think that the
rings are water ice. If so, particle sizes are 1–10cm;[12] but another set of
observations suggests 42m. Infrared spectrometry by Kuiper in 1951 and
1957 suggested that the rings were carbon dioxide ice, covered with
hoarfrost,[7] but in 1970 he announced that the rings were in fact ammonia
ice.[13]

The rings are cold enough for water ice to be stable in space, but
ammonia ice should sublime away. Kuiper suggested that possibly some
water ice was present, giving a misleading figure for the ammonia temperature. In 1966, Kozyrev studied the shadow of the rings on the planet
spectroscopically and found that the ammonia band was stronger and
the methane one weaker than elsewhere on the planet; i.e., the shadow
of the rings was *warmer* than the rest of the disk (like the shadows of
the Galileans on Jupiter), apparently due to the greenhouse effect of an
atmosphere over the upper face of the rings. Furthermore, the apparent

atmosphere consisted at least partly of water vapour.[7] If water were subliming from the rings then ammonia should be given off as well, if Kuiper's 1970 conclusions are correct, and the strength of the Kozyrev ammonia absorption might therefore be directly due in part to the ring atmosphere; but Kuiper failed to find any evidence of ammonia in Saturn's spectrum, in the infrared.[13] There seems to be a straightforward contradiction here.

Some of the other apparent contradictions might be explained if the ring particles were regular in shape, presenting different aspects to Earth-based observers at different times. Dollfus suggested, to explain the polarization of ring B, that its elements were cigar-shaped and aligned parallel to the orbital plane.[8] An even more striking suggestion, dramatically portrayed by Ludek Pesek for the *National Geographic Magazine*, is that innumerable collisions might have reduced the fragments to cylinders aligned *perpendicularly* to the orbital plane.[14]

James Campbell suggested at ASTRA that such a situation might explain the disparity in estimates of the particle sizes. It might also explain the disagreement about their composition, given that solar radiation causes small particles in the rings to be swept out, or to be deposited on to larger pieces. Small particles either freeze to the larger ones, or are driven off again by the energy of the collisions.[7] Presumably, then, in the process leading to the alignment shown in the Pesek painting, cylinders of rock, ammonia ice or carbon dioxide could be expected to acquire hoarfrost caps; and, if rock and all three ices are present, quite a number of combinations would be possible and would show up in the appropriate wavelengths. After Campbell advanced this notion, it was reported in *Sky & Telescope* that ring A has a fixed pattern of brightness asymmetry, perhaps due to clustering waves of particles. The investigators considered the possibility that the effect might be an artefact of trapped rotation on the part of the ring particles, but rejected it because either the particles would have to be inclined at 45° to the Saturn line, which tidal forces would prevent, or else would have to change brightness in unison – "an implausible situation".[55] Not so implausible, perhaps, if Campbell's idea is correct.

First plans are for Pioneer 11 to pass between the rings and the planet, in September 1979. The red/blue monochrome pictures will show interesting contrasts, because Saturn's disk is brighter than the rings in red light and the rings are brighter than the disk in violet. The manoeuvre will be no less dangerous than the Jupiter pass "through the dragon's mouth", because there are indications that the Crepe Ring may extend right down to the edge of the atmosphere.[7] The same would apply to a passage through ring E, however, and a flyby beyond it would be too far out to be of much use. Pioneer 11 will therefore be a pathfinder for the Voyager missions, following only 6–12 months behind although they did not leave Earth until 1977 (flight time from Jupiter to Saturn is halved by the improved relative positions of the planets).

One daring option was to take Pioneer back through the rings *via* Cassini's Division, the clear zone between ring A and ring B caused by the pull of Janus or Mimas. Certainly the Cassini Division is about the only place where a spacecraft would have a chance to get through the rings proper : it is a true gap in the rings, whereas lesser "ripples" like Encke's Division in ring A are only attenuations, still containing detectable material.[7] (No less than ten minor divisions were reported by Lyot and others, although some observers contest their reality.[15] Fascinatingly, when the shadow side of the rings faces Earth the divisions appear *bright*, because of diffusion of light within the rings; they should therefore shine by diffused Saturn-light when edge-on to Earth.[7])

Still another possibility was to retarget Pioneer, by Saturn flyby, to a Uranus encounter; but this was discarded because spacecraft power would be too low for good results by the time it reached Uranus.[16] The alternative plan was that, after passing only 3,700km above the clouds (ten times closer than its Jupiter flyby) it would go out in the equatorial plane and pass within 19,000km of Titan – rapidly becoming the most interesting place in the Solar System. In this respect it would again be a valuable predecessor to the Voyager missions, which are scheduled to scan Titan, Rhea, Tethys and Dione.[17] But meantime the Uranus option has assumed greater scientific importance with the discovery that it, too, has rings, not all that much like Saturn's. Pioneer 11 is now expected to act as a pathfinder for Voyager 2 instead and cut the ring plane outside ring A, after which it cannot pass Titan. Whether NASA will send it to Uranus on the offchance that it may be useful again as a pathfinder remains to be seen.

Saturn's moons are a fascinating collection – not least because of their beautiful names (Janus, Mimas, Enceladus, Tethys, Dione, Rhea, Titan, Hyperion, Iapetus and Phoebe – fig. 21). Mimas, Enceladus, Tethys and Dione orbit as a near-rigid system, with commensurable orbits whose periods are in the ratio 6 : 4 : 3 : 2;[3] but Janus doesn't fit into the scheme. Hyperion and Iapetus likewise have orbits closely locked to Titan's; Rhea's orbit is subject to extensive perturbation by Titan; and, as mentioned before, Phoebe has a retrograde orbit and is probably a captured asteroid. (Phoebe is close to the plane of Saturn's orbit around the Sun, while the other moons are in the plane of the equator.[8]) The great advantage of the situation, from the viewpoint of future exploration and development, is that there will be frequent, *regular*, recurring opportunities for inter-moon journeys. Since Titan will be the base of such activities the situation would be complicated by a possible asteroid belt between Rhea and Titan;[18] but since the Pioneers didn't find the belt between Io and Amalthea, predicted on the same basis, all may be well.

Because of its distance and eccentric orbit, Phoebe probably doesn't keep the same face to Saturn. The other moons have captured rotations, although large areas of Rhea and Hyperion would see the planet rise and set, growing or shrinking, as they trace their elliptical paths around it. Unlike the Galilean satellites, Saturn's inner moons are small and their densities increase with distance from the planet (it remains to be seen whether Janus fits that pattern. Indeed, there are suggestions that the

1966 observations leading to the discovery of "Janus" might be interpreted as the discovery of several small satellites.[56]) In fact Mimas, Enceladus and Tethys have such high albedos and low densities that they may well consist entirely of ice; they have been described as "cosmic snowballs".

Rhea, Dione and Tethys are all brighter on the leading hemisphere than on the trailing side – an interesting comparison with Callisto. Still more interestingly, Iapetus is very much brighter on its *trailing* hemisphere; it appears to be mostly snow-covered, with one large patch of bare dark rock.[12] Perhaps in these moons we have more evidence of a final bombardment phase in the early formation of the Solar System: Rhea and Dione might have bright craters and ejecta (like Tycho on the Moon and Kuiper on Mercury), while perhaps Iapetus received a glancing impact which formed a dark mare and temporarily put its rotation out of Saturn-lock. In other words, has Iapetus been *turned round*?

When we come to Titan, however, again we have a world in every sense, a place fully entitled to be called a planet if it didn't happen to go around Saturn. It is larger than Mercury, and since 1948 it has been known that Titan has an atmosphere of methane. In the early 1950s, long before liquid-hydrogen technology, methane seemed to be the ideal reaction mass for nuclear-powered rockets and it was predicted that Saturn might be reached by Man before Jupiter, since refuelling facilities were guaranteed on Titan. It was also noted that Titan was orange-red, like Mars; and, if the temperature rose from the calculated $100°K$ to $200°K$, the atmosphere would be likely to escape into space.[8]

Well, continuing observation established that Titan's temperature *is* $200°K$, twice the predicted value, and the atmosphere *is* escaping rapidly. But it is escaping in the form of free hydrogen, which takes some explaining: perhaps it comes from the dissociation of methane and ammonia by sunlight with more complex hydrocarbons forming at the same time by photochemical action.[19] Io's torus-atmosphere suggests why the process hasn't gone to completion with all the hydrogen long since gone: it seems that Titan must maintain a hydrogen ring right around Saturn, at ten times the diameter of the ring system, and be constantly recapturing and recycling the atmosphere.[20] The high surface temperature can't be explained by carbon dioxide/water vapour greenhouse effect, because the atmosphere is still cold enough to freeze them out; but hydrogen greenhouse effect could account for them, if the atmosphere is highly opaque to infrared radiation.[21] Sure enough, it emerges that Titan's colour is due to clouds covering most of the surface;[22] *deep red* clouds, the familiar colour of the organic compounds synthesized from methane, ethane, ammonia and hydrogen sulphide by long-wavelength ultraviolet radiation, resembling organic matter from carbonaceous chondrites in composition, and Jupiter's red spots and Saturn's equator in colour.[5] Many artists have portrayed Saturn in a blue Titan sky since the first classic representation by Chesley Bonestell;[22] at the moment of writing Ed Buckley was the first (plate 15) to show Titan's sky as red.

Titan's atmosphere is much denser than Mars'; surface pressure may

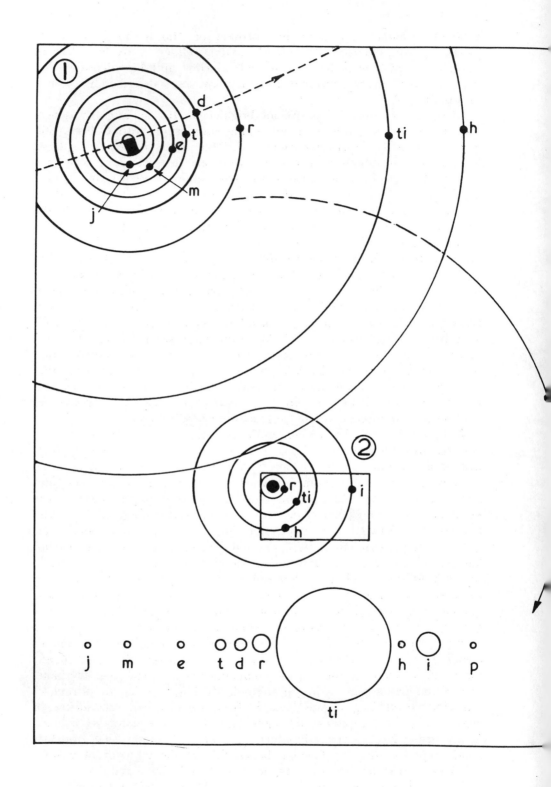

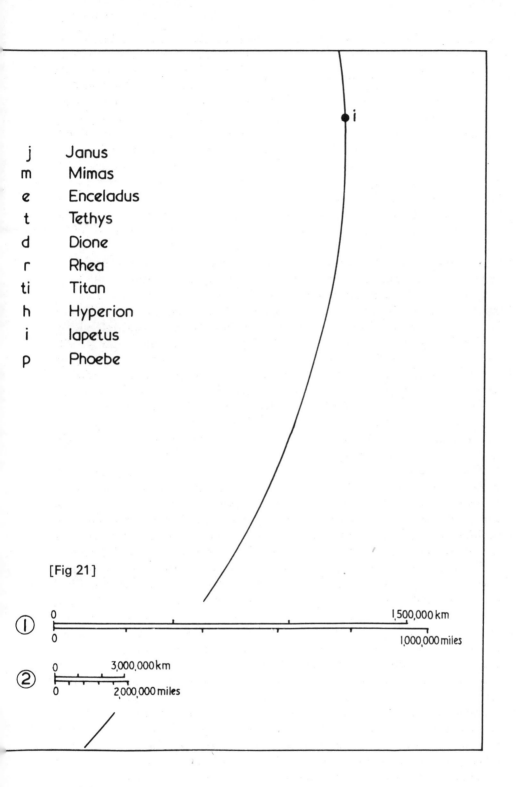

j	Janus
m	Mimas
e	Enceladus
t	Tethys
d	Dione
r	Rhea
ti	Titan
h	Hyperion
i	Iapetus
p	Phoebe

[Fig 21]

① 0 ——————— 1,500,000 km
0 ——————— 1,000,000 miles

② 0 —— 3,000,000 km
0 —— 2,000,000 miles

be nearly half Earth's. (Robert Shaw suggested that hot-air balloons may be a very effective transport system on Titan.) The 200°K temperature is only 10° below the coldest recorded on Earth. The general composition may be comet-like, with water, methane and ammonia ice in the interior;[23] the atmosphere is apparently rich in organic compounds, similar layers may be present on or/and below the surface, and the chemical factory of the *upper* atmosphere may have laid down tarry deposits in addition.[19] In short, the surface conditions of Titan are more like the primal Earth's than any other place in the known Solar System, and the chemistry exists for life to appear there. To evolve on the surface, it might have to use methane or ammonia as a "working fluid" rather than water.[24] But, if Titan has significant internal heat, life might evolve in underground lakes or volcanic springs and develop ways to withstand the surface cold – e.g., using glycerine, as some terrestrial organisms do.[25]

It might seem at first that Titan's colour implies that there is no life to gobble up the "naturally" formed organic compounds. Studies of Titan during lunar occultations, however, suggest that the "chemical factory" may be really high up – 150km![26] But even more intriguing possibilities were raised by a NASA release announcing "a new kind of photo-synthesis". Bacteriorhodopsin, a reddish-purple compound, has a rôle similar to chlorophyll in converting solar energy to electrical energy and storing it in such compounds as ATP. Chlorophyll, termed by Kraft Ehricke "the basic solar-powered molecule of life",[27] marks the evolutionary transition from "planetogenic" life, feeding on chemical energy in the environment, to "astrogenic" life, nourished by the Sun. Just as chlorophyll makes Earth's landmasses green, bacteriorhodopsin could make a planet reddish-purple.

There is no evidence yet for volcanic activity on Titan – although Robert Shaw suggested that "ice volcanoes" releasing water vapour might provide an alternative source for the hydrogen escaping into the torus. Such activity might be chemically triggered, if for instance potassium or sodium-enriched dust came into contact with water. At nightfall, or during eclipse, no doubt the rising columns of vapour would freeze.

There is a hypothesis that volcanic outbreaks on the larger moons of Jupiter, Saturn, Uranus and Neptune might have created the "families" of short-period comets associated with the giant planets.[28] Beyond doubt, violent eruptions (like Krakatoa, for example) *could* expel enough rock and ice from a large moon into orbit around the Sun to make a comet; but whether such lumps would be expelled in one piece and in sufficient numbers to account for the short-period comets is a different question. The notion is very far from universal acceptance. Relatively minor volcanic activity, however, could cause interesting effects on Titan: for example, water-ice formations such as glaciers and cliffs might surround volcanoes in rings at respectful distances. Full-scale eruptions releasing lava would move the ice formations further out. On the cold stretches, other phenomena might arise: Ed Buckley suggested, for instance, that in Titan's atmosphere there would be time for very big hailstones to form and settle. At night, even with the greenhouse effect, there should be a considerable temperature drop – would there be ammonia rain? Oceans of methane have even been suggested, if surface pressures are high enough.[19] Given surface deposits of organic compounds, and occasional releases of liquid water or vapour, even odder features might accumulate – sugar mountains, for example. As Shakespeare said, "That is, hot ice and wondrous strange snow."

Until much more advanced propulsion systems are developed, all Saturn missions are likely to involve Jupiter. A minimum-energy (Hohmann) mission to Saturn would take six years,[29] but using Jupiter gravity assist it can take as little as three – as in the Voyager missions. On the other hand, using Jupiter flyby to *slow* the spacecraft would allow Saturn and Titan, in combination, to decelerate a minimum-energy probe into orbit around Saturn.[30] 1978 gave the first optimum launch window for such a mission, which would take seven years; the USA has no such plans, but the National Academy of Sciences has suggested a Mariner-Saturn orbiter for 1985.[31] Titan flyby would bring a probe into elliptical orbit around Saturn with a 200–400 day period, but successive Titan encounters could reduce it to 29 days or less.[30] Alternatively, the satellite could be shifted into an inclined orbit to look down on the rings. Using Jupiter and Saturn flyby, a minimum-energy probe could be placed in orbit around Uranus (see later); Jupiter *or* Saturn could slow a probe enough to allow Neptune capture. The 1978 "Grand Tour" launch window would have allowed a probe to scan Jupiter and Saturn, passing between the rings and the planet, then on to Uranus and finally to Neptune. That project was abandoned for lack of funds, but Voyager, although less sophisticated, could pull it off. We may hope so, since there seems no chance for a Pioneer Saturn–Uranus mission suggested for 1980.[31] Useful photographic studies of Saturn might also be made from a space probe orbiting Jupiter.[32]

In *Search the Solar System*, Strong suggests landing an automated observatory on Janus and firing instrumented sub-probes from there across the rings.[29] The proposal has a number of merits. Janus orbits precisely in the plane of the rings and the equator and is 160–480km in diameter; a unit landed even a few km north of the equator would be in a permanent position to launch probes into elliptical orbits skimming the rings on the inward leg, passing through the thinnest part of the Crepe Ring and skirting the underside of the rings on the return. The probes' orbital periods would be synchronized with Janus's to relay data to Earth.

An approach to Janus might be dangerous because of ring E, as already mentioned. (The northern hemisphere would almost certainly be selected, since small particles and dust tend to be depressed to the underside of the rings and swept out by sunlight pressure.[7]) The safest technique might be to position the spacecraft (partly or wholly by Titan braking) in equatorial orbit beyond ring E, then spiral inwards slowly using low thrust. It would take a long time to reach Janus and would not be suitable for manned missions but would mean that encounters with ring E particles would be at low relative velocities. If Saturn's rings are primal Solar System material, if they were never united into a solid differentiated body, then sample collection and analysis would be extremely important. Already the search for such samples has taken us to the Moon and lures us towards Deimos and Phobos; it may lead us from planet to planet, and finally to the halo of comets beyond, and even then curiosity may not be satisfied.

> *No man has seen it; nor the lensed eye*
> *That pin-points week by week the same patch of sky*
> *Records even a blur across its pupil; only*
> *The errantry of Saturn, the wry*
> *Retarding of Uranus, speak*
> *Of the pull beyond the pattern:–*
> *The unknown is shown*
> *Only by a bend in the known.*
>
> Norman Nicholson, "The Undiscovered Planet"

Once we pass Saturn, the colossal distances of the Solar System show themselves by the sudden falling off in our knowledge. Uranus, Neptune and Pluto remained undiscovered until the invention of the telescope; Neptune and Pluto might not be known yet but for Sir Isaac Newton and the mathematicians who followed him. Although Pluto's dimensions would class it with the inner planets, there are good reasons to include it in discussing the giant worlds and their satellites; and, as we shall see, there is a great deal of argument about what (if anything other than comets) circles the Sun beyond the orbit of Pluto.

Between Saturn and Uranus, in 1977, Charles Kowal, the discoverer of Jupiter satellites 13 and 14, found an object he named "Chiron". 160–640km across,[57] with a highly elliptical orbit,[58] it may be the first of a new asteroid belt or a stray which has been repositioned by multiple flybys. If the former, the orbit is *very* elliptical; if the latter, the diameter is astonishingly large. It was the second unexpected find in the outer System that spring and it suggests that a whole new bag of jigsaws is about to be spilled on the table before us.

Uranus and Neptune are both giant worlds, both greenish-blue in colour, both very cold in their outer atmospheres. It has been assumed for a considerable time that they, too, would have metal/rock cores overlaid with ices; but ammonia would be added to the ice layers. (Spectroscopy confirmed the presence of hydrogen and methane.) It shouldn't be too great a surprise by now that both Uranus and Neptune are instead hotter than they should be. Recent infrared studies have shown Uranus at 120°K and Neptune at 100°K, confirming earlier radio measurements.[33] Greenhouse effect may be part of the explanation, but tides raised by the retrograde satellite Triton may have a significant heating effect within Neptune.[12] Triton may be more massive than Ganymede and larger than Titan;[26] like Titan it has an atmosphere of methane.

Now that our models of Jupiter and Saturn have been completely revised, however, it would take a brave man to predict that there are no hotter layers within Uranus and Neptune. Both planets are too far away to show much surface detail; but both rotate rapidly, and Uranus has a definite equatorial zone and dark belts. Furthermore, Uranus varies enough in overall bightness to indicate as much activity as Saturn has.[34] Well, it seems that Saturn has high internal temperatures, and its activity is similar to Jupiter's, which seems to be almost entirely convective . . .

Uranus' other similarity to Saturn brought it into the news in 1977, and made the Voyager 2 redirection a much higher priority. The dramatic story is told in *Sky & Telescope* for June 1977: briefly, NASA's Kuiper Airborne Observatory was over the Indian Ocean on March 10 to watch Uranus occult the star SAO 158687 in Libra. Before the event, however, and again after it, the star's brightness showed matching unexpected drops.[59] The observers had found five narrow rings of dark, chunky material orbiting Uranus in the equatorial plane; just as predicted by Ed Buckley four years before in his painting "Golgotha Moon" (plate 18). The rings Alpha to Delta are less than 10km wide and 1–2 thousand km apart; ring Epsilon (outermost) may be double. The discovery implies that the history of the Solar System can be read more easily in its outer reaches, and Voyager 2 can be there by 1986. Meanwhile still another major development has emerged: the accepted value since 1930 for Uranus's day is 50–100% too low,[60, 61] and the same may be true for Neptune. Their days are like the Earth's or Mars' rather than Jupiter's or Saturn's.

There is one respect, however, in which Uranus is wholly different from Saturn, Neptune and every other world in the Solar System. It has an axial tilt of 98°; or, if you prefer, a retrograde rotation and an axial tilt of 82°. In other words, Uranus rotates on its side: it is the only planet whose poles lie almost in the plane of its orbit, while its moons, orbiting in the plane of the equator, are describing a course which would be impossible anywhere else, even in polar orbit. As Uranus circles the Sun, with its poles always pointing to the same stars, the changes in illumination correspond to Earth's Midnight Sun and Arctic night – except that the full cycle takes 84 Earth years, and only the equatorial zone is unaffected. Meantime, the satellites remain in the plane of the equator, star-locked in inclination, with the same 84-year seasons superimposed on their synchronous rotation; spiralling around the planet's path in spring and autumn, arcing over and under it at midsummer and midwinter . . . and thereby hangs a tale.

The most favoured explanation for Uranus's axial tilt is that during its formation, one or more collisions were violent enough to lay the planet on its side.[35] Part of the problem seems to be that the event happened before the formation of the satellites, so the entire cloud of matter agglomerating around the planet would be turned over as well – not an easy event to envisage. Perhaps the moons are fragments of the colliding body, later drawn into precise equatorial orbits by the planet's rotational bulge. Whipple suggested that Uranus and Neptune might have been built of comets;[36] the hypothesis might be modified to allow at least one major collision between two accreting bodies, but it could also tie in with a more speculative suggestion.

Over the years, the SF magazine *Analog* (formerly *Astounding*) has produced many remarkable articles in its science-fact department; several have already been listed as references in this book. Some, notably those on giant meteor impacts, have advanced notions now far more acceptable than they were at the time. One which made a great impression on me was "The Problem of the Gyroscopic Earth", by Captain J. P. Kirton,[37] and, since I've never seen it mentioned elsewhere, it seems worth a paragraph or two here.

Kirton remarked that the plane of the ecliptic, and therefore of the Solar System as a whole, passes very close to the Galactic Centre in the sky at present. The coincidence is striking because the ecliptic and the Galactic Equator cut at a very large angle – i.e., the Solar System is revolving around the Galactic Centre on its side, as Uranus goes round the Sun, and the plane of the planetary orbits will cross the Galactic Centre only twice in a Galactic Year. As it happens, Man's awareness of the situation – which began only a few years ago, when the Sun's position in the Milky Way was finally determined – has come about during one of these short spells, little longer than Man's entire stay on Earth so far.

Of course, the alignment may be coincidental – "everyone's got to be somewhere". But, Kirton asked, what if the ecliptic plane is locked to the Galactic Centre and slews round with it during the Galactic Year (200 million Earth years)? Because of the gyroscopic effects of their rotations the planets' poles would continue to point in the same direction (or to precess around it, in the cases of Earth, Moon and Mars) while their axial tilts slowly changed by roughly half a degree in each million years. Thus we would see why Earth's last ice age cycle before the present one was 200 million years ago: we could only have icecaps when the Earth is near-upright in its orbit. The Sun's orbit around the Galactic Centre then has to be elliptical, so that the Solar System turns over through 360° once in every 400 million years instead of 200 million. (Since then we have learned that Mercury, with its elliptical orbit, turns *round* once in two of its years.)

If Venus was formed a Galactic Year earlier or later than the other planets, probably earlier, its retrograde rotation would have been in the prevailing direction of orbital motion at the time; 200 million years from now, Venus would be the only planet to spin "directly". The high argon content of Venus' atmosphere, according to Pioneer Venus 2, might be confirmation that the planet formed well before Earth. Uranus would then have been formed 100 million years earlier or later than the rest – probably later – and 100 million years from now Uranus would be upright while the other planets lie on their sides.

To that we can now add that, if Uranus and Neptune were built up out of comets, after the rest of the Solar System had taken shape, then Uranus might well be 100 or 300 million years younger than the inner worlds and Neptune 400 or 800 million, because of the enormous volume of space to be swept out and the very long orbital periods of comets. The formation of Neptune could therefore coincide with the final bombardment phase in the history of the inner planets. Coincidence – or the effect of a new perturbing body in the outer System? If the Moon were formed out of meteor-type planetesimals' rocky crusts, torn off as they passed by the Earth (see Chapter 4), then the analogous effect on comets (if they have rocky cores – see Chapter 8) would be to tear off the ice and redirect the rock – much of it sunward. Rocky pieces left over from Uranus' formation could likewise be redirected in Neptune flybys. The notion may gain some support from the discovery of thin rings – possibly debris torn from passing planetesimals – orbiting Uranus.

All this is pure speculation, unless any mechanism can be suggested to account for the Solar System's turning over. Kirton himself suggested that the gravitational differential of the Galactic Centre across the width of the Solar System might be enough to slew the orbital planes around. A. E. Roy was sufficiently interested to calculate the effect, but informed ASTRA that the galactic pull was insufficient to explain the plane change required. Since then, however, serious work has been done on the possibility that the Solar System may have one or more planets beyond Pluto. Joseph L. Brady has suggested that a massive tenth planet may exist 10,000 million kilometres from the Sun, in a highly inclined orbit. The notion has not gained acceptance – a major objection being that such a planet would cause the whole plane of the Solar System to turn over! On the characteristics given by Brady, indeed (inclination to the Ecliptic 120°, longitude of descending node 295°.75[38]) it seems that Poseidon (as it has unofficially become known) should cut the ecliptic quite close to the Galactic Centre, once every 464 years.

It would be very interesting if more precise calculations of Poseidon's orbit moved the descending node (one of the two points where it crosses the ecliptic) nearer to the Galactic Centre. If Poseidon reinforces the Centre's pull every 464 years, Kirton's hypothesis would have to be taken seriously. But, on the other hand, if *Poseidon's* orbital plane is the one locked to the Galactic Centre, and the rest of the Solar System follows it in a precessional cycle, and the Sun's galactic orbit *is* elliptical, then as the Sun goes through its galactic pericentron the Poseidon node would drift away from the Galactic Centre, and the ecliptic would approach it. The limit of the rock might be the present situation. In other words, the node may now be as far from the Galactic Centre as it can get, in the sky, and the Sun may be physically at its nearest to the Galactic Centre. If so, estimates of the mass of the Milky Way from the Sun's current velocity may be too large, if they assume that the Sun is in circular orbit at the present distance. The difference might be large enough to account for at least some of the "missing mass" of the Galaxy which some astrophysicists think is located in "black holes".

Still another consequence of the hypothesis would be that Poseidon would be the eldest of the planets, apart perhaps from Mercury; but we have seen that Mercury may originally have been a moon of Venus, and therefore contemporary with it in origin (Chapter 7). Perhaps, then,

Poseidon's retrograde, highly inclined orbit indicates that it was captured from another star, or more probably that it was a "stray" world which happened to fall into orbit around the new, condensing, Sun. (Several astronomers have suggested that stray planets, ranging in size up to near-stellar masses, may be very common in the Galaxy.[39]) We would then have to ask how such a body, orbiting on the fringe of the condensing disk of protoplanetary material, would affect the initial formation of the "natural" planets. Could we have a dynamic explanation for Bode's Law at last, in terms of resonances between the Sun's gravity and Poseidon's? Neptune and Pluto don't fit simply into Bode's Law; but Harper has pointed out that they are correctly placed if for some reason the outer planets of the system fit Bode's Law at *half*-intervals.[40]

There have been several astronomical speculations earlier in this book – carbonaceous dust on Mars, recent Venus impacts (me), Sun-synchronous Vulcan (Robert Shaw), ice caps on cylindrical fragments in Saturn's rings (James Campbell). The association of the tenth planet with the Kirton Hypothesis is the biggest one to date – at least comparable with Lawton's hypothesis in Chaper 12 – and is worth summarizing in hopes that someone will follow it up. The suggestion is that the tenth planet exists and its orbital plane is locked to the Galactic Centre, turning over once in 400 million years, with the rest of the Solar System precessing behind; that the Sun is now at Galactic pericentron; and that the tenth planet may be a "stray" captured early in the history of the Sun. The consequences would be as follows: (1) the retrograde rotation of Venus would be explained; (2) the 98° tilt of Uranus and its moons would be explained; (3) the final bombardment of the inner planets would coincide with the formation of Neptune; (4) the 200-million year "break" between ice-age cycles would be explained without recourse to cosmic dust or changes in the Sun; (5) the "missing mass" of the Galaxy would be accounted for without invoking "black holes" or other invisible entities; and (6) the Bode's Law distribution of the planetary orbits could be explained in terms of resonance between the tenth planet's pull and the Sun's. The case against the tenth planet's existence is summarized by Anthony Lawton in Chapter 12. A probe mission to Neptune, and telescopic studies of Pluto over the next few years, could provide supporting evidence for his hypothesis and/or mine.

Following detailed studies of a possible Mariner Jupiter–Uranus space-craft, launched in 1979 to arrive in 1986,[35] NASA applied for funds for

14: The new look of Saturn. Even before the 1979 Pioneer II flyby our ideas about Saturn were changing. Titan, the largest moon in the Solar System, is now known to be extensively covered by red clouds—possibly organic compounds. *(Painting by Ed Buckley.)*

the mission. There would be a possibility of extending the flight to a Neptune flyby, since the outer planets would then be in the Grand Tour configuration. "Start funding" was refused, however, even when the launch date was put back to 1981. If Voyager 2 opts for a close look at the planet in 1986, only one of the moons can be studied close up in addition. If the Neptune option is chosen, that encounter would be in 1990.[50] With a flyby of Jupiter *and* Saturn, it would be possible to place a minimum-energy space probe in orbit around Uranus by means of a capture encounter with Titania, the fourth satellite.[30] The flight would take more than twenty-six years just to get into orbit, however, so the Uranus orbiter is likely to wait until we have the launchers for a faster outward journey and a retrofire.

Relatively little has been said so far about Pluto, partly because so little is known and partly because it is still − just − the outermost world of the Solar System. But Pluto's orbit is so elliptical that it comes nearer the Sun than Neptune, and from 1979 to 1999 Neptune will in fact be the outermost known planet.[29] Because of Triton's retrograde orbit around Neptune, and Nereid's highly eccentric one, it is often suggested that Pluto could be a moon which escaped from Neptune altogether. At present Pluto's orbit is so inclined that there is no chance of an encounter with Neptune, but, tracing back its path, taking account of perturbations by other planets, it seems that they could have met in the past.[41] One of the few things we know about Pluto is its day, 6.38737 Earth days[42] − an odd figure, quite unlike the rotational period of any other known planet, but quite reasonable for a former satellite with a trapped rotation. Triton's situation, on the other hand, is drastic − the orbit is decaying due to tidal interaction and in a few million years the moon will disintegrate.[51] How long has that been going on?

In 1973 Pluto's axial tilt was found to be 50°, relative to the orbital plane.[1] The tilt relative to the ecliptic is therefore 67° or 33°, depending on the orientation of the axis; 33° would be appropriate for a satellite orbiting Neptune with a 4° inclination to the equator. Pluto may therefore have been expelled from Neptune by an encounter with Triton. A current value of 67° still suits the argument, since a Triton slingshot could have given Pluto's axis a large precession. Furthermore, Pluto and Triton have very similar orbital inclinations to the ecliptic, differing by at most 3.5°.[40] It seems, then, that either Triton and Pluto were twin moons which perturbed one another up to a final slingshot separation, or Triton was originally a planet in its own right, but encountered Neptune

15: The new look of Titan. Saturn in Titan's blue or sometimes green sky has been a favourite subject for artists since Titan's atmosphere was discovered. The true colour, however, is now known to be red. Surface atmosphere pressure may be half Earth's, with mean temperature about Earth's coldest. *(Painting by Ed Buckley.)*

and hurled Pluto away – being swung round itself, in the encounter, into a retrograde orbit still closer to the planet than Pluto's had been. The highly eccentric orbit of Nereid, the outer moon, may testify to these dramatic events – or Nereid may be a captured asteroid.[29]

But where did Triton come from, if independent? In *Search for Solar System* Strong has it "spiralling inwards" – strange behaviour, not noted in any of the other planets. There's no reason to think that Triton evolved naturally in an orbit crossing Neptune's, and, furthermore, the encounter took place far enough into the System's history for Neptune to have captured Pluto's rotation. Is it possible, then, that Triton is another stray planet, snatched from another passing system or a wanderer in interstellar space already – perhaps older than all the rest of the Solar System, depending on the reality and age of Poseidon? Alternatively, it might be a really distant member of our own Solar System and have been turned inwards by encounter with some other star. Whatever its origin, Triton seems a high-priority candidate for scientific investigation. If Voyager 2 reaches Neptune or Mariner Jupiter–Uranus flies, and is redirected to Neptune after the Uranus encounter, every effort should be made to photograph Triton during the Neptune flyby.

At any rate, it seems fair to discuss Pluto in the giant worlds chapter because it was possibly a satellite of Neptune at birth. Because of its great distance, Pluto is just about the least known and most mysterious body in the Solar System, and (once again) what we think we know is contradictory. It will be interesting to see whether any of the problems can be cleared up in 1987, when Pluto will be at perihelion and 26 million km nearer the Sun than Neptune.

Pluto's diameter is extremely uncertain. Estimates vary from 4,100km up to 6,000km.[9] The problem may be partly due to a low albedo, but even that is uncertain. *Prima facie* one would expect Pluto to have a high albedo, since it is large enough to have held an atmosphere like Triton's, and with Pluto's transfer to the *outer* reaches all gases except neon would have frozen, since the mean temperature is $43°$ K. If the atmospheric pressure were high enough, neon oceans could exist during most of Pluto's year, evaporating near perihelion; but surface pressure would have to be three times as high as Earth's, and there are no indications that Pluto has such a dense atmosphere.[43] But Kitt Peak observatory studies have located frozen methane, at temperatures below $225°C$, and suggest that Pluto may be brighter than had been supposed.[52]

Pluto was discovered in 1930, after its existence had been predicted (like Neptune's in the 19th century) by analysis of the observed perturbations experienced by Uranus. Lowell predicted that "planet P" would lie 6,400 million kilometres from the Sun and have six times the mass of the Earth; Pluto's mean distance from the Sun is 5,866,000,000km, but, with the supposed mass, even a 5,760km diameter would give it fifty times the density of water and a surface gravity of 17g![44]

No ordinary material known to science could give Pluto so high a density. A core of "condensed matter" – nuclei stripped of their electrons and packed together, as in white dwarf stars – might provide a solution, but could it be contained against electrostatic repulsion, by a total mass only six times that of the Earth's? There is no evidence that even Jupiter contains condensed matter; Pioneer 10 data indicate the contrary, that density increases smoothly to the centre.

A more plausible explanation might be that Pluto is mostly covered with some smooth liquid or ice, probably methane, which reflects the Sun and causes the planet's diameter to be underestimated. A dramatic painting on this theme by Mel Hunter appears in Alan E. Nourse's book *Nine Planets*.[45] The ASTRA discussions turned up a number of variations on that theme, particularly in relation to different versions of A. T. Lawton's dust hypothesis (Chapter 12). My own favourite was a still, clear methane ocean, with a dark layer of dust over deep layers of ices on its floor. Ammonia and (presumably) methane-ice would sink.[47] But while Pluto obstinately declines to occult a star and give a firm value for its diameter,[48] each near miss brings down the possible maximum figure. Pluto cannot be bigger than Mercury, perhaps no bigger than our Moon, and cannot apparently be the source of the "planet P" perturbations. But, most strangely, it is now reported that Pluto may be smaller still and have a moon a third of its own size. Is that the source for the measured "rotation"? And if so how did such a situation arise? It seems incompatible with the notion that Pluto was a moon of Neptune – satellites of satellites crash.[53] Perhaps Pluto was the core of a third planetesimal which lost its crust in a Neptune flyby between Roche Limits, and Triton embodies that crustal material. If so, Pluto should be a relatively dense world – though not, thank God, fifty times as dense as water!

Neptune, the outermost world for the next few years (as far as we know) is beginning to yield up a secret or two of its own. For some years it has been alleged that Neptune showed no markings or activity, and Uranus and Neptune were studied for variations which would indicate changes in the Sun. At last Neptune underwent a brightness change not shared by Uranus and it had to be admitted that there was a high-altitude cloud layer – possibly frozen methane or argon.[60]

As to what may lie beyond Neptune and Pluto, we are literally in the dark. Harper has suggested that the perturbations attributed first to Pluto, then to a tenth planet, may actually be caused by a huge ring of asteroids, totalling up to 26 times the mass of Jupiter, orbiting from 100AU outwards between the planets and the main cometary halo 30,000–50,000AU from the Sun.[40] (The effect of such a belt would be to advance the perihelion of a body orbiting within it, like the relativistic effect of Mercury's motion[49] – which at one time was attributed to the perturbing influence of a hypothetical planet, Vulcan.) Perhaps the Harper asteroids and the cometary halo might be the result of a fractionating process, within a shell of material captured by the Sun after a nearby supernova – see Chapter 12's appendix. Pending missions into interstellar space, such as the Daedalus probes mentioned in Chapter 6, our best indications about conditions "out there" come from visiting comets and once again, thanks to artificial satellites and manned observations from Skylab, the whole picture has changed in recent years.

11　The Comets and the Outer System

There are as many comets in the heavens as there are fish in the sea.

Johannes Kepler

When beggars die, then are no comets seen:
The heavens themselves blaze forth the death of princes.

William Shakespeare

The known members of the outer Solar System, the comets, have been mentioned repeatedly in earlier chapters because of their intrusions, not just across the orbits of the outer worlds but into the inner System and up to the face of the Sun itself. Indeed, since we are unable to track comets far beyond the orbit of Jupiter, and usually they are among the inner worlds before they are detected, there might seem to be a case for including them among the resources of the *inner* System; the Soviet astronomer Vsekhsvyatskiy has argued that such classification would reflect the true state of affairs.[1]

Vsekhsvyatskiy's argument (which, it must be emphasized, is at odds with the generally accepted view) is that comets are the result of violent volcanic eruptions on the moons of the giant planets. It is a well-known fact that the better known comets occur in planetary "families", with their aphelion distances grouped around the orbits of the giant worlds. Thus their orbital periods are relatively short and their reappearances can be predicted – Halley's Comet, recorded at 76-year intervals throughout the Christian era, being the most famous example. Comets not "belonging" to any planet, such as Comet Kohoutek, have much longer orbital periods ranging into millions of years. Kohoutek's period was a strangely short 75,000 years – of which more anon.

The general view at present was first put forward by Oort, that there is a cloud of 100 billion or more comets orbiting the Sun in a "halo" with perihelion distances at 100,000–150,000AU, "close to the boundary region where the domain dominated by solar gravity gives way to the gravitational realm of other nearby stars".[2] (100,000AU approximately equals 1.66 light-years. The nearest known star, Proxima Centauri, is 4.2 light-years away. Proxima is a red dwarf companion of Alpha Centauri, itself a double star, at 4.3 light-years). The origin of the cloud is controversial: Oort himself thought that comets were fragments of the original "asteroid planet" which, after its disruption, had been thrown by

Jupiter flyby into highly elliptical orbits.[2] Since it now seems unlikely that there ever was an asteroid planet, the general view is that comets formed at their present distances, perhaps at the very beginning of the Solar System, and the influence of passing stars has thrown some of them into elliptical orbits; a few of these comets, again, have been "captured" by the giant planets and form the present "families".

Vsekhsvyatskiy maintains that it is reasonable to suppose that the "families" are the main body of comets, that those with very long periods are the result of slingshots, and that no outer System "halo" exists. Part of his argument is that, if the boundaries of the System lie at 100,000–150,000AU, they should be grazed by another star on average once every 25,000–110,000 years. Up to 10,000 such approaches might have occurred during the history of the Solar System, and on that basis a halo of comets should not survive more than a few hundred million years. The argument loses its force if the comet halo is younger than the rest of the System, however, and we have already suggested that they and Harper's postulated asteroids[3] belong to a fractionated cloud of supernova material captured by the Sun. Fernie,[4] and Hughes and Routledge,[5] have argued on different grounds that the Sun is located within an expanding cloud of dust and gas from a supernova which occurred about 1,000 parsecs (3,260 light years) from us, 30–90 million years ago.

The make-up of comets has already been discussed in general terms. When first observed a comet is usually only a small disk, resembling an asteroid. As it approaches the Sun a fuzzy cloud known as the "coma" surrounds the nucleus, and under the pressure of the Solar Wind one or more "tails" are then driven out from the comet, away from the Sun. The head of a comet (nucleus and coma) can expand to more than the volume of the Earth, while tails can grow to many million km in length and often take on a curved, scimitar-like shape owing to the different orbital speeds of the particles. It isn't always realized by illustrators that a comet's tail *always* streams away from the Sun, and therefore comets recede from the Sun tail-first. Some comets also produce an "antitail", a bright spike projecting sunwards. Comet Arend-Roland (1957 III), one of the last bright comets to be well seen from the British Isles, was an example, while Kohoutek was another. It seems that "antitails" may be made up of particles too large to be driven back by radiation pressure breaking away from the nucleus into independent orbits around the Sun – perhaps a source for meteor showers.[6]*

The composition of comets had been described by Whipple as "dirty ice", since the meteor showers associated with comets showed that they contained solid matter – even if it was mostly in the form of dust. Dust was found to be escaping in large quantities from Comet Arend-Roland in 1957, and was observed in the tail of Wilson-Hubbard (1961 V). Comet Seki-lines (1962 III) produced a split tail indicating a sudden outburst of dust near perihelion;[8] Kohoutek also showed fine dust in the

---

*I was rather pleased about that suggestion, since it ties in with the description of a comet's head in a story I called "The Comet, the Cairn and the Capsule", published (slightly altered) in 1972.[7]

tail, and three of these comets had larger, heavier dust particles in their sunward "spikes".[1] Spectroscopy showed that the main component of comets had to be water ice, subliming from the nuclei and dissociated by sunlight into hydrogen and hydroxyl (OH) ions. Satellite studies of Comets Tago-Sato-Kosaka (1969-g) and Bennett (1969-i) revealed huge hydrogen atmospheres;[9] Tago-Sato-Kosaka's was as large as the Sun, according to OAO-2, but OGO-V found that the Bennett halo was 13 million km across![10] Until then the gas production of comets had been drastically underestimated; now the comets had to consist primarily of ice. "Deabsorption" of gases from porous rock, the process depicted by Arthur C. Clarke in "Into the Comet",[11] would be far too slow to explain the observed emissions.

Although the "dirty ice" model is still in circulation – e.g., as an explanation for the absence of impact craters after the Tunguz explosion of 1908[12] – there are nevertheless arguments that comets have solid interiors. We have already mentioned the idea that the "Earth-grazing" asteroids are the nuclei of "dead" comets (Chapter 12);[13] sightings of "star-like objects" in nuclei support the hypothesis.[14] Comet Pereira (1963 V) passed the Sun at only 20,000km, passing through the inner corona and grazing the chromosphere; almost all gases were driven off, but the comet remained intact,[1] although some have split up near the Sun or disappeared entirely.[12] Wilson-Harrington, discussed in Chapter 12, may well have been a comet surrendering the last of its gases and joining the Earth-grazing asteroid class.

Evidence of complex surface chemistry is building up. A variety of compounds of carbon, oxygen, nitrogen and hydrogen have been detected in molecular form in the heads of comets, and as ions in the tails.[13] Presumably methane, ammonia and carbon dioxide are all present in the mixed ices of the cometary nuclei; but, in addition, ions of sodium, calcium, chromium, cobalt, iron, nickel, manganese, copper and vanadium have been observed in comets near the Sun. Comet Ikeya-Saki (1965-f), another "non-event" as far as British observers were concerned, was an example.[1] Kohoutek's comet provided the first direct spectral evidence of the presence of water, and radio studies identified the compounds hydrogen cyanide and methyl cyanide;[15] helium was found in Kohoutek's tail by Mariner 10.[16] Over the next few years, the list of compounds detected in comets may grow as steadily as the tally of organic molecules found in interstellar space.

In general, the evolution of a comet's appearance as it swings around the Sun is very hard to predict. Comet Kohoutek is an outstanding example: detected relatively far from the Sun, and therefore expected to become a spectacular object in the skies, it completely failed to develop the expected brilliance. Even if the weather in January 1974 had been better, the comet could not have been seen from ground level in the UK without binoculars or a telescope. The Skylab astronauts had a far better view in space, and Sky and Telescope for October 1974 featured detailed drawings by Edward Gibson of the changes in the comet's appearance. From above the atmosphere, Kohoutek's colour was bright yellow and, after it passed perihelion, with the sunward spike rapidly fading from view, it took on the appearance of an expanding high-altitude rocket exhaust. The colour faded gradually to white and became whitish-violet.[17] There seemed to be no detail within the coma apart from the faint blur of the nucleus – as compared with, say, Comet Bennett, which had a brilliant nucleus surrounded by spikes like the star on a Christmas tree. The biggest surprise about Kohoutek was that, although brightness flared up at perihelion, much less gas was released than had been predicted; most of the comet's glow was sunlight reflected by dust.[12] This is a case of an unexpectedly *small* change in brilliance, whereas comets are often subject to sharp increases or decreases in brightness. Various models have been put forward to account for such rapid changes: speaking at an ASTRA lecture in Hamilton, A. T. Lawton introduced us to "Rudge's flat comets", which were supposed to have taken up the form of rapidly spinning disks (by conservation of angular momentum) in the final stage of contraction. Another suggestion is that comets are loosely compacted from clouds of billions of small particles, coated with interstellar "frost".[18] (The presence of ice crystals in interstellar space has been established for many years.[19]) Surface deposits of frozen gases would be used up quickly near perihelion, but would have been replenished by the next time the comet approached the Sun.

Harper, who has suggested the existence of a massive asteroid belt 30–50,000AU from the Sun,[3] has a similar explanation for Kohoutek's non-brilliance. In his view Kohoutek, with its unusual mean distance of 1,800AU from the Sun, was such an asteroid, overlaid with dust and ice, pushed sunwards by a slingshot encounter. Most of the ice was driven off at an early stage, hence Kohoutek's unusual brightness when first detected; as the body drew closer to the Sun its brightness became more and more dependent on dust dislodged by radiation pressure and electro-static forces.[12] Thus, the difference between Harper asteroids and Oort comets would lie only in the proportions of rock and ice in their makeup.

It is often suggested that the comets represent the earliest solid matter of the Solar System, too far from the Sun and too widely dispersed to have coalesced into planets. F. L. Whipple suggested that "cometesimals" originally formed in great numbers beyond the orbit of Saturn and drew together to form Uranus and Neptune, while about 1% of survivors were thrown into long-period elliptical orbits and now form the Oort cloud.[20] Other astronomers believe that comets are far more numerous and follow more or less circular orbits in the outer reaches, with only occasional "casualties" plunging towards the Sun as a result of slingshot encounters.[21] But, attractive as it is to suppose that these flimsy, beautiful visitors are the outer rings of the material from which the Sun and planets are made, there is the persistent problem of passing stars. However many comets there are, how could they have survived out there for so long? Without interruptions other than chance encounters among themselves, 23% of them would have been hurled out of the System altogether or sent sunwards to eventual death.[21] 10,000 passing stars should surely have wreaked havoc with the remainder.

On the other hand, the evidence is clear that comets *do* belong to the Solar System. To date there is not one established case of a comet entering the System with hyperbolic velocity, which would prove that it had come from some other star or from interstellar space. Nor do cometary approaches show any bias towards the direction of the Sun's Way[21]. Several astronomers have been led to suggest, therefore, that comets are formed – continuously or intermittently – out of interstellar matter captured by the Sun. Interstellar dust has been blamed for variations in climate on Earth; if the Sun passes through a cloud of dust and ice, just how much activity does it stir up and how much matter does it trail away with it? It is expected that the Solar Wind will make a shockwave with interstellar gas at around 100AU[22] – how far to either side will that spread, and how will it affect floating dust and ice crystals already being stirred by the Sun's gravitational field? The gravitational tug is itself far from insignificant: even at 126,000AU, with an orbital period of 45 million years, a captured particle would be moving at 0.083km per second, more than 290kph.[23]

In the 1950s R. A. Lyttleton suggested an interesting model for comets: they might be clouds of interstellar dust, loosely held together by gravitational attraction but as fluid as the "dust-oceans" once thought of as a danger to spaceships on the Moon. We know that dust particles which escape from comets take up their own closely similar orbits, but Lyttleton argued that the condition was permanent: every grain in the shifting mass was in its own elliptical orbit around the Sun, and near perihelion they collided with enough violence to turn the mass incandescent.[24] Kohoutek could well have fitted the description, but most comets must contain a great deal of ice as well as dust and should therefore be well glued together. Furthermore, it has been shown that dust grains orbiting a star can glue themselves together into planetesimals relatively rapidly, over mere thousands of years;[25] most of the heavier elements in interstellar space are already locked up in such grains.[26]

In the appendix to Chapter 12 it will be suggested that the Sun is in fact ploughing into a cloud of interstellar dust, leaving a clear lane behind it. It is therefore possible that we are currently in a "comet-building" phase, with a disk of material surrounding the Solar System in the plane of the Ecliptic. By a fractionating process, like that of the primeval Solar System, ices may be concentrating in the outermost reaches and more dusty bodies forming closer to us. Whether there has been time for comets and asteroids to form in large numbers, whether the larger bodies will be differentiated, and whether their cores will be sufficiently impacted to hold together in due course as Earth-grazing asteroids, are questions which might in principle be settled mathematically; but the importance of the topic is quite enough to justify spaceprobe missions to the comets.

The elliptical orbits of the comets make them difficult targets for space missions, unless all that is wanted is a flyby at high relative speed. One early proposal from the NASA Office of Space Study was for a Cometary Explorer to be launched in 1976.[27] The spacecraft would have met Comet Grigg-Skjellerup in 1977 and been retargeted to encounter Comet

Giacobini-Zinner in 1979. Another option not adopted was a Pioneer mission in 1977 taking in two asteroids and Comet Forbes.[28] Despite higher costs in energy terms, most attention has been concentrated on a possible mission to Comet Encke, the shortest-period comet known as of 1972.[9] In 1980 Comet Encke could be observed at perihelion by a Helios spacecraft, launched by Titan III, and a second encounter would be possible in 1984 near minimum solar activity. That one is still on the National Academy of Sciences' list of possibilities, as is a rendezvous mission in 1982.[29]

The most important single fact required from a comet mission is the diameter of the nucleus.[13] That alone will be of great value in choosing between conflicting models, and the more photographic detail obtained the better. Unfortunately, current models of Explorer and Helios spacecraft do not carry cameras and modification would be costly: for the 1976 Explorer mission a Pioneer-type sensor was envisaged.[27] Helios and the Explorer IMP series (Interplanetary Monitoring Platforms) are otherwise well equipped to study the comet's bow shock, plasma turbulence behind it and the ionized tail (a two-probe mission would be ideal).[30] It is important to compare the plasma activity around the comet with the Earth's "magnetosheath", for whose mapping the IMP spacecraft take much of the credit. Helios spacecraft, of course, are specifically designed for exploration near the Sun; Encke has the closest known short-period perihelion, at 0.34AU.

Rendezvous with a comet is likely to involve solar-electric propulsion (ion-drive). Low-thrust ion-drives, in which the reaction mass is propelled from the ship by electric fields instead of chemical energy, have been on the drawing-board for many years and have been tested in Earth orbit, but have still to be tried on long space missions. They are likely to be used extensively in unmanned exploration – e.g., for out-of-the-Ecliptic missions, or the Janus landing discussed in Chapter 10 – but, because of the very low accelerations and long journey times they produce, their role in manned spaceflight is more uncertain. For unmanned approaches to comets, with a high collision risk from dust particles and bigger lumps, perhaps, ion-drive is well suited – apart from the electrical interference with plasma studies! The pull of the nucleus itself is expected to be trivial and the lander will probably harpoon the nucleus and winch itself down. At least on that approach, if the nucleus is a boiling dust cloud on the Lyttleton model, the harpoon will not hold and the lander will not vanish from view. Jets of gas have been observed from nuclei at angles to the Sun-comet line, however, implying nucleus rotation,[22] so many of the Chapter 8 problems with asteroid landings will recur.

Most missions to short-period comets, however, are frankly described as rehearsals. The biggest comet which we *know* is due back is Halley's in 1986. "Wherefore if it should return according to our prediction about the year 1758, impartial posterity will not refuse to acknowledge that this was first discovered by an Englishman." There is a particular mystique about Halley's Comet, partly because its 76-year period lets few people see it more than once in a lifetime, partly because of its association with the Norman Conquest and the Bayeux Tapestry, partly because for many people it represents the mysterious predictive powers of science. It will be a demanding mission : to get a probe to it required a launch in 1978 and then a Jupiter flyby in 1979, to be in the right plane to meet the comet respectfully in 1985 and ride with it through perihelion in 1986.[30] ("Respectfully" is a key word : it is to be hoped that the Test Ban Treaty will be forcefully invoked if there are any more suggestions to use a nuclear weapon on the nucleus.[31]) No funding emerged for such a mission, however, so instead of escorting the comet through perihelion it may be possible to spend only a few minutes near the nucleus in a high-speed flyby. For a more prolonged encounter the Jupiter flyby is virtually essential, because Halley's Comet is retrograde.

In 1977, however, NASA was engaged in design studies for a Halley mission. Considerable publicity was given to solar-sail designs being considered, but NASA has now decided to opt for the better tried technology of the ion-drive.

If all else fails, there will be another opportunity in 2062 or there-abouts. There may well have been bigger comets in the meantime, although whether they can be detected in time for rendezvous missions from Earth is another matter. A comet from the outer reaches might be more valuable, after all, in being less damaged by frequent battles with the Sun. (In 1910, Halley's Comet was suspected of being dimmer than of old.) The most valuable information, the surface deposits spelling out what's happening in the outer system, may be long gone from Halley by now. By the early years of next century there may be ships permanently fuelled and waiting – probably unmanned, in view of the punitive accelerations involved – to scramble for that record, from some rare bird on its first visit, before the Sun wipes it away.

PART IV
Now where do we stand?

12 Beyond Pluto

A. T. LAWTON, FRAS, FBIS

Who lights the heavens with glittering starlight,
Who sets the Sun ablaze on high?
In fiery radiance, he rises and greets us,
And goes his way a victor bold.
And goes his way, a victor bold.

Beethoven, Creation's Hymn

If we ask "Are there planets beyond Pluto?" at present we must answer, "Probably not, but we don't really know", in spite of a false alarm in 1972 by Brady, who, when investigating the orbit of Halley's Comet in order to provide accurate predictions of its expected return in 1986, announced that cyclic residuals in the orbit could be attributed to a massive planet moving in a retrograde orbit inclined at an angle of 60° to the ecliptic. The period of the orbit was estimated at 464 years, and the mean distance from the Sun as 63.5AU, or 9,400 million km. The planet was estimated as 85% of the mass of Jupiter and was therefore a gas giant, possibly the first of another series out to about 200AU or 30,000 million km. There were hints of such possibilities since there were traces of further cyclic residuals suggesting yet another planet with a period of about 1,000 years and therefore a mean distance of some 90AU. Alas, these predictions have proved false. The area quoted by Brady was carefully photographed and checked by Dewhirst of Cambridge with negative results. Goldred and Ward showed that, if such a planet existed, then the whole plane of rotation of the Solar System would precess (tilt) by a measurable amount, and, since no such precession is observed, it seemed unlikely that the planet existed.* The "coup de grace" was delivered by Kiang who was able to prove that the undoubted cyclic residual discovered by Brady was due to the combined perturbing effects of the Sun, Jupiter and Halley's Comet itself. Since the mass of the latter is minute compared to the other bodies, it is cyclically tweaked every 270 years first one way then the other, giving a pseudo 550-year orbital period with all the appearances of being caused by a massive

---

*Or does it? (see Chapter 10). As for visibility – a gas giant without ammonia clouds (frozen out) would be dark, even before dust infall is considered . . . DL.

planet. Brady agreed with these conclusions and the present consensus in that, if there are any planets beyond Pluto, they are very small indeed.

The key questions then are really: "What is the dominant force through the vast regions beyond Pluto, how far does it extend, and what does it control?" Apart from their astronomical importance, I hope to show that the answers point to a future for technological civilization, different from those postulated by Dyson, Kardashev and others. Professor Nikolai Kardashev has argued that technological civilizations can be classified under three primary headings: *Type 1* civilizations, which control the full resources of a planet, *Type 2* civilizations, which control the full resources of a solar system, and *Type 3* civilizations, which control the full resources of a galaxy. (Our own Milky Way Galaxy contains about 150 thousand million suns, a significant number of which may possess planetary systems.) Professor Freeman Dyson has considered the evolution of Type 2 and Type 3 cultures in some detail (see below): his approach assumes that the evolutionary pressures are Malthusian, i.e., that the chief motivation is population growth.

In Chapter 5, A. F. Nimmo mentioned a model of population growth which assumed extensive interplanetary migration and a flow of food and mineral resources to Earth, first put forward by the physicist Gerard O'Neill. O'Neill suggests that the numbers of the human race could be stabilized at about twice the present level, with more than half the population living in "Space Habitats" – huge cylinders orbiting Earth at the distance of the Moon, each housing many millions of people. Although O'Neill's ideas have received a great deal of attention they are in effect a modified form of Dyson's plans, to which we would have to revert if population growth was *not* halted. The strength of constructional materials ultimately sets a limit to the dimensions of a hollow cylinder, whereas a hollow sphere can be made much larger – it can be internally reinforced and structured until it reaches the dimensions of the smaller satellites and largest asteroids, i.e., 800 to 1,000km in diameter.

Dyson has argued that the continued increase in population will eventually force us to dismantle the planets and build huge numbers of hollow asteroids, in order to use the available matter of the Solar System and the Sun's energy output as efficiently as possible. As already noted, however, the largest part of the planetary system's mass is tied up in the planet Jupiter, and by the time we have the capability to convert Jupiter into more useful materials and dismantle it, we can expect that the Moon, Venus, Mercury and Mars will have been extensively settled, exploited, and adapted into the best possible imitation of Earth-surface conditions. Such "terraforming" may save the inner planets from being dismantled because they will acquire large populations during the thousands of years it takes to pull Jupiter apart. It may not be worth the effort of evacuating them for the (relatively) small number of asteroids to be gained by dismantling them.

Even with all the inner planets made habitable, and Jupiter dismantled and reformed into pseudo Earth-like planets occupying suitable orbits without too much mutual interference, it is difficult to imagine the complex being able to support more than about 300 billion human beings. The reasons are not far to seek for the problem is one of ecological balance. A very simple calculation which equates the total amount of oxygen regenerated by the plant life on land and in the oceans *today* shows that the counterbalancing human population on Earth consuming that oxygen cannot and *must* not exceed 10 billion people. This calculation is optimistic, for it does not take into account the negating effects of urban development, of chemically propelled oxygen consuming vehicles and power systems, and of oceanic poisoning and pollution which kills off the plant life.

Using Jupiter's resources to build asteroids, as Dyson suggested, rather than worlds, would make more living space and raw materials available and allow more solar energy to be intercepted. Progressively smaller gains would come from the destruction of Saturn, Uranus, Neptune and finally the inner planets. The logical end to the process, suggested by Dyson in an earlier paper, is to reshape all the available matter into a thin shell completely enclosing the Sun – at which point the living area gained is enormous, the Sun's full output is trapped, but there are no raw materials left to work with! More seriously, detailed examination shows that a complete sphere would be unstable. The Solar System is basically thin and flat because this is a stable configuration. At the "poles" of a rotating mass, gravity wins and squashes downwards and inwards, whereas at the "equator" centrifugal force wins and pushes radially outwards. As a result the initial Dyson shell would be a band or belt extending about 25° above and below the plane of the Ecliptic, covering about 14% of a complete sphere – no more; and it would collapse after a few million years into an ecliptic pancake, forcing the inhabitants to flee from "home" long before – if they still had the means.

If we cannot or will not restrict our numbers large-scale emigration may be the only alternative to chaos and collapse. It may well be, however, that no habitable planets exist within a distance of at least 30 parsecs. Before the human population exceeds 300 billion and we have re-modelled the Solar System we almost certainly will have launched sophisticated unmanned probes to explore the possible systems of the nearest stars. Nevertheless the problems of human interstellar travel at present seem so difficult in terms of engineering technology, environmental preservation and human and material lifetimes that I think they may take longer to solve than remodelling our Solar System. It is not a question of blindly hopping over to Alpha Centauri or Barnard's Star in the hope of finding a planet and condemning (say) 2,000 top-quality specimens to certain death if you don't! Such colonization must be done on a basis of certainty – not chance. The Pilgrim Fathers and the *Mayflower* founded colonies in the certain knowledge that land with good agricultural properties existed and that they could manage that land. In similar vein, I firmly believe that the first interstellar colonists will go to a chosen destination with the certainty that they will find planets which they can terraform (if necessary) *with the equipment they bring with them*. It cannot be otherwise, for once on their way there is no turning back : a colony fleet *must* plan for as many contingeneies as it can.

This leads to the interesting conclusion that terraforming and its developments *must* precede true human interstellar travel and colonization. A society that was experienced in such matters would not be too concerned if it found semi-terran planets. It would seem logical for the colony to select the best candidate as a working base, transform it to a suitable environmental home, and then set about terraforming the other planets. Such projects will take a great deal of time, however : they are appropriate to relatively small task forces with very high technology, not to a vast and unceasing flow of emigrants from the Solar System.

Where then is the expanding population of a Kardashev Type 2 civilization to turn for the raw materials it needs – with living surfaces, in whatever form, rapidly becoming the biggest priority? Dyson and others have suggested various ways of producing new materials by "star busting"; e.g., projecting an intense beam of coherent gamma radiation into the core of a star and creating a supernova, then harvesting the materials. To me the idea is morally abhorrent, for what effect would such an operation have on a planet with an emerging civilization say 100 parsecs away? In any case, before the explosion would be triggered, the advanced civilization would be forced to retreat several tens of parsecs in order to be away from the worst effects; without the warped hyper-drive beloved of SF the whole operation could take several of our generations (longer for the method suggested by Dyson, which involved perpetrating multiple stellar collisions). Furthermore, how do you harvest such a mass of intensely radioactive energetic material? And also how do you rescue the "core" of the supernova explosion? Here we have the most valuable part of the potential harvest, namely heavy metals and possibly uranic and transuranic elements, essential for power-yielding purposes and for use as catalysts in other nuclear reactions.

However, the aim is to create a supernova, and the operation is much more critical then may have been thought when the idea was first postulated. I think that the energy balance required is too delicate for even a very advanced civilization to undertake. Although to us a heavy metal yield of 2×10^{29}kg, the likely yield from a B or A Main Sequence star two to three times the mass of the Sun, may seem stupendous it may be only 2 years' supply for an advanced Kardashev civilization! This leads me to consider that the civilization progression as conceived by Kardashev

16 and 17: Missions to the strays. Comets *(above)* and asteroids have the widest-ranging orbits in the Solar System, although the asteroids with highly eccentric orbits may be the nuclei of "dead" comets. Advanced propulsion systems such as ion-drive will be needed for manned missions to the main Asteroid Belt *(below).* Try turning this painting around for some remarkable shifts of perspective. *(Paintings by Ed Buckley.)*

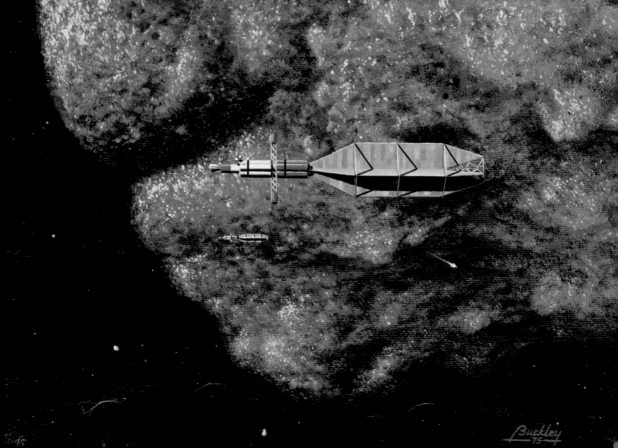

may not apply, and that advanced civilizations may choose alternative methods of providing equable surroundings.

So, if a society of 300 billion people is under extreme pressure to expand, fully developed in Solar System remodelling, with no immediately available outlets for mass emigration and without any short-time solution in terms of material derived from other stars, what is it to do? I hope to show that a detailed inventory of the outer resources of our own Solar System may allow it to build *other* Solar Systems! Furthermore, the activities outlined are on such a scale that other civilizations may possibly see the birth of the new Solar System, and in studying it detect the radio traffic necessary to direct and coordinate such an operation. Communication or even Contact itself could then follow, and I personally think that such events are more likely as an accidental result of such operations rather than the outcome of deliberately planned radiotelescope searches.

So what *are* the limits of the Solar System "beyond Pluto" and how are they set? The answer lies in the gravitational field of the Sun and its interaction with the gravitational fields of the neighbouring stars.

These act very much like a set of weighing scales with the Sun in one pan and each of the nearby stars in the other. At some point along the scale's beam the forces will balance – and so it is with the gravitational fields. If we take for example Barnard's Star, which has a mass 0.15 that of the Sun, and is situated at approximately 1.84 parsecs, then the point of balance is set at $1.84 - (0.15 \times 1.84) = 1.56$ parsecs from the Sun, whose gravitational field dominates the scene for 5/6 or over 80% of the distance, with Barnard's Star having its say only over the last 17%. If we consider a spherical radius of 3.68 parsecs from the Sun, 21 star systems lie within that distance, but only 3 other star systems have gravitational fields comparable to our Sun. Thus the region of equal gravitational force, which I call the "isogravisphere", surrounding the Sun may be likened to a vast balloon with a large number of dents or valleys in its surface produced by the majority of the surrounding stars, and three very large dents produced by Alpha Centauri, Sirius and Procyon. These are heavier than the Sun with masses as follows: Alpha Centauri 1.8 x solar mass, Sirius 3.2 x solar mass, Procyon 1.35 x solar mass. They are also comparatively nearby stars: Alpha Centauri is 1.3 parsecs from the Sun, Sirius 2.7 parsecs and Procyon 3.47 parsecs. Applying the "weighing scale" formula we obtain the following "gravitational isocline" distances from the Sun: Alpha Centauri 0.58 parsecs, Sirius 0.83 parsecs, and

18: Golgotha Moon. In this 1973 painting Ed Buckley predicted that the outer planets Uranus and Neptune might be surrounded by belts of small satellites —some, perhaps, of striking appearance—as shown surrounding Uranus in the background. In March 1977 a NASA airborne observatory discovered five rings of dark chunky debris orbiting Uranus. *(Painting by Ed Buckley.)*

[Fig 22]

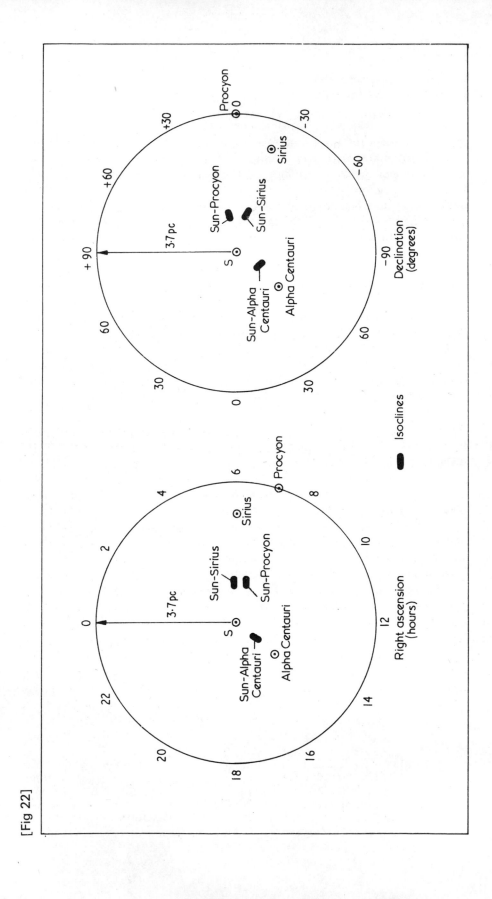

Procyon 0.89 parsecs. These deep dents in an otherwise smooth surface are not symmetrical; their disposition is as shown in fig. 22.

I should also point out that these stars also will have gravitational balance points between them as well as with the Sun; once again I stress that these four stars utterly dominate and control any material that may exist in the immediate neighbourhood up to a distance of (say) 4 parsecs. This raises the question "Is there any material about?". The answer is "Yes".

We can easily calculate the volume in a spherical radius of 4 parsecs from $V = 4/3\pi r^3$ where $V =$ volume, $r =$ radius and $\pi = 3,1416$. This gives us about 268 cubic parsecs – a colossal volume; if we expressed this in cubic centimetres we would have a figure of 10^{58} – that is, 10 followed by 58 noughts. This is a number which is so huge that it is almost impossible to grasp, but, if we could imagine each cubic centimetre occupied by just one poppy seed and then imagine that all these seeds were brought together, they would fill the Solar System entirely to beyond Pluto and, more than that, they would crush together and form an enormous red giant star! The seeds (mainly carbon and hydrogen) would crush together under their own tiny individual masses and the carbon/hydrogen atoms thus forced together would duplicate the reactions in a star and blaze forth with a fury that would be hundreds of times more intense than the Sun.

Obviously this space is not occupied by billions upon billions of poppy seeds, but it *is* occupied by material built up of dust, hydrogen gas, some odd fragments of ice, ammonia, methane and other particles. And it is not difficult to show that, if only one hydrogen atom occupied each cubic centimetre, we would have a very large amount of raw material. A hydrogen atom weights 10^{-27}g; the volume we are discussing is 10^{58}cm^3; so the total weight is 10^{58} x 10^{-27}g $= 10^{31}$g $= 10^{28}$kg. This is the direct equivalent of the mass of ten Jupiter-type planets and we aren't yet really trying!

Here is the beginning of rich picking indeed. For if it can be shown that dust and gas does exist in quantity then we really do have the possibility of collecting it and literally making a star. And if we make a star then the making of planets to surround it would be almost kindergarten stuff to a race of experienced terran engineers who had restructured their Solar System and saturated it with O'Neill cylinders.

Fortunately, several authorities quote densities for interstellar gas and dust in the immediate neighbourhood of the Sun and they give values which are very much higher than our original assumption of one hydrogen atom per cubic centimetre. The dust and gas concentrations out to Jupiter and responsible for the Zodiacal Light have an average density of 10^{-18}g/cm^3 according to Zdenek Kopal. However, in the Halley Lecture of May 1975 Professor W. McCrea of Sussex University discussed the formation of comets in gas and dust clouds formed as the Solar System swept through varying material densities in the Galactic Spiral. McCrea advanced strong arguments for the formation of comets from such clouds. Most interesting of all, he quoted densities of 10^5 to

10^7 particles per cubic centimetre. These figures of particle density can be easily converted to equivalents in terms of mass, and densities of 10^5 to 10^7 particles per cm^3 become masses of 10^{-22} up to 10^{-20} g/cm^3. When this last set of figures is multiplied by our "gravitational isocline" volume we have total masses of between 1,000 and 100,000 Suns!

If the Sun does pass through such areas the advanced society would have all the material it needed and much much more as a very generous bounty! This colossal potential of raw material to create 1,000 to 100,000 Suns allows us to say: "Perhaps there is a lot less dust than 100,000 Suns' worth, but perhaps there is enough to make one Sun, and perhaps if we know where to look we might find that local concentrations are much higher – so high that we may be able to sweep them up and compress them to form a star."

How do we know that if we compress gas and dust a star will form? Simply because this is the way Nature does it! A large cloud of gas and dust several parsecs across slowly collapses and condenses over millions of years becaue of gravitational forces and forms a large bubble. As the gas condensation goes on, it collapses faster and becomes more dense. This is important for, the more dense it is, the more it acts like a blanket and traps any heat generated by the compression of the gas at the centre of the balloon. Things now happen *very* quickly indeed. The ball of gas suddenly collapses and, impelled by the gravitational forces which are now so powerful they dominate *everything*, the atoms of the gas are crushed together so hard that they fuse and weld together in pairs and form helium. The enormous amount of heat that is released from this pushes back the remainder of the gas and leaves a glowing ball about 1.6 million km (and in some cases up to 16 million km) in diameter. A star has been born! This final collapse is sudden and drastic, taking only a few minutes to ignite the hydrogen fires which will keep the star burning for anything from 1 million to 100,000 million years. We can be confident that this really does happen, for astronomers have observed warm dark bubbles (called "Bok Globules") which seem to be clouds just about to collapse and "light up", while other objects (known as "T Tauri stars" from the first one observed) appear to be stars which actually have just lit up. They are always found in clouds of dust and gas and appear to be surrounded by thick but flat belts of dust in similar manner to a gigantic version of Saturn's rings, and they flicker and quiver like new born infants.

Our advanced society skilled in terraforming needs to seek out a dust cloud which requires "nudging" into a ball of the right density. I would suggest that such cloud concentrations may be found at the gravitational balance points of the four major stars mentioned earlier. If we could send probes to the areas of 0.58 parsecs towards Alpha Centauri, 0.83 parsecs towards Sirius and 0.89 parsecs towards Procyon, we could well find concentrations of dust and gas particles trapped more or less like Balaam's Ass, not knowing in which direction to drift. Professor Lyttleton of Cambridge believes that comets are born in concentrations of dust which are gathered in the gravitational isocline of Sirius and the Sun.

If this be true then here is our first dust and gas concentration waiting to be swept up! And it possibly follows that the other areas mentioned could be similarly explored and treated.

Such exploration and measurement of dust and gas cloud densities is almost within the present technical ability of Man, for the British Interplanetary Society has recently conceived a starship propulsion system and associated structure which could travel to Sirius in about 80 years. This means it would reach the Sirius isocline in about 27 years, and transmit back its findings on the particle cloud concentrations. With luck and determination we could begin to know some of these answers by 2050 – under a hundred years from now – a figure which nicely matches the idea of a human population of (say) 12 billion, nearly 30% of whom would be living in O'Neill cylinders and on the Moon and Mars.

How could we sweep up the dust and gas?

I would suggest that this may be done by using a modified form of Bussard ramscoop. Normally the ramscoop is conceived as passing interstellar hydrogen through a magnetic scoop, which compresses it and heats it to form a thermonuclear jet of helium mixed with hydrogen; the jet is allowed to escape from the rear of the ship, thus pushing it forward much like a conventional present-day jet aircraft. If we built a specialized form of Bussard ramjet which allowed only a *very small* amount of hydrogen to pass through it, but actually *pushed* the rest ahead of it, then we have a very effective interstellar sweeping brush. By positioning (say) six such ships at selected points around a cloud and literally sweeping in, all at the same time, a roughly spherical ball of gas and dust would be created and gradually compressed. The gas has to be compressed to the point where it self-collapses. There should be plenty of power extricable from the gas, and the energy produced is *not* used to drive the ship faster but to increase the strength of the magnetic field and thus compress the gas still further. Eventually temperature sensors would note that the centre of the gas ball was heating up. Simultaneously the ships' captains would note that the gas was beginning to *stream past the ships*! In other words, the drastic collapse to a star has begun! The signal now is to get turned around, face the stream of inrushing gas and "Get the Hell out of it or we'll be fried alive" as the artificially created star flares into life.

A B-type star of solar mass created at the isocline of the Sun and Sirius would easily be the brightest star in the night sky. It would have a visual magnitude of -8 to -10, far brighter than Venus (mag -4) and nearly as bright as the full moon (mag -11). It would also have a very peculiar spectrum rich in silicon from the excess of dust collected with the gas. Just such a silicon rich B-type star has recently been identified and has been reported in *Nature*. The authors are frankly puzzled as to the star type. Although a perfectly natural explanation will probably be forthcoming, the possibility of its being a star made by an intelligent race cannot be entirely ruled out. I would like to think that one day we may well find a star that really *is* artificial. And if we turned radiotelescopes onto it we would find the area "alive" with radio chatter as the operation was being directed and monitored. It is also likely that the "new" star would be an O or B type with the Old Homeland G type somewhere around nearby.

Thus interstellar communication may be by accident, not design. The quotation of Kepler (Chapter 8) as modified by Future Man may cause him to say : "Behold, between Sirius and the Sun I place a new star !" If we create stars at will whenever the need arises, the human race automatically eliminates all the problems of finding stars with planets that are habitable. Man ultimately really does become the Creator of his Universe.

Appendix to Chapter 12
(Duncan Lunan)

Presenting his ideas at a lecture to ASTRA in 1974, Anthony Lawton went in some detail into the processes by which the Sun might capture and concentrate interstellar material. If the present situation had lasted undisturbed since the origin of the Solar System, then the Sun would have dominated most of the volume shown in fig. 23a, with areas of dispute surrounding the "funnels" generated by our three most massive neighbour stars. Over thousands of millions of years, all the dust contained in that volume at first would tend to settle into a disk in the plane of the Ecliptic, as shown in fig. 23b. In terms of density, a "fried egg" distribution pattern would develop, with the layers growing thicker towards the centre, as the dust continued to contract under the influence of gravity and as a result of collisions between the particles. Since the isogravisphere is not smooth, the gravitational "funnels" of Alpha Centauri, Sirius and Procyon would upset the symmetrical contraction of the dust and a density profile like fig. 23c might take shape. Meantime, however, the entire spherical volume would constantly be replenished by fresh dust penetrating the isogravisphere and draining towards the disk in its turn.

The true situation is more dynamic. To begin with, Sirius is a type AO star and its stable lifetime is probably less than a thousand million years, so its rôle in the game is relatively new. Furthermore, the Sun and all the stars are orbiting around the Galactic Centre, each on its own path, and as we saw in Chapter 11 thousands of stars may have passed within 0.6 parsecs of the Sun during the history of the Solar System, giving dust envelopes no chance to form. In addition the Soviet astronomer Chebotarev has calculated that there should be a Lagrange L_1 point, a "balance point" if not an actual "funnel", generated by the Galactic Centre at 200,000 AU (1.02 parsecs) from the Sun. Particles beyond 100,000 AU would therefore not remain in orbit for longer than 400 million years. In Chapter 10 I suggested that the mass of the Galaxy may have been overestimated, and G. W. Morgenthaler has pointed out that local stellar spheres of influence are not mapped accurately with respect to the Galactic Centre[1]; but whatever the details, it is obvious that the Sun has not been calmly sweeping out the present isogravisphere since birth.

[Fig 23]

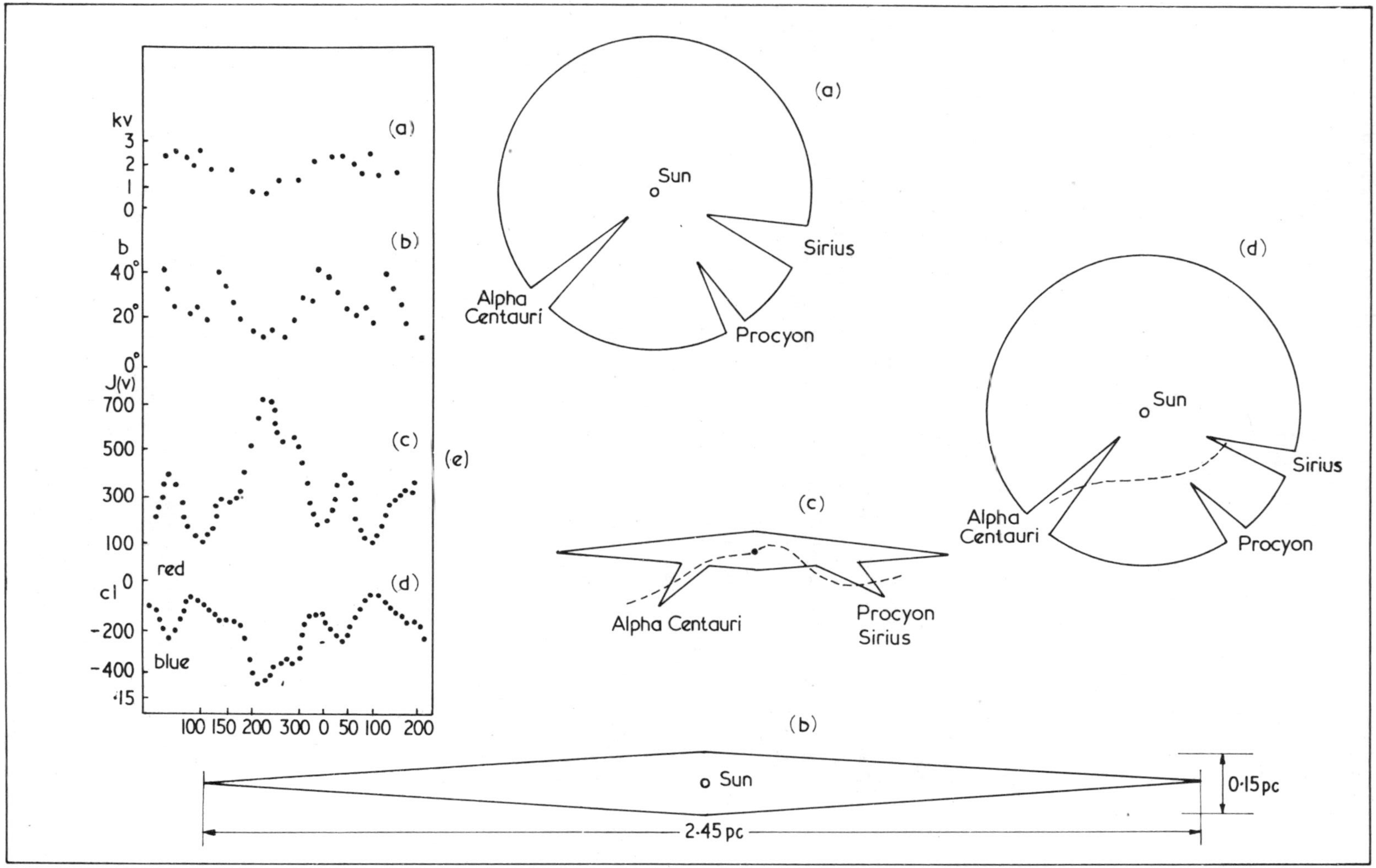
(a)
kv
3
2
1
0
(b)
b
40°
20°
0°
J(v)
700
500
(c)
300
100
red
0
c1
(d)
-200
blue
-400
·15
100 150 200 300 0 50 100 200
(e)
(a)
Sun
Sirius
Alpha
Centauri
Procyon
(d)
Sun
Sirius
Alpha
Centauri
Procyon
(c)
Alpha Centauri
Procyon
Sirius
(b)
Sun
0·15pc
2·45pc

Lawton's suggestion, however, following McCrea, is that the "big four" stars have *jointly* been sweeping up dust – especially when passing through interstellar clouds. To test the notion, he suggested space probe missions, on trajectories like fig. 23c's, to map the dust profiles surrounding the Sun. It should also be noted that the present configuration of the stars allows low-energy, free-flight transfers (taking millions of years) through the Sun's isogravisphere from, say, Alpha Centauri to Sirius (fig. 23d). That may partly explain why, although two comets (Lexell and Morehouse) are known to have *left* the Solar System owing to slingshots, none have so far been detected on hyperbolic orbits indicating they come from outside. Comets are more likely to be exchanged between Sirius and Alpha Centauri than for either to exchange them with us.

Attempts have already been made to map the dust profiles around us, however, using interstellar absorption and polarization.[2] The correlation was made by J. D. Fernie, who concluded that the Sun is near the edge of a dust envelope 490–610 parsecs across. Dust density within the segments, perhaps part of a dark lane within a galactic spiral arm, was three times that in surrounding space. Hughes and Routledge later found[3] that the Sun was likewise located within a ring of gas, about 610pc in radius, still expanding at 10km/sec. Noting that the youngest stars in the Sun's neighbourhood likewise seem to be concentrated within a 610pc radius, they concluded that the gas, and the dust trailing behind it, had been generated by a very rare, very violent Type 3 supernova 30–90 million years ago, expelling much more solid matter than the "normal" super-novae discussed above by Lawton. Although the Sun was probably 1,000pc from the explosion, the initial shockwaves and radiation bombardment might have ended the Mezozoic Era of life on Earth, killing off the dinosaurs.

Behind the gas would have come the dust, and there the dramatic point is made by fig. 24 (after Fernie). Since the explosion, it seemed that the Sun had moved three-quarters of the way towards the cloud centre

[Fig 24]

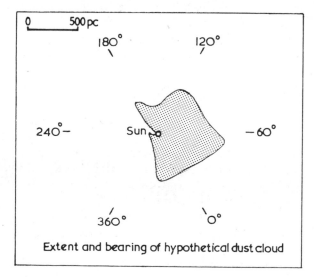

Extent and bearing of hypothetical dust cloud

and its advance was very plainly at the vertex of what could only be called a "Lawton funnel". With or without help from its friends, the Sun had been sweeping up dust for several million years at least. Where was it going? If it was settling into a disk in the plane of the Ecliptic, there should be peaks of Fernie's absorption curves where the Galactic Equator cuts the Ecliptic, at longitudes 5° and 185°. The Galactic Longitude of Sirius is 228°, that of Alpha Centauri 302°, and both stars are close to the Galactic Equator, the plane of the Milky Way, along which Fernie's curves are drawn.

Fig. 23e (after Fernie) shows the results obtained. The curves represent different types of observations, with curves (c) and (d) in particular being complementary. There is, indeed, an absorption peak at about 5° longitude, while at 185° the absorption level forms a "shoulder", higher than it would be if the curve were following a smooth sinusoidal variation with longitude. At 228°, however, absorption is right at its lowest – Sirius lies in the clear zone "behind" the Sun as it advances into the cloud. At 302° absorption is again lower than a sine curve would predict. On the face of it, there seems to be a concentration of dust in the plane of the ecliptic, with *clear* lanes near Alpha Centauri and Sirius. But there might be dust clouds at the centres of those clear lanes, just too far off the Galactic Equator to show up in these curves: there could be a peak in absorption at 0°, which is of course the longitude of the Galactic Centre; and, if that "balance point" can have a dust cloud, so too presumably can the stars. Clearly a great deal of further work would have to be done to produce clear answers from Earth-based studies alone.

If there is a disk in the plane of the ecliptic, its origin depends to a great extent on its distance. At 126,000AU, for example, a dust particle would have an orbital period of 45 million years and could not yet have circled the Sun twice since capture, if it were part of the dust cloud from the postulated supernova. It seems very unlikely that a disk could have formed at such distances in so "short" a time. If the comets formed out of material captured at the same time, then it's significant that they don't show any preference for the plane of the ecliptic.

Still another possibility is that the present distribution of dust around the Solar System is not the tidy, concentric system of fig. 23c but considerably more dynamic. If Hughes and Routledge are correct, the outer rim of the dust from "their" supernova is presumably moving now at less than 10km/sec, having initially been ejected at perhaps 10,000km/sec: if the first wave was moving at 100km/sec when it reached us, 50,000 years would be enough time for individual particles to pass through the Solar System, travel to Sirius and make a slingshot return to us; 25–26,000 years would suffice for Alpha Centauri. Fernie's curves show an absorption low near 48°, *opposite* Sirius, and a high near 122°, opposite Alpha Centauri. How are these details to be interpreted, and in particular what to do they do to fig. 24? Instead of a relatively static situation, the curves may represent a great wave of dust breaking over us in three dimensions.

The odd thing is, however, when the situation is viewed on a celestial

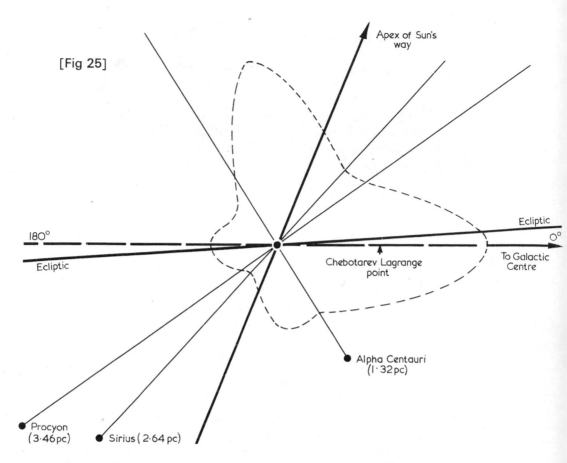

[Fig 25]

Apex of Sun's way

Ecliptic

180°

0°

Ecliptic

Chebotarev Lagrange point

To Galactic Centre

Alpha Centauri (1·32 pc)

Procyon (3·46 pc)

Sirius (2·64 pc)

sphere, that it comes near to being *two*-dimensional. Sirius, Procyon and Alpha Centauri all lie relatively close to the plane of the Galactic Equator; furthermore, as, Lawton points out, they are all on the same side of us. Roughly opposite to the midpoint of the three of them lies the Apex of the Sun's Way, near Vega – right in the direction that the Sun is moving, in fig. 24. If we regard fig. 25 as a disk about 20° of Galactic Latitude in thickness, all the points and directions mentioned so far can be plotted within it.* When Fernie's curves for the variation of interstellar absorption with Galactic Longitude are superimposed on it, it is obvious that the relation is anything but random.

Can the profile of fig. 25 be related to the Sun's movement through space? Linda Lunan summed up the problem with the concise statement, "There should be some simple process to account for that." The first suggestion to emerge was that the absorption peaks at 5° and 185° might *not* represent a disk of dust in the plane of the Ecliptic. The Ecliptic plane passes so close to the Galactic Centre that the peak around 5° might actually indicate a cloud in the Chebotarev Lagrange point at about 1.02pcs. Perhaps there might be an L_2 cloud on the far side of

*The line marked "Ecliptic" is the intersection of the ecliptic plane, at nearly 90°, with the plane of the Galactic Equator.

the Sun from the Galactic Centre. If so, Alpha Centauri and Sirius-Procyon might by analogy sweep out *clear* lanes on both sides of the Sun, but why should there be a peak in absorption at 100° longitude? The clue seemed to lie in the relationship of the three big neighbour stars to the Sun's Way, as if we were breaking up the flow of interstellar dust and spreading it over them like a cloak – and suddenly the dynamic flow of fig. 26 took shape on the page.

Lawton has pointed out that away from the isogravisphere dents generated by those three stars, the Sun's pull dominates the whole volume of space for several parsecs. It is entirely possible that we could be pushing a shock-wave of dust ahead of us at about 1pc distance. The peak of absorption at 100° indicates that we are meeting the flow of interstellar dust at 32° to our line of flight – or cutting across an expanding supernova cloud at a similar angle. Alpha Centauri, Procyon and most of all Sirius are sweeping out clear zones, apparently accentuating eddy effects in the shockwave rather than capturing clouds of their own. Some of the dust turned back towards the Sun will presumably fall into the Solar System, but most will rise or fall out of the plane of the diagram

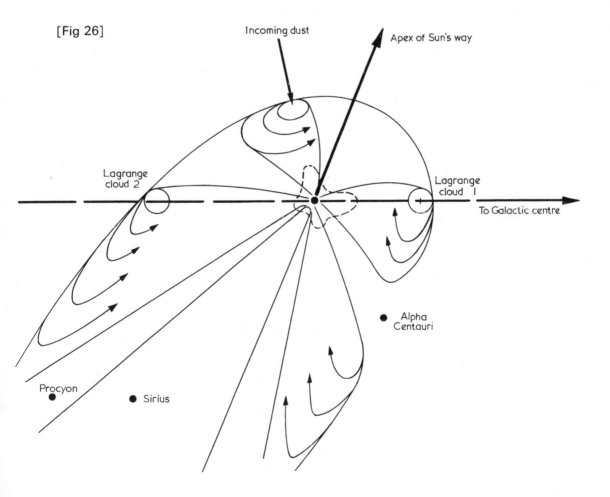

[Fig 26]

Incoming dust

Apex of Sun's way

Lagrange cloud 2

Lagrange cloud 1

To Galactic centre

Alpha Centauri

Procyon

Sirius

and rejoin the prevailing stream back along the Sun's Way. The formation of comets and Harper asteroids may be explained in terms of eddy flows converging "beyond Pluto"; and the best places to look for "balance-point" clouds may be in line with the Galactic Centre, not between us and our neighbour stars.

Since that hypothesis was drafted, two possibly related developments have come to light. The Pioneer spacecraft have discovered that, for reasons not understood, neutral hydrogen and helium are streaming into the Solar System at 72,400kph, in the Ecliptic plane, from a direction inclined at 60° to the Sun's Way.[4] The direction in relation to fig. 26 isn't specified in ref. 4, but the 60° angle suggests that the flow may be coming from the Chebotarev point. The velocity is interestingly close to the Sun's own velocity through space. Furthermore, French astronomers have found a dust cloud in the position indicated, about 1pc away, and apparently moving towards us with precisely the velocity quoted for the incoming gas.[5] If the report is accurate, I would strongly suggest that the apparent velocity is a turbulence effect generated by our own movement through the interstellar medium.

Some answers may come from planetary astronomy and astronautics, meantime. The replenishment of the Zodiacal Light dust obviously comes at least in part from comets, but some at least of it may be direct infall. If the comets are after all the newest members of the Solar System, virgin samples of their dust might prove the point. The moons of the outer planets may also sweep up dust, as suggested in Chapters 9 and 10; in particular, Robert Shaw suggested that Triton's retrograde orbit would cause dust to be collected at low relative velocities at the appropriate times of the month. Atmospheric processes would lay down deep deposits at the poles, perhaps resembling the "laminated terrain" of the Martian polar caps: ice core samples would be of great value. On Io, with its alternatively frozen and gaseous atmosphere, a fractionating process may have laid down particularly valuable strata, virtually a "neat" history of the Solar System's dust intake. Pluto should also be watched, for similar reasons: if methane lines appear in the spectrum near perihelion, and the planet turns significantly brighter as it moves away again, it would suggest a fractionating process there too and an infall of dark dust coming from *somewhere* in the outer part of Pluto's orbit. Unlikely as it now seems, a star occultation still might indicate that Pluto is larger than anticipated – perhaps with a dark reflecting surface, due to dust accumulation in a still methane ocean.

As for the Solar System beyond Pluto, then – we don't know what's out there, we don't know how much there is of it, and we don't know exactly where it is. The observations we can make from here are mere curtain-raisers. But they are beginning to suggest, yet again, that things in the outer System are not as we supposed – and may prove to be of the utmost importance.

13 Life and the Solar System

John W. Macvey, FRAS, FBIS

Is it probable for Europe to be inhabited and not the other parts of
the world? Can one island have inhabitants and numerous other
islands have none? Is it conceivable for one apple-tree in the infinite
orchard of the Universe to bear fruit, while innumerable other trees
have nothing but foliage?

Konstantin Tsiolkovsky,
"Dreams of Earth and Sky", 1895

Before we can think of life evolving either in the other planets of the
Solar System or in other stellar systems we must take a close look at
what we believe happened here on Earth. We have sound reasons for
believing that all life on Earth evolved from a single primitive origin.
Could what happened here have occurred on other planets as well?

In 1976 the American Viking spacecraft landed on Mars.
Although equipped to carry out a variety of observations on the red
planet its unique purpose was to land on the Martian surface and look
for life. What could be expected? Here it is appropriate to quote the
words of Carl Sagan: "There was a time not so long ago when most
scientists considered the possibility of life elsewhere as a kind of science-
fiction subject to be readily dismissed. You don't come upon this so often
any more. The tide of thought has changed somewhat and people are
going to consider it as a serious scientific question. There is good reason
for that. For thousands of years we could only guess. Now there are
experiments that can be done."

The Viking experiments were designed to analyze the Martian soil and
to search for microscopic life. Microbes are known to cover the surface
of the Earth and, if it is found that similar conditions exist on Mars, a
certain parallel may be drawn. The Martian experiments are, in fact,
developed from our knowledge of the origins of life on Earth.

Earth and Mars are roughly 4.6 billion years old. By now we have a
reasonable (though certainly not complete) picture of the way life evolved
on Earth. Geologists have attempted with a fair measure of success to
trace the path of evolution from animal fossils found in the rocks. Five
million years ago Man as a species is not found. Going back beyond that
all other mammals disappear. Continuing backwards into pre-history we

find the disappearance of reptiles, then of fishes, plants, insects, shell-fish and corals. Finally, around 600 million years ago, the earliest sea-creatures also disappear. Beyond this point geologists find virtually nothing. They have reached the oldest of the rocks – those deposited or formed during the Precambrian ages.

In this backward run through Earth's history from the present time we have covered less than one tenth of Earth's existence. Did no life exist at all in these incredibly remote ages? Occasionally odd traces occur in these rocks but whether or not they are the fossil remains of living organisms is difficult to say.

At Harvard University recently it was decided to carry out a more thorough scrutiny of these Precambrian rocks using a different technique. This involved grinding down slices of rock samples until they were as thin as paper. When this was done details were observed which had hitherto gone unnoticed. Microscopic examination revealed obscure shapes which *might* have been primitive single-cell organisms. Emphasis must be put on the word "might", for there was no proof that these had ever been alive.

It was decided the matter must, if possible, be put to the test. In a salt marsh on the Pacific coast of Mexico there is found a thick mass of blue-green algae. These are minute single-cell plants which grow in water anywhere. They provide convenient food for fish and for this reason are generally unable to amass. The high salt content of this marsh precludes any possibility of fish life and so the algae accumulate. Organisms of this nature are seen as possible evolutionary precursors of more complex life.

During the early years of this century Walcock discovered certain laminated rock structures and suggested that these had probably formed as a result of fossilisation of microscopic plant life (i.e., algae). At the time this idea resulted in considerable debate. However, the question was pretty well settled when it was discovered that the structure of the supposed algae in these ancient rocks matched up very closely to that of the matted algal mass in the Mexican swamp. Algae thus existed 1,000 million years ago. Similar fossils have been discovered in other parts of the world. Although these are only shadowy shapes they are almost certainly the petrified remains of single-celled organisms. Probably the oldest of all have been found in South Africa. Their age is about 3 billion years!

Earth was formed some 4.6 billion years ago. During the first billion years it remained unsuited for the origin of life. We know from the crater-festooned surface of the Moon that quite a lot of debris gathering-up by the planets must have taken place. The existence of craters on Mars and Mercury confirms this and there seems little doubt that Earth must have suffered in this respect too. Here, however, the healing effect of eons of wind, rain, frost and snow have virtually erased all traces. But such conditions as then existed were hardly conducive to life initiation.

Life then probably started on our planet around 4 billion years ago. Its origin was almost certainly a quick process on the geological timescale and was probably completed in a couple of hundred million years or less. It took place in a period sandwiched between the earliest fossils and the tempestuous primeval age of meteorites and molten lava. As our planet cooled down gases which were liberated created a primitive atmosphere while water vapour formed and then condensed. Somewhere at the interface between early seas and primitive atmosphere critical chemical reactions began. In sheltered regions, such as beaches or pools, conditions eventually became just right for the formation of the complex molecules of life. Here they were constituted and here they coalesced.

A prominent researcher in this field is S. L. Miller of the University of California. There he has created, under laboratory conditions, a model of Earth's primitive environment. Says Miller: "The primitive environment was very different from that of the present day. The form of carbon chiefly present was CH_4 (methane) instead of CO_2 (carbon dioxide) as at present. Nitrogen was in the form of NH_3 (ammonia) instead of molecular nitrogen as it is today. There was water, no oxygen but an abundance of hydrogen. Nobody had ever tried experimenting to see what would happen in such an atmosphere." The basis of Miller's now classic experiment was the construction of a model ocean, a model atmosphere and provision of the necessary apparatus to reproduce the torrential rain of primeval times. To simulate lightning an electric discharge was suitably arranged.

After being in operation for only a week the hitherto clear model ocean had turned a muddy brown. Miller promptly dubbed this as "primeval soup". The next step was to discover the formula (or should it be recipe?) of this "soup". Chemical analysis showed it to consist of an assortment of amino acids. Since these are in effect the "building blocks" for proteins and since they were present in large concentrations this constituted a truly historic result.

The next, and logical, step was to try a similar type of experiment with nucleic acid. Nucleic acid (or DNA) carries the genetic code and is essential to life since it contains the chemical "information" which arranges amino acids into chains of proteins. This work was carried out by Orgell of the Salk Institute in California. In order to secure conditions reasonably analogous with those of primitive Earth, he and his co-workers conducted their experiments out in the desert where they could be sure of hot, dry days and cold, wet nights. Using sunlight to heat simple chemicals they succeeded in producing the beginning of nucleotides – DNA "building blocks". The result, although undoubtedly interesting and not without promise, could be considered only partially successful. At best they were able to produce a chain 6 nucleotides long. On average, however, a DNA molecule is 20 *metres* long!

Experiments carried out by Fox and his co-workers at the University of Miami embody a different approach.[7] On the Hawaiian volcano Mt Kilauea they dropped amino acids onto pieces of hot lava. Here again we have an attempt to assemble proteins from amino acids under primitive Earth conditions. In the first instance there is the simulation of hot lava meeting primordial "soup" (largely amino acids). The water boils off leaving a sticky brown residue or proteinoid. Washing this off the hot

rock with water is analogous to the action of rain or sea by an early
sterile Earth. The result was something of a milestone, since contact with
water resulted in the proteinoid molecules assembling themselves into
some kind of order. Under the microscope the assembled proteinoids were
seen to resemble tiny transparent spheres roughly the size of living cells.
Fox was able to photograph a growth sequence extending over three days.
Moreover, it was apparent that in some instances proteinoids were dividing into pairs of "daughter" cells. How analogous was this to the process
taking place in living tissue?

It was known that proteinoids did not contain DNA whereas living
cells do. Living cells also contain chromosomes. The problem now was
how to link DNA with protein; to ascertain how DNA produced the
"information" by which proteins are made and by which life is co-
ordinated, controlled and caused to evolve.

It was easy enough to make the appropriate molecules. The problem
centred on the genetic code. None of the researchers believed they could
start with a mixture of gases and water and eventually produce some
recognizable living creature. For this, evolution is essential and the
principal requirement of evolution is time, something which certainly
cannot be simulated.

It was clear by now that life had originated with relative rapidity over
a period of about 200 million years. The circumstances all indicated that
it was probably not an uncommon event and because of this could be
expected on other planets as well, depending of course, on the same or
similar conditions obtaining.

The next piece of the metabolic jigsaw was supplied by meteorites.
In September 1969 a meteorite fall occurred in Australia. It was picked
up almost immediately and placed in a sterilized environment. Here at
last was a golden opportunity to look for organic compounds in a meteorite
uncontaminated by terrestrial biology.

The meteorite (a carbonaceous chondrite) was taken to the Ames
Research Centre in the United States. When it was broken up and its
contents analysed amino acids were found to be present. In fact a whole
series was identified that was totally different from any ever found by
previous investigators. But – and here in a sense lay the crux of the entire
matter – that very same series had previously been found in the mixture
formed during the electric discharge experiment. The implication was
very plain. If this process could go on in the Solar System (proven by
the meteorite analysis) it would also go on in other solar systems. Life
based on chemical evolution was *not* unique to Earth.

. Mars had long been considered the most likely planet in the Solar
System (apart from Earth) to contain life of one form or another. At
first, thanks to Lowell and others, this was seen in terms of an enlightened
master race of scientists and engineers. Witness for example this account
by R. A. Proctor in his *Poetry of Astronomy* published in 1881:
"Undoubtedly wide seas and oceans with many straits and bays and
inland seas exist on Mars. We see in the telescope long white shore lines,
the clearing mists of morning, the gathering mists of night – and we

know that there must be air-currents in an atmosphere undergoing such changes. There must be rain and snow and hail, electrical storms, tornadoes and hurricanes."

With the passing of time the pendulum swung completely in the opposite direction. The first Mariner to fly past Mars and send back photographs of the surface seemed to confirm the latter trend. The planet showed no canals, only many craters. Mars was apparently lifeless and dry. But in 1971–72 Mariner 9 found, as well as chasms and volcanoes, what looked suspiciously like vast, dried-up river systems! This was of immediate and intense interest in a metabolic context since water is essential to life and is present in every living cell. It has also been shown to be essential in all the simulated "primitive Earth" experiments. These "river" systems were compared with photographs taken from satellites of the great river systems on Earth such as the Amazon, Orinoco, Mississippi, Ganges and Yangtze. The similarity was quite astonishing.

As a consequence of all this, biologists now see the possibility of life on Mars as much less remote than they did a few years ago. The burning question now is whether or not there might exist on Mars a low-order *dormant* life which merely awaits the coming of the next warm cycle to be rendered active. In an attempt to find a pointer NASA scientists have taken soil samples from certain high valleys in the Antarctic. This part of our own planet does not really duplicate conditions on Mars at the present time. It merely represents the closest we can get. These Antarctic soil samples all yielded negative results. Here at least there was no life in the soil.

Despite this the possibility of low-order, dormant life on Mars has not been abandoned for the parallel is very far from complete. Our polar regions have been frozen for most of the period of Earth's existence whereas there may have been (probably was) a period in early Martian history during which conditions were much more favourable – a time when water was reasonably abundant and when other gases were present in the atmosphere – i.e., conditions were appropriate to life initiation. Perhaps then life *did* originate. Unlike on Earth, however, conditions gradually deteriorated, the environment becoming ever more rigorous. In such circumstances Martian life may have mutated and evolved in a manner that enabled it to survive.

We know that nothing has adapted to Antarctic conditions in 100,000 years. What we do *not* know is how long an organism would have had on Mars to adapt to climatic deterioration. If the theory that Mars has alternated between warm/wet and cold/dry environments is valid then there may be dormant life (not to be construed as hibernating "Rip Van Winkle" Martians!). Such small, low-order organisms could exist in the Martian soil. Were we able to remove some of this soil to warm, wet conditions the results might be highly instructive.

It should be stated at this point that the solar radiation at the surface of Mars is very rich in ultraviolet below 2,000 angstroms and thus able to cleave organic polymers of a biological nature. Moreover, fairly recent experiments in a sealed chamber containing simulated Martian conditions in respect of surface, atmosphere and radiation flux showed that hardy terrestrial bacteria were unable to survive. On the other hand Martian bacteria may well have adapted to the rigorous conditions.

Venus, for long an enigma especially in regard to life, would appear now also to have been given the thumbs down. The passing of the years has produced many speculative models of the Venusian surface. These have ranged from a boiling CO_2 ocean through a world still in a hot swampy "Carboniferous" age, a great morass of seething hydrocarbons to a bleak and terrible wind-swept desert. The desert concept seems at the present time to be the most likely. The planet is now known to be extremely hot – much hotter than was hitherto supposed. It seems hardly an ideal spot for any form of advanced life, although here too we may be able to think in terms of much more lowly organisms.

It is more than a little ironical that in past times, when both Mars and Venus were being looked upon favourably as abodes of life, planets such as Jupiter were automatically debarred – except perhaps in the pages of SF, where "Jovians" were not infrequent visitors. While we still cannot accept Jovians there has nevertheless been a subtle change in outlook.

As in the case of Venus, several models of Jupiter have been postulated over the years. The present picture is that of an outer layer of gas clouds and ammonia-ice suspended in a matrix of hydrogen, methane, ammonia and helium.[1] Pressure and temperature are seen as increasing towards the planet's centre, resulting eventually in a super-critical liquid ocean due to condensation of hydrogen. As depth increases this becomes "metallic" hydrogen, which could in turn overlie a small solid silicate and metal core.

This hardly seems like a habitat for life – any kind of life. However, it is as well to consider the possibilities in a little more depth. Earlier we looked at possible agents responsible for life initiation here on Earth. On Jupiter, despite its basically different features, there exists a distinct parallel. Radiation, electrical discharges, radioactivity (and perhaps forms of volcanism) are present. These could have acted on atmospheric gases to produce a large variety of simple organic compounds which could, in due course, have given rise to the various polymers necessary for the creation of living cells. From this point on, evolution might have taken over but, of necessity, along a very different path from that followed on Earth.[2] The obvious course is to carry out experiments of a similar nature to those of Miller and his associates but on this occasion to adapt them, so far as is possible, to the conditions known to prevail within the Jovian atmosphere. The gaseous mixture must in this instance be one comprizing hydrogen, helium, methane and ammonia. Water could not exist in the liquid phase in the upper reaches of that atmosphere but does so in the warmer lower layers. Should organic evolution be feasible on Jupiter such experiments should at least serve to indicate the path, or paths, it might follow.

Some experiments along these lines have already been carried out with interesting results. These involved the subjection of methane/ammonia mixtures to electrical discharges of differing forms (spark and semi-corona) at room temperatures but at pressures lower than atmospheric.[3, 4] It should be noted that such conditions only approximate to those of Jupiter. Despite this the results were intriguing. The products resulting included hydrogen cyanide and a number of organic cyanides. The latter, on acid hydrolysis, yielded the familiar amino acids glycine, sarcosine and aspartic – common and essential terrestrial biological compounds. Apart from the volatile compounds a peculiar reddish "tar" was also produced in considerable quantity. An intriguing feature of this material was that its colour bore a marked resemblance to that of the Red Spot on Jupiter, and to the clouds, if not also the surface, of Titan. Although spacecraft landings on Titan are unlikely before the 1990s at the earliest, Saturn's largest moon is now one of the best candidates for "life as we know it".

Farther experiments have been carried out following the suggestion that the gas hydrogen sulphide(H_2S) might occur in the lower layers of the Jovian atmosphere. This entailed subjecting methane, ammonia *and* H_2S to a spark discharge. On hydrolysis of the resultant tarry mixture the sulphur-containing amino acids cysteine and methonine were not formed.[5] It could be shown that these amino acids *were* produced if a similar gaseous mixture were irradiated by ultraviolet radiation.[6] These acids are oxidized very easily in the presence of water. Their formation would not, however, be inhibited in the upper Jovian atmosphere by virtue of the absence of liquid water.

Internal heat (which undoubtedly Jupiter possesses) might also lead to the production of organic compounds from methane/ammonia mixtures.[7] More, however, would require to be known of the intensity and nature of the Jovian heat source as well as the concentration of the ammonia/methane mixture surrounding it. We are unlikely to come by this information in the foreseeable future.

The production of organic compounds by irradiation of the Jovian atmosphere is also a distinct possibility. There would certainly be no lack of irradiating agents – uv and X-rays from the Sun, cosmic rays and "solar wind" protons to name but three. How enduring such compounds would be is, however, still a matter of conjecture.[8]

Whatever the process (it may in fact be due to all three), there can be little doubt that organic compounds are being actively synthesized in the Jovian atmosphere. It now remains to be seen whether or not biopolymers analogous or similar to those in terrestrial organic polymers can be formed. This represents the crux of the matter for, however interesting may be the evolution of simple organic compounds from inorganic materials, this interest remains purely chemical unless and until more complex organic molecules of a biopolymeric nature are known to be forming. Then and then only can a biological interest arise.

The reddish tar already mentioned could (theoretically at least) replace proteins in a Jovian life-form.[2] True proteins are not formed as a result of electric discharges – at least they do not appear to be. Nucleic acids also constitute a very real difficulty when we come to consider Jovian life. These are essential metabolic compounds containing pyrimidine and

purine polymers linked by phosphates and which also contain carbo-
hydrate (sugar) residues. The difficulty lies with the essential phosphate
linkage since phosphate groups would be highly unstable in the reducing
Jovian atmosphere (in chemical terms reduction is the converse of
oxidation). This means that nucleic acids must be ruled out. These are
utterly essential to terrestrial life. Consequently we must speculate on an
alternative type of compound which does not suffer from this drawback.
Unfortunately such speculation has at present little real basis.

It is of interest in the circumstances, however, to assess how terrestrial
cells would react under Jovian conditions. If it can be shown that they
would not stand up it would mean that life on Earth is after all of a
more specialized type – not necessarily unique but certainly less general
than we have hitherto allowed ourselves to suppose.

It is undoubtedly true that in the course of Earth's history conditions
for life – and therefore for cells – have changed considerably. Organisms
which today cannot survive in a different atmosphere must at one time
have been able to do so. The answer of course, is bound up in the word
"adaptability". Terrestrial organisms, terrestrial cells were able (in time)
to adapt. When our planet changed from one having a primary hydrogen/
ammonia atmosphere to one with a secondary oxygen/nitrogen atmosphere
over a (geologically) short period of time considerable powers of adaptability must have been necessary for the various organisms then in
existence.[9]

To this day there are examples of terrestrial plants which show an
amazing degree of tolerance to a radically changed environment; e.g.,
onion plants in a predominantly ammoniacal atmosphere and certain
species of cacti under water. A number of terrestrial micro-organisms are
also very hardy. At least four are known which are capable of with-
standing at least 24 hours of simulated Jovian conditions. Perhaps after
all terrestrial conditions are much less critical than it seemed just a few
lines back.

But if these lowly organisms could exist in the Jovian atmosphere could
they also *grow* under such conditions? Clearly this is a different question.
The principal factors are high ammonia concentration and very high
pressures (probably in the region of 100 atmospheres). Most would agree
these are extreme enough by any standards.

Certainly pressures of this order do not adversely affect survival
characteristics. At such pressures the temperature is likely to be in the
region of 20°C, which can hardly be described as too cold. And what
of the necessary nutrients? These could be nitrogenous organic compounds
synthesized by electrical discharges in the upper reaches of the atmosphere.
In conjunction with liquid water droplets a rain could result which was
simply a dilute solution of these compounds. A source of essential minerals
is less obvious. It has been suggested, however, that this might be provided
by the large amounts of meteoric dust trapped as a result of the planet's
high gravity.[2] We know that raindrops condense around solid particles
so that minerals would also constitute part of the "organic rain".

There are alternative biochemical systems – i.e., systems based not on carbon/oxygen as is the case on Earth but on other elements. This seems an appropriate point to introduce these ideas. It cannot be too strongly stressed, however, that these must of necessity be speculative since we have, as yet, no actual knowledge or experience of anything along such lines. Moreover, by so speculating it might seem that we are tacitly admitting that the terrestrial organic "template" is not, after all, the universal standard. This does not follow. The terrestrial pattern may still be fairly universal – but with exceptions.

The composition of space is such that condensing stars and planets have a composition and distribution similar to that of the Solar System. This means that the elements available for life initiation and development are fairly standard throughout the Universe.[10, 11] Since, therefore, terrestrial life is essentially carbon/oxygen based there is a reasonable case for assuming that life throughout the Universe, including of course the Solar System in its entirety, is so based. The exceptions are most likely to arise in the case of certain stars known to contain an abundance of the elements manganese, mercury, silicon and calcium. These are generally also oxygen deficient.[12] Any planets possessed by such stars are presumably going to reflect this state of affairs. The implications in respect of less usual lifeforms are therefore obvious.

This however, is extrapolating our present theme considerably. At the moment our brief is a consideration of the life possibilities within our own small solar family of worlds. These other stars of which we spoke have an *abundance* of these less usual elements. Our Sun also possesses them, although to a much lesser extent. Our planet possesses them too as we are all well aware. We cannot therefore eliminate entirely the possibility of less usual elements being biochemically involved in certain of our sister worlds around the Sun. This is the basis of our case for considering alternative life chemistries within the Solar System.

The first alternative we might consider is that of lifeforms utilizing ammonia instead of water. Until quite recently this was regarded as rather implausible on the following grounds: since liquid ammonia boils at $-33°C$ any lifeform would have to be a low-temperature one; liquid ammonia freezes at $-77°C$, i.e., ammonia exists in liquid form over a temperature range of only $44C°$; enzymes would be inactive in liquid ammonia because of its high alkalinity.

The first two points almost certainly arise from the fact that ammonia possesses these properties at $0°C$ and an atmospheric pressure of 1. Increasing the pressure to 60 atmospheres *raises* the effective boiling point and also *lowers* the freezing point. This extends the liquid temperature range from $44C°$ to $131C°$. In such circumstances the range compares more than favourably with water, which has a liquid temperature range of only $100C°$. At this pressure (60 atmospheres) the boiling point of ammonia is $98.3°C$ and the freezing point $-32.7°C$. We can see that liquid ammonia-based life need not necessarily have low-temperature connotations.

The third point is based on the premise that the pH (acid/alkaline) scale of values must be that of water. However, in any ammonia system the pH scale would be that of *ammonia*, not of water. We regard ammonia very rightly as alkaline. We must also remember that in the compound ammonia chloride $[(NH_4)^+ Cl^-]$ it acts as an *acid*.

· In denying the possibilities of ammonia-based lifeforms we are allowing ourselves to be blinded by the conditions obtaining in *our* environment. Certainly the *bio*chemistries of water and ammonia-based life would show a wide divergence; e.g., in the regulation of cell membrane potentials. In the case of terrestrial organisms, sodium chloride and potassium chloride are utilized; these compounds are very water-soluble and consequently suitable. They are, however, much less soluble in liquid ammonia and because of this are unsuited to such a rôle. Their function in ammonia-containing cells could probably be taken by the chlorides of caesium and rubidium, both of which are easily soluble in such a medium.[12]

Ammonia-based life is therefore not outside the bounds of possibility and so far as the Solar System is concerned we must inevitably turn our thoughts to the giant planets Jupiter and Saturn and their ammonia-rich atmospheres.

The element silicon has for long been regarded as an alternative to carbon in possible alien biochemistries. In a number of respects this is not unreasonable. On our own planet silicon is the second most common element known and it may well enjoy equal pre-eminence on other planets including those of the Solar System. Chemically it is akin to carbon in a number of ways, notably in its ability to link up with other elements.

Closer examination of silicon in this context reveals a number of apparent deficiences. Its abundance is beyond dispute but so far as Earth is concerned it is largely locked up as silicates in the rocks, a state of affairs quite likely to prevail on the Moon, Mercury, Venus and Mars as well. Carbon atoms link up to form long chains. Such links are stable to a degree not found in any other element. Though silicon has this power also it is to a much lesser degree.

Life on Earth is based on three essential carbon polymers – proteins, carbohydrates and nucleic acids. In these the principal "skeleton" of each molecule contains only up to *two* carbon atoms, although the side or subsidiary arms of the chain may contain eight carbon-to-carbon linkages. High multiple linkages of carbon atoms are not therefore mandatory in the polymers essential to terrestrial life. There may consequently be an analogy in the case of silicon polymers essential to any silicon-based life.

Such polymers must be stable. Here again silicon fulfills the necessary requirements. The rocks of our planet are composed to a very large extent of silicon/oxygen polymers. The silicon/oxygen bond is extremely stable – more so in fact than the carbon/carbon bond which is so essential a feature of terrestrial life. Even the silicon/silicon bond has a reasonable strength, although less than that of carbon/carbon.[13]

In view of all these facts it might seem rather surprising that life on Earth did not elect to become silicon-based. Was the selection of carbon purely arbitrary? This is most unlikely and it is now that we come to the most damaging deficiency of silicon. On Earth there is an abundance of water and in the presence of water any *complex* silicon compound is hydrolyzed to silicon dioxide (SiO_2). In these circumstances water could hardly serve its rôle of medium and essential solvent. We can fairly safely assume that lifeforms based on silicon polymers could not exist on worlds where water in one form or another was present. This rules out terrestrial-type planets anywhere. Even the minute amounts present on Mars or in the Martian atmosphere would probably be too much. Silicon-based life would seem a possibility only on worlds where water, ammonia and other polar solvents are not present. The possibilities of finding such life within the Solar System are therefore rather remote.

Another possibility is life based on certain of that group of elements known as the halogens: fluorine, chlorine, bromine, iodine and astatine. Fluorine and chlorine are the two most likely to be involved, as the atoms of the others are regarded as being too large; the former are also the most chemically reactive – indeed, fluorine is the second most reactive element known and because of this is rather difficult to handle. Both it and chlorine are most unpleasant corrosive elements and it is rather difficult for us to imagine any lifeform based on either of these elements, although chemically a certain case may be made for both of them in such a rôle.[12] It seems at best most unlikely that any of the solar planets could nurture life of this type and consequently there is little point in going into the matter here.

Today we stand at something of a crossroads so far as extraterrestrial life in the Solar System is concerned. Within the last century we have come from an era when advanced, intelligent beings were seen as a strong possibility on at least two of our sister worlds to one in which all except our own were regarded as virtually sterile. Now, with more accurate information at our disposal, the pendulum is slowly moving back the way it has come. Where will it stop?

14 The Case for Continuation

We shall not cease from exploration
And the end of all our exploring
Will be to arrive where we started
And know the place for the first time.
Through the unknown, remembered gate
When the last of earth left to discover
Is that which was the beginning;
At the source of the longest river
The voice of the hidden waterfall
And the children in the apple-tree
Not known, because not looked for,
But heard, half-heard, in the stillness
Between two waves of the sea.

T. S. Eliot, "Little Gidding"

In Parts 2 and 3 of this book we followed in detail the Solar System exploration of the 1960s and early 1970s, and I hope there are no readers left still asking, "After we'd landed on the Moon, what was the point of doing it again and again?" Preaching to the converted, there would be little need to summarize the position by hinting at the uses to which the findings may be put. But with science and technology under increasing attack year by year, with space exploration so easily singled out for misleading but oft-repeated criticism, we can't close a book like this without marshalling our arguments for the next round.

New Worlds for Old is intended for the level of argument which runs, "They haven't found anything up there that we didn't expect, and it's all irrelevant anyway." The first answer to that is that we cannot hope to live in harmony with our own world until we fully understand its origin, its history, its present composition and character, and its interactions with the interplanetary environment. To reach that understanding, we have to examine the other worlds of the Solar System as well as Earth itself. Until our neighbour worlds, the asteroids, the comets and the interplanetary medium have been studied in detail we cannot say with any confidence that we understand how our world came into being. Until our past is illuminated by comparative knowledge of theirs, we cannot be sure that we know the forces which shaped our past and will influence the future. We need to know about the geology and weather systems of the other planets to understand fully the surface and atmosphere of our own. To understand Earth's interaction with the interplanetary medium there is no substitute for putting spacecraft into it. Most critical of all, perhaps, we need to know everything the other planets can teach us about the behaviour of the Sun.

The record of exploration to date is as follows:

Mercury has been studied by radar and flown past three times by spacecraft, with photographic coverage of nearly half its surface. *Results*: rotation relative to the Sun takes two Hermian years, not one; one hemisphere is significantly different from the other; the planet has a large metal core and an intrinsic magnetic field, and may have shrunk after formation; the final bombardment phase in the origin of the Solar System affected *all* the inner planets; the Sun is not subject to occasional cataclysmic "flare-ups". *We need* full photographic coverage and sample return, especially from terrain apparently not "saturated" by bombardment. There are tentative plans for an Orbiter mission, but no funding.

Venus has sustained radar mapping and five flyby missions, three of them failures; nine atmosphere entry probes, one a failure; five orbiters; and six soft landings, two at least with photographic coverage. *Results*: rotation is retrograde and longer than the year; atmosphere rotates retrograde in four days; surface temperatures and pressures are much higher than expected; atmosphere is nearly all carbon dioxide; clouds are sulphuric acid droplets; despite big impacts and volcanic activity surface is nearly flat, yet shows no sign of wind erosion; no magnetic field or radiation belts. *We need* much more surface exploration and sample return, also atmosphere circulation studies. France and USSR jointly have tentative plans for atmosphere floating station. Manned flyby missions abandoned.

The Moon has been subjected to radar mapping and detailed photography over the visible hemisphere and the Farside equator, with less detailed photography of the rest of the Farside. The possibilities of flyby probes and hard and soft landers have virtually been exhausted; unmanned sample return and mobile explorers still have minor contributions to make; manned exploration halted in mid-stride after six successful landings with geological exploration, scientific station deployment and extensive sample return. *Results*: Moon apparently formed separately from Earth, internally differentiated with a semi-liquid core, initially with a magnetic field, now gone; severe bombardment melted entire original crust, final bombardment phase followed re-solidification; one hemisphere significantly different from the other; lunar core displaced towards Earth; crust exceptionally rigid; moonquakes generated at core boundary; core more thermally active than Earth's; possible surface evidence of supernova radiation bombardment; possible evidence of solar flare-ups, ruled out by Mercury flyby pictures. *We need* surface exploration and sample return from big craters and possible volcanic regions, and extension of orbital scientific study from equator to entire surface, also Farside and polar landings. US and Europe plan unmanned Polar Orbiter Explorer, not yet funded; Soviet unmanned sample returns will presumably continue.

Mars has had equatorial radar mapping, six flybys, six orbiters, three atmosphere entry probes and two successful landings. *Results* : extensive surface cratering by bombardment; one hemisphere significantly different from the other; large-scale volcanic activity in the past, polar caps water ice; widespread evidence of liquid water action in the past; atmosphere mostly carbon dioxide, thinner than expected; violent erosion in intermittent planet-wide dust storms; partially formed core, possible weak magnetic field, possible beginnings of plate tectonics, but no marsquakes detected by landers; positive results in lander tests for biological action, but no living matter detected in soil samples; possible organic compounds in soil shaded by rocks from solar ultraviolet radiation. The Martian moons are dark, dust-covered, chipped and cratered by bombardment, possibly differentiated crustal fragments of primal body. *We need* extensive surface exploration and sample return, including deep cores from polar ice, and lunar sample return. Manned orbiter and landing missions abandoned; tentative plans for surface rovers and sample return, orbiters and lunar sample return, but no funds as yet.

The Asteroids have had radar-studies of Earth-grazers, and two penetrations of the main Belt not passing near any large bodies. Crustal samples studied after reaching Earth as meteorite falls. *Results* : Belt asteroids apparently fragments of primal bodies shattered by multiple collisions; evidence that original planetesimals were partly melted and differentiated, but formed at lower temperatures than lunar material; increased dust impacts on spacecraft within three main bands of Belt; relatively thick interplanetary dust out to Belt but origin probably comets rather than asteroid collisions. *We need* flyby missions, orbiters, landers, and returned samples of known origin. Tentative plans for Earth-grazer flyby and landing missions, but no funding; no plans for missions to main Belt.

Jupiter has had two flyby missions with photographic studies of the planet and Galilean moons; high-altitude aircraft spectroscopic studies; radiotelescope studies, including RAE 2 in lunar orbit; star occultation studies (planet and moons); and radar mapping of the Galileans has begun. *Results* : planet generates great internal heat, with an intense magnetic field and radiation belts; belt particles swept up by Galilean moons; magnetic "tail" stretches to beyond orbit of Saturn; atmosphere mostly hydrogen, with helium, methane and ammonia; aerosols including organic compounds in upper atmosphere; water vapour in depths; metallic hydrogen in core, possibly no solid core at all; equatorial atmosphere dominated by Coriolis forces, polar regions by convection; Red Spot apparently atmospheric storm, but explanation obscure; Io possibly salt-covered, violent electrical activity in atmosphere, generates hydrogen cloud which envelops planet; Ganymede has ice fields, maria, extensive cratering, interior may be entirely liquid water; relatively thick dust cloud surrounds planet and moons. *We need* orbiters, especially in inclined orbits; atmosphere entry probes; lunar flybys, orbiters, landers and sample return, especially polar ice cores from Io. Two US flybys pending (Voyagers) and orbiter/entry probe planned (Galileo). Tentative plans for another flyby (Mariner Jupiter-Uranus), Ganymede orbiter and lander; but no funds yet.

Saturn and its moons have been studied by radiotelescope (including RAE 2), aircraft, star and lunar occultations, and radar studies of Titan have begun. *Results*: there is some evidence for high internal temperatures, a magnetic field and radiation belts; nature and origin of the ring particles remains obscure; Titan has twice the expected mean surface temperature, high-altitude red clouds (possibly organics), surface atmospheric pressure half Earth's, and hydrogen escaping from the atmosphere to form a ring completely surrounding Saturn. Pioneer 11 flyby to come, Voyagers 1 and 2 to follow. *We need* all the same investigations as for the Jupiter system, plus a polar station on Janus for investigation of the rings, and most of all we need surface exploration on Titan. Pioneer 11's path will be outside ring A, ruling out the possibility of a Titan flyby. Flybys of Titan, Rhea and Dione are planned for the two Voyager probes; ring studies will depend on the experience of Pioneer 11. Tentative plans for an orbiter mission, no funding yet.

Uranus has had the same study program as Saturn, but no radar studies as yet. *Results*: some internal heat; may have magnetic field, but not necessarily radiation belts; five dark rings of "chunky" debris discovered; rotation revised. *We need* a full study program, particularly of the moons and rings to learn their history and find reasons for the 98° tilt of the Uranus system. Grand Tour flyby missions cancelled; Voyager 2 flyby likely; detailed plans for Mariner Jupiter-Uranus, but no "start funding" yet; tentative plans for Pioneer Saturn-Uranus, Mariner Uranus-Neptune, likewise not funded yet.

Neptune study program, as for Uranus. *Results*: some internal heat, possibly due partly to Triton tides; high clouds, but no belt structures; rotation under review; Triton orbit decaying. *We need* full study program, particularly thorough exploration of Triton to determine its history, and polar samples to look for dust deposits. Grand Tour flyby cancelled; Voyager 2 flyby possible; Mariner Jupiter-Uranus could be sent on to Neptune, if it goes ahead; tentative plans only for Mariner Uranus-Neptune.

Pluto studies mostly ground-based, particularly at Kitt Peak Observatory. *Results*: may be as small as the Moon; methane ice detected, possibly others; mean temperature about 40°K; may be former moon of Neptune, but may alternatively have its own large moon; apparently cannot be responsible for observed perturbation of Uranus. *We need* detailed studies, correlated with Triton and Nereid findings, to determine Pluto's origin (and Triton's), also mapping and analysis of surface dust. Grand Tour flyby cancelled; no other missions planned yet.

Poseidon, a hypothetical tenth planet responsible for the perturbations first attributed to Pluto, has been sought for by ground-based telescopes but not found.

Comets have been studied optically from the ground, from aircraft and from Skylab; also spectroscopically from artificial satellites and from

Mariner 10; radar experiments unsuccessful so far. *Results*: some comets have very extensive hydrogen haloes, indicating that they are composed mainly of ices; others show copious dust emissions; increasing evidence of complex chemistry including organic compounds. *We need* detailed observations within tails and comae to compare with Earth's magneto-sphere, measurements of nucleus diameter, detailed nucleus photography, nucleus flyby to determine interior structure, nucleus landing and sample return. Tentative plans for comet encounter and comet rendezvous, but no funds. Halley ion-drive mission actively being studied.

Beyond Pluto we can only study absorption of starlight, and for increased effectiveness we need comparison with observations made in the outer Solar System. Pioneers 10 and 11 will eventually leave the Solar System, likewise Voyagers 1 and 2, but for effective studies we need interstellar probes moving at significant fractions of the speed of light, as in the British Interplanetary Society's Project Daedalus study. NASA has given financial support to the Daedalus enquiry, but costs of the project are estimated to be similar to those of the Vietnam War.

There is a long way to go, particularly in the light of Chapter 1's suggestion that manned exploration will be needed to make our under-standing of the Solar System comprehensive. As stated above, the first application of such knowledge is to better understanding of the Earth and our survival on it. But beyond that, we have to face the fact that in exploring the system we are also surveying its *usable* resources; having done so, it seems logical to ask what use we will actually make of them.

In *Man and the Stars* the foreseeable dangers to the human race were listed under eight headings; weapons of mass destruction, overpopulation, pollution of the environment, destruction of irreplaceable natural resources, long-term genetic breakdown, giant meteor impact, Sun change or nearby supernova, and Contact with other intelligence (not necessarily with malignant intent). With the understanding gained from the "new" Solar System, much can be done to counter the second, third and fourth threats, but space technology (as in Earth Resources, communications and weather satellites) will also be needed. In my own opinion, effective long-term solutions will include moving industry into space, deriving raw materials from elsewhere in the Solar System, and interplanetary settle-ments on the general lines suggested by O'Neill (see Chapter 12). To counter the first, fifth and sixth threats and begin on the seventh will likewise require such a prolonged space effort; and any action program aimed at guaranteering human survival against all eight will have inter-stellar colonization as its long-term objective, whether or not it follows the *Man and the Stars* outlines in detail. *Man and the Planets* will discuss the intermediate phase, from the first Shuttle launches in 1979 to full Kardashev 2 status, controlling the resources of the Solar System, over the next 200 years.

What then of the last lines of the Eliot quotation, the "half-heard" voices in the apple tree? – the same image as in the Tsiolkovsky quotation heading Chapter 13, as it happens. Although we may find life on Mars, on Titan or at the poles of Jupiter we will have to go beyond the Solar

System to find voices we can converse with; but the understanding we gain from other life in the Solar System may help us to hear those voices more quickly. In Chapter 12, Anthony Lawton suggested that Contact may come from positive action, laying claim to the natural resources around us, rather than from passive listening. The implications are beyond the scope of this book – but beyond doubt there will be more books, whether or not they come out of ASTRA discussion projects. The new look of the Solar System, 1979, is anything but the last word.

References

Chapter 1

1 Sir Robert Ball, *The Earth's Beginning*, Cassell, 1909
2 James Strong, *Search the Solar System*, David & Charles, 1973
3 Robert S. Richardson, *Mars*, Allen & Unwin, 1965
4 Douglas Arnold, "The Likeness of Apollo", in *Beyond this Horizon*, ed Christopher Carrel, Ceolfrith Arts, Sunderland Arts Centre, 1973
5 Kenneth W. Gatland, *The Pocket Encyclopedia of Spaceflight in Colour*, vols 1–4, Blandford Press (continuing series)
6 Brian W. Aldiss, "Who Can Replace a Man?" (short story), in *The Canopy of Time*, Faber & Faber, 1959
7 " 'Cockroach' on Mars", *Spaceflight*, vol 17, no 1, p 15, Jan 1975; "NASA's Smart Robot", *op cit*, pp 16–17
8 John W. Campbell, "Colloid v. Crystalloid", *Analog Science Fiction/Science Fact*, vol LXXVI, no 3, pp 6–9, 156–62, Nov 1965
9 Carl Sagan, *The Cosmic Connection*, Doubleday, 1973
10 Eric Burgess, "A Hat-trick for Mariner", *New Scientist*, vol 66, no 943, pp 15–18, 3 Apr 1975
11 Carl Sagan, "Viking to Mars: the Mission Strategy", *Sky & Telescope*, vol 50, no 1, pp 15–19 and 23, July 1975
12 David Baker, "Financial Setbacks in the US Space Programme", *Spaceflight*, vol 15, no 8, pp 306–8, Aug 1973
13 "Space Shuttle Workforce", *Spaceflight*, vol 14, no 12, p 456, Dec 1972
14 E. H. Wells, "Small Optical Telescopes on the Moon", *Spaceflight*, vol 14, no 3, pp 90–94, Mar 1972
15 "BAC and the Space Telescope", *Spaceflight*, vol 20, no 3, pp 105–6, Mar 1978
16 "Launches for Cash Customers", *Spaceflight*, vol 18, no 6, pp 218–19, June 1976
17 Robert Edgar, "Payloads for the Shuttle", *Spaceflight*, vol 18, no 9, pp 327–30, Sept 1976
18 Jerry Pournelle, "Halfway to Anywhere", *Galaxy*, vol 34, no 7, pp 94–101, Apr 1974

Chapter 2

1 Willy Ley and Chesley Bonestell, *The Conquest of Space*, Sidgwick & Jackson, 1951
2 Arthur C. Clarke, *The Exploration of Space*, Temple Press, 1951
3 Kenneth W. Gatland and Anthony M. Kunesch, *Space Travel*, Allan Wingate, 1953
4 Arthur C. Clarke and R. A. Smith, *The Exploration of the Moon*, Frederick Muller, 1954
5 Cornelius Ryan (ed), *Across the Space Frontier*, Sidgwick & Jackson, 1953
6 Cornelius Ryan (ed), *The Conquest of the Moon*; UK edition: *Man on the Moon*, Sidgwick & Jackson, 1953
7 James McGovern, *Crossbow and Overcast*, Hutchinson, 1965
8 J. Gordon Vaeth, "Personal Profile", *Spaceflight*, vol 12, no 8, pp 326–9, Aug 1970
9 John L. Chapman, *Atlas, the Story of a Missile*, Gollancz, 1960
10 Jonathon Norton Leonard, *Flight into Space*, Sidgwick & Jackson, 1953
11 Arthur C. Clarke, *The Making of a Moon*, Muller, 1957
12 Desmond King-Hele, *Satellites and Scientific Research*, revised edition, Routledge & Kegan Paul, 1962
13 Lloyd Mallan, *Space Satellites*, Fawcett Publications, Greenwich, Connecticut, 1958
14 Werner Buedeler, *Operation Vanguard*, Union Verlag, Stuttgart, 1956; translation: A. L. Helm, Burke; revised edition, 1958
15 Milton W. Rosen, *The Viking Rocket Story*, Faber & Faber, 1956

16 A. Scott Crossfield and Clay Blair Jr, *Always Another Dawn*, Hodder & Stoughton, 1961

17 Walter Dornberger, *V2*, 1952; translation: James Clough and Geoffrey Halliday, Hurst & Blackett, 1954

18 Frank K. Everest, *The Fastest Man Alive*, Cassell, 1958

19 W. R. Lundgren, *Across the High Frontier*, Gollancz, 1956

20 William Bridgeman, *The Lonely Sky*, Cassell, 1956

21 Martin Caidin, *Race for the Moon*, William Kimber, 1965

22 Lloyd Mallan, *Space Science*, Fawcett Publications, 1961

23 Martin Caidin, *Worlds in Space*, Sidgwick & Jackson, 1954

24 Irmgard Gröttrup, *Rocket Wife*, André Deutsch, 1959

25 M. Vassiliev and V. V. Dobronravov, *Sputnik into Space*, State Publishing House, Moscow; translation: Souvenir Press, 1958

26 C. M. Green, M. Lomask, *Vanguard – a History*, NASA SP-4202, US Govt Printing Office, 1970

27 "Go! Colonel Glenn in Orbit", *Daily Express* record, in collaboration with NBC News, 1962

28 David G. Simons and Don A. Schanche, *Man High: 24 hours on the edge of space*, Doubleday, 1960

29 David Baker, "The X-15 in Retrospect", *Spaceflight*, vol 13, no 6, pp 216-19, June 1971

30 Kenneth F. Weaver, "Project Mercury: Countdown for Space", *National Geographic Magazine*, vol 119, no 5, pp 702-34, May 1961

31 Kenneth W. Gatland, *Spacecraft and Boosters*, vol 1, Iliffe, 1964

32 *Into Orbit*, by the seven astronauts of Project Mercury, Cassell, 1962

33 Joseph N. Bell, *Seven into Space*, Ebury Press, 1960

34 John Noble Winford, *We Reach the Moon*, Bantam Books, 1969

35 Martin Caidin, *Rendezvous in Space*, Dutton, 1962

36 Lloyd Mallan, *Man into Space*, Fawcett Publications, 1960

37 Kenneth F. Weaver, "Space Rendezvous, Milestone on the Way to the Moon", *National Geographic Magazine*, vol 129, no 4, pp 538-53, Apr 1966

38 "The Glorious Walk in the Cosmos", *Life International*, 28 June 1965

39 James E. Oberg, "The Voshkod Programme: Krushev's Folly?", *Spaceflight*, vol 16, no 4, pp 145-9, Apr 1974

Chapter 3 (A. E. Roy)

Ehricke, K. A., *Space Flight, Vol. II, Dynamics*, Chapter 9, Van Nostrand and Company, Inc, 1962

Hohmann, W., *Die Erreichbarkeit der Himmelskörper*, R. Oldensbourg Publishing Co, Munich, 1925

Roy, A. E., *The Foundations of Astrodynamics*, The Macmillan Company, New York, 1965

Vortregt, M., "Interplanetary Navigation", *Journal of the British Interplanetary Society*, vol 15, 1956

Chapter 4

1 John Nobel Wilford, *We Reach the Moon*, Bantam Books, 1969

2 Dave Dooling, "The Evolution of the Apollo Spacecraft", *Spaceflight*, vol 16, no 4, pp 127-36, Apr 1974

3 Homer E. Newell, "First Colour Photographs on the Moon's Rocky Face", *National Geographic Magazine*, vol 136, no 4, pp 578-92, Oct 1966

4 *Surveyor Program Results*, NASA SP-184, US Govt Printing Office, 1969

5 James Nasmyth and James Carpenter, *The Moon, considered as a planet, a world, and a satellite*, John Murray, 1874

6 Adrian Berry, *The Next Ten Thousand Years*, Jonathan Cape, 1974

7 Arthur C. Clarke, *The Exploration of Space*, Temple Press, 1951

8 Joseph Sadil and Ludek Pesek, *The Moon and the Planets*, Paul Hamlyn, 1963

9 Kenneth F. Weaver, "Apollo 15 Explores the Mountains of the Moon", *National Geographic Magazine*, vol 141, no 2, pp 230-65, Feb 1972

10 David R. Scott, "What Is It Like to Walk on the Moon?", *National Geographic Magazine*, vol 144, no 3, pp 327-9, Sept 1973

11 James B. Irwin and William A. Emerson Jr, *To Rule the Night*, Hodder & Stoughton, 1973

12 Harrison M. Schmitt, "Exploring Taurus-Littrow", *National Geographic Magazine*, vol 144, no 3, pp 290–307, Sept 1973

13 J. F. Culver, "The Human Eye in Space Exploration", in *Fourth International Symposium on Bioastronautics and the Exploration of Space*, ed Roadman, Strughold and Mitchell, Aerosphere Medical Division (AFSC), Brook Air Force Base, Texas, 1968

14 "Work on the Moon", *Spaceflight*, vol 12, no 4, p 186, Apr 1970

15 C. S. Lewis, *Out of the Silent Planet*, John Lane, The Bodley Head, 1938

16 Hal Clement, "Mistaken for Granted" (short story), *If*, vol 22, no 3, Jan/Feb 1974

17 "Apollo 16 Brings Us Visions from Space", *National Geographic Magazine*, vol 142, no 6, pp 856–65, Dec 1972

18 *Splendour of the Heavens*, Hutchinson, nd

19 Gene Simmons, *On the Moon with Apollo 17, a guidebook to Taurus-Littrow*, NASA EP-101, US Govt Printing Office, Dec 1972

20 P. J. Parker, "The Triumph of Apollo 12", (Part 1), *Spaceflight*, vol 12, no 2, pp 77–81, Feb 1970

21 "LM Effects on Surveyor 3", *Spaceflight*, vol 12, no 7, pp 279–80, July 1970

22 P. M. Molton, "Survival of Micro-Organisms on the Moon", *Spaceflight*, vol 15, no 2, p 51, Feb 1973

23 "Germs on the Moon", *Spaceflight*, vol 12, no 11, p 451, Nov 1970

24 "Nuclear Power Triumph", *Spaceflight*, vol 16, no 3, p 107, Mar 1974

25 P. J. Parker, "We Have a Problem!", *Spaceflight*, vol 12, no 9, pp 356–8, Sept 1970

26 "Cause of Apollo 13 Mishap", *op cit*, p 358

27 J. O. Cappellari Jr and W. I. McLaughlin, "Telescopic Observations of Lunar Missions", *Spaceflight*, vol 13, no 10, pp 363–9, Oct 1971

28 *Astronautics and Aeronautics, 1970: Chronology on Science, Technology and Policy*, NASA SP-4015, US Govt Printing Office, 1972

29 David Baker, "Apollo 14: a Visit to Fra Mauro" (Part 1), *Spaceflight*, vol 13, no 5, pp 164–9, May 1971

30 David Baker, "Apollo 14: a Visit to Fra Mauro" (Part 2), *Spaceflight*, vol 13, no 6, pp 210–12, June 1971

31 David Baker, "Expedition to Hadley-Apennine – 1", *Spaceflight*, vol 13, no 10, pp 358–62, Oct 1971

32 David Baker, "Lunar Roving Vehicle: Design Report", *Spaceflight*, vol 13, no 7, pp 234–40, July 1971

33 Isaac Asimov, "The Great Borning", *Fantasy & Science Fiction*, vol 33, no 13, pp 106–16, Sept 1967

34 V. A. Firsoff, *Strange World of the Moon*, Hutchinson, 1959

35 "The Lunar Rocks", *Spaceflight*, vol 12, no 4, p 183, Apr 1970

36 J. E. Davies, "Preliminary Examination of the Apollo 12 Lunar Samples", *Spaceflight*, vol 13, no 1, pp 24–29, Jan 1971

37 Anthony J. Calio, "What Apollo Achieved on the Moon", *Spaceflight*, vol 16, no 12, pp 462–3, Dec 1974

38 Edwin B. Aldrin Jr and Wayne Warga, *Return to Earth*, Random House, New York, 1973

39 Kenneth F. Weaver, "Have We Solved the Mysteries of the Moon?", *National Geographic Magazine*, vol 144, no 3, pp 309–25, Sept 1973

40 "Transient Lunar Phenomena", *Spaceflight*, vol 14, no 9, p 353, Sept 1972

41 R. S. Richardson and N. A. Kozyrev, "A Volcano on the Moon?"/"Observations of a Volcanic Process on the Moon", in *Man and the Moon*, ed R. S. Richardson, World Publishing Company, 1961

42 Joseph F. Goodavage, "What Strange – and Frightening – Discoveries Did Our Astronauts Make on the Moon?", *Saga*, vol 47, no 6, pp 30–3, 36, and 38–40, Mar 1974

43 J. E. Davies, "Apollo Seismic Experiments", *Spaceflight*, vol 13, no 10, pp 370–3, Oct 1971

44 P. J. Parker, "The Triumph of Apollo 12" (Part 2), *Spaceflight*, vol 12, no 3, pp 118–20, Mar 1970; Photographs p 123

45 Robert Sheckley, "Ask a Foolish Question" (short story), *Science Fiction Stories*, 1953; also in *Citizen in Space*, Ballantine Books, 1955

46 "Heat-Flow Experiment", Section 11, *Apollo 15 Preliminary Science Report*, NASA SP-289, US Govt Printing Office, 1972

47 David Baker, "Mission to Descartes – 2", *Spaceflight*, vol 14, no 8, pp 287–91, Aug 1972

48 David Baker, "The Last Apollo – 2", *Spaceflight*, vol 15, no 3, pp 87–91, Mar 1973
49 "Has the Moon a Core?", *Spaceflight*, vol 14, no 10, p 380, Oct 1972
50 "Moon-Strike Recorded", *Spaceflight*, vol 14, no 8, p 301, Aug 1972
51 "Rock of Lunar Mountains", *Spaceflight*, vol 14, no 8, p 300, Aug 1972
52 R. L. Lomas, "Estimates of the Moon's Geometry using Lunar Orbiter Imagery and Apollo Laser Altimeter Data", NASA TR R–407, US Govt Printing Office, Oct 1973
53 C. W. Wolfe, "Secondary Relief Features as Clues to Planetary Formation", in *Second Conference on Planetology and Space Mission Planning*, Annals of the New York Academy of Sciences, vol 163, Article 1, pp 1–558
54 E. A. Steinhoff, "Importance of the Use of Extraterrestrial Resources to the Economy of Space Flight beyond Near-Earth Orbit", in *Fourth International Symposium on Bioastronautics and the Exploration of Space, op cit*
55 "Titanium on the Moon", *Spaceflight*, vol 12, no 2, p 67, Feb 1970
56 "Tektites and the Origin of the Moon", *Journal of the British Interplanetary Society*, vol 27, no 11, p 866, Nov 1974
57 "Tektites – terrestrial or lunar?", *Spaceflight*, vol 14, no 8, p 313, Aug 1972
58 T. Page, "Notes on Lunar Research", *Sky & Telescope,* vol 48, no 2, pp 88–90, Aug 1974
59 "The Fate of Satellites of the Moon", *Journal of the British Interplanetary Society*, vol 27, no 5, p 385, May 1974
60 R. J. Fryer, "Apollo Mission Plans", *Spaceflight*, vol 12, no 3, pp 120–1, Mar 1970
61 D. T. Schowalter and T. B. Malone, "The Development of a Lunar Habitability System", NASA CR–1676, US Govt Printing Office, Feb 1972
62 "Awesome Views of the Forbidding Moonscape", *National Geographic Magazine*, vol 135, no 2, pp 233–9, Feb 1969
63 Edgar D. Mitchell, "Space Experiment in ESP", *Spaceflight*, vol 14, no 1, pp 20–21, Jan 1972
64 S. C. Phillips, "Apollo 8: A Most Fantastic Voyage", *National Geographic Magazine*, vol 135, no 5, pp 593–631, May 1969
65 Virgil "Gus" Grissom, *Gemini!: a personal account of man's venture into space*, 1968
66 Ben Bova, "Giant Step Backward", *Analog Science Fiction/Science Fact*, vol XCI, no 6, pp 5–9 and 177–8, Aug 1973
67 "The Apollo 15 Investigation", *Spaceflight*, vol 15, no 2, pp 71–2, Feb 1973
68 David Baker, "Implications of the 1975 NASA Budget", *Spaceflight*, vol 16, no 10, pp 362–5, Oct 1974

Chapter 5 (A. F. Nimmo)
Arthur C. Clarke, *The Promise of Space*, Pelican Books, 1970
Arthur C. Clarke, *Profiles of the Future*, Pan Books, 1973
Duncan Lunan, *Man and the Stars*, Souvenir Press, 1974
John McHale, *World Facts and Trends*, The Macmillan Company, New York, 1972
Roland Pressat, *Demographic Analysis*, E. Arnold, 1972
Mahmood Mamdani, "The Myth of Population Control", *Monthly Review Press*, 1972
Tomas Frejka, *The Future of Population Growth*, Interscience, 1973
Gordon Rattray Taylor, *The Biological Time Bomb*, Signet Books, 1969
E. A. Steinhoff, "Importance of the Use of Extraterrestrial Resources to the Economy of Space Flight beyond Near-Earth Orbit", in *Fourth International Symposium on Bioastronautics and the Exploration of Space, op cit*, Chapter 4

UNITED NATIONS PUBLICATIONS (NEW YORK):
"A Concise Summary of the World Population in the 1970s; Population and Vital Statistics, Data Available as of 1st Oct", 1972
"The Determinants and Consequences of Population Trends, vol 1", 1973
"The United Nations Demographic Yearbook 1973", 1974
"Asia: an Area Assessment", Raphael M. Salas, 1974
"World Population Year Bulletin No. 11", Mar–Apr 1974

UNITED NATIONS PUBLICATIONS (GENEVA):
"Development Forum", Dec 1974 issue

SCIENTIFIC AMERICAN:
John B. Calhoun, "Population Density and Social Pathology", Feb 1962
Geoffrey Eglinton, James R. Maxwell, and Colin T. Pillinger, "The Carbon Chemistry of the Moon" (Apollo 11), Oct 1972

SPACEFLIGHT:
"Titanium on the Moon" (Apollo 11), Feb 1970
"Lunar Science Results" (Apollo 11), Aug 1970
"Preliminary Examinations of the Apollo 12 Lunar Samples", J. E. Davies (Apollo 12), Jan 1971
"Space Report: Luna 16 Samples", Feb 1971
"Space Report: the Fra Mauro Samples" (Apollo 14), Nov 1971
"Space Report: the Moon Found Serene" (Apollo 15), Dec 1971
"Space Report: Apollonius Crater", Aug 1972
R. C. Parkinson, "Takeoff Point for a Lunar Colony", pp 322-6, Sept 1974
"Lunar Water Process", p 131, Apr 1971

JOURNAL OF THE BRITISH INTERPLANETARY SOCIETY:
G. L. Matloff and A. J. Fennelly, "A Superconducting Ion Scoop and its Application to Interstellar Flight", vol 27, pp 663-73, Sept 1974

ANALOG:
G. Harry Stine, "The Third Industrial Revolution (Conclusion)", Feb 1973

NEW SCIENTIST:
Graham Chedd, "Colonization at Lagrangea", 24 Oct 1974

NEW INTERNATIONALIST, MAY 1974:
"The Myth of Population Control"
Peter Adamson, "A Population Policy and a Development Policy Are One and the Same Thing"
Pierre Pradervand, "The Malthusian Man"
Pi-Chao Chen, "The Largest Nation on Earth"
Sue Tuckwell, "Abortion: the Hidden Plague"
Mahl, "The Super Gadjet"

Chapter 6
1 Arthur Koestler, *The Sleepwalkers*, Hutchinson, 1959
2 Richard C. Hoagland, "Why We *Won't* Find Life on Mars", *Analog Science Fiction/Science Fact*, vol XCIV, no 4, pp 51-70, Dec 1974
3 Patrick Moore, *Guide to Mars*, Frederick Muller, 1956
4 Kenneth F. Weaver, "Journey to Mars", *National Geographic Magazine*, vol 143, no 2, pp 231-63, Feb 1973
5 " 'Red Planet' Mars is Really Blue, Green and Orange", *The Daily Telegraph*, p 19, 12 Nov 1974
6 Robert S. Richardson, *Mars*, George Allen & Unwin, 1965
7 Bruce Murray (ed), *Mars and the Mind of Man*, Harper & Row, 1973
8 Patrick Moore and Charles Cross, *Mars*, Mitchell Beazley, 1973
9 Lee Correy, "Twin-Planet Probe", *Analog Science Fiction/Science Fact*, vol LXXVI, no 6, pp 86-98, Feb 1966
10 W. H. Pickering, "Mars in Focus", *Spaceflight*, vol 12, no 3, pp 98-103, Mar 1970
11 Charles A. Cross, "Mapping the Surface of Mars", *Spaceflight*, vol 13, no 11, pp 402-7, Nov 1971
12 David Baker, "Orbiters to Mars", *Spaceflight*, vol 13, no 5, pp 187-92, May 1971
13 Kenneth F. Weaver, "Voyage to the Planets", *National Geographic Magazine*, vol 138, no 2, pp 147-93, Aug 1970
14 Carl Sagan, *The Cosmic Connection*, Doubleday, 1973
15 *Spaceflight*, vol 14, no 2, p 68, Feb 1972
16 W. K. Hartmann, "A 1974 Tour of the Planets", *Sky & Telescope*, vol 48, no 2, pp 78-80, Aug 1974

17 "Solar System Chemistry", *Journal of the British Interplanetary Society*, vol 27, no 2, pp 148–9, Feb 1974
18 E. C. Slipher, "New Light on the Changing Face of Mars", *National Geographic Magazine*, vol CVIII, no 3, pp 427–36, Sept 1955
19 Carl Sagan, "Exobiology" in *New Science and the Solar System: a New Scientist Special Review*, IPC Magazines Ltd, 1975
20 James Strong, *Search the Solar System*, David & Charles, 1973
21 Carl Sagan, O. B. Toon, and P. J. Gierasch, "Climatic Change on Mars", Cornell University Centre for Radiophysics and Space Research
22 Willy Ley and Wernher von Braun, *The Exploration of Mars*, Sidgwick & Jackson, 1956
23 "Mars Probes Off Target", *Spaceflight*, vol 16, no 6, pp 213–14, June 1974
24 "The Past and Present of Mars" (Novosti Press Agency), *Spaceflight*, vol 16, no 8, pp 291–3, Aug 1974
25 Richard Goody, "Weather on the Inner Planets", in *New Science in the Solar System, op cit*
26 Carl Sagan, "Viking to Mars: the Mission Strategy", *Sky & Telescope*, vol 50, no 1, pp 15–19 and 23 July 1975
27 "The Landing Sites", *Spaceflight*, vol 18, nos 7–8, pp 238–40, July–Aug 1976
28 Carl Sagan and I. S. Shlovskii, *Intelligent Life in the Universe*, Holden-Day, 1966
29 "Viking on Mars", *Spaceflight*, vol 18, no 9, pp 332–4, Sept 1976
30 *Sky & Telescope*, vol 52, no 2 (Aug 1976)
31 "Surface of Mars", *Spaceflight*, vol 15, no 1, p 22, Jan 1973
32 Richard S. Lewis, "On the Golden Plains of Mars", *Spaceflight*, vol 18, no 10, pp 356–64, Oct 1976
33 J. Kelly Beatty, "Viking 1 Lands on a Very Red Planet", *Sky & Telescope*, vol 52, no 3, pp 156–61, Sept 1976
34 Eric Burgess, "First Days on Mars", *New Scientist*, vol 71, no 1011, pp 214–17, 29 July 1976
35 *Splendour of the Heavens*, Hutchinson, nd
36 Willy Ley and Chesley Bonestell, *The Conquest of Space*, Sidgwick & Jackson, 1951
37 Roger Lewin, "Life on Mars: curiouser and curiouser", *New Scientist*, vol 71, no 1013, pp 328–30, 12 Aug 1976
38 Eric Burgess, "Space Scientists Still Optimistic about Life on Mars", *New Scientist*, vol 71, no 1015, p 439, 26 Aug 1976
39 "Mars Looks a Little Livelier Each Day", *New Scientist*, vol 71, no 1016, p 476, 2 Sept 1976
40 Eric Burgess, "Life on Mars Creeps Closer", *New Scientist*, p 480, 2 Sept 1976
41 "Viking 2 on Mars: 'A Forest of Rocks' ", *Sky & Telescope*, vol 52, no 4, pp 252–3, Oct 1976
42 "Stream Bed on the Surface of Mars?", *New Scientist*, vol 72, no 1024, p 214, 28 Oct 1976
43 "Milestones", *Spaceflight*, vol 16, no 5, p 161, May 1974
44 Carl Sagan, "Science Horizons", US Information Service, April 1972 (abridged from *Times* magazine)
45 Richard S. Lewis, "The Puzzle of the Martian Soil", *Spaceflight*, vol 18, no 11, pp 391–5, Nov 1976
46 "Life but No Bodies on Mars", *New Scientist*, vol 72, no 1022, p 78, 14 Oct 1976
47 "Viking Update", *Sky & Telescope*, vol 52, no 5, p 333, Nov 1976
48 "Mars Viewed from the Viking 1 Orbiter", *Sky & Telescope*, vol 52, no 3, pp 171–4, Sept 1976
49 Robert L. Staehle, "Mars Polar Ice Sample Return Mission – 1", *Spaceflight*, vol 18, no 11, pp 383–90, Nov 1976
50 Eric Burgess, "Mars – a Water Planet?", *New Scientist*, vol 72, no 1023, pp 152–3, 21 Oct 1976
51 K. A. Ehricke, "A Strategic Approach to Interplanetary Flight", in *Fourth International Symposium on Bioastronautics and the Exploration of Space, op cit*
52 "Project Daedalus, an Interim Report on the BIS Starship Study", *Spaceflight*, vol 16, no 9, pp 356–8, Sept 1974
53 S. F. Singer, "The Martian Satellites", in *Physical Studies of Minor Planets*, ed T. Gehrels, NASA SP-267, US Govt Printing Office, 1971
54 "The Surface of Deimos", *Spaceflight*, vol 14, no 9, p 356, Sept 1972
55 "Viking Looks at Phobos in Detail", *New Scientist*, vol 72, no 1023, p 158, 21 Oct 1976

56 "75 Miles from Phobos", *New Scientist*, vol 74, no 1046, p 19, 7 May 1977
57 "Zooming in on Phobos", *Scientific American*, vol 236, no 4, p 57, Apr 1977
58 Geraint Day, "Martian Dust Storms – a Mechanism for Transportation of Life?" *Spaceflight*, vol 20, no 3, pp 83–8, Mar 1978
59 "Viking Amid Martian Frost", *Sky & Telescope*, vol 55, no 2, p 106, Feb 1978
60 J. Kelly Beatty, "Vikings to Earth: 'It's Cold Up Here!' ", *Sky & Telescope*, vol 53, no 6, pp 417–20, June 1977
61 James A. Cutts *et al*, "North Polar Region of Mars: Imaging Results from Viking 2", *Science*, vol 194, no 4271, pp 1329–37, 17 Dec 1976
62 Michael A. Michaud, "Spaceflight, Colonization and Independence: a Synthesis", Part One, *Journal of the British Interplanetary Society*, vol 30, no 3, pp 83–95, Mar 1977
63 Joseph Veverka, "Phobos and Deimos", *Scientific American*, vol 236, no 2, pp 30–7, Feb 1977
64 Ian Ridpath, *Messages from the Stars*, Fontana/Collins, 1978
65 "Moons of Mars", *Spaceflight*, vol 19, nos 7–8, p 265, July–Aug 1977
66 "Striations on Phobos", *Sky & Telescope*, vol 54, no 4, p 269, Oct 1977
67 "Zooming in on Phobos and Deimos", *Sky & Telescope*, vol 54, no 6, p 469, Dec 1977

Chapter 7

1 Svante Arrhenius, *The Destinies of the Stars*, Putnam, 1918
2 Jet Propulsion Laboratory, California Institute of Technology, *Mariner: Mission to Venus*, McGraw-Hill, 1963
3 Patrick Moore, *The Planet Venus*, Faber & Faber, 1961
4 "The Fate of Satellites of the Moon", *Journal of the British Interplanetary Society*, vol 27, no 5, p 385, May 1974
5 Isaac Asimov, *The Tragedy of the Moon*, Coronet Books, Hodder & Stoughton, 1975
6 Isaac Asimov, "Four Steps to Salvation", *Fantasy & Science Fiction* (British edition), vol II, no 11, pp 44–54, Oct 1961
7 Lucien Radaux and G. de Vaucouleurs, *Larousse Encyclopedia of Astronomy*, Batchworth Press, 1959
8 Patrick Moore, *Science and Fiction*, Harrap, 1957
9 Ray Bradbury, "The Long Rain", *The Illustrated Man*, Doubleday, 1951
10 John Wyndham (with Lucas Parkes), *The Outward Urge*, Science Fiction Book Club, 1961
11 John Christopher, *The 22nd Century*, Grayson & Grayson, 1954
12 Henry Kuttner, *Fury*, Mayflower-Dell, 1963
13 Carl Sagan, "The Planet Venus", *Science*, vol 133, 24 Mar 1961
14 J. D. Strong, 'Conditions on the Planet Venus", in *Fourth International Symposium on Bioastronautics and the Exploration of Space, op cit*
15 Zdenek Kopal, *Man and his Universe*, Rupert Hart-Davis, 1972
16 *Mariner-Venus 1967: Final Project Report*, NASA SP–190, US Govt Printing Office, 1971
17 Carl Sagan and I. S. Shlovskii, *Intelligent Life in the Universe*, Holden-Day, 1966
18 "Rotation of Venus", *Spaceflight*, vol 12, no 12, p 491, Dec 1970
19 D. Ya. Martynov, *The Planets: Solved and Unsolved Problems*, "Nauka" Press, Moscow, 1970; trans NASA TT F–698, US Govt Printing Office, May 1972
20 James Strong, *Search the Solar System*, David & Charles, 1973
21 Garry Hunt, "Venus", in *New Science in the Solar System, op cit*
22 T. Ransome, "Investigations of the Atmosphere of Venus", *Spaceflight*, vol 12, no 10, pp 415–17, Oct 1970
23 K. L. Plummer, "1970: a Soviet Space Year", *Spaceflight*, vol 13, no 5, pp 175–9, May 1971
24 "Design of Venera 8", *Spaceflight*, vol 14, no 12, p 460, Dec 1972
25 "New Generation Venera", *Spaceflight*, vol 15, no 11, p 428, Nov 1973
26 "Venera 8 Results", *Spaceflight*, vol 15, no 1, p 23, Jan 1973
27 "Milestones", *Spaceflight*, vol 15, no 3, p 161, May 1973
28 Carl Sagan, *The Cosmic Connection*, Doubleday, 1973
29 "Pulsating Clouds of Venus", *Spaceflight*, vol 15, no 10, p 376, Oct 1973
30 "Solar System Chemistry", *Journal of the British Interplanetary Society*, vol 27, no 2, pp 148–9, Feb 1974
31 Harold C. Urey, "Some Remarks on the Evolution of the Atmosphere and Oceans", in *Fourth International Symposium on Bioastronautics and the Exploration of Space*

32 *Flight International*, p 544, 4 Oct 1973
33 *Journal of the British Interplanetary Society*, vol 25, p 669, 1972
34 "Earthquakes and the Earth's Magnetism", *Journal of the British Interplanetary Society*, vol 27, no 2, p 150, Feb 1974
35 J. E. Enever, "Giant Meteor Impact", *Analog Science Fact/Science Fiction*, vol LXXVII, no 1, pp 61–84, Mar 1966
36 "The Atmosphere of Venus", JBIS vol 27, no 2, pp 150–1, Feb 1974
37 R. G. Perel'man, *Goals and Means in the Conquest of Space*, "Nauka" Press, Moscow, 1967; translation NASA TT F-595, US Govt Printing Office
38 "Venus Unveiled", *Spaceflight*, vol 18, no 1, pp 20–1 and 40, Jan 1976
39 "Veneras 9 and 10 on Venus", *Sky & Telescope*, vol 50, no 6, pp 374–5, Dec 1975
40 "Veneras 9 and 10 Create a Sensation", *New Scientist*, vol 68, no 973, p 260, 30 Oct 1975
41 "Milestones", *Spaceflight*, vol 18, no 4, p 117, Apr 1976
42 "Experiments for 1978 Venus Probe", *Spaceflight*, vol 16, no 10, p 389, Oct 1974
43 "1978 Venus Probe", *Spaceflight*, vol 15, no 11, p 428, Nov 1973
44 "Plans for Venus", *Spaceflight*, vol 14, no 6, p 224, June 1972
45 Isaac Asimov, "Not as We Know It", in *View from a Height*, Dobson, 1964
46 N. W. Pirie, "Germanium as a Carbon Analogue", in *The Scientist Speculates*, ed I. J. Good, Heinemann, 1962
47 Stanislaw Lem, *Solaris*, Faber & Faber, 1971
48 F. J. Dyson, "The Search for Extraterrestrial Technology", in *Perspectives in Modern Physics*, ed R. E. Marshak, Interscience, 1966
49 G. Colombo, *Feasibility of a Combined Jupiter Fly-by and Out-of-the-Ecliptic Mission*, ESRO Report SN-15, Dec 1967
50 Werner Sandner, *The Planet Mercury*, Faber, 1963
51 Alan E. Nourse, "Brightside Crossing" (short story), in *Tiger by the Tail*, Dobson, 1962
52 Roger Zelazny, *Jack of Shadows*, Faber & Faber, 1971
53 Arthur C. Clarke, "The Wall of Darkness" (short story), in *The Other Side of the Sky*, Gollancz, 1961
54 Kenneth F. Weaver, "Voyage to the Planets", *National Geographic Magazine*, vol 138, no 2, pp 147–93, Aug 1970
55 "Surface of Mercury", *Spaceflight*, vol 14, no 8, p 314, Aug 1972
56 "Radar Probes Mercury", *Spaceflight*, vol 16, no 4, pp 150–1, Apr 1974
57 G. R. Hollenbeck, D. G. Roos and P. S. Lewis, *Ballistic Mode Mercury Orbiter Mission Opportunity Handbook*, NASA CR-2298, US Govt Printing Office, Aug 1973
58 John Guest, "Mercury", in *New Science in the Solar System*, op cit
59 "Mission to Mercury", *Spaceflight*, vol 16, no 7, pp 265–9, July 1974
60 C. A. Cross, "Encounter with Mercury", *Spaceflight*, vol 16, no 8, pp 282–90, Aug 1974
61 J. Kelly Beatty, "Mariner 10's Second Look at Mercury", *Sky & Telescope*, vol 48, no 5, pp 307–14, Nov 1974
62 "Mariner 10 and Mercury", *Sky & Telescope*, vol 48, no 3, pp 157–9, Sept 1974
63 V. A. Firsoff, "Could Mercury have Ice-Caps?", *The Observatory*, Apr 1971
64 Eric Burgess, "A Hat-trick for Mariner", *New Scientist*, vol 66, no 943, pp 15–18, 3 April 1975
65 "Mercury's Surface", JBIS, vol 28, no 5, p 347, May 1975
66 Larry Niven, "Inconstant Moon" (short story), in *Inconstant Moon*, Gollancz, 1973
67 "Mercury a Past Satellite of Venus?" JBIS, vol 28, no 5, pp 347–8, May 1975
68 Patrick Moore, *Guide to the Planets*, Collins, 1957
69 Ian Ridpath, *Stars and Space 77*, Independent Newspapers Ltd, 1977
70 "Lava Flows on Venus", *Spaceflight*, vol 10, no 1, pp 18–20, Jan 1977

Chapter 8

1 Dandridge M. Cole and Donald W. Cox, *Islands in Space: the Challenge of the Planetoids*, Chilton Books, 1964
2 Willy Ley, *Satellites, Rockets and Outer Space*, Signet Key Books, 1958
3 "Evolution of the Asteroids", *Sky & Telescope*, vol 46, no 6, p 367, Dec 1973
4 Jerry Pournelle, "A Step Farther Out", *Galaxy*, vol 35, no 5, pp 105–13, May 1974
5 F. Yu. Ziegel, *The Minor Planets*, NASA TT F-700, US Govt Printing Office, May 1972

6 David Baker, "Report from Jupiter, part 1", *Spaceflight*, vol 16, no 4, pp 140–4, Apr 1974

7 Anthony R. Martin, "The Detection of Extrasolar Planetary Systems", Part 2, JBIS, vol 27, no 12, pp 881–907, Dec 1974

8 S. K. Vsekhsvyatskiy, *The Nature and Origin of Comets and Meteors*, 'Prosveshcheniye Press, Moscow, 1967; translation NASA TT F–608, US Govt Printing Office, Apr 1970

9 F. L. Whipple, "Why Missions to Comets and Asteroids?", *Astronautics and Aeronautics*, pp 12–16, Oct 1972

10 "The Early Solar System", *Spaceflight*, vol 14, no 9, p 354, Sept 1972

11 Clark R. Chapman, "The Nature of Asteroids", *Scientific American*, vol 232, no 1, pp 24–34, Jan 1975

12 C. P. Sonett, "The Relationship of Meteoritic Parent Body Thermal Histories and Electromagnetic Heating by a Pre-main Sequence T Tauri Sun", in *Physical Studies of Minor Planets*, ed T. Gehrels, NASA SP–267, US Govt Printing Office, 1971

13 Thornton Page, "Notes on Lunar Research", *Sky & Telescope*, vol 48, no 2, pp 88–90, Aug 1974

14 "The Surface of Deimos", *Spaceflight*, vol 14, no 9, p 356, Sept 1972

15 "A New Interior Planet", *Sky & Telescope*, vol 51, no 3, p 158, Mar 1976

16 A. C. Macey and J. Niehoff, "Sample Return Missions to the Asteroid Eros", in *Physical Studies of Minor Planets*, op cit

17 James Strong, *Search the Solar System*, David & Charles, 1973

18 B. Zellner, "New Findings About Eros", *Sky & Telescope*, vol 50, no 6, pp 376–9, Dec 1975

19 H. F. Meissinger and E. W. Greenstadt, "Design and Science Instrumentation of an Unmanned Vehicle for Sample Return from the Asteroid Eros", in *Physical Studies of the Minor Planets*, op cit

20 Jean Maeus, "Minor Planet's Orbit" (letter), *Spaceflight*, vol 14, no 12, p 479, Dec 1972

21 "The Triplet System, Earth–Moon–Toro", *Spaceflight*, vol 14, no 8, pp 312–13, Aug 1972

22 P. M. Janiczek, P. K. Seidelmann and R. L. Dunscombe, "A Minor Planet on an Inner Grand Tour", abstract in programme of the third regular meeting of the Division on Dynamical Astronomy, American Astronomical Society, University of Maryland, 2–3 March 1972

23 Isaac Asimov, "The Rocks of Damocles", in *Asimov on Astronomy*, Macdonald & Jane's, 1974

24 Luigi G. Jacchia, "A Meteorite that Missed the Earth", *Sky & Telescope*, vol 48, no 1, pp 4–9, July 1974

25 Arthur C. Clarke, *Rendezvous with Rama*, Gollancz, 1973

26 Ralph A. Hall, "Secondary Meteorites", *Analog Science Fiction/Science Fact*, vol LXXII, no 5, pp 8–16 and 81–5, Jan 1964

27 Ralph A. Hall, "Giant Meteor Impact", *Analog Science Fiction/Science Fact*, vol LXXVII, no 1, pp 61–84, Mar 1966

28 G. Harry Stine, "The Third Industrial Revolution: the Exploitation of the Space Environment", *Spaceflight*, vol 16, no 9, pp 327–34, Sept 1974

29 Ian Ridpath, *Messages from the Stars*, Fontana/Collins, 1978

30 Keith Hindley, "Fireball Networks – a Mixed Blessing", *New Scientist*, vol 72, no 1032, pp 695–8, Dec 23–30 1976

Chapter 9

1 R. D. Enzmann, "Introduction to the Section on Environments", in *Second Conference on Planetology and Space Mission Planning*, op cit

2 D. Ya. Martynov, *The Planets: Solved and Unsolved Problems*, op cit

3 S. K. Vesekhsvyatskiy, *The Nature and Origin of Comets and Meteors*, op cit

4 S. Fred Singer, "The Martian Satellites – discussion", in *Physical Studies of Minor Planets*, op cit

5 "Notes on Jupiter's Moons", *Sky & Telescope*, vol 50, no 6, p 380, Dec 1975

6 V. A. Firsoff, *Strange World of the Moon*, Hutchinson, 1959

7 Anthony R. Martin, "Missions to Jupiter – 1", *Spaceflight*, vol 14, no 8, pp 294–9, Aug 1972

8 F. Graham Smith, *Radio Astronomy*, Penguin Books, 1960

9 James Strong, *Search the Solar System*, David & Charles, 1973

10 Isaac Asimov, "By Jove!", in *View from a Height*, Dobson, 1964

11 K. A. Ehricke, "Astrogenic Environments", *Spaceflight*, vol 14, no 1, pp 2–14, Jan 1972
12 JBIS, vol 25, p 672, 1972
13 David Baker, "Report from Jupiter – 2", *Spaceflight*, vol 17, no 3, pp 102–7, Mar 1975
14 "Jupiter XIII", *Sky & Telescope*, vol 48, no 6, p 378, Dec 1974
15 Garry Hunt, "Jupiter", in *New Science in the Solar System, op cit*
16 A. E. Roy, "Brief Moment of Glory", *The Glasgow Herald*, 8 Dec 1973
17 Duncan Lunan, "The Galilean Problem" (short story), *Galaxy*, vol 32, no 2, Sept 1971
18 "Energy Sources in Jupiter", JBIS, vol 27, no 6, pp 466–7, June 1974
19 "Preliminary Pioneer 10 Findings", *op cit*, pp 473–4
20 "Ice on Callisto?" *Spaceflight*, vol 16, no 8, p 290, Aug 1974
21 Thornton Page, "Notes on Lunar Research", *Sky & Telescope*, vol 48, no 2, pp 88–90, Aug 1974
22 "Triumph of Pioneer 11", *Spaceflight*, vol 17, no 3, pp 108–9, Mar 1975
23 "Ganymede from Pioneer 10", *Sky & Telescope*, vol 49, no 1, p 8, Jan 1975
24 J. G. Hills, "On the Formation of the Asteroids", in *Physical Studies of Minor Planets*
25 Brian O'Leary, "Occultations of Stars by Planetary Satellites and Asteroids", *Sky & Telescope*, vol 48, no 2, pp 91–3, Aug 1974
26 M. S. Bobrov, *The Rings of Saturn*, "Nauka" Press, Moscow, 1970; translation: NASA TT F–701, US Govt Printing Office, June 1972
27 "Pioneer 11: through the Dragon's Mouth", *Sky & Telescope*, vol 49, no 2, pp 72–8, Feb 1975
28 "Jupiter's Glittering Moon", *Spaceflight*, vol 17, no 3, p 114, Mar 1975
29 "Sodium Emission from Io", JBIS, vol 27, no 8, p 629, Aug 1974
30 "Satellites of the Outer Planets", *Spaceflight*, vol 14, no 9, p 356, Sept 1972
31 William K. Hartmann, "A 1974 Tour of the Planets", *Sky & Telescope*, vol 48, no 2, pp 78–81, Aug 1974
32 "Jovian Magnetic Field", *Spaceflight*, vol 17, no 7, pp 255–6, July 1975
33 *Exploration of the Solar System*, ed A. Henderson Jr, J. Grey, NASA EP–122, US Govt Printing Office, 1974
34 "Slingshot to Saturn", *Spaceflight*, vol 15, no 5 pp 181–2, May 1973
35 "International Space Plan", *Spaceflight*, vol 16, no 11, pp 432–3, Nov 1974
36 Vernor Vinge and Arthur Sorkin, "Titan as a Gravitational Brake", JBIS, vol 27, no 2, pp 129–31, Feb 1974
37 R. C. Parkinson, "The Resources of the Solar System", *Spaceflight*, vol 17, no 4, pp 124–8, Apr 1975
38 R. C. Parkinson, "Planetary Spacecraft for the 1980s", *Spaceflight*, vol 17, no 10, pp 346–51, Oct 1975
39 Anthony R. Martin, "Missions to Jupiter – 2", *Spaceflight*, vol 14, no 9, pp 325–32, Sept 1972
40 Robert Edgar, "Payloads for the Shuttle", *Spaceflight*, vol 18, no 9, pp 327–30, Sept 1976
41 Ben Bova, "1974 – the Year That Was", *Analog Science Fiction/Science Fact*, vol XCIV, no 5, pp 5–11, Jan 1975
42 Jerry Pournelle, "A Step Farther Out – This Generation of Wonder", *Galaxy*, vol 35, no 7, pp 116–23, July 1974
43 "Radar Probes Ganymede", *Spaceflight*, vol 17, no 10, pp 369–70, Oct 1975
44 W. B. Hubbard and J. R. Jokipii, "New Studies of Jupiter", *Sky & Telescope*, vol 50, no 4, pp 212–16, Oct 1975
45 NASA Staff, "Discovering Jupiter"; Part 1, *Spaceflight*, vol 18, no 12, pp 438–447, Dec 1976; Part 2, vol 19, no 1, pp 21–8, Jan 1977
46 John H. Wolfe, "Jupiter", *Scientific American*, vol 233, no 6, pp 119–26, Sept 1975
47 "The Sounds of Earth", *Spaceflight*, vol 20, no 4, pp 123–6 and 160, Apr 1978
48 Kenneth W. Gatland, *Astronautics in the Sixties*, Iliffe, 1962
49 "Space Highlights from around the World", *Sky & Telescope*, vol 51, no 3, pp 169–71, Mar 1976
50 "House OK's JOP", *L5 News*, vol 2, no 8, pp 2 and 4, Aug 1977
51 "Jupiter Probe Reference Design Mission", *L5 News*, vol 2, no 8, pp 3 and 16, Aug 1977
52 G. E. Hunt, "Space Exploration of the Jovian Atmosphere", *JBIS*, vol 30, no 1, pp 15–19, Jan 1977

53 "Jovian Internal Structure", *JBIS*, vol 29, nos 7–8, p 519, July–Aug 1976
54 C. Sagan, "Exobiology", in *New Science in the Solar System, op cit*

Chapter 10
 1 Simon Mitton, "Saturn and Beyond", in *New Science in the Solar System, op cit*
 2 J. K. Alexander, "New Vistas in Planetary Radio Astronomy", *Sky & Telescope*, vol 51, no 3, pp 148–53, Mar 1976
 3 "Gravitational Fields of the Giant Planets", *Spaceflight*, vol 14, no 9, p 354, Sept 1972
 4 Anthony Michaelis, "Saturn's Secrets Come to Light", *The Daily Telegraph*, 22 May 1972
 5 "Organic Molecules in the Atmospheres of the Giant Planets", JBIS, vol 27, no 9, pp 703–4, Sept 1974
 6 R. D. Enzmann, "Introduction to the Section on Environments", in *Second Conference on Planetology and Space Mission Planning, op cit*
 7 M. S. Bobrov, *The Rings of Saturn, op cit*
 8 A. F. O'D. Alexander, *The Planet Saturn*, Faber & Faber, 1962
 9 D. Ya. Martynov, *The Planets: Solved and Unsolved Ploblems, op cit*
10 "Particle Size in the Rings of Saturn", JBIS, vol 27, no 6, p 466, June 1974
11 "Saturn's Rings", JBIS, vol 27, no 5, p 386, May 1974
12 William K. Hartmann, "A 1974 Tour of the Planets", *Sky & Telescope*, vol 48, no 2, 78–81, Aug 1974
13 "Rings of Saturn", *Spaceflight*, vol 12, no 5, p 219, May 1970
14 Kenneth F. Weaver, "Voyage to the Planets", *National Geographic Magazine*, vol 138, no 3, pp 147–93, Aug 1970
15 W. C. Livingstone, "Saturn's Rings and Perfect Seeing", *Sky & Telescope*, vol 49, no 4, pp 207 and 215, Apr 1975
16 "Pioneer 11: through the Dragon's Mouth", *Sky & Telescope*, vol 49, no 2, pp 72–8, Feb 1975
17 R. F. Freitag, "Man's Future in Astronautics", *Spaceflight*, vol 17, no 3, pp 82–7, Mar 1975
18 S. Fred Singer, "The Martian Satellites", discussion in *Physical Studies of Minor Planets, op cit*
19 "Titan: a Satellite which Recycles its Atmosphere", in *New Science in the Solar System, op cit*
20 "Saturn's Gas Ring", JBIS, vol 27, no 5, p 386, May 1974
21 "Titan's Green House", JBIS, vol 27, no 1, p 69, Jan 1974
22 Willy Ley and Chesley Bonestell, *The Conquest of Space*, Sidgwick & Jackson, 1951
23 Bruce Murray (ed), *Mars and the Mind of Man*, Harper & Row, 1973
24 Isaac Asimov, "Not as We Know It", in *View from a Height*, Dobson, 1964
25 Ye. V. Belikova, G. S. Komolova ond I. A. Yegerov, "Influence of a Set of External Factors on Biologically Active Substances", in *Extraterrestrial Life and its Detection Methods*, ed A. A. Imshenetskiy, "Nauka" Press, Moscow, 1970; translation NASA TT F-710, US Govt Printing Office, May 1972
26 J. Veverka, J. Elliot and J. Goguen, "Measuring the Sizes of Saturn's Satellites", *Sky & Telescope*, vol 50, no 6, pp 356–9, Dec 1975
27 K. A. Ehricke, "Astrogenic Environments", *Spaceflight*, vol 14, no 1, pp 2–14, Jan 1972
28 S. K. Vesekhsvyatskiy, *The Nature and Origin of Comets and Meteors, op cit*
29 James Strong, *Search the Solar System*, David & Charles, 1973
30 Vernor Vinge and Arthur Sorkin, "Titan as a Gravitational Brake", *op cit*
31 Robert Edgar, "Payloads for the Shuttle", *op cit*
32 Anthony R. Martin, "Missions to Jupiter – 2", *op cit*
33 "Pacific Astronomers Convene", *Sky & Telescope*, vol 48, no 3, pp 143–7, Sept 1974
34 Patrick Moore, *Guide to the Planets*, Collins (Comet Books), 1957
35 "Exploration of Uranus", JBIS, vol 28, no 7, pp 490–2, July 1975
36 F. L. Whipple, "Why Missions to Comets and Asteroids?", *Astronautics & Aeronautics*, pp 12–16, Oct 1972
37 J. P. Kirton, "The Problem of the Gyroscopic Earth", *Analog Science Fiction/ Science Fact*, vol LXXIII, no 3, pp 8–16 and 81, May 1964
38 Joseph L. Brady, "The Effect of a Trans-Plutonian Planet on Halley's Comet", *Publications Astronomical Society of the Pacific*, vol 84, pp 314–22, Apr 1972
39 A. T. Lawton, "'Stray' Planets, their Formation and the Possibilities of CETI", *Spaceflight*, vol 16, no 5, pp 188–9, May 1974

40 George W. Harper, "Styx and Stones: and Maybe Charon Too", *Analog Science Fiction/Science Fact*, vol XCII, no 3, pp 64–81, Nov 1973
41 "The Neptune-Pluto System", *Spaceflight*, vol 14, no 1, p 32, Jan 1972
42 "Pluto's Rotation", *Sky & Telescope*, vol 48, no 1, p 22, July 1974
43 "Atmosphere of Pluto?" JBIS, vol 27, no 11, p 865, Nov 1974
44 Robert S. Richardson, *Mars*, Allen & Unwin, 1965
45 Alan E. Nourse, *Nine Planets*, Harper & Bros, 1960
46 Walter Sullivan, *We Are Not Alone*, Pelican Books, 1970
47 P. Molton, "Non-Aqueous Biosystems: the Case for Liquid Ammonia as a Solvent", JBIS, vol 27, no 4, pp 243–62, Apr 1974
48 Brian O'Leary, "Occultations of Stars by Planetary Satellites and Asteroids", *op cit*
49 Shin Yabushita, *Perturbations of the Orbit of a Space Probe by the Ring of Asteroids*, ESRO, SR-19, Sept 1972
50 *New Scientist*, p 403, 18 Aug 1977
51 "Mission to Jupiter/Saturn", no 2, JPL S-22-82, 11/77
52 Ian Ridpath, *Stars and Space 77*, Independent Newspapers Ltd, 1977
53 "The Fate of Satellites of the Moon", *Journal of the British Interplanetary Society*, vol 27, no 5, p 385, May 1974
54 Keith Hindley, "Iapetus Probes the Rings of Saturn", *New Scientist*, pp 140–1, 20 Oct 1977
55 "Asymmetry of Saturn's Ring A", *Sky & Telescope*, vol 53, no 5, pp 357–8, May 1977
56 "How Many Satellites Has Saturn?", *Sky & Telescope*, vol 55, no 4, p 294, Apr 1978
57 Ian Ridpath, "The Mini-Planet", *New Scientist*, pp 406–7, 17 Nov 1977
58 *New Scientist*, p 817, 22–29 Dec 1977
59 J. L. Elliot, E. Dunham and R. L. Millis, "Discovering the Rings of Uranus", *Sky & Telescope*, vol 53, no 6, pp 412–16 and 430, June 1977
60 "Reports on Uranus and Neptune", *op cit*, pp 429–30
61 *New Scientist*, p 221, 27 Oct 1977

Chapter 11

1   S. K. Vsekhsvyatskiy, *The Nature and Origin of Comets and Meteors*, *op cit*
2   Sir Harold Spencer-Jones, *General Astronomy*, third edition, E. Arnold, 1951
3   George W. Harper, *Styx and Stones: and Maybe Charon Too*, *op cit*, Chapter 10
4   J. D. Fernie, "Interstellar Absorption in the Galactic Neighbourhood of the Sun", *Astronomical Journal*, vol 67, no 4, pp 224–8, May 1962
5   V. A. Hughes and D. Routledge, "An Expanding Ring of Interstellar Gas with Centre Close to the Sun", *Astronomical Journal*, vol 77, p 210, 1973
6   "Observations of Comet Kohoutek", JBIS, vol 27, no 11, pp 865–6, Nov 1974
7   Duncan Lunan, "The Comet, the Cairn and the Capsule" (short story), *If*, vol 21, no 6, pp 118–33, July–Aug 1972
8   "Split Tails of Comets", JBIS, vol 27, no 3, p 226, March 1974
9   R. W. Farquhar and N. F. Ness, "Two Early Missions to the Comets", *Astronautics & Aeronautics*, pp 32–7, Oct 1972
10 *Astronautics & Aeronautics, 1970: Chronology on Science, Technology and Policy*, *op cit*
11 Arthur C. Clarke, "Into the Comet" (short story), in *Tales of Ten Worlds*, Gollancz, 1963
12 George W. Harper, "Kohoutek: a Failure that Wasn't", *Analog Science Fiction/Science Fact*, vol XCIII, no 5, pp 40–51, July 1974
13 F. L. Whipple, "Why Missions to Comets and Asteroids?", *Astronautics & Aeronautics*, pp 12–16, Oct 1972
14 F. Yu. Zigel, *The Minor Planets*, *op cit*
15 "Water Molecules in Kohoutek", *Spaceflight*, vol 16, no 4, p 151, Apr 1974
16 "Does Mercury Have an Atmosphere", JBIS, vol 27, no 6, p 476, June 1974
17 Edward G. Gibson, "Comet Kohoutek Drawings from Skylab", *Sky & Telescope*, vol 48, no 4, pp 208–12, Oct 1974
18 "Cometary Nuclei", JBIS, vol 27, no 1, p 68, Jan 1974
19 Jean Dufay, *Galactic Nebulae and Interstellar Matter*, Hutchinson, 1957
20 F. L. Whipple, *Earth, Moon and Planets*, third edition, Pelican Books, 1971
21 Isaac Asimov, "Steppingstones to the Stars", in *Asimov on Astronomy*, *op cit*
22 *Exploration of the Solar System*, *op cit*

23 Isaac Asimov, "Harmony in Heaven", in *Asimov on Astronomy, op cit*
24 Simon Mitton, "Prospects for Comet Kohoutek", *New Scientist*, pp 464–6, 15 Nov 1973
25 "Planetesimal Formation", JBIS, vol 27, no 2, p 149, Feb 1974
26 "Comets", *Spaceflight*, vol 13, no 8, p 303, Aug 1971
27 Craig Covault, "NASA Studies Explorers for Missions to Comets", *Aviation Week & Space Technology*, p 20, 9 April 1973
28 "Industry Observer", *Aviation Week & Space Technology*, p 9, 18 Sept 1972
29 Robert Edgar, "Payloads for the Shuttle", *op cit*
30 Richard C. Hoagland, "Rendezvous in 1985", *Analog Science Fiction/Science Fact*, vol XCV, no 9, pp 59–76, Sept 1975
31 Robert A. Park, "Intercepting a Comet", *Astronautics & Aeronautics*, pp 54–8, Aug 1964
32 "Solar Sailing", *Spaceflight*, vol 19, no 4, pp 124–5, Apr 1977

Chapter 12 (A. T. Lawton)
PLANETS BEYOND PLUTO:

J. L. Brady, *Publications Astronomical Society of the Pacific*, 84, pp 314–22, 1972
J. L. Brady and E. Carpenter, *Astronomical Journal*, 76, pp 728–39, 1971
A. T. Lawton, *Spaceflight*, 14, pp 454–5, 1972
T. Kiang, *Monthly Notices of the Royal Astronomical Society*, 182, pp 271–87

DYSON SPHERES AND O'NEILL CYLINDERS:

F. J. Dyson, *Science*, 131, p 1667, 1960
F. J. Dyson, "Intelligent Life in the Universe", Lecture given in San Francisco, 18 Sept 1972
G. O'Neill, excerpts from symposium at Princeton 1975, reported in London *Sunday Telegraph, Nature*, etc.
G. O'Neill, "The Colonisation of Space", *Physics Today*, Sept 1974
A. Berry, "Pioneers Who Aim to Live in the Sky", *Sunday Telegraph*, 29 June 1975

STAR BUSTING:

G. R. Burbidge, "Galactic Explosions as Sources of Radio Emission", *Nature*, 190, 1961
C. Sagan and I. S. Shlovskii, *Intelligent Life in the Universe*, pp 475–6, Holden–Day, 1966

GAS DENSITY:

Zdenek Kopal, *Telescopes in Space*, p 124, Faber & Faber, 1968
W. McCrea, "The 1975 Halley Memorial Lecture", *Nature*, 225, p 136, 1975

STAR FORMATION:

Fred Hoyle, *Astronomy*, pp 269–81, Macdonald & Co, 1962

BUSSARD RAM SCOOPS:

R. W. Bussard, *Acta Astronautica*, 6, pp 179–94, 1960
C. Sagan, *Planetary and Space Science*, 11, pp 485–98, 1963; also *Intelligent Life in the Universe, op cit*
A. R. Martin, "Structural Limitations on Interstellar Spaceflight", *Acta Astronautica*, 16, pp 353–7, 1971
A. R. Martin, "Magnetic Intake Limitations on Interstellar Ramjets", *Acta Astronautica*, 18, pp 1–10, 1973

Appendix (D. Lunan)

1 G. W. Morgenthaler, "Interstellar Exploration Mission Profiles", in *Second Conference on Planetology and Space Mission Planning, op cit*
2 J. D. Fernie, "Interstellar Absorption in the Galactic Neighbourhood of the Sun", *op cit*
3 V. A. Hughes and D. Routledge, "An Expanding Ring of Interstellar Gas with Centre Close to the Sun", *op cit*

4   NASA Staff, "Discovering Jupiter – 2", *Spaceflight*, vol 19, no 1, pp 21–8, Jan 1977
5   "Is the Solar System Heading into an Interstellar Cloud?", *Sky & Telescope*, vol 56, no 3, pp 211–12, Sept 1978

Chapter 13 (John Macvey)

1   C. M. Michaux, NASA Report SP–3031, Chapter 13
2   P. M. Molton, "Exobiology, Jupiter and Life", *Spaceflight*, vol 14, no 6, pp 220–3
3   F. Woeller and C. Ponnamperuma, *Icarus*, vol 10, p 386, 1969
4   M. S. Chadha *et al*, *Icarus*, vol 15, p 39, 1971
5   P. Molton *et al*, *Space Life Science*, 1972
6   B. H. Khare and C. Sagan, *Nature*, vol 232, p 577, 1971
7   S. W. Fox and K. Harada, *Nature*, vol 201, p 335, 1964
8   P. M. Molton and J. C. Gilbert, *Icarus*, 1972
9   S. M. Siegal, *Spaceflight*, vol 12, p 128, 1970
10 L. H. Aller, "Some Aspects of the Abundance Problem in Planetary Nebulae", *Publications Astronomical Society of the Pacific*, vol 76, pp 279–88, 1964
11 L. F. Herzog, "Determining the Composition and History of the Solar System", in *Analytical Chemistry in Space*, p 8, Pergamon, 1970
12 P. M. Molton, "Terrestrial Biochemistry in Perspective: Some Other Possibilities", *Spaceflight*, vol 15, no 4, p 139
13 R. A. Horne, "On the Unlikelihood of Non-Aqueous Biosystems", *Space Life Science*, vol 3, pp 34–41, 1971

Index

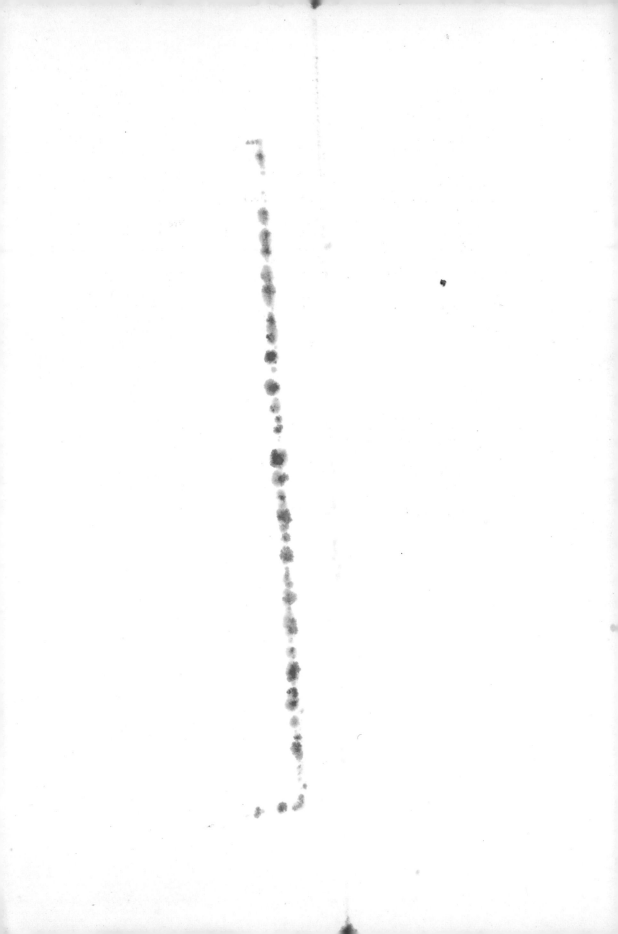

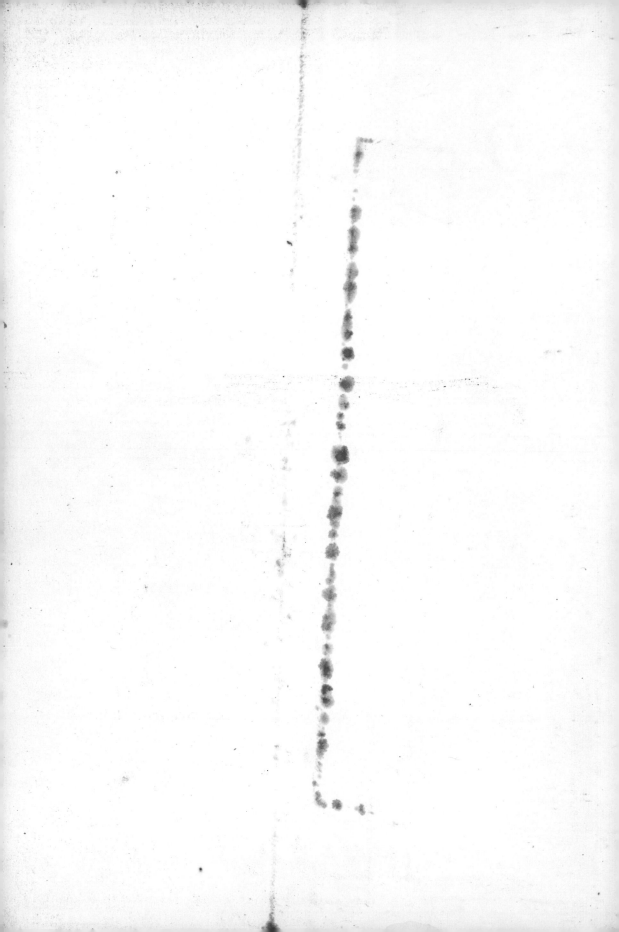